Taxing Wages 2017

OECD
BETTER POLICIES FOR BETTER LIVES

This work is published under the responsibility of the Secretary-General of the OECD. The opinions expressed and arguments employed herein do not necessarily reflect the official views of OECD member countries.

This document and any map included herein are without prejudice to the status of or sovereignty over any territory, to the delimitation of international frontiers and boundaries and to the name of any territory, city or area.

Please cite this publication as:
OECD (2017), *Taxing Wages 2017*, OECD Publishing, Paris.
http://dx.doi.org/10.1787/tax_wages-2017-en

ISBN 978-92-64-27076-3 (imprimé)
ISBN 978-92-64-27080-0 (PDF)
ISBN 978-92-64-27081-7 (epub)

Annual
ISSN 1995-3844 (print)
ISSN 2072-5124 (online)

The statistical data for Israel are supplied by and under the responsibility of the relevant Israeli authorities. The use of such data by the OECD is without prejudice to the status of the Golan Heights, East Jerusalem and Israeli settlements in the West Bank under the terms of international law.

Corrigenda to OECD publications may be found on line at: *www.oecd.org/about/publishing/corrigenda.htm*.

© OECD 2017

You can copy, download or print OECD content for your own use, and you can include excerpts from OECD publications, databases and multimedia products in your own documents, presentations, blogs, websites and teaching materials, provided that suitable acknowledgment of the source and copyright owner is given. All requests for public or commercial use and translation rights should be submitted to *rights@oecd.org*. Requests for permission to photocopy portions of this material for public or commercial use shall be addressed directly to the Copyright Clearance Center (CCC) at *info@copyright.com* or the Centre français d'exploitation du droit de copie (CFC) at *contact@cfcopies.com*.

Foreword

This annual publication provides details of taxes paid on wages in all 35 member countries of the OECD. The information contained in the Report covers the personal income tax and social security contributions paid by employees, the social security contributions and payroll taxes paid by their employers and cash benefits received by families. The objective of the Report is to illustrate how personal income taxes, social security contributions and payroll taxes are calculated and to examine how these levies and cash family benefits impact on net household incomes. The results also allow quantitative cross-country comparisons of labour cost levels and of the overall tax and benefit position of single persons and families.*

The Report shows the amounts of taxes, social security contributions, payroll taxes and cash benefits for eight family-types, which differ by income level and household composition. It also presents the resulting average and marginal tax rates. Average tax rates show that part of gross wage earnings or total labour costs which are taken in personal income taxes (before and after cash benefits), social security contributions and payroll taxes. Marginal tax rates show the part of an increase of gross earnings or total labour costs that is paid in these levies.

The focus of the Report is the presentation of new data on the tax/benefit position of employees in 2016. In addition, the new data is compared with corresponding data for the year 2015. The average worker is designated as a full-time employee (including manual and non-manual) in either industry sectors B-N inclusive with reference to the International Standard Industrial Classification of All Economic Activities, Revision 4 (ISIC Rev.4) or industry sectors C-K inclusive with reference to the International Standard Industrial Classification of All Economic Activities, Revision 3 (ISIC Rev.3).

The Report is structured as follows:

- *Chapter 1 contains an overview of the main results for 2016.*
- *Chapter 2 contains the Special Feature on "Taxation and Skills".*
- *Part I (International Comparisons) reviews the main results for 2015 and 2016 and is divided into 3 chapters (Nos. 3 to 5). Chapter 3 reviews the main results for 2016, which are summarised in comparative tables and figures included at the end of that section. Chapter 4 presents a graphical exposition of the estimated tax burden on labour income in 2016 for gross wage earnings between 50% and 250% of the average wage. Then Chapter 5 reviews the main results for 2015, which are summarised in the comparative tables at the end of the chapter and compares them with the 2016 figures.*
- *Part II (Chapter 6) focuses on the historical trends in the tax burden for the period 2000-16.*
- *Part III contains individual country tables specifying the wage levels considered and the associated tax burdens for eight separate family types, together with descriptions of each tax/benefit system.*
- *The Annex describes the methodology and its limitations.*

* *Previous editions were published under the title* The Tax/Benefit Position of Employees *(1996-98 editions) and* The Tax/Benefit Position of Production Workers *(editions published before 1996).*

The Report has been prepared under the auspices of the Working Party on Tax Policy Analysis and Tax Statistics of the Committee on Fiscal Affairs. This document has been produced with the financial assistance of the European Union Programme for Employment and Social Innovation "EaSI" (2014-20). The views expressed herein can in no way be taken to reflect the official opinion of the European Union.

Table of contents

Part III

Country details, 2016

Tables

Figures

Follow OECD Publications on:

http://twitter.com/OECD_Pubs

http://www.facebook.com/OECDPublications

http://www.linkedin.com/groups/OECD-Publications-4645871

http://www.youtube.com/oecdilibrary

http://www.oecd.org/oecddirect/

This book has... *StatLinks*

A service that delivers Excel® files from the printed page!

Look for the *StatLinks* at the bottom of the tables or graphs in this book. To download the matching Excel® spreadsheet, just type the link into your Internet browser, starting with the *http://dx.doi.org* prefix, or click on the link from the e-book edition.

Executive summary

After falling during the financial crisis, the effective tax rate on the labour costs of the average worker increased by 1 percentage point between 2009 and 2013 before decreasing slightly over the last few years and reaching 36.0% on average in OECD countries in 2016. The effective tax rate, or tax wedge, as a percentage of labour costs, is measured by taking the total taxes and social security contributions (SSCs) paid by employees and employers, minus family benefits received as a proportion of the total labour costs for employers.

Although the OECD average decreased slightly in 2016, 20 OECD countries experienced a higher tax wedge on the average worker compared with 2015, while 14 countries experienced reductions. For 18 of the countries with an increasing tax wedge, the changes were less than 0.50 percentage points.

In most of the countries where the tax wedge on the average worker increased, the main reason for the increase was due to changes to personal income taxes (PIT), even though only two countries increased their statutory rates (Denmark and Greece). Most of the PIT increases were driven by a higher proportion of earnings becoming subject to tax as the value of tax free allowances and tax credits fell relative to earnings. In most countries where there was a fall in the tax wedge, reductions in PIT were the key factor, however, lower SSCs also played a significant role in France, Iceland, Italy and Switzerland.

Since 2009, the year where the OECD average tax wedge was at its lowest level since the *Taxing Wages* series commenced in 2000, the tax wedge has increased in 20 OECD countries, fallen in 14 others and remained unchanged in one country (Chile). In this time, PIT has risen in 13 of the countries with increasing tax wedges: among those countries three countries had higher statutory PIT rates for workers on average earnings in 2016 than in 2009; six had increased or introduced surtaxes; and two had abolished basic tax credits. This report considers how these changes affect various types of households, including single earners, families with or without children, and single parents. In all OECD countries, the tax wedge for families with children is either lower or, in two cases, the same, as single earners without children.

The report also contains a special feature examining how the labour income tax system can provide incentives or disincentives for workers to invest in human capital and skills. Investment in skills is a key factor in fostering inclusive growth and in raising productivity in OECD economies. The special feature presents effective tax rates on skills investments, incorporating PIT and employees' SSCs for the sample case of a 32-year-old single worker undertaking a short course of training. In this case, the average effective tax rate on skills is 24.9%, which represents the amount by which the tax system reduces the net present value of the skills investment made by this individual. Overall, tax levels on skills are progressive; those on higher incomes and those who earn a higher return on skills investments are taxed at higher effective rates. While tax expenditures designed to encourage worker training can reduce the effective tax rate on skills, in many countries this support is provided in the form of tax deductions for training expenses related to a workers' current job. As a result, the benefits of such support are often limited for those seeking to change careers and those on low incomes.

Key findings

The average tax wedge in the OECD decreased in 2016 relative to 2015

- Across OECD countries, the average PIT and SSCs on employment incomes was 36.0% in 2016, a decrease of 0.07 percentage points relative to 2015.
- In 2016, the highest average tax wedges for childless single workers earning the average national wage were in Belgium (54.0%), Germany (49.4%), Hungary (48.2%) and France (48.1%). The lowest were in Chile (7%), New Zealand (17.9%) and Mexico (20.1%).
- Between 2015 and 2016, the tax wedge increased in 20 of 35 countries, fell in 14 and remained unchanged in Chile. Changes to the PIT were the main contributor to an increasing total tax wedge in 16 of the 20 countries.
- There was an increase of more than 1 percentage point in the tax wedge in only one country; Greece (1.06 percentage points), which was driven by an increase in both PIT and SSCs.
- A decline of one percentage point or more was experienced in two countries, which both implemented reforms – Austria (2.47 percentage points) and Belgium (1.32 percentage points). The change in Austria was mainly due to lower PIT, whereas in Belgium it was caused by lower PIT and employer's SSCs.
- Changes to PIT were also the primary contributing factor in most countries where the tax wedge fell in 2016. The exceptions were France, Italy, Iceland and Switzerland. Decreasing employer's SSCs were the main factor in France and Italy.

Tax wedges for families with children

- In 2016, the highest tax wedge for one-earner families with two children at the average wage was in France (40.0%). Belgium, Finland, Greece, Italy and Sweden had tax wedges of between 38% and 40%. New Zealand had the lowest tax wedge for these families (6.2%), followed by Chile (7%), Ireland (8.3%) and Switzerland (9.1%). The average for OECD countries was 26.6%.
- Between 2015 and 2016, the largest increase in the tax wedge for one earner families with children was in New Zealand (1.24 percentage points). The largest decreases were in Austria (2.68 percentage points), Portugal (2.50 percentage points), Belgium (1.73 percentage points), Hungary (1.60 percentage points) and Ireland (1.03 percentage points).
- The tax wedge for families with children is lower than that for single individuals without children in all OECD countries except in Chile and Mexico, where both family types face the same tax levels. No PIT is payable at the average wage level in Chile and no tax provisions for families with children exist in Mexico. The differences are more than 15% of labour costs in Canada, the Czech Republic, Germany, Ireland, Luxembourg and Slovenia.

© OECD 2017

Chapter 1

Overview

This chapter presents the main results of the analysis of the taxation of labour income across OECD member countries in 2016. Most emphasis is given to the tax wedge – a measure of the difference between labour costs to the employer and the corresponding net take-home pay of the employee – which is calculated by expressing the sum of personal income tax, employee plus employer social security contributions together with any payroll tax, minus benefits as a percentage of labour costs. The calculations also focus on the net personal average tax rate. This is the term used when the personal income tax and employee social security contributions net of cash benefits are expressed as a percentage of gross wage earnings. The analysis focuses on the single worker, with no children, at average earnings and makes a comparison with the single earner married couple with two children.

The statistical data for Israel are supplied by and under the responsibility of the relevant Israeli authorities. The use of such data by the OECD is without prejudice to the status of the Golan Heights, East Jerusalem and Israeli settlements in the West Bank under the terms of international law.

This Report provides unique information for each of the thirty-five OECD countries on the income taxes paid by workers, their social security contributions, the family benefits they receive in the form of cash transfers, as well as the social security contributions and payroll taxes paid by their employers. Results reported include the marginal and average tax burden for one- and two-earner households, and the implied total labour costs for employers. These data are widely used in academic research and in the formulation and evaluation of social and economic policies. The taxpayer-specific detail in this Report enables it to complement the information provided annually in *Revenue Statistics*, a publication providing internationally comparative data on tax levels and tax structures in OECD countries. The methodology followed in this Report is described briefly in the introduction section below and in more detail in the Annex.

The tables and charts present estimates of tax burdens and of the tax "wedge" between labour costs and net take-home pay for eight illustrative family types on comparable levels of income. The key results for 2016 are summarised in second section below. Part I of the Report presents more detailed results for 2016, together with comparable results for 2015 and discusses the changes between the two years. Part II of the Report reviews historical changes in tax burdens between 2000 and 2016.

The present Chapter 1 begins with an introduction to the *Taxing Wages* methodology that is followed by a review of the results of tax burden indicators for 2016. The review includes the tax wedge and the personal average tax rates results for a single worker, without children, earning the average wage, and also the corresponding indicators for a one-earner couple at the average wage level, with two children. Finally, the chapter ends with a section on the change in the average wage levels by country and the industry classification on which they are based.

Introduction

This section briefly introduces the methodology employed for this Report, which focuses on full-time employees. It is assumed that their annual income from employment is equal to a given percentage of the average full-time adult gross wage earnings for each OECD economy, referred to as the *average wage* (AW). This covers both manual and non-manual workers for either industry sectors C-K inclusive with reference to the International Standard Industrial Classification of All Economic Activities, Revision 3 (ISIC Rev.3) or industry sectors B-N inclusive with reference to the International Standard Industrial Classification of All Economic Activities, Revision 4 (ISIC Rev.4).[1] Further details are provided in Table 1.6 as well as in the Annex of this Report. Additional assumptions are made about the personal circumstances of these wage earners in order to determine their tax/benefit position.

In the Report, the term *tax* includes the personal income tax, social security contributions and payroll taxes (which are aggregated with employer social contributions in the calculation of tax rates) payable on gross wage earnings. Consequently, any income tax that might be due on non-wage income and other kinds of taxes – e.g. corporate income tax, net wealth tax and consumption taxes – are not taken into account. The benefits included are those paid by general government as cash transfers, usually in respect of dependent children.

For most OECD countries, the tax year is equivalent to the calendar year, the exceptions being Australia, New Zealand and the United Kingdom. In the case of New Zealand and the United Kingdom, where the tax year starts in April, the calculations apply a "forward-looking" approach. This implies that, for example, the tax rates reported for 2016 are those for the tax year 2016-17. However, in Australia, where the tax year starts in July, it has been decided to take a "backward looking" approach in order to present more reliable results. So, for example, the year 2016 in respect of Australia has been defined to mean its tax year 2015-16.

The Report presents several measures of taxation on labour. Most emphasis is given to the tax wedge – a measure of the difference between labour costs to the employer and the corresponding net take-home pay of the employee – which is calculated by expressing the sum of personal income tax, employee plus employer social security contributions together with any payroll tax, minus benefits as a percentage of labour costs. Employer social security contributions and – in some countries – payroll taxes are added to gross wage earnings of employees in order to determine a measure of total labour costs. However, it should be recognised that this measure may be less than the true labour costs faced by employers because, for example, employers may also have to make non-tax compulsory payments.[2] The average tax wedge measures identify that part of total labour costs which is taken in tax and social security contributions net of cash benefits. In contrast, the marginal tax wedge measures identify that part of an increase of total labour costs that is paid in taxes and social security contributions less cash benefits.

The calculations also focus on the net personal average tax rate. This is the term used when the personal income tax and employee social security contributions net of cash benefits are expressed as a percentage of gross wage earnings. The net personal marginal tax rate shows that part of an increase of gross wage earnings that is paid in personal income tax and employee social security contributions net of cash benefits.

Review of results for 2016

Tax wedge

Table 1.1 shows that the tax wedge between total labour costs to the employer and the corresponding net take-home pay for single workers without children, at average earnings levels, varied widely across OECD countries in 2016 (see column 1). While in Austria, Belgium, France, Germany, Hungary and Italy, the tax wedge is over 45%, it is 20% or lower in Chile, Mexico and New Zealand. The highest tax wedge is observed in Belgium (54.0%) and the lowest in Chile (7.0%). Table 1.1 shows that the average tax wedge in OECD countries was 36.0% in 2016.

The changes in tax wedge between 2015 and 2016 for the average worker without children are described in column 2 of Table 1.1. The tax wedge increased in twenty countries, fell in fourteen and remained unchanged in one. The tax wedge increased by more than one percentage point only in Greece, where it changed by 1.06 percentage point. In contrast, decreases of one percentage point or more were observed in Austria (2.47 percentage points) and Belgium (1.32 percentage points). There was no change in the tax wedge for Chile.

In general, the rises in tax wedge rates were driven by higher income taxes (see column 3). This was the major factor in sixteen of the countries showing an overall

Table 1.1. **Comparison of total tax wedge**

As % of labour costs

Country[1]	Total Tax wedge 2016	Annual change 2016/15 (in percentage points)[2]			
		Tax wedge	Income tax	Employee SSC	Employer SSC[3]
	(1)	(2)	(3)	(4)	(5)
Belgium	54.0	-1.32	-0.80	0.07	-0.59
Germany	49.4	0.05	-0.12	0.17	0.00
Hungary	48.2	-0.78	-0.78	0.00	0.00
France	48.1	-0.34	0.19	0.17	-0.70
Italy	47.8	-0.08	0.02	0.01	-0.11
Austria	47.1	-2.47	-2.40	-0.06	-0.01
Finland	43.8	0.22	-0.60	0.38	0.44
Czech Republic	43.0	0.19	0.19	0.00	0.00
Sweden	42.8	0.21	0.21	0.00	0.00
Slovenia	42.7	0.09	0.09	0.00	0.00
Latvia	42.6	0.10	0.10	0.00	0.00
Slovak Republic	41.5	0.12	0.12	0.00	0.00
Portugal	41.5	-0.60	-0.60	0.00	0.00
Greece	40.2	1.06	0.67	0.20	0.19
Spain	39.5	0.09	0.09	0.00	0.00
Estonia	38.9	-0.12	-0.12	0.00	0.00
Luxembourg	38.4	0.05	0.12	0.01	-0.08
Turkey	38.1	-0.09	-0.09	0.00	0.00
Netherlands	37.5	0.40	-0.42	0.35	0.47
Denmark	36.5	0.02	0.09	0.00	-0.07
Norway	36.2	-0.40	-0.40	0.00	0.00
Poland	35.8	0.05	0.05	0.00	0.00
Iceland	34.0	-0.21	-0.07	-0.02	-0.12
Japan	32.4	0.12	0.01	0.06	0.06
United States	31.7	0.15	0.19	0.00	-0.05
Canada	31.4	-0.13	-0.17	0.01	0.02
United Kingdom	30.8	-0.03	-0.11	0.04	0.04
Australia	28.6	0.23	0.23	0.00	0.00
Ireland	27.1	-0.24	-0.24	0.00	0.00
Korea	22.2	0.18	0.13	0.02	0.02
Israel	22.1	0.57	0.41	0.02	0.13
Switzerland	21.8	-0.05	-0.01	-0.02	-0.02
Mexico	20.1	0.33	0.35	0.00	-0.02
New Zealand	17.9	0.33	0.33	0.00	0.00
Chile	7.0	0.00	0.00	0.00	0.00
Unweighted average OECD-Average	36.0	-0.07	-0.09	0.04	-0.01

Note: Single individual without children at the income level of the average worker.

1. Countries ranked by decreasing total tax wedge.
2. Due to rounding, the changes in tax wedge in column (2) may differ by one hundredth of a percentage point from the sum of columns (3)-(5). For Denmark, the Green Check (cash benefit) contributes to the difference as it is not included in columns (3)-(5).
3. Includes payroll taxes where applicable.

Source: Country submissions, *OECD Economic Outlook Volume 2016* (No. 100).

StatLink http://dx.doi.org/10.1787/888933460943

increase. The largest increase in income taxes as a percentage of labour costs was in Greece (0.67 percentage points), as a result of the reduction in the basic tax credit.

By contrast, higher social security contributions account for virtually all of the increased tax wedge in Finland, Germany, Japan and the Netherlands. Increasing employer social security contributions account for the largest part in the increase in the tax wedges in the Netherlands[3] (0.47 percentage points) and in Finland (0.44 percentage points). The increase in Germany's tax wedge is mainly driven by higher employee social security contributions (0.17 percentage points).

Table 1.2 and Figure 1.1 show the constituent components of the tax wedge in 2016, i.e. income tax, employee and employer social security contributions (including payroll taxes

Table 1.2. **Income tax plus employee and employer social security contributions**

As % of labour costs, 2016

Country[1]	Total tax wedge[2]	Income tax	Social security contributions		Labour costs[4]
			Employee	Employer[3]	
	(1)	(2)	(3)	(4)	(5)
Belgium	54.0	20.8	10.9	22.3	74 913
Switzerland	21.8	10.0	5.9	5.9	74 439
Germany	49.4	15.9	17.3	16.2	73 683
Luxembourg	38.4	16.2	11.4	10.8	73 489
Austria	47.1	10.8	13.9	22.4	71 776
Netherlands	37.5	15.2	12.2	10.1	70 665
Norway	36.2	17.5	7.3	11.5	67 823
France	48.1	10.8	10.5	26.8	65 294
Iceland	34.0	26.9	0.3	6.8	63 384
Sweden	42.8	13.6	5.3	23.9	62 359
Australia	28.6	23.0	0.0	5.6	60 112
Finland	43.8	17.9	7.1	18.7	59 663
United Kingdom	30.8	12.6	8.4	9.7	58 714
Japan	32.4	6.8	12.5	13.1	57 882
Denmark	36.5	35.9	0.0	0.8	57 759
United States	31.7	16.9	7.1	7.7	56 956
Italy	47.8	16.4	7.2	24.2	55 609
Korea	22.2	5.2	7.6	9.4	54 053
Spain	39.5	11.6	4.9	23.0	52 319
Ireland	27.1	13.8	3.6	9.7	49 547
Canada	31.4	13.8	6.8	10.8	45 998
Greece	40.2	7.7	12.6	19.9	41 169
New Zealand	17.9	17.9	0.0	0.0	39 687
Israel	22.1	9.4	7.5	5.3	39 359
Portugal	41.5	13.4	8.9	19.2	37 058
Slovenia	42.7	9.8	19.0	13.9	36 499
Czech Republic	43.0	9.4	8.2	25.4	34 697
Estonia	38.9	12.5	1.2	25.3	34 173
Turkey	38.1	10.4	12.8	14.9	33 017
Hungary	48.2	11.7	14.4	22.2	32 930
Poland	35.8	6.1	15.3	14.4	31 931
Slovak Republic	41.5	7.5	10.2	23.8	29 981
Latvia	42.6	15.0	8.5	19.1	25 391
Chile	7.0	0.0	7.0	0.0	20 517
Mexico	20.1	8.5	1.2	10.4	14 638
Unweighted average					
OECD-Average	36.0	13.4	8.2	14.4	50 214

Note: Single individual without children at the income level of the average worker.

1. Countries ranked by decreasing labour costs.
2. Due to rounding, the total in column(1) may differ by one tenth of a percentage point from the sum of columns (2)-(4). For Denmark, the Green Check (cash benefit) contributes to the difference as it is not included in columns (2)-(4).
3. Includes payroll taxes where applicable.
4. US dollars with equal purchasing power.

Source: Country submissions, *OECD Economic Outlook Volume 2016* (No. 100).

StatLink http://dx.doi.org/10.1787/888933460952

Figure 1.1. **Income tax plus employee and employer social security contributions, 2016**

As a % of labour costs

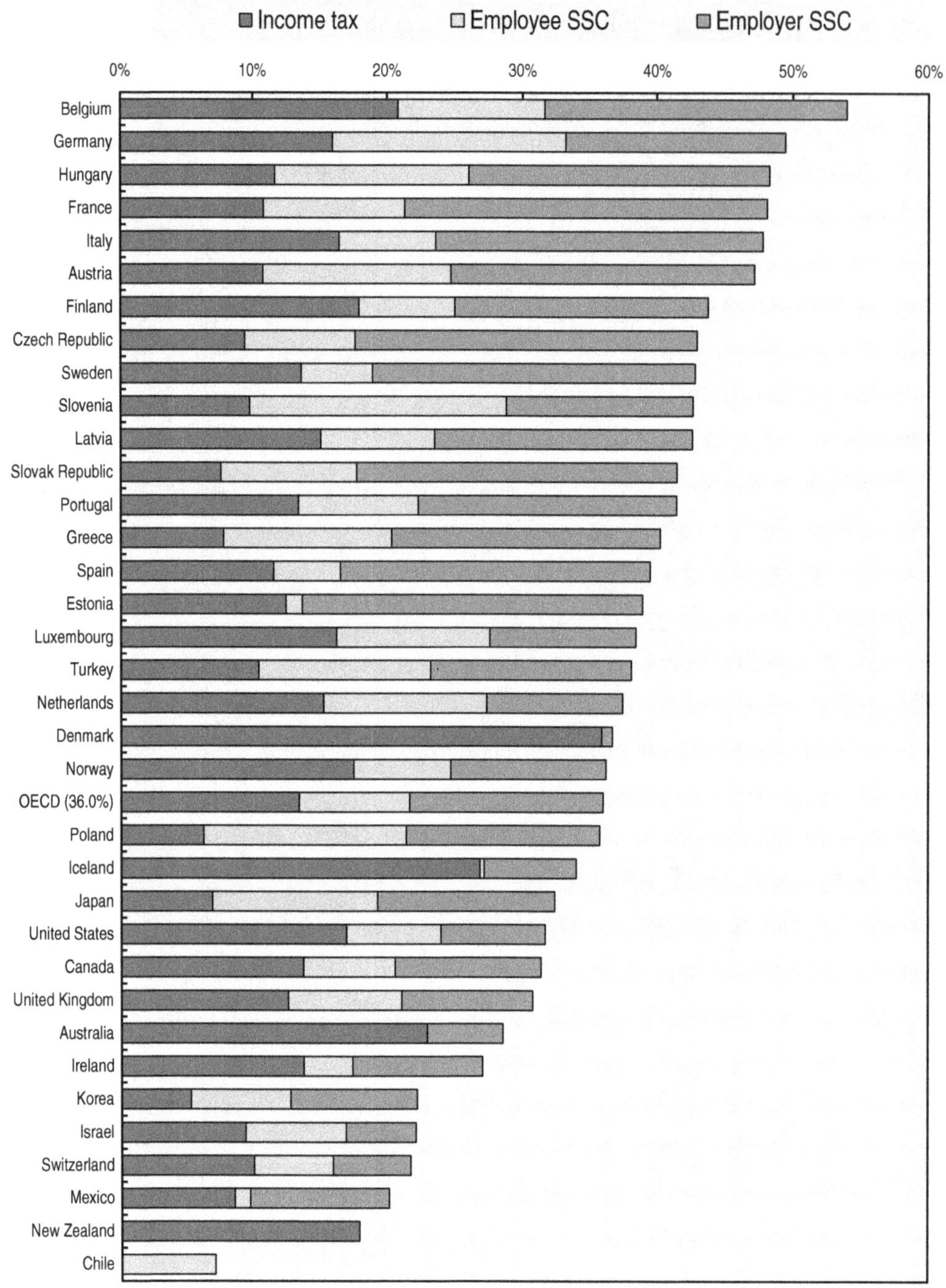

Notes:

Single individual without children at the income level of the average worker.

Includes payroll taxes where applicable.

StatLink http://dx.doi.org/10.1787/888933460105

where applicable), as a percentage of labour costs for the average worker without children. The labour costs in Table 1.2 are expressed in US dollars with equivalent purchasing power.

The percentage of labour costs paid in income tax varies considerably within OECD countries. The lowest figures are in Chile (zero) and Korea (5.2%). The highest values are in

Denmark (35.9%), with Australia, Belgium and Iceland all over 20%. The percentage of labour costs paid in employee social security contributions also varies widely, ranging from zero in Australia, Denmark and New Zealand to 17.3% in Germany and 19.0% in Slovenia. Employers in France pay 26.8% of total labour costs in social security contributions, the highest amongst OECD countries. The corresponding figures are also more than 20% in nine other countries – Austria, Belgium, the Czech Republic, Estonia, Hungary, Italy, the Slovak Republic, Spain and Sweden.

As a percentage of labour costs, the total of employee and employer social security contributions exceeds 20% in more than half of the OECD countries. It also represents at least one-third of total labour costs in eight OECD countries: Austria, Belgium, the Czech Republic, France, Germany, Hungary, the Slovak Republic and Slovenia.

Personal average tax rates

The personal average tax rate is defined as income tax plus employee social security contributions as a percentage of gross wage earnings. Table 1.3 and Figure 1.2 show the personal average tax rates in 2016 for a single worker without children at the average earnings level. The average workers' gross wage earnings figures in Table 1.3 are expressed in terms of US dollars with equivalent purchasing power. Figure 1.2 provides a graphical representation of the personal average tax rate decomposed between income tax and employee social security contributions.

Table 1.3 and Figure 1.2 show that on average, the personal average tax rate for a single worker at average earnings in OECD countries is 25.5%. Belgium at 40.7% of gross earnings has the highest rate with Denmark and Germany being the only other countries with rates of more than 35%. Chile and Mexico have the lowest personal average tax rates at 7.0 and 10.8% of gross average earnings respectively. Korea is the only other country with a rate of less than 15%.

The impact of taxes and benefits on a worker's take-home pay varies greatly among OECD countries. Such wide variations in the size and make-up of tax wedges reflect in part differences in:

- the overall ratio of aggregate tax revenues to Gross Domestic Product; and,
- the share of personal income tax and social security contributions in national tax mixes.

The mix of income tax and social security contributions paid out of gross wage earnings also varies greatly between countries as illustrated in Figure 1.2.

In 2016, the share of income tax within the personal average tax rate is higher than the share of the employee social security contributions for 23 of the 35 OECD member countries. No employee social security contributions are levied in Australia, Denmark and New Zealand and the rates are 4% or less of gross earnings in Estonia, Iceland, Ireland and Mexico. In contrast, the single worker at the average wage level paid substantially more (i.e., over 6 percentage points) in employee social security contributions than in personal income tax in five countries – Greece, Japan, Poland, Slovenia and Chile. In Chile, the average worker did not pay personal income tax in 2016. In six countries – the Czech Republic, France, Germany, Israel, Korea and Turkey – the shares of personal income tax and employee social security contributions as percentages of gross earnings are very close (i.e., differences of 3 percentage points or less).

Table 1.3. **Income tax plus employee social security contributions, 2016**
As % of gross wage earnings

Country[1]	Total payment[2]	Income tax	Empoyee social security contributions	Gross wage earnings[3]
	(1)	(2)	(3)	(4)
Switzerland	16.9	10.7	6.2	70 077
Luxembourg	31.0	18.1	12.8	65 522
Netherlands	30.4	16.9	13.5	63 549
Germany	39.7	19.0	20.7	61 750
Norway	27.9	19.7	8.2	60 020
Iceland	29.2	28.9	0.3	59 044
Belgium	40.7	26.8	14.0	58 214
Denmark	36.2	36.2	0.0	57 310
Australia	24.3	24.3	0.0	56 727
Austria	31.9	13.9	18.0	55 680
United Kingdom	23.3	14.0	9.4	53 020
United States	26.0	18.3	7.7	52 543
Japan	22.2	7.8	14.4	50 278
Korea	14.1	5.7	8.4	48 979
Finland	30.8	22.0	8.8	48 479
France	29.1	14.8	14.3	47 817
Sweden	24.9	17.9	7.0	47 450
Ireland	19.2	15.2	4.0	44 737
Italy	31.1	21.6	9.5	42 166
Canada	23.1	15.4	7.7	41 021
Spain	21.4	15.0	6.4	40 276
New Zealand	17.9	17.9	0.0	39 687
Israel	17.8	9.9	7.9	37 286
Greece	25.4	9.6	15.8	32 974
Slovenia	33.4	11.3	22.1	31 437
Portugal	27.6	16.6	11.0	29 946
Turkey	27.3	12.3	15.0	28 099
Poland	25.0	7.2	17.8	27 343
Czech Republic	23.6	12.6	11.0	25 893
Hungary	33.5	15.0	18.5	25 627
Estonia	18.3	16.7	1.6	25 540
Slovak Republic	23.2	9.8	13.4	22 852
Latvia	29.1	18.6	10.5	20 537
Chile	7.0	0.0	7.0	20 517
Mexico	10.8	9.5	1.4	13 112
Unweighted average				
OECD-Average	25.5	15.7	9.8	43 015

Note: Single individual without children at the income level of the average worker.
1. Countries ranked by decreasing gross wage earnings.
2. Due to rounding total may differ by one tenth of a percentage point from aggregate of columns for income tax and social security contributions
3. US dollars with equal purchasing power.

Source: Country submissions, *OECD Economic Outlook Volume 2016* (No. 100).

StatLink http://dx.doi.org/10.1787/888933460962

Family tax rates

Table 1.4 compares the tax wedges for a one-earner married couple with two children and a single individual without children, at average earnings levels. These tax wedges varied widely across OECD countries in 2016 (see columns 1 and 2). The size of the tax wedge for the family is generally lower than the one observed for the individual without

Figure 1.2. **Percentage of gross wage earnings paid in income tax and employee social security contributions, 2016**

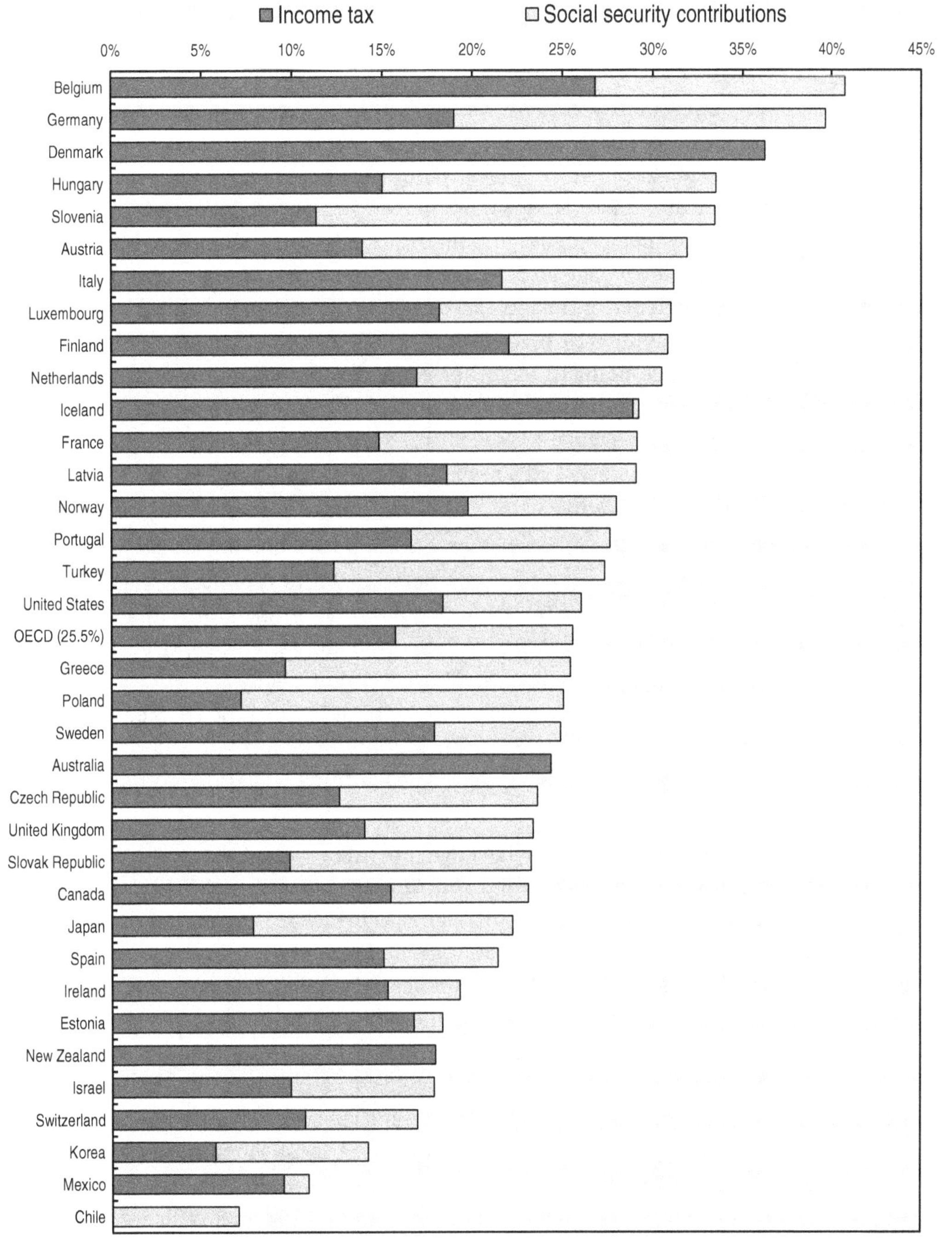

Notes:

Countries ranked by decreasing tax burden.

Single workers at the income level of the average worker.

StatLink http://dx.doi.org/10.1787/888933460115

children, since many OECD countries provide a fiscal benefit to families with children through advantageous tax treatment and/or cash transfers. Hence, the OECD average tax wedge for the one-earner couple with two children was 26.6% compared to 36.0% for the single average worker.

The tax savings realised by a one-earner married couple compared to a single worker are greater than 20% of labour costs in Luxembourg, and greater than 15% of labour costs in six other countries – Belgium, Canada, the Czech Republic, Germany, Ireland and Slovenia. The tax burdens are the same in Chile and Mexico and different by less than three percentage points in Greece, Israel, Korea and Turkey (see columns 1 and 2).

In 28 of the 35 OECD countries, there was only a small change (not exceeding plus or minus one percentage point) in the tax wedge of an average one-earner married couple with two children between 2015 and 2016 (see column 3). There is no change in Chile. There is an increase of greater than 1 percentage point in New Zealand (1.24) only. In 2016, the tax wedge for families fell by 2.68 percentage points in Austria mainly due to the reformed income tax schedule. The tax wedge also decreased by more than two percentage points in Portugal (2.50) as a consequence of the increased child tax credit. It decreased by more than one percentage point in Belgium (1.73), in Hungary (1.60) and in Ireland (1.03). It decreased by less than one percentage point in six other countries: Estonia, France, Italy, Norway, Switzerland and Turkey. By comparison, the change in the tax wedge of a single taxpayer without children at the average wage level was greater than one percentage point in three OECD countries (Austria, Belgium and Greece). Detailed explanations on the latter are given in the section on the tax wedge above.

A comparison of the changes in tax wedges between 2015 and 2016 for the one-earner married couples with two children and single persons without children, at the average wage level, is shown in column 5 of Table 1.4. The fiscal preference for families increased in twelve OECD member countries: Austria, Belgium, Estonia, France, Greece, Hungary, Ireland, Israel, Italy, Portugal, Switzerland and Turkey. Additionally, the effects of changes in the tax system on the tax wedge were the same for both family types in Mexico. In seven other countries; Australia, Italy, Japan, Korea, Luxembourg, Spain and the United States, the change in the tax wedge for the two family types differed by 0.05 percentage points or less. There were no changes at all in Chile.

Figure 1.3 compares the net personal average tax rate for the average worker between single individuals and a one-earner married couple with two children. These results show the same pattern as the tax wedge results. This is because employer social security contributions, which are not taken into account in the former but included in the latter, are independent of family type. Due to tax reliefs and cash benefits for families with children, the one-earner married couple's disposable income is higher than the single individual's by 20% or more of earnings in six countries – Luxembourg (25.1%), Canada (21.9%), Slovenia (21.8%) the Czech Republic (21.2%), Ireland (20.8%) and Belgium (19.8%). In contrast, the disposable income is higher by less than 10% of earnings in twelve countries – Spain (7.3%), Sweden (6.4%), Japan (6.1%), the Netherlands and Poland (5.8%), Finland (5.6%), the United Kingdom (5.5%), Norway (5.2%), Israel (2.9%), Greece and Korea (both 2.4%) and Turkey (2.0%). The burden is the same for both family types in Chile and in Mexico. It is also interesting to note that when cash benefits are taken into account, the net personal average tax rate for the average one-earner married couples with two children in Ireland becomes negative (-1.6%) as cash benefits exceed the income tax and social security contributions.

Wages

Table 1.5 shows the gross wage earnings in national currency of the average worker in each OECD member country for 2015 and 2016. The figures for 2016 are estimated by the OECD Secretariat by applying the change in the compensation per employee in the total

Table 1.4. **Comparison of total tax wedge by family type**

As % of labour costs

Country[1]	Family[2] total tax wedge 2016	Single[3] total tax wedge 2016	Annual change 2016/15 (in percentage points)		
			Family tax wedge	Single tax wedge	Difference between single and family (4)-(3)
	(1)	(2)	(3)	(4)	(5)
France	40.0	48.1	-0.47	-0.34	0.13
Finland	39.2	43.8	0.30	0.22	-0.08
Italy	38.6	47.8	-0.10	-0.08	0.02
Belgium	38.6	54.0	-1.73	-1.32	0.41
Greece	38.3	40.2	0.73	1.06	0.34
Sweden	38.0	42.8	0.31	0.21	-0.11
Austria	36.5	47.1	-2.68	-2.47	0.21
Turkey	36.4	38.1	-0.33	-0.09	0.24
Germany	34.0	49.4	0.17	0.05	-0.11
Spain	33.8	39.5	0.10	0.09	-0.01
Hungary	33.7	48.2	-1.60	-0.78	0.82
Netherlands	32.2	37.5	0.65	0.40	-0.24
Latvia	31.7	42.6	0.30	0.10	-0.20
Norway	31.6	36.2	-0.24	-0.40	-0.16
Poland	30.8	35.8	0.23	0.05	-0.18
Slovak Republic	28.9	41.5	0.42	0.12	-0.30
Portugal	28.2	41.5	-2.50	-0.60	1.90
Estonia	28.1	38.9	-0.53	-0.12	0.41
Czech Republic	27.2	43.0	0.45	0.19	-0.26
Japan	27.1	32.4	0.15	0.12	-0.03
Denmark	26.1	36.5	0.16	0.02	-0.14
United Kingdom	25.8	30.8	0.05	-0.03	-0.08
Slovenia	23.9	42.7	0.22	0.09	-0.13
Iceland	23.9	34.0	0.73	-0.21	-0.94
United States	20.8	31.7	0.18	0.15	-0.03
Mexico	20.1	20.1	0.33	0.33	0.00
Korea	20.0	22.2	0.23	0.18	-0.05
Israel	19.4	22.1	0.49	0.57	0.07
Australia	18.1	28.6	0.26	0.23	-0.03
Luxembourg	16.1	38.4	0.07	0.05	-0.02
Canada	11.9	31.4	0.86	-0.13	-0.99
Switzerland	9.1	21.8	-0.10	-0.05	0.05
Ireland	8.3	27.1	-1.03	-0.24	0.79
Chile	7.0	7.0	0.00	0.00	0.00
New Zealand	6.2	17.9	1.24	0.33	-0.90
Unweighted average					
OECD-Average	26.6	36.0	-0.08	-0.07	0.01

1. Countries ranked by decreasing tax wedge of the family.
2. One earner married couple with two children and earnings at the average wage level.
3. Single individual without children and earnings at the average wage level.

Source: Country submissions, *OECD Economic Outlook Volume 2016* (No. 100).

StatLink http://dx.doi.org/10.1787/888933460977

economy as presented in the OECD Economic Outlook (No 100) database to the final average wage values provided by OECD member countries. More information on the values of the average wage and the estimation methodology is included in the Annex of this Report.

The annual change in 2016 – shown in column 3 – varied between a decrease of 0.6% in Switzerland and an increase of 18.0% in Turkey. To a large extent, the changes reflect the

Figure 1.3. **Income tax plus employee contributions less cash benefits, 2016**

As % of gross wage earnings, by family-type

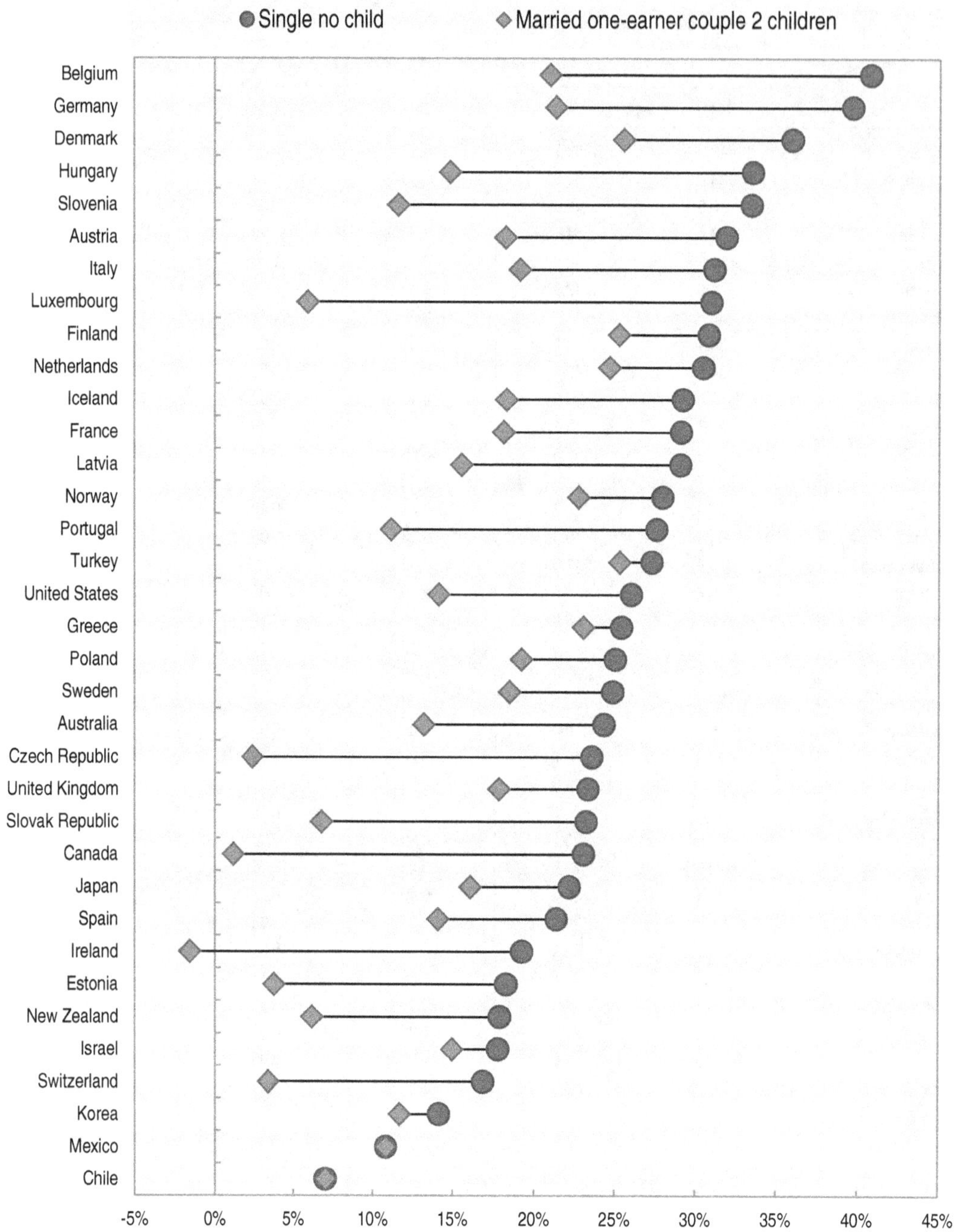

Notes:

Countries ranked by decreasing rates for single taxpayer without children.

Family types: a single individual without children and earnings at the average wage level and a one earner married couple with two children and earnings at the average wage level.

StatLink http://dx.doi.org/10.1787/888933460128

different inflation levels of individual OECD countries – see column 4 of Table 1.5. The annual change in real wage levels (before personal income tax and employee social security contributions) is within the range of -2% to +2% for 23 countries; see column 5 of Table 1.5. Twelve countries show changes that are outside this range: Mexico (2.1%),

Table 1.5. **Comparison of wage levels**

Country	Gross wage in national currency		Annual change 2016/15 (percentage)			
	2015	2016	Gross wage	Inflation[1]	Real wage before tax	Change in personal average tax rate[2]
	(1)	(2)	(3)	(4)	(5)	(6)
Australia	80 774	82 114	1.7	1.3	0.3	1.0
Austria	43 911	44 409	1.1	0.9	0.2	-9.0
Belgium	46 479	46 570	0.2	1.7	-1.5	-3.0
Canada	50 350	50 997	1.3	1.5	-0.2	-0.7
Chile	7 557 360	8 003 491	5.9	3.9	1.9	0.0
Czech Republic	319 162	330 072	3.4	0.6	2.9	1.1
Denmark	403 600	412 555	2.2	0.3	1.9	0.2
Estonia	13 045	13 640	4.6	0.8	3.7	-0.9
Finland	43 382	43 816	1.0	0.3	0.7	-0.3
France	37 648	38 049	1.1	0.3	0.8	0.7
Germany	46 800	47 809	2.2	0.3	1.9	0.2
Greece	20 107	20 074	-0.2	0.1	-0.2	4.8
Hungary	3 169 128	3 312 081	4.5	0.1	4.4	-2.9
Iceland	7 644 000	8 456 409	10.6	1.7	8.8	-0.5
Ireland	34 674	35 592	2.6	0.0	2.7	-1.4
Israel[3]	137 990	142 247	3.1	-0.5	3.6	2.8
Italy	30 654	30 642	0.0	-0.1	0.0	0.0
Japan	5 083 906	5 110 601	0.5	-0.3	0.8	0.4
Korea	42 908 652	43 857 243	2.2	0.9	1.3	1.3
Latvia	9 588	10 173	6.1	-0.2	6.3	0.4
Luxembourg	55 858	56 197	0.6	-0.1	0.7	0.4
Mexico	107 551	112 827	4.9	2.8	2.1	3.8
Netherlands	50 009	50 853	1.7	0.0	1.7	0.3
New Zealand	56 110	57 649	2.7	0.5	2.2	1.9
Norway	551 198	564 218	2.4	3.6	-1.2	-1.6
Poland	46 136	47 782	3.6	-0.8	4.4	0.2
Portugal	17 298	17 521	1.3	0.7	0.6	-2.6
Slovak Republic	10 661	10 918	2.4	-0.5	3.0	0.7
Slovenia	18 092	18 292	1.1	-0.2	1.3	0.3
Spain	26 475	26 710	0.9	-0.3	1.2	0.5
Sweden	414 105	423 065	2.2	0.9	1.2	1.1
Switzerland	86 017	85 536	-0.6	-0.4	-0.2	-0.2
Turkey	31 191	36 806	18.0	7.9	9.4	-0.4
United Kingdom	35 947	36 571	1.7	0.6	1.1	-0.3
United States	51 509	52 543	2.0	1.2	0.8	0.2

1. Estimated percentage change in the total consumer price index.
2. Difference in the personal average tax rate of the average worker (single without children) between 2016 and 2015.
Source: Country submissions, *OECD Economic Outlook Volume 2016* (No. 100).

StatLink http://dx.doi.org/10.1787/888933460988

New Zealand (2.2%), Ireland (2.7%), the Czech Republic (2.9%), the Slovak Republic (3.0%), Israel (3.6%), Estonia (3.7%), Hungary and Poland (both with 4.4%), Latvia (6.3%), Iceland (8.8%) and Turkey (9.4%). In 29 out of the 35 OECD countries, taxpayers had higher real post-tax income in 2016 than in 2015 as real wages before tax increased faster or decreased slower than personal average tax rates (see column 6), the exceptions being Australia, Greece, Italy, Korea, Mexico and Switzerland. In Australia, the real wage before tax increased by 0.3%, whereas the personal average tax rate increased by 1.0%. In Greece, while the real wage before tax decreased by 0.2%, the personal average tax rate rose by 4.8%. In Mexico, the increase in the personal average tax rate was higher than the increase of the real gross wage;

the percentage changes were respectively 3.8% and 2.1%. Finally, in Italy, Korea and Switzerland, the percentage changes were the same in both the real wage before tax and the personal average tax rate.

When comparing wage levels, it is important to note that the definition of average wage earnings can vary between countries due to data limitations. For instance, some countries do not include the wages earned by supervisory and managerial workers and not all countries exclude wage earnings from part-time workers (see Table A.4 in the Annex).

Table 1.6 provides more information on whether the average wages for the years 2000 to 2016 are based on industry sectors C-K inclusive with reference to the International Standard Industrial Classification of All Economic Activities, Revision 3 (ISIC Rev.3) or industry sectors B-N inclusive with reference to the International Standard Industrial Classification of All Economic Activities, Revision 4 (ISIC Rev.4).

Most OECD countries have calculated average wage earnings on the basis of sectors B-N in the ISIC Rev. 4 Industry Classification at least since 2008. The exceptions are Chile and Mexico. Some countries have revised the average wage values for prior years as well. Average wage values based on the ISIC Rev. 4 Classification or any variant are available for all years for Australia, Canada, the Czech Republic, Estonia, Finland, Greece, Hungary, Iceland, Italy, Japan, Latvia, the Slovak Republic, Slovenia, Spain and Switzerland.

Australia (for all years) and New Zealand (years 2004 to 2016) have provided values based on the 2006 ANZSIC industry classification, divisions B to N, which substantially overlaps the ISIC Rev.4, sectors B to N. For New Zealand, the years prior to 2004 continue to be based on sectors C-K in ANZSIC. Turkey has provided values based on the NACE Rev.2 classification sectors B-N for years 2007 to 2016. Values for the years prior to 2007 are based on the average production worker wage (ISIC rev.3.1, sector D).

Table 1.6. **Average Wage Industry Classification**

	years for which ISIC Rev. 3.1 or any variant (Sectors C-K) has been used to calculate the AW	years for which ISIC Rev. 4 or any variant (Sectors B-N) has been used to calculate the AW
Australia[1]		2000-16
Austria[2]	2004-07	2008-16
Belgium	2000-07	2008-16
Canada		2000-16
Chile[3]	2000-16	
Czech Republic		2000-16
Denmark[4]	2000-07	2008-16
Estonia		2000-16
Finland		2000-16
France	2000-07	2008-16
Germany	2000-05	2006-16
Greece[5]		2000-16
Hungary		2000-16
Iceland[6]		2000-16
Ireland[7]	2000-07	2008-16
Israel[8]	2000-12	2013-16
Italy		2000-16
Japan		2000-16
Korea[9]	2000-07	2008-16
Latvia[10]		2000-16
Luxembourg	2000-04	2005-16
Mexico[11]		

Table 1.6. **Average Wage Industry Classification** *(cont.)*

	years for which ISIC Rev. 3.1 or any variant (Sectors C-K) has been used to calculate the AW	years for which ISIC Rev. 4 or any variant (Sectors B-N) has been used to calculate the AW
Netherlands[12]	2000-07	2008-11
New Zealand[13]	2000-03	2004-16
Norway	2000-08	2009-16
Poland	2000-06	2007-16
Portugal	2000-05	2006-16
Slovak Republic[14]		2000-16
Slovenia		2000-16
Spain		2000-16
Sweden	2000-07	2008-16
Switzerland		2000-16
Turkey[15]		2007-16
United Kingdom	2000-07	2008-16
United States	2000-06	2007-16

1. Australia: based on ANZSIC06 such that the categories substantially overlap with ISIC 4, sectors B-N.
2. Austria: 2000-03 average wage values are not based on the NACE (ISIC) classification.
3. Chile: the AW values are based on sectors C to O from years 2006 to 2016. From 2010 onwards sectors L (7522) and L (7523) are excluded.
4. Denmark: The AW values are based on sectors B-N and R-S (NACE rev 2).
5. Greece: the average annual earnings refer to full time employees for the sectors B to N of NACE Rev 2, including Division 95 and excluding Divisions 37, 39 and 75 for 2008 onwards.
6. Iceland: using national classification system that corresponds with the NACE rev. 2 classification system.
7. Ireland: values from 2000 to 2007 are based on sectors C-E (NACE). From 2008 onwards, they are based on sectors B-E (NACE rev.2).
8. Israel: Information on data for Israel: http://oe.cd/israel-disclaimer.
9. Korea: average wage values are based on 6th Korean Standard Industrial Classification (KSIC) C-K for 2000-01, 8th KISC C-M for 2002 to 2007 and 9th KISC B-N except E for 2008 onwards.
10. Latvia: Values are based on NACE rev.2 and cover the private sector that includes commercial companies with central or local government capital participation up to 50%, commercial companies of all types without central or local government capital participation, individual merchants, and peasant and fishermen farms with 50 and more employees.
11. Mexico: 2000-16 AW values are based on the Mexican Classification of Economic Activities (Clasificación Mexicana de Actividades Económicas (CMAE)) which is based on one of the first versions of ISIC.
12. Netherlands: The average wages from 2012 onwards include the private and the public sectors, since values on the private sectors only (sectors B to N) are not available.
13. New Zealand: see the note for Australia which applies from 2004.
14. Slovak Republic: average wage values based on ISIC Rev. 4 classification (B to N) and still include the self-employment data.
15. Turkey: the average wage is based on the average production worker wage ISIC rev. 3.1 sector D for years 2000 to 2006.

StatLink http://dx.doi.org/10.1787/888933460996

Notes

1. Not all national statistical agencies use ISIC Rev.3.1 or ISIC Rev.4 to classify industries. However, the Statistical Classification of Economic Activities in the European Community (NACE), the North American Industry Classification System (NAICS) and the Australian and New Zealand Standard Industrial Classification (ANZSIC) include a classification which is broadly in accordance with industries C-K in ISIC Rev.3.1 or industries B-N in ISIC Rev.4.
2. Non-tax compulsory payments are requited and unrequited compulsory payments to privately-managed funds, welfare agencies or social insurance schemes outside general governments and to public enterprises (*www.oecd.org/tax/tax-policy/tax-database.htm#NTCP*).
3. Following a comprehensive tax reform package, tax wedges for 6 out of the 8 household types decreased in the Netherlands in 2016, ranging from 0.16 percentage points to 2.99 percentage points.

© OECD 2017

Chapter 2

Special feature: Taxation and skills

This special feature examines how the labour income tax system can provide incentives or disincentives for workers to invest in human capital and skills. It provides effective tax rates on skills investments incorporating personal income taxes and employees' social security contributions for the sample case of a 32-year-old single worker undertaking a short course of training. Social security contributions increase the tax burden on skills compared to a scenario where only personal income taxes are considered. The tax burden on skills is also progressive; those on higher incomes and those who earn a higher return on skills investments are taxed at higher effective rates. Analysing the impact of labour taxation on skills investments should be borne in mind by policymakers when considering the taxation of labour.

The statistical data for Israel are supplied by and under the responsibility of the relevant Israeli authorities. The use of such data by the OECD is without prejudice to the status of the Golan Heights, East Jerusalem and Israeli settlements in the West Bank under the terms of international law.

Introduction

Ensuring that all individuals can develop the skills needed to productively participate in the economy is necessary for inclusive economic growth. Skills investments raise wages and employment, and so can reduce inequality while at the same time expanding the economy's productive capacity. Improving the level of skills across the economy has positive impacts for individuals and society as a whole.

The taxation of labour income has a key role to play in ensuring that individuals have the right incentives to invest in skills. The labour tax wedge in OECD countries is on average 36.0% of a single workers' income at the average wage in 2016. The key return to skills investments for workers is better jobs and better wages, so the way these returns are taxed by the labour income tax system is a central determinant of whether individuals in OECD countries face the right incentives to invest in skills.

Previous work by the OECD has used the *Taxing Wages* models to analyse the impact of the tax system on incentives to invest in skills and to activate skills in the labour market. In particular, the Tax Policy Study *Taxation and Skills* (OECD, 2017) has outlined a series of indicators of the tax system's impact on skills. This special feature builds on the methodology presented in that study to estimate Marginal Effective Tax Rates (METRs) and Average Effective Tax Rates (AETRs) on skills investments. They measure how much taxes increase or reduce the net returns to skills investments for an individual, and are key statistics in assessing taxation and skills policies in OECD countries.

The *Taxation and Skills* study focused only on the impact of the personal income tax (PIT) on skills, and largely omitted a discussion of social security contributions (SSCs) and how they can incentivise or dis-incentivise skills investment decisions. This special feature extends the results of the OECD (2017) study by presenting results for 29 OECD countries for METRs and AETRs on skills incorporating employees' SSCs for the sample case of a 32-year-old individual undertaking a short course of job-related training.[1] Results are presented for 2011[2] Examining employees' SSCs is a key component of understanding the overall impact of the tax system on skills investment because in many OECD countries employees' SSCs make up a substantial portion of the overall labour tax wedge.

The special feature proceeds as follows. The following section briefly introduces the different channels through which the PIT and SSC systems can impact financial incentives to invest in skills; for a more in depth discussion of the ETR methodology, see OECD, 2017. The next section provides the main results for METRs and AETRs for the stylised case of a 32-year old individual engaging in a short skills investment. The penultimate section examines how these tax rates change with income. The last section concludes.

Personal income taxes, social contributions, and financial incentives to invest in skills

Taxation and spending policies create incentives or disincentives for the development and activation of skills in a variety of ways. Higher government spending support for skills can make these investments cheaper for individuals, which may cause them to invest more in skills. Conversely, higher taxes on wages can reduce the benefits of investment in skills for individuals and employers, which may induce them to invest less. Similarly, raising taxes on labour income can reduce the returns to skills investments and discourage labour market activation; this in itself will reduce incentives to invest in skills. Table 2.1 shows how the costs and returns to skills investment are shared between governments and individuals.

Table 2.1. **How the financial costs and returns to skills are apportioned**

	Government	Individuals
Costs	• Foregone taxes during periods of study • Education spending • Costs of scholarships and grants • Cost of skills tax expenditures for individuals and businesses	• Foregone after-tax earnings during education • Direct costs such as fees
Benefits	• Higher taxes paid after education • Reduced spending on social benefits, including unemployment benefits • Higher economic growth and productivity	• Higher after-tax wages • Better employment prospects • Better social and health outcomes

How the tax system can impact financial incentives to invest in skills

The METR and AETR on skills summarise the overall positive and negative effects of the tax system on the incentives of an individual to invest in skills. They can be thought of as the difference between the returns to skills in a world with taxes compared to a world without taxes. Analysing the difference in the returns to education in a world with and without taxes is the approach taken to calculating effective tax rates for physical capital by Devereux and Griffith (2003). The work undertaken by Brys and Torres (2013), and further developed in OECD (2017), to develop METRs and AETRs for skills builds on this approach. Using the *Taxing Wages* models, the tax burden on skills can be calculated for stylised examples in OECD countries.

The difference between the METR and the AETR is a function of the returns to education with and without taxes. In the marginal case, this difference is measured when an individual earns just enough returns on their skills investment to break even (i.e. when the after-tax returns are equal to the costs borne by the individual). The tax burden on such a breakeven skills investment is the METR. The AETR is the difference between the value of a skills investment with and without taxes assuming some other (usually higher) level of skills returns.

These two tax rates are a function of how the tax system both subsidises the costs of an investment in skills, and taxes away the returns to skills. Considering costs first, it can be noted that PITs and SSCs reduce the cost of investing in skills by reducing foregone earnings, a key cost component of a skills investment. Skills investments are time-consuming, which reduces the time available to work and therefore reduces income. Foregone income is often a significant cost of skills investments. However, the amount of income foregone during education is offset by the fact that the government also foregoes the taxes which would have been paid by the individual on this income. This means that the tax system reduces the cost of skills investments relative to what would be the case in a world without taxes, which in turn means that the rate at which foregone earnings would have been taxed is a key component of the METR and AETR.

A second channel by which the tax system impacts the financial incentives to invest in skills is through tax expenditures designed to offset the direct costs of skills. Direct costs of skills investments are the costs other than foregone earnings, and include tuition fees, books and materials. These skills tax expenditures can come in the form of reductions in taxable income of the amounts spent on education or reductions in tax liability in some proportion to education spending. They can also come in the form of tax benefits that reduce or exempt scholarship income from taxation. They can also come in the form of lower levels of PITs or SSCs rates on student wage income. The tax system therefore reduces the cost of skills in two ways. Reduced taxes offset foregone earnings, and tax expenditures can help offset direct costs. As these forms of tax offsetting increase in value, the METR and AETR on skills fall.

A third channel through which the tax system impacts incentives to invest in skills is by reducing the returns to skills by taxing them away. Individuals can earn more after education – they earn an "earnings premium" for their extra skills. These returns are taxed away through PITs and SSCs, reducing the returns to skills. In addition, tax progressivity implies that those whose earnings increase more after a skills investment pay taxes at steadily higher rates. In addition to a fraction of the returns to skills being taxed away, which might occur in a flat-rate tax system, tax progressivity means that a steadily higher fraction of the returns is taxed away. Increasing the tax rate on the earnings increment will increase the METR and AETR. Higher skills may also increase a worker's employment prospects, but this channel has not been included in the Taxation and Skills models.

In sum, the tax system affects the financial incentives to invest in skills both positively and negatively. It reduces the costs of skills but also reduces the returns; the former through the tax rate on foregone earnings (TFE) and skills tax expenditures (STEs), and the latter through the tax rate on the earnings increment (TEI). Each of these components can be calculated using the *Taxing Wages* models. These three components will be important in explaining the results in the next sections.

The relative value of the TFE, STEs and the TEI is a function of the PIT and SSC tax schedules, which in turn drive the effective tax rates on skills. In a proportional tax system for example, the marginal tax rate on labour is the same regardless of the income level. This means that the TFE and the TEI will be the same in such a system. If the direct costs of a skills investment are fully tax deductible, then the tax system should be neutral with respect to skills investments: the METR on skills will be zero. This is because the costs of a skills investment are being subsidised by the tax system at the same rate at which the returns to skills are being taxed away. Moreover, this will be the case whether the tax rate is low or high. At a high tax rate, the TEI and TFE will both be high. At a low tax rate, the TEI and the TFE will both be low. In both cases, where the rate at which the tax system reduces costs in the same way as the rate at which it taxes away returns, the tax system is neutral with regard to the skills investment. In such instances skills investments that would be profi from the individual's perspective in the absence of taxes will still be profitable in the presence of taxes (Brys and Torres, 2013).

Both the AETR and METR are weighted averages of these positive and negative effects of the tax system on incentives to invest in skills, where the weight depends on the level of the earnings increment. Where returns to skills are high, the way these returns are taxed is more important. In such cases the tax rate on the earnings increment is a larger determinant of the overall effective tax rate on skills. Where returns are low, the costs of skills come to matter more. In these cases, the impact of the tax system on foregone earnings is a larger determinant. These impacts are summarised in Table 2.2.

Table 2.2. **Components of the METR and AETR**

Name	Effect on METR and AETR	Dominates the METR and AETR when:
Tax expenditures for skills costs	Decreases	Direct costs of skills are high
Tax rate on foregone earnings	Decreases	Foregone earnings are high
Tax rate on earnings increment	Increases	Returns to skills are high

How employees' social security contributions can impact financial incentives to invest in skills

SSCs are a significant factor to take into account when analysing the financial incentives to invest in skills. This report shows that in 2016 for a single childless individual earning the average wage, an average of 9.8% of pre-tax income is paid in employees' SSCs in OECD countries. This is compared to 15.7% in income being paid in the form of PIT. Given the size of employees' SSCs in the overall tax wedge on labour, employees' SSCs may significantly alter the financial incentives to invest in skills.

Some of the channels through which employees' SSCs can impact skills are the same as in the case of the PIT. SSCs can increase the TFE and so reduce the tax burden on skills. They can also increase the TEI and so increase the overall taxation on skills. In addition, there may be tax expenditures for skills that exist specifically in the SSC system, such as reduced SSC rates on student income.

The impact of employees' SSCs on incentives to invest in skills may also differ from the impact of PIT in a variety of ways. SSCs can be less progressive than income taxes, as they are generally levied at a flat rate. A previous *Taxing Wages* special feature finds that for single taxpayers, the progressivity of the labour income tax system when considering income taxes alone differed from the progressivity of the labour income tax when PIT and SSCs were combined (OECD, 2013a).

Progressivity of the PIT and SSC schedule will increase the effective taxation of skills investments, as higher returns from skills investments will be taxed away at higher rates, reducing the returns and the incentives to invest in skills. The *Taxation and Skills* Tax Policy Study (OECD, 2017) has pointed out that it is the "local" progressivity of the tax system which is important in assessing the tax impact on incentives to invest in skills. The joint effect of the PIT and the SSC schedule on local progressivity (i.e. at different earning levels) will therefore have an impact on the financial incentives to invest in skills.

SSCs are also important because they entitle taxpayers to social benefits. Income taxes alter the returns to skills investments in part by taxing them away, reducing the increase in after-tax income that a taxpayer earns after increasing their skills. SSCs do this as well; taxpayers pay more SSCs when their earnings rise, so the increase in after-tax income that comes with a skills investment is reduced. However the increased SSCs paid often also increase a taxpayers' entitlement to social benefits. These can include unemployment insurance, pensions or disability benefits. These positive impacts of increased skills on increased future social benefits through the mechanism of paying increased SSCs are not accounted for in this model. This means that the negative impact of the SSC system on financial incentives to invest in skills may be overstated by the results in this special feature. This is particularly the case for those countries where SSCs form a significant part of the labour income tax wedge, and where social benefits received are closely tied to contributions paid. In this respect, the results presented in this special feature should therefore be interpreted with caution. Incorporating these impacts is challenging, as the relationship between SSCs paid and benefit entitlement is complex and highly non-linear in many OECD countries. These issues are left for future research.

A further channel through which SSCs may impact the financial incentives to invest in skills in a way that is different from the impact of PIT is through impacts on employment. As is well known, high taxes on labour can introduce barriers to the activation of skills in the labour market by reducing the returns to work and the returns to hiring new workers (OECD, 2011). But labour supply responses may differ with respect to PIT and SSCs. Lehmann et al. (2013), for example, provide evidence that labour supply responses are different for PIT and payroll taxes. These tax-induced disincentives to participation in the formal labour market also significantly reduce the incentives to develop skills. This means that the impact of SSCs on labour activation and on incentives to invest in skills may be different from those of PIT.

METRs and AETRs incorporating social security contributions

This section presents the key results of the special feature; the tax rates on skills incorporating employees' SSCs. Results in this section are presented for a taxpayer at the average wage. In the next section, results are presented for an individual at 70%, 100% and 170% of the average wage. Results are presented at these levels to maintain comparability with the results presented in the *Taxation and Skills* study, while at the same time approximating the income levels used in *Taxing Wages*. This special feature focuses on employees' SSCs, and does not present the results for employers' SSCs. This is in part due to the more complicated questions of economic incidence of employers' SSCs on labour, and thus on the impact of employers' SSCs on skills financing decisions.

To understand these results, it is important to understand some of the key assumptions made in the model. It is assumed that skills are financed by individuals and not employers. It is also assumed that the skills investment is not financed by borrowing; it is assumed that the skills investment is financed by an individual's prior savings. See the *Taxation and Skills* Tax Policy Study for an in-depth discussion on the assumptions underlying the model calculations.

The ETRs on skills depend on a wide variety of factors and are affected through a variety of channels. This means that the specifics of the stylised skills investment considered will also significantly drive the results. The results presented should be understood as being specific to the stylised skills scenario presented, and may not be the same for other skills scenarios in a country. For example, because the ETRs are a function of the returns to skills, they vary with the amount of time an individual will remain in the workforce. Because the foregone earnings are a key factor through which the tax system offsets the returns to skills, the individual's foregone income is a key driver of the ETRs. The additional income that will be earned after studying matters too. Individuals might be taxed differently depending on whether they are single or married, and whether they have children and dependants; the ETRs on skills depend on these factors as well.

This special feature focuses on a 32-year-old single taxpayer with no children, who undertakes a short course of job-related education and earns the average wage before making the skills investment. The results are presented based on tax systems as they existed in 2011. To incorporate the fact that earning is time-consuming, it is assumed that the individual earns 95% of the average wage over the year that they study (i.e. the worker foregoes 5% of income when following the course of training).

Part of the motivation for the use of in-career training is to further examine incentives for individuals to engage in lifelong learning. Lifelong learning is a key concern in ensuring that individuals are adaptable to technological change and globalisation (OECD, 2012). Continuous training is particularly important for individuals whose jobs are placed in jeopardy by these forces. Furthermore, continuous training is important for the development of a knowledge-based, high-productivity economy. Ensuring that the fruits of this productivity are available to all is a core part of driving an inclusive growth agenda (OECD, 2016). This motivates the particular focus on the taxation of lifelong learning.

A second motivating factor in the choice of stylised case to present the METRs is the kinds of tax provisions that exist in OECD countries. Specifically, a course of job-related training is chosen to examine the most common forms of tax support for skills in OECD countries. Many OECD countries that have tax deductions for training require that the training be related to an individual's current employment. This is designed to prevent inefficient subsidisation of skills spending that is in reality consumption spending. It also however means that in many OECD countries training that is not job-related is not tax deductible or tax-creditable.

METRs incorporating employees' social security contributions

A METR on skills is defined as the tax burden on a skills investment that just breaks even for the individual who makes the investment. Results for METRs in this scenario incorporating PIT have been presented in the previous OECD tax policy study *Taxation and Skills* (OECD, 2017). When compared to these results, the inclusion of employees' SSCs raises METRs on skills on average, as can be seen in Figure 2.1. The average METR across 29 OECD countries where only PIT is included is 9.1% for a stylised in-work training example. When employees' SSCs are included as well as PIT, the METR rises to 19.7%.

In the case where only PIT is considered, the highest METR on skills occurs in Denmark which has a METR of 41.7%. Denmark has no employees' SSCs of SSCs while income taxes are high and progressive, which explains Denmark's high income tax burden on skills. When employees' SSCs are incorporated, the highest METR can be found in Hungary with a METR of 52.4%. In the case where only PIT is considered, the lowest METR on skills can be observed for Mexico which has a METR of -49.7%. When employees' SSCs are incorporated Mexico continues to face the lowest METR, but the inclusion of SSCs causes the METR to rise slightly to -47.1%.[3]

The extent to which incorporating employees' SSCs raises METRs on skills varies by country; the sizes of the increases depend on the significance of SSCs in a given country's labour taxation system, and also on the specific shape of the SSC and PIT schedule around the average wage (where the results are measured). The highest increase in the METR on skills can be found in Austria, where METRs increased from -16.2% when only PIT is considered, to 13.5%, which is still one of the lowest METRs on skills in the sample of countries considered.

The lowest increase in the METRs is zero; this is the case in countries which levy no employees' SSCs such as Australia, Denmark, and New Zealand. Amongst those countries where an increase is recorded, employees' SSCs increase METRs by the lowest amount in the Netherlands, where they increase the METR by 0.5%.

The inclusion of employees' SSCs into the analysis can impact the METR through the TFE and the TEI; that is, through the ways in which the SSC system subsidises costs and

Figure 2.1. **Marginal effective tax rates on skills with personal income taxes alone and with both personal income taxes and employees' social security contributions, 2011**

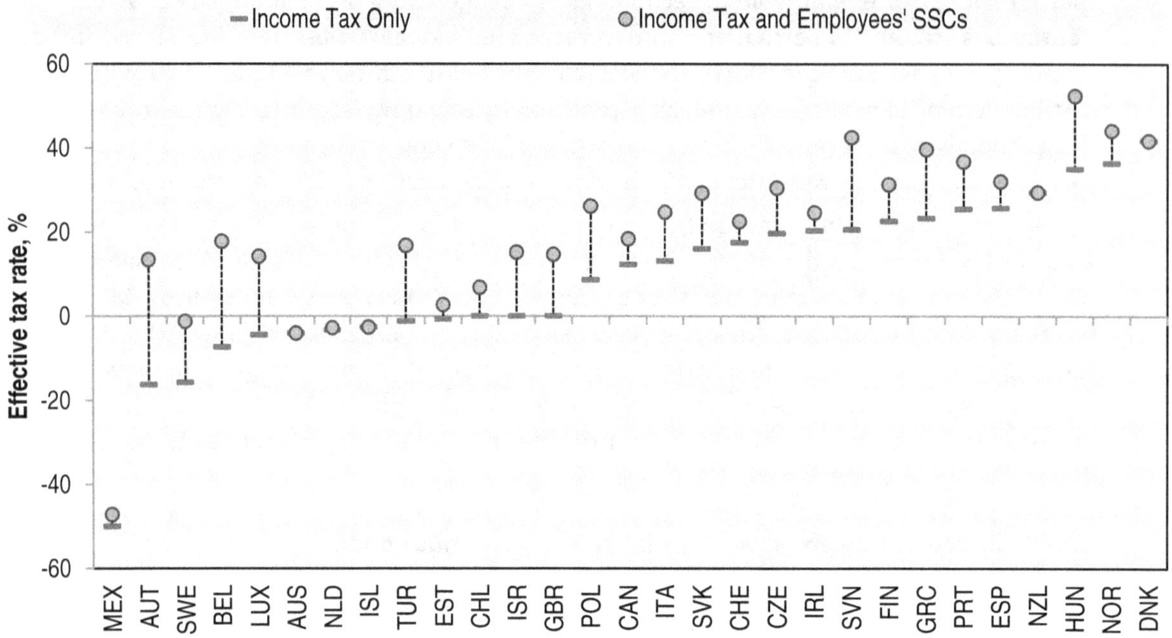

Note: Data are for a 32-year-old single taxpayer with no children, who undertakes a short course of job-related education, earning 95% of the average wage over the year while they study. This figure shows results that incorporate tax deductions for direct costs, tax exemptions for scholarship income, and reduced taxes on student wage income. STEs that subsidise parental spending on education or that subsidise firm spending on education are not included. It is assumed that the skills investment is financed wholly with savings: students do not incur any debt to make a skills investment. Data are presented for 2011.

StatLink http://dx.doi.org/10.1787/888933460135

reduces returns of skills investments. Where the rate of SSCs is flat, the inclusion of SSCs into the analysis will not alter the overall effective tax burden on skills investments. This is seldom the case, however. For example, in some instances there are ceilings above which an extra currency unit of income may not be liable for additional SSCs. This may mean that SSCs increase the TFE, but not the TEI. In these cases, accounting for SSCs may reduce the tax burden on skills substantially. While this is not observed in Figure 2.1, it may occur at other income levels depending on the location of ceilings in countries' SSC schedules.

In other cases SSC liability may rise with income. SSC schedules may be progressive due to either higher rates on higher incomes or due to allowances below which SSCs are not levied or are levied at reduced rates. In these cases, accounting for SSCs will raise the TEI by more than the increase in the TFE. In these cases, the overall effective tax rate on skills may be higher where SSCs are taken into account.

Tax expenditures also influence the differential impact of PIT and SSC systems on financial incentives to invest in skills. Skills tax expenditures in many countries often include deductibility of the costs of skills from the PIT base. This reduces the costs of skills and so reduces METRs on skills. These costs are however seldom deductible from the SSC base. This means that, holding other factors constant, AETRs and METRs are likely to be higher when SSCs are incorporated than when PIT alone is considered.

It is also important to consider the ways in which the SSC system interacts with the PIT system. In many countries, employees' SSCs are deductible from the PIT base. In this special feature the results presented for PIT factor in these deductions of SSCs from the PIT base. This approach follows that taken throughout *Taxing Wages*. When employees' SSCs are incorporated, they will add to the tax burden on the earnings increment, but this effect may be partly offset by the fact that the SSCs paid will be deductible from the PIT base and the PIT burden will be reduced. So SSCs cannot necessarily be considered to be levied directly 'on top' of the PIT schedule, as the imposition of employees' SSCs affects PIT liability as well. As PIT schedules are more progressive at lower income levels, employees' SSCs will reduce significantly the PIT that will have to be paid at lower income levels. Employees' SSCs will therefore result in a smaller increase in the TFE than that they will increase the TEI, resulting in an increase in the METR on skills investments.

AETRs incorporating social security contributions

The AETR on skills differs from the METR on skills in that while the METR examines the tax burden where an individual is just breaking even on a skills investment, the AETR examines the tax burden when an individual is earning a fixed return on a skills investment. The AETR in this skills investment scenario is based on an assumed 15% increase in earnings after a skills investment is made. So an individual that earns 100% of the average wage before a skills investment is assumed to earn 115% of the average wage afterwards.

The AETR in the case where only PIT is included has a cross-country average of 16.1% for the stylised example. This is higher than the METR, as is the case throughout the *Taxation and Skills* study. The AETR is higher than the METR because as individuals earn higher and higher earnings premiums after a skills investment, they are pushed into higher tax brackets and their returns to skills are taxed away at higher rates. In addition, an average skills investment is assumed to yield a higher pre-tax return compared to a marginal skills investment. Both factors together explain why AETRs are higher than METRs on average.

When employees' SSCs are included as well as PIT the AETR rises from an average of 16.1% to 24.9% across the countries considered, as is shown in Figure 2.2. As is the case with the METR, there are similar reasons why the AETR on skills is higher when SSCs are incorporated. However, the increase in the AETR is smaller than the increase in the METR when employees' SSCs are included. In the case where only PIT is considered, the highest AETR on skills can be found in Denmark which has an AETR of 41.7%, as is the case with a marginal skills investment. When employees' SSCs are incorporated, the highest AETR is observed in Hungary – as with the marginal case – with an AETR of 52.2%. In the case where only PIT is considered, the lowest AETR on skills is observed in Mexico which has an AETR of -11.7%. When employees' SSCs are incorporated, Mexico continues to face the lowest AETR although it slightly rises to -10.1%.

The extent to which incorporating employees' SSCs into the analysis raises AETRs on skills varies by country. As with METRs, this depends on the significance of SSCs in a given country's labour taxation system. The highest increase in the AETR on skills can be observed in Slovenia, where AETRs increased by 21.7 percentage points, from 20.6% when only PIT is considered, to 42.4%. Slovenia has one of the highest shares of SSCs in their labour taxation system, which the analysis suggests increases the financial burden on skills investments.

As with the METRs on skills, the lowest increase in the indicators is zero, which occurs in those OECD countries which have no employees' SSCs. Among those countries where an increase is recorded, SSCs increase by the lowest amount in the Netherlands, where the AETRs increase by 0.6%. This is due to the fact that the average wage is above the ceiling for most employees' SSCs in the Netherlands. Some SSCs are levied in the first two tax brackets,

Figure 2.2. **Average effective tax rates on skills with personal income taxes alone and with both personal income taxes and employees' social security contributions, 2011**

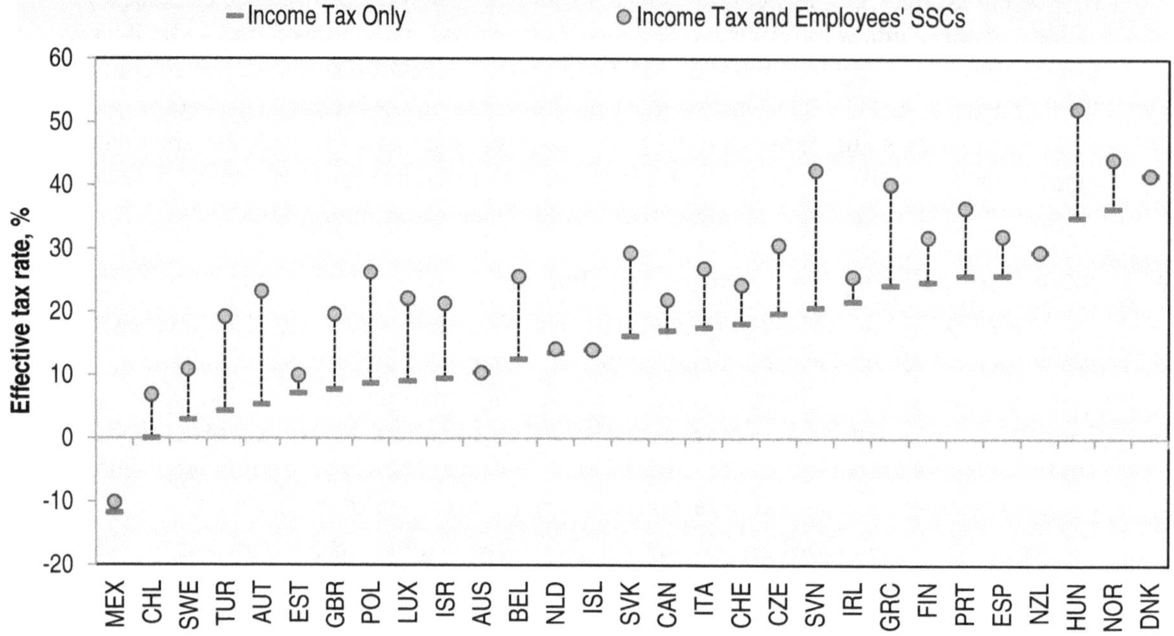

Note: Data are for a 32-year-old single taxpayer with no children, who undertakes a short course of job-related education, earning 95% of the average wage over the year while they study. This figure shows results that incorporate tax deductions for direct costs, tax exemptions for scholarship income, and reduced taxes on student wage income. STEs that subsidise parental spending on education or that subsidise firm spending on education are not included. It is assumed that the skills investment is financed wholly with savings: students do not incur any debt to make a skills investment. Data are presented for 2011.

StatLink http://dx.doi.org/10.1787/888933460148

but an individual at the average wage receiving a pay increase of 15% will pass over the ceiling for these contributions as well. This result highlights the fact that local features in the tax schedule can have substantial impacts on incentives to invest in skills with a view to increasing income. By contrast, ceilings in the SSC system may mean than effective tax rates on skills are lower for those on higher incomes than for those on lower incomes.

Progressivity of effective tax rates on skills

This section explores how the results vary depending on the income of the taxpayer making the skills investment. The previous section focused on a taxpayer earning the average wage, but highlighted the extent to which local features in the tax schedule could impact incentives to invest in skills. This suggests that comparing the tax burden on skills across the income tax schedule could be instructive. In addition it is important to examine differing incentives to invest in skills across income levels. OECD research has suggested that those with higher incomes are more likely to invest in skills, as are those with higher initial levels of education (OECD, 2013b). Skills beget skills for many individuals. This raises issues regarding the inclusiveness of the tax system with respect to skills which can be informed by examining tax rates on skills across income levels.

Progressivity of METRs incorporating social security contributions

Figure 2.3a suggests that PIT METRs on skills are modestly progressive, though this average conceals significant within-country variation. The increase in the taxation of skills investments in OECD countries is shown in Figure 2.3a. On average, the METR is 10.4% at

Figure 2.3. **Marginal effective tax rate on skills across income levels, 2011**

A. Personal income taxes only

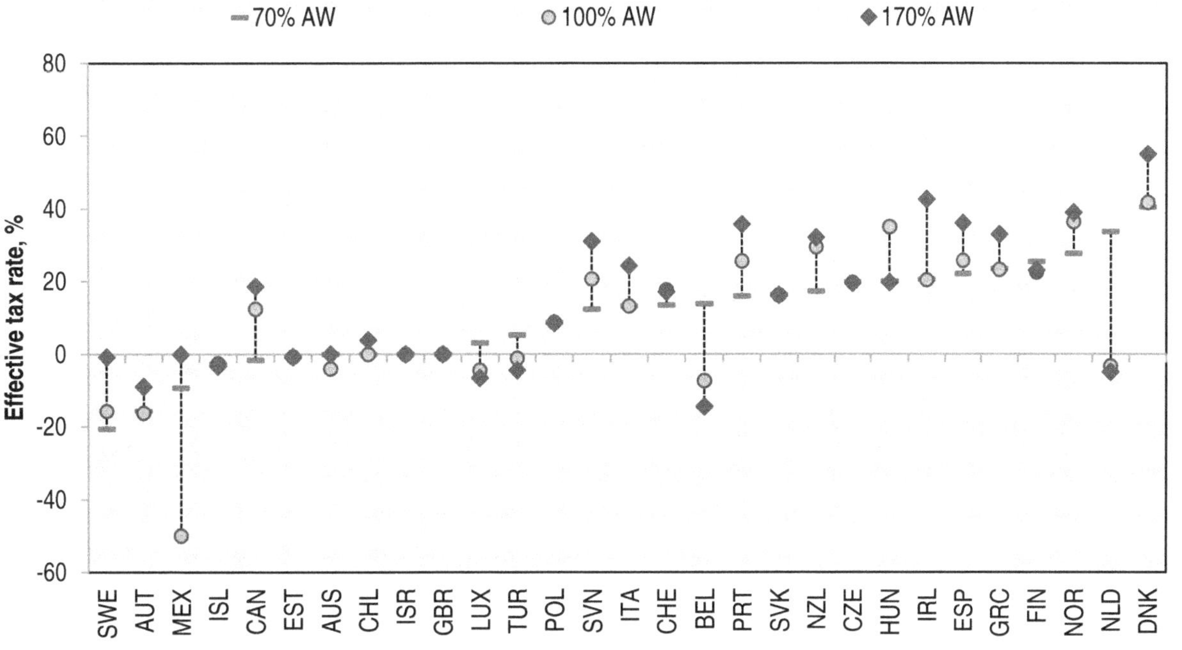

B. Personal income taxes and employees' social security contributions

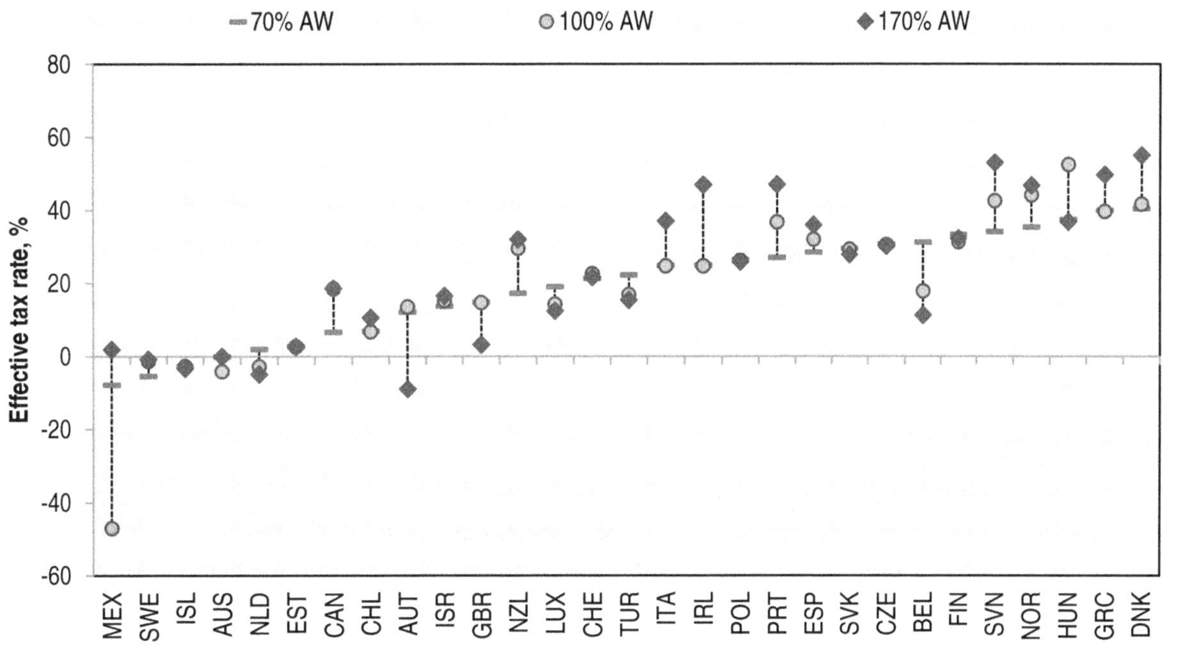

Note: Data are for a 32-year-old single taxpayer with no children, who undertakes a short course of job-related education, earning 95% of the average wage over the year while they study. This figure shows results that incorporate tax deductions for direct costs, tax exemptions for scholarship income, and reduced taxes on student wage income. STEs that subsidise parental spending on education or that subsidise firm spending on education are not included. It is assumed that the skills investment is financed wholly with savings: students do not incur any debt to make a skills investment. Data are presented for 2011

StatLink http://dx.doi.org/10.1787/888933460155

70% of the average wage, 9.1% at 100% of the average wage, and 14.2% at 170% of the average wage when only PIT is considered. Thirteen of the 29 countries considered see an increase in the METR on skills between 70% and 100% of the average wage, and 16 of the countries see an increase between 100% and 170%. The largest increase in the METR between 70% and 170% can be observed in Ireland, where the METR rises by 22 percentage points. Ireland has one of the most progressive tax systems in the OECD, which means that at each stage in the income distribution the TEI may be higher than TFE, which in turn means that the METR will rise with income.

In several countries the METR falls over the income range. Significant decreases are noted in Belgium and the Netherlands. In Belgium, the METR falls from 13.8% at 70% of the average wage to -14.4% at 170% of the average wage. In the Netherlands, the METR falls from 33.7% at 70% of the average wage to -4.9% at 170% of the average wage. This significant fall in the tax burden in the Netherlands is due to the ceiling on employees' SSCs, above which they no longer impact the METR on skills. Individuals pass above the SSC threshold just above the 70% of the average wage. This means that as individuals earn more income after education, SSCs are no longer paid on a marginal euro of income. This in turn means that SSCs are not deductible from the PIT tax base, and so PIT liability rises somewhat sharply. This in turn means that the PIT system taxes away the returns to skills quite sharply in the Netherlands at 70% of the average wage specifically. Further up the income distribution, this ceiling effect no longer exists. In this instance the tax burden on skills falls significantly; the tax system reduces the returns and subsidises the costs at a similar rate. These effects show that ceilings and thresholds can have a significant impact on incentives to invest in skills at various points in the income distribution.

Progressivity of METRs when incorporating employees' SSCs is more mixed, as can be seen in Figure 2.3b. On average, the METR is 19.5% at 70% of the average wage, 19.7% at 100% of the average wage, and 22.5% at 170% of the average wage when PIT and employees' SSCs are considered. Increases in the progressivity of METRs when employees' SSCs are incorporated are mostly of a smaller degree. The largest increase in METR between 70% and 170% can be observed in Ireland, where the METR on skills increases by 22 percentage points from 70% of the average wage to 170%. Ireland has no ceiling for SSCs, unlike many other countries with SSCs, which could raise the TEI for those on high incomes when SSCs are incorporated, in addition to the high levels of tax progressivity previously mentioned.

It is important to bear in mind that more than one kind of progressivity matters when it comes to skills. Progressivity can exist with respect to income prior to and after a skills investment. On the one hand the tax system can be progressive with respect to income before making a skills investment, which will mean that those on higher incomes before education pay higher rates of tax on their skills investments. On the other hand, the tax system can be progressive with respect to incomes after a skills investment, which will mean that those skills investments that earn higher returns pay higher rates of tax. Many tax systems will feature both forms of progressivity. These figures examine progressivity with respect to income before making a skills investment. Those on higher incomes in most countries pay higher rates of tax on skills investments. The latter form of progressivity – progressivity with respect to the returns to skills – can be seen from the fact that AETRs on skills are usually higher than METRs on skills; those skills investments yielding higher returns are taxed more heavily than those skills investments that simply break even.

Progressivity of AETRs incorporating social security contributions

As discussed previously, the AETRs on skills are higher than the METRs; skills investments are more heavily taxed when they earn higher returns than when they earn lower returns. As with METRs, AETRs on skills are also rising with income, though this rise is more uniform across countries and often larger than is the case with the METRs. These results are shown in Figure 2.4a.

On average across the 29 countries the AETR is 11.5% at 70% of the average wage, 16.1% at 100% of the average wage, and 26.1% at 170% of the average wage when only PIT is considered. All but two of the countries see an increase in the AETR on skills between 70% and 100% of the average wage, and all but one of the countries see an increase between 100% and 170%. The largest increase in AETR between 70% and 170% is in Sweden, where the AETR increases by 42 percentage points. The smallest is in the Netherlands, where increases in the AETR on skills between 70% of the average wage and 170% is close to zero.

These increases in the AETR across income levels stem in part from the closeness of AETRs to the TEI. Where the costs of skills are comparatively low relative to the returns, the way that the returns to skills are taxed is a more important component of the overall impact of the tax system on skills than the way the tax system subsidises costs. In such instances, the AETR on skills will closely resemble the TEI, which in turn closely follows the income tax schedule in most OECD countries and so is progressive.

Progressivity of AETRs when incorporating employees' SSCs is not substantially increased or decreased relative to the case where income taxes alone are considered, as can be seen in Figure 2.4b. This is in part due to the lack of progressivity in the average SSC schedule near the average wage compared to the PIT schedule. The results may be different at other points in the income distribution not considered in this special feature. On average, the AETR is 19.4% at 70% of the average wage, 24.9% at 100% of the average wage, and 33.2% at 170% of the average wage when PIT and employees' SSCs are considered. Only one country (Mexico) sees a decline in the AETR on skills between 70% and 100% of the average wage, only three of the countries sees a decline between 100% and 170%. The largest increase in AETR between 70% and 170% is in Sweden. Only the Slovak Republic sees a decline over the income range, but only by 0.1%.

Conclusion

This special feature has outlined effective tax rates on skills for both a marginal and average skills investment for a mid-career individual undergoing a period of job-related training. The effective tax rates on skills are indicators of the overall extent to which the tax system encourages or discourages skills investment. Overall the incorporation of employees' SSCs into the analysis raises the tax burden on skills relative to the case where only PIT is taken into account. This is true for both marginal and average skills investments. When employees' SSCs are taken into account the AETR on skills for the stylised example is 24.9%. For a marginal skills investment, the effective tax rate is 19.7%.

Recent OECD publications have highlighted the crucial role productivity plays in fostering growth that is inclusive and sustainable in OECD economies. Raising productivity levels is a key component in delivering wage increases and increases in standards of living to workers across OECD countries (OECD, 2016). Increasing skills is a key component of raising productivity, and better skills are also associated with a wide variety of positive life outcomes in areas such as employment, longevity and health.

Figure 2.4. **Average effective tax rates on skills across income levels, 2011**

A. Personal income taxes only

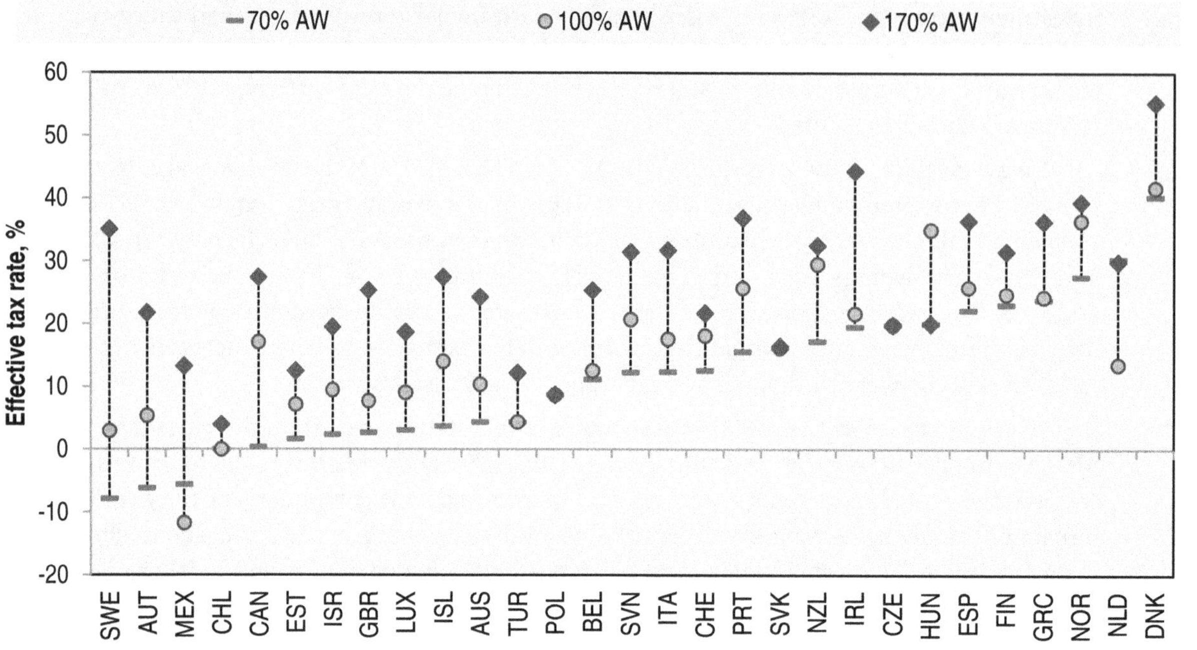

B. Personal income taxes and employees' social security contributions

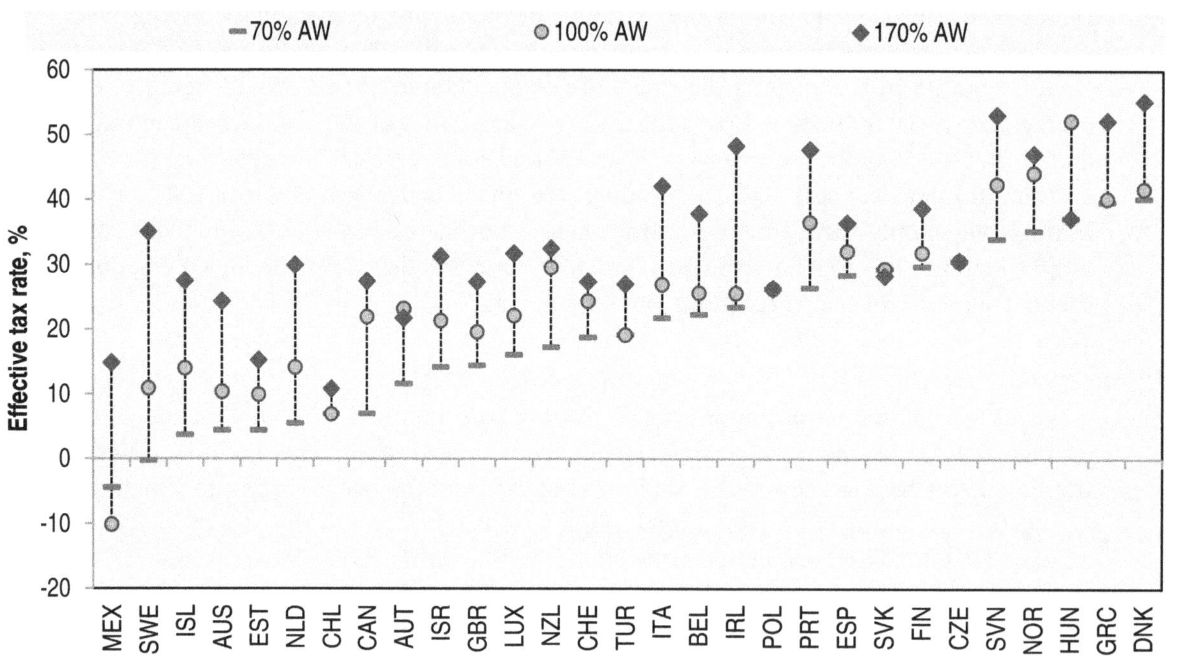

Note: Data are for a 32-year-old single taxpayer with no children, who undertakes a short course of job-related education, earning 95% of the average wage over the year while they study. This figure shows results that incorporate tax deductions for direct costs, tax exemptions for scholarship income, and reduced taxes on student wage income. STEs that subsidise parental spending on education or that subsidise firm spending on education are not included. It is assumed that the skills investment is financed wholly with savings: students do not incur any debt to make a skills investment. Data are presented for 2011.

StatLink http://dx.doi.org/10.1787/888933460167

While skills investments are important, they do not receive as much attention from tax policymakers as physical capital investments. This special feature, as well as the OECD (2017) *Taxation and Skills* Tax Policy Study has sought to address this disparity. This work has shown that, as with taxation of labour income, assessment of the overall impact of both SSCs and PIT needs to be considered when examining incentives to invest in skills.

In most of the examples considered, employees' SSCs increase the burden on skills. While the impact of the PIT system on financial incentives to invest in skills can be positive, negative or even neutral in differing OECD countries under different skills scenarios, this is not the case with SSCs. This is in part due to the fact that while skills expenditures are often deductible from the PIT base, they are not deductible from the SSC base. This creates a tax distortion in the financial incentives to invest in skills. In some countries however, the inclusion of SSCs reduces the overall burden on skills. This is due to the fact that some SSC systems have ceilings above which no further contributions are paid, which reduces the burden on the financial returns to skills. These ceilings can mean that financial incentives to invest in skills can be higher for those on higher incomes.

This special feature has shown that the combination of the deductibility of SSCs from the PIT base, ceilings and thresholds for SSCs, and changes in rate schedules can all impact individuals' incentives to invest in skills. These incentives depend on the ways in which the tax system reduces the returns and offsets the costs of skills investments. This means that features in the PIT and SSC schedules can impact individuals' incentives to invest in skills both above and below an individuals' current income level. These factors highlight the importance of designing both the PIT and SSC schedules in a coherent way.

Further research is needed to examine the impacts of tax-benefit systems on skills incentives. This special feature presented results for only one stylised case; many other cases could be considered regarding adult education, including skills investments financed by firms as well as vocational skills investments in the form of apprenticeships. In addition, this special feature considered only employees' SSCs; future research could consider employers' SSCs as well. Finally, the analysis here has considered the payments into the social security system, not receipts from it such as healthcare benefits, pensions or unemployment insurance. Factoring these into the analysis could greatly change the results on the incentives around skills investments for some countries.

Notes

1. The countries covered are Australia, Austria, Belgium, Canada, Chile, the Czech Republic, Denmark, Estonia, Finland, Greece, Hungary, Iceland, Ireland, Israel, Italy, Luxembourg, Mexico, the Netherlands, New Zealand, Norway, Poland, Portugal, the Slovak Republic, Slovenia, Spain, Sweden, Switzerland, Turkey, and the United Kingdom. France, Germany, Japan, Korea and the United States are omitted due to data limitations. Data are presented for 2011.
2. This lag is due in part due to data limitations with regarding to data on the costs of education. Data on the costs of education are taken from *Education at a Glance* (OECD, 2014) which is published with a time lag.
3. Following the revision to the system of national accounts in Denmark in 2014 with respect to the implementation of ESA 2010, the contributions to unemployment funds are not classified as taxes any longer as they are not mandatory. The change has been retroactive.

References

Brys, B. and C. Torres (2013), "Effective Personal Tax Rates on Marginal Skills Investments in OECD Countries: A New Methodology", *OECD Taxation Working Papers*, No. 16, *https://doi.org/10.1787/22235558*.

Devereux, M.P. and R. Griffith (2003), "Evaluating Tax Policy Decisions for Location Decisions", *International Tax and Public Finance*, Vol. 10, pp. 107-126.

Lehmann, E., F. Marical and L. Rioux (2013), "Labor income responds differently to income-tax and payroll-tax reforms", *Journal of Public Economics*, Vol. 99, pp. 66-84.

OECD (2011), *Taxation and Employment*, OECD Publishing, Paris, *http://dx.doi.org/10.1787/9789264120808-en*.

OECD (2012), *Better Skills, Better Jobs, Better Lives: The OECD Skills Strategy*, *http://dx.doi.org/10.1787/9789264177338-en*.

OECD (2013a), *Taxing Wages 2013*, OECD Publishing, Paris, *http://dx.doi.org/10.1787/tax_wages-2013-en*.

OECD (2013b), *OECD Skills Outlook 2013 - First Results from the Survey of Adult Skills*, OECD Publishing, Paris, *https://doi.org/10.1787/9789264204256-en*.

OECD (2014), *Education at a Glance 2014: OECD Indicators*, OECD Publishing, Paris, *https://doi.org/10.1787/eag-2013-en*.

OECD (2016), The Productivity-Inclusiveness Nexus: Preliminary version, OECD Publishing, Paris, *http://dx.doi.org/10.1787/9789264258303-en*.

OECD (2017), "Taxation and Skills", *OECD Tax Policy Study*, OECD, Paris, Vol. 24.

PART I

International comparisons

This section provides unique information for each of the OECD countries on the income taxes paid by workers, their social security contributions, the family benefits they receive in the form of cash transfers as well as the social security contributions and payroll taxes paid by their employers. It provides results for 2016 and 2015 and discusses the changes between the two years. Results reported cover the marginal and average tax burden for eight different family types.

© OECD 2017

PART I

Chapter 3

2016 Tax burdens

The 2016 tax burden results based on the eight model family types are presented in Tables 3.1 to 3.11 and Figures 3.1 to 3.7. The model family types vary by marital status, number of children and economic status: single taxpayers, without children, earning 67%, 100% and 167% of the average wage (AW); a single parent, with two children, earning 67% of the AW; a single earner couple at the AW level with two children; two-earner couples at 133% and 167% of the AW with two children; and a two-earner couple, without children, at 133% of the AW.

The chapter presents different measures for the average tax burdens (tax wedge, personal tax rate, net personal tax rate, personal income tax rate and employee social security contribution rate) and marginal rates (tax wedge and net personal tax rate). The results for two measures of tax progressivity are also considered: tax elasticity on gross earnings and labour costs.

The statistical data for Israel are supplied by and under the responsibility of the relevant Israeli authorities. The use of such data by the OECD is without prejudice to the status of the Golan Heights, East Jerusalem and Israeli settlements in the West Bank under the terms of international law.

Average tax burdens

Table 3.1 and Figure 3.1 show the average tax wedge (combined burden of income tax, employee and employer social security contributions) taking into account the amount of cash benefits each specific family type is entitled to. Total taxes due minus transfers received are expressed as a percentage of total labour costs, defined as gross wage *plus* employers' social security contributions (including payroll taxes). In the case of a single person on average wage the tax wedge ranges from 7.0% (Chile) and 17.9% (New Zealand) to 49.4% (Germany) and 54.0% (Belgium). For a one-earner married couple, with two children, at the same wage level the tax wedge is lowest in New Zealand (6.2%) and Chile (7.0%) and highest in France (40.0%) and Finland (39.2%). As stated in Chapter 1, the tax wedge tends to be lower for a married couple, with two-children, at this wage level than for a single individual without children due to both receipt of cash benefits and/or more advantageous tax treatment. It is also interesting to note that the tax wedge for a single parent, with two children, earning 67% of the average wage is negative in Australia (-1.1%), New Zealand (-13.0%), Canada (-14.9%) and Ireland (-18.8%). This is due to the amount of cash benefits received by these families plus any applicable non-wastable tax credits that exceed the sum of the total tax and social security contributions that are due.

Table 3.2 and Figure 3.2 present the combined burden of the personal income tax and employee social security contributions, expressed as a percentage of gross wage earnings (the corresponding measures for income tax and employee contributions separately are shown in Tables 3.4 and 3.5). A single person at the average wage level without children is liable to an average tax plus contributions burden of more than 40% only in Belgium (40.7%). The lowest average rates were in Chile (7.0%), Mexico (10.8%), Korea (14.1%), Switzerland (16.9%), Israel (17.8%), New Zealand (17.9%), Estonia (18.3%) and Ireland (19.2%).

Table 3.3 shows the combined burden of income tax and employee social security contributions with the taxes due being reduced by the entitlement to cash benefits for each family-type. Figure 3.3 illustrates this burden for single individuals without children and one-earner married couples with two children, with both family types on average earnings. Comparing Tables 3.2 and 3.3, the average tax rates for families with children (columns 4 -7) are lower in Table 3.3 because most OECD countries support families with children through cash benefits.

A lower burden is also observed for a single individual, without children, at 67% of the average wage in Canada because of a cash transfer paid to mitigate the burden imposed by the federal consumption tax (i.e. the *Goods and Services Tax Credit*; further details can be found in the country chapter contained in Part III of this Report). The same is true in Denmark for single taxpayers at 67% and 100% of the average wage and two-earner married couples, without children, at 133% of the average wage who receive a *Green Check* to compensate for increased environmental taxes.

Comparing Tables 3.2 and 3.3, for single parents, with two children, earning 67% of the average wage, 28 countries provide cash benefits. In Canada and Ireland these represent respectively 39.3% and 38.1% of income and they are at least 25% of income in four other countries: New Zealand (28.0%), Slovenia (26.2%), Australia (25.9%) and Denmark (25.6%). 27 countries provide benefits for a one-earner married couple, with two children, earning the average wage level, although these are less generous relative to income, ranging up to 17.1% (Canada). The lower level of cash benefits for the married couple can be attributed to three reasons: single parents may be eligible for more generous treatment; the benefits themselves may be fixed in absolute amount; or the benefits may be subject to income testing.

Table 3.4 shows personal income tax due as a percentage of gross wage earnings. For single persons, without children, at the average wage (column 2) – the income tax burden varies between 0% (Chile) and 36.2% (Denmark). In most OECD member countries, at the average wage level, the income tax burden for one-earner married couples with two children is substantially lower than that faced by single persons (compare columns 2 and 5). These differences are clearly illustrated in Figure 3.4. In twelve OECD countries, the income tax burden faced by a one-earner married couple with two children is less than half that faced by a single individual (the Czech Republic, Germany, Hungary, Ireland, Latvia, Luxembourg, Poland, Portugal, the Slovak Republic, Slovenia, Switzerland and the United States). In contrast, there is no difference in six countries – Australia, Chile, Israel, Mexico, New Zealand and Sweden. In Finland, the average personal income tax rate for the single worker was one tenth of a percentage point higher than for the one-earner married couple.

There are only two OECD member countries where a married average worker with two children has a negative personal income tax burden. This is due to the presence of nonhwastable tax credits, whereby credits are paid in excess of the taxes otherwise due. This results in tax burdens of -4.2% in the Czech Republic and -1.5% in the Slovak Republic. Similarly, single parents, with two children, earning 67% of the average wage show a negative tax burden in seven countries – the Czech Republic, Germany, Israel, the Slovak Republic, Spain, the United Kingdom and the United States. In four other countries – Chile, Korea, Poland and Portugal – this family-type pays no income tax.

A comparison of columns 5 and 6 in Table 3.4 demonstrates that if the previously non-employed spouse finds a job which pays 33% of the average wage, the income tax burden of the family (now expressed as 133% of the average wage) is slightly higher in nineteen countries, the largest differences being in the Czech Republic (6.7 percentage points) with Germany (5.6 percentage points) and the Slovak Republic (5.4 percentage points). At the same time, the income tax burden is lower in fourteen countries, the largest differences being in Finland (-5.0 percentage points), Australia (-4.4 percentage points) and Mexico (-4.3 percentage points). There is no impact on the tax burden in Chile and France.

An important consideration in the design of an income tax is the level of progressivity – the rate at which the income tax burden increases with income. A comparison of columns 1 to 3 in Table 3.4 provides an insight into the levels of progressivity in the income tax systems of OECD countries. Comparing the income tax burden of single individuals at the average wage level with their counterparts at 167% of the average wage (columns 2 and 3), the lower paid worker faces a lower tax burden in all countries except in Hungary. There, a flat tax rate is applied on labour income and all households without children pay the same percentage of income tax. The same is true for single individuals at 67% of the average wage level compared with their counterparts at the average wage level, with an additional exception in Chile where neither pay income tax. Finally the burden faced by single individuals at 67% of the average wage level represents less than 25% of the burden faced by their counterparts at 167% in four OECD countries: Chile (0%), Mexico (18%), Korea (21%) and the Netherlands (23%).

The addition of social security contributions to the average tax rate reduces this progressivity as well as the proportional tax savings (i.e. tax savings of the low income workers relative to the higher income workers). When comparing Table 3.2 with Table 3.4, we observe that the OECD personal average tax burden of single individuals at 67% of the average wage level is only 31% lower than their counterparts at 167% compared to the OECD average tax savings of 47% for personal income taxes alone. The OECD average tax savings observed for one-earner married couples with two children at the average wage level relative to the average single workers falls from 35% to 22%. These lower figures reflect that there is little variation between social security contribution rates across family types, as shown in Table 3.5.

Table 3.5 shows employee social security contributions as a percentage of gross wage earnings. For a single worker without children at the average wage (column 2) the contribution rate varies between zero (Australia, Denmark and New Zealand) and 22.1% (Slovenia). Australia, Denmark and New Zealand do not levy any employee social security contributions paid to general government and there are three other countries with very low rates – Iceland (0.3%), Mexico (1.4%) and Estonia (1.6%). Social security contributions are usually levied at a flat rate on all earnings, i.e. without any exempt threshold. In a number of OECD member countries a ceiling applies. However, this "capping" provision usually applies to wage levels higher than 167% of the average wage. The flat rates result in a constant average burden of employee social security contributions for most countries between 33% and 167% of average wage earnings. Some examples of a constant proportional burden for employee social security contributions for over the eight model family types, are (in decreasing order of rates) Slovenia (22.1%), Hungary (18.5%), Poland (17.8%), Greece (15.8%), Turkey (15.0%), the Czech Republic and Portugal (11.0%), Latvia (10.5%), Norway (8.2%), the United States (7.7%), Chile (7.0%), Switzerland (6.2%) and Estonia (1.6%).

In addition, at the average wage level only Germany and the Netherlands impose different burdens of social security contributions on employees according to their family status (see Figure 3.5).

Marginal tax burdens

Table 3.6 and Figure 3.6 show the percentage of the marginal increase in labour costs that is deducted through the combined effect of increasing personal income tax, employee and employer (including payroll taxes) social security contributions and decreasing cash transfers. It is assumed that the gross earnings of the principal earner rise by 1 currency unit. This is the marginal tax wedge. In most cases, it absorbs 25% to 55% of an increase in labour costs for single individuals on average wage without children. However, in eight OECD countries these individuals face higher marginal wedges – Belgium (66.7%), Germany (60.1%), France (58.9%), Austria (56.0%), Finland (55.9%) and Luxembourg (55.5%). Mexico (25.2%) and Chile (7.0%) have the lowest marginal tax rates.

In twenty-three OECD member countries, the marginal tax wedge for one-earner married couples at average earnings with two children is either the same or within 5 percentage points as that for single persons at average wage earnings with no children. The marginal tax wedge is more than 5 percentage points lower for one-earner married couples in eight countries: Ireland (18.1 percentage points), Luxembourg (16.1 percentage points), France (15.9 percentage points), Portugal (12.1 percentage points), the United States (9.3 percentage points), Germany (7.8 percentage points), Slovenia (7.4 percentage points) and Switzerland (5.8 percentage points). In contrast, the marginal rate for one-earner married couples with two children is more than 5 percentage points higher than it is for single workers with no children in Canada (35.8 percentage points), New Zealand (21.3 percentage points), Australia (18.9 percentage points) and Iceland (9.0 percentage points). These higher marginal rates arise because of the phase out of income-tested tax reliefs and/or cash transfers. When an income-tested measure is being phased out, the reduction in the relief or benefit compounds the increase in the tax otherwise payable. These programmes are set out in greater detail in the relevant country chapters in Part III of the Report.

Table 3.7 and Figure 3.7 show the incremental change to personal income tax and employee social security contributions less cash benefits when gross wage earnings increase at the margin (it is assumed that the gross earnings of the principal earner rise by 1 currency unit). As in the case of the tax wedge, in most cases personal income tax and employee social security contributions absorb 25% to 55% of a worker's pay rise for single individuals without children at the average wage level. The marginal tax rate is lower than 25% only in Chile (7.0%), Mexico (19.5%), Korea (21.0%), Estonia (21.3%) and Switzerland (23.3%).

In twenty-two OECD member countries, the net marginal personal tax rate for one-earner married couples with two children at the average wage level is either the same or within 5 percentage points as that for single persons with no children. The marginal rate is more than 5 percentage points lower for the one-earner married couples in nine countries: France (21.7 percentage points), Ireland (20.0 percentage points), Luxembourg (18.1 percentage points), Portugal (15.0 percentage points), the United States (10.0 percentage points), Germany (9.3 percentage points), Slovenia (8.5 percentage points), Switzerland (6.1 percentage points) and Spain (5.6 percentage points). In contrast, the marginal rate for one-earner married couples with two children is more than 5 percentage points higher than it is for single persons with no children in Canada (39.4 percentage points), New Zealand (21.3 percentage points), Australia (20.0 percentage points) and Iceland (9.6 percentage points). Similar to the marginal tax wedges, these higher marginal rates arise because of the phase out of income-tested tax reliefs and/or cash transfers.

Table 3.8 shows the percentage increase in net income relative to the percentage increase in gross wages when the latter increases by 1 currency unit, i.e. the elasticity of after-tax income.[1] Under a proportional tax system, net income would increase by the same percentage as the increase in gross earnings, in which case the elasticity is equal to 1. The more progressive the system is – at the income level considered – the lower this elasticity will be. In the case of the one-earner married couples, with two children, at the average wage , column 5 of Table 3.8 shows that Canada (0.27), Australia (0.47), New Zealand (0.52) and Belgium (0.56) have, on this measure, the most progressive systems of income tax plus employee social security contributions taking into account tax provisions and cash transfers for children at this income level. In contrast, Chile (1.00), France (0.95), Poland (0.91) and Mexico (0.90) either implement or are close to a proportional system of income tax plus employee social security contributions – at least for this family type.

It is interesting to note that the elasticity exceeds one for a single individual at 167% of the average earnings in Austria (1.01), indicating that the income tax system at this point in the income scale is regressive. In other words, a percentage increase in gross pay leads to an increase in net income in excess of the percentage increase in gross wage earnings.

Table 3.9 provides a different elasticity measure: the percentage increase in net income relative to the percentage increase in labour costs (i.e. gross wage earnings plus employer social security contributions and payroll taxes) when the latter rises by 1 currency unit.[2] In this case, taxes and social security contributions paid by employers are also part of the analysis. In more than half of the OECD member countries the value of this elasticity lies between 0.5 and 0.97 for the eight selected family-types. This elasticity is below 0.5 for single parents earning 67% of the average wage level in Canada (0.42), Australia (0.41), France (0.35), Ireland (0.28) and the United Kingdom (0.25), for one-earner married couples at the average wage level with two children in Australia (0.47) and Canada (0.28) and for two-earner married couples where one spouse earns the average wage and the other 33% of it with two children in Australia (0.39). In contrast, the elasticity is between 0.97 and 1.0 for all family types in Chile and some family types in Hungary, Japan, Latvia, Mexico and Poland, and one family type in Estonia (single worker earning 167% of the average wage; i.e. 0.98) and Korea (single parent with two children earning 67% of the average wage; i.e. 1.0). Under this elasticity measure the income tax system is regressive for a single individual at 167% of average earnings in Spain (1.12), Germany (1.15) and Austria (1.19).

Table 3.10 sets out figures for gross wage earnings and net income for the eight family-types after all amounts have been converted into U.S. dollars with the same purchasing power. Single workers with the average wage take home (see Table 3.10, column 4) over USD 37 000 in twelve countries: Switzerland (USD 58 246), Luxembourg (USD 45 239), the Netherlands (USD 44 200), Norway (USD 43 258), Australia (USD 42 930), Korea (USD 42 051), Iceland (USD 41 806), the United Kingdom (USD 40 646), Japan (USD 39 118), the United States (USD 38 894), Austria (USD 37 934) and Germany (USD 37 260). The corresponding lowest levels were in Mexico (USD 11 691), Latvia (USD 14 571), Hungary (USD 17 042) and the Slovak Republic (USD 17 542). In the case of a one-earner married couple with two children at the average earnings level, families take home over USD 50 000 in Luxembourg and Switzerland; with the lowest level again being in Mexico. With the exceptions of Chile and Mexico, the one-earner married couple takes home more than the single individual at the average wage due to the favourable tax treatment of this family and/or the cash transfers to which they are entitled.

Table 3.11 shows the corresponding figures to Table 3.10 for labour costs and net income. Thus, the "net" columns in Tables 3.10 and 3.11 are identical. Usually, labour costs are much higher than gross wages, because any employer social security contributions (including payroll taxes) are taken into account. If measured in US dollars with equal purchasing power, labour costs for single workers earning the average wage level are highest in Belgium (USD 74 913) and Switzerland (USD 74 439), and lowest in Mexico (USD 14 638) and Chile (USD 20 517). Annual labour costs are equal to annual gross wage in Chile and New Zealand. In those countries neither compulsory employer social security contributions nor payroll taxes are levied on wages. However, employers in Chile are subject to non-tax compulsory payments related notably to pension schemes.

Notes

1. The reported elasticities in Table 3.8 are calculated as (100-METR)/(100-AETR), where METR is the marginal rate of income tax plus employee social security contributions less cash benefits reported in Table 3.7 and AETR is the average rate plus employee social security contributions less cash benefits reported in Table 3.3.
2. The reported elasticities in Table 3.9 are calculated as (100-METR)/(100-AETR), where METR is the marginal rate of income tax plus employee and employer social security contributions less cash benefits reported in Table 3.6 and AETR is the average rate plus employee and employer social security contributions less cash benefits reported in Table 3.1.

Table 3.1. **Income tax plus employee and employer contributions less cash benefits, 2016**

As % of labour costs, by family-type and wage level

	Single no ch 67 (% AW)	Single no ch 100 (% AW)	Single no ch 167 (% AW)	Single 2 ch 67 (% AW)	Married 2 ch 100-0 (% AW)	Married 2 ch 100-33 (% AW)[2]	Married 2 ch 100-67 (% AW)[2]	Married no ch 100-33 (% AW)[2]
Australia	23.4	28.6	34.1	-1.1	18.1	24.4	26.5	24.4
Austria	42.8	47.1	50.8	27.0	36.5	36.3	39.6	43.4
Belgium	47.5	54.0	59.9	33.6	38.6	38.8	46.4	45.2
Canada	26.5	31.4	32.7	-14.9	11.9	20.5	24.7	28.3
Chile	7.0	7.0	8.0	6.1	7.0	4.6	6.6	7.0
Czech Republic	40.2	43.0	45.2	25.0	27.2	33.0	35.8	40.6
Denmark	34.3	36.5	42.4	7.7	26.1	29.8	31.9	34.5
Estonia	37.8	38.9	39.8	21.2	28.1	31.5	33.3	38.0
Finland	37.9	43.8	49.8	27.5	39.2	36.1	38.6	39.6
France	43.0	48.1	54.4	24.5	40.0	37.5	42.6	42.7
Germany	45.3	49.4	51.4	31.0	34.0	38.8	42.4	45.2
Greece	36.1	40.2	45.8	31.7	38.3	37.8	38.3	38.9
Hungary	48.2	48.2	48.2	25.3	33.7	37.3	39.5	48.2
Iceland	30.5	34.0	38.7	21.6	23.9	29.6	32.6	30.6
Ireland	21.2	27.1	38.0	-18.8	8.3	13.4	19.1	19.9
Israel[1]	15.1	22.1	31.3	-0.4	19.4	16.3	15.7	18.4
Italy	40.8	47.8	54.1	25.3	38.6	38.4	41.5	42.7
Japan	31.0	32.4	35.0	24.9	27.1	28.5	29.4	31.6
Korea	19.0	22.2	24.5	17.0	20.0	19.6	19.8	20.9
Latvia	41.8	42.6	43.3	25.5	31.7	33.6	35.7	41.8
Luxembourg	31.2	38.4	45.3	7.5	16.1	20.5	26.3	29.5
Mexico	15.3	20.1	23.1	15.3	20.1	18.0	18.2	18.0
Netherlands	30.6	37.5	42.1	7.6	32.2	27.9	29.8	32.8
New Zealand	13.6	17.9	23.6	-13.0	6.2	13.0	16.7	16.5
Norway	33.2	36.2	42.0	22.0	31.6	30.8	32.8	33.5
Poland	35.1	35.8	36.4	29.6	30.8	32.1	33.1	35.1
Portugal	36.3	41.5	47.0	21.4	28.2	29.8	35.9	36.2
Slovak Republic	39.0	41.5	43.5	27.8	28.9	31.9	36.0	37.7
Slovenia	38.7	42.7	46.1	10.4	23.9	30.9	34.3	40.2
Spain	35.9	39.5	43.7	24.4	33.8	35.6	36.4	36.6
Sweden	40.8	42.8	51.4	33.6	38.0	37.4	39.1	41.1
Switzerland	19.0	21.8	26.3	3.9	9.1	12.1	15.2	19.6
Turkey	35.5	38.1	42.0	33.9	36.4	35.0	36.4	35.8
United Kingdom	25.9	30.8	37.3	6.2	25.8	22.4	26.2	25.8
United States	29.3	31.7	36.5	12.7	20.8	24.5	26.5	29.2
Unweighted average								
OECD-Average	**32.3**	**36.0**	**40.4**	**16.6**	**26.6**	**28.2**	**30.9**	**32.8**
OECD-EU 22	**37.7**	**41.7**	**46.2**	**20.7**	**30.8**	**32.3**	**35.5**	**38.0**

Note: ch = children

1. Information on data for Israel: http://oe.cd/israel-disclaimer.
2. Two-earner family.

StatLink http://dx.doi.org/10.1787/888933461095

Figure 3.1. **Income tax plus employee and employer contributions less cash benefits, 2016**

As a % of labour costs, by family-type

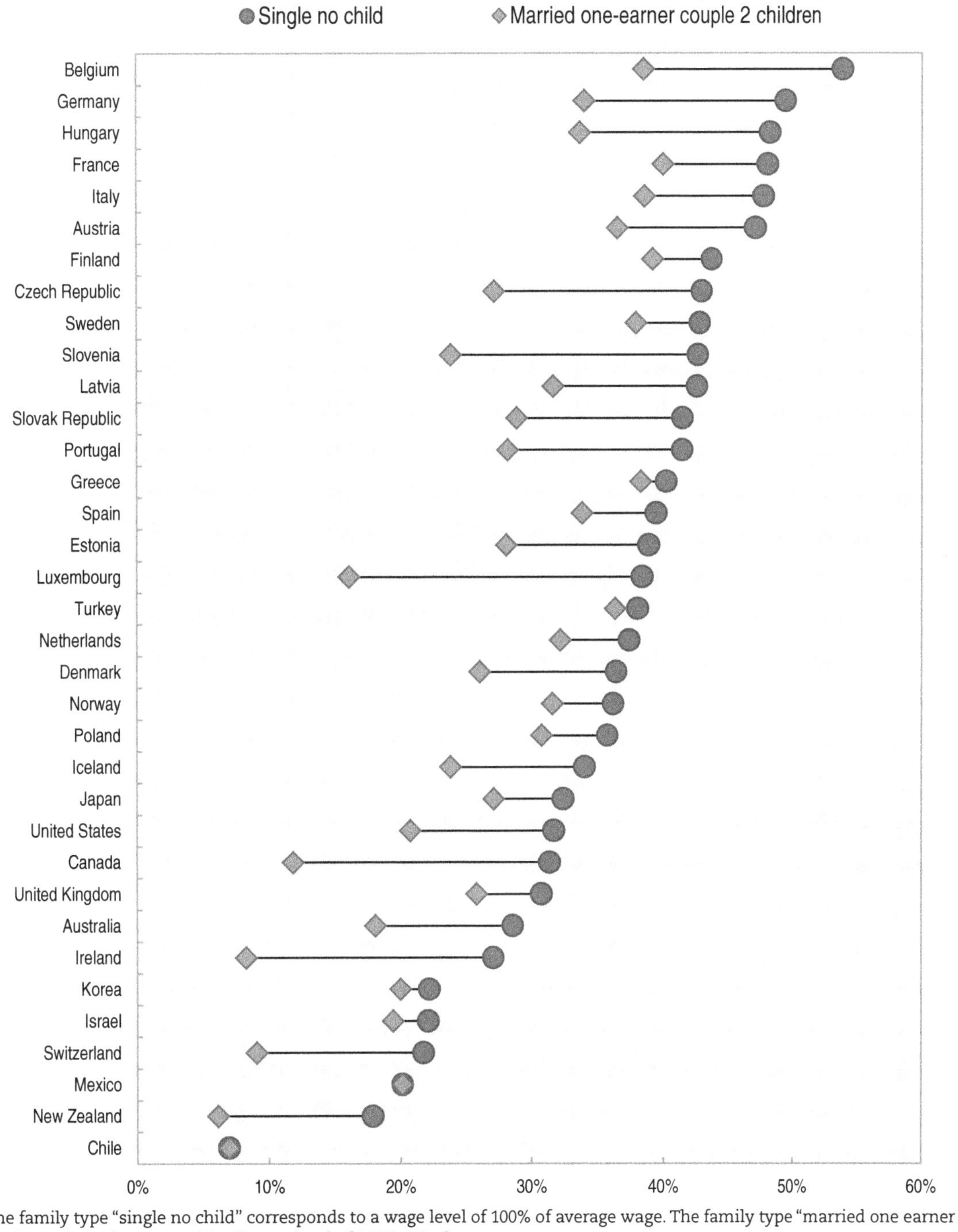

Note: The family type "single no child" corresponds to a wage level of 100% of average wage. The family type "married one earner couple 2 children" corresponds to a combined wage level of 100%-0% of average wage.

Source: OECD calculations based on country submissions and *OECD Economic Outlook, Volume 2016* (No. 100).

StatLink *http://dx.doi.org/10.1787/888933460173*

Table 3.2. Income tax plus employee contributions, 2016

As % of gross wage earnings, by family-type and wage level

	Single no ch 67 (% AW)	Single no ch 100 (% AW)	Single no ch 167 (% AW)	Single 2 ch 67 (% AW)	Married 2 ch 100-0 (% AW)	Married 2 ch 100-33 (% AW)[2]	Married 2 ch 100-67 (% AW)[2]	Married no ch 100-33 (% AW)[2]
Australia	18.8	24.3	30.2	18.8	24.3	19.9	22.1	19.9
Austria	26.3	31.9	37.5	23.0	29.7	26.5	29.1	27.0
Belgium	33.4	40.7	48.5	27.9	29.1	30.1	36.4	32.0
Canada	19.0	23.1	26.3	10.7	18.3	19.7	21.4	19.7
Chile	7.0	7.0	8.0	7.0	7.0	7.0	7.0	7.0
Czech Republic	19.9	23.6	26.6	6.1	6.8	13.5	16.6	20.5
Denmark	33.8	36.2	42.2	32.3	32.2	34.1	35.2	34.1
Estonia	16.8	18.3	19.5	12.8	12.6	14.7	16.1	16.8
Finland	23.6	30.8	38.2	22.9	30.7	25.5	27.7	25.7
France	25.3	29.1	34.5	22.2	22.2	22.2	25.3	25.8
Germany	34.7	39.7	43.9	17.6	21.3	26.9	31.2	34.6
Greece	20.2	25.4	32.4	19.4	25.9	23.4	23.9	23.7
Hungary	33.5	33.5	33.5	20.0	24.4	26.7	28.1	33.5
Iceland	25.4	29.2	34.2	25.4	21.8	25.5	27.7	25.5
Ireland	12.7	19.2	31.4	6.5	10.8	11.7	16.0	11.7
Israel[1]	11.2	17.8	26.9	2.5	17.8	14.3	13.0	14.3
Italy	21.9	31.1	39.5	14.2	24.2	21.0	24.5	24.5
Japan	20.5	22.2	25.9	20.5	20.8	21.2	21.5	21.2
Korea	10.6	14.1	17.7	8.4	11.7	11.3	11.5	12.7
Latvia	28.0	29.1	29.9	13.9	19.6	20.9	23.0	28.0
Luxembourg	22.8	31.0	38.6	16.2	19.3	20.9	25.3	20.9
Mexico	3.7	10.8	15.4	3.7	10.8	6.5	8.0	6.5
Netherlands	22.8	30.4	37.9	14.7	28.4	22.6	24.1	25.2
New Zealand	13.6	17.9	23.6	15.0	17.9	16.5	16.7	16.5
Norway	24.5	27.9	34.4	21.1	26.8	24.9	26.6	24.9
Poland	24.2	25.0	25.7	17.8	19.2	20.7	21.9	24.2
Portugal	21.2	27.6	34.4	11.0	15.3	15.9	20.7	21.0
Slovak Republic	20.0	23.2	25.9	13.0	11.9	16.3	19.1	19.8
Slovenia	28.8	33.4	37.4	22.2	25.1	26.0	27.9	30.6
Spain	16.8	21.4	27.3	1.8	14.1	16.3	17.4	17.7
Sweden	22.2	24.9	36.1	22.2	24.9	22.6	23.8	22.6
Switzerland	14.0	16.9	21.7	8.3	10.4	11.9	14.2	14.6
Turkey	24.2	27.3	31.9	22.4	25.3	23.6	25.3	24.5
United Kingdom	19.1	23.3	29.8	4.9	22.7	19.0	21.6	19.0
United States	23.0	26.0	31.3	5.0	14.1	17.9	20.2	23.0
Unweighted average								
OECD-Average	**21.2**	**25.5**	**30.8**	**15.2**	**19.9**	**19.9**	**22.0**	**22.0**
OECD-EU 22	**24.0**	**28.6**	**34.1**	**16.5**	**21.4**	**21.7**	**24.3**	**24.5**

Note: ch = children

1. Information on data for Israel: http://oe.cd/israel-disclaimer.
2. Two-earner family.

StatLink http://dx.doi.org/10.1787/888933461107

Figure 3.2. **Income tax plus employee contributions, 2016**

As % of gross wage earnings, by family-type and wage level

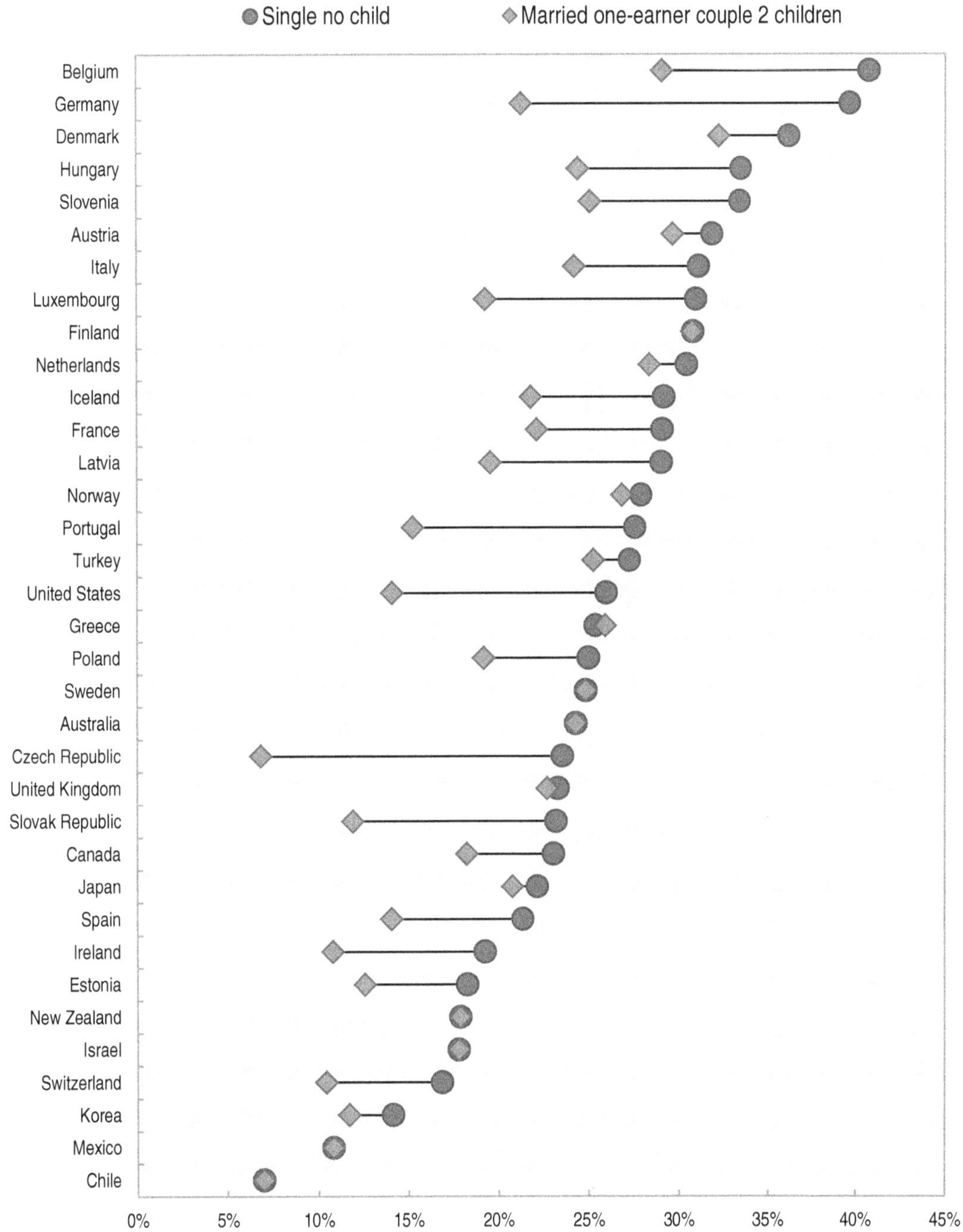

Note: The family type "single no child" corresponds to a wage level of 100% of average wage. The family type "married one earner couple 2 children" corresponds to a combined wage level of 100%-0% of average wage.

Source: Country submissions, *OECD Economic Outlook Volume 2016* (No. 100).

StatLink http://dx.doi.org/10.1787/888933460180

Table 3.3. **Income tax plus employee contributions less cash benefits, 2016**

As % of gross wage earnings, by family-type and wage level

	Single no ch 67 (% AW)	Single no ch 100 (% AW)	Single no ch 167 (% AW)	Single 2 ch 67 (% AW)	Married 2 ch 100-0 (% AW)	Married 2 ch 100-33 (% AW)[2]	Married 2 ch 100-67 (% AW)[2]	Married no ch 100-33 (% AW)[2]
Australia	18.8	24.3	30.2	-7.1	13.2	19.9	22.1	19.9
Austria	26.3	31.9	37.5	5.8	18.2	17.8	22.2	27.0
Belgium	33.4	40.7	48.5	15.8	20.9	24.0	31.5	32.0
Canada	17.7	23.1	26.3	-28.7	1.2	11.0	15.6	19.7
Chile	7.0	7.0	8.0	6.1	7.0	4.6	6.6	7.0
Czech Republic	19.9	23.6	26.6	-0.5	2.4	10.2	13.9	20.5
Denmark	33.5	36.0	42.2	6.6	25.5	29.0	31.2	33.7
Estonia	16.8	18.3	19.5	-5.4	3.8	8.1	10.8	16.8
Finland	23.6	30.8	38.2	10.7	25.2	21.3	24.4	25.7
France	25.3	29.1	34.5	1.0	18.1	19.1	22.9	25.8
Germany	34.7	39.7	43.9	17.6	21.3	26.9	31.2	34.6
Greece	20.2	25.4	32.4	14.7	23.0	22.3	23.0	23.7
Hungary	33.5	33.5	33.5	4.0	14.8	19.4	22.3	33.5
Iceland	25.4	29.2	34.2	15.8	18.3	24.4	27.7	25.5
Ireland	12.7	19.2	31.4	-31.5	-1.6	4.6	10.4	11.7
Israel[1]	11.2	17.8	26.9	-5.1	14.9	12.1	11.3	14.3
Italy	21.9	31.1	39.5	1.4	19.1	18.7	22.8	24.5
Japan	20.5	22.2	25.9	13.5	16.1	17.7	18.7	21.2
Korea	10.6	14.1	17.7	8.4	11.7	11.3	11.5	12.7
Latvia	28.0	29.1	29.9	7.9	15.5	17.9	20.6	28.0
Luxembourg	22.8	31.0	38.6	-3.8	5.9	10.9	17.3	20.9
Mexico	3.7	10.8	15.4	3.7	10.8	6.5	8.0	6.5
Netherlands	22.8	30.4	37.9	-2.8	24.6	19.8	21.9	25.2
New Zealand	13.6	17.9	23.6	-13.0	6.2	13.0	16.7	16.5
Norway	24.5	27.9	34.4	11.8	22.7	21.8	24.1	24.9
Poland	24.2	25.0	25.7	17.8	19.2	20.7	21.9	24.2
Portugal	21.2	27.6	34.4	2.7	11.2	13.1	20.7	21.0
Slovak Republic	20.0	23.2	25.9	5.2	6.7	12.4	16.0	19.8
Slovenia	28.8	33.4	37.4	-4.0	11.6	19.7	23.8	30.6
Spain	16.8	21.4	27.3	1.8	14.1	16.3	17.4	17.7
Sweden	22.2	24.9	36.1	12.7	18.5	17.8	20.0	22.6
Switzerland	14.0	16.9	21.7	-2.1	3.4	6.6	10.0	14.6
Turkey	24.2	27.3	31.9	22.4	25.3	23.6	25.3	24.5
United Kingdom	19.1	23.3	29.8	-2.4	17.8	15.3	18.7	19.0
United States	23.0	26.0	31.3	5.0	14.1	17.9	20.2	23.0
Unweighted average								
OECD-Average	**21.2**	**25.5**	**30.8**	**3.0**	**14.3**	**16.4**	**19.5**	**22.0**
OECD-EU 22	**24.0**	**28.6**	**34.1**	**3.4**	**15.3**	**17.5**	**21.1**	**24.5**

Note: ch = children

1. Information on data for Israel: http://oe.cd/israel-disclaimer.
2. Two-earner family.

StatLink http://dx.doi.org/10.1787/888933461116

Figure 3.3. **Income tax plus employee contributions less cash benefits, 2016**

As % of gross wage earnings, by family-type and wage level

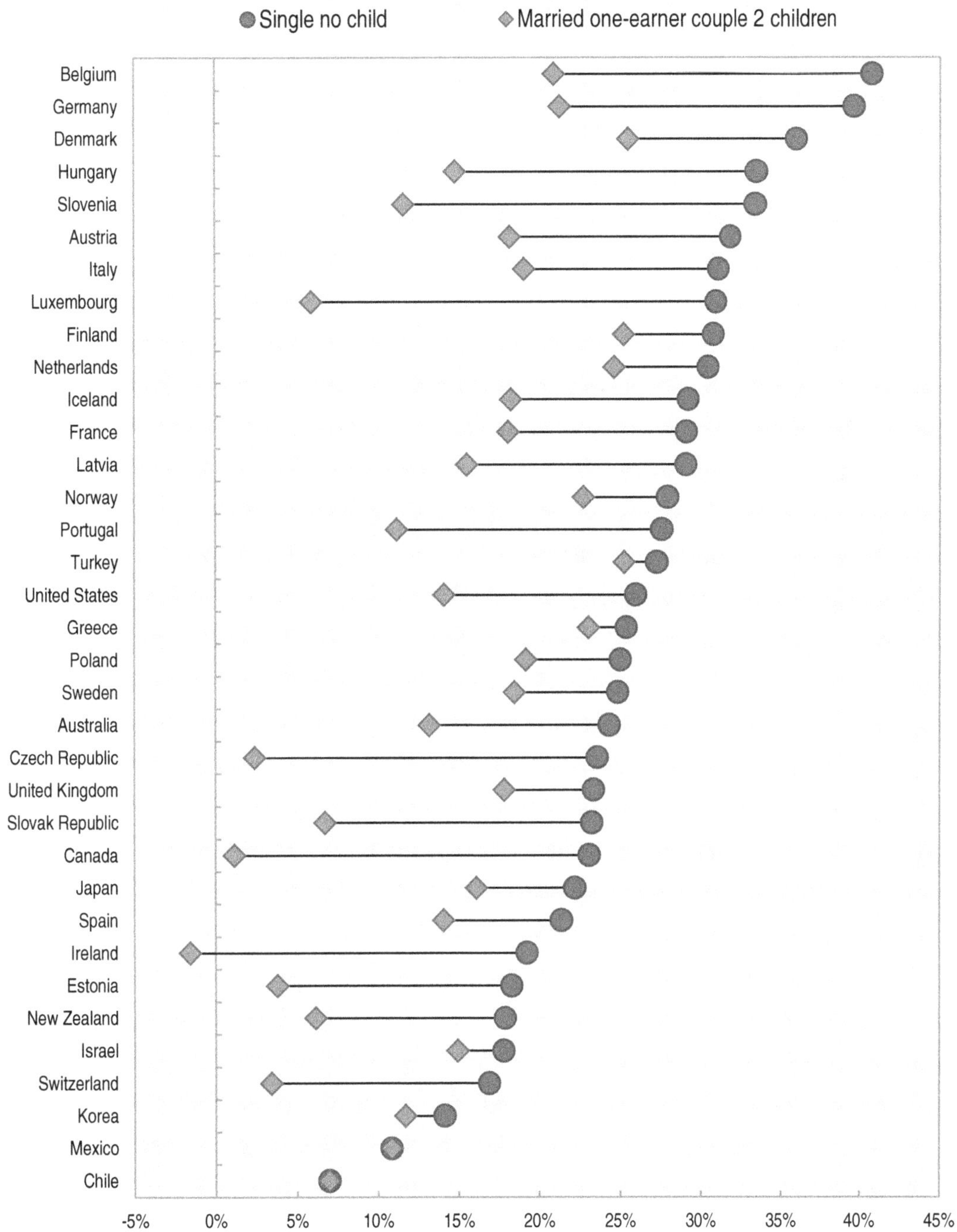

Note: The family type "single no child" corresponds to a wage level of 100% of average wage. The family type "married one earner couple 2 children" corresponds to a combined wage level of 100%-0% of average wage.

Source: OECD calculations based on country submissions and *OECD Economic Outlook, Volume 2016* (No. 100)

StatLink *http://dx.doi.org/10.1787/888933460197*

Table 3.4. **Income tax, 2016**

As % of gross wage earnings, by family-type and wage level

	Single no ch 67 (% AW)	Single no ch 100 (% AW)	Single no ch 167 (% AW)	Single 2 ch 67 (% AW)	Married 2 ch 100-0 (% AW)	Married 2 ch 100-33 (% AW)[2]	Married 2 ch 100-67 (% AW)[2]	Married no ch 100-33 (% AW)[2]
Australia	18.8	24.3	30.2	18.8	24.3	19.9	22.1	19.9
Austria	8.3	13.9	21.0	5.0	11.7	9.2	11.1	9.8
Belgium	19.5	26.8	34.5	14.1	15.1	19.3	22.4	21.2
Canada	11.8	15.4	21.4	3.5	10.6	12.5	13.9	12.5
Chile	0.0	0.0	1.0	0.0	0.0	0.0	0.0	0.0
Czech Republic	8.9	12.6	15.6	-4.9	-4.2	2.5	5.6	9.5
Denmark	33.8	36.2	42.2	32.3	32.2	34.1	35.2	34.1
Estonia	15.2	16.7	17.9	11.2	11.0	13.1	14.5	15.2
Finland	15.0	22.0	29.4	14.4	21.9	16.9	19.0	17.1
France	11.0	14.8	20.9	7.9	7.9	7.9	11.0	11.5
Germany	14.0	19.0	27.5	-2.8	0.9	6.5	10.8	13.9
Greece	4.4	9.6	16.6	3.7	10.1	7.6	8.1	8.0
Hungary	15.0	15.0	15.0	1.5	5.9	8.2	9.6	15.0
Iceland	25.0	28.9	34.0	25.0	21.5	25.0	27.3	25.0
Ireland	8.7	15.2	27.4	2.5	6.8	8.7	12.0	8.7
Israel[1]	5.3	9.9	17.3	-3.5	9.9	7.4	5.9	7.4
Italy	12.4	21.6	29.9	4.7	14.7	11.5	15.0	15.0
Japan	6.2	7.8	12.7	6.2	6.4	6.9	7.2	6.9
Korea	2.2	5.7	10.6	0.0	3.3	2.9	3.1	4.3
Latvia	17.5	18.6	19.4	3.4	9.1	10.4	12.5	17.5
Luxembourg	10.1	18.1	25.8	3.5	6.5	8.2	12.5	8.2
Mexico	2.5	9.5	14.0	2.5	9.5	5.2	6.7	5.2
Netherlands	6.4	16.9	27.9	4.5	16.4	12.7	11.9	13.2
New Zealand	13.6	17.9	23.6	15.0	17.9	16.5	16.7	16.5
Norway	16.3	19.7	26.2	12.9	18.6	16.7	18.4	16.7
Poland	6.4	7.2	7.8	0.0	1.4	2.8	4.1	6.3
Portugal	10.2	16.6	23.4	0.0	4.3	4.9	9.7	10.0
Slovak Republic	6.6	9.8	12.5	-0.4	-1.5	3.9	5.7	7.4
Slovenia	6.7	11.3	15.3	0.1	3.0	3.9	5.8	8.5
Spain	10.4	15.0	21.0	-4.6	7.7	9.9	11.0	11.3
Sweden	15.2	17.9	31.4	15.2	17.9	15.6	16.8	15.6
Switzerland	7.8	10.7	15.5	2.1	4.2	5.7	7.9	8.3
Turkey	9.2	12.3	16.9	7.4	10.3	8.6	10.3	9.5
United Kingdom	11.0	14.0	22.3	-3.2	13.4	11.0	12.8	11.0
United States	15.4	18.3	23.7	-2.6	6.5	10.2	12.5	15.4
Unweighted average								
OECD-Average	**11.4**	**15.7**	**21.5**	**5.6**	**10.1**	**10.5**	**12.3**	**12.4**
OECD-EU 22	**12.1**	**16.8**	**22.9**	**4.9**	**9.6**	**10.4**	**12.6**	**13.1**

Note: ch = children

1. Information on data for Israel: http://oe.cd/israel-disclaimer.
2. Two-earner family.

StatLink http://dx.doi.org/10.1787/888933461120

Figure 3.4. **Income tax, 2016**

As % of gross wage earnings, by family-type

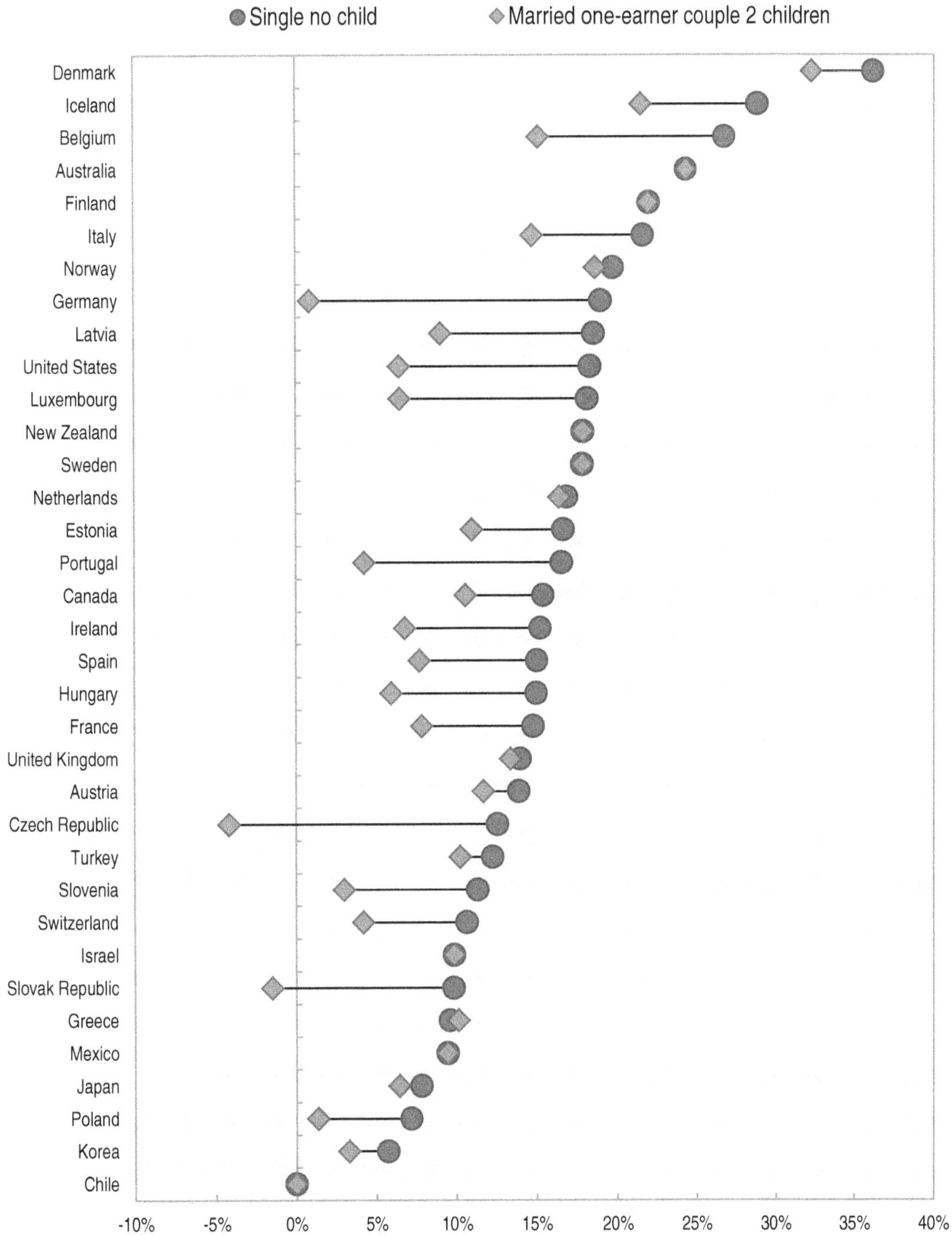

Note: The family type "single no child" corresponds to a wage level of 100% of average wage. The family type "married one earner couple 2 children" corresponds to a combined wage level of 100%-0% of average wage.

Source: OECD calculations based on country submissions and *OECD Economic Outlook, Volume 2016* (No. 100)

StatLink *http://dx.doi.org/10.1787/888933460202*

Table 3.5. **Employee contributions, 2016**

As % of gross wage earnings, by family-type and wage level

	Single no ch 67 (% AW)	Single no ch 100 (% AW)	Single no ch 167 (% AW)	Single 2 ch 67 (% AW)	Married 2 ch 100-0 (% AW)	Married 2 ch 100-33 (% AW)[2]	Married 2 ch 100-67 (% AW)[2]	Married no ch 100-33 (% AW)[2]
Australia	0.0	0.0	0.0	0.0	0.0	0.0	0.0	0.0
Austria	18.0	18.0	16.5	18.0	18.0	17.2	18.0	17.2
Belgium	13.9	14.0	14.0	13.9	14.0	10.8	14.0	10.8
Canada	7.2	7.7	5.0	7.2	7.7	7.2	7.5	7.2
Chile	7.0	7.0	7.0	7.0	7.0	7.0	7.0	7.0
Czech Republic	11.0	11.0	11.0	11.0	11.0	11.0	11.0	11.0
Denmark	0.0	0.0	0.0	0.0	0.0	0.0	0.0	0.0
Estonia	1.6	1.6	1.6	1.6	1.6	1.6	1.6	1.6
Finland	8.6	8.8	8.8	8.6	8.8	8.5	8.7	8.5
France	14.3	14.3	13.6	14.3	14.3	14.3	14.3	14.3
Germany	20.7	20.7	16.4	20.4	20.4	20.4	20.4	20.7
Greece	15.8	15.8	15.8	15.8	15.8	15.8	15.8	15.8
Hungary	18.5	18.5	18.5	18.5	18.5	18.5	18.5	18.5
Iceland	0.5	0.3	0.2	0.5	0.3	0.5	0.4	0.5
Ireland	4.0	4.0	4.0	4.0	4.0	3.0	4.0	3.0
Israel[1]	5.9	7.9	9.6	5.9	7.9	6.8	7.1	6.8
Italy	9.5	9.5	9.6	9.5	9.5	9.5	9.5	9.5
Japan	14.4	14.4	13.2	14.4	14.4	14.4	14.4	14.4
Korea	8.4	8.4	7.1	8.4	8.4	8.4	8.4	8.4
Latvia	10.5	10.5	10.5	10.5	10.5	10.5	10.5	10.5
Luxembourg	12.7	12.8	12.9	12.7	12.8	12.7	12.8	12.7
Mexico	1.3	1.4	1.5	1.3	1.4	1.3	1.3	1.3
Netherlands	16.4	13.5	10.1	10.2	12.0	10.0	12.2	12.0
New Zealand	0.0	0.0	0.0	0.0	0.0	0.0	0.0	0.0
Norway	8.2	8.2	8.2	8.2	8.2	8.2	8.2	8.2
Poland	17.8	17.8	17.8	17.8	17.8	17.8	17.8	17.8
Portugal	11.0	11.0	11.0	11.0	11.0	11.0	11.0	11.0
Slovak Republic	13.4	13.4	13.4	13.4	13.4	12.4	13.4	12.4
Slovenia	22.1	22.1	22.1	22.1	22.1	22.1	22.1	22.1
Spain	6.4	6.4	6.2	6.4	6.4	6.4	6.4	6.4
Sweden	7.0	7.0	4.7	7.0	7.0	7.0	7.0	7.0
Switzerland	6.2	6.2	6.2	6.2	6.2	6.2	6.2	6.2
Turkey	15.0	15.0	15.0	15.0	15.0	15.0	15.0	15.0
United Kingdom	8.1	9.4	7.5	8.1	9.4	8.0	8.8	8.0
United States	7.7	7.7	7.7	7.7	7.7	7.7	7.7	7.7
Unweighted average								
OECD-Average	**9.8**	**9.8**	**9.3**	**9.6**	**9.8**	**9.5**	**9.7**	**9.5**
OECD-EU 22	**11.9**	**11.8**	**11.2**	**11.6**	**11.7**	**11.3**	**11.7**	**11.4**

Note: ch = children

1. Information on data for Israel: http://oe.cd/israel-disclaimer.
2. Two-earner family.

StatLink http://dx.doi.org/10.1787/888933461132

Figure 3.5. **Employee contributions, 2016**

As % of gross wage earnings, by family-type

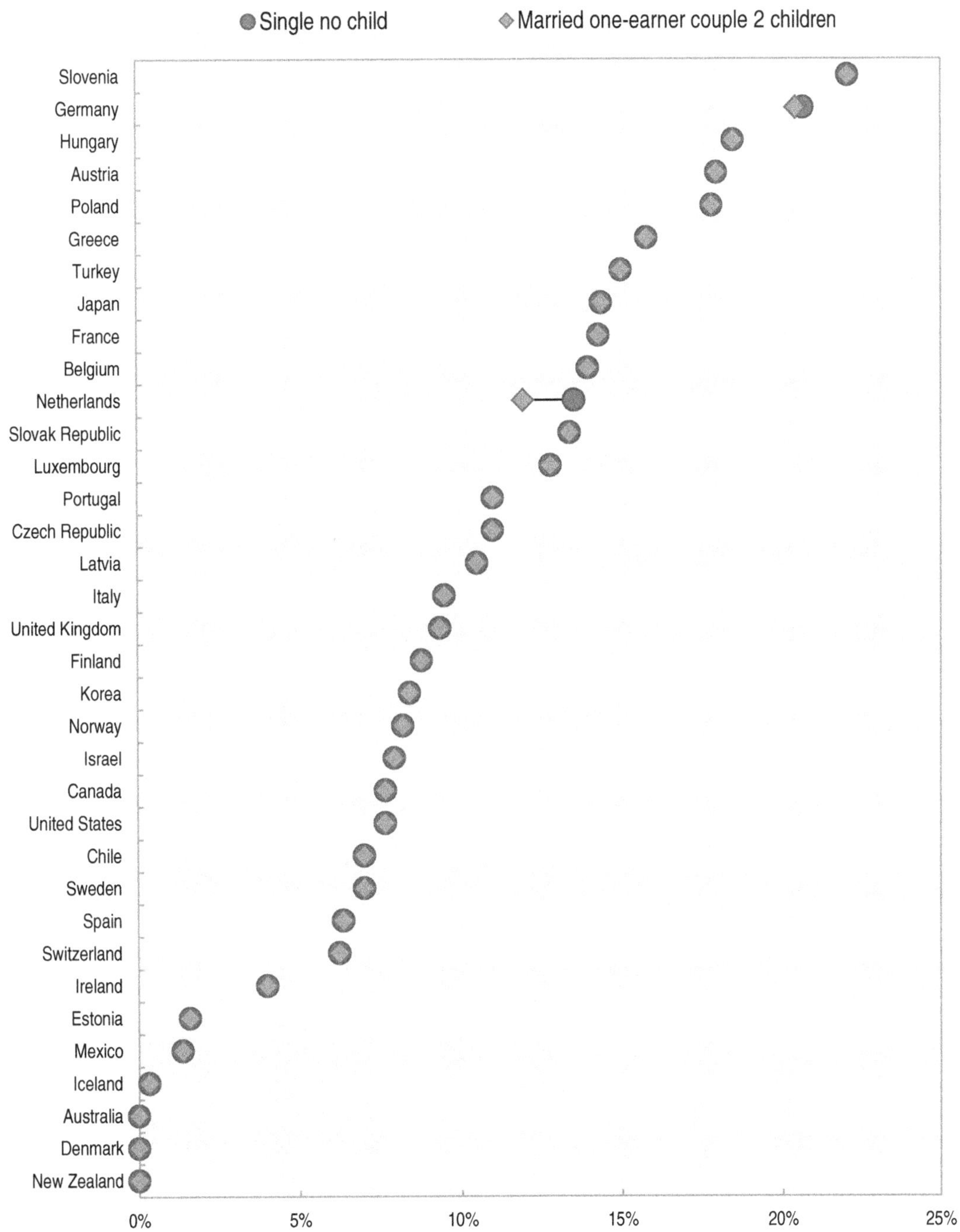

Note: The family type "single no child" corresponds to a wage level of 100% of average wage. The family type "married one earner couple 2 children" corresponds to a combined wage level of 100%-0% of average wage.

Source: OECD calculations based on country submissions and *OECD Economic Outlook, Volume 2016* (No. 100)

StatLink *http://dx.doi.org/10.1787/888933460212*

Table 3.6. Marginal rate of income tax plus employee and employer contributions less cash benefits, 2016

As % of labour costs, by family-type and wage level

	Single no ch 67 (% AW)	Single no ch 100 (% AW)	Single no ch 167 (% AW)	Single 2 ch 67 (% AW)	Married 2 ch 100-0 (% AW)	Married 2 ch 100-33 (% AW)[2]	Married 2 ch 100-67 (% AW)[2]	Married no ch 100-33 (% AW)[2]
Australia	39.6	42.4	42.4	58.5	61.3	70.7	42.4	42.4
Austria	56.0	56.0	41.3	56.0	56.0	56.0	56.0	56.0
Belgium	65.7	66.7	67.9	65.7	66.7	66.7	66.7	66.7
Canada	33.8	39.6	37.0	52.3	75.4	44.7	44.7	39.6
Chile	7.0	7.0	10.2	7.0	7.0	7.0	7.0	7.0
Czech Republic	48.6	48.6	48.6	48.6	48.6	48.6	48.6	48.6
Denmark	39.7	42.0	55.8	38.2	42.0	42.0	42.0	42.0
Estonia	41.2	41.2	41.2	41.2	41.2	41.2	41.2	41.2
Finland	54.8	55.9	59.0	54.8	56.8	56.8	56.8	55.9
France	69.3	58.9	59.9	73.6	43.0	43.0	60.5	53.4
Germany	55.6	60.1	44.3	53.6	52.3	55.3	57.6	55.5
Greece	47.4	48.9	56.2	47.4	48.9	48.9	48.9	48.9
Hungary	48.2	48.2	48.2	48.2	48.2	48.2	48.2	48.2
Iceland	41.1	41.1	48.2	50.1	50.1	46.5	41.1	41.1
Ireland	36.3	54.4	54.4	67.3	36.3	36.3	36.3	36.3
Israel[1]	31.2	37.7	47.0	34.3	37.7	37.7	37.7	37.7
Italy	54.8	54.8	63.2	56.0	56.0	56.0	55.4	54.8
Japan	32.9	37.1	35.1	32.9	37.1	37.1	37.1	37.1
Korea	29.0	28.5	31.9	17.0	28.5	28.5	28.5	28.5
Latvia	44.2	44.2	44.2	44.2	44.2	44.2	44.2	44.2
Luxembourg	47.8	55.5	55.5	50.4	39.4	44.5	52.9	44.5
Mexico	17.5	25.2	28.4	17.5	25.2	25.2	25.2	25.2
Netherlands	48.2	51.6	52.7	48.7	51.6	51.6	51.6	51.6
New Zealand	17.5	30.0	33.0	38.8	51.3	51.3	30.0	30.0
Norway	42.4	42.4	53.0	42.4	42.4	42.4	42.4	42.4
Poland	37.2	37.2	37.2	29.6	37.2	37.2	37.2	37.2
Portugal	51.9	51.9	59.4	28.1	39.8	51.1	51.1	51.9
Slovak Republic	46.5	46.5	46.5	46.5	46.5	46.5	46.5	46.5
Slovenia	43.6	51.0	60.4	43.6	43.6	43.6	43.6	51.0
Spain	45.2	49.5	37.0	45.2	45.2	49.5	49.5	49.5
Sweden	45.6	48.3	69.6	45.6	48.3	48.3	48.3	48.3
Switzerland	26.3	27.8	36.6	18.8	22.0	26.1	29.4	26.9
Turkey	42.8	47.8	47.8	42.8	47.8	47.8	47.8	47.8
United Kingdom	40.2	40.2	49.0	76.3	40.2	40.2	40.2	40.2
United States	34.3	43.6	43.6	55.1	34.3	34.3	34.3	34.3
Unweighted average								
OECD-Average	**41.8**	**44.6**	**47.0**	**45.0**	**44.3**	**44.4**	**43.8**	**43.2**
OECD-EU 22	**48.6**	**50.5**	**52.3**	**50.4**	**46.9**	**48.0**	**49.3**	**48.8**

Note: ch = children

It is assumed that gross earnings of the principal earner in the household rise. The outcome may differ if the wage of the spouse g especially if partners are taxed individually.

1. Information on data for Israel: http://oe.cd/israel-disclaimer.
2. Two-earner family.

StatLink http://dx.doi.org/10.1787/888933461143

Figure 3.6. **Marginal rate of income tax plus employee and employer contributions less cash benefits, 2016**

As % of labour costs, by family-type

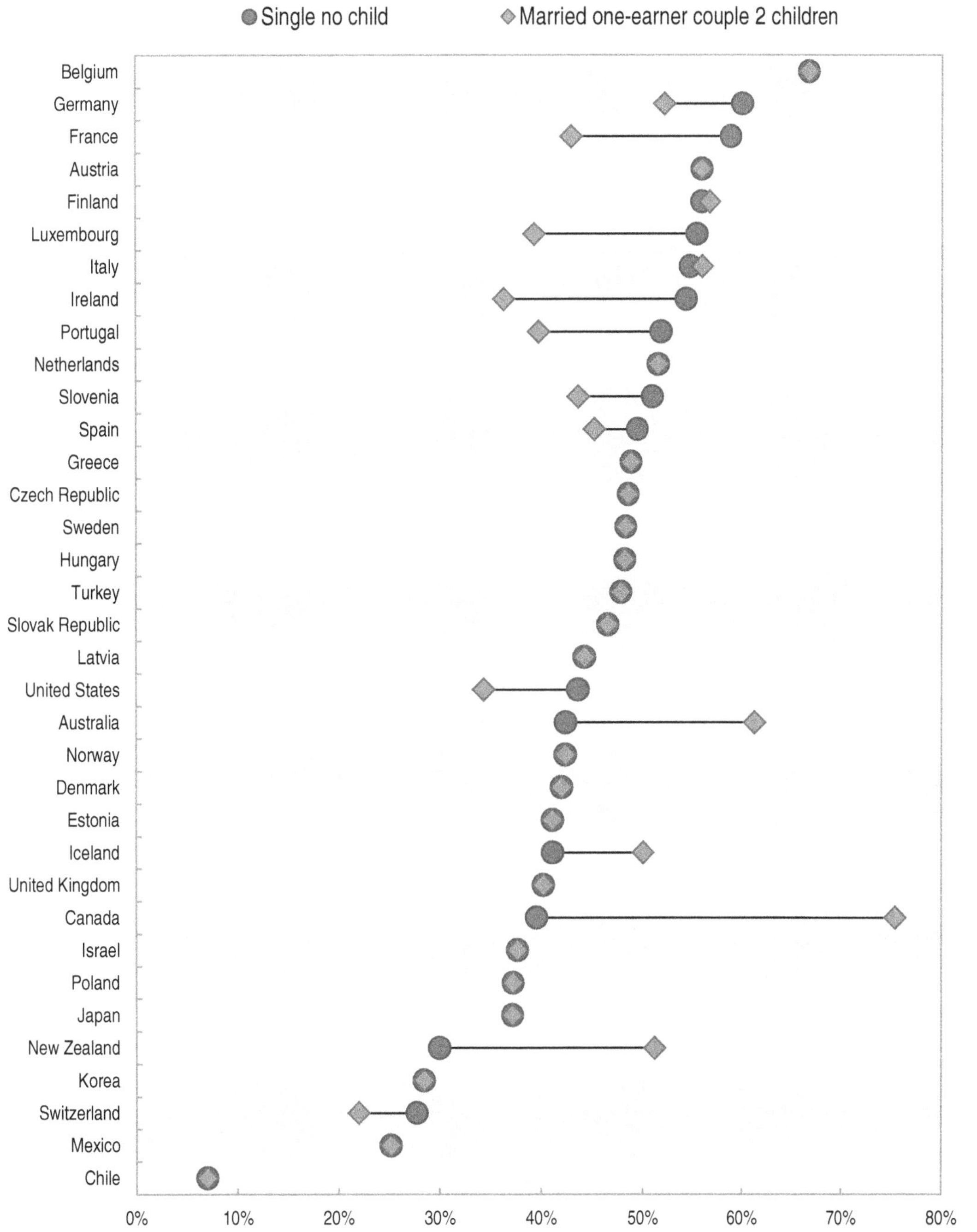

Note: The family type "single no child" corresponds to a wage level of 100% of average wage. The family type "married one earner couple 2 children" corresponds to a combined wage level of 100%-0% of average wage.

Source: OECD calculations based on country submissions and *OECD Economic Outlook, Volume 2016* (No. 100)

StatLink http://dx.doi.org/10.1787/888933460220

Table 3.7. **Marginal rate of income tax plus employee contributions less cash benefits, 2016**

As % of gross wage earnings, by family-type and wage level

	Single no ch 67 (% AW)	Single no ch 100 (% AW)	Single no ch 167 (% AW)	Single 2 ch 67 (% AW)	Married 2 ch 100-0 (% AW)	Married 2 ch 100-33 (% AW)[2]	Married 2 ch 100-67 (% AW)[2]	Married no ch 100-33 (% AW)[2]
Australia	36.0	39.0	39.0	56.0	59.0	69.0	39.0	39.0
Austria	43.3	43.3	36.9	43.3	43.3	43.3	43.3	43.3
Belgium	54.6	55.9	59.4	54.6	55.9	55.9	55.9	55.9
Canada	25.5	33.6	33.9	46.3	73.0	39.3	39.3	33.6
Chile	7.0	7.0	10.2	7.0	7.0	7.0	7.0	7.0
Czech Republic	31.1	31.1	31.1	31.1	31.1	31.1	31.1	31.1
Denmark	39.7	42.0	55.8	38.2	42.0	42.0	42.0	42.0
Estonia	21.3	21.3	21.3	21.3	21.3	21.3	21.3	21.3
Finland	44.3	45.8	49.5	44.3	46.8	46.8	46.8	45.8
France	43.6	43.9	42.6	51.6	22.2	22.2	46.1	36.4
Germany	47.0	52.4	44.3	44.7	43.1	46.6	49.4	46.9
Greece	34.3	36.2	45.3	34.3	36.2	36.2	36.2	36.2
Hungary	33.5	33.5	33.5	33.5	33.5	33.5	33.5	33.5
Iceland	36.8	36.8	44.4	46.4	46.4	42.6	36.8	36.8
Ireland	29.5	49.5	49.5	63.8	29.5	29.5	29.5	29.5
Israel[1]	26.0	33.0	43.0	29.4	33.0	33.0	33.0	33.0
Italy	40.4	40.4	51.5	42.0	42.0	42.0	41.2	40.4
Japan	22.8	27.6	31.1	22.8	27.6	27.6	27.6	27.6
Korea	21.7	21.0	28.0	8.4	21.0	21.0	21.0	21.0
Latvia	31.1	31.1	31.1	31.1	31.1	31.1	31.1	31.1
Luxembourg	41.5	50.1	50.1	44.4	32.0	37.7	47.2	37.7
Mexico	12.1	19.5	22.9	12.1	19.5	19.5	19.5	19.5
Netherlands	42.5	46.3	52.7	43.1	46.3	46.3	46.3	46.3
New Zealand	17.5	30.0	33.0	38.8	51.3	51.3	30.0	30.0
Norway	34.9	34.9	46.9	34.9	34.9	34.9	34.9	34.9
Poland	26.7	26.7	26.7	17.8	26.7	26.7	26.7	26.7
Portugal	40.5	40.5	49.8	11.0	25.5	39.5	39.5	40.5
Slovak Republic	29.9	29.9	29.9	29.9	29.9	29.9	29.9	29.9
Slovenia	34.6	43.1	54.0	34.6	34.6	34.6	34.6	43.1
Spain	28.8	34.4	37.0	28.8	28.8	34.4	34.4	34.4
Sweden	28.5	32.1	60.1	28.5	32.1	32.1	32.1	32.1
Switzerland	21.7	23.3	32.6	13.8	17.2	21.5	25.0	22.3
Turkey	32.8	38.7	38.7	32.8	38.7	38.7	38.7	38.7
United Kingdom	32.0	32.0	42.0	73.0	32.0	32.0	32.0	32.0
United States	29.3	39.3	39.3	51.6	29.3	29.3	29.3	29.3
Unweighted average								
OECD-Average	**32.1**	**35.6**	**39.9**	**35.6**	**35.0**	**35.1**	**34.6**	**34.0**
OECD-EU 22	**36.3**	**39.2**	**43.4**	**38.4**	**34.8**	**36.1**	**37.7**	**37.1**

Note: ch = children

It is assumed that gross earnings of the principal earner in the household rise. The outcome may differ if the wage of the spouse g especially if partners are taxed individually.

1. Information on data for Israel: http://oe.cd/israel-disclaimer.
2. Two-earner family.

StatLink http://dx.doi.org/10.1787/888933461152

Figure 3.7. **Marginal rate of income tax plus employee contributions less cash benefits, 2016**

As % of gross wage earnings, by family-type

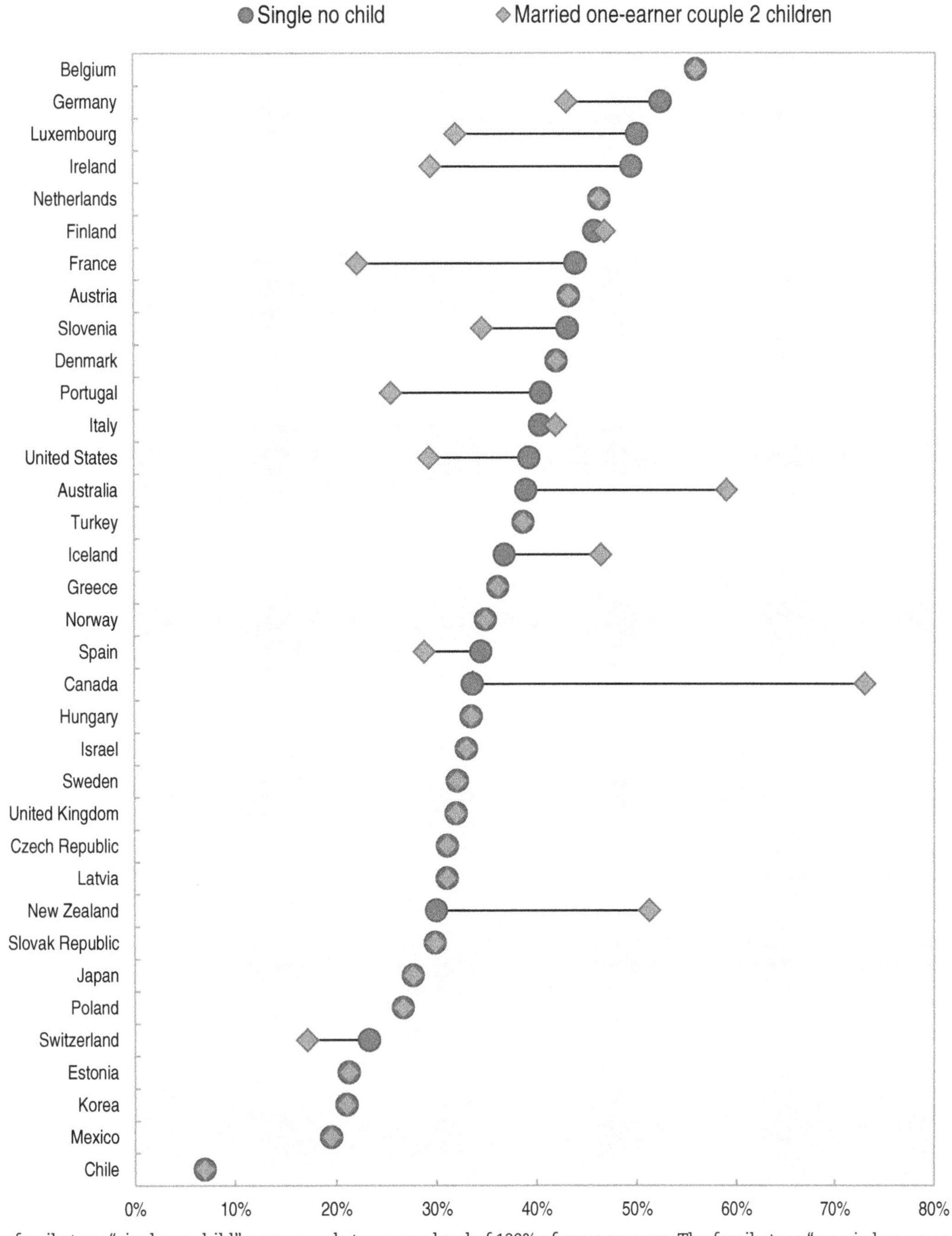

Note: The family type "single no child" corresponds to a wage level of 100% of average wage. The family type "married one earner couple 2 children" corresponds to a combined wage level of 100%-0% of average wage.

Source: OECD calculations based on country submissions and *OECD Economic Outlook, Volume 2016* (No. 100)

StatLink *http://dx.doi.org/10.1787/888933460233*

Table 3.8. **Percentage increase in net income relative to percentage increase in gross wages, 2016**

After an increase of 1 currency unit in gross wages, by family-type and wage level

	Single no ch 67 (% AW)	Single no ch 100 (% AW)	Single no ch 167 (% AW)	Single 2 ch 67 (% AW)	Married 2 ch 100-0 (% AW)	Married 2 ch 100-33 (% AW)[2]	Married 2 ch 100-67 (% AW)[2]	Married no ch 100-33 (% AW)[2]
Australia	0.79	0.81	0.87	0.41	0.47	0.39	0.78	0.76
Austria	0.77	0.83	1.01	0.60	0.69	0.69	0.73	0.78
Belgium	0.68	0.74	0.79	0.54	0.56	0.58	0.64	0.65
Canada	0.91	0.86	0.90	0.42	0.27	0.68	0.72	0.83
Chile	1.00	1.00	0.98	0.99	1.00	0.98	1.00	1.00
Czech Republic	0.86	0.90	0.94	0.69	0.71	0.77	0.80	0.87
Denmark	0.91	0.91	0.76	0.66	0.78	0.82	0.84	0.87
Estonia	0.95	0.96	0.98	0.75	0.82	0.86	0.88	0.95
Finland	0.73	0.78	0.82	0.62	0.71	0.68	0.70	0.73
France	0.75	0.79	0.88	0.49	0.95	0.96	0.70	0.86
Germany	0.81	0.79	0.99	0.67	0.72	0.73	0.74	0.81
Greece	0.82	0.86	0.81	0.77	0.83	0.82	0.83	0.84
Hungary	1.00	1.00	1.00	0.69	0.78	0.83	0.86	1.00
Iceland	0.85	0.89	0.85	0.64	0.66	0.76	0.87	0.85
Ireland	0.81	0.63	0.74	0.28	0.69	0.74	0.79	0.80
Israel[1]	0.83	0.82	0.78	0.67	0.79	0.76	0.76	0.78
Italy	0.76	0.87	0.80	0.59	0.72	0.71	0.76	0.79
Japan	0.97	0.93	0.93	0.89	0.86	0.88	0.89	0.92
Korea	0.88	0.92	0.88	1.00	0.89	0.89	0.89	0.90
Latvia	0.96	0.97	0.98	0.75	0.82	0.84	0.87	0.96
Luxembourg	0.76	0.72	0.81	0.54	0.72	0.70	0.64	0.79
Mexico	0.91	0.90	0.91	0.91	0.90	0.86	0.87	0.86
Netherlands	0.74	0.77	0.76	0.55	0.71	0.67	0.69	0.72
New Zealand	0.96	0.85	0.88	0.54	0.52	0.56	0.84	0.84
Norway	0.86	0.90	0.81	0.74	0.84	0.83	0.86	0.87
Poland	0.97	0.98	0.99	1.00	0.91	0.92	0.94	0.97
Portugal	0.76	0.82	0.77	0.92	0.84	0.70	0.76	0.75
Slovak Republic	0.88	0.91	0.95	0.74	0.75	0.80	0.84	0.87
Slovenia	0.92	0.85	0.73	0.63	0.74	0.82	0.86	0.82
Spain	0.86	0.83	0.87	0.72	0.83	0.78	0.79	0.80
Sweden	0.92	0.90	0.62	0.82	0.83	0.83	0.85	0.88
Switzerland	0.91	0.92	0.86	0.84	0.86	0.84	0.83	0.91
Turkey	0.89	0.84	0.90	0.87	0.82	0.80	0.82	0.81
United Kingdom	0.84	0.89	0.83	0.26	0.83	0.80	0.84	0.84
United States	0.92	0.82	0.88	0.51	0.82	0.86	0.89	0.92
Unweighted average								
OECD-Average	**0.86**	**0.86**	**0.86**	**0.68**	**0.76**	**0.78**	**0.81**	**0.84**
OECD-EU 22	**0.84**	**0.85**	**0.86**	**0.65**	**0.77**	**0.77**	**0.79**	**0.83**

Note: ch = children

Net income is calculated as gross earnings minus personal income tax and employees' social security contributions plus family benefits. The increase reported in the Table represents a form of elasticity. In a proportional tax system the elasticity would equal 1. The more progressive the system at these income levels, the lower is the elasticity. The reported elasticities in Table 3.8 are calculated as (100 - METR) / (100 - AETR), where METR is the marginal rate of income tax plus employee social security contributions less cash benefits reported in Table 3.7 and AETR is the average rate plus employee social security contributions less cash benefits reported in Table 3.3.

1. Information on data for Israel: http://oe.cd/israel-disclaimer.
2. Two-earner family. Assumes a rise in the labour costs associated with the principal earner in the household.

StatLink http://dx.doi.org/10.1787/888933461165

Table 3.9. Percentage increase in net income relative to percentage increase in gross labour cost, 2016

After an increase of 1 currency unit in gross labour cost, by family-type and wage level

	Single no ch 67 (% AW)	Single no ch 100 (% AW)	Single no ch 167 (% AW)	Single 2 ch 67 (% AW)	Married 2 ch 100-0 (% AW)	Married 2 ch 100-33 (% AW)[2]	Married 2 ch 100-67 (% AW)[2]	Married no ch 100-33 (% AW)[2]
Australia	0.79	0.81	0.87	0.41	0.47	0.39	0.78	0.76
Austria	0.77	0.83	1.19	0.60	0.69	0.69	0.73	0.78
Belgium	0.65	0.72	0.80	0.52	0.54	0.54	0.62	0.61
Canada	0.90	0.88	0.94	0.42	0.28	0.69	0.73	0.84
Chile	1.00	1.00	0.98	0.99	1.00	0.98	1.00	1.00
Czech Republic	0.86	0.90	0.94	0.69	0.71	0.77	0.80	0.87
Denmark	0.92	0.91	0.77	0.67	0.78	0.83	0.85	0.88
Estonia	0.95	0.96	0.98	0.75	0.82	0.86	0.88	0.95
Finland	0.73	0.78	0.82	0.62	0.71	0.68	0.70	0.73
France	0.54	0.79	0.88	0.35	0.95	0.91	0.69	0.81
Germany	0.81	0.79	1.15	0.67	0.72	0.73	0.74	0.81
Greece	0.82	0.86	0.81	0.77	0.83	0.82	0.83	0.84
Hungary	1.00	1.00	1.00	0.69	0.78	0.83	0.86	1.00
Iceland	0.85	0.89	0.85	0.64	0.66	0.76	0.87	0.85
Ireland	0.81	0.63	0.74	0.28	0.69	0.74	0.79	0.79
Israel[1]	0.81	0.80	0.77	0.65	0.77	0.74	0.74	0.76
Italy	0.76	0.87	0.80	0.59	0.72	0.71	0.76	0.79
Japan	0.97	0.93	1.00	0.89	0.86	0.88	0.89	0.92
Korea	0.88	0.92	0.90	1.00	0.89	0.89	0.89	0.90
Latvia	0.96	0.97	0.98	0.75	0.82	0.84	0.87	0.96
Luxembourg	0.76	0.72	0.81	0.54	0.72	0.70	0.64	0.79
Mexico	0.98	0.94	0.93	0.98	0.94	0.91	0.91	0.91
Netherlands	0.75	0.77	0.82	0.55	0.71	0.67	0.69	0.72
New Zealand	0.96	0.85	0.88	0.54	0.52	0.56	0.84	0.84
Norway	0.86	0.90	0.81	0.74	0.84	0.83	0.86	0.87
Poland	0.97	0.98	0.99	1.00	0.91	0.92	0.94	0.97
Portugal	0.76	0.82	0.77	0.92	0.84	0.70	0.76	0.75
Slovak Republic	0.88	0.91	0.95	0.74	0.75	0.79	0.84	0.86
Slovenia	0.92	0.85	0.73	0.63	0.74	0.82	0.86	0.82
Spain	0.86	0.83	1.12	0.72	0.83	0.78	0.79	0.80
Sweden	0.92	0.90	0.62	0.82	0.83	0.83	0.85	0.88
Switzerland	0.91	0.92	0.86	0.84	0.86	0.84	0.83	0.91
Turkey	0.89	0.84	0.90	0.87	0.82	0.80	0.82	0.81
United Kingdom	0.81	0.86	0.81	0.25	0.81	0.77	0.81	0.81
United States	0.93	0.83	0.89	0.51	0.83	0.87	0.89	0.93
Unweighted average								
OECD-Average	**0.85**	**0.86**	**0.89**	**0.67**	**0.76**	**0.77**	**0.81**	**0.84**
OECD-EU 22	**0.83**	**0.85**	**0.89**	**0.64**	**0.77**	**0.77**	**0.79**	**0.83**

Note: ch = children

Net income is calculated as gross earnings minus personal income tax and employees' social security contributions plus family benefits. The increase reported in the Table represents a form of elasticity. In a proportional tax system the elasticity would equal 1. The more progressive the system at these income levels, the lower is the elasticity. The reported elasticities in Table 3.9 are calculated as (100 - METR) / (100 - AETR), where METR is the marginal rate of income tax plus employee and employer social security contributions less cash benefits reported in Table 3.6 and AETR is the average rate plus employee and employer social security contributions less cash benefits reported in Table 3.1.

1. Information on data for Israel: http://oe.cd/israel-disclaimer.
2. Two-earner family. Assumes a rise in the labour costs associated with the principal earner in the household.

StatLink http://dx.doi.org/10.1787/888933461177

Table 3.10a. Annual gross wage and net income, single person, 2016

In US dollars using PPP, by family-type and wage level

	Single no ch 67 (% AW)		Single no ch 100 (% AW)		Single no ch 167 (% AW)		Single 2 ch 67 (% AW)	
	Total gross earnings before taxes	Net income after taxes	Total gross earnings before taxes	Net income after taxes	Total gross earnings before taxes	Net income after taxes	Total gross earnings before taxes	Net income after taxes
Australia	38 007	30 855	56 727	42 930	94 733	66 114	38 007	40 706
Austria	37 305	27 507	55 680	37 934	92 985	58 142	37 305	35 125
Belgium	39 003	25 979	58 214	34 492	97 217	50 060	39 003	32 859
Canada	27 484	22 618	41 021	31 554	68 505	50 455	27 484	35 367
Chile	13 746	12 784	20 517	19 081	34 263	31 518	13 746	12 908
Czech Republic	17 348	13 902	25 893	19 789	43 242	31 742	17 348	17 436
Denmark	38 398	25 541	57 310	36 701	95 709	55 367	38 398	35 851
Estonia	17 112	14 234	25 540	20 869	42 652	34 340	17 112	18 035
Finland	32 481	24 809	48 479	33 551	80 960	50 004	32 481	28 996
France	32 037	23 939	47 817	33 904	79 854	52 274	32 037	31 716
Germany	41 372	27 011	61 750	37 260	103 122	57 892	41 372	34 085
Greece	22 093	17 632	32 974	24 602	55 067	37 244	22 093	18 848
Hungary	17 170	11 418	25 627	17 042	42 797	28 460	17 170	16 487
Iceland	39 560	29 495	59 044	41 806	98 604	64 864	39 560	33 291
Ireland	29 974	26 168	44 737	36 126	74 711	51 263	29 974	39 430
Israel[1]	24 981	22 190	37 286	30 649	62 267	45 519	24 981	26 247
Italy	28 251	22 071	42 166	29 045	70 418	42 609	28 251	27 848
Japan	33 687	26 773	50 278	39 118	83 965	62 201	33 687	29 134
Korea	32 816	29 336	48 979	42 051	81 794	67 343	32 816	30 056
Latvia	13 760	9 901	20 537	14 571	34 297	24 054	13 760	12 678
Luxembourg	43 900	33 872	65 522	45 239	109 421	67 154	43 900	45 552
Mexico	8 785	8 456	13 112	11 691	21 897	18 516	8 785	8 456
Netherlands	42 578	32 873	63 549	44 200	106 126	65 870	42 578	43 783
New Zealand	26 590	22 969	39 687	32 586	66 277	50 656	26 590	30 053
Norway	40 213	30 363	60 020	43 258	100 233	65 724	40 213	35 456
Poland	18 320	13 889	27 343	20 506	45 663	33 940	18 320	15 054
Portugal	20 064	15 811	29 946	21 691	50 009	32 828	20 064	19 513
Slovak Republic	15 311	12 252	22 852	17 542	38 162	28 282	15 311	14 509
Slovenia	21 063	14 998	31 437	20 927	52 500	32 882	21 063	21 914
Spain	26 985	22 459	40 276	31 664	67 261	48 926	26 985	26 507
Sweden	31 791	24 727	47 450	35 658	79 241	50 598	31 791	27 755
Switzerland	46 951	40 381	70 077	58 246	117 028	91 594	46 951	47 954
Turkey	18 827	14 272	28 099	20 438	46 926	31 977	18 827	14 611
United Kingdom	35 524	28 748	53 020	40 646	88 544	62 182	35 524	36 390
United States	35 204	27 090	52 543	38 894	87 747	60 263	35 204	33 430
Unweighted average								
OECD-Average	**28 820**	**22 495**	**43 015**	**31 607**	**71 834**	**48 653**	**28 820**	**27 944**
OECD-EU 22	**28 265**	**21 352**	**42 187**	**29 725**	**70 453**	**45 278**	**28 265**	**27 290**

Note: ch = children

1. Information on data for Israel: http://oe.cd/israel-disclaimer.

StatLink http://dx.doi.org/10.1787/888933461184

Table 3.10b. Annual gross wage and net income, married couple, 2016

In US dollars using PPP, by family-type and wage level

	Married 2 ch 100-0 (% AW)		Married 2 ch 100-33 (% AW)[2]		Married 2 ch 100-67 (% AW)[2]		Married no ch 100-33 (% AW)[2]	
	Total gross earnings before taxes	Net income after taxes	Total gross earnings before taxes	Net income after taxes	Total gross earnings before taxes	Net income after taxes	Total gross earnings before taxes	Net income after taxes
Australia	56 727	49 245	75 446	60 459	94 733	73 784	75 446	60 415
Austria	55 680	45 552	74 054	60 837	92 985	72 361	74 054	54 058
Belgium	58 214	46 026	77 425	58 880	97 217	66 611	77 425	52 676
Canada	41 021	40 547	54 558	48 571	68 505	57 790	54 558	43 814
Chile	20 517	19 081	27 287	26 018	34 263	31 989	27 287	25 377
Czech Republic	25 893	25 271	34 438	30 928	43 242	37 225	34 438	27 394
Denmark	57 310	42 706	76 223	54 108	95 709	65 816	76 223	50 534
Estonia	25 540	24 572	33 968	31 207	42 652	38 043	33 968	28 268
Finland	48 479	36 258	64 477	50 733	80 960	61 179	64 477	47 915
France	47 817	39 173	63 596	51 456	79 854	61 604	63 596	47 165
Germany	61 750	48 603	82 127	60 012	103 122	70 922	82 127	53 696
Greece	36 272	27 922	48 241	37 476	60 574	46 628	48 241	36 786
Hungary	25 627	21 833	34 084	27 456	42 797	33 251	34 084	22 666
Iceland	59 044	48 265	78 529	59 390	98 604	71 302	78 529	58 502
Ireland	44 737	45 438	59 501	56 758	74 711	66 968	59 501	52 535
Israel[1]	37 286	31 712	49 590	43 586	62 267	55 214	49 590	42 522
Italy	42 166	34 122	56 081	45 592	70 418	54 345	56 081	42 361
Japan	50 278	42 186	66 870	55 034	83 965	68 252	66 870	52 673
Korea	48 979	43 249	65 142	57 776	81 794	72 400	65 142	56 855
Latvia	20 537	17 348	27 315	22 437	34 297	27 249	27 315	19 660
Luxembourg	65 522	61 658	87 144	77 680	109 421	90 488	87 144	68 910
Mexico	13 112	11 691	17 483	16 338	21 853	20 109	17 483	16 338
Netherlands	63 549	47 907	84 520	67 780	106 126	82 920	84 520	63 193
New Zealand	39 687	37 244	52 783	45 941	66 277	55 197	52 783	44 065
Norway	60 020	46 386	79 827	62 458	100 233	76 097	79 827	59 981
Poland	27 343	22 097	36 366	28 851	45 663	35 668	36 366	27 578
Portugal	29 946	26 605	39 828	34 622	50 009	39 671	39 828	31 444
Slovak Republic	22 852	21 311	30 393	26 631	38 162	32 051	30 393	24 374
Slovenia	31 437	27 792	41 812	33 554	52 500	40 023	41 812	29 008
Spain	40 276	34 610	53 567	44 842	67 261	55 584	53 567	44 111
Sweden	47 450	38 686	63 108	51 882	79 241	63 413	63 108	48 854
Switzerland	70 077	67 688	93 202	87 037	117 028	105 369	93 202	79 641
Turkey	28 099	21 004	37 372	28 539	46 926	35 050	37 372	28 199
United Kingdom	53 020	43 565	70 517	59 736	88 544	71 994	70 517	57 135
United States	52 543	45 133	69 882	57 392	87 747	70 022	69 882	53 808
Unweighted average								
OECD-Average	**43 109**	**36 643**	**57 336**	**47 486**	**71 990**	**57 331**	**57 336**	**44 358**
OECD-EU 22	**42 337**	**35 412**	**56 308**	**46 066**	**70 703**	**55 182**	**56 308**	**42 287**

Note: ch = children

1. Information on data for Israel: http://oe.cd/israel-disclaimer.
2. Two-earner family.

StatLink http://dx.doi.org/10.1787/888933461199

Table 3.11a. Annual labour costs and net income, single person, 2016

In US dollars using PPP, by family-type and wage level

	Single no ch 67 (% AW)		Single no ch 100 (% AW)		Single no ch 167 (% AW)		Single 2 ch 67 (% AW)	
	Total gross labour costs before taxes	Net income after taxes	Total gross labour costs before taxes	Net income after taxes	Total gross labour costs before taxes	Net income after taxes	Total gross labour costs before taxes	Net income after taxes
Australia	40 275	30 855	60 112	42 930	100 387	66 114	40 275	40 706
Austria	48 090	27 507	71 776	37 934	118 222	58 142	48 090	35 125
Belgium	49 459	25 979	74 913	34 492	124 820	50 060	49 459	32 859
Canada	30 775	22 618	45 998	31 554	74 984	50 455	30 775	35 367
Chile	13 746	12 784	20 517	19 081	34 263	31 518	13 746	12 908
Czech Republic	23 247	13 902	34 697	19 789	57 944	31 742	23 247	17 436
Denmark	38 846	25 541	57 759	36 701	96 157	55 367	38 846	35 851
Estonia	22 896	14 234	34 173	20 869	57 068	34 340	22 896	18 035
Finland	39 974	24 809	59 663	33 551	99 637	50 004	39 974	28 996
France	42 016	23 939	65 294	33 904	114 613	52 274	42 016	31 716
Germany	49 368	27 011	73 683	37 260	119 115	57 892	49 368	34 085
Greece	27 583	17 632	41 169	24 602	68 752	37 244	27 583	18 848
Hungary	22 063	11 418	32 930	17 042	54 994	28 460	22 063	16 487
Iceland	42 467	29 495	63 384	41 806	105 851	64 864	42 467	33 291
Ireland	33 196	26 168	49 547	36 126	82 743	51 263	33 196	39 430
Israel[1]	26 132	22 190	39 359	30 649	66 214	45 519	26 132	26 247
Italy	37 258	22 071	55 609	29 045	92 867	42 609	37 258	27 848
Japan	38 781	26 773	57 882	39 118	95 696	62 201	38 781	29 134
Korea	36 216	29 336	54 053	42 051	89 205	67 343	36 216	30 056
Latvia	17 015	9 901	25 391	14 571	42 397	24 054	17 015	12 678
Luxembourg	49 238	33 872	73 489	45 239	122 727	67 154	49 238	45 552
Mexico	9 988	8 456	14 638	11 691	24 091	18 516	9 988	8 456
Netherlands	47 383	32 873	70 665	44 200	113 854	65 870	47 383	43 783
New Zealand	26 590	22 969	39 687	32 586	66 277	50 656	26 590	30 053
Norway	45 441	30 363	67 823	43 258	113 264	65 724	45 441	35 456
Poland	21 394	13 889	31 931	20 506	53 325	33 940	21 394	15 054
Portugal	24 829	15 811	37 058	21 691	61 886	32 828	24 829	19 513
Slovak Republic	20 087	12 252	29 981	17 542	50 069	28 282	20 087	14 509
Slovenia	24 454	14 998	36 499	20 927	60 953	32 882	24 454	21 914
Spain	35 053	22 459	52 319	31 664	86 965	48 926	35 053	26 507
Sweden	41 780	24 727	62 359	35 658	104 139	50 598	41 780	27 755
Switzerland	49 874	40 381	74 439	58 246	124 313	91 594	49 874	47 954
Turkey	22 121	14 272	33 017	20 438	55 138	31 977	22 121	14 611
United Kingdom	38 803	28 748	58 714	40 646	99 140	62 182	38 803	36 390
United States	38 291	27 090	56 956	38 894	94 853	60 263	38 291	33 430
Unweighted average								
OECD-Average	**33 564**	**22 495**	**50 214**	**31 607**	**83 626**	**48 653**	**33 564**	**27 944**
OECD-EU 22	**34 274**	**21 352**	**51 346**	**29 725**	**85 563**	**45 278**	**34 274**	**27 290**

Note: ch = children

1. Information on data for Israel: http://oe.cd/israel-disclaimer.

StatLink http://dx.doi.org/10.1787/888933461208

Table 3.11b. **Annual labour costs and net income, married couple, 2016**

In US dollars using PPP, by family-type and wage level

	Married 2 ch 100-0 (% AW)		Married 2 ch 100-33 (% AW)[2]		Married 2 ch 100-67 (% AW)[2]		Married no ch 100-33 (% AW)[2]	
	Total gross labour costs before taxes	Net income after taxes	Total gross labour costs before taxes	Net income after taxes	Total gross labour costs before taxes	Net income after taxes	Total gross labour costs before taxes	Net income after taxes
Australia	60 112	49 245	79 949	60 459	100 387	73 784	79 949	60 415
Austria	71 776	45 552	95 462	60 837	119 866	72 361	95 462	54 058
Belgium	74 913	46 026	96 147	58 880	124 371	66 611	96 147	52 676
Canada	45 998	40 547	61 085	48 571	76 773	57 790	61 085	43 814
Chile	20 517	19 081	27 287	26 018	34 263	31 989	27 287	25 377
Czech Republic	34 697	25 271	46 147	30 928	57 944	37 225	46 147	27 394
Denmark	57 759	42 706	77 120	54 108	96 605	65 816	77 120	50 534
Estonia	34 173	24 572	45 560	31 207	57 068	38 043	45 560	28 268
Finland	59 663	36 258	79 352	50 733	99 637	61 179	79 352	47 915
France	65 294	39 173	82 285	51 456	107 310	61 604	82 285	47 165
Germany	73 683	48 603	97 998	60 012	123 051	70 922	97 998	53 696
Greece	45 286	27 922	60 230	37 476	75 627	46 628	60 230	36 786
Hungary	32 930	21 833	43 797	27 456	54 994	33 251	43 797	22 666
Iceland	63 384	48 265	84 301	59 390	105 851	71 302	84 301	58 502
Ireland	49 547	45 438	65 565	56 758	82 743	66 968	65 565	52 535
Israel[1]	39 359	31 712	52 087	43 586	65 490	55 214	52 087	42 522
Italy	55 609	34 122	73 960	45 592	92 867	54 345	73 960	42 361
Japan	57 882	42 186	76 983	55 034	96 663	68 252	76 983	52 673
Korea	54 053	43 249	71 891	57 776	90 269	72 400	71 891	56 855
Latvia	25 391	17 348	33 775	22 437	42 405	27 249	33 775	19 660
Luxembourg	73 489	61 658	97 741	77 680	122 727	90 488	97 741	68 910
Mexico	14 638	11 691	19 925	16 338	24 580	20 109	19 925	16 338
Netherlands	70 665	47 907	94 043	67 780	118 048	82 920	94 043	63 193
New Zealand	39 687	37 244	52 783	45 941	66 277	55 197	52 783	44 065
Norway	67 823	46 386	90 204	62 458	113 264	76 097	90 204	59 981
Poland	31 931	22 097	42 468	28 851	53 325	35 668	42 468	27 578
Portugal	37 058	26 605	49 287	34 622	61 886	39 671	49 287	31 444
Slovak Republic	29 981	21 311	39 121	26 631	50 069	32 051	39 121	24 374
Slovenia	36 499	27 792	48 543	33 554	60 953	40 023	48 543	29 008
Spain	52 319	34 610	69 584	44 842	87 372	55 584	69 584	44 111
Sweden	62 359	38 686	82 937	51 882	104 139	63 413	82 937	48 854
Switzerland	74 439	67 688	99 004	87 037	124 313	105 369	99 004	79 641
Turkey	33 017	21 004	43 912	28 539	55 138	35 050	43 912	28 199
United Kingdom	58 714	43 565	77 003	59 736	97 517	71 994	77 003	57 135
United States	56 956	45 133	76 016	57 392	95 247	70 022	76 016	53 808
Unweighted average								
OECD-Average	**50 331**	**36 643**	**66 673**	**47 486**	**83 973**	**57 331**	**66 673**	**44 358**
OECD-EU 22	**51 533**	**35 412**	**68 097**	**46 066**	**85 933**	**55 182**	**68 097**	**42 287**

Note: ch = children

1. Information on data for Israel: http://oe.cd/israel-disclaimer.
2. Two-earner family.

StatLink http://dx.doi.org/10.1787/888933461219

© OECD 2017

PART I

Chapter 4

Graphical exposition of the 2016 tax burden

The chapter presents a graphical exposition of the tax burdens on labour income in 2016 for gross wage earnings ranging from 50% to 250% of the average wage. These are illustrated in separate graphs for each of four family types and for each OECD member country. The family types are single taxpayers without children; single parents with two children; one-earner married couples without children and one-earner married couples with two children.

The graphs are divided in two sets showing the average and the marginal tax wedge components as percentage of total labour costs (central and local income taxes; employee and employer social security contributions and family benefits). The graphs also show the net personal average and marginal tax rates.

The statistical data for Israel are supplied by and under the responsibility of the relevant Israeli authorities. The use of such data by the OECD is without prejudice to the status of the Golan Heights, East Jerusalem and Israeli settlements in the West Bank under the terms of international law.

The graphs in this section show the tax burden on labour income in 2016 for gross wage earnings between 50% and 250% of the average wage (AW). For each OECD member country, there are separate graphs for four family types: single taxpayers without children, single parents with two children, one-earner married couples without children and one-earner married couples with two children. The net personal average and marginal tax rates ([the change in] personal income taxes and employee social security contributions net of cash benefits as a percentage of [the change in] gross wage earnings) are included in the graphs that show respectively the average and the marginal tax wedge.[1]

The graphs illustrate the relative importance of the different components of the tax wedges: central government income taxes, local government income taxes, employee social security contributions, employer social security contributions (including payroll taxes where applicable) and family benefits as a percentage of total labour costs. It should be noted that a decreasing share in total labour costs implies that the values of tax payments less benefits are not increasing as rapidly as the corresponding total labour costs. It does not necessarily imply that the values of payments less benefits are decreasing in cash terms.

Low-income households are treated favourably by the tax-benefit system in many OECD countries. Negative central government income taxes are observed in Belgium because of the non-wastable tax credits for low income workers and for dependent children; in the Czech Republic, Germany, the Slovak Republic and the United Kingdom because of non-wastable child tax credits; in Canada because of the non-wastable working income tax benefit; in Israel because of the non-wastable earned income tax credit (EITC) for families with children (since 2016, single parents have been eligible for the EITC for a wider income range); in Italy because of the Fiscal Bonus targeting low income workers; in Luxembourg and Spain because of non-wastable tax credits for single parents; in Mexico because of the non-wastable employment subsidy credit and in the United States because of the non-wastable EITC and the child tax credit. Concerning Sweden, the charts show negative central government income taxes due to an EITC. However, the tax credit is wastable in the sense that it cannot reduce the total individual's tax payments to less than zero. As a matter of fact, the EITC is also deducted from the local government income tax.

When cash benefits are also taken into account, single parents and/or one-earner married couples with two children do not pay income taxes and employee social security contributions at income levels between 50% and 101% of the AW in twenty-one OECD member countries. For example, the net personal average tax rate for single parents with two children becomes positive at 89% of the AW in New Zealand, 97% of the AW in Ireland and 98% of the AW in Canada. The corresponding measure for one-earner married couples with two children becomes positive at 89% of the AW in New Zealand, 93% of the AW in the Czech Republic, 99% of the AW in the Canada and at 101% of the AW level in Ireland.

There are large variations in family benefit levels across OECD countries. They represent about a quarter or more of total labour costs for low-income single parents and/or one-earner married couples with two children in Australia, Canada, Denmark, Estonia, France, Ireland, Luxembourg, the Netherlands, New Zealand and Slovenia.

The marginal tax wedge is relatively flat across the earnings distribution in some countries because of the flat social security contribution and personal income tax rates. Single taxpayers without children face a flat marginal tax wedge all over the 50% to 250% of AW income range in the Czech Republic (48.6%), Hungary (48.3%) and Latvia (44.2%). The marginal tax wedge is also relatively constant in Chile, Estonia, Iceland, Poland, Turkey and the United Kingdom. In Chile, it is 7.0% on earnings below 115% of the AW and then 10.3% on higher earnings up to 250% of the AW. In Estonia, it is 41.2% on earnings ranging from 58% to 250% of the AW. In Iceland, the marginal tax wedge is 41.1% on earnings from 50% to 123% of the AW and then 48.2% on earnings from 124% of the AW to 250% of the AW. In Poland, it is 37.2% between 50% and 209% of the AW, and then 47.6% up to 250% of the AW. In Turkey, it is 42.8% on earnings below 95% of the AW and 47.8% on earnings between 96% and 250% of the AW. In the United Kingdom, it is 40.3% on earnings below 117% of the AW and then 49.0% on earnings between 118% and 250% of the AW.

Social security contributions are levied at flat rates in many OECD countries. Some countries have an earnings ceiling above which no additional social security contributions have to be paid. The variations in the marginal social security contributions are in general the same for the four family types, since the contribution rates or income ceilings do not vary depending on the marital status or the number of dependent children. Nevertheless, in Hungary the marginal employee social security contributions are higher for the families with children, at low income levels, due to the impact of the withdrawal of the child tax allowance with increasing earnings. Families whose combined personal income tax base is not sufficient to claim the maximum amount of the family tax allowance can deduct the remaining sum from the health insurance and pension contributions.

Within the income range of 50% to 250% of the AW, the marginal employer social security rates fall to zero as a result of income ceilings in Germany (at 156% of the AW), Luxembourg (at 206% of the AW), the Netherlands (at 109% of the AW) and Spain (164% of the AW). The marginal employee social security rates fall to zero in Austria (at 154% of the AW), Canada (at 108% of the AW), Germany (at 156% of the AW), the Netherlands (at 230% of the AW), Spain (at 164% of the AW) and Sweden (at 113% of the AW).

In addition, taxpayers experience declining marginal employee and/or employer social security contribution rates as percentage of total labour costs over some parts of the earnings range as income increases. This can be observed in Austria, Belgium, Canada, France, Germany, Japan, Korea, Luxembourg, the Netherlands, the Slovak Republic, Switzerland, the United Kingdom and the United States. Large decreases in the marginal rates as percentage of total labour costs were observed in Luxembourg where the marginal employee social security contribution rate drops from 11.55% to 1.9% on earnings above 205% of the AW, in the United Kingdom where the marginal employee social security contribution rate drops from 10.54% to 1.76% of earnings above 117% of the AW and in the United States where the marginal employer and employee social security contribution rates drop from 7.11% to 1.43% on earnings above 225% of the AW.

Taxpayers face marginal tax rates and wedges of about 80% or more in several of OECD countries at particular earnings levels. This is the case for low-income taxpayers without children in Australia, Austria, Belgium, France, Ireland, Italy, Mexico, Portugal, Slovenia and the United Kingdom. They also apply to families with children in Australia, Austria,

Belgium, Canada, Chile, the Czech Republic, Estonia, Finland, France, Greece, Ireland, Italy, Japan, Luxembourg, Mexico, Poland, Portugal, the Slovak Republic, Slovenia, Spain and the United Kingdom. In many countries, these high marginal tax rates are partly the result, as income rises, in reductions in benefits, allowances or tax credits that are targeted at low-income taxpayers.

The zigzag movement in the marginal tax burdens observed in some of the graphs arises when the changes in taxes, social security contributions, and/or cash benefits for small rises in income vary over the income range in a non-continuous way. This is the case because of rounding rules in Germany, Luxembourg, Sweden and Switzerland; the discrete characteristics of the PAYE (Pay As You Earn) tax credit, the spouse tax credit and the child transfers in Italy; and in the United States because of the truncation of gross earnings in the calculation of the child tax credit.

Notes

1. The marginal tax wedges in the graphs are calculated in a slightly different manner than the marginal tax rates that are included in the rest of the Taxing Wages publication. In Taxing Wages, marginal rates are usually calculated by increasing gross earnings by one currency unit (except for the spouse in the one-earner married couple whose earnings increase by 33% of the average wage). However, the "+1 currency unit" approach requires the calculation of marginal rates for every single currency unit within the income range included in the graphs. It otherwise would not be correct to draw a line through the different data points because the data for the income levels in between the different points would be missing. In order to reduce the required number of calculations, the marginal rates that are shown in the graphs are calculated by increasing gross earnings by 1 percentage point – each line in the graph therefore consists of 200 data points – instead of 1 currency unit.

TAXING WAGES 2017 © OECD 2017

Australia 2016: Average tax wedge decomposition

By level of gross earnings expressed as a % of the average wage

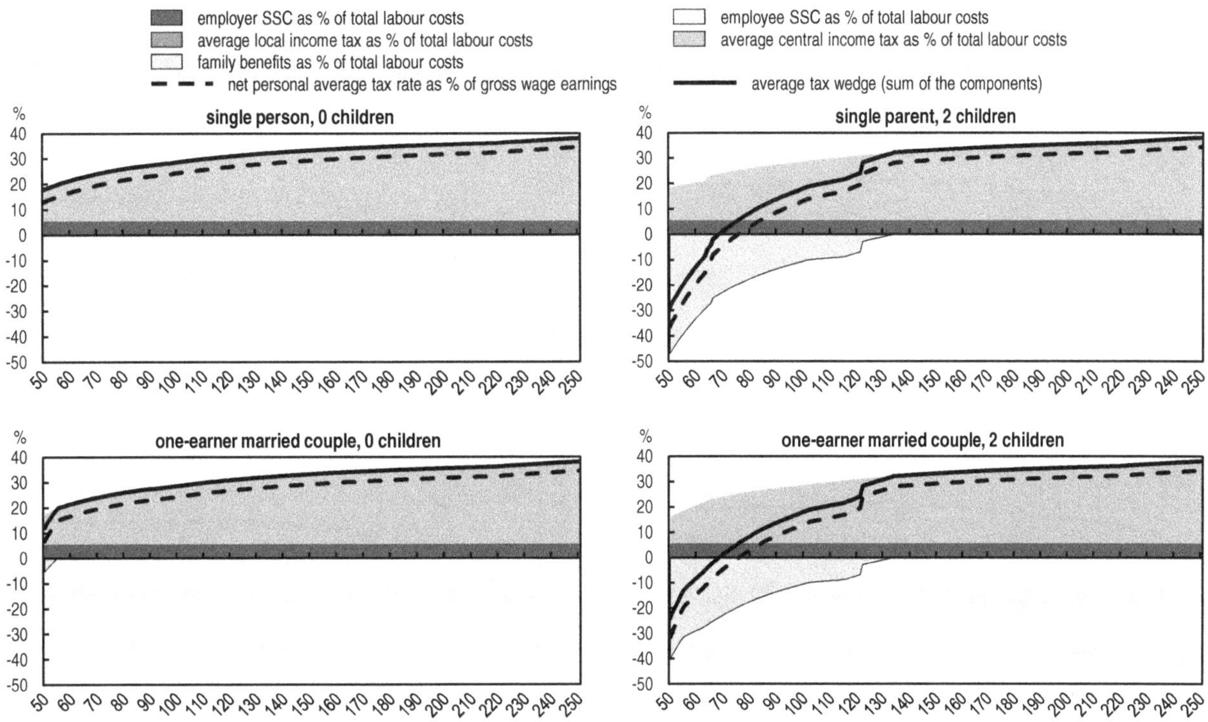

StatLink http://dx.doi.org/10.1787/888933460242

Australia 2016: Marginal tax wedge decomposition

By level of gross earnings expressed as a % of the average wage

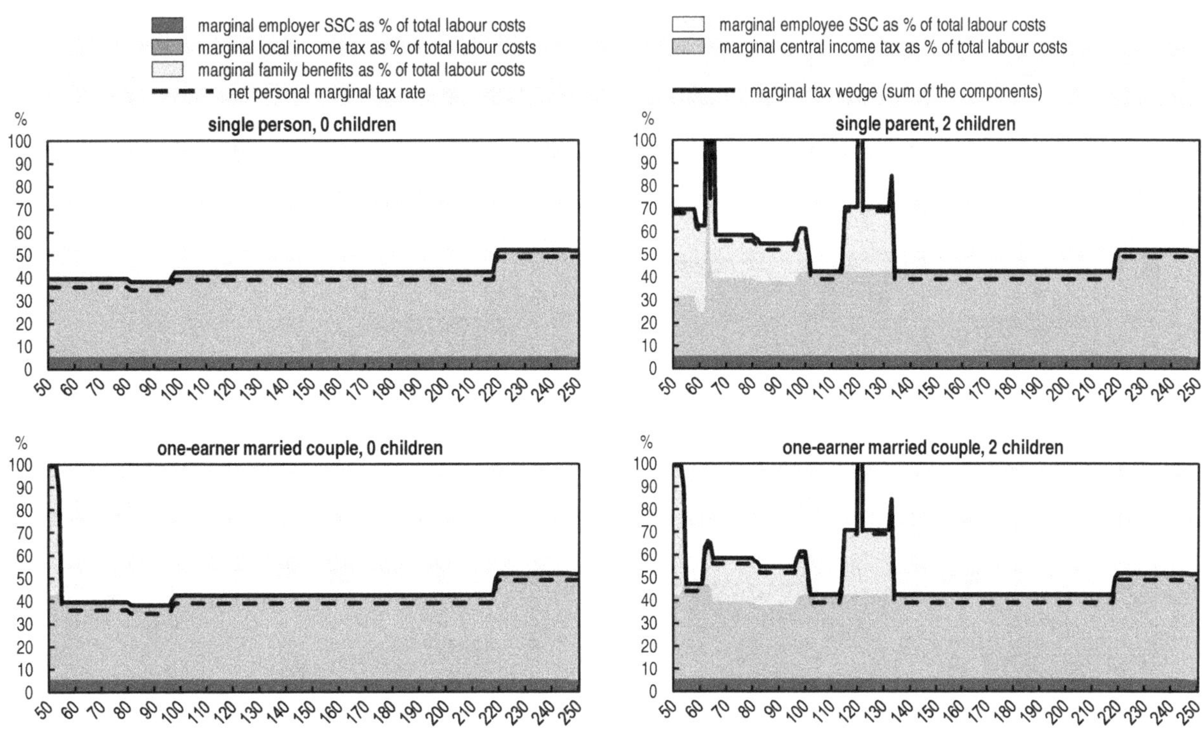

StatLink http://dx.doi.org/10.1787/888933460253

Austria 2016: Average tax wedge decomposition

By level of gross earnings expressed as a % of the average wage

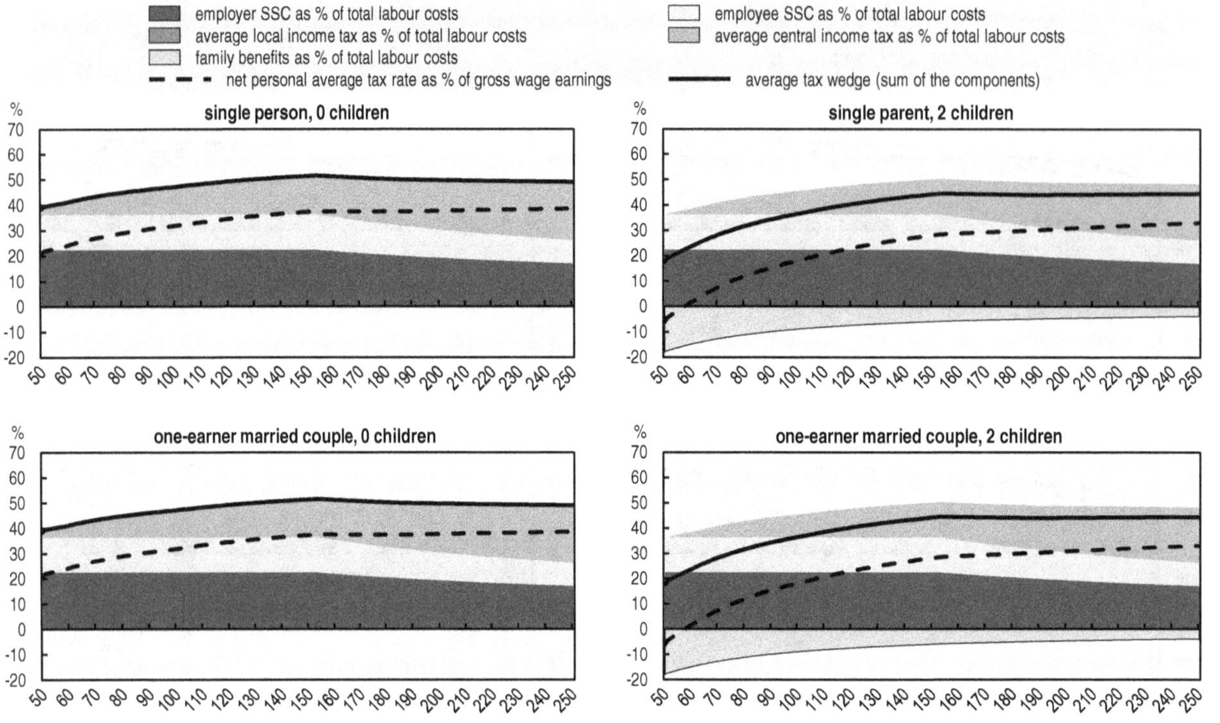

StatLink http://dx.doi.org/10.1787/888933460264

Austria 2016: Marginal tax wedge decomposition

By level of gross earnings expressed as a % of the average wage

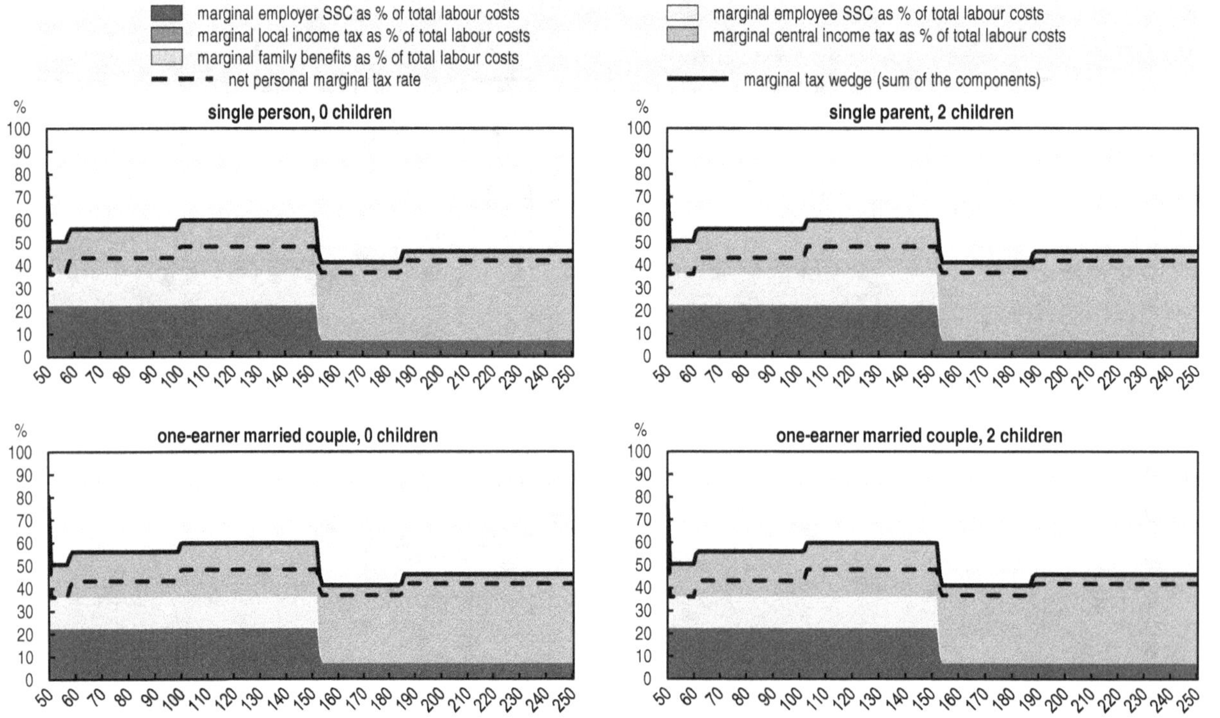

StatLink http://dx.doi.org/10.1787/888933460279

Belgium 2016: Average tax wedge decomposition

By level of gross earnings expressed as a % of the average wage

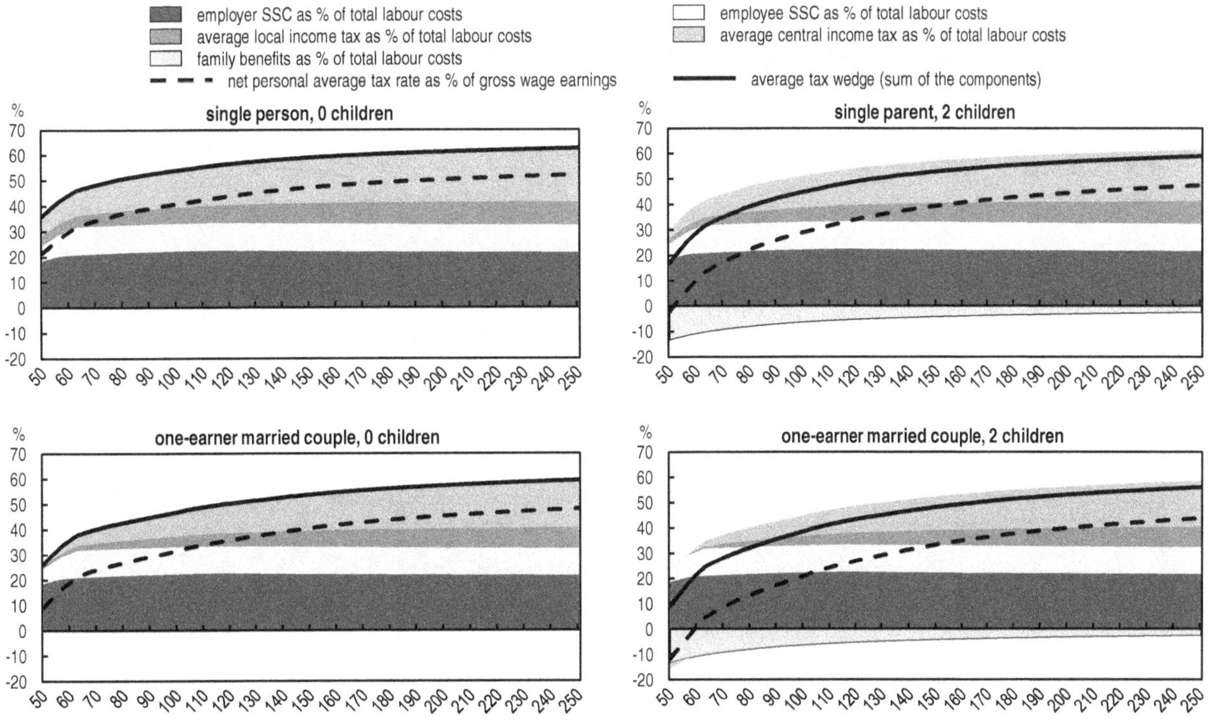

StatLink http://dx.doi.org/10.1787/888933460282

Belgium 2016: Marginal tax wedge decomposition

By level of gross earnings expressed as a % of the average wage

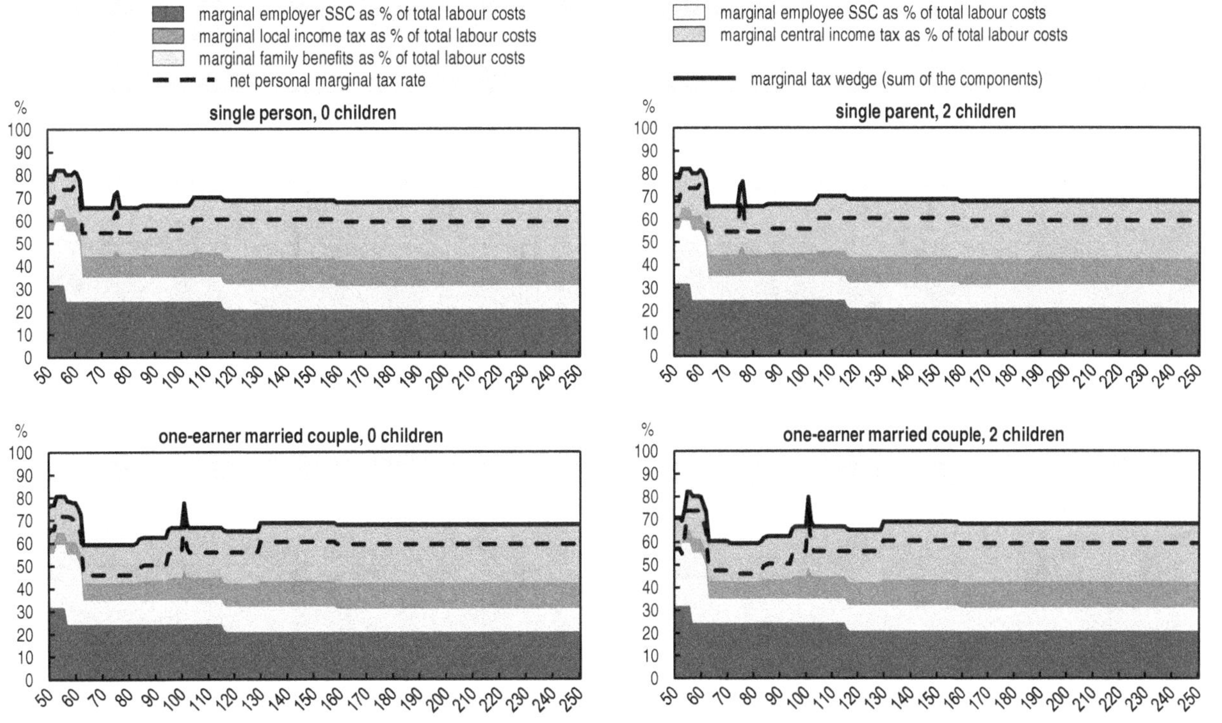

StatLink http://dx.doi.org/10.1787/888933460298

Canada 2016: Average tax wedge decomposition

By level of gross earnings expressed as a % of the average wage

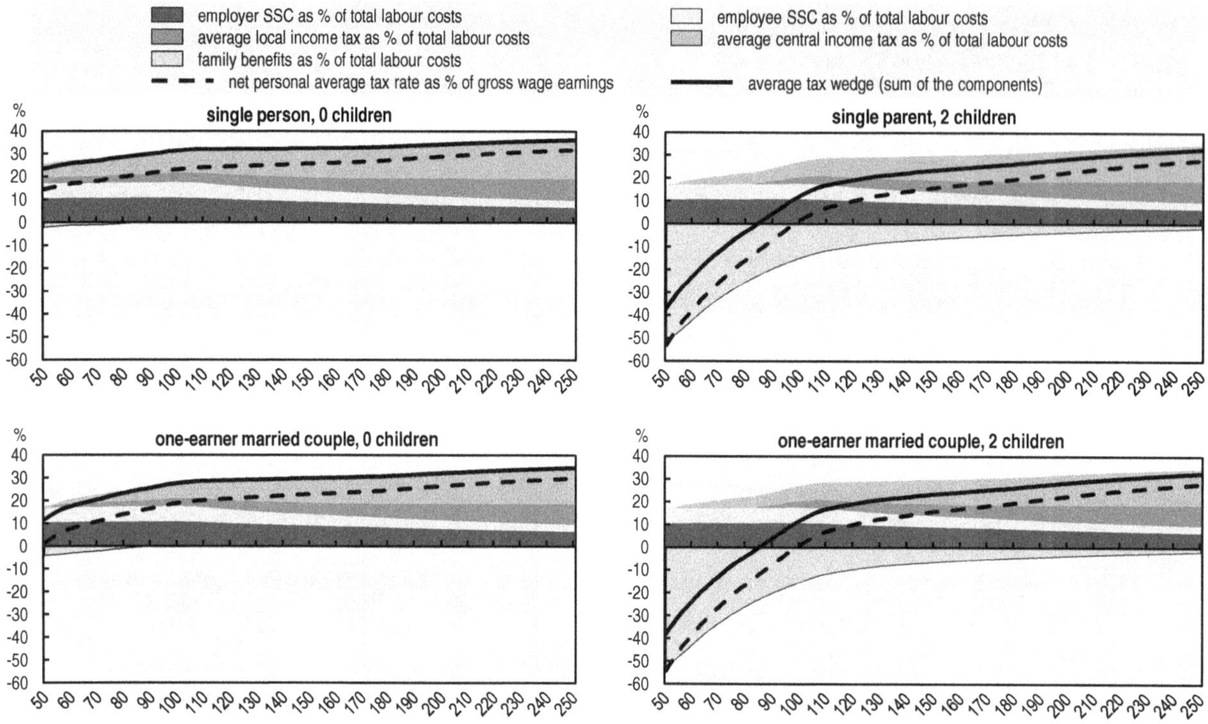

StatLink http://dx.doi.org/10.1787/888933460302

Canada 2016: Marginal tax wedge decomposition

By level of gross earnings expressed as a % of the average wage

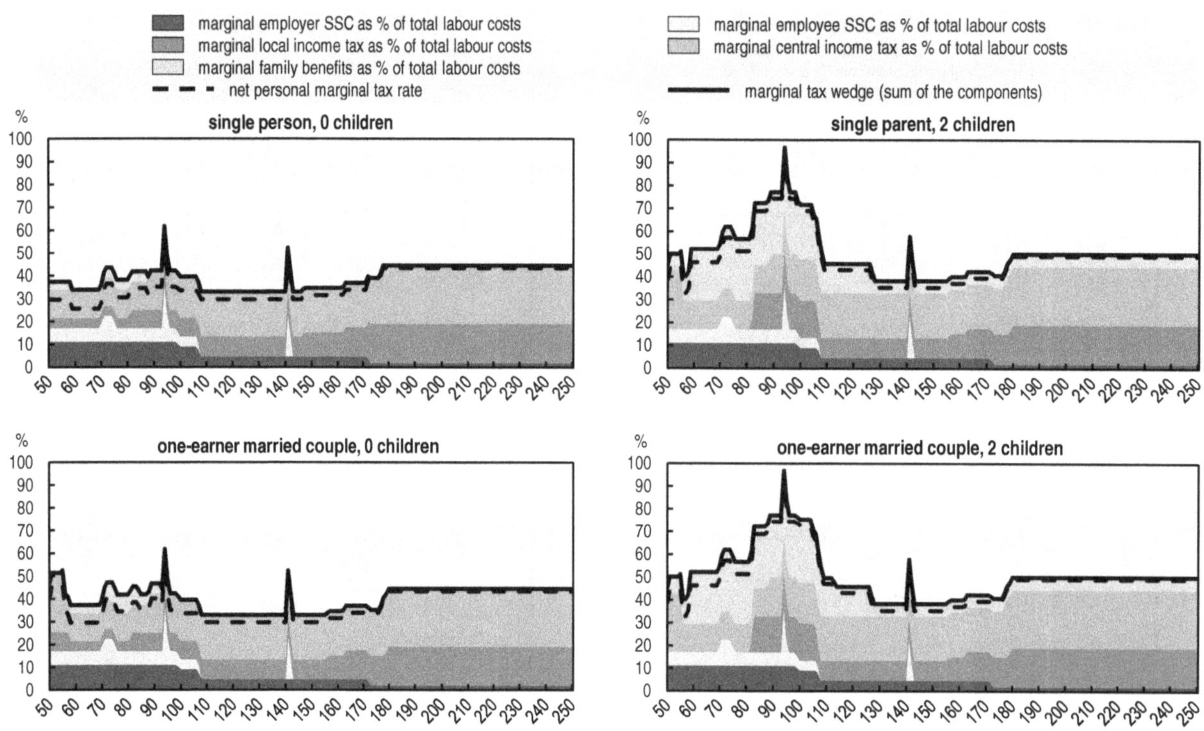

StatLink http://dx.doi.org/10.1787/888933460317

Chile 2016: Average tax wedge decomposition

By level of gross earnings expressed as a % of the average wage

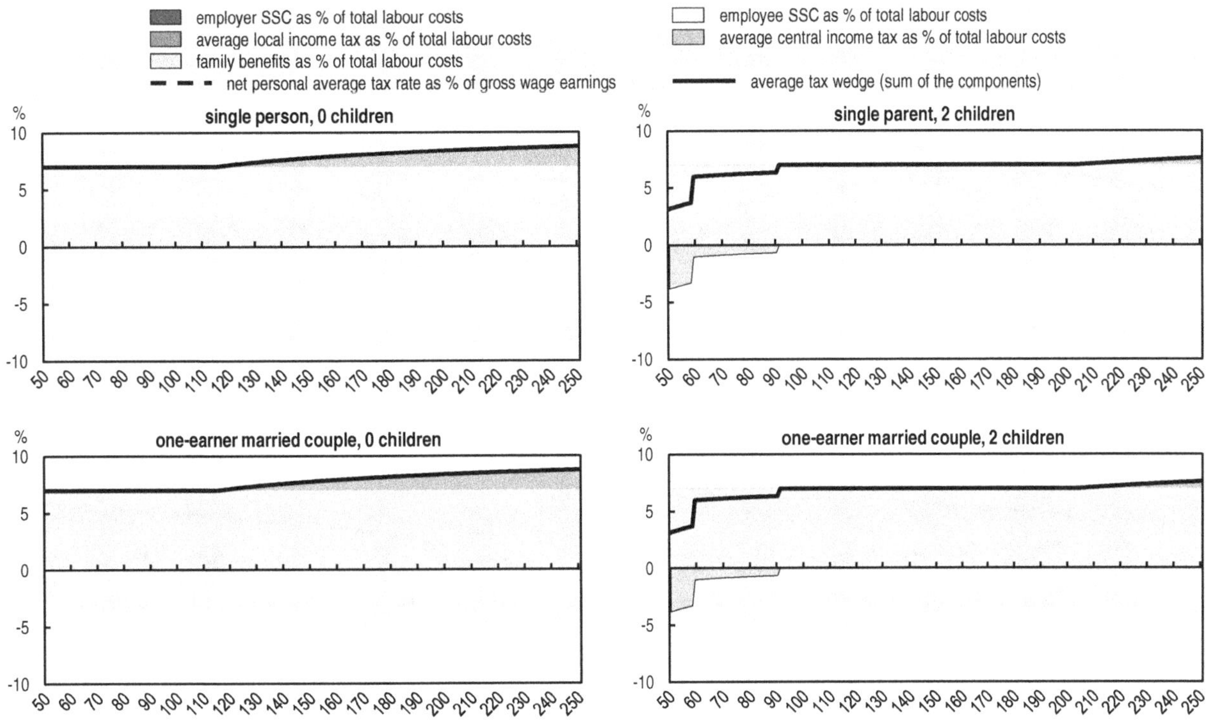

StatLink http://dx.doi.org/10.1787/888933460324

Chile 2016: Marginal tax wedge decomposition

By level of gross earnings expressed as a % of the average wage

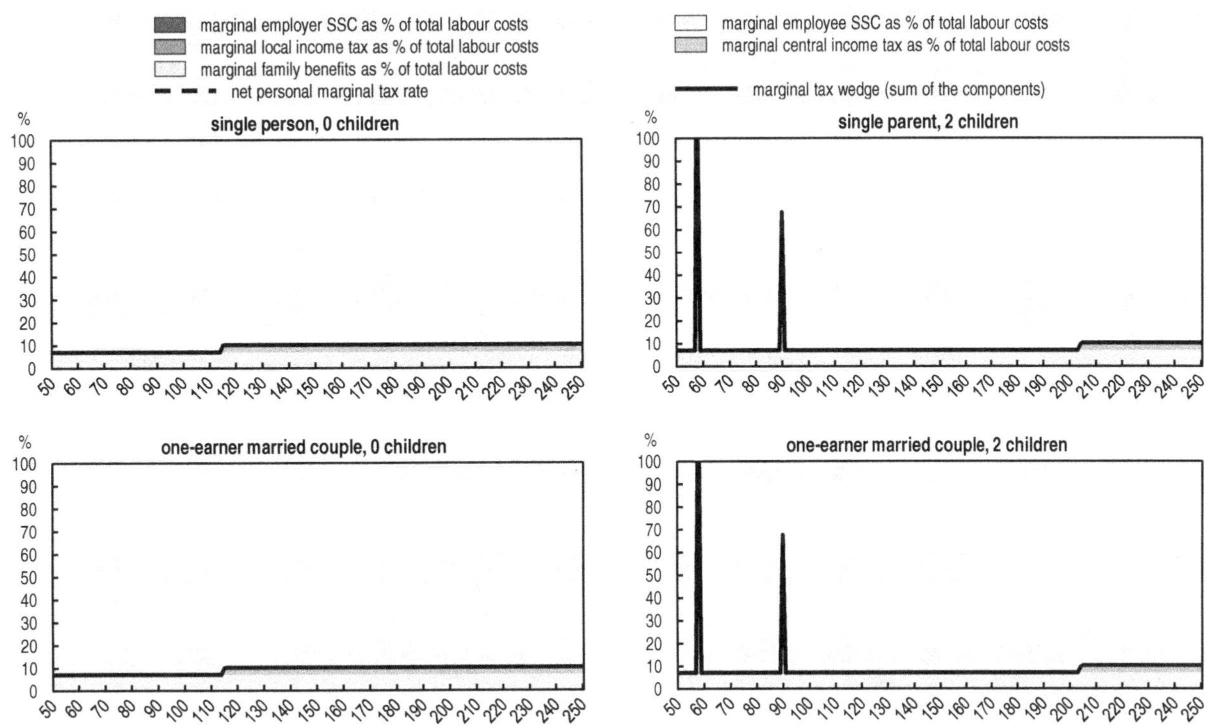

StatLink http://dx.doi.org/10.1787/888933460330

Czech Republic 2016: Average tax wedge decomposition

By level of gross earnings expressed as a % of the average wage

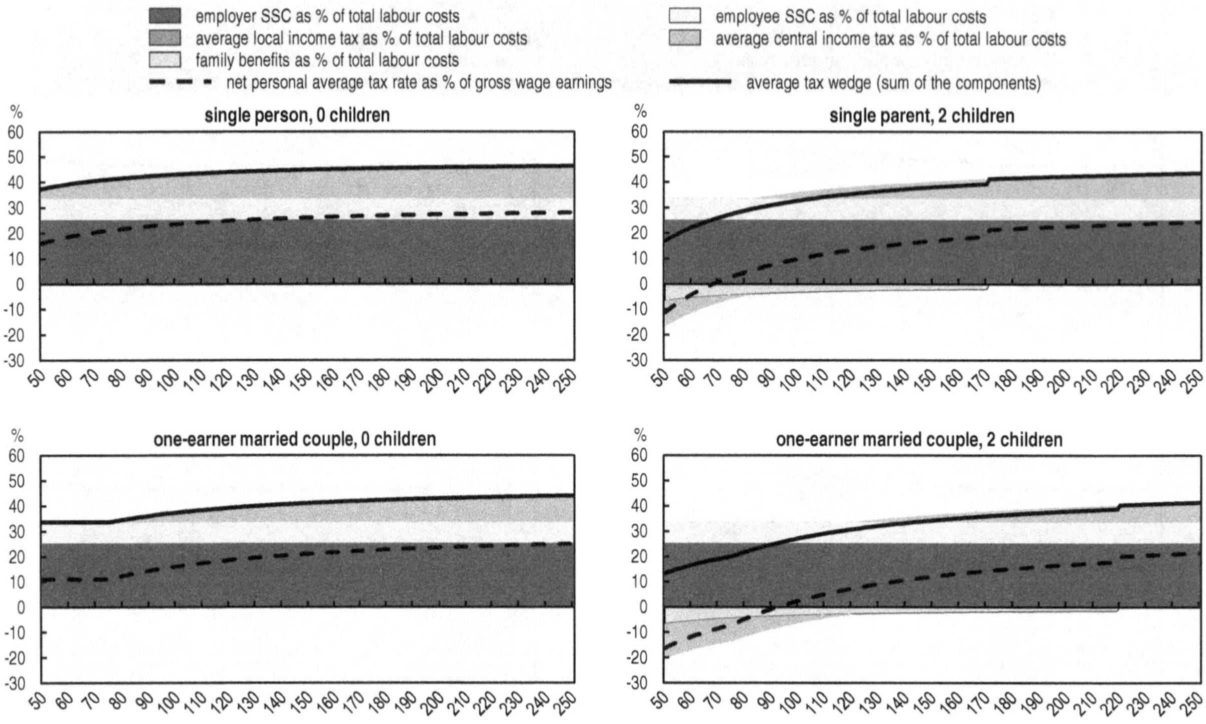

StatLink http://dx.doi.org/10.1787/888933460348

Czech Republic 2016: Marginal tax wedge decomposition

By level of gross earnings expressed as a % of the average wage

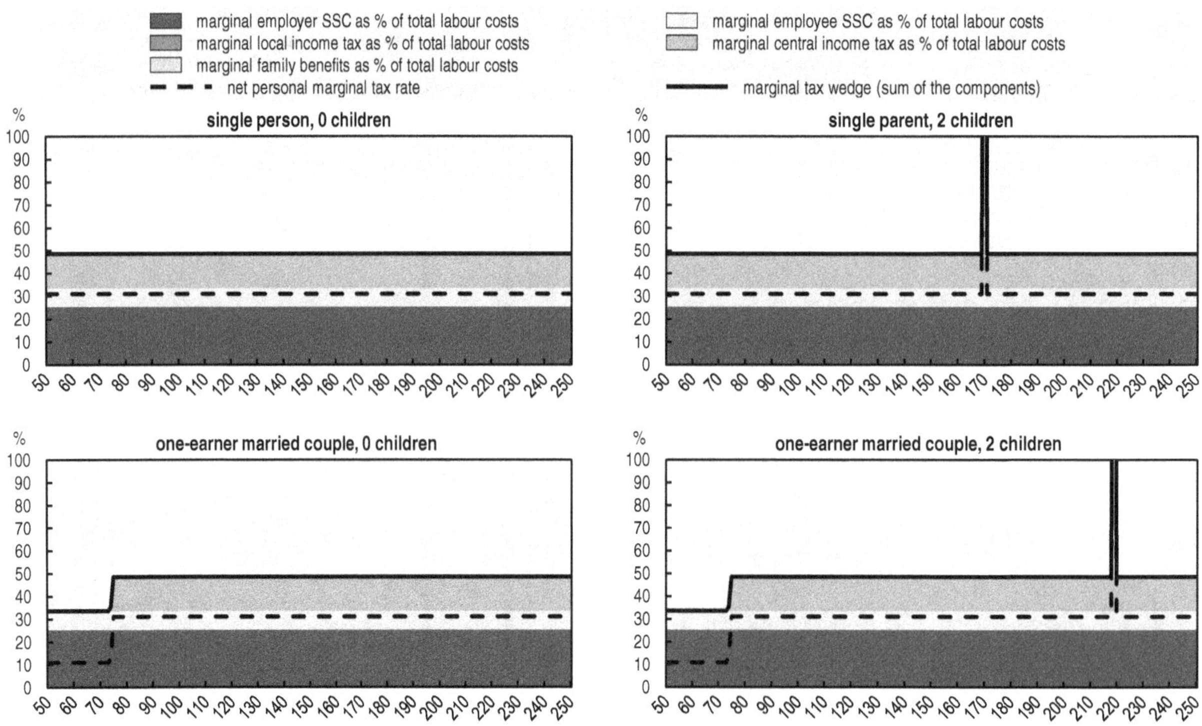

StatLink http://dx.doi.org/10.1787/888933460358

Denmark 2016: Average tax wedge decomposition

By level of gross earnings expressed as a % of the average wage

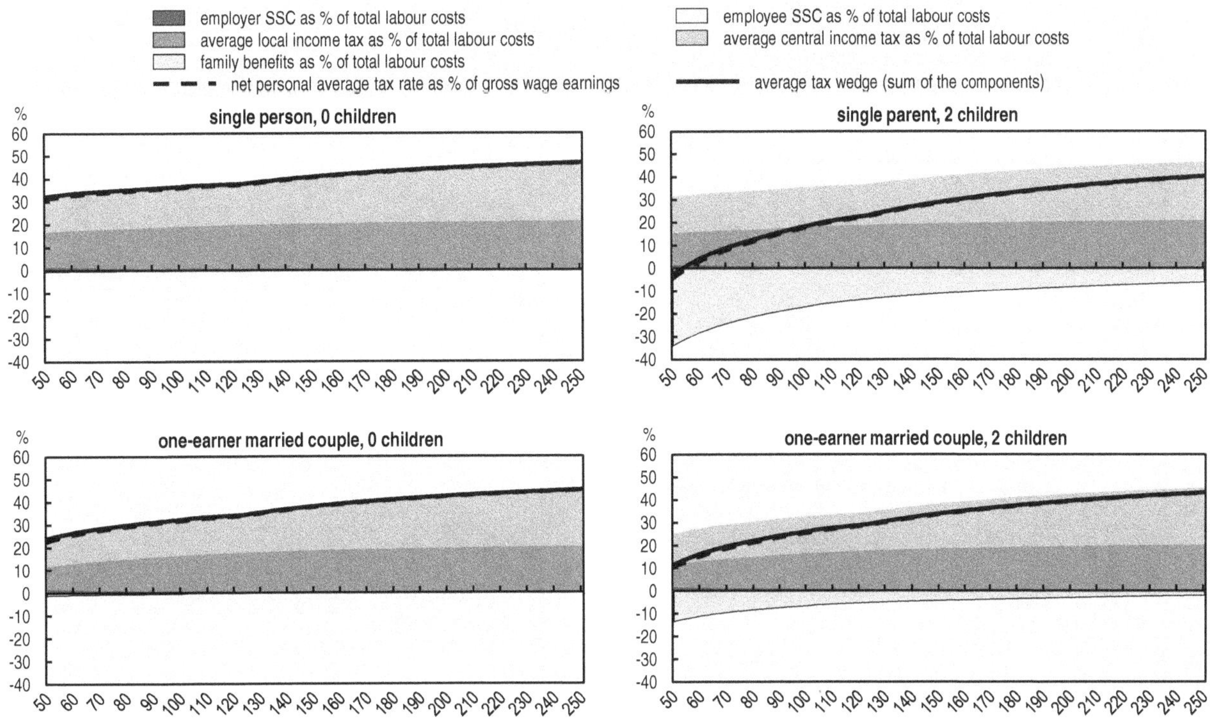

StatLink http://dx.doi.org/10.1787/888933460362

Denmark 2016: Marginal tax wedge decomposition

By level of gross earnings expressed as a % of the average wage

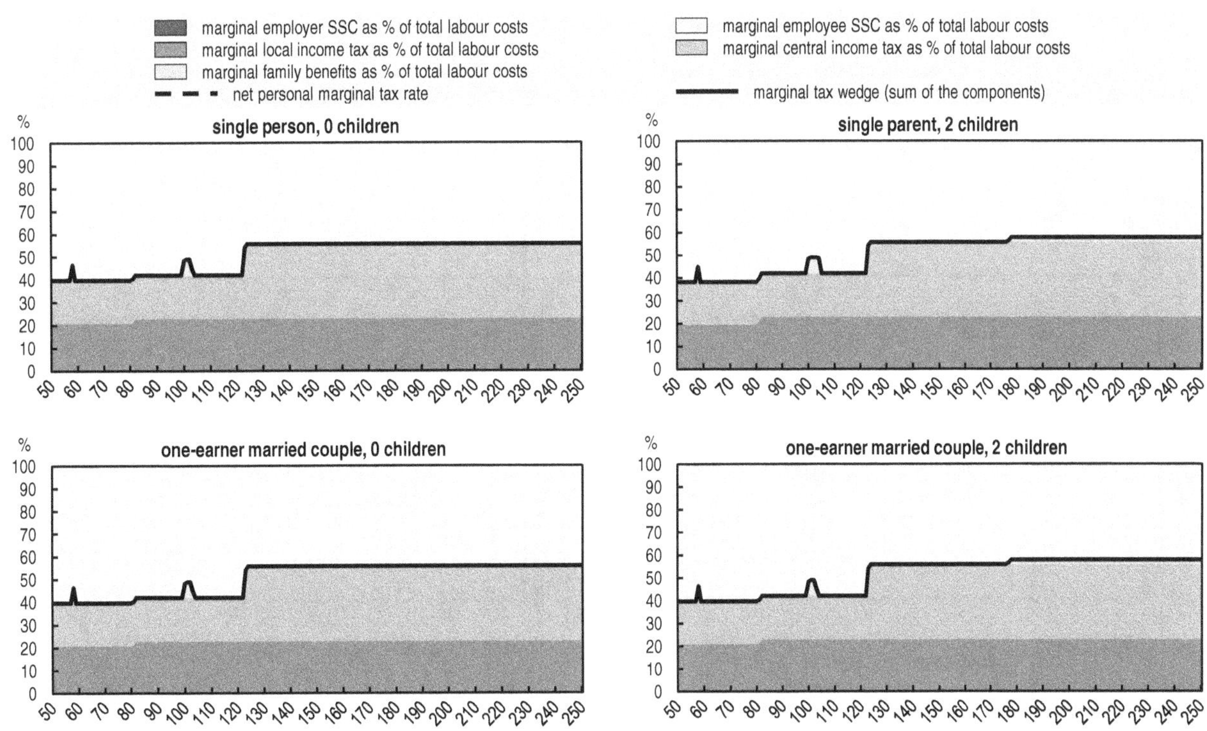

StatLink http://dx.doi.org/10.1787/888933460376

Estonia 2016: Average tax wedge decomposition

By level of gross earnings expressed as a % of the average wage

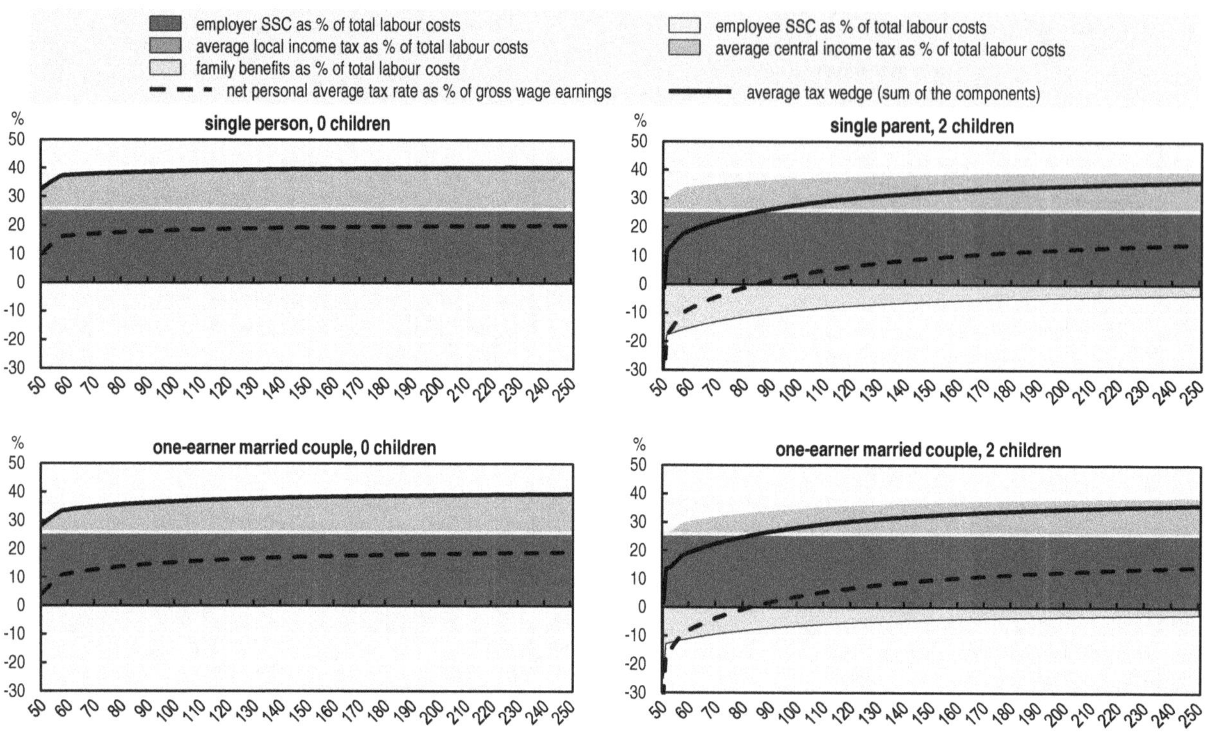

StatLink http://dx.doi.org/10.1787/888933460382

Estonia 2016: Marginal tax wedge decomposition

By level of gross earnings expressed as a % of the average wage

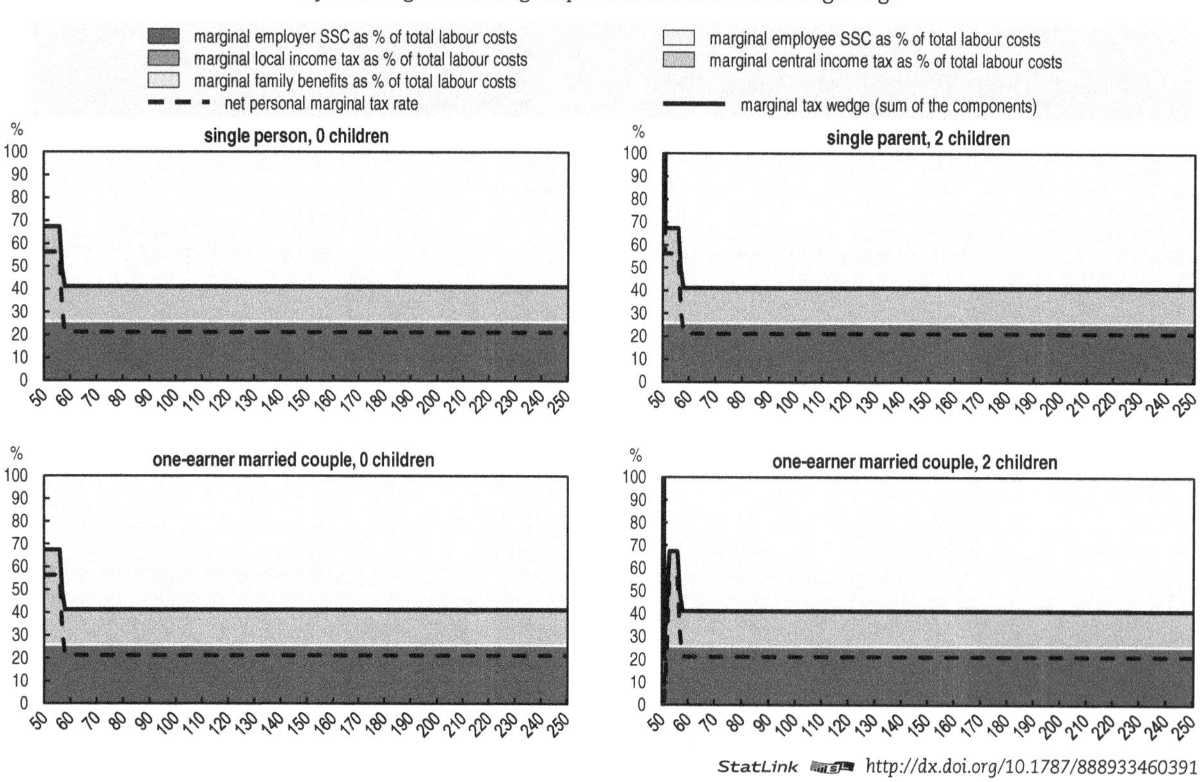

StatLink http://dx.doi.org/10.1787/888933460391

Finland 2016: Average tax wedge decomposition

By level of gross earnings expressed as a % of the average wage

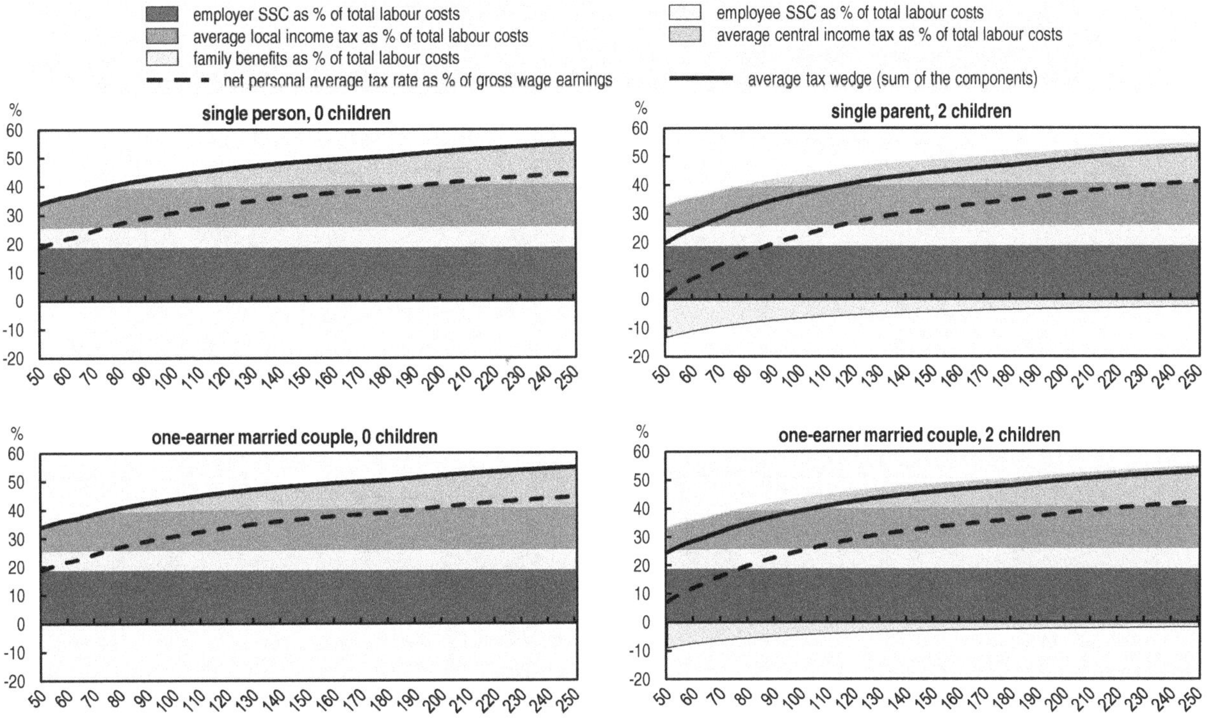

StatLink http://dx.doi.org/10.1787/888933460409

Finland 2016: Marginal tax wedge decomposition

By level of gross earnings expressed as a % of the average wage

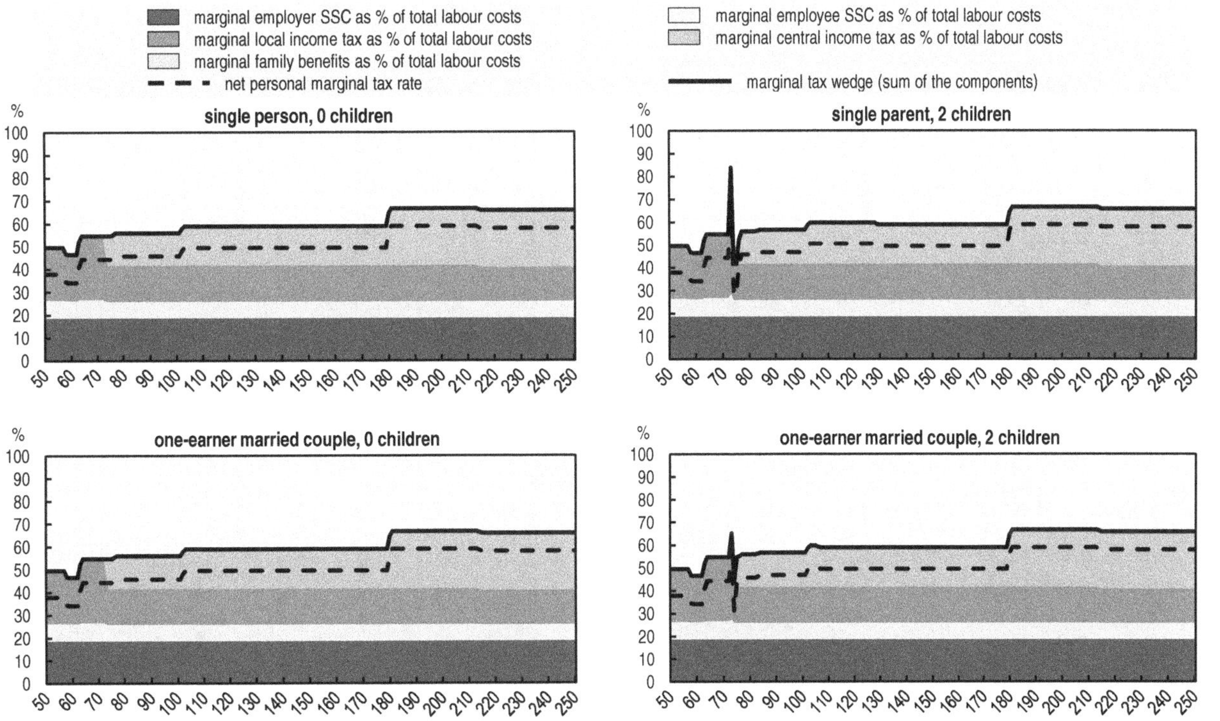

StatLink http://dx.doi.org/10.1787/888933460418

France 2016: Average tax wedge decomposition

By level of gross earnings expressed as a % of the average wage

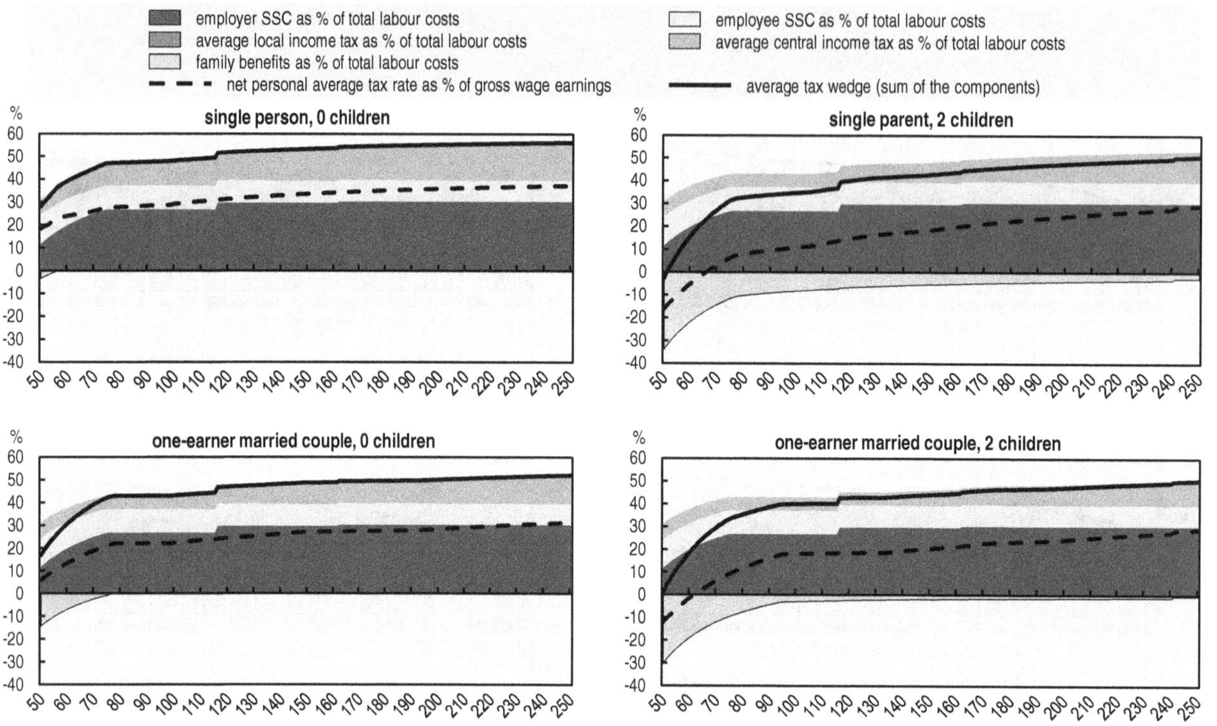

StatLink http://dx.doi.org/10.1787/888933460420

France 2016: Marginal tax wedge decomposition

By level of gross earnings expressed as a % of the average wage

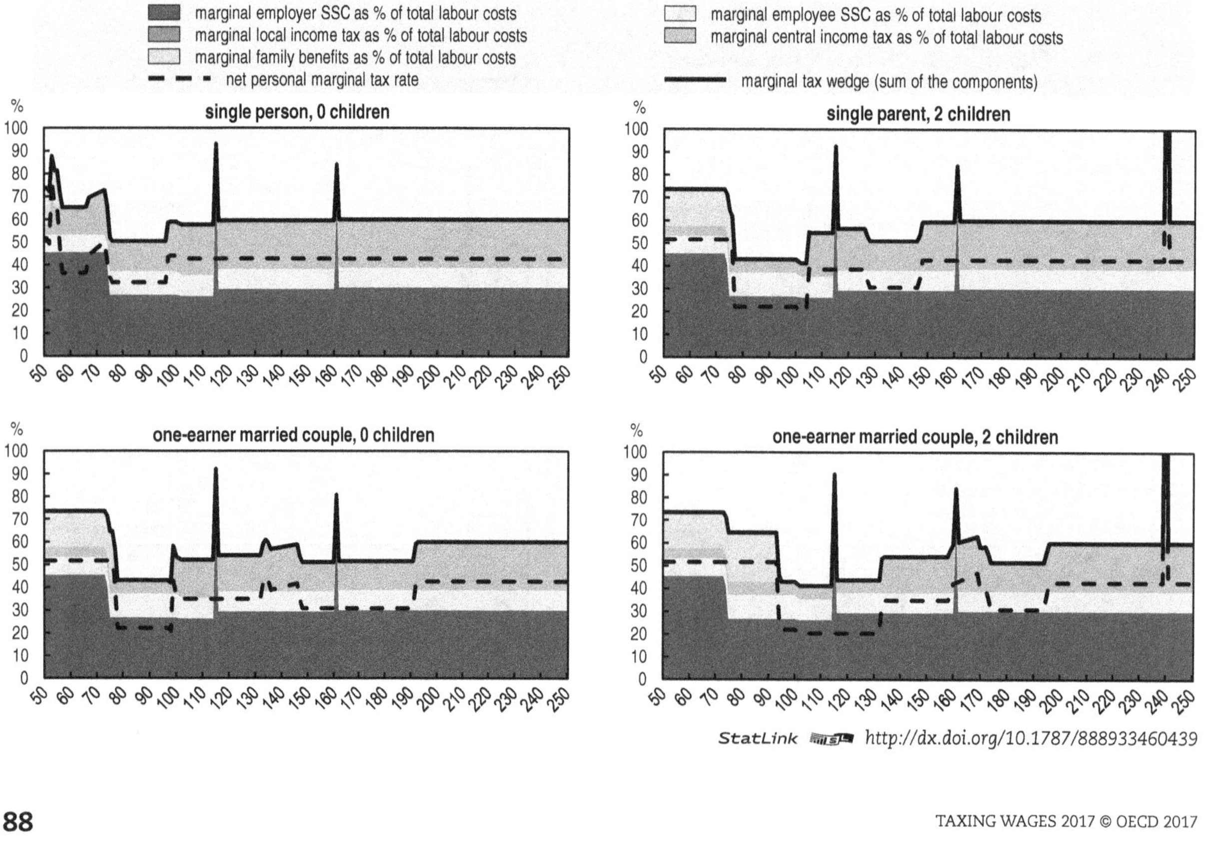

StatLink http://dx.doi.org/10.1787/888933460439

Germany 2016: Average tax wedge decomposition

By level of gross earnings expressed as a % of the average wage

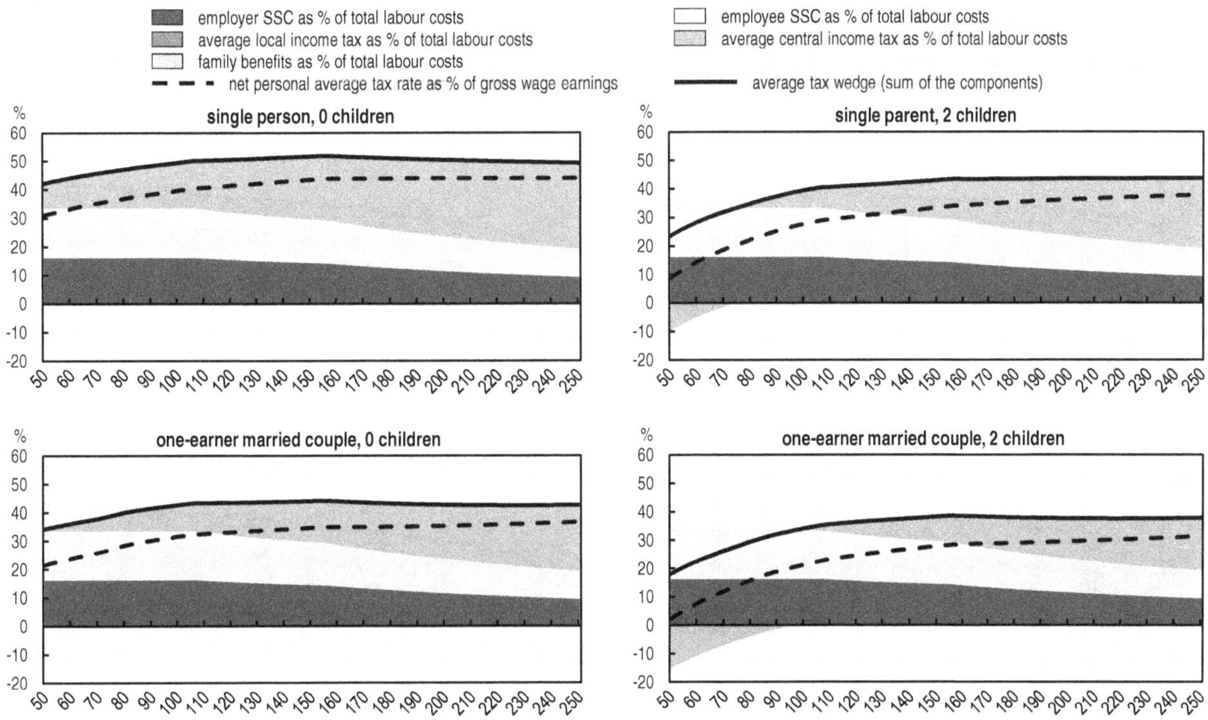

StatLink http://dx.doi.org/10.1787/888933460448

Germany 2016: Marginal tax wedge decomposition

By level of gross earnings expressed as a % of the average wage

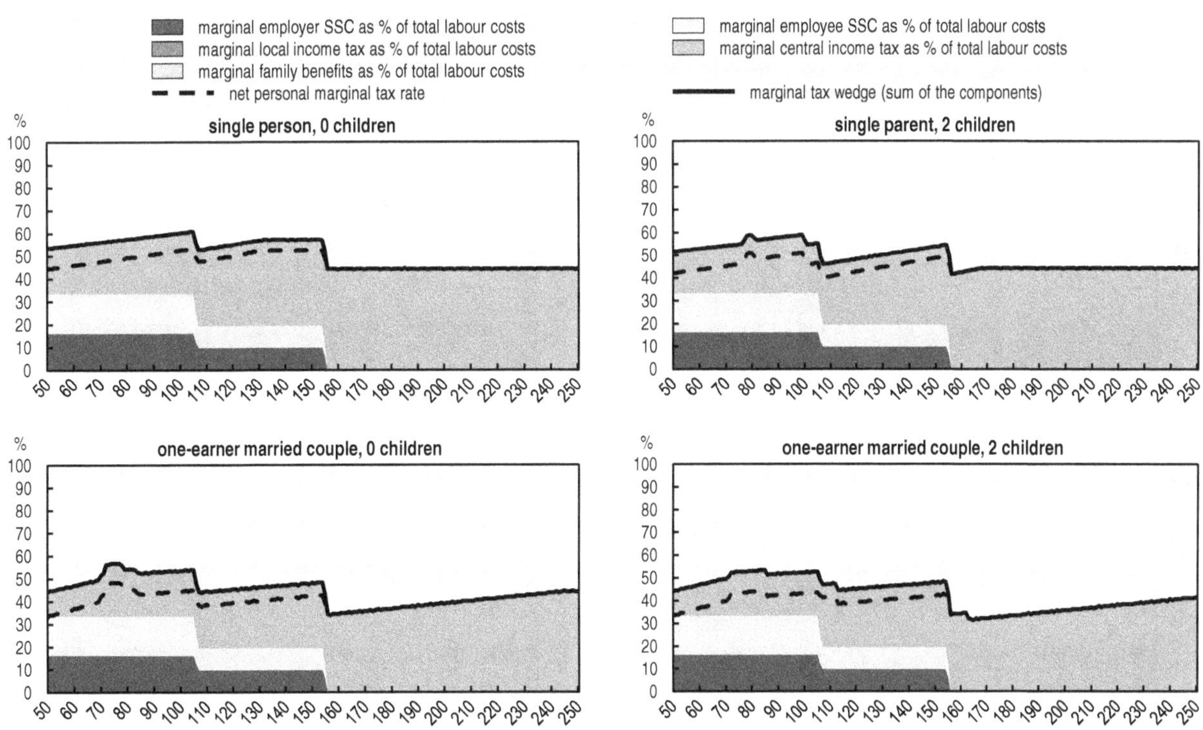

StatLink http://dx.doi.org/10.1787/888933460453

Greece 2016: Average tax wedge decomposition

By level of gross earnings expressed as a % of the average wage

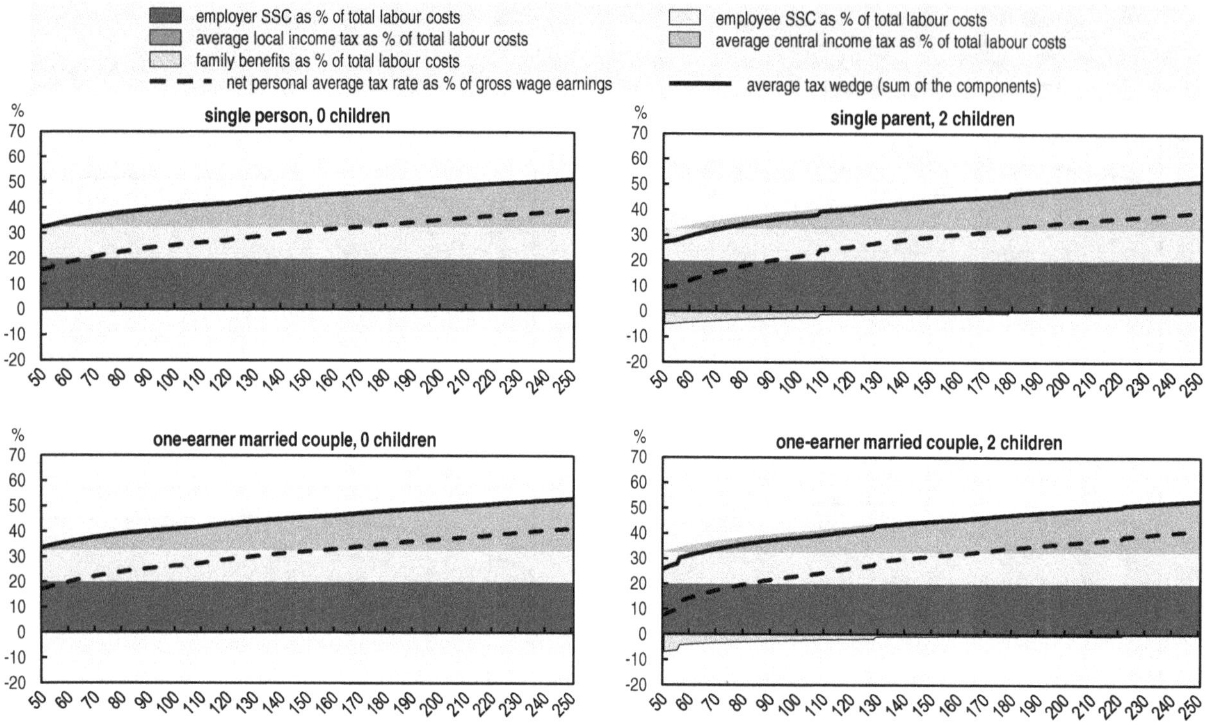

StatLink http://dx.doi.org/10.1787/888933460467

Greece 2016: Marginal tax wedge decomposition

By level of gross earnings expressed as a % of the average wage

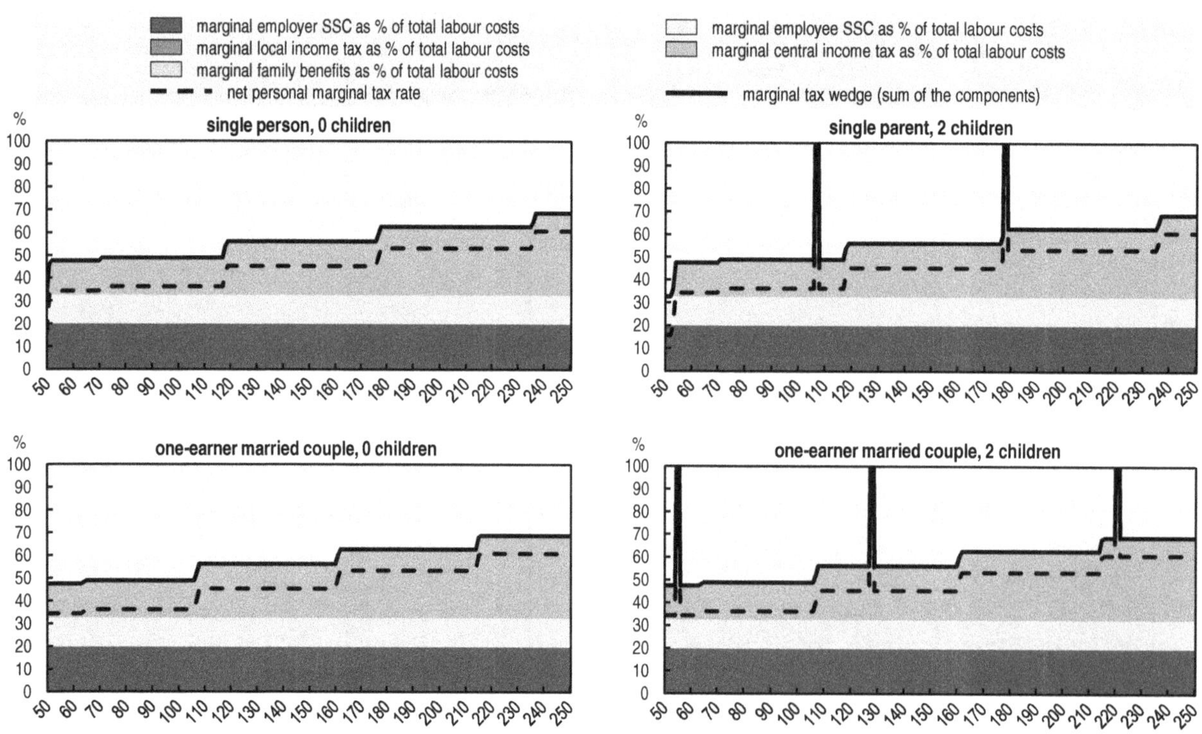

StatLink http://dx.doi.org/10.1787/888933460471

Hungary 2016: Average tax wedge decomposition

By level of gross earnings expressed as a % of the average wage

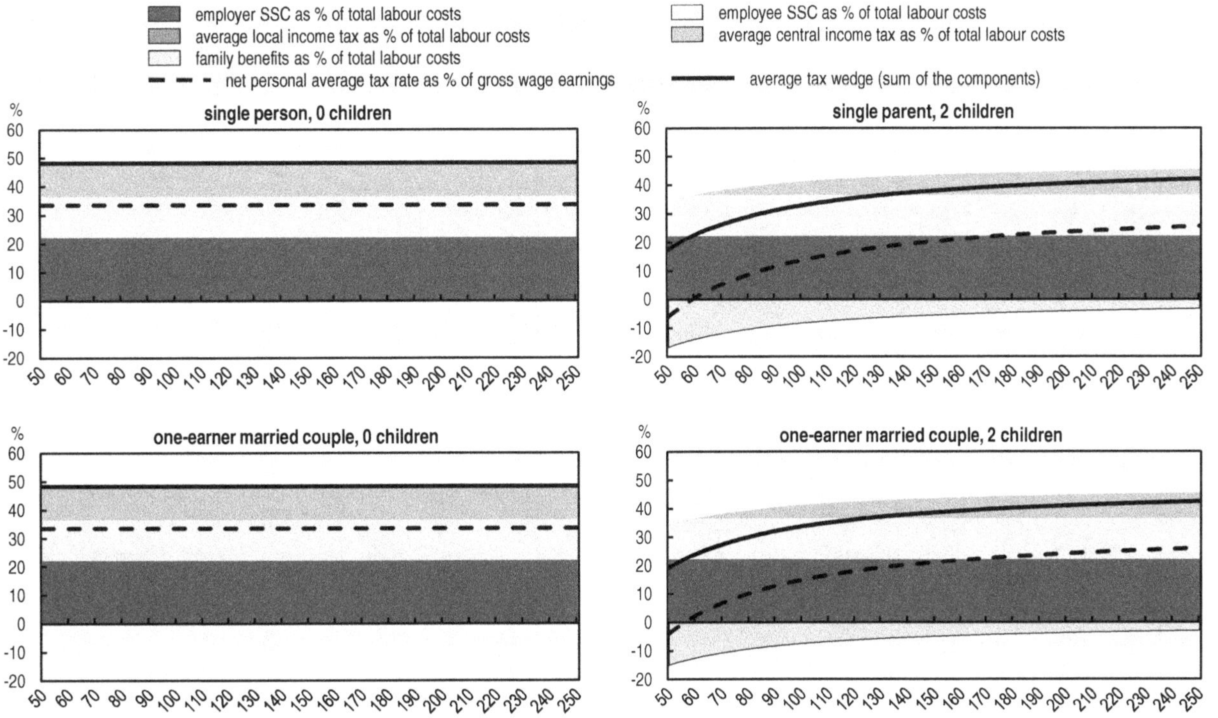

StatLink http://dx.doi.org/10.1787/888933460488

Hungary 2016: Marginal tax wedge decomposition

By level of gross earnings expressed as a % of the average wage

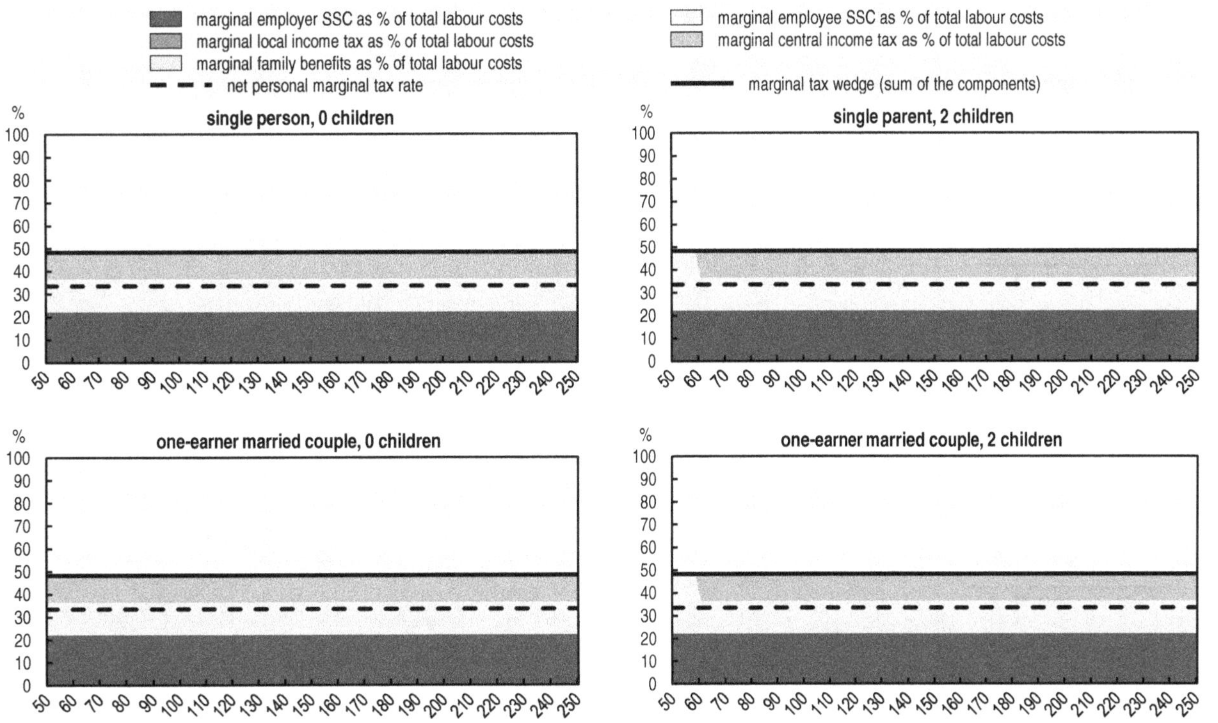

StatLink http://dx.doi.org/10.1787/888933460495

Iceland 2016: Average tax wedge decomposition

By level of gross earnings expressed as a % of the average wage

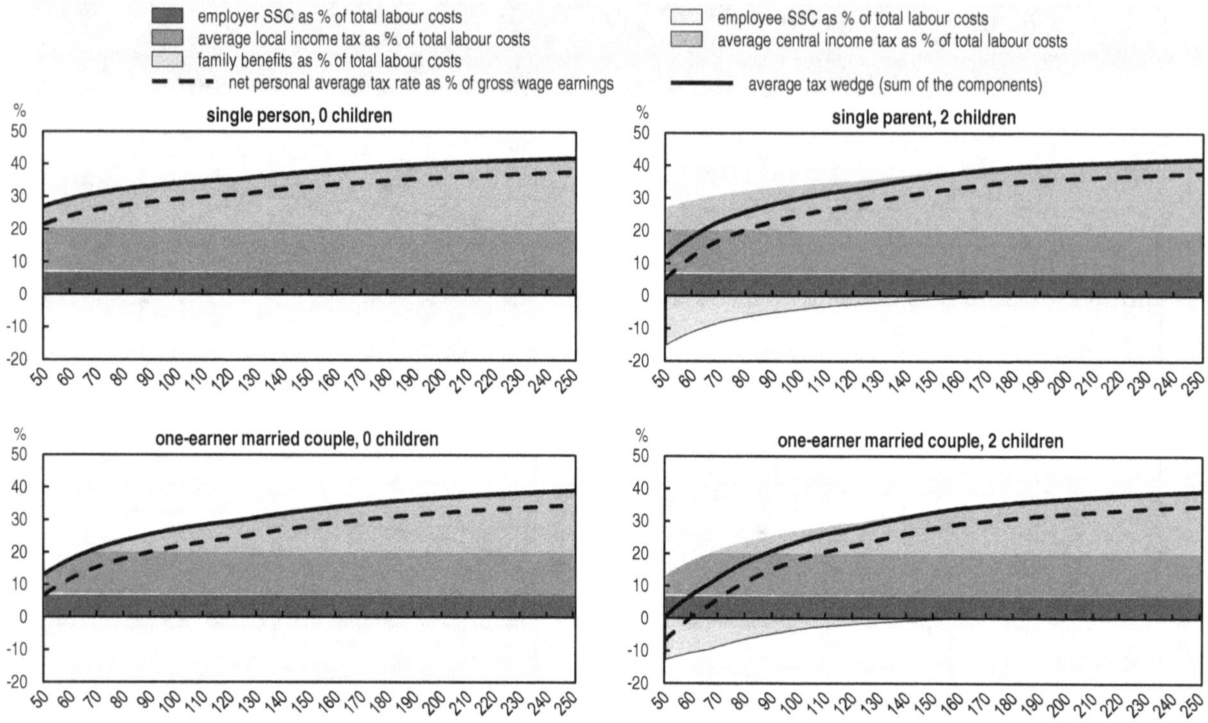

StatLink http://dx.doi.org/10.1787/888933460508

Iceland 2016: Marginal tax wedge decomposition

By level of gross earnings expressed as a % of the average wage

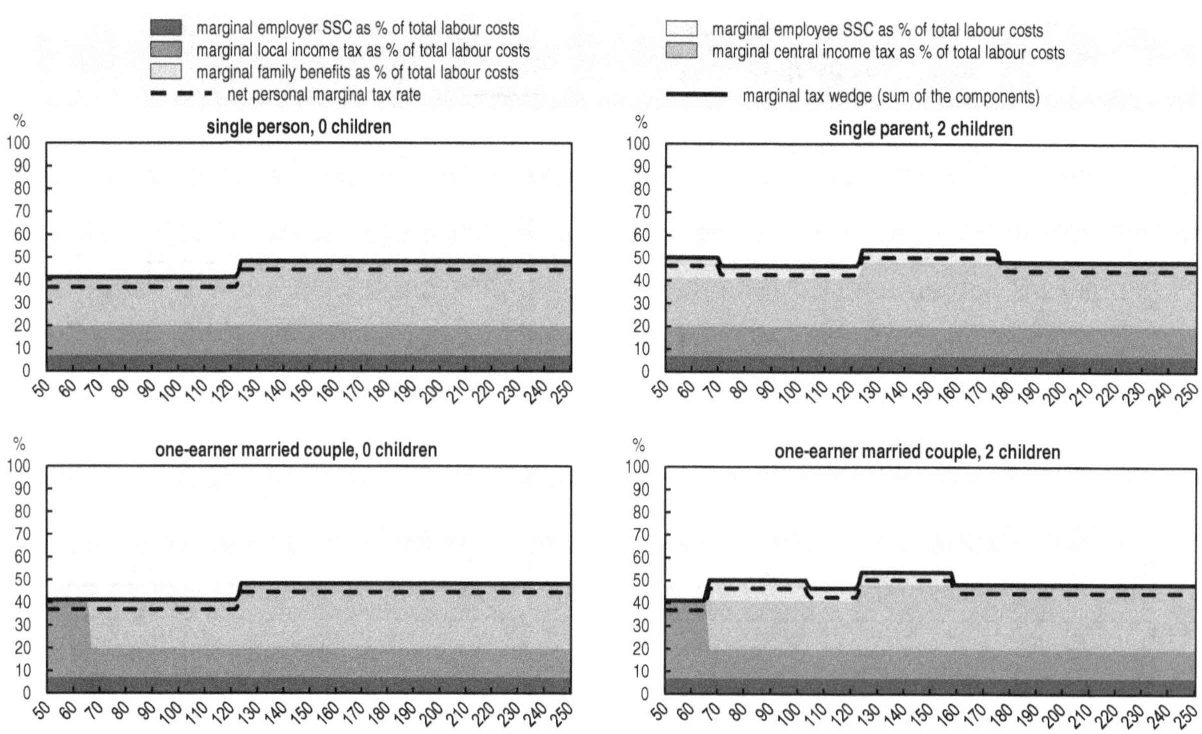

StatLink http://dx.doi.org/10.1787/888933460516

Ireland 2016: Average tax wedge decomposition

By level of gross earnings expressed as a % of the average wage

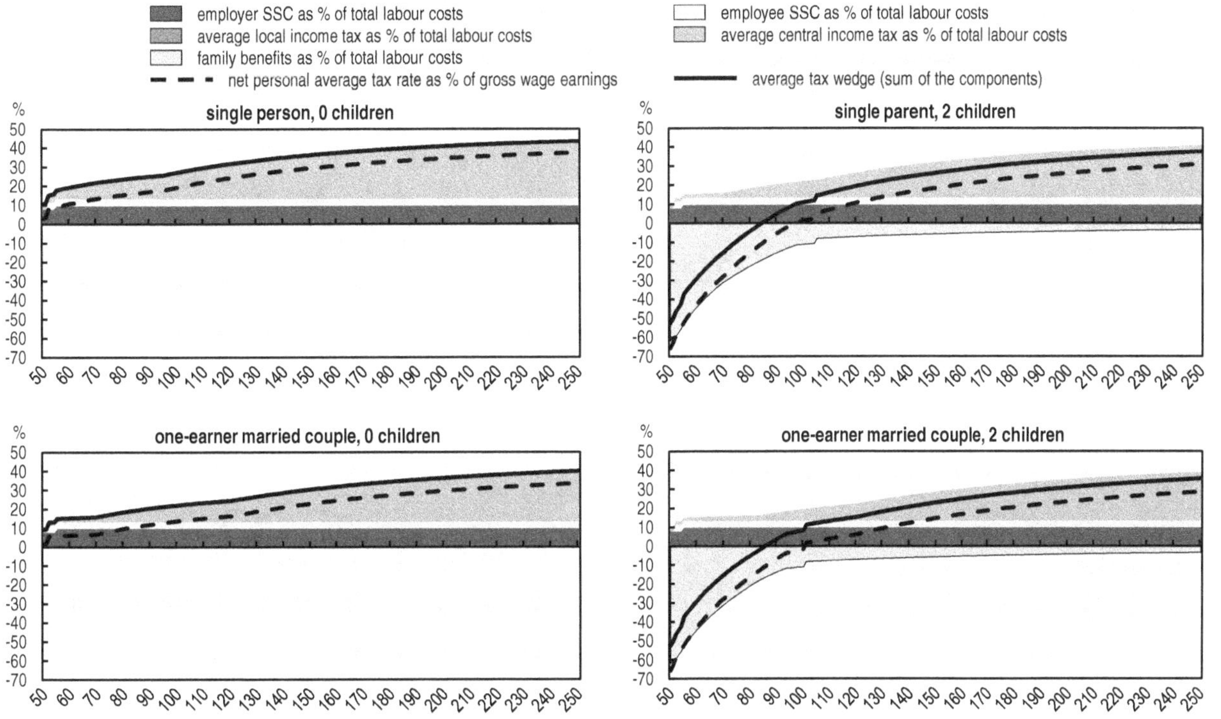

StatLink http://dx.doi.org/10.1787/888933460527

Ireland 2016: Marginal tax wedge decomposition

By level of gross earnings expressed as a % of the average wage

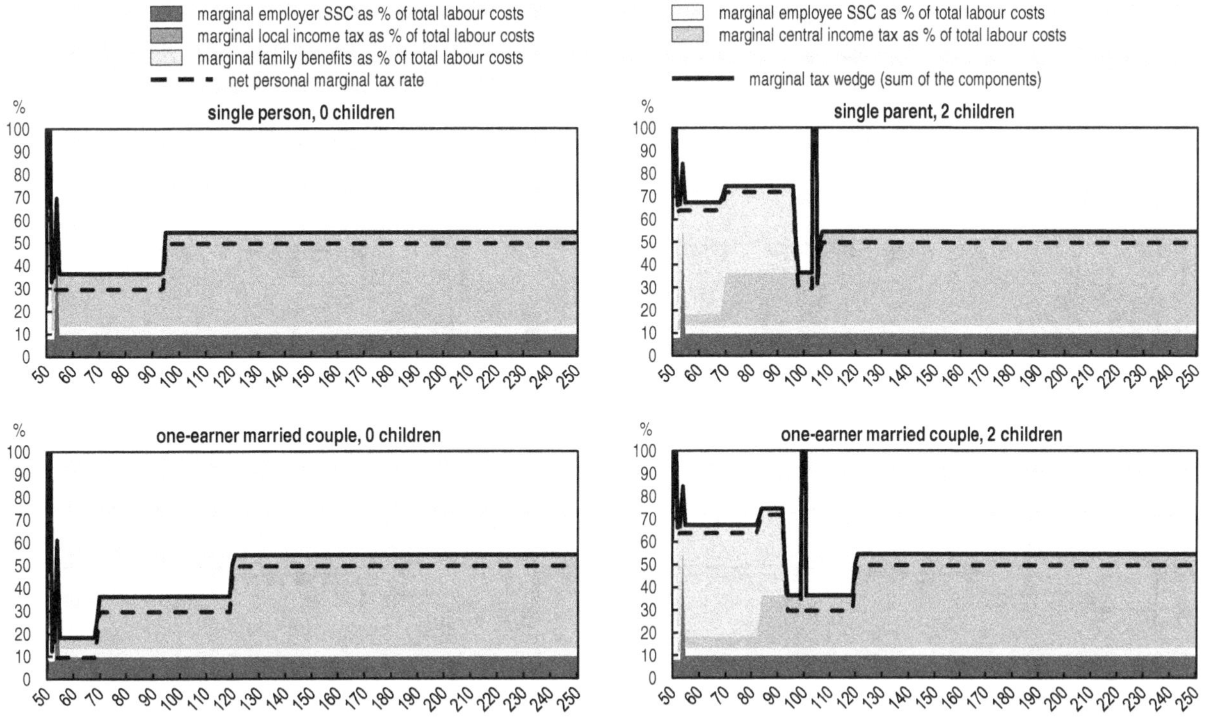

StatLink http://dx.doi.org/10.1787/888933460533

Israel 2016: Average tax wedge decomposition

By level of gross earnings expressed as a % of the average wage

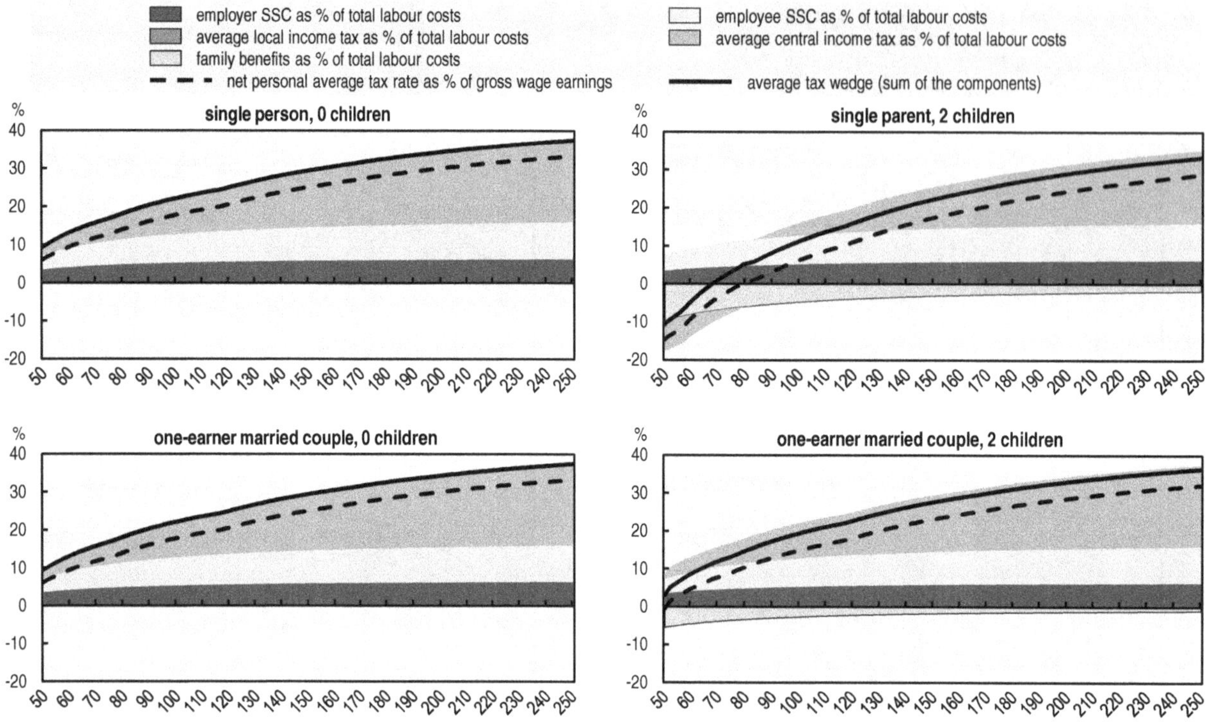

StatLink http://dx.doi.org/10.1787/888933460540

Israel 2016: Marginal tax wedge decomposition

By level of gross earnings expressed as a % of the average wage

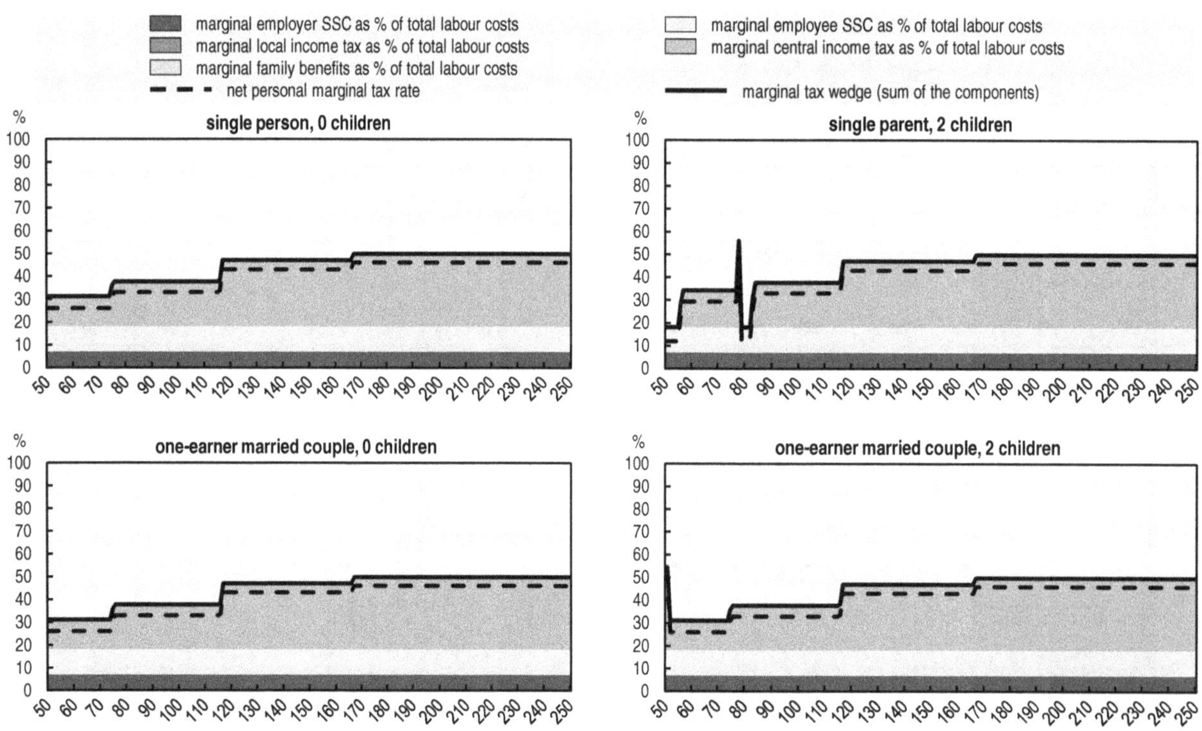

StatLink http://dx.doi.org/10.1787/888933460557

Italy 2016: Average tax wedge decomposition

By level of gross earnings expressed as a % of the average wage

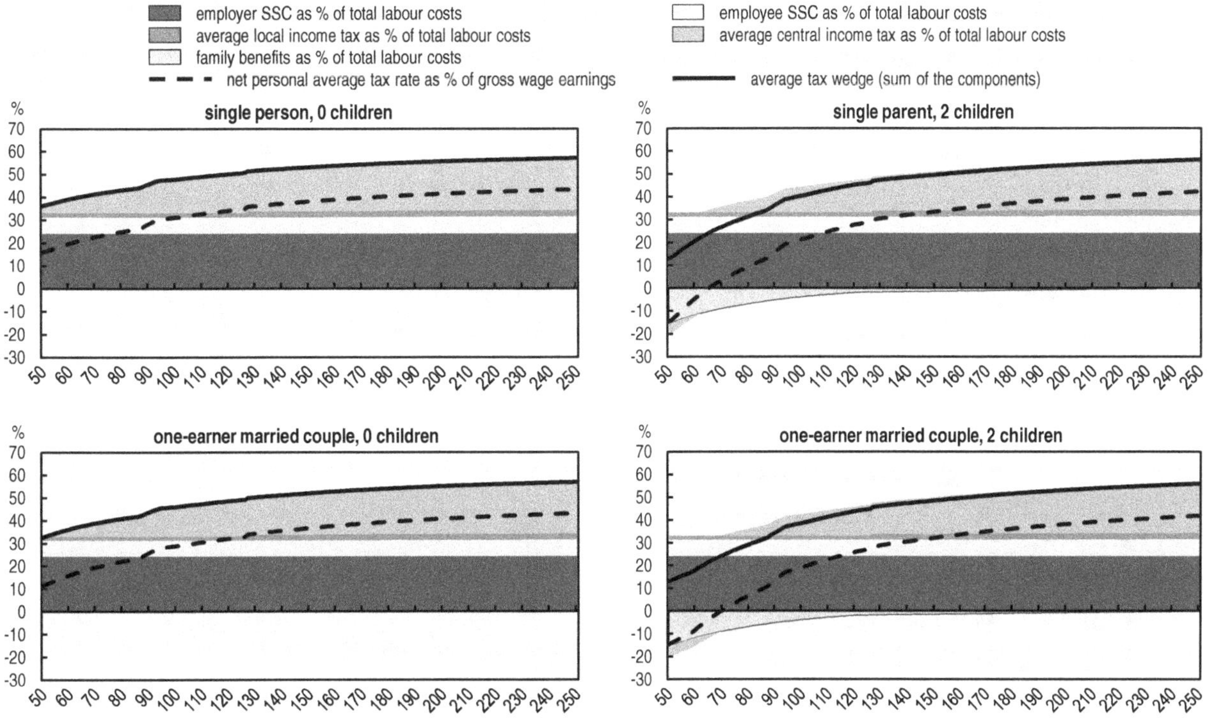

StatLink http://dx.doi.org/10.1787/888933460562

Italy 2016: Marginal tax wedge decomposition

By level of gross earnings expressed as a % of the average wage

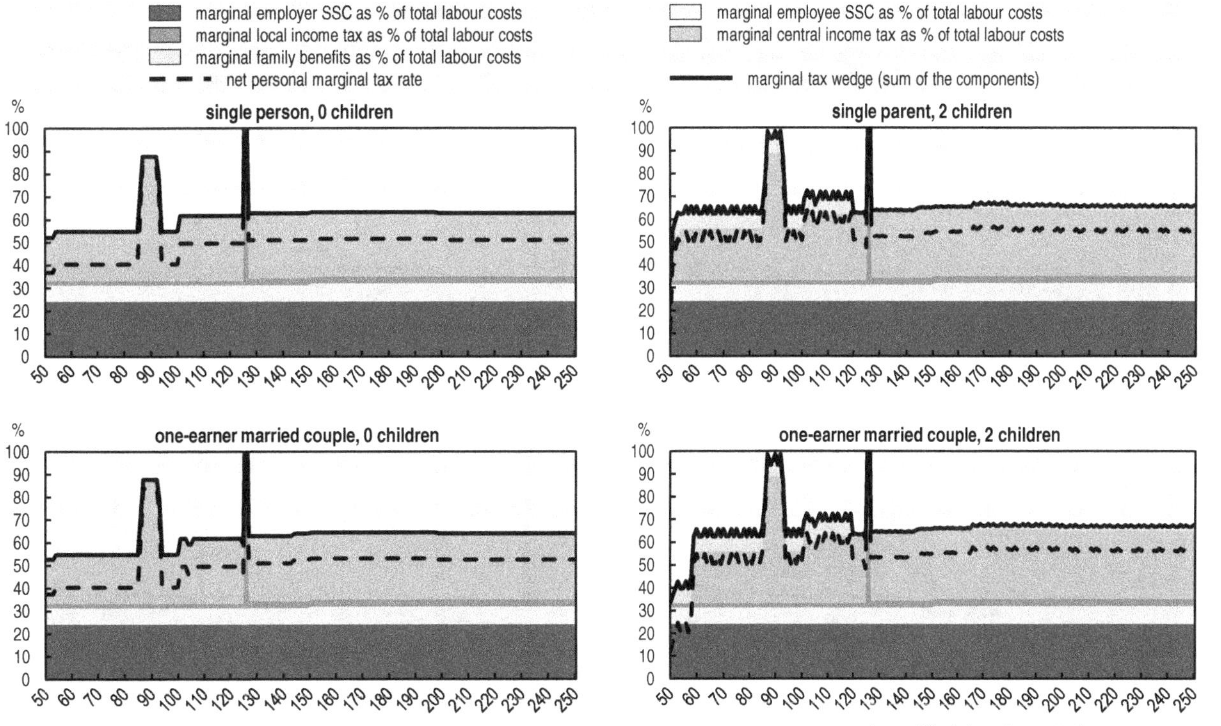

StatLink http://dx.doi.org/10.1787/888933460571

Japan 2016: Average tax wedge decomposition

By level of gross earnings expressed as a % of the average wage

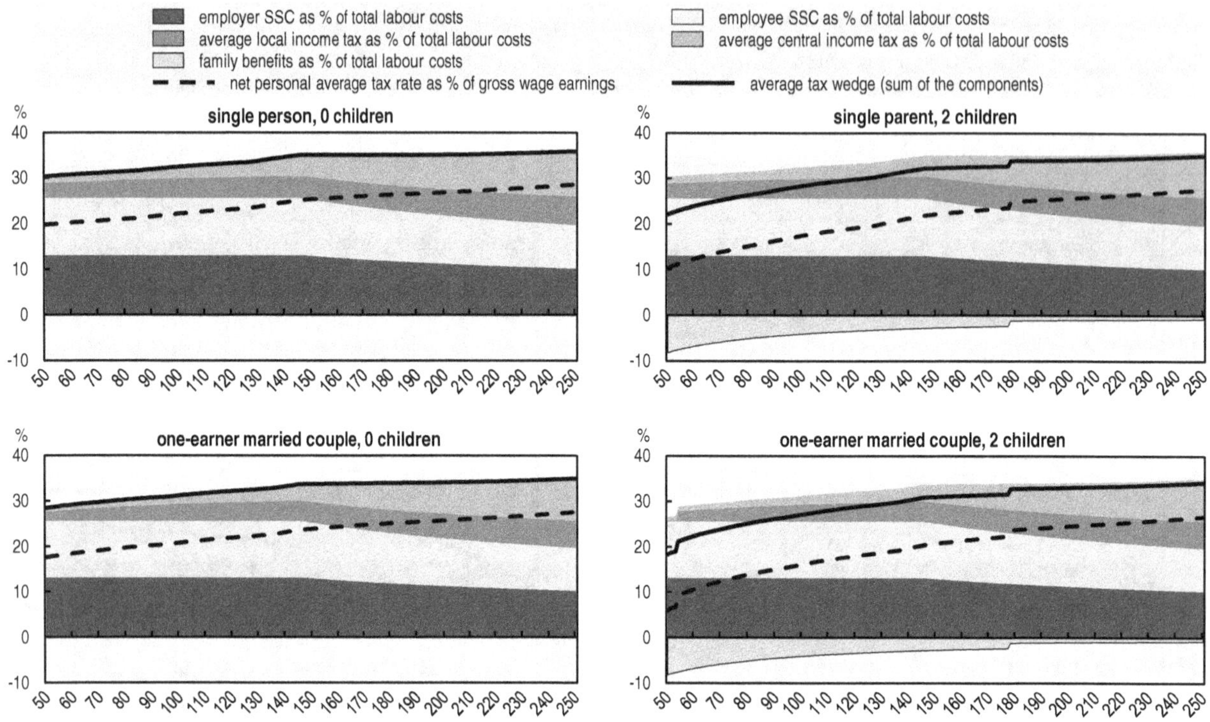

StatLink http://dx.doi.org/10.1787/888933460588

Japan 2016: Marginal tax wedge decomposition

By level of gross earnings expressed as a % of the average wage

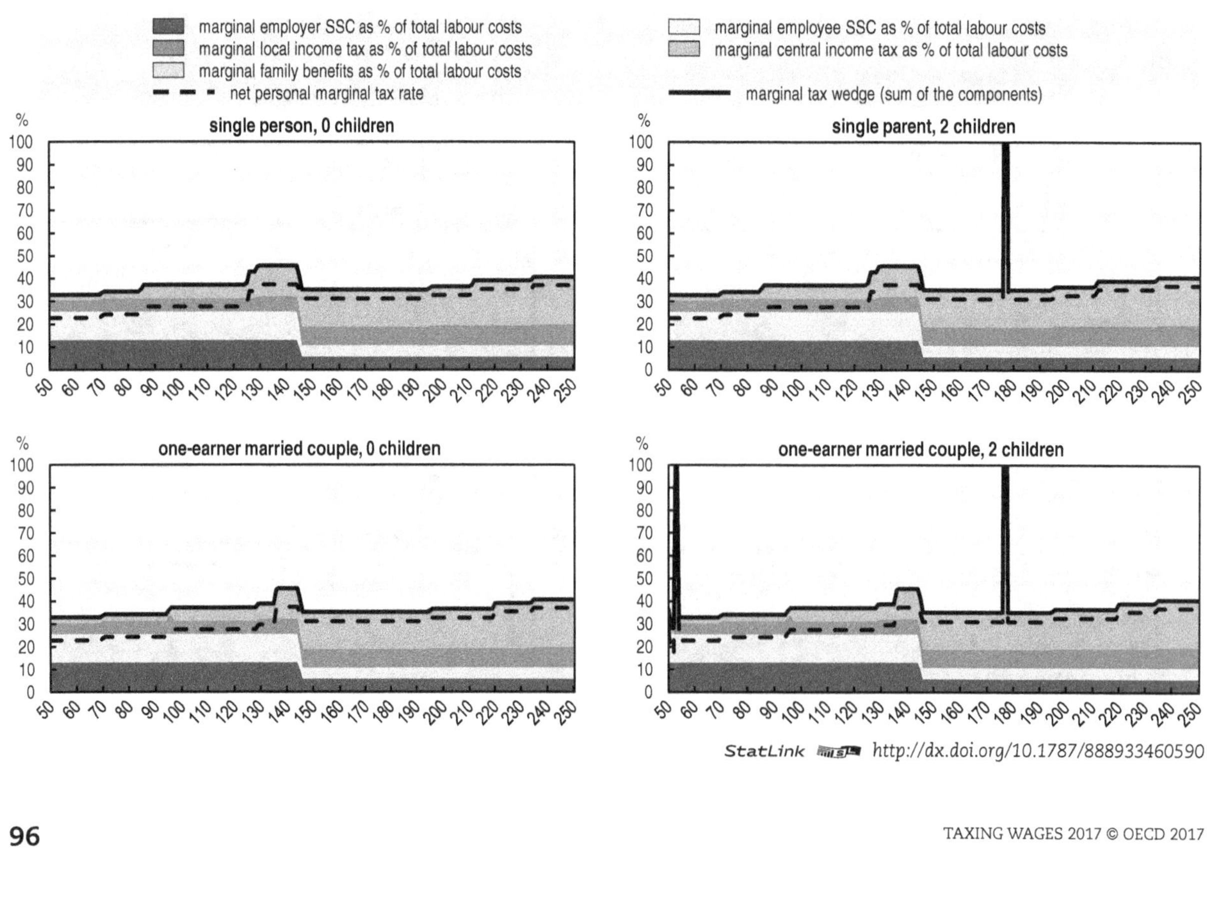

StatLink http://dx.doi.org/10.1787/888933460590

Korea 2016: Average tax wedge decomposition

By level of gross earnings expressed as a % of the average wage

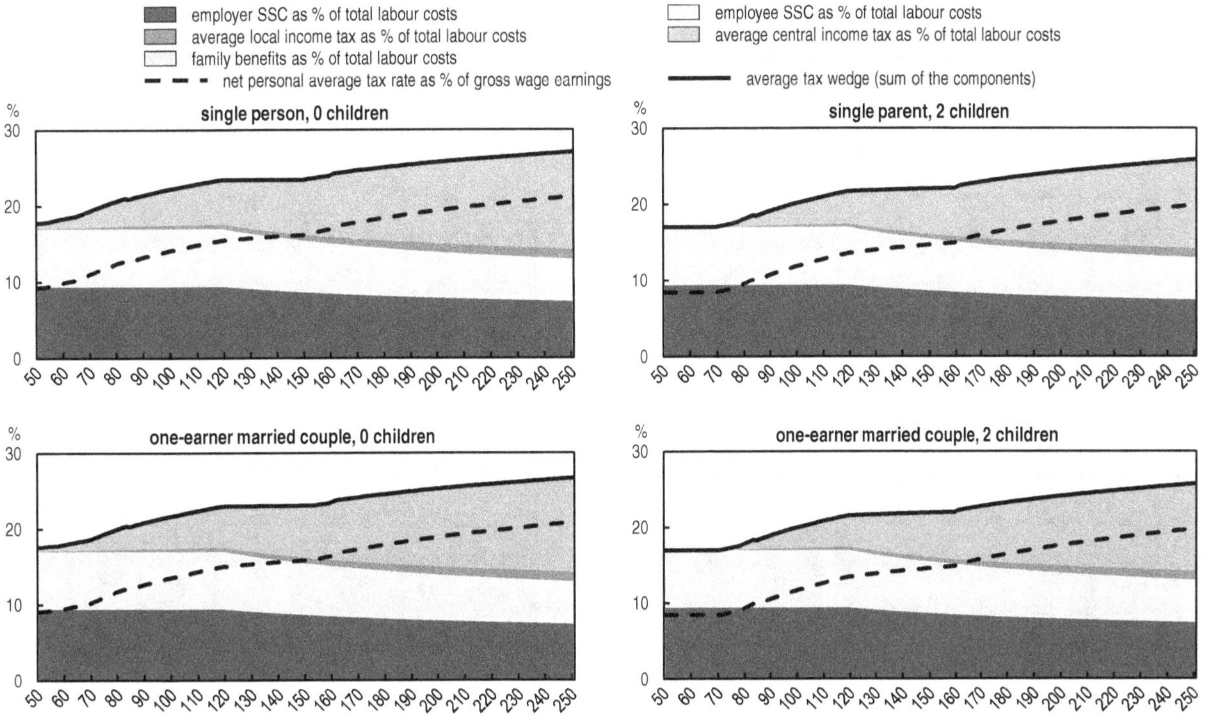

StatLink http://dx.doi.org/10.1787/888933460604

Korea 2016: Marginal tax wedge decomposition

By level of gross earnings expressed as a % of the average wage

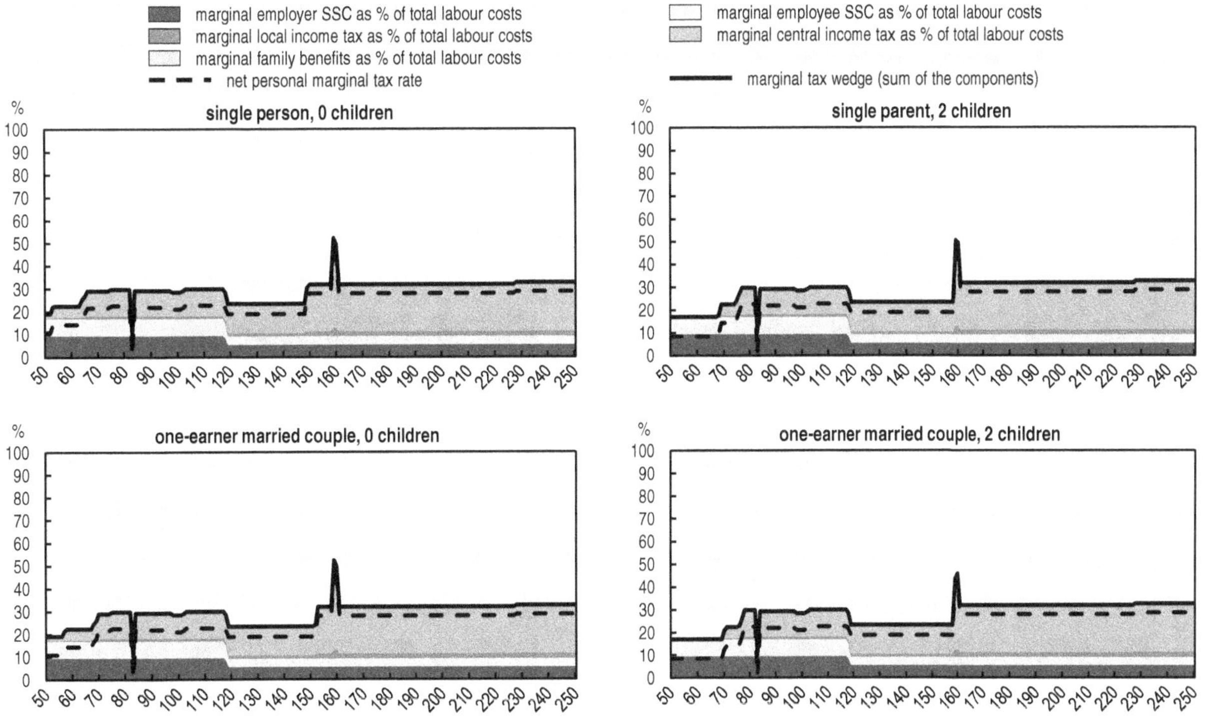

StatLink http://dx.doi.org/10.1787/888933460617

Latvia 2016: Average tax wedge decomposition

By level of gross earnings expressed as a % of the average wage

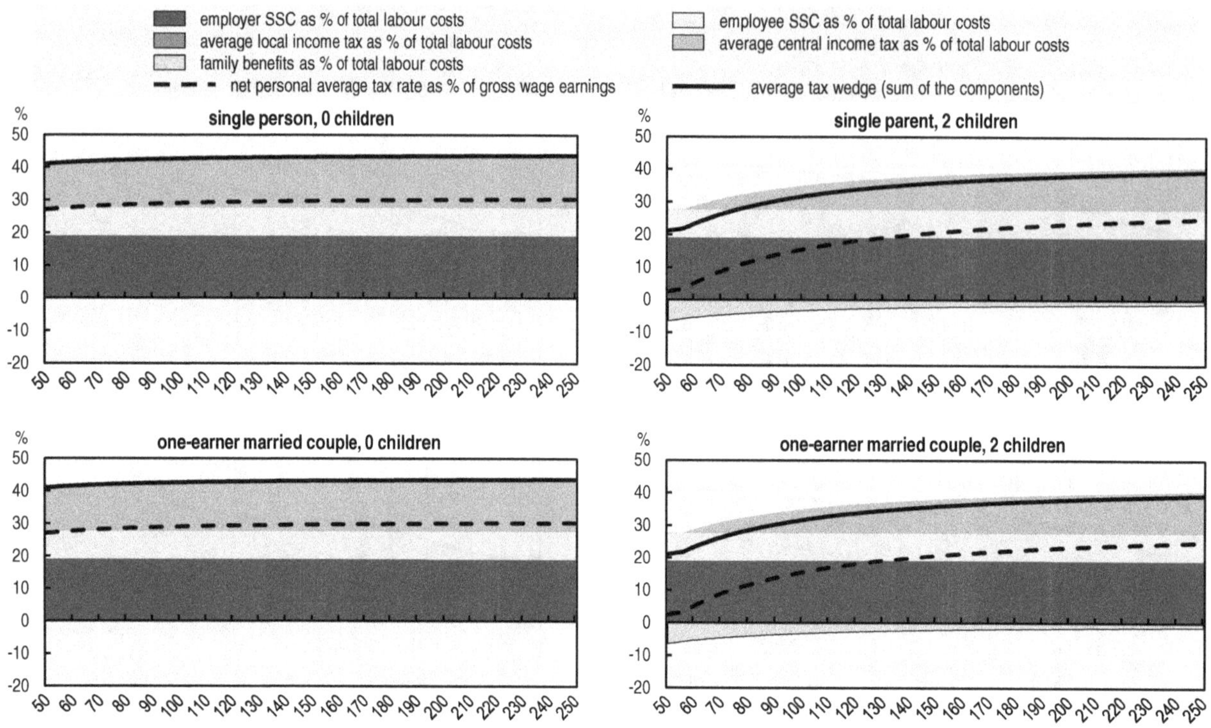

StatLink http://dx.doi.org/10.1787/888933460622

Latvia 2016: Marginal tax wedge decomposition

By level of gross earnings expressed as a % of the average wage

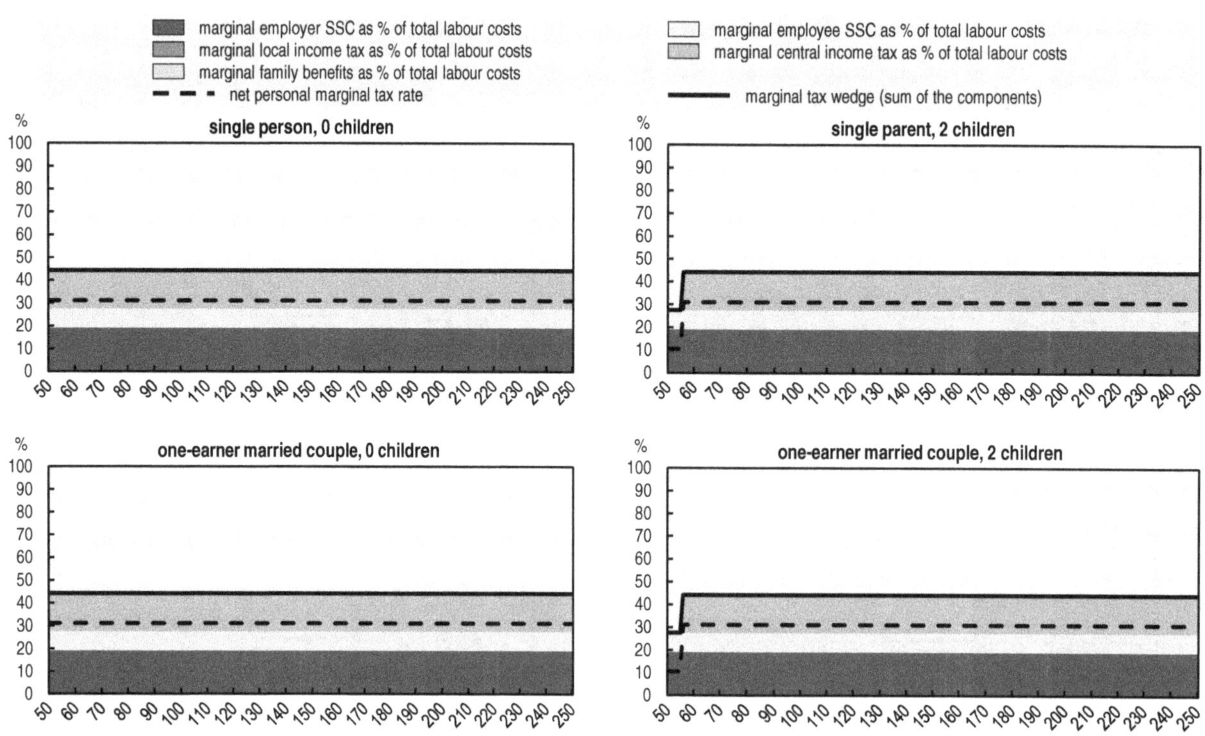

StatLink http://dx.doi.org/10.1787/888933460633

Luxembourg 2016: Average tax wedge decomposition

By level of gross earnings expressed as a % of the average wage

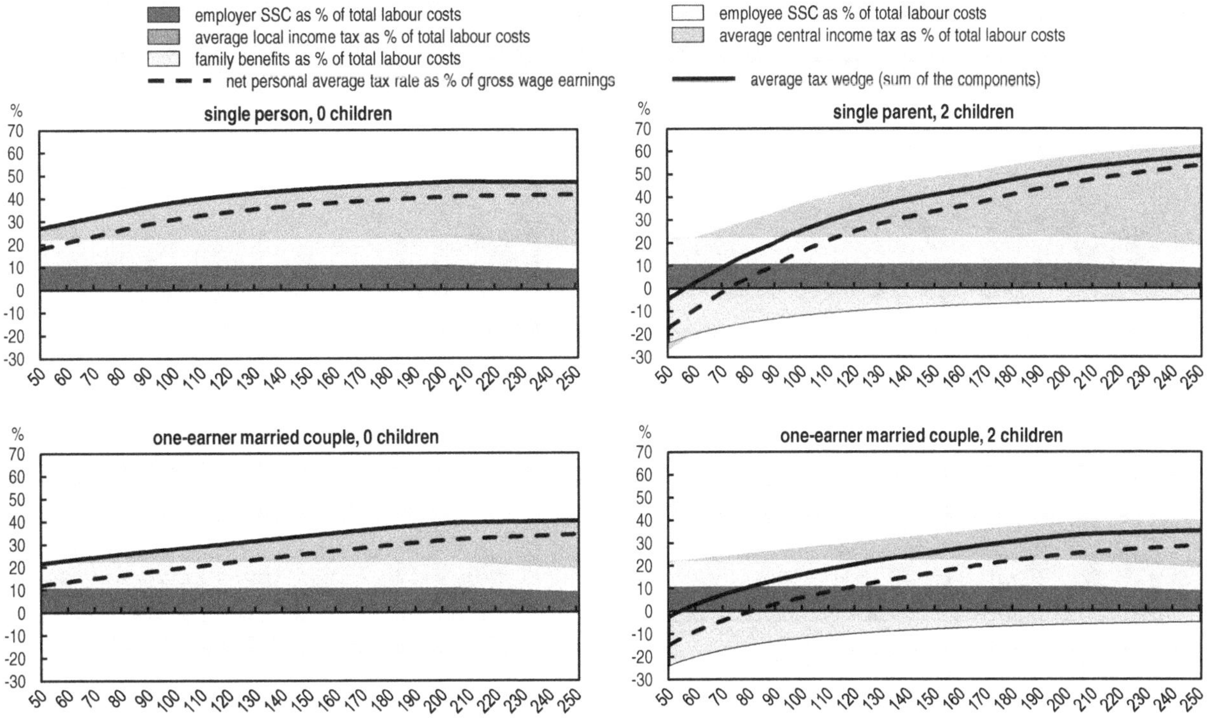

StatLink http://dx.doi.org/10.1787/888933460648

Luxembourg 2016: Marginal tax wedge decomposition

By level of gross earnings expressed as a % of the average wage

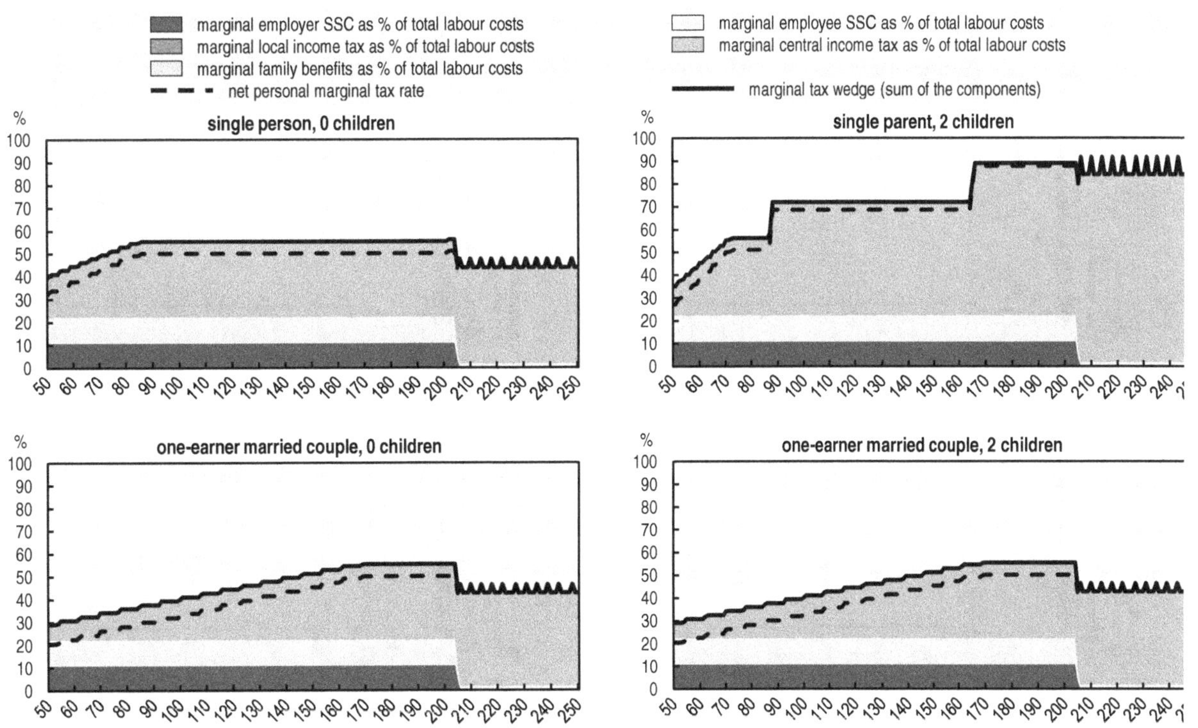

StatLink http://dx.doi.org/10.1787/888933460654

Mexico 2016: Average tax wedge decomposition

By level of gross earnings expressed as a % of the average wage

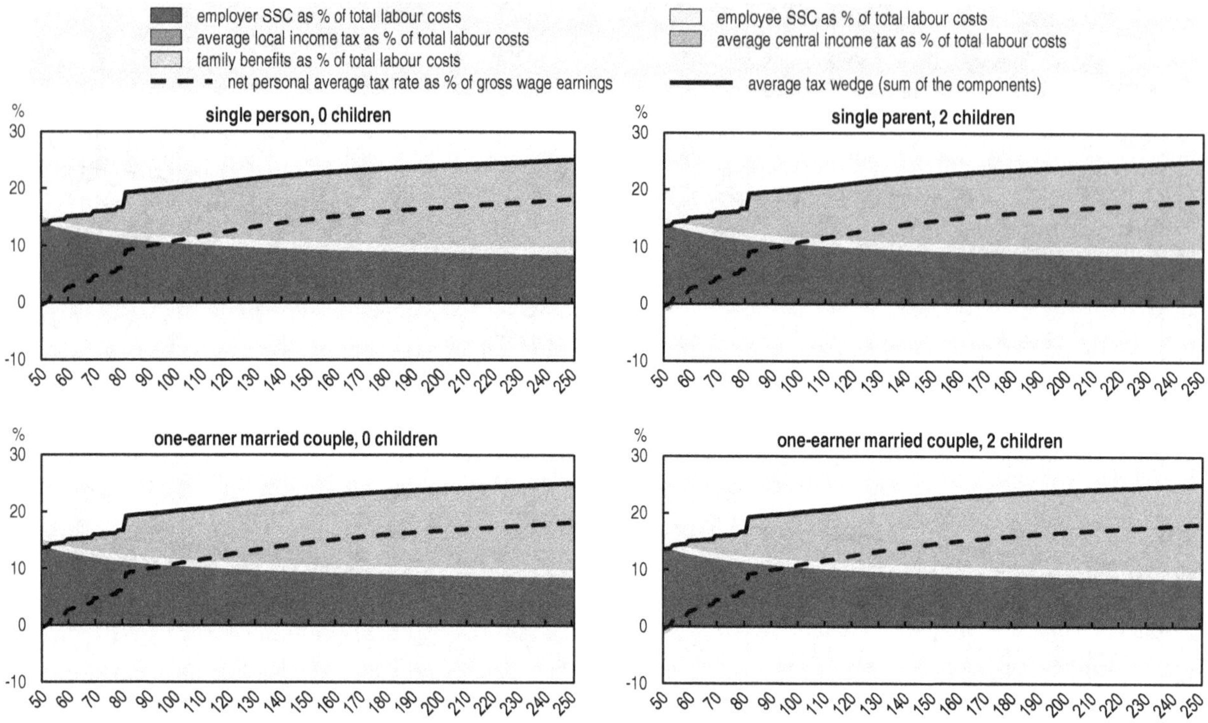

StatLink http://dx.doi.org/10.1787/888933460668

Mexico 2016: Marginal tax wedge decomposition

By level of gross earnings expressed as a % of the average wage

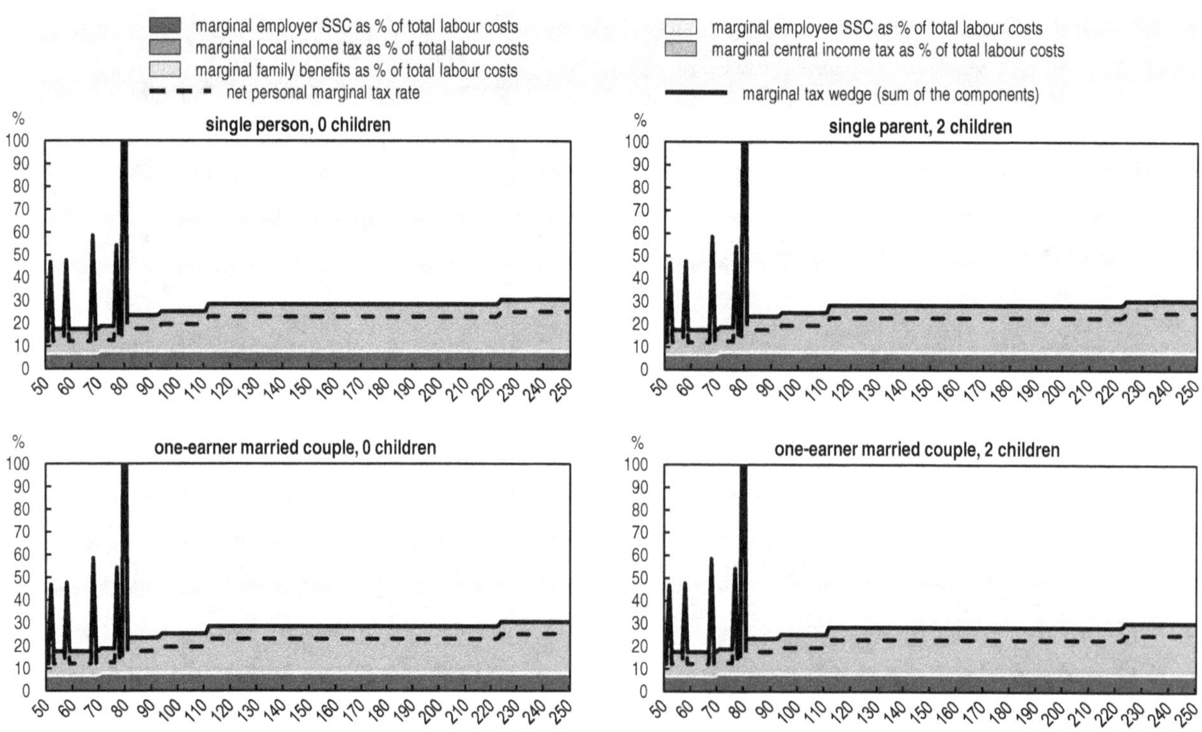

StatLink http://dx.doi.org/10.1787/888933460672

Netherlands 2016: Average tax wedge decomposition

By level of gross earnings expressed as a % of the average wage

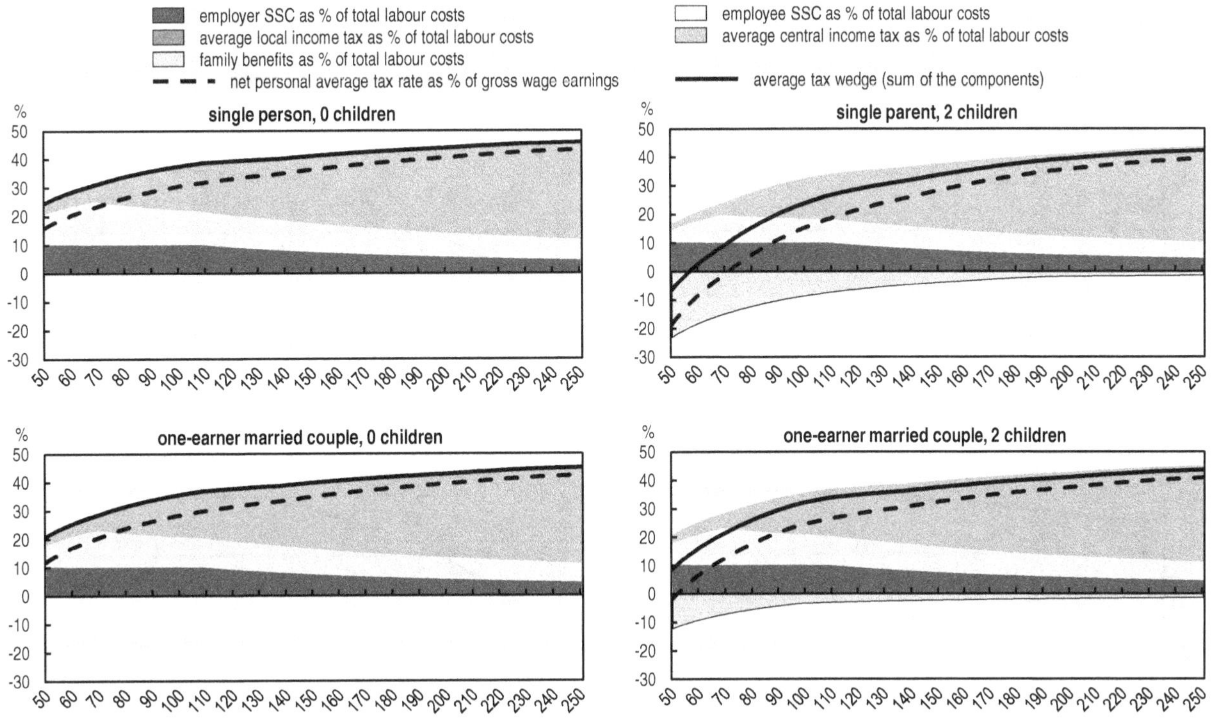

StatLink http://dx.doi.org/10.1787/888933460686

Netherlands 2016: Marginal tax wedge decomposition

By level of gross earnings expressed as a % of the average wage

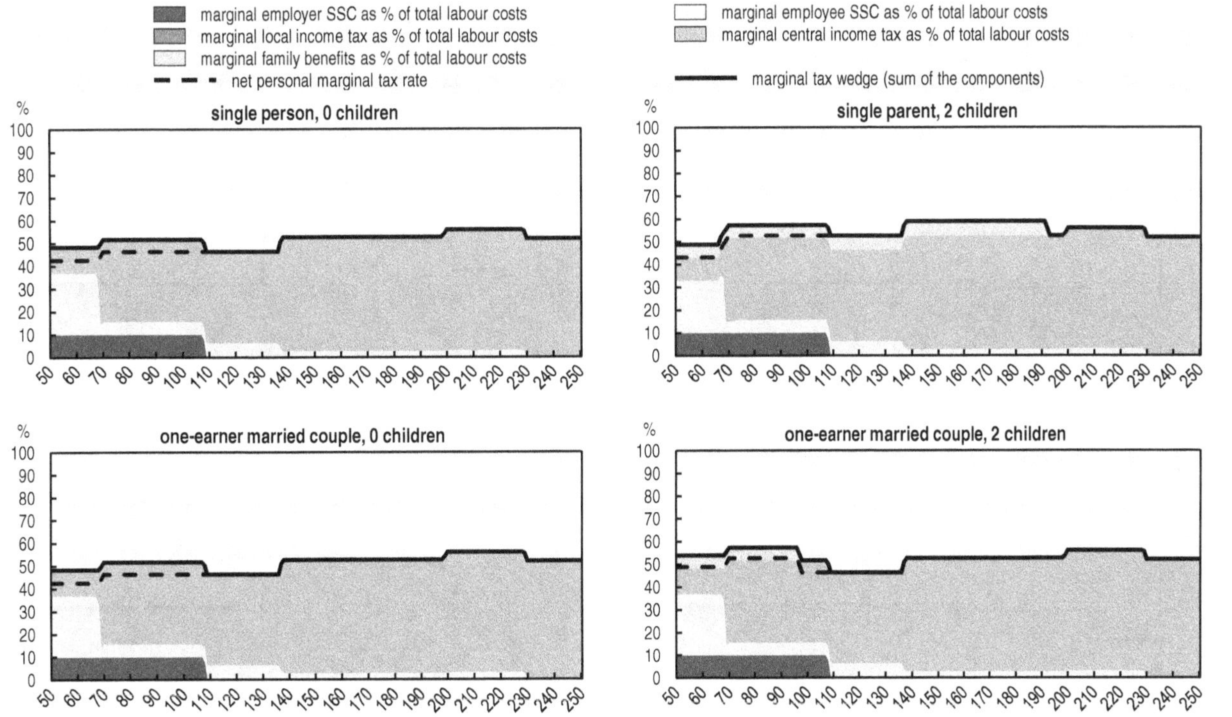

StatLink http://dx.doi.org/10.1787/888933460698

New Zealand 2016: Average tax wedge decomposition

By level of gross earnings expressed as a % of the average wage

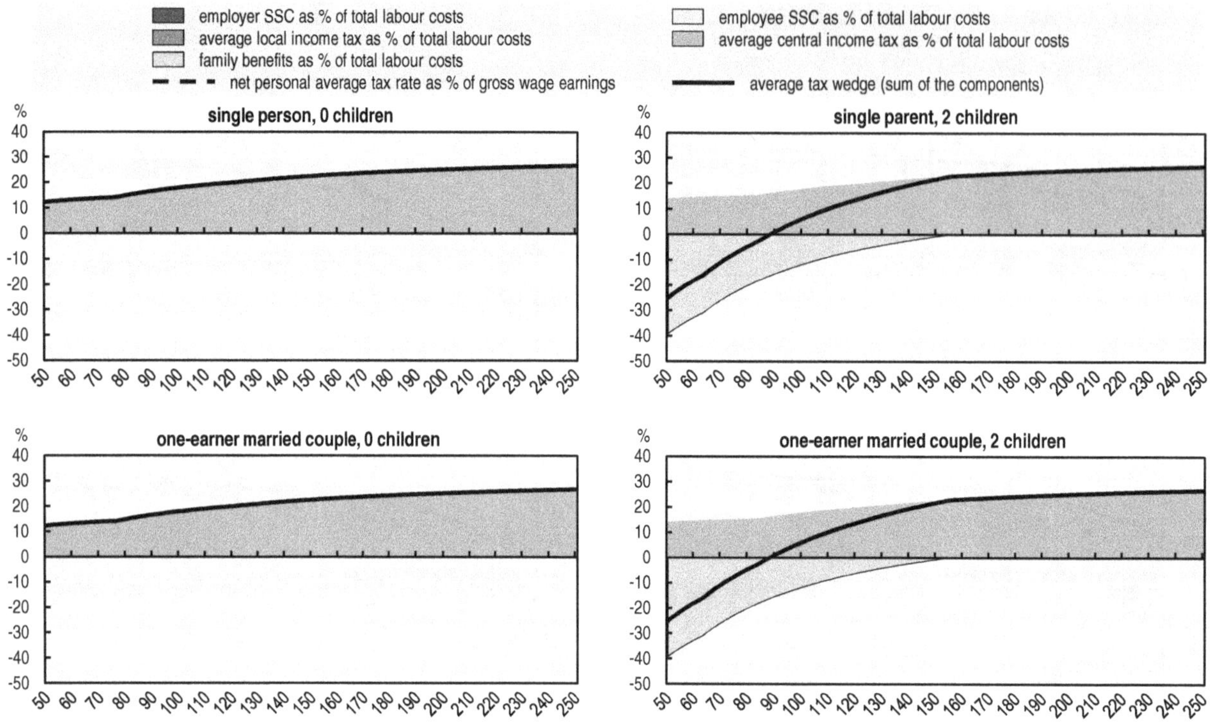

StatLink http://dx.doi.org/10.1787/888933460702

New Zealand 2016: Marginal tax wedge decomposition

By level of gross earnings expressed as a % of the average wage

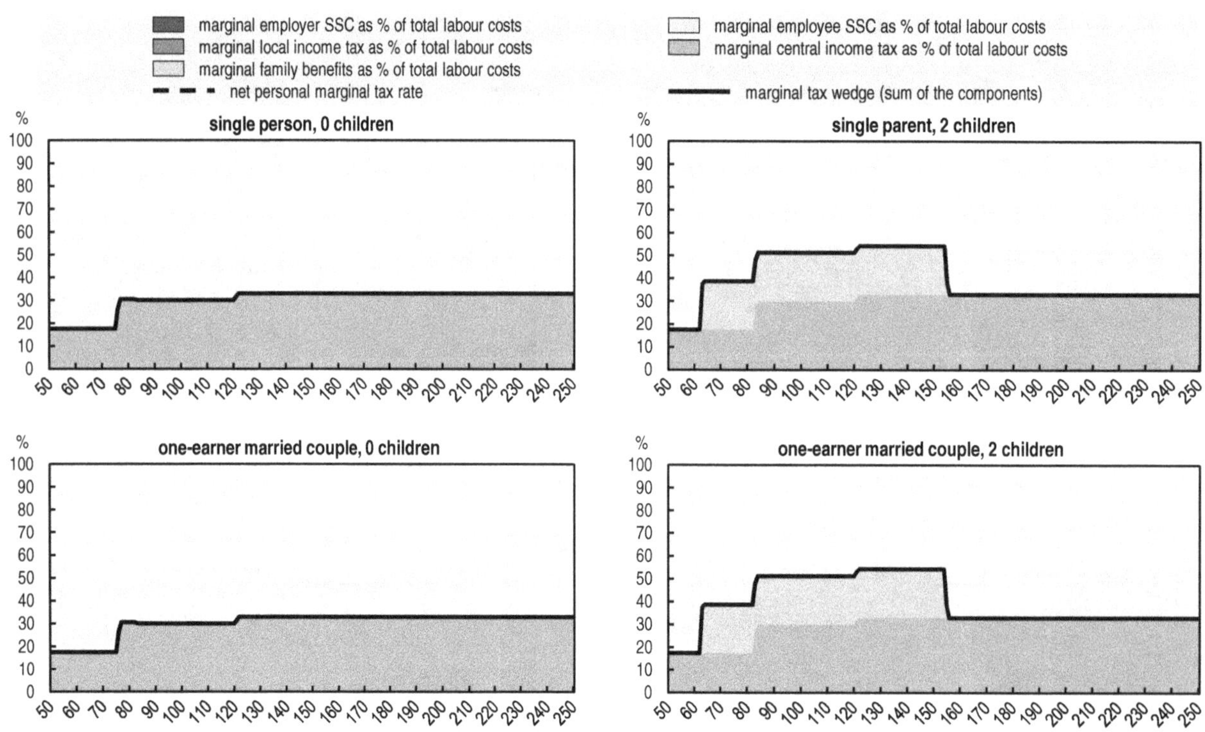

StatLink http://dx.doi.org/10.1787/888933460715

Norway 2016: Average tax wedge decomposition

By level of gross earnings expressed as a % of the average wage

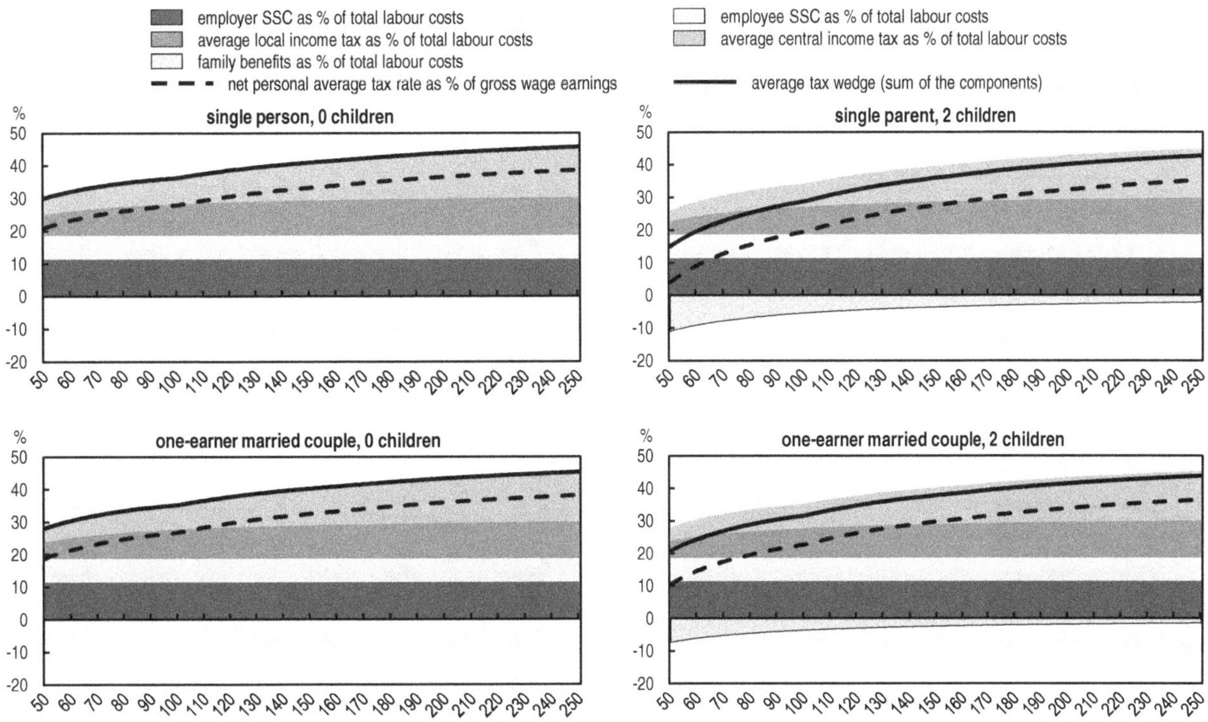

StatLink http://dx.doi.org/10.1787/888933460725

Norway 2016: Marginal tax wedge decomposition

By level of gross earnings expressed as a % of the average wage

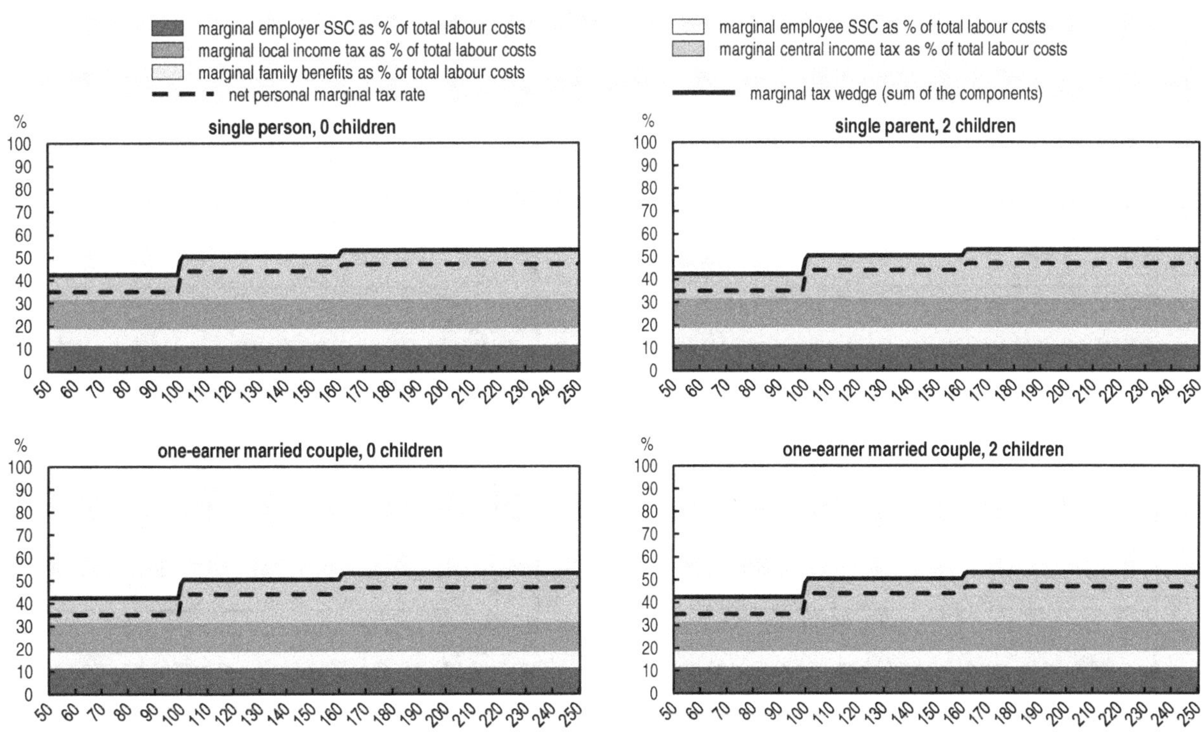

StatLink http://dx.doi.org/10.1787/888933460739

Poland 2016: Average tax wedge decomposition

By level of gross earnings expressed as a % of the average wage

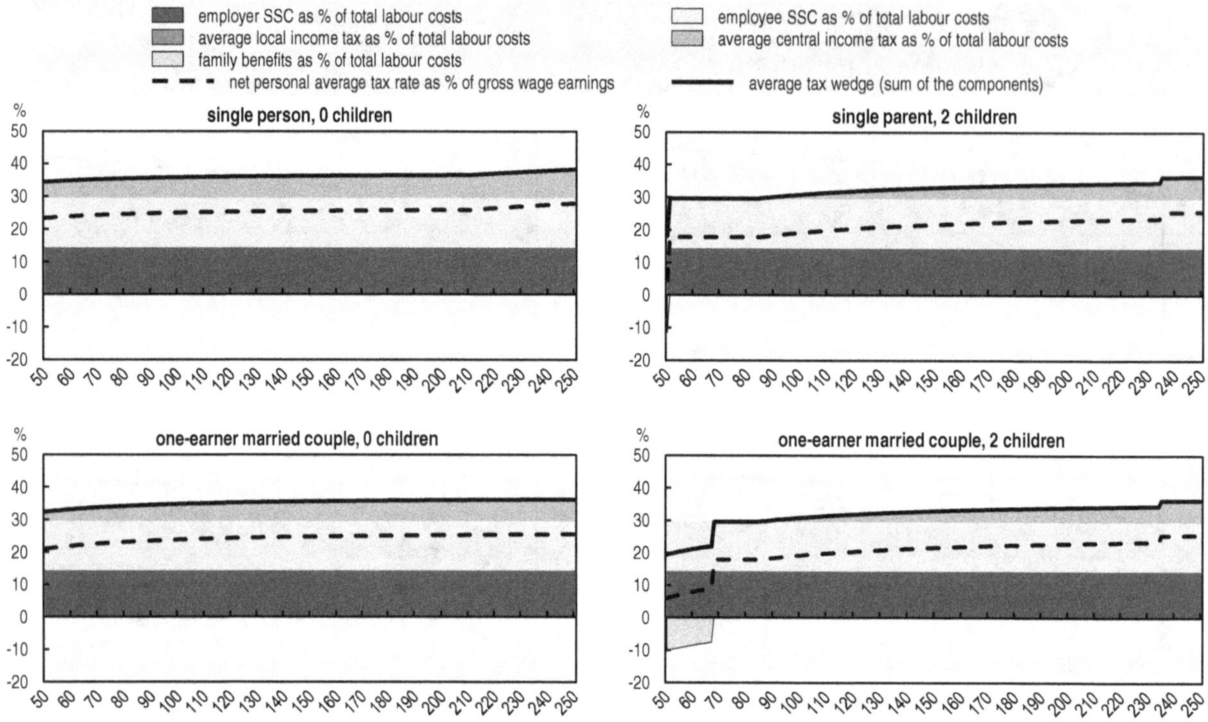

StatLink http://dx.doi.org/10.1787/888933460744

Poland 2016: Marginal tax wedge decomposition

By level of gross earnings expressed as a % of the average wage

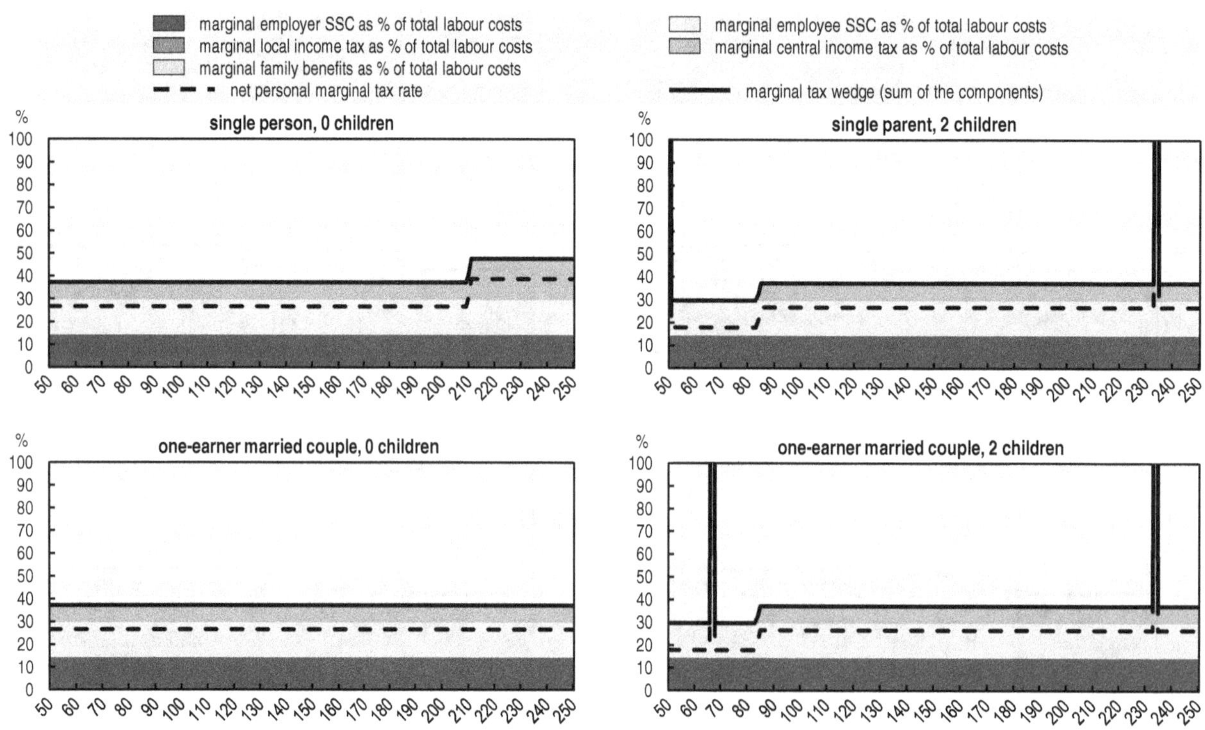

StatLink http://dx.doi.org/10.1787/888933460755

TAXING WAGES 2017 © OECD 2017

Portugal 2016: Average tax wedge decomposition

By level of gross earnings expressed as a % of the average wage

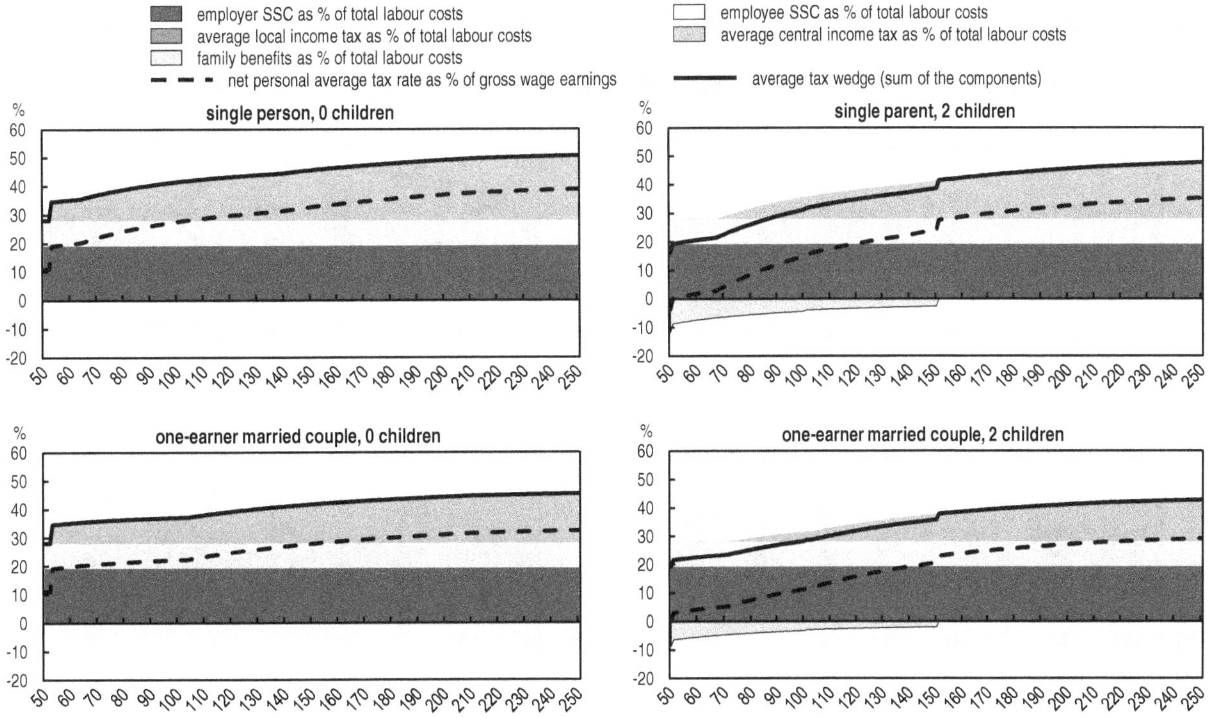

StatLink http://dx.doi.org/10.1787/888933460764

Portugal 2016: Marginal tax wedge decomposition

By level of gross earnings expressed as a % of the average wage

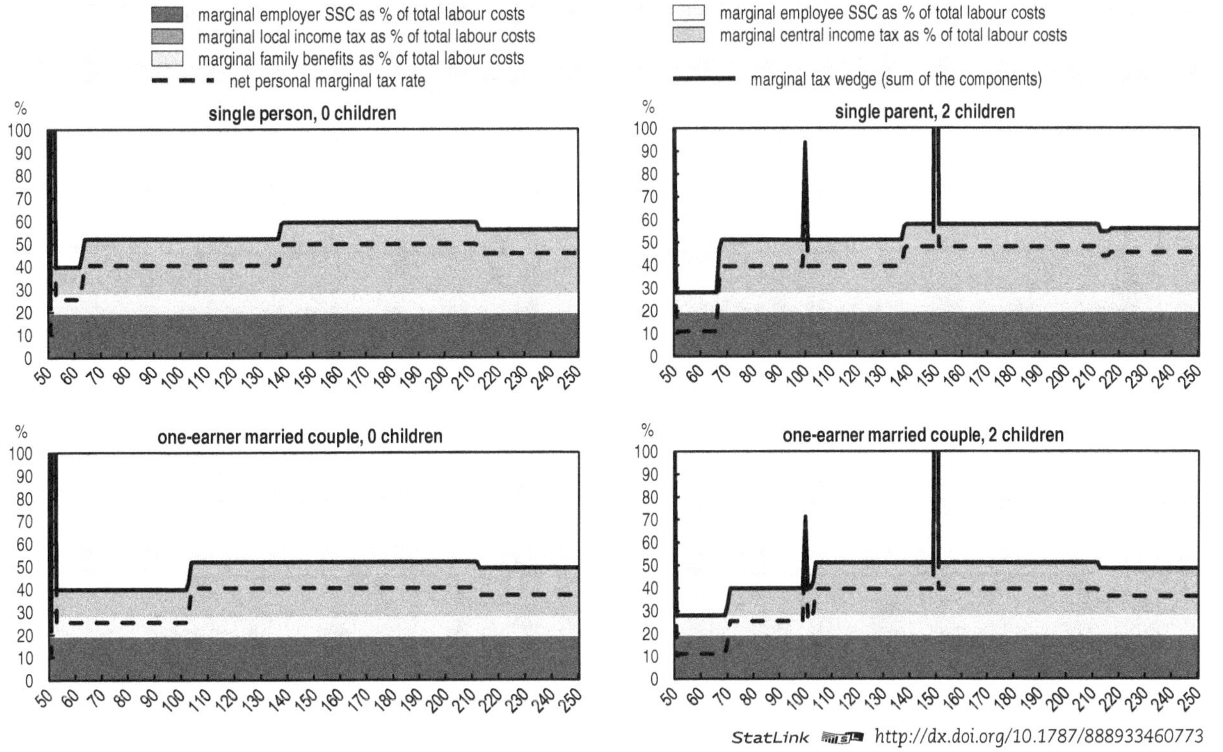

StatLink http://dx.doi.org/10.1787/888933460773

Slovak Republic 2016: Average tax wedge decomposition

By level of gross earnings expressed as a % of the average wage

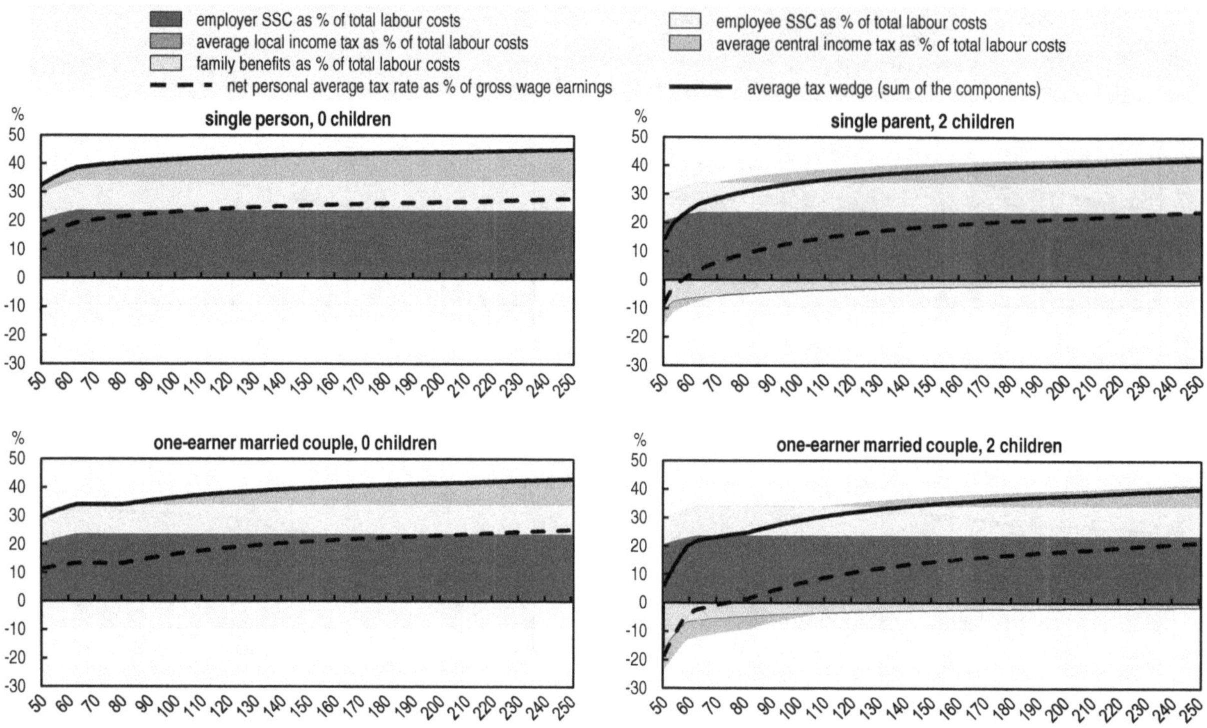

StatLink http://dx.doi.org/10.1787/888933460781

Slovak Republic 2016: Marginal tax wedge decomposition

By level of gross earnings expressed as a % of the average wage

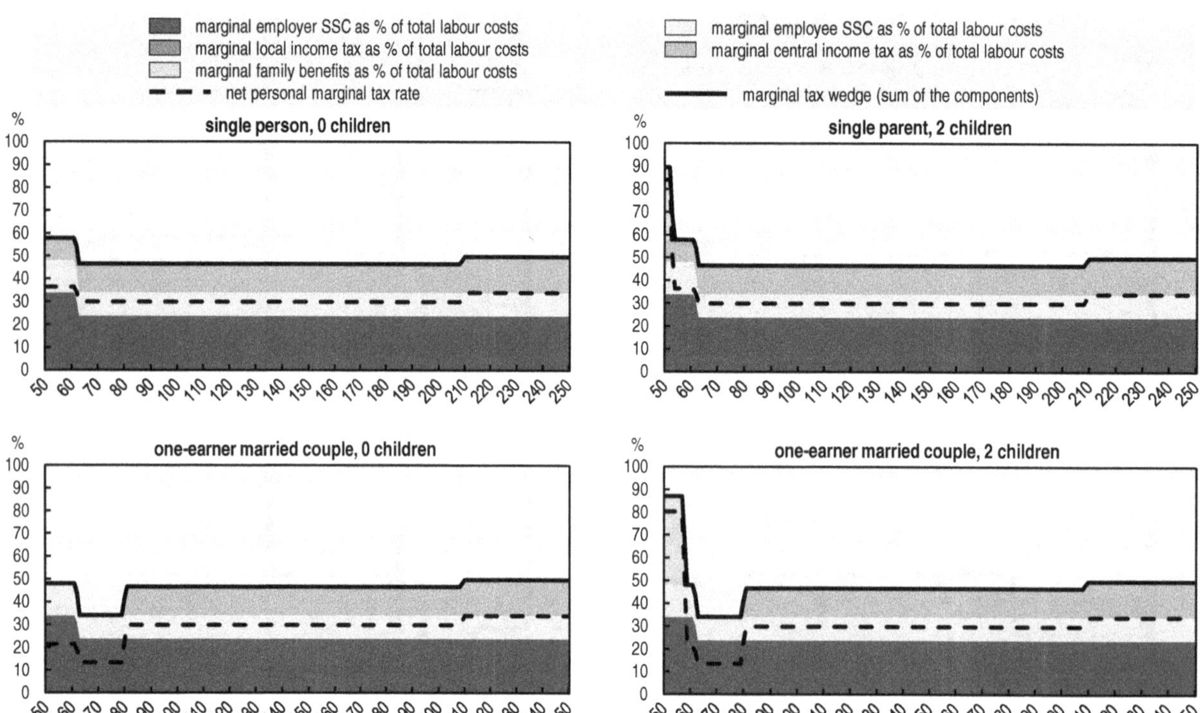

StatLink http://dx.doi.org/10.1787/888933460794

Slovenia 2016: Average tax wedge decomposition

By level of gross earnings expressed as a % of the average wage

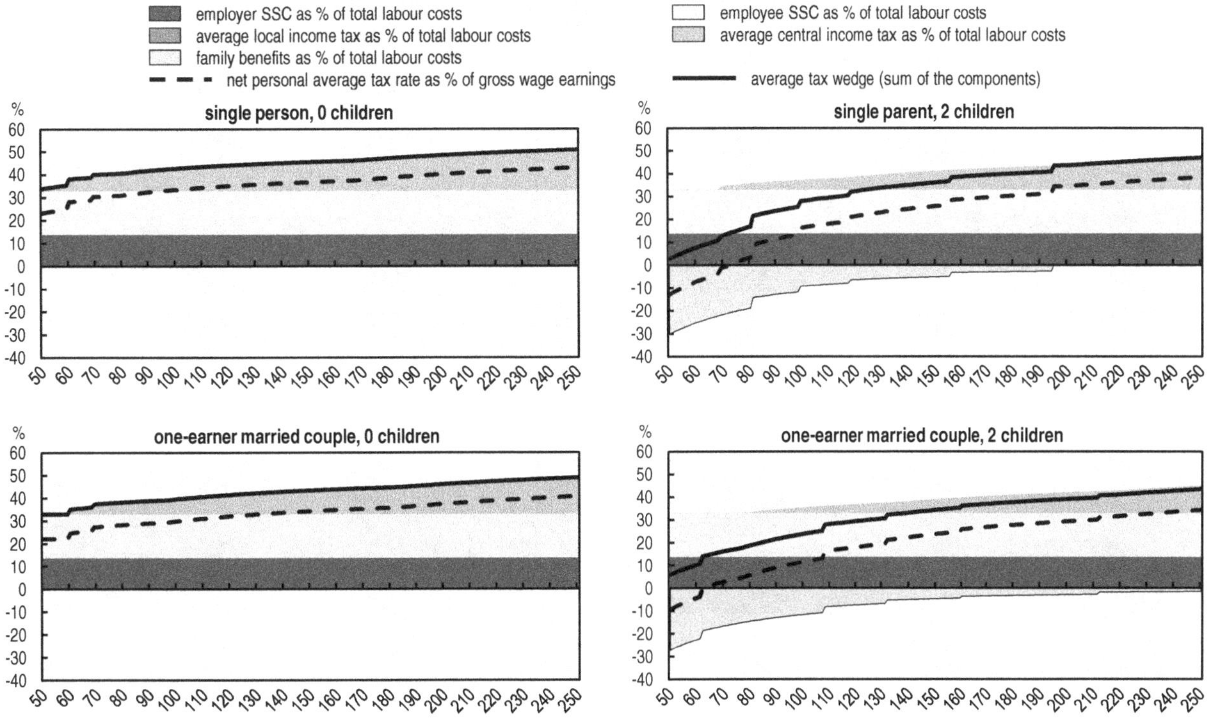

StatLink http://dx.doi.org/10.1787/888933460805

Slovenia 2016: Marginal tax wedge decomposition

By level of gross earnings expressed as a % of the average wage

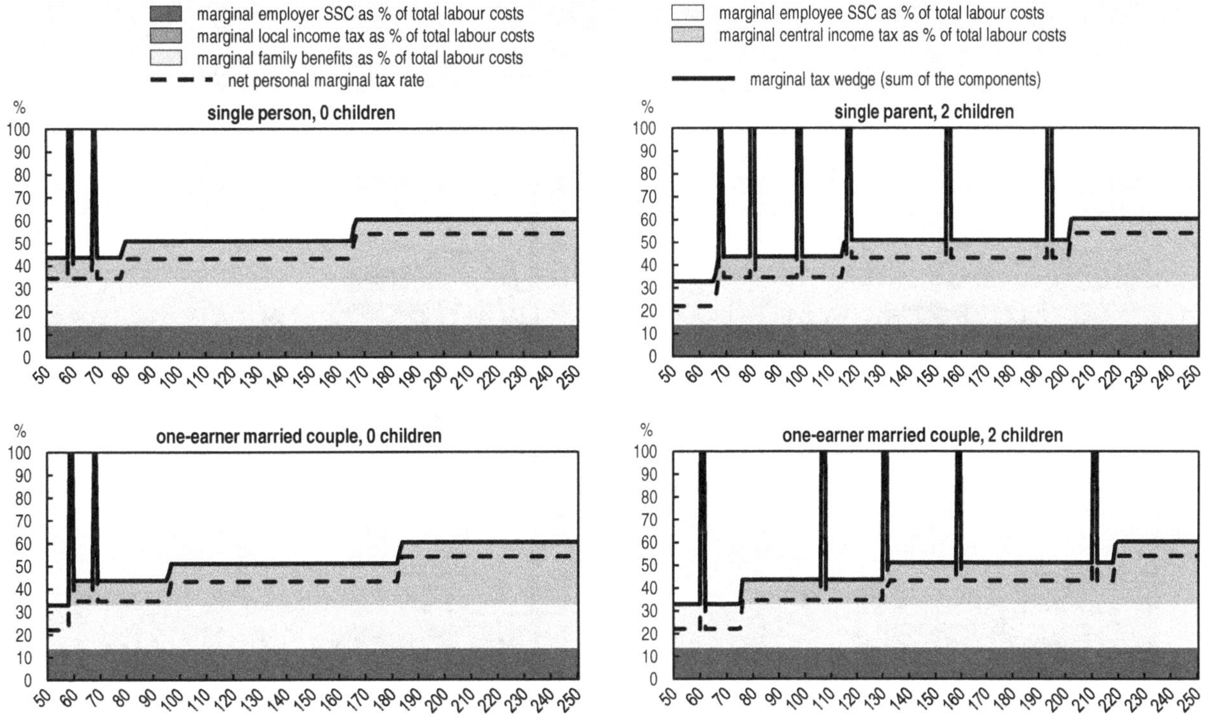

StatLink http://dx.doi.org/10.1787/888933460817

Spain 2016: Average tax wedge decomposition

By level of gross earnings expressed as a % of the average wage

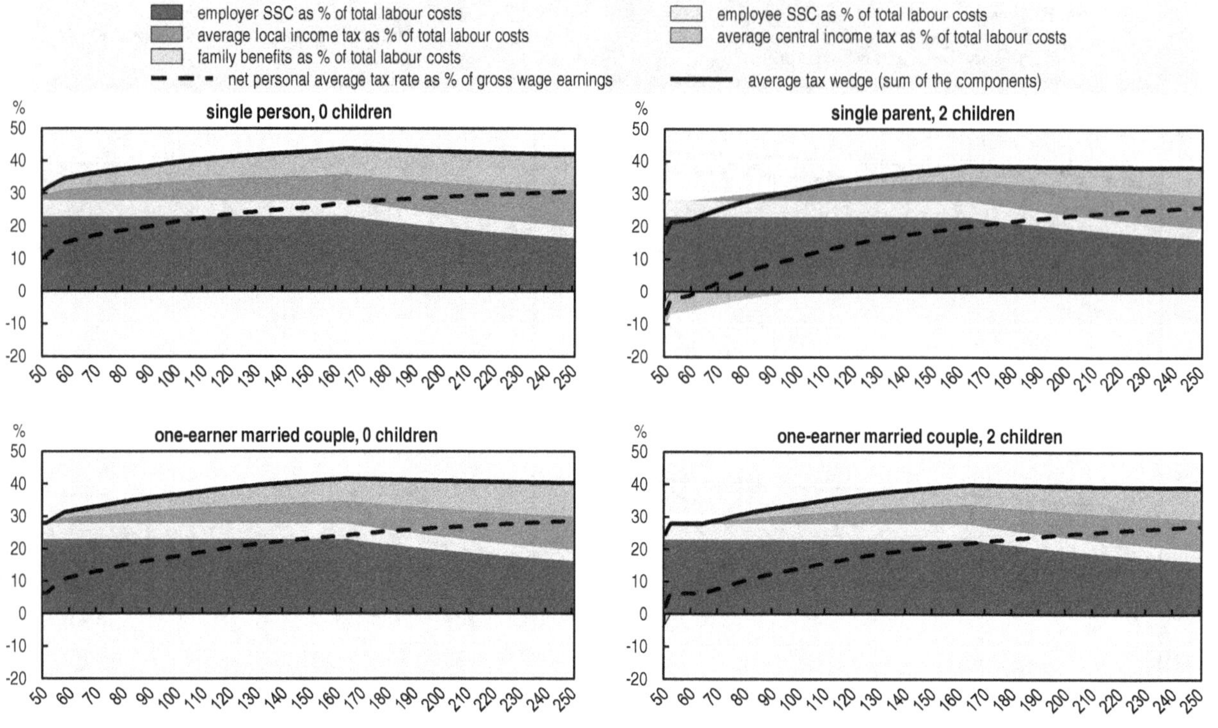

StatLink http://dx.doi.org/10.1787/888933460825

Spain 2016: Marginal tax wedge decomposition

By level of gross earnings expressed as a % of the average wage

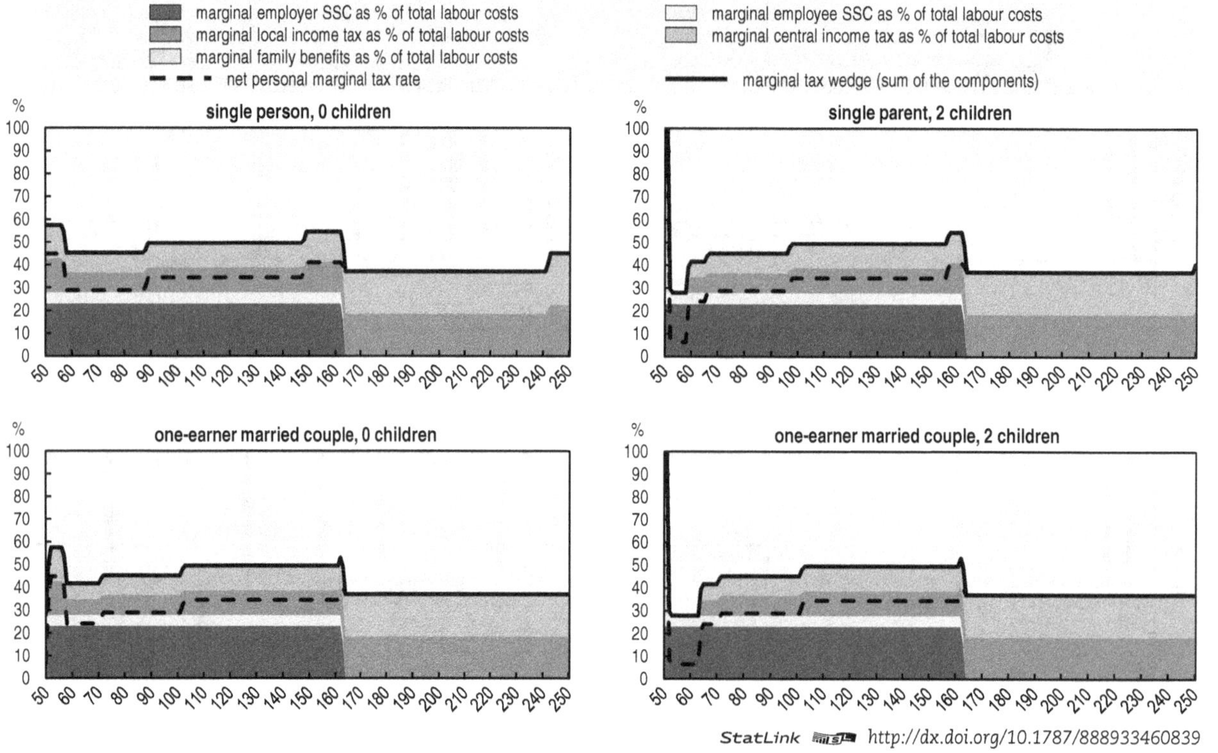

StatLink http://dx.doi.org/10.1787/888933460839

Sweden 2016: Average tax wedge decomposition

By level of gross earnings expressed as a % of the average wage

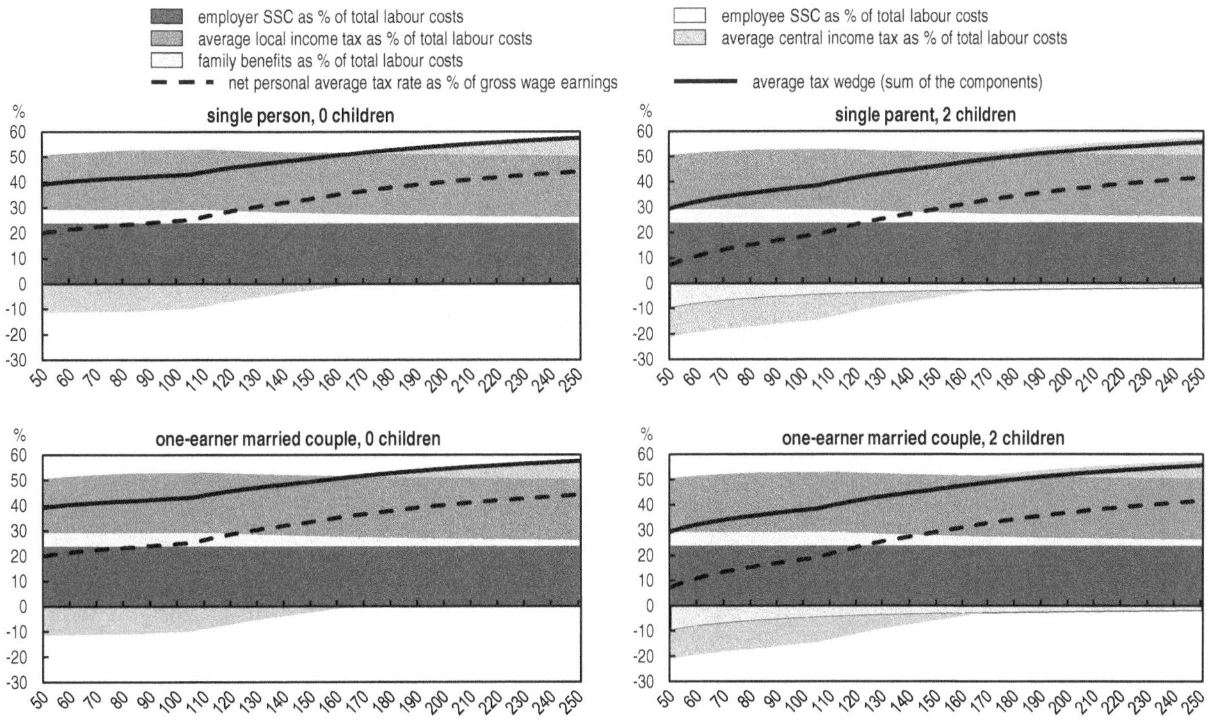

StatLink http://dx.doi.org/10.1787/888933460845

Sweden 2016: Marginal tax wedge decomposition

By level of gross earnings expressed as a % of the average wage

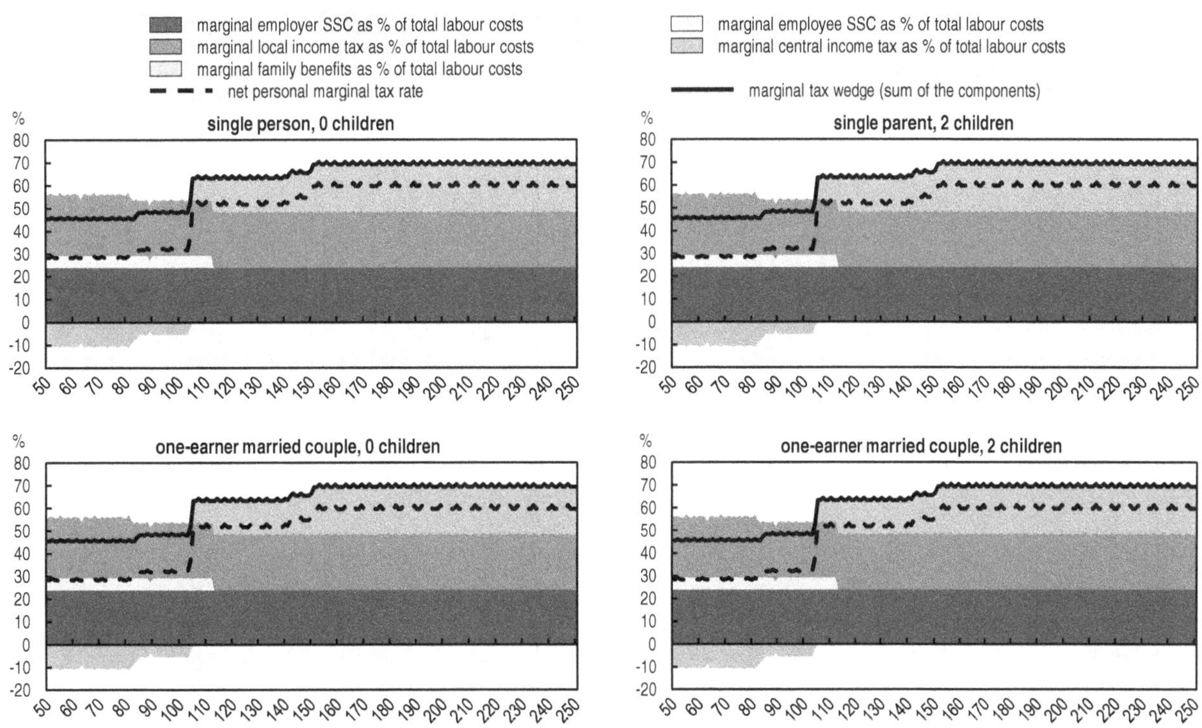

StatLink http://dx.doi.org/10.1787/888933460858

Switzerland 2016: Average tax wedge decomposition

By level of gross earnings expressed as a % of the average wage

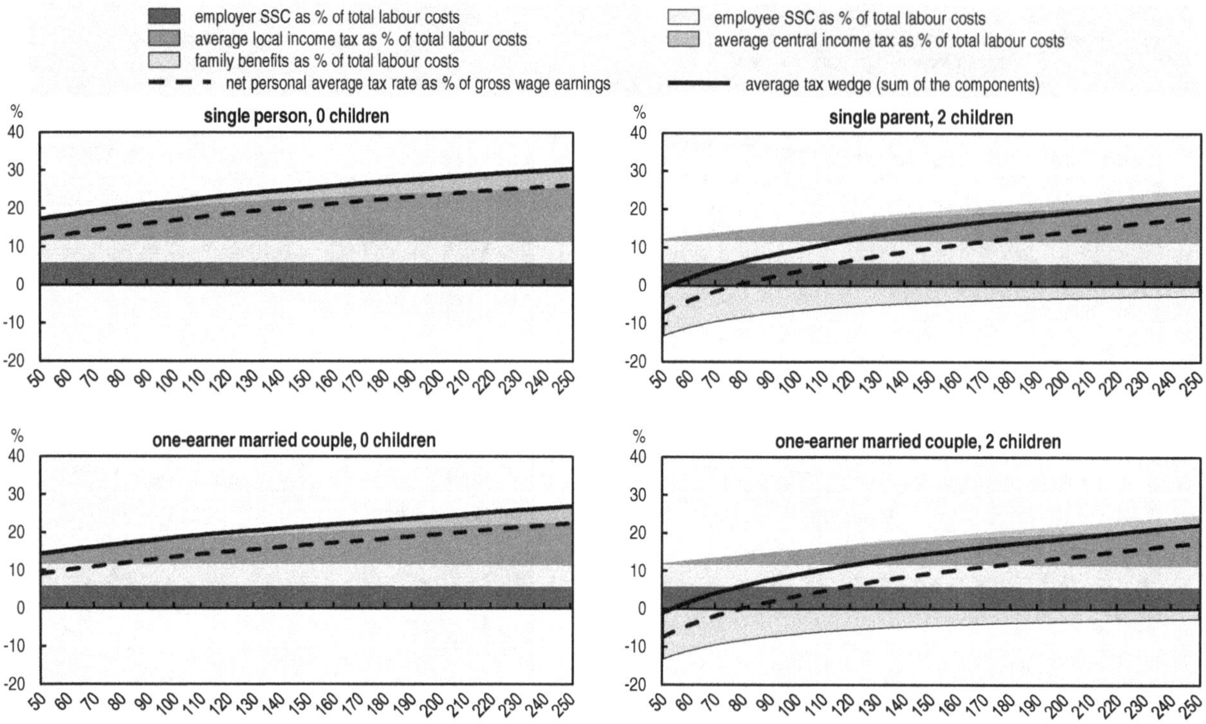

StatLink http://dx.doi.org/10.1787/888933460868

Switzerland 2016: Marginal tax wedge decomposition

By level of gross earnings expressed as a % of the average wage

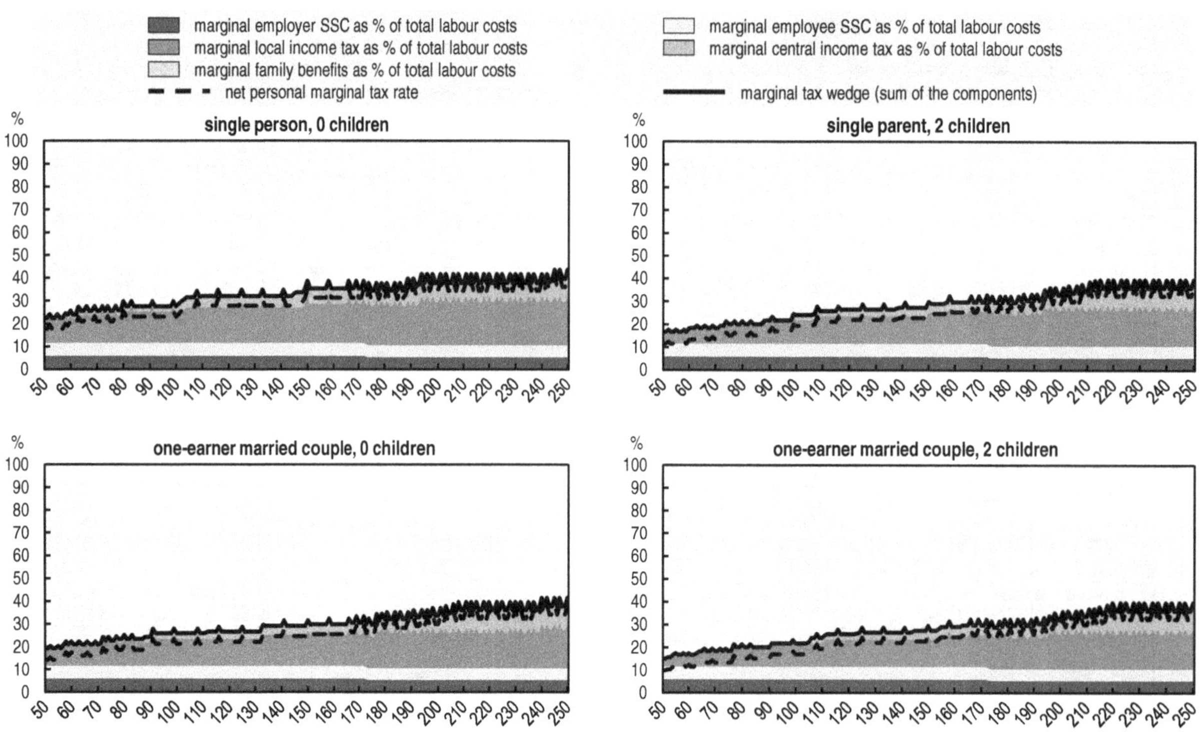

StatLink http://dx.doi.org/10.1787/888933460875

Turkey 2016: Average tax wedge decomposition

By level of gross earnings expressed as a % of the average wage

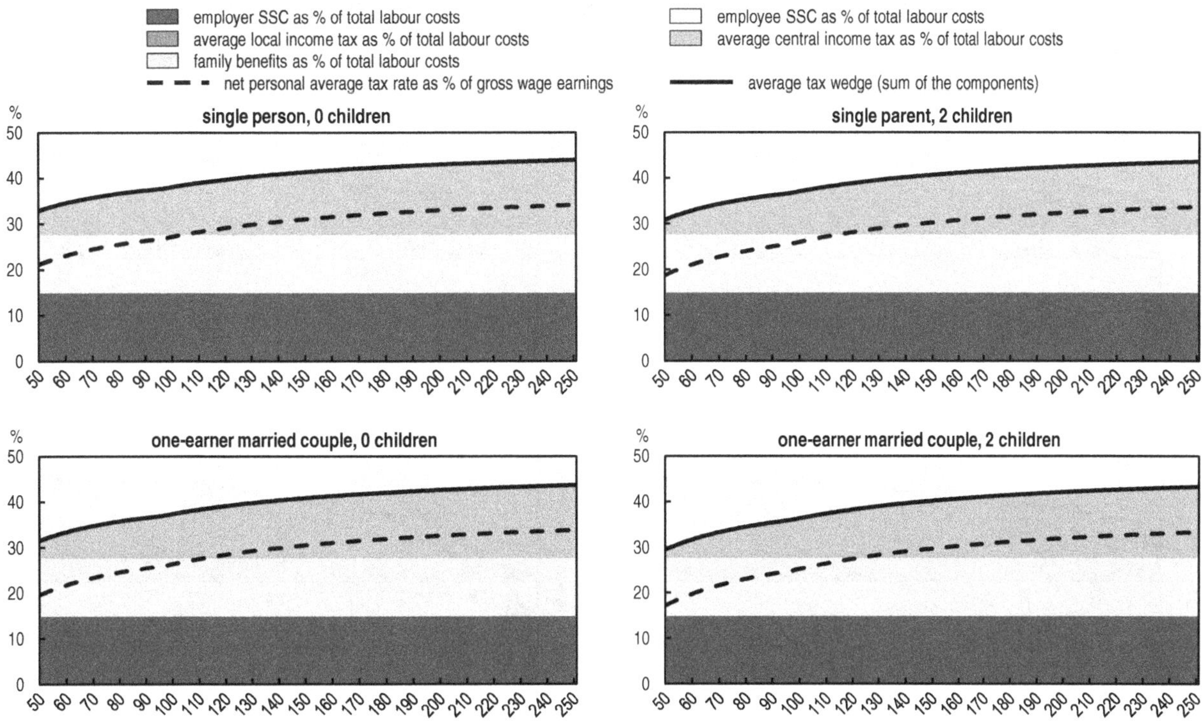

StatLink http://dx.doi.org/10.1787/888933460882

Turkey 2016: Marginal tax wedge decomposition

By level of gross earnings expressed as a % of the average wage

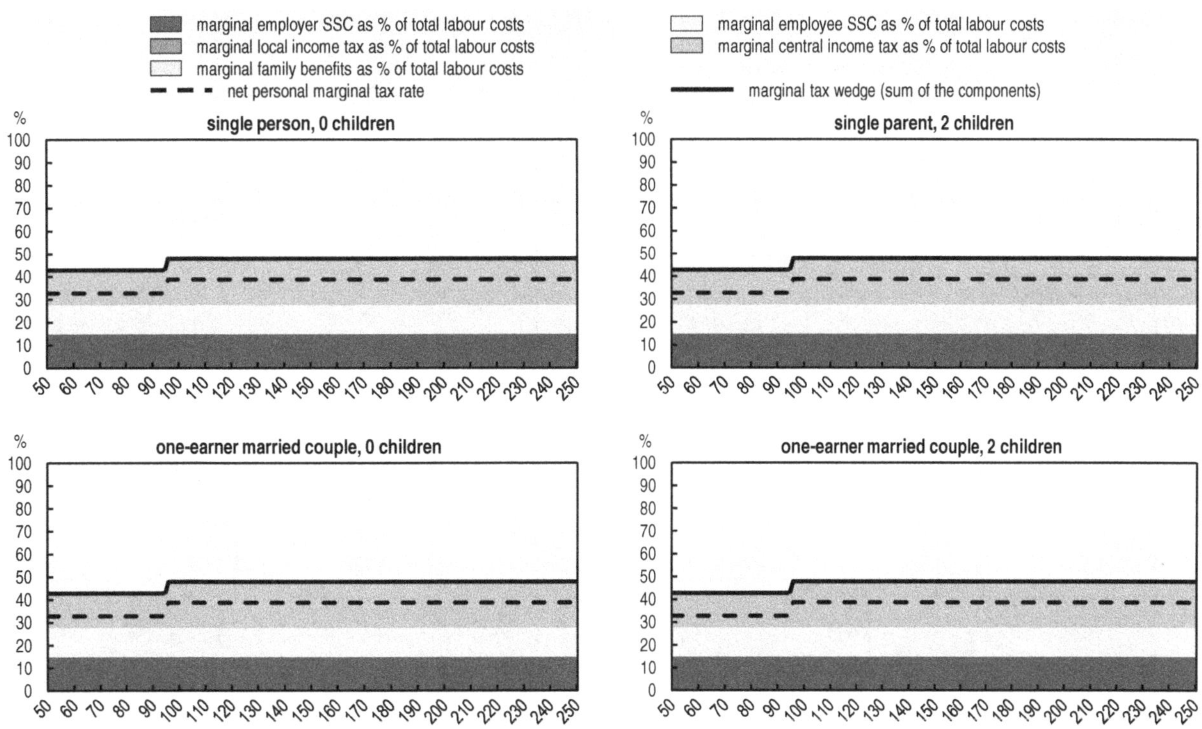

StatLink http://dx.doi.org/10.1787/888933460892

United Kingdom 2016: Average tax wedge decomposition

By level of gross earnings expressed as a % of the average wage

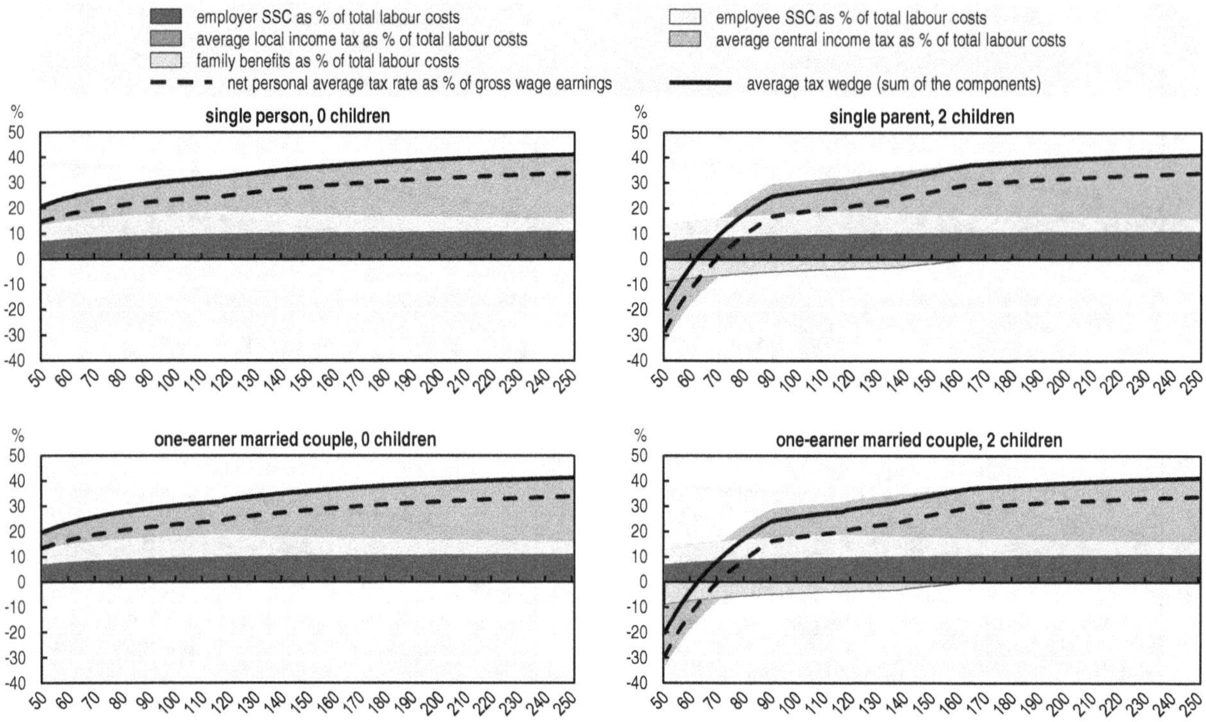

StatLink http://dx.doi.org/10.1787/888933460906

United Kingdom 2016: Marginal tax wedge decomposition

By level of gross earnings expressed as a % of the average wage

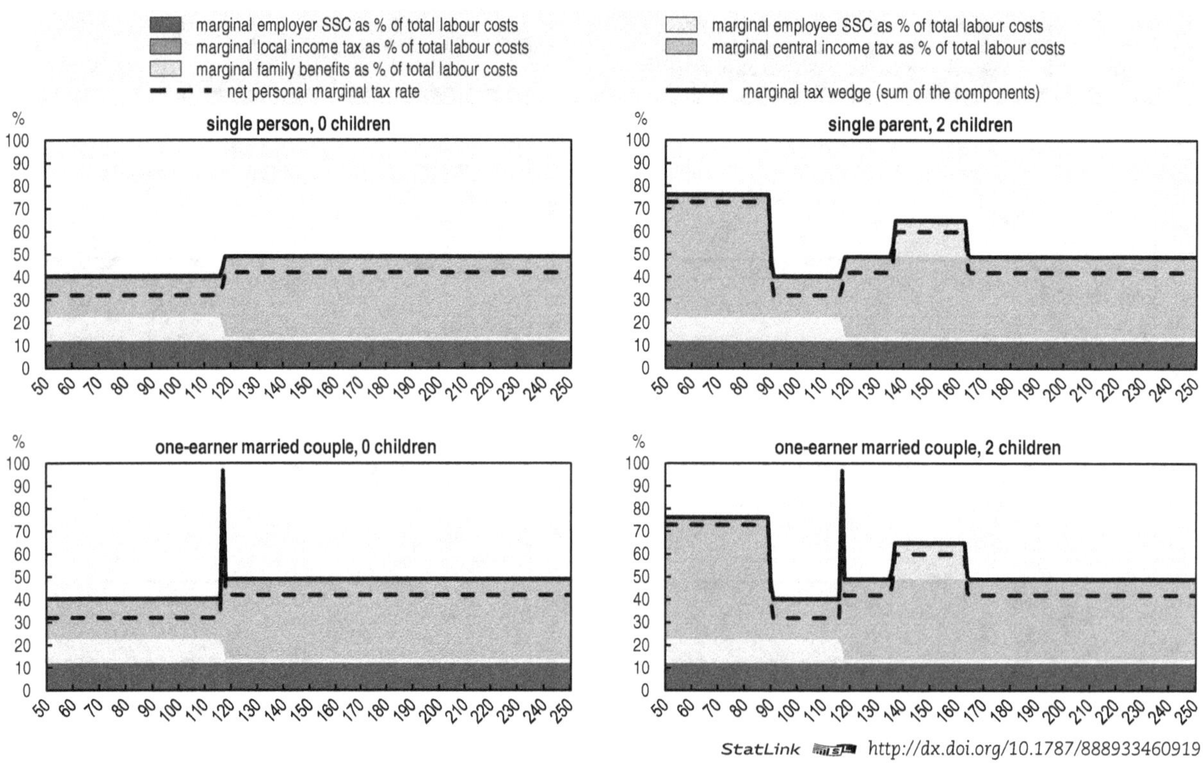

StatLink http://dx.doi.org/10.1787/888933460919

United States 2016: Average tax wedge decomposition

By level of gross earnings expressed as a % of the average wage

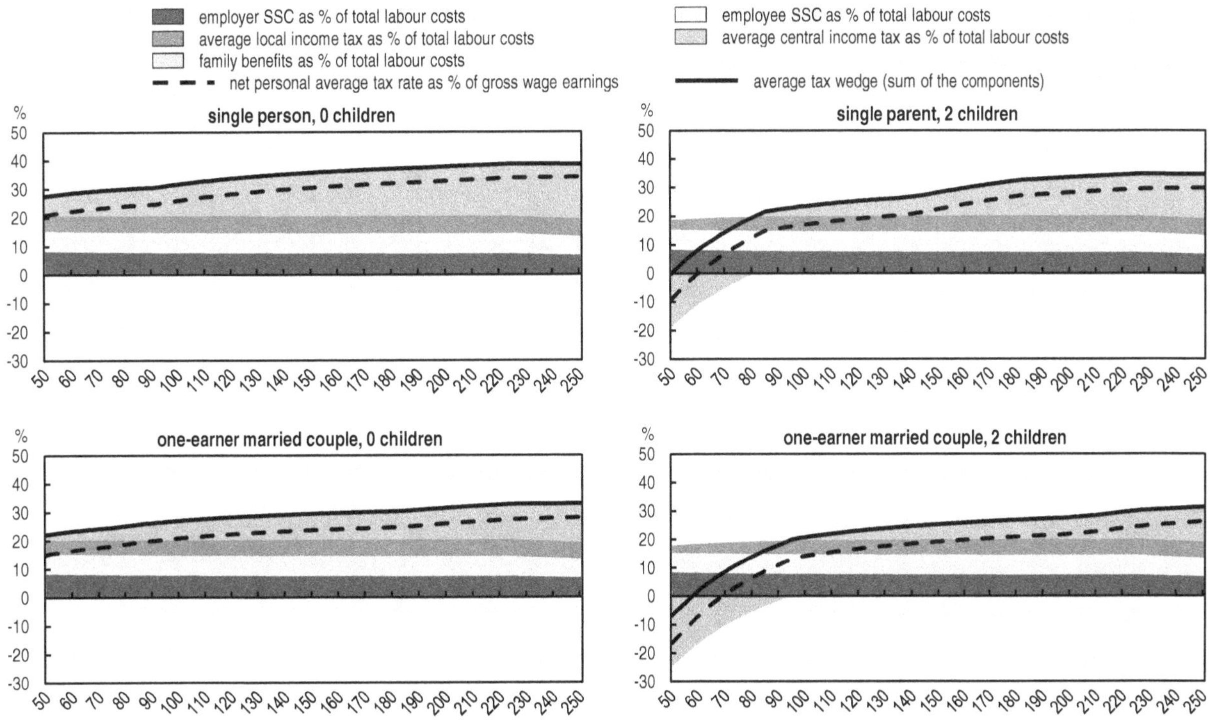

StatLink http://dx.doi.org/10.1787/888933460926

United States 2016: Marginal tax wedge decomposition

By level of gross earnings expressed as a % of the average wage

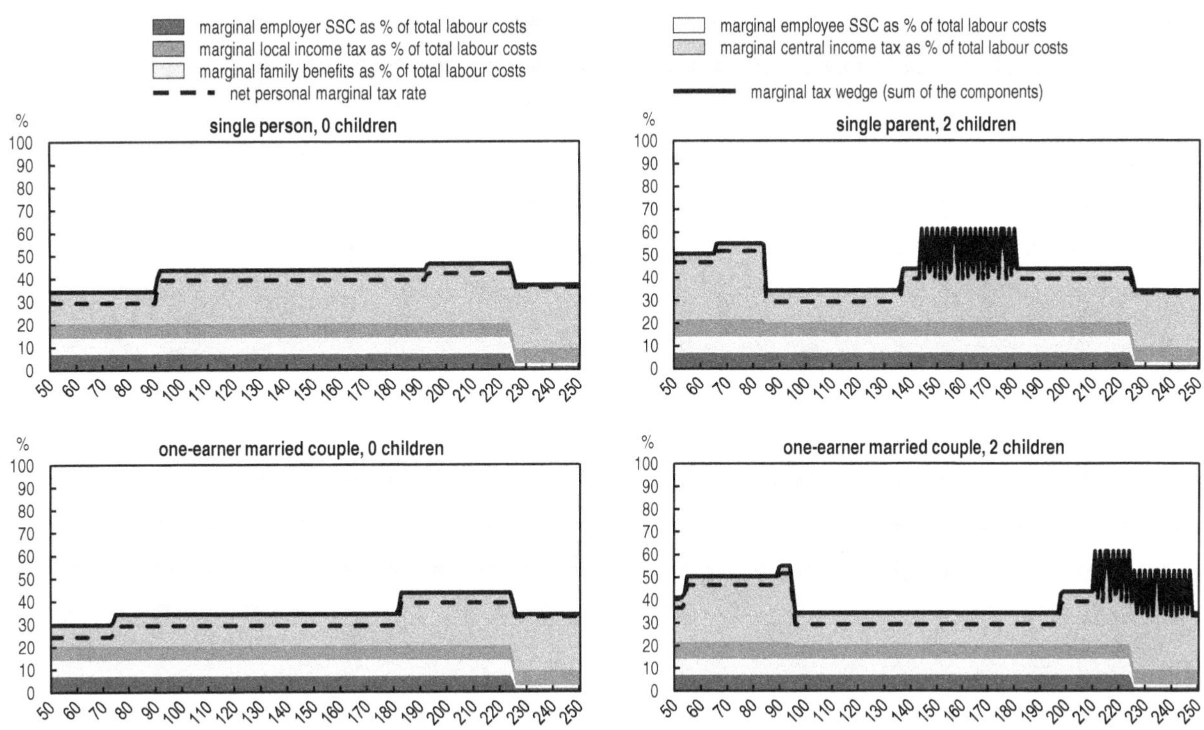

StatLink http://dx.doi.org/10.1787/888933460931

Taxing Wages 2017
© OECD 2017

PART I

Chapter 5

2015 Tax burdens (and changes to 2016)

The chapter presents the results of tax burden measures on labour income for the eight model family types for 2015. The chapter includes Tables 5.1 to 5.11 that show a number of measures of the average tax burdens (tax wedge, personal tax rate, net personal tax rate, personal income tax rate and employee social security contribution rate) and the marginal rates (tax wedge and net personal tax rate). The results for two measures of tax progressivity are also considered: tax elasticity on gross earnings and labour costs.

The table formats are identical to Tables 3.1 to 3.11 which are discussed in Chapter 3 on tax burden results on labour income for 2016. This chapter compares the two sets of tables and analyses the changes in tax burden between 2015 and 2016.

The statistical data for Israel are supplied by and under the responsibility of the relevant Israeli authorities. The use of such data by the OECD is without prejudice to the status of the Golan Heights, East Jerusalem and Israeli settlements in the West Bank under the terms of international law.

The following commentary on the changes in tax burdens and marginal tax rates between 2015 and 2016 focuses on two of the eight family-types – single employees, without children, at the average wage (column 2 of the tables) and one-earner married families, with two children, at the average wage (column 5). Comparisons with the columns 1, 3-4 and 6-8 of the tables give corresponding results for the six other family-types. Generally, only those changes exceeding 1 percentage point for average effective rates and 5 percentage points for marginal effective rates are flagged in this chapter. Most of these are due to tax reforms or changes in the tax systems. Further detailed information on the countries' tax systems is given in the Part III of the Report that is entitled "Country details, 2016".

Table 5.1 presents the total tax wedge (described as income tax plus employee and employer's social security contributions less cash benefits) by family-type as a percentage of total labour costs (gross wage plus employers' social security contributions [including payroll taxes]). In the majority of countries, changes in the gap between total labour costs and the corresponding net take-home pay in 2016 as compared with 2015 were within plus or minus one percentage point.

Comparing column 2 in Tables 3.1 and 5.1, the OECD average tax wedge decreased by 0.1 percentage point from 36.1% to 36.0% for a single average worker between 2015 and 2016. It fell by more than one percentage point in Austria (2.5 percentage points) and Belgium (1.3 percentage points). In Austria, there was a tax reform in 2016 that decreased the marginal tax rates within the income tax schedule and increased the tax credit for employees. During that year, in Belgium, changes in tax system also had an impact on the tax wedge. Among others, the tax allowance for work-related expenses and the income tax schedules were reformed, and the employer social security contribution rates were reduced. In contrast, there were no increases in the tax wedge of more than one percentage point for the single average worker across the OECD member countries.

For one-earner married couples (comparing column 5 of Tables 3.1 and 5.1) the OECD average tax wedge also decreased by 0.1 percentage point during this period, although the rate remained at 26.6% as rounded to the first decimal. The tax wedge increased by more than one percentage point only in New Zealand (1.3 percentage points), where the tax system remained unchanged. As a result, due to frozen *Family Tax Credit* and *In-Work Tax Credit* for families with children, the payments of the income-tested cash benefits decreased relative to increasing earnings between 2015 and 2016. In contrast, the tax wedge decreased by more than one percentage point in Austria (2.7 percentage points), Portugal (2.5 percentage points), Belgium (1.7 percentage points) and Hungary (1.6 percentage points). In Austria, in addition to the changes in the tax system that are mentioned in the previous paragraph, there was an increase in the tax allowances for children. In Portugal, the surtax became progressive and the tax credit for dependent children was increased in 2016. In the same year, in Hungary, the single statutory personal income tax rate was reduced from 16% to 15%. Also, families with children benefited from an increased *Family Tax Allowance*.

Table 5.2 shows the combined burden of income tax and employee social security contributions in the form of personal average tax rates as a percentage of gross wage earnings. For single persons on average earnings, it increased by more than one percentage point between 2015 and 2016 in Greece (1.2 percentage points) where the basic income tax credit was reduced and the employee social security contribution rate was increased. The personal average tax rates decreased by more than one percentage point in Austria (3.1 percentage points) and in Belgium (1.3 percentage points). For one-earner married couples with two children, there were no increases of more than one percentage point. In contrast, the personal average tax rates decreased by more than one percentage point in Austria (3.4 percentage points), Portugal (3.0 percentage points), Hungary (2.5 percentage points), Belgium (1.6 percentage points) and Ireland (1.1 percentage point). In Ireland, the *Home Carers Allowance*, a tax credit paid to the one-earner married couple on average earnings with two children, was increased. In addition, the marginal tax rates of the *Universal Social Charge* were reduced.

Table 5.3 provides the combined burden of income tax and employee social security contributions less the amount of cash family benefits as a percentage of gross wage earnings. This is the measure of the net personal average tax rate. Comparing column 2 of Tables 3.3 and 5.3, for single persons on average earnings, there were changes of more than one percentage point between 2015 and 2016 in Austria (-3.1 percentage points), Belgium (-1.3 percentage points) and Greece (+1.2 percentage points). Comparing column 5 of Tables 3.3 and 5.3, an increase in the net personal average tax rate of one-earner married couples exceeding one percentage point occurred in New Zealand (1.3 percentage points) only. It decreased by more than one percentage point in Austria (3.4 percentage points), Portugal (3.1 percentage points), Hungary (2.1 percentage points), Belgium (1.7 percentage points) and Ireland (1.2 percentage points).

Table 5.4 presents information on income tax due as a percentage of gross wage earnings. Comparing column 2 of Tables 3.4 and 5.4, in most OECD member countries, the average income tax rates for single persons on average earnings changed only slightly between 2015 and 2016 and the OECD average income tax rate decreased by 0.1 percentage point. The average income tax rate did not increase by more than one percentage point in any OECD member countries. In contrast, it decreased by more than one percentage point in Austria (3.1 percentage points) and in Belgium (1.2 percentage points). Comparing column 5 of Tables 3.4 and 5.4, the OECD average income tax rate for the one-earner married couples with two children decreased by 0.3 percentage points during that period. As for the single workers, there were no increases of more than one percentage point across the OECD member countries. However, the average income tax rates decreased by more than one percentage point in Austria (3.3 percentage points), Portugal (3.0 percentage points), Hungary (2.5 percentage points), Belgium (1.6 percentage points) and Ireland (1.1 percentage points).

Table 5.5 shows information on employee social security contributions as a percentage of gross wage earnings. Comparing columns 2 and 5 of Tables 3.5 and 5.5, there were no changes of more than one percentage point across the OECD member countries between 2015 and 2016 for either of these family types. The OECD average employee social security contribution rate increased by 0.1 percentage point for the one-earner married couples with two children during that period. It remained unchanged for the single workers.

Table 5.6 shows the marginal tax wedge (rate of income tax plus employee and employer social security contributions and payroll taxes where applicable minus benefits) as percentage of total labour costs, when the gross earnings of the principal earner rise by 1 currency unit in 2015. Comparing columns 2 and 5 respectively in Tables 3.6 and 5.6, changes between 2015 and 2016 in the marginal tax wedge were generally within the range of plus or minus 5 percentage points. There were changes of more than 5 percentage points in two OECD countries: Belgium (-20.0 percentage points for the one-earner married couple with two children) and Norway (-8.2 percentage points for the two family types). In the latter country, the Central Government income tax schedule was reformed and extended with two additional lower income tax brackets.

Table 5.7 presents the marginal rate of income tax plus employee social security contributions minus benefits by family-type and wage level, when the gross earnings of the principal earner rise by 1 currency unit in 2015. Comparing columns 2 and 5 respectively in Tables 3.7 and 5.7, the pattern of changes between 2015 and 2016 in the net personal marginal tax rates were similar to that for the marginal tax wedge discussed above. The examples of changes outside the range of plus or minus 5 percentage points were in Belgium (-26.3 percentage points for the one-earner married couple with two children) and Norway (-9.3 percentage points for the two family types). In addition, there were also changes of more than 5 percentage points in Austria (-5.8 percentage points for the two family types), Canada (+5.5 percentage points for the one-earner married couple with two children) and Turkey (+5.9 percentage points for the two family types). In Canada, the change in the net personal marginal tax rate is notably due to the removal of the *Family Tax Cut*, via which couples with minor children could transfer a part of taxable income from the higher-income spouse to a spouse in a lower tax bracket.

Table 5.8 shows the percentage increase in net income relative to the percentage increase in gross wages when the latter increases by 1 currency unit.[1] Table 5.9 provides the percentage increase in net income relative to the percentage increase in labour costs (i.e. gross wage earnings plus employer social security contributions and payroll taxes) when the latter rises by 1 currency unit.[2] The results shown in these two tables are directly dependent upon the marginal and average tax rates that have been discussed in the paragraphs above. Tables 5.10 and 5.11 report background information on levels of labour costs plus gross and net wages in 2015.

Notes

1. The reported elasticities in Table 5.8 are calculated as (100-METR)/(100-AETR), where METR is the marginal rate of income tax plus employee social security contributions less cash benefits reported in Table 5.7 and AETR is the average rate plus employee social security contributions less cash benefits reported in Table 5.3.
2. The reported elasticities in Table 5.9 are calculated as (100-METR)/(100-AETR), where METR is the marginal rate of income tax plus employee and employer social security contributions less cash benefits reported in Table 5.6 and AETR is the average rate plus employee and employer social security contributions less cash benefits reported in Table 5.1.

Table 5.1. **Income tax plus employee and employer contributions less cash benefits, 2015**

As % of labour costs, by family-type and wage level

	Single no ch 67 (% AW)	Single no ch 100 (% AW)	Single no ch 167 (% AW)	Single 2 ch 67 (% AW)	Married 2 ch 100-0 (% AW)	Married 2 ch 100-33 (% AW)[2]	Married 2 ch 100-67 (% AW)[2]	Married no ch 100-33 (% AW)[2]
Australia	23.1	28.4	34.0	-1.4	17.8	22.7	26.3	24.2
Austria	45.1	49.6	52.1	29.6	39.2	38.5	42.2	45.5
Belgium	49.4	55.3	60.7	35.6	40.3	41.3	48.1	47.6
Canada	26.5	31.5	33.3	-15.4	11.0	19.9	24.3	28.4
Chile	7.0	7.0	7.9	6.1	7.0	4.7	6.6	7.0
Czech Republic	39.9	42.8	45.1	24.6	26.7	32.8	35.5	40.5
Denmark	34.3	36.4	42.4	7.5	25.9	29.8	31.8	34.5
Estonia	38.0	39.0	39.9	21.7	28.6	31.7	33.7	38.0
Finland	37.9	43.5	49.4	27.3	38.9	36.0	38.4	39.6
France	43.3	48.4	54.3	35.8	40.5	37.8	43.0	43.7
Germany	45.2	49.4	51.3	30.7	33.9	38.6	42.2	45.1
Greece	34.6	39.2	45.6	30.8	37.6	37.1	37.7	38.0
Hungary	49.0	49.0	49.0	27.2	35.3	38.7	40.8	49.0
Iceland	30.2	34.3	38.6	20.4	23.1	29.1	32.6	30.4
Ireland	21.5	27.3	38.7	-19.1	9.3	13.9	19.7	20.2
Israel[1]	14.6	21.6	30.6	2.8	18.9	15.9	15.3	17.9
Italy	40.9	47.9	54.2	25.4	38.7	38.5	41.6	42.8
Japan	30.9	32.3	34.9	24.7	27.0	28.4	29.3	31.5
Korea	18.7	22.0	24.2	17.0	19.8	19.5	19.6	20.8
Latvia	41.7	42.5	43.2	25.0	31.4	33.3	35.5	41.6
Luxembourg	31.2	38.4	45.3	7.3	16.0	20.5	26.2	29.5
Mexico	15.0	19.8	22.8	15.0	19.8	17.6	17.9	17.6
Netherlands	32.2	37.0	42.3	10.6	31.6	28.6	30.8	33.2
New Zealand	13.5	17.6	23.3	-14.4	4.9	12.0	16.5	16.2
Norway	33.6	36.6	42.3	22.1	31.8	31.1	33.2	33.9
Poland	35.0	35.7	36.3	29.6	30.6	31.9	33.0	35.0
Portugal	36.2	42.1	48.0	25.3	30.7	31.1	35.6	36.1
Slovak Republic	38.8	41.4	43.4	27.3	28.5	31.7	35.7	37.6
Slovenia	38.6	42.6	46.5	10.1	23.6	30.8	34.6	40.2
Spain	35.8	39.4	43.8	24.2	33.7	35.5	36.3	36.5
Sweden	40.6	42.6	50.7	33.2	37.7	37.1	38.8	40.9
Switzerland	19.1	21.8	26.3	4.0	9.2	12.2	15.4	19.6
Turkey	35.9	38.2	41.8	34.6	36.7	35.5	36.7	36.2
United Kingdom	26.0	30.8	37.3	5.2	25.8	22.4	26.2	25.8
United States	29.2	31.6	36.4	12.1	20.6	24.4	26.4	29.2
Unweighted average								
OECD-Average	**32.4**	**36.1**	**40.5**	**17.2**	**26.6**	**28.3**	**31.1**	**33.0**
OECD-EU 22	**38.0**	**41.8**	**46.3**	**21.6**	**31.1**	**32.6**	**35.8**	**38.2**

Note: ch = children

1. Information on data for Israel: http://oe.cd/israel-disclaimer.
2. Two-earner family.

StatLink http://dx.doi.org/10.1787/888933461222

Table 5.2. Income tax plus employee contributions, 2015

As % of gross wage earnings, by family-type and wage level

	Single no ch 67 (% AW)	Single no ch 100 (% AW)	Single no ch 167 (% AW)	Single 2 ch 67 (% AW)	Married 2 ch 100-0 (% AW)	Married 2 ch 100-33 (% AW)[2]	Married 2 ch 100-67 (% AW)[2]	Married no ch 100-33 (% AW)[2]
Australia	18.5	24.1	30.1	18.5	24.1	19.7	21.9	19.7
Austria	29.2	35.0	39.4	26.4	33.1	29.4	32.4	29.7
Belgium	35.4	42.0	49.1	29.9	30.7	32.2	37.9	34.1
Canada	19.0	23.2	27.0	10.7	17.7	19.2	21.1	19.8
Chile	7.0	7.0	7.9	7.0	7.0	7.0	7.0	7.0
Czech Republic	19.5	23.3	26.4	5.8	6.4	13.4	16.3	20.3
Denmark	33.8	36.1	42.1	32.2	32.2	34.0	35.2	34.0
Estonia	17.1	18.4	19.6	12.8	12.8	14.9	16.2	17.0
Finland	24.0	30.9	38.1	23.4	30.8	25.8	28.0	26.1
France	25.8	28.9	34.4	22.1	22.1	22.1	25.5	26.5
Germany	34.6	39.6	43.8	17.3	21.1	26.8	31.1	34.5
Greece	18.5	24.2	32.2	18.5	25.2	22.8	23.3	22.8
Hungary	34.5	34.5	34.5	23.2	26.9	28.8	30.0	34.5
Iceland	25.0	29.3	34.0	25.0	21.3	25.2	27.6	25.2
Ireland	13.1	19.5	32.1	7.3	11.9	12.1	16.6	12.1
Israel[1]	10.8	17.3	26.3	5.9	17.3	13.9	12.7	13.9
Italy	21.9	31.1	39.5	14.2	24.2	21.0	24.5	24.5
Japan	20.4	22.1	25.9	20.4	20.7	21.1	21.4	21.1
Korea	10.3	14.0	17.3	8.4	11.5	11.1	11.3	12.6
Latvia	27.9	28.9	29.8	13.7	19.4	20.7	22.8	27.8
Luxembourg	22.7	30.8	38.6	16.0	19.2	20.8	25.2	20.8
Mexico	3.3	10.4	15.1	3.3	10.4	6.1	7.6	6.1
Netherlands	24.9	30.4	38.3	18.5	28.0	23.8	25.6	26.0
New Zealand	13.5	17.6	23.3	14.9	17.6	16.2	16.5	16.2
Norway	25.0	28.4	34.8	21.4	27.2	25.3	27.0	25.3
Poland	24.1	24.9	25.6	17.8	18.9	20.5	21.7	24.1
Portugal	21.1	28.3	35.6	14.8	18.3	17.5	20.3	20.9
Slovak Republic	19.7	23.1	25.8	12.5	11.5	16.1	18.9	19.7
Slovenia	28.7	33.3	37.9	22.1	25.0	25.9	27.8	30.5
Spain	16.7	21.3	27.3	1.5	13.9	16.2	17.2	17.6
Sweden	22.0	24.6	35.2	22.0	24.6	22.3	23.5	22.3
Switzerland	14.0	16.9	21.7	8.4	10.5	12.0	14.2	14.6
Turkey	24.7	27.4	31.6	23.2	25.6	24.3	25.7	25.0
United Kingdom	19.2	23.4	29.8	4.0	22.8	19.1	21.7	19.1
United States	23.0	25.8	31.2	4.3	13.9	17.7	20.1	22.9
Unweighted average								
OECD-Average	**21.4**	**25.6**	**30.9**	**15.6**	**20.1**	**20.1**	**22.2**	**22.1**
OECD-EU 22	**24.3**	**28.8**	**34.3**	**17.1**	**21.8**	**22.1**	**24.6**	**24.8**

Note: ch = children

1. Information on data for Israel: http://oe.cd/israel-disclaimer.
2. Two-earner family.

StatLink http://dx.doi.org/10.1787/888933461235

Table 5.3. Income tax plus employee contributions less cash benefits, 2015

As % of gross wage earnings, by family-type and wage level

	Single no ch 67 (% AW)	Single no ch 100 (% AW)	Single no ch 167 (% AW)	Single 2 ch 67 (% AW)	Married 2 ch 100-0 (% AW)	Married 2 ch 100-33 (% AW)[2]	Married 2 ch 100-67 (% AW)[2]	Married no ch 100-33 (% AW)[2]
Australia	18.5	24.1	30.1	-7.4	12.9	18.1	21.9	19.7
Austria	29.2	35.0	39.4	9.3	21.6	20.8	25.5	29.7
Belgium	35.4	42.0	49.1	17.8	22.6	26.1	33.1	34.1
Canada	17.7	23.2	27.0	-29.2	0.2	10.3	15.1	19.8
Chile	7.0	7.0	7.9	6.1	7.0	4.7	6.6	7.0
Czech Republic	19.5	23.3	26.4	-1.0	1.8	9.9	13.6	20.3
Denmark	33.4	35.9	42.1	6.3	25.3	28.8	31.1	33.6
Estonia	17.1	18.4	19.6	-4.8	4.5	8.7	11.2	17.0
Finland	24.0	30.9	38.1	11.0	25.2	21.6	24.6	26.1
France	25.8	28.9	34.4	15.9	17.9	19.0	23.0	26.5
Germany	34.6	39.6	43.8	17.3	21.1	26.8	31.1	34.5
Greece	18.5	24.2	32.2	13.8	22.3	21.7	22.4	22.8
Hungary	34.5	34.5	34.5	6.5	16.9	21.2	23.9	34.5
Iceland	25.0	29.3	34.0	14.4	17.4	23.8	27.6	25.2
Ireland	13.1	19.5	32.1	-31.9	-0.4	5.1	11.1	12.1
Israel[1]	10.8	17.3	26.3	-1.6	14.5	11.8	11.1	13.9
Italy	21.9	31.1	39.5	1.4	19.1	18.7	22.8	24.5
Japan	20.4	22.1	25.9	13.4	16.0	17.6	18.6	21.1
Korea	10.3	14.0	17.3	8.4	11.5	11.1	11.3	12.6
Latvia	27.9	28.9	29.8	7.3	15.2	17.5	20.3	27.8
Luxembourg	22.7	30.8	38.6	-4.1	5.7	10.7	17.1	20.8
Mexico	3.3	10.4	15.1	3.3	10.4	6.1	7.6	6.1
Netherlands	24.9	30.4	38.3	1.0	24.3	21.0	23.4	26.0
New Zealand	13.5	17.6	23.3	-14.4	4.9	12.0	16.5	16.2
Norway	25.0	28.4	34.8	12.0	23.0	22.2	24.5	25.3
Poland	24.1	24.9	25.6	17.8	18.9	20.5	21.7	24.1
Portugal	21.1	28.3	35.6	7.5	14.3	14.7	20.3	20.9
Slovak Republic	19.7	23.1	25.8	4.6	6.2	12.1	15.7	19.7
Slovenia	28.7	33.3	37.9	-4.4	11.3	19.6	24.1	30.5
Spain	16.7	21.3	27.3	1.5	13.9	16.2	17.2	17.6
Sweden	22.0	24.6	35.2	12.2	18.1	17.4	19.6	22.3
Switzerland	14.0	16.9	21.7	-2.0	3.5	6.7	10.1	14.6
Turkey	24.7	27.4	31.6	23.2	25.6	24.3	25.7	25.0
United Kingdom	19.2	23.4	29.8	-3.5	17.8	15.3	18.7	19.1
United States	23.0	25.8	31.2	4.3	13.9	17.7	20.1	22.9
Unweighted average								
OECD-Average	**21.3**	**25.6**	**30.9**	**3.8**	**14.4**	**16.6**	**19.7**	**22.1**
OECD-EU 22	**24.3**	**28.8**	**34.3**	**4.6**	**15.6**	**17.9**	**21.4**	**24.8**

Note: ch = children

1. Information on data for Israel: http://oe.cd/israel-disclaimer.
2. Two-earner family.

StatLink http://dx.doi.org/10.1787/888933461249

Table 5.4. **Income tax, 2015**

As % of gross wage earnings, by family-type and wage level

	Single no ch 67 (% AW)	Single no ch 100 (% AW)	Single no ch 167 (% AW)	Single 2 ch 67 (% AW)	Married 2 ch 100-0 (% AW)	Married 2 ch 100-33 (% AW)[2]	Married 2 ch 100-67 (% AW)[2]	Married no ch 100-33 (% AW)[2]
Australia	18.5	24.1	30.1	18.5	24.1	19.7	21.9	19.7
Austria	11.1	17.0	23.4	8.3	15.0	12.1	14.3	12.4
Belgium	21.5	28.0	35.1	16.0	16.7	21.4	23.9	23.3
Canada	11.8	15.6	22.1	3.5	10.0	12.0	13.6	12.6
Chile	0.0	0.0	0.9	0.0	0.0	0.0	0.0	0.0
Czech Republic	8.5	12.3	15.4	-5.2	-4.6	2.4	5.3	9.3
Denmark	33.8	36.1	42.1	32.2	32.2	34.0	35.2	34.0
Estonia	15.5	16.8	18.0	11.2	11.2	13.3	14.6	15.4
Finland	15.9	22.6	29.8	15.2	22.5	17.8	19.7	18.0
France	11.6	14.7	20.9	7.9	7.9	7.9	11.3	12.3
Germany	14.2	19.1	27.7	-2.9	0.9	6.5	10.9	14.1
Greece	3.0	8.7	16.7	3.0	9.7	7.3	7.8	7.3
Hungary	16.0	16.0	16.0	4.7	8.4	10.3	11.5	16.0
Iceland	24.5	29.0	33.8	24.5	21.0	24.7	27.2	24.7
Ireland	9.1	15.5	28.1	3.3	7.9	9.1	12.6	9.1
Israel[1]	4.9	9.4	16.8	0.0	9.4	7.1	5.6	7.1
Italy	12.4	21.6	29.9	4.7	14.7	11.5	15.0	15.0
Japan	6.2	7.8	12.6	6.2	6.4	6.8	7.1	6.8
Korea	2.0	5.6	10.3	0.0	3.1	2.8	2.9	4.2
Latvia	17.4	18.4	19.3	3.2	8.9	10.2	12.3	17.3
Luxembourg	10.0	18.0	25.7	3.3	6.4	8.1	12.4	8.1
Mexico	2.1	9.1	13.6	2.1	9.1	4.7	6.3	4.7
Netherlands	7.3	17.3	29.1	5.8	16.7	13.2	12.7	13.7
New Zealand	13.5	17.6	23.3	14.9	17.6	16.2	16.5	16.2
Norway	16.8	20.2	26.6	13.2	19.0	17.1	18.8	17.1
Poland	6.3	7.1	7.8	0.0	1.1	2.6	3.9	6.2
Portugal	10.1	17.3	24.6	3.8	7.3	6.5	9.3	9.9
Slovak Republic	6.3	9.7	12.4	-0.9	-1.9	3.7	5.5	7.3
Slovenia	6.6	11.2	15.8	0.0	2.9	3.8	5.7	8.4
Spain	10.3	14.9	21.1	-4.8	7.6	9.8	10.9	11.2
Sweden	15.0	17.6	30.4	15.0	17.6	15.3	16.5	15.3
Switzerland	7.8	10.7	15.6	2.1	4.2	5.7	8.0	8.4
Turkey	9.7	12.4	16.6	8.2	10.6	9.3	10.7	10.0
United Kingdom	11.2	14.1	22.3	-4.0	13.5	11.1	12.9	11.1
United States	15.3	18.1	23.6	-3.3	6.2	10.0	12.4	15.3
Unweighted average								
OECD-Average	**11.6**	**15.8**	**21.6**	**6.0**	**10.4**	**10.7**	**12.4**	**12.6**
OECD-EU 22	**12.4**	**17.0**	**23.3**	**5.4**	**10.1**	**10.8**	**12.9**	**13.4**

Note: ch = children

1. Information on data for Israel: http://oe.cd/israel-disclaimer.
2. Two-earner family.

StatLink http://dx.doi.org/10.1787/888933461250

Table 5.5. Employee contributions, 2015

As % of gross wage earnings, by family-type and wage level

	Single no ch 67 (% AW)	Single no ch 100 (% AW)	Single no ch 167 (% AW)	Single 2 ch 67 (% AW)	Married 2 ch 100-0 (% AW)	Married 2 ch 100-33 (% AW)[2]	Married 2 ch 100-67 (% AW)[2]	Married no ch 100-33 (% AW)[2]
Australia	0.0	0.0	0.0	0.0	0.0	0.0	0.0	0.0
Austria	18.1	18.1	16.0	18.1	18.1	17.3	18.1	17.3
Belgium	13.9	14.0	14.0	13.9	14.0	10.8	14.0	10.8
Canada	7.2	7.6	4.9	7.2	7.6	7.2	7.5	7.2
Chile	7.0	7.0	7.0	7.0	7.0	7.0	7.0	7.0
Czech Republic	11.0	11.0	11.0	11.0	11.0	11.0	11.0	11.0
Denmark	0.0	0.0	0.0	0.0	0.0	0.0	0.0	0.0
Estonia	1.6	1.6	1.6	1.6	1.6	1.6	1.6	1.6
Finland	8.2	8.3	8.3	8.1	8.3	8.0	8.2	8.0
France	14.2	14.2	13.5	14.2	14.2	14.2	14.2	14.2
Germany	20.5	20.5	16.2	20.2	20.2	20.2	20.2	20.5
Greece	15.5	15.5	15.5	15.5	15.5	15.5	15.5	15.5
Hungary	18.5	18.5	18.5	18.5	18.5	18.5	18.5	18.5
Iceland	0.5	0.4	0.2	0.5	0.4	0.5	0.4	0.5
Ireland	4.0	4.0	4.0	4.0	4.0	3.0	4.0	3.0
Israel[1]	5.9	7.9	9.5	5.9	7.9	6.8	7.1	6.8
Italy	9.5	9.5	9.6	9.5	9.5	9.5	9.5	9.5
Japan	14.3	14.3	13.2	14.3	14.3	14.3	14.3	14.3
Korea	8.4	8.4	7.1	8.4	8.4	8.4	8.4	8.4
Latvia	10.5	10.5	10.5	10.5	10.5	10.5	10.5	10.5
Luxembourg	12.7	12.8	12.9	12.7	12.8	12.7	12.8	12.7
Mexico	1.3	1.4	1.5	1.3	1.4	1.3	1.3	1.3
Netherlands	17.6	13.1	9.2	12.7	11.3	10.6	12.9	12.3
New Zealand	0.0	0.0	0.0	0.0	0.0	0.0	0.0	0.0
Norway	8.2	8.2	8.2	8.2	8.2	8.2	8.2	8.2
Poland	17.8	17.8	17.8	17.8	17.8	17.8	17.8	17.8
Portugal	11.0	11.0	11.0	11.0	11.0	11.0	11.0	11.0
Slovak Republic	13.4	13.4	13.4	13.4	13.4	12.4	13.4	12.4
Slovenia	22.1	22.1	22.1	22.1	22.1	22.1	22.1	22.1
Spain	6.4	6.4	6.2	6.4	6.4	6.4	6.4	6.4
Sweden	7.0	7.0	4.7	7.0	7.0	7.0	7.0	7.0
Switzerland	6.3	6.3	6.2	6.3	6.3	6.3	6.3	6.3
Turkey	15.0	15.0	15.0	15.0	15.0	15.0	15.0	15.0
United Kingdom	8.0	9.3	7.4	8.0	9.3	8.0	8.8	8.0
United States	7.7	7.7	7.7	7.7	7.7	7.7	7.7	7.7
Unweighted average								
OECD-Average	**9.8**	**9.8**	**9.3**	**9.7**	**9.7**	**9.5**	**9.7**	**9.5**
OECD-EU 22	**11.9**	**11.7**	**11.1**	**11.6**	**11.7**	**11.3**	**11.7**	**11.4**

Note: ch = children

1. Information on data for Israel: http://oe.cd/israel-disclaimer.
2. Two-earner family.

StatLink http://dx.doi.org/10.1787/888933461263

Table 5.6. Marginal rate of income tax plus employee and employer contributions less cash benefits, 2015

As % of labour costs, by family-type and wage level

	Single no ch 67 (% AW)	Single no ch 100 (% AW)	Single no ch 167 (% AW)	Single 2 ch 67 (% AW)	Married 2 ch 100-0 (% AW)	Married 2 ch 100-33 (% AW)[2]	Married 2 ch 100-67 (% AW)[2]	Married no ch 100-33 (% AW)[2]
Australia	39.6	42.4	42.4	58.5	61.3	70.7	42.4	42.4
Austria	56.8	60.5	42.2	56.8	60.5	60.5	60.5	60.5
Belgium	66.3	66.3	68.5	66.3	86.7	66.3	65.5	66.3
Canada	33.8	40.9	38.4	52.3	70.4	39.7	39.7	40.9
Chile	7.0	7.0	10.2	7.0	7.0	7.0	7.0	7.0
Czech Republic	48.6	48.6	48.6	48.6	48.6	48.6	48.6	48.6
Denmark	39.7	42.0	55.8	38.1	42.0	42.0	42.0	42.0
Estonia	41.2	41.2	41.2	41.2	41.2	41.2	41.2	41.2
Finland	54.2	55.2	58.3	54.2	56.0	56.0	56.0	55.2
France	67.2	59.3	59.8	57.5	43.5	43.5	56.4	56.4
Germany	55.6	60.1	44.3	53.6	52.2	55.3	57.6	55.5
Greece	47.1	47.6	61.6	47.1	47.6	47.6	47.6	47.6
Hungary	49.0	49.0	49.0	49.0	49.0	49.0	49.0	49.0
Iceland	42.5	42.5	48.3	51.4	51.4	47.8	42.5	42.5
Ireland	37.7	55.8	55.8	67.9	37.7	37.7	37.7	37.7
Israel[1]	31.0	37.5	46.9	17.9	37.5	37.5	37.5	37.5
Italy	54.9	54.9	63.3	56.1	56.1	56.1	55.5	54.9
Japan	32.8	37.0	35.3	32.8	37.0	37.0	37.0	37.0
Korea	25.4	29.2	31.9	17.0	29.2	29.2	29.2	29.2
Latvia	44.2	44.2	44.2	44.2	44.2	44.2	44.2	44.2
Luxembourg	47.9	55.5	55.5	50.4	39.4	44.5	53.0	44.5
Mexico	17.5	25.2	28.4	17.5	25.2	25.2	25.2	25.2
Netherlands	47.0	47.0	52.7	49.3	47.0	47.0	47.0	47.0
New Zealand	17.5	30.0	33.0	38.8	51.3	51.3	30.0	30.0
Norway	42.7	50.6	53.3	42.7	50.6	50.6	50.6	50.6
Poland	37.2	37.2	37.2	29.6	37.2	37.2	37.2	37.2
Portugal	53.9	53.9	60.8	39.8	39.8	39.8	51.1	53.9
Slovak Republic	46.5	46.5	46.5	46.5	46.5	46.5	46.5	46.5
Slovenia	43.6	51.0	60.4	32.9	43.6	43.6	43.6	51.0
Spain	45.2	49.5	37.0	45.2	45.2	49.5	49.5	49.5
Sweden	45.5	48.2	67.3	45.5	48.2	48.2	48.2	48.2
Switzerland	26.3	27.8	35.9	18.9	22.1	26.1	29.4	26.9
Turkey	42.8	42.8	47.8	42.8	42.8	42.8	42.8	42.8
United Kingdom	40.2	40.2	49.0	76.3	40.2	40.2	40.2	40.2
United States	34.3	43.6	43.6	55.1	34.3	34.3	34.3	34.3
Unweighted average								
OECD-Average	**41.8**	**44.9**	**47.3**	**44.2**	**44.9**	**44.1**	**43.6**	**43.5**
OECD-EU 22	**48.6**	**50.6**	**52.7**	**49.8**	**47.8**	**47.5**	**49.0**	**49.0**

Note: ch = children

It is assumed that gross earnings of the principal earner in the household rise. The outcome may differ if the wage of the spouse goes up, especially if partners are taxed individually.

1. Information on data for Israel: http://oe.cd/israel-disclaimer.
2. Two-earner family.

StatLink http://dx.doi.org/10.1787/888933461271

Table 5.7. Marginal rate of income tax plus employee contributions less cash benefits, 2015

As % of gross wage earnings, by family-type and wage level

	Single no ch 67 (% AW)	Single no ch 100 (% AW)	Single no ch 167 (% AW)	Single 2 ch 67 (% AW)	Married 2 ch 100-0 (% AW)	Married 2 ch 100-33 (% AW)[2]	Married 2 ch 100-67 (% AW)[2]	Married no ch 100-33 (% AW)[2]
Australia	36.0	39.0	39.0	56.0	59.0	69.0	39.0	39.0
Austria	44.4	49.1	37.9	44.4	49.1	49.1	49.1	49.1
Belgium	55.0	55.0	59.8	55.0	82.2	55.0	53.9	55.0
Canada	25.5	35.1	35.4	46.3	67.5	33.8	33.8	35.1
Chile	7.0	7.0	10.2	7.0	7.0	7.0	7.0	7.0
Czech Republic	31.1	31.1	31.1	31.1	31.1	31.1	31.1	31.1
Denmark	39.7	42.0	55.8	38.1	42.0	42.0	42.0	42.0
Estonia	21.3	21.3	21.3	21.3	21.3	21.3	21.3	21.3
Finland	44.0	45.2	48.9	44.0	46.2	46.2	46.2	45.2
France	39.9	43.9	42.6	22.1	22.1	22.1	39.9	39.9
Germany	47.0	52.4	44.3	44.6	43.0	46.6	49.4	46.9
Greece	34.1	34.7	52.2	34.1	34.7	34.7	34.7	34.7
Hungary	34.5	34.5	34.5	34.5	34.5	34.5	34.5	34.5
Iceland	38.2	38.2	44.4	47.8	47.8	43.9	38.2	38.2
Ireland	31.0	51.0	51.0	64.4	31.0	31.0	31.0	31.0
Israel[1]	26.0	33.0	43.0	12.0	33.0	33.0	33.0	33.0
Italy	40.4	40.4	51.5	42.0	42.0	42.0	41.2	40.4
Japan	22.7	27.6	31.2	22.7	27.6	27.6	27.6	27.6
Korea	17.7	21.9	27.9	8.4	21.9	21.9	21.9	21.9
Latvia	31.1	31.1	31.1	31.1	31.1	31.1	31.1	31.1
Luxembourg	41.5	50.1	50.1	44.4	32.0	37.7	47.2	37.7
Mexico	12.1	19.5	22.9	12.1	19.5	19.5	19.5	19.5
Netherlands	41.5	41.5	52.7	44.1	41.5	41.5	41.5	41.5
New Zealand	17.5	30.0	33.0	38.8	51.3	51.3	30.0	30.0
Norway	35.2	44.2	47.2	35.2	44.2	44.2	44.2	44.2
Poland	26.7	26.7	26.7	17.8	26.7	26.7	26.7	26.7
Portugal	43.0	43.0	51.5	25.5	25.5	25.5	39.5	43.0
Slovak Republic	29.9	29.9	29.9	29.9	29.9	29.9	29.9	29.9
Slovenia	34.6	43.1	54.0	22.1	34.6	34.6	34.6	43.1
Spain	28.8	34.4	37.0	28.8	28.8	34.4	34.4	34.4
Sweden	28.4	32.0	57.0	28.4	32.0	32.0	32.0	32.0
Switzerland	21.7	23.3	32.2	13.8	17.2	21.5	25.0	22.3
Turkey	32.8	32.8	38.7	32.8	32.8	32.8	32.8	32.8
United Kingdom	32.0	32.0	42.0	73.0	32.0	32.0	32.0	32.0
United States	29.3	39.3	39.3	51.6	29.3	29.3	29.3	29.3
Unweighted average								
OECD-Average	**32.0**	**35.9**	**40.2**	**34.4**	**35.7**	**34.7**	**34.4**	**34.3**
OECD-EU 22	**36.4**	**39.3**	**43.8**	**37.3**	**36.0**	**35.5**	**37.4**	**37.4**

Note: ch = children

It is assumed that gross earnings of the principal earner in the household rise. The outcome may differ if the wage of the spouse goes up, especially if partners are taxed individually.

1. Information on data for Israel: http://oe.cd/israel-disclaimer.
2. Two-earner family.

StatLink http://dx.doi.org/10.1787/888933461286

Table 5.8. Percentage increase in net income relative to percentage increase in gross wages, 2015

After an increase of 1 currency unit in gross wages, by family-type and wage level

	Single no ch 67 (% AW)	Single no ch 100 (% AW)	Single no ch 167 (% AW)	Single 2 ch 67 (% AW)	Married 2 ch 100-0 (% AW)	Married 2 ch 100-33 (% AW)[2]	Married 2 ch 100-67 (% AW)[2]	Married no ch 100-33 (% AW)[2]
Australia	0.79	0.80	0.87	0.41	0.47	0.38	0.78	0.76
Austria	0.79	0.78	1.03	0.61	0.65	0.64	0.68	0.72
Belgium	0.70	0.78	0.79	0.55	0.23	0.61	0.69	0.68
Canada	0.91	0.85	0.89	0.42	0.33	0.74	0.78	0.81
Chile	1.00	1.00	0.97	0.99	1.00	0.98	1.00	1.00
Czech Republic	0.86	0.90	0.94	0.68	0.70	0.76	0.80	0.86
Denmark	0.91	0.90	0.76	0.66	0.78	0.81	0.84	0.87
Estonia	0.95	0.97	0.98	0.75	0.82	0.86	0.89	0.95
Finland	0.74	0.79	0.83	0.63	0.72	0.69	0.71	0.74
France	0.81	0.79	0.87	0.93	0.95	0.96	0.78	0.82
Germany	0.81	0.79	0.99	0.67	0.72	0.73	0.73	0.81
Greece	0.81	0.86	0.71	0.76	0.84	0.83	0.84	0.85
Hungary	1.00	1.00	1.00	0.70	0.79	0.83	0.86	1.00
Iceland	0.82	0.88	0.84	0.61	0.63	0.74	0.85	0.83
Ireland	0.79	0.61	0.72	0.27	0.69	0.73	0.78	0.79
Israel[1]	0.83	0.81	0.77	0.87	0.78	0.76	0.75	0.78
Italy	0.76	0.87	0.80	0.59	0.72	0.71	0.76	0.79
Japan	0.97	0.93	0.93	0.89	0.86	0.88	0.89	0.92
Korea	0.92	0.91	0.87	1.00	0.88	0.88	0.88	0.89
Latvia	0.96	0.97	0.98	0.74	0.81	0.84	0.86	0.96
Luxembourg	0.76	0.72	0.81	0.53	0.72	0.70	0.64	0.79
Mexico	0.91	0.90	0.91	0.91	0.90	0.86	0.87	0.86
Netherlands	0.78	0.84	0.77	0.56	0.77	0.74	0.76	0.79
New Zealand	0.95	0.85	0.87	0.54	0.51	0.55	0.84	0.84
Norway	0.86	0.78	0.81	0.74	0.72	0.72	0.74	0.75
Poland	0.97	0.98	0.99	1.00	0.90	0.92	0.94	0.97
Portugal	0.72	0.80	0.75	0.81	0.87	0.87	0.76	0.72
Slovak Republic	0.87	0.91	0.95	0.74	0.75	0.80	0.83	0.87
Slovenia	0.92	0.85	0.74	0.75	0.74	0.81	0.86	0.82
Spain	0.85	0.83	0.87	0.72	0.83	0.78	0.79	0.80
Sweden	0.92	0.90	0.66	0.82	0.83	0.82	0.85	0.88
Switzerland	0.91	0.92	0.87	0.84	0.86	0.84	0.83	0.91
Turkey	0.89	0.93	0.90	0.88	0.90	0.89	0.90	0.90
United Kingdom	0.84	0.89	0.83	0.26	0.83	0.80	0.84	0.84
United States	0.92	0.82	0.88	0.51	0.82	0.86	0.88	0.92
Unweighted average								
OECD-Average	**0.86**	**0.86**	**0.86**	**0.69**	**0.75**	**0.78**	**0.81**	**0.84**
OECD-EU 22	**0.84**	**0.85**	**0.85**	**0.67**	**0.76**	**0.78**	**0.80**	**0.83**

Note: ch = children

Net income is calculated as gross earnings minus personal income tax and employees' social security contributions plus family benefits. The increase reported in the Table represents a form of elasticity. In a proportional tax system the elasticity would equal 1. The more progressive the system at these income levels, the lower is the elasticity. The reported elasticities in Table 5.8 are calculated as (100 - METR) / (100 - AETR), where METR is the marginal rate of income tax plus employee social security contributions less cash benefits reported in Table 5.7 and AETR is the average rate plus employee social security contributions less cash benefits reported in Table 5.3.

1. Information on data for Israel: http://oe.cd/israel-disclaimer.
2. Two-earner family. Assumes a rise in the labour costs associated with the principal earner in the household.

StatLink http://dx.doi.org/10.1787/888933461294

Table 5.9. **Percentage increase in net income relative to percentage increase in gross labour cost, 2015**

After an increase of 1 currency unit in gross labour cost, by family-type and wage level

	Single no ch 67 (% AW)	Single no ch 100 (% AW)	Single no ch 167 (% AW)	Single 2 ch 67 (% AW)	Married 2 ch 100-0 (% AW)	Married 2 ch 100-33 (% AW)[2]	Married 2 ch 100-67 (% AW)[2]	Married no ch 100-33 (% AW)[2]
Australia	0.79	0.80	0.87	0.41	0.47	0.38	0.78	0.76
Austria	0.79	0.78	1.21	0.61	0.65	0.64	0.68	0.72
Belgium	0.67	0.75	0.80	0.52	0.22	0.57	0.66	0.64
Canada	0.90	0.86	0.92	0.41	0.33	0.75	0.80	0.82
Chile	1.00	1.00	0.97	0.99	1.00	0.98	1.00	1.00
Czech Republic	0.86	0.90	0.94	0.68	0.70	0.76	0.80	0.86
Denmark	0.92	0.91	0.77	0.67	0.78	0.83	0.85	0.88
Estonia	0.95	0.97	0.98	0.75	0.82	0.86	0.89	0.95
Finland	0.74	0.79	0.83	0.63	0.72	0.69	0.71	0.74
France	0.58	0.79	0.88	0.66	0.95	0.91	0.77	0.77
Germany	0.81	0.79	1.14	0.67	0.72	0.73	0.73	0.81
Greece	0.81	0.86	0.71	0.76	0.84	0.83	0.84	0.85
Hungary	1.00	1.00	1.00	0.70	0.79	0.83	0.86	1.00
Iceland	0.82	0.88	0.84	0.61	0.63	0.74	0.85	0.83
Ireland	0.79	0.61	0.72	0.27	0.69	0.72	0.78	0.78
Israel[1]	0.81	0.80	0.77	0.84	0.77	0.74	0.74	0.76
Italy	0.76	0.87	0.80	0.59	0.72	0.71	0.76	0.79
Japan	0.97	0.93	1.00	0.89	0.86	0.88	0.89	0.92
Korea	0.92	0.91	0.90	1.00	0.88	0.88	0.88	0.89
Latvia	0.96	0.97	0.98	0.74	0.81	0.84	0.86	0.96
Luxembourg	0.76	0.72	0.81	0.53	0.72	0.70	0.64	0.79
Mexico	0.97	0.93	0.93	0.97	0.93	0.91	0.91	0.91
Netherlands	0.78	0.84	0.82	0.57	0.77	0.74	0.77	0.79
New Zealand	0.95	0.85	0.87	0.54	0.51	0.55	0.84	0.84
Norway	0.86	0.78	0.81	0.74	0.72	0.72	0.74	0.75
Poland	0.97	0.98	0.99	1.00	0.90	0.92	0.94	0.97
Portugal	0.72	0.80	0.75	0.81	0.87	0.87	0.76	0.72
Slovak Republic	0.87	0.91	0.95	0.74	0.75	0.78	0.83	0.86
Slovenia	0.92	0.85	0.74	0.75	0.74	0.81	0.86	0.82
Spain	0.85	0.83	1.12	0.72	0.83	0.78	0.79	0.80
Sweden	0.92	0.90	0.66	0.82	0.83	0.82	0.85	0.88
Switzerland	0.91	0.92	0.87	0.84	0.86	0.84	0.83	0.91
Turkey	0.89	0.93	0.90	0.88	0.90	0.89	0.90	0.90
United Kingdom	0.81	0.86	0.81	0.25	0.80	0.77	0.81	0.81
United States	0.93	0.82	0.89	0.51	0.83	0.87	0.89	0.93
Unweighted average								
OECD-Average	**0.86**	**0.86**	**0.88**	**0.69**	**0.75**	**0.78**	**0.81**	**0.84**
OECD-EU 22	**0.83**	**0.85**	**0.88**	**0.66**	**0.76**	**0.78**	**0.79**	**0.83**

Note: ch = children

Net income is calculated as gross earnings minus personal income tax and employees' social security contributions plus family benefits. The increase reported in the Table represents a form of elasticity. In a proportional tax system the elasticity would equal 1. The more progressive the system at these income levels, the lower is the elasticity. The reported elasticities in Table 5.9 are calculated as (100 - METR) / (100 - AETR), where METR is the marginal rate of income tax plus employee and employer social security contributions less cash benefits reported in Table 5.6 and AETR is the average rate plus employee and employer social security contributions less cash benefits reported in Table 5.1.

1. Information on data for Israel: http://oe.cd/israel-disclaimer.
2. Two-earner family. Assumes a rise in the labour costs associated with the principal earner in the household.

StatLink http://dx.doi.org/10.1787/888933461305

Table 5.10a. Annual gross wage and net income, single person, 2015

In US dollars using PPP, by family-type and wage level

	Single no ch 67 (% AW)		Single no ch 100 (% AW)		Single no ch 167 (% AW)		Single 2 ch 67 (% AW)	
	Total gross earnings before taxes	Net income after taxes	Total gross earnings before taxes	Net income after taxes	Total gross earnings before taxes	Net income after taxes	Total gross earnings before taxes	Net income after taxes
Australia	37 003	30 146	55 229	41 931	92 233	64 503	37 003	39 751
Austria	36 929	26 155	55 118	35 804	92 047	55 767	36 929	33 512
Belgium	39 032	25 229	58 256	33 783	97 288	49 511	39 032	32 078
Canada	26 915	22 146	40 172	30 832	67 087	48 950	26 915	34 773
Chile	13 369	12 433	19 953	18 556	33 322	30 675	13 369	12 550
Czech Republic	16 707	13 452	24 937	19 122	41 644	30 633	16 707	16 878
Denmark	37 134	24 728	55 424	35 531	92 559	53 622	37 134	34 803
Estonia	16 433	13 631	24 526	20 002	40 959	32 938	16 433	17 222
Finland	32 137	24 412	47 966	33 149	80 103	49 599	32 137	28 596
France	31 538	23 390	47 071	33 477	78 609	51 575	31 538	26 521
Germany	40 537	26 501	60 504	36 545	101 041	56 758	40 537	33 513
Greece	21 870	17 823	32 641	24 730	54 511	36 947	21 870	18 862
Hungary	16 251	10 644	24 255	15 887	40 506	26 531	16 251	15 200
Iceland	36 494	27 377	54 468	38 494	90 962	60 038	36 494	31 240
Ireland	28 870	25 084	43 090	34 679	71 960	48 825	28 870	38 070
Israel[1]	24 330	21 710	36 313	30 025	60 643	44 680	24 330	24 728
Italy	28 241	22 060	42 150	29 032	70 391	42 590	28 241	27 833
Japan	33 211	26 420	49 569	38 610	82 779	61 377	33 211	28 760
Korea	32 276	28 940	48 173	41 444	80 449	66 492	32 276	29 570
Latvia	12 980	9 364	19 374	13 770	32 354	22 715	12 980	12 032
Luxembourg	42 442	32 794	63 346	43 810	105 788	64 996	42 442	44 162
Mexico	8 533	8 250	12 799	11 463	21 332	18 115	8 533	8 250
Netherlands	41 568	31 228	62 042	43 206	103 611	63 920	41 568	41 152
New Zealand	26 043	22 524	38 870	32 044	64 913	49 782	26 043	29 804
Norway	38 142	28 605	56 928	40 772	95 070	61 947	38 142	33 572
Poland	17 526	13 303	26 158	19 633	43 683	32 484	17 526	14 401
Portugal	19 854	15 669	29 633	21 243	49 487	31 863	19 854	18 364
Slovak Republic	14 725	11 819	21 978	16 906	36 702	27 235	14 725	14 042
Slovenia	20 730	14 774	30 940	20 628	51 670	32 112	20 730	21 638
Spain	26 576	22 147	39 666	31 231	66 243	48 142	26 576	26 170
Sweden	31 097	24 262	46 414	35 005	77 511	50 243	31 097	27 288
Switzerland	46 212	39 725	68 974	57 304	115 186	90 135	46 212	47 152
Turkey	16 832	12 672	25 123	18 247	41 955	28 704	16 832	12 934
United Kingdom	34 985	28 274	52 216	39 991	87 200	61 217	34 985	36 193
United States	34 511	26 590	51 509	38 232	86 020	59 180	34 511	33 017
Unweighted average								
OECD-Average	**28 058**	**21 837**	**41 880**	**30 718**	**69 938**	**47 280**	**28 058**	**26 989**
OECD-EU 22	**27 644**	**20 761**	**41 259**	**28 962**	**68 903**	**44 101**	**27 644**	**26 297**

Note: ch = children

1. Information on data for Israel: http://oe.cd/israel-disclaimer.

StatLink http://dx.doi.org/10.1787/888933461315

Table 5.10b. **Annual gross wage and net income, married couple, 2015**

In US dollars using PPP, by family-type and wage level

	Married 2 ch 100-0 (% AW)		Married 2 ch 100-33 (% AW)[2]		Married 2 ch 100-67 (% AW)[2]		Married no ch 100-33 (% AW)[2]	
	Total gross earnings before taxes	Net income after taxes	Total gross earnings before taxes	Net income after taxes	Total gross earnings before taxes	Net income after taxes	Total gross earnings before taxes	Net income after taxes
Australia	55 229	48 096	73 455	60 151	92 233	72 077	73 455	58 998
Austria	55 118	43 198	73 307	58 084	92 047	68 539	73 307	51 530
Belgium	58 256	45 108	77 481	57 232	97 288	65 127	77 481	51 064
Canada	40 172	40 084	53 428	47 911	67 087	56 937	53 428	42 838
Chile	19 953	18 556	26 538	25 286	33 322	31 107	26 538	24 680
Czech Republic	24 937	24 489	33 166	29 872	41 644	36 000	33 166	26 446
Denmark	55 424	41 420	73 714	52 449	92 559	63 774	73 714	48 934
Estonia	24 526	23 423	32 620	29 794	40 959	36 358	32 620	27 068
Finland	47 966	35 859	63 795	49 996	80 103	60 381	63 795	47 176
France	47 071	38 628	62 605	50 735	78 609	60 520	62 605	45 985
Germany	60 504	47 742	80 470	58 936	101 041	69 628	80 470	52 681
Greece	35 905	27 901	47 754	37 393	59 962	46 504	47 754	36 874
Hungary	24 255	20 167	32 259	25 410	40 506	30 811	32 259	21 130
Iceland	54 468	45 008	72 443	55 193	90 962	65 872	72 443	54 194
Ireland	43 090	43 272	57 309	54 399	71 960	64 007	57 309	50 372
Israel[1]	36 313	31 032	48 297	42 596	60 643	53 933	48 297	41 589
Italy	42 150	34 105	56 060	45 570	70 391	54 319	56 060	42 341
Japan	49 569	41 650	65 926	54 327	82 779	67 371	65 926	51 987
Korea	48 173	42 648	64 070	56 935	80 449	71 375	64 070	56 009
Latvia	19 374	16 438	25 767	21 262	32 354	25 802	25 767	18 594
Luxembourg	63 346	59 710	84 250	75 237	105 788	87 674	84 250	66 707
Mexico	12 799	11 463	17 066	16 027	21 332	19 713	17 066	16 027
Netherlands	62 042	46 974	82 516	65 185	103 611	79 386	82 516	61 030
New Zealand	38 870	36 959	51 697	45 494	64 913	54 208	51 697	43 305
Norway	56 928	43 841	75 714	58 936	95 070	71 781	75 714	56 532
Poland	26 158	21 209	34 790	27 675	43 683	34 197	34 790	26 414
Portugal	29 633	25 409	39 412	33 605	49 487	39 425	39 412	31 170
Slovak Republic	21 978	20 619	29 230	25 700	36 702	30 948	29 230	23 477
Slovenia	30 940	27 431	41 150	33 076	51 670	39 238	41 150	28 582
Spain	39 666	34 138	52 756	44 215	66 243	54 830	52 756	43 489
Sweden	46 414	38 031	61 731	51 000	77 511	62 293	61 731	47 974
Switzerland	68 974	66 562	91 735	85 575	115 186	103 597	91 735	78 332
Turkey	25 123	18 682	33 413	25 306	41 955	31 181	33 413	25 045
United Kingdom	52 216	42 912	69 447	58 805	87 200	70 878	69 447	56 193
United States	51 509	44 367	68 507	56 385	86 020	68 766	68 507	52 816
Unweighted average								
OECD-Average	**41 973**	**35 632**	**55 825**	**46 164**	**70 093**	**55 673**	**55 825**	**43 074**
OECD-EU 22	**41 408**	**34 463**	**55 072**	**44 801**	**69 151**	**53 665**	**55 072**	**41 147**

Note: ch = children

1. Information on data for Israel: http://oe.cd/israel-disclaimer.
2. Two-earner family.

StatLink http://dx.doi.org/10.1787/888933461323

Table 5.11a. **Annual labour costs and net income, single person, 2015**

In US dollars using PPP, by family-type and wage level

	Single no ch 67 (% AW)		Single no ch 100 (% AW)		Single no ch 167 (% AW)		Single 2 ch 67 (% AW)	
	Total gross labour costs before taxes	Net income after taxes	Total gross labour costs before taxes	Net income after taxes	Total gross labour costs before taxes	Net income after taxes	Total gross labour costs before taxes	Net income after taxes
Australia	39 212	30 146	58 525	41 931	97 737	64 503	39 212	39 751
Austria	47 612	26 155	71 063	35 804	116 461	55 767	47 612	33 512
Belgium	49 847	25 229	75 540	33 783	125 900	49 511	49 847	32 078
Canada	30 139	22 146	45 034	30 832	73 399	48 950	30 139	34 773
Chile	13 369	12 433	19 953	18 556	33 322	30 675	13 369	12 550
Czech Republic	22 388	13 452	33 415	19 122	55 803	30 633	22 388	16 878
Denmark	37 610	24 728	55 900	35 531	93 034	53 622	37 610	34 803
Estonia	21 987	13 631	32 816	20 002	54 803	32 938	21 987	17 222
Finland	39 339	24 412	58 715	33 149	98 055	49 599	39 339	28 596
France	41 283	23 390	64 897	33 477	112 815	51 575	41 283	26 521
Germany	48 371	26 501	72 196	36 545	116 648	56 758	48 371	33 513
Greece	27 241	17 823	40 658	24 730	67 899	36 947	27 241	18 862
Hungary	20 882	10 644	31 168	15 887	52 050	26 531	20 882	15 200
Iceland	39 227	27 377	58 548	38 494	97 775	60 038	39 227	31 240
Ireland	31 974	25 084	47 722	34 679	79 696	48 825	31 974	38 070
Israel[1]	25 427	21 710	38 279	30 025	64 373	44 680	25 427	24 728
Italy	37 300	22 060	55 672	29 032	92 972	42 590	37 300	27 833
Japan	38 208	26 420	57 027	38 610	94 334	61 377	38 208	28 760
Korea	35 611	28 940	53 151	41 444	87 694	66 492	35 611	29 570
Latvia	16 051	9 364	23 953	13 770	39 995	22 715	16 051	12 032
Luxembourg	47 645	32 794	71 112	43 810	118 758	64 996	47 645	44 162
Mexico	9 709	8 250	14 293	11 463	23 474	18 115	9 709	8 250
Netherlands	46 026	31 228	68 634	43 206	110 788	63 920	46 026	41 152
New Zealand	26 043	22 524	38 870	32 044	64 913	49 782	26 043	29 804
Norway	43 100	28 605	64 329	40 772	107 429	61 947	43 100	33 572
Poland	20 466	13 303	30 547	19 633	51 013	32 484	20 466	14 401
Portugal	24 569	15 669	36 671	21 243	61 240	31 863	24 569	18 364
Slovak Republic	19 319	11 819	28 835	16 906	48 154	27 235	19 319	14 042
Slovenia	24 067	14 774	35 921	20 628	59 988	32 112	24 067	21 638
Spain	34 523	22 147	51 527	31 231	85 628	48 142	34 523	26 170
Sweden	40 868	24 262	60 997	35 005	101 865	50 243	40 868	27 288
Switzerland	49 101	39 725	73 284	57 304	122 300	90 135	49 101	47 152
Turkey	19 778	12 672	29 519	18 247	49 297	28 704	19 778	12 934
United Kingdom	38 186	28 274	57 795	39 991	97 608	61 217	38 186	36 193
United States	37 567	26 590	55 866	38 232	93 017	59 180	37 567	33 017
Unweighted average								
OECD-Average	**32 687**	**21 837**	**48 927**	**30 718**	**81 435**	**47 280**	**32 687**	**26 989**
OECD-EU 22	**33 525**	**20 761**	**50 261**	**28 962**	**83 690**	**44 101**	**33 525**	**26 297**

Note: ch = children

1. Information on data for Israel: http://oe.cd/israel-disclaimer.

StatLink http://dx.doi.org/10.1787/888933461336

Table 5.11b. Annual labour costs and net income, married couple, 2015

In US dollars using PPP, by family-type and wage level

	Married 2 ch 100-0 (% AW)		Married 2 ch 100-33 (% AW)[2]		Married 2 ch 100-67 (% AW)[2]		Married no ch 100-33 (% AW)[2]	
	Total gross labour costs before taxes	Net income after taxes	Total gross labour costs before taxes	Net income after taxes	Total gross labour costs before taxes	Net income after taxes	Total gross labour costs before taxes	Net income after taxes
Australia	58 525	48 096	77 838	60 151	97 737	72 077	77 838	58 998
Austria	71 063	43 198	94 513	58 084	118 675	68 539	94 513	51 530
Belgium	75 540	45 108	97 513	57 232	125 387	65 127	97 513	51 064
Canada	45 034	40 084	59 808	47 911	75 173	56 937	59 808	42 838
Chile	19 953	18 556	26 538	25 286	33 322	31 107	26 538	24 680
Czech Republic	33 415	24 489	44 442	29 872	55 803	36 000	44 442	26 446
Denmark	55 900	41 420	74 665	52 449	93 510	63 774	74 665	48 934
Estonia	32 816	23 423	43 646	29 794	54 803	36 358	43 646	27 068
Finland	58 715	35 859	78 091	49 996	98 055	60 381	78 091	47 176
France	64 897	38 628	81 630	50 735	106 180	60 520	81 630	45 985
Germany	72 196	47 742	96 021	58 936	120 567	69 628	96 021	52 681
Greece	44 724	27 901	59 482	37 393	74 689	46 504	59 482	36 874
Hungary	31 168	20 167	41 453	25 410	52 050	30 811	41 453	21 130
Iceland	58 548	45 008	77 869	55 193	97 775	65 872	77 869	54 194
Ireland	47 722	43 272	63 150	54 399	79 696	64 007	63 150	50 372
Israel[1]	38 279	31 032	50 676	42 596	63 706	53 933	50 676	41 589
Italy	55 672	34 105	74 044	45 570	92 972	54 319	74 044	42 341
Japan	57 027	41 650	75 845	54 327	95 234	67 371	75 845	51 987
Korea	53 151	42 648	70 691	56 935	88 762	71 375	70 691	56 009
Latvia	23 953	16 438	31 863	21 262	40 004	25 802	31 863	18 594
Luxembourg	71 112	59 710	94 579	75 237	118 758	87 674	94 579	66 707
Mexico	14 293	11 463	19 458	16 027	24 001	19 713	19 458	16 027
Netherlands	68 634	46 974	91 348	65 185	114 660	79 386	91 348	61 030
New Zealand	38 870	36 959	51 697	45 494	64 913	54 208	51 697	43 305
Norway	64 329	43 841	85 557	58 936	107 429	71 781	85 557	56 532
Poland	30 547	21 209	40 627	27 675	51 013	34 197	40 627	26 414
Portugal	36 671	25 409	48 772	33 605	61 240	39 425	48 772	31 170
Slovak Republic	28 835	20 619	37 625	25 700	48 154	30 948	37 625	23 477
Slovenia	35 921	27 431	47 775	33 076	59 988	39 238	47 775	28 582
Spain	51 527	34 138	68 530	44 215	86 049	54 830	68 530	43 489
Sweden	60 997	38 031	81 126	51 000	101 865	62 293	81 126	47 974
Switzerland	73 284	66 562	97 468	85 575	122 385	103 597	97 468	78 332
Turkey	29 519	18 682	39 260	25 306	49 297	31 181	39 260	25 045
United Kingdom	57 795	42 912	75 778	58 805	95 982	70 878	75 778	56 193
United States	55 866	44 367	74 580	56 385	93 433	68 766	74 580	52 816
Unweighted average								
OECD-Average	**49 043**	**35 632**	**64 970**	**46 164**	**81 808**	**55 673**	**64 970**	**43 074**
OECD-EU 22	**50 446**	**34 463**	**66 667**	**44 801**	**84 095**	**53 665**	**66 667**	**41 147**

Note: ch = children

1. Information on data for Israel: http://oe.cd/israel-disclaimer.
2. Two-earner family.

StatLink http://dx.doi.org/10.1787/888933461341

PART II

Tax burden trends 2000-16

This section presents detailed results of the evolution of the tax burden between 2000 and 2016. It provides information for each of the OECD countries on the income taxes paid by workers, their social security contributions, the family benefits they receive in the form of cash transfers as well as the social security contributions and payroll taxes paid by their employers over this period.

The statistical data for Israel are supplied by and under the responsibility of the relevant Israeli authorities. The use of such data by the OECD is without prejudice to the status of the Golan Heights, East Jerusalem and Israeli settlements in the West Bank under the terms of international law.

Taxing Wages 2017
© OECD 2017

PART II

Chapter 6

Evolution of the tax burden (2000-16)

The chapter presents the evolution of the tax burdens on labour income between 2000 and 2016. The chapter contains Tables 6.1 to 6.8, each corresponding to a particular model family type and divided into three parts: part a.-tables containing the (average) tax wedge comprising income taxes plus employee and employer social security contributions (including any applicable payroll taxes) less cash benefits; part b.-tables providing the (average) burden of personal income taxes; and the part c.-tables depicting the (average) burden of income taxes plus employee social security contributions less cash benefits (net personal average tax rates).

The statistical data for Israel are supplied by and under the responsibility of the relevant Israeli authorities. The use of such data by the OECD is without prejudice to the status of the Golan Heights, East Jerusalem and Israeli settlements in the West Bank under the terms of international law.

Historical trends

The evolution of the tax burden for the eight family types over the period 2000 to 2016 is presented in Tables 6.1 to 6.8 in the last section of this chapter titled "Tables showing income taxes, social security contributions and cash benefits". Each of the Tables 1 to 8 corresponds to a particular family type and each is divided into three parts.

The discussion focuses on the main observable trends over the period and highlights selected important year-to-year changes.

Important trends

The OECD average tax wedge, the income tax burden and the net tax burden (personal income tax plus social security contributions less cash benefits) have all declined between 2000 and 2016 for each of the selected family types.

The reductions over the period in the OECD average tax wedge ranged from 1.0 percentage point (for single persons on average earnings or earning 167% of the average wage [AW]) to 2.4 percentage points (for single parents at 67% of the AW).

The decrease in the OECD average income tax burden ranged from 0.4 percentage points (for single persons on AW) to 1.9 percentage points (for single parents at 67% of the AW).

The OECD net personal average tax burden has also declined for all family types in the period considered. The reduction ranged from 0.6 percentage points (for single persons on AW) to 1.9 percentage points (for single parents at 67% of the AW).

Tax wedge

Focusing on the overall (average) tax wedge (a.-tables), there are fifteen OECD member countries with a reduction of more than 5 percentage points between 2000 and 2016 for at least one family type – Australia, Belgium, Canada, Denmark, Finland, France, Hungary, Ireland, Israel, the Netherlands, New Zealand, Portugal, Sweden, Turkey and the United Kingdom.

The largest decline is observed in the Netherlands where the single parent benefited from a reduction in the tax wedge of 18.8 percentage points. The single person, without children, at 67% of the AW also enjoyed a reduction of 11.7 percentage points. In Ireland the single parent at 67% of the AW experienced a reduction of 18.1 percentage points in the tax wedge.

A reduction of 7 percentage points or more in the tax wedge for at least one family-type was observed in eight other countries – Canada, Denmark, France, Hungary, Israel, New Zealand, Sweden and the United Kingdom. In Canada, the tax wedge decreased by 14.5 percentage points for the single parent at 67% of the AW and by 11.2 percentage points for the one-earner married couple on the AW with two children. In Denmark, the largest decrease was for the single person earning 167% of the AW (7.6 percentage points). In France, the single parent experienced the largest decrease in the tax wedge (10.0 percentage points) among the other family types. In Hungary, there were reductions of more than 7 percentage points for five out of the eight family types. The largest decreases were for the single person earning 167% of the AW (11.0 percentage points) and the one-earner married couple, with two children, earning the AW (10.2 percentage points). In Israel, the tax wedge decreased by more than 7 percentage points for the single persons, without children, earning 67% of the AW (8.1 percentage points) and earning the AW (7.5 percentage points). In New Zealand, the single parent earning 67% of the AW benefited the most from the reduction in the tax wedge (10.0 percentage points). It also decreased by 7.4 percentage points for the one-earner married couple earning the AW with two children. In Sweden, the tax wedge decreased by more than 7 percentage points for half of the family types: by 8.0 percentage points for the two-earner married couple with total earnings at 133% of the AW without children, by 7.8 percentage points for the single person, without children, earning 67% of the AW and by 7.3 percentage points for the single person on the AW and the two-earner married couple with total earnings at 133% of the AW with two children.

The tax wedge has decreased for all family types in thirteen of the OECD member countries (Australia, Belgium, Canada, Denmark, Finland, Germany, Hungary, Israel, New Zealand, Poland, Slovenia, Sweden and Switzerland) while it has increased across all family types in three countries (Korea, Luxembourg and Mexico).

Average income tax rate

Between 2000 and 2016, the average income tax burden (b.-tables) has decreased for all family types in thirteen of the OECD member countries: Belgium, Canada, Estonia, Finland, Germany, Hungary, Israel, New Zealand, Slovenia, Sweden, Switzerland, Turkey and the United Kingdom. Among those countries, the most significant reductions affecting most of the family types are noted in Sweden where seven out of the eight family types enjoyed decreases of around 9-10 percentage points except the single taxpayer earning 167% of the AW for whom the decrease was 4.9 percentage points. In Estonia, the average income tax burden has decreased by more than 6 percentage points for all families with children, with the single parent at 67% of the AW enjoying an income tax reduction of 8.7 percentage points. In Hungary, there were significant decreases of 15.3 percentage points for the single person earning 167% of the AW and 12.5 percentage points for the one-earner married couple, with children, earning the AW. In Israel, the average income tax rate decreased by 6 to around 9 percentage points in all family types except for the single parent at 67% of the AW who had a reduction of 4.6 percentage points. Other decreases of more than 5 percentage points were observed in Finland (for the single parent earning 67% of the AW by 6.5 percentage points and for the married couples at 133% of the AW with and without children by 6.5 and 6.3 percentage points), in Turkey (by 5.8 percentage points for the single parent earning 67% of the AW and by 5.4 percentage points for the two-earner married couple at 133% of the AW with two children), and in the United Kingdom where there was a reduction of 11.8 percentage points for the single parent at 67% of the AW. Reductions of less than 5 percentage points in average income tax rates are observed for all family types in Belgium, Canada, Germany, New Zealand, Slovenia and Switzerland.

There are sixteen other OECD member countries with reductions in the personal income tax in some family types: Australia, Austria, the Czech Republic, France, Iceland, Ireland, Italy, Korea, Latvia, Luxembourg, Norway, Poland, Portugal, the Slovak Republic, Spain and the United States. In two of those countries the reductions in average income tax rates exceeded 6 percentage points: the Czech Republic (by 8.2 percentage points for the one-earner married couple, with children, earning the AW and by 7.2 percentage points for the single parent earning 67% of the AW) and the Slovak Republic (by 6.3 percentage points for the one-earner married couple earning the AW with children).

At the other extreme, the personal income tax burden has increased across all family types in five OECD member countries: Denmark, Greece, Japan, Mexico and the Netherlands. In Mexico the increases were in the range of 6 to 9 percentage points over the eight family types. In the Netherlands, there were increases of 11.6 percentage points for the one-earner married couple with two children and 7.3 percentage points for the single person on AW.

In contrast, in Chile the average income tax burden slightly increased only in the case of the single person earning 167% of the AW (0.5 percentage points). The average income tax rates stayed constant for the other family types since they did not pay income taxes between 2000 and 2016.

Net personal average tax rate

The *net* tax burden takes into account personal income taxes and employee social security contributions as well as cash benefits (c.-tables). It decreased between 2000 and 2016 for all family types in nine OECD countries: Belgium, Canada, Denmark, Germany, Israel, New Zealand, Poland, Sweden and Switzerland. Of these, the most significant reductions were observed in Sweden, where seven out of the eight family types had reductions exceeding 7 percentage points. In Sweden, the net personal average tax rate decreased the most for the two-earner married couple, without children, with total earnings at 133% of the AW (9.7 percentage points). Reductions ranging between 5 and 8 percentage points were observed in Israel for all but one family type, the exception being single parents earning 67% of the average wage where the reduction was only 3.6 percentage points. In Canada, the net personal average tax rate significantly decreased for half of the family types, notably by 16.9 percentage points for the single parents and 13.0 percentage points for the one-earner married couple, with two children, earning the AW. In Denmark, the tax burden also significantly declined for half of the family types by percentage points ranging from 5.1 (for the two-earner married couple with total earnings at 167% of the AW and with two children) to 7.7 (for the single person earning 167% of the AW).

The net personal average tax rate also decreased strongly in Ireland and New Zealand for most families with children and especially for single parents at 67% of the AW (by 22.2 percentage points in Ireland and by10.0 percentage points in New Zealand). There were also substantial changes for the single parents earning 67% of the AW in the Netherlands (-17.3 percentage points) and the United Kingdom (-10.1 percentage points). There are eight other OECD member countries with reductions in the net personal average tax rate of 5 percentage points or more in at least one family type: Australia, Belgium, Estonia, France, Hungary, Poland, Portugal and Spain. In Australia, there was a reduction of 5.2 percentage points for the one-earner married couple with two children and 5.0 percentage points for the single parent. For the latter, the net personal average tax rate declined by 12.5 percentage points in France, by 6.4 percentage points in Portugal and by 5.0 percentage points in Spain. A significant decrease was observed in Hungary for the single person earning 167% of the AW (9.3 percentage points) and the one-earner married couple with two children (5.7 percentage points). In Estonia, married couples with children had their net tax burden decreased by more than 5 percentage points: 6.8 percentage points for the one-earner couple earning the AW, 6.3 percentage points for the two-earner married couple at 133% of the AW with two children and 6.0 percentage points for the two-earner couple at 167% of the AW with two children. In Belgium, the net personal average tax rate decreased by more than 5 percentage points for the two-earner married couples at 133% of the AW without children (6.1 percentage points) and with children (5.3 percentage points). In Poland, it decreased by 5.4 percentage points for the two-earner married couples at 167% of the AW with two children.

Between 2000 and 2016, an increase of 5 or more percentage points in the net personal average tax rate for one or more family types was only observed in seven countries. In five of these countries, the Czech Republic, Iceland, Mexico, Norway and the Slovak Republic, the single parents earning 67% of the average wage saw increases of between 6 and 17 percentage points. There were also increases of similar size for other family types. For example, in Mexico there were increases of between 8 and 9 percentage points for each of the family types except the single person earning 167% of the AW (+5.3 percentage points). In Iceland, the net personal average tax rate increased by 8.0 percentage points for the two-earner married couple at 133% of the AW with children and by 9.4 percentage points for the one-earner married couple with children. For the latter, it also increased significantly in the Czech Republic (7.7 percentage points).

Progressivity

The discussion of the 2016 results in Part I of this publication gave some consideration to their use in assessing the progressivity of personal income taxes and the results presented in Part IIcan also be used to look at the evolution of this measure.

The degree of progressivity of the personal income tax system can be assessed by comparing the burden faced by single persons earning 67% of the AW with that faced by their counterparts earning 167% of the AW. Hence Table 6.1b is compared with Table 6.3b. For all OECD countries (except Hungary and Mexico) and for all years between 2000 and 2016 the lower paid worker always pays a lower percentage of income in personal income tax than the higher paid worker. In Hungary, the exceptions are that the levels are the same for both workers from 2013 onwards. In Mexico, from 2000 to 2010, the personal income tax is negative for the single persons earning 67% of the AW due to non-wastable tax credits.

On average, the progressivity of the personal income taxes has not changed very much in OECD countries. On average (excluding Mexico), the single worker earning 67% of the AW paid 53% of the tax burden of the worker earning 167% of the AW in 2000 and 52% in 2016.

Comparing the situation in each OECD country, personal income taxes have become more progressive in sixteen countries. The most significant changes were in New Zealand where the burdens on lower paid worker fell from 77% to 58%, in Sweden where it fell from about 68% to 48% and in Turkey where it decreased from 73% to 54%.

Personal income taxes have become slightly less progressive (using this measure) in fourteen OECD countries: Australia, Austria, Denmark, Greece, Hungary, Iceland, Korea, Latvia, the Netherlands, Poland, Portugal, the Slovak Republic, Spain and the United States. The most significant change occurred in Hungary where the ratio rose from about 58% of the higher paid worker in 2000 to 100% from 2013 onwards. The tax burden ratio remained at the same level in Chile, Estonia, Japan and Luxembourg in 2000 and 2016.

Families

The results presented in Tables 6.5 and 6.2 can be used to compare the tax burdens faced by a one-earner married couple, with two children, earning the AW and the single worker, without children, at the same income level. Focusing on the net tax burden (personal income tax plus employee social security contributions less cash benefits which can be found in Part c of the Tables), one observes that the OECD average tax savings for the married couple compared with the single worker represented 11.0% of gross income in 2000 and 11.2% in 2016.

The savings for the one-earner married couple have increased in eighteen countries and declined in sixteen others. There were four countries where the tax savings have increased by more than 5 percentage points: in Canada increasing by 11.0 percentage points from 10.9% to 21.9%, in Portugal increasing by 7.6 percentage points from 8.8% to 16.4%, in Ireland and New Zealand increasing both by 5.9 percentage points from 14.9% to 20.8% and from 5.8% to 11.7% of gross income. There were corresponding reductions of more than 5 percentage points in the Czech Republic where the tax savings decreased by 6.6 percentage points from 27.8% to 21.2% of income, in Norway where the decrease was of 6.2 percentage points from 11.4% to 5.2%, in Iceland where the decrease was of 5.6 percentage points from 16.5% to 10.9% and in the Netherlands with a reduction in the tax savings by 5.4 percentage points from 11.2% to 5.8% of gross income.

Tables showing the income taxes, social security contributions and cash benefits

The evolution of the income taxes, social security contributions and cash benefits for the eight family types across the OECD over the period 2000 to 2016 is presented in Tables 6.1 to 6.8. Each of the Tables 1 to 8 corresponds to a particular family type and each is divided into three parts.

- Part a.-tables containing the (average) tax wedge comprising income taxes plus employee and employer social security contributions (including any applicable payroll taxes) less cash benefits,
- Part b.-tables providing the (average) burden of personal income taxes, and the
- Part c.-tables depicting the (average) burden of income taxes plus employee social security contributions less cash benefits (*net* personal average tax rates).

Tables 6.9 and 6.10 show the average gross and net earnings of a single individual between 2000 and 2016 in US dollar using purchasing power parities of national currencies and in national currencies.

Table 6.1a. **Income tax plus employee and employer contributions less cash benefits, single persons at 67% of average earnings**

Tax burden as a % of labour costs, single persons without children

	2000	2006	2009	2010	2011	2012	2013	2014	2015	2016
Australia	25.9	24.8	20.8	21.0	20.7	21.7	21.9	22.4	23.1	23.4
Austria	43.2	43.8	43.3	43.5	43.9	44.2	44.6	44.8	45.1	42.8
Belgium	51.4	49.5	50.0	50.4	50.6	50.5	50.0	49.9	49.4	47.5
Canada	27.7	27.3	26.1	25.8	26.0	26.2	26.3	26.5	26.5	26.5
Chile	7.0	7.0	7.0	7.0	7.0	7.0	7.0	7.0	7.0	7.0
Czech Republic	41.3	40.1	38.8	39.0	39.7	39.4	39.4	39.7	39.9	40.2
Denmark	38.2	36.2	35.4	34.2	34.5	34.6	34.3	34.1	34.3	34.3
Estonia	39.8	37.3	37.8	38.7	39.0	39.2	38.8	38.9	38.0	37.8
Finland	42.7	38.9	37.2	36.8	36.8	36.8	37.6	38.0	37.9	37.9
France	43.9	46.3	46.6	46.8	47.0	46.9	45.5	45.0	43.3	43.0
Germany	47.6	47.5	45.9	44.9	45.6	45.5	45.1	45.1	45.2	45.3
Greece	36.0	36.5	36.6	35.8	40.0	39.8	37.0	35.8	34.6	36.1
Hungary	51.4	43.3	46.2	43.8	45.2	47.9	49.0	49.0	49.0	48.2
Iceland	23.8	28.3	26.1	28.4	29.4	29.3	29.7	29.3	30.2	30.5
Ireland	18.2	16.1	16.2	16.8	20.0	20.8	21.8	22.0	21.5	21.2
Israel[1]	23.2	16.4	14.5	14.1	13.9	13.8	13.6	14.2	14.6	15.1
Italy	43.6	42.8	43.5	44.0	44.5	44.7	44.9	41.9	40.9	40.8
Japan	28.7	27.5	27.8	28.9	29.5	29.9	30.2	30.6	30.9	31.0
Korea	15.0	16.0	16.9	17.4	17.8	18.0	18.4	18.5	18.7	19.0
Latvia	41.7	41.6	39.6	43.2	43.2	43.3	42.8	42.1	41.7	41.8
Luxembourg	29.8	27.8	27.4	27.7	29.5	29.2	30.1	30.5	31.2	31.2
Mexico	7.6	10.6	11.9	12.9	13.2	13.6	14.4	14.7	15.0	15.3
Netherlands	42.3	33.2	33.3	33.6	33.5	33.5	33.1	32.3	32.2	30.6
New Zealand	18.6	18.9	15.5	14.3	13.0	13.1	13.3	13.4	13.5	13.6
Norway	35.1	34.4	34.1	34.1	34.3	34.2	34.1	33.8	33.6	33.2
Poland	37.0	37.9	33.1	33.3	33.4	34.7	34.8	34.9	35.0	35.1
Portugal	33.2	32.8	31.9	32.2	32.3	32.6	35.2	34.9	36.2	36.3
Slovak Republic	40.6	35.3	34.4	34.7	36.1	36.9	38.5	38.6	38.8	39.0
Slovenia	42.6	41.4	39.7	38.6	38.7	38.6	38.5	38.6	38.6	38.7
Spain	34.9	36.0	34.4	36.5	36.8	37.2	37.2	37.3	35.8	35.9
Sweden	48.6	46.0	41.3	40.7	40.7	40.8	40.9	40.5	40.6	40.8
Switzerland	20.2	19.4	19.2	19.3	19.6	19.4	19.4	19.2	19.1	19.0
Turkey[2]	39.1	41.8	34.1	34.4	34.5	34.6	34.9	35.8	35.9	35.5
United Kingdom	29.1	30.6	29.1	29.4	28.5	27.9	26.8	26.2	26.0	25.9
United States	29.0	28.8	28.0	28.3	27.8	27.8	29.4	29.5	29.2	29.3
Unweighted average										
OECD-Average	**33.7**	**32.6**	**31.5**	**31.7**	**32.2**	**32.4**	**32.5**	**32.4**	**32.4**	**32.3**
OECD-EU 22	**39.9**	**38.2**	**37.4**	**37.5**	**38.1**	**38.4**	**38.4**	**38.2**	**38.0**	**37.7**

1. Information on data for Israel: http://oe.cd/israel-disclaimer.
2. Wage figures are based on the old definition of average worker (ISIC D, rev3.) for years 2000 to 2006.

StatLink http://dx.doi.org/10.1787/888933461357

Table 6.1b. **Income tax, single persons at 67% of average earnings**

Tax burden as a % of gross wage earnings, single persons without children

	2000	2006	2009	2010	2011	2012	2013	2014	2015	2016
Australia	21.1	20.3	15.8	16.0	16.0	17.1	17.3	17.7	18.5	18.8
Austria	7.6	9.4	8.7	9.0	9.5	9.9	10.4	10.7	11.1	8.3
Belgium	22.8	21.7	21.9	22.5	22.6	22.5	22.1	22.0	21.5	19.5
Canada	15.0	13.0	11.9	11.5	11.6	11.6	11.6	11.8	11.8	11.8
Chile	0.0	0.0	0.0	0.0	0.0	0.0	0.0	0.0	0.0	0.0
Czech Republic	8.3	6.6	6.9	7.2	8.2	7.8	7.8	8.2	8.5	8.9
Denmark	28.9	27.6	34.8	34.0	34.2	34.3	33.8	33.6	33.8	33.8
Estonia	19.9	15.8	14.9	14.8	15.2	15.5	16.0	16.2	15.5	15.2
Finland	20.9	17.6	16.5	15.7	15.5	14.9	15.9	15.8	15.9	15.0
France	12.5	12.0	12.2	12.2	12.4	12.6	12.6	12.6	11.6	11.0
Germany	16.3	15.0	14.8	13.8	13.9	14.1	14.1	14.1	14.2	14.0
Greece	2.3	2.6	2.8	1.8	6.6	6.1	3.2	3.2	3.0	4.4
Hungary	17.6	9.0	11.8	10.8	12.1	16.0	16.0	16.0	16.0	15.0
Iceland	20.0	23.9	20.8	21.5	22.6	23.1	23.7	23.3	24.5	25.0
Ireland	11.2	4.4	4.5	5.1	8.6	9.4	9.4	9.6	9.1	8.7
Israel[1]	12.1	6.5	5.0	4.4	4.4	4.4	4.2	4.7	4.9	5.3
Italy	15.2	15.2	15.9	16.6	17.2	17.5	17.7	13.8	12.4	12.4
Japan	5.1	5.7	6.3	6.1	6.1	6.1	6.1	6.1	6.2	6.2
Korea	0.8	1.1	1.3	1.4	1.4	1.5	1.8	1.7	2.0	2.2
Latvia	17.0	18.4	16.0	20.5	18.5	18.6	18.0	17.9	17.4	17.5
Luxembourg	10.3	7.8	6.9	7.3	7.8	8.2	9.3	9.7	10.0	10.1
Mexico	-5.7	-2.7	-1.4	-0.4	0.0	0.4	1.4	1.8	2.1	2.5
Netherlands	5.3	4.4	5.4	5.3	5.3	5.3	5.8	5.3	7.3	6.4
New Zealand	18.6	18.9	15.5	14.3	13.0	13.1	13.3	13.4	13.5	13.6
Norway	19.0	17.9	17.8	17.8	17.9	17.8	17.8	17.0	16.8	16.3
Poland	5.3	5.3	5.4	5.6	5.8	5.9	6.0	6.2	6.3	6.4
Portugal	6.4	5.9	4.7	5.1	5.2	5.6	8.8	8.4	10.1	10.2
Slovak Republic	6.0	4.9	3.8	4.2	5.9	5.9	5.9	6.1	6.3	6.6
Slovenia	10.2	8.1	7.9	6.6	6.7	6.6	6.5	6.6	6.6	6.7
Spain	8.6	10.0	8.4	11.2	11.5	12.0	12.1	12.2	10.3	10.4
Sweden	24.7	21.5	15.9	15.0	15.1	15.2	15.3	14.8	15.0	15.2
Switzerland	8.4	8.5	8.2	8.3	8.3	8.1	8.1	7.9	7.8	7.8
Turkey[2]	13.2	14.3	8.2	8.6	8.7	8.8	9.2	9.5	9.7	9.2
United Kingdom	15.1	15.5	14.2	14.4	13.5	13.1	12.0	11.5	11.2	11.0
United States	15.0	14.4	13.6	13.8	15.2	15.3	15.1	15.2	15.3	15.4
Unweighted average										
OECD-Average	**12.4**	**11.4**	**10.8**	**10.9**	**11.3**	**11.5**	**11.7**	**11.6**	**11.6**	**11.4**
OECD-EU 22	**13.3**	**11.8**	**11.6**	**11.8**	**12.3**	**12.6**	**12.7**	**12.5**	**12.4**	**12.1**

1. Information on data for Israel: http://oe.cd/israel-disclaimer.
2. Wage figures are based on the old definition of average worker (ISIC D, rev3.) for years 2000 to 2006.

StatLink http://dx.doi.org/10.1787/888933461360

Table 6.1c. **Income tax plus employee contributions less cash benefits, single persons at 67% of average earnings**

Tax burden as a % of gross wage earnings, single persons without children

	2000	2006	2009	2010	2011	2012	2013	2014	2015	2016
Australia	21.1	20.3	15.8	16.0	16.0	17.1	17.3	17.7	18.5	18.8
Austria	25.6	27.4	26.7	27.0	27.6	28.0	28.5	28.8	29.2	26.3
Belgium	35.8	35.2	35.8	36.4	36.5	36.4	36.0	35.9	35.4	33.4
Canada	19.5	18.9	17.7	17.4	17.4	17.5	17.6	17.8	17.7	17.7
Chile	7.0	7.0	7.0	7.0	7.0	7.0	7.0	7.0	7.0	7.0
Czech Republic	20.8	19.1	17.9	18.2	19.2	18.8	18.8	19.2	19.5	19.9
Denmark	37.9	35.6	34.8	33.5	33.7	33.8	33.3	33.1	33.4	33.5
Estonia	19.9	16.4	16.7	17.6	18.0	18.3	18.0	18.2	17.1	16.8
Finland	27.8	24.3	22.7	22.7	22.6	22.4	23.4	23.7	24.0	23.6
France	25.9	25.7	25.9	25.9	26.1	26.3	26.4	26.7	25.8	25.3
Germany	36.8	36.7	35.4	34.3	34.8	34.9	34.5	34.5	34.6	34.7
Greece	18.2	18.6	18.8	17.8	22.8	22.6	19.7	19.2	18.5	20.2
Hungary	30.1	23.3	28.8	27.8	29.6	34.5	34.5	34.5	34.5	33.5
Iceland	20.2	24.1	21.6	22.2	23.3	23.8	24.3	23.9	25.0	25.4
Ireland	11.2	7.1	7.2	7.9	11.4	12.3	13.4	13.6	13.1	12.7
Israel[1]	19.4	12.1	10.9	10.4	10.3	10.2	10.0	10.5	10.8	11.2
Italy	24.4	24.4	25.4	26.1	26.7	27.0	27.2	23.3	21.9	21.9
Japan	18.4	17.9	18.5	19.1	19.5	19.8	20.0	20.2	20.4	20.5
Korea	7.5	8.3	8.9	9.2	9.5	9.7	10.0	10.1	10.3	10.6
Latvia	26.0	27.4	25.0	29.5	29.5	29.6	29.0	28.4	27.9	28.0
Luxembourg	21.8	19.5	19.1	19.4	20.8	20.4	21.5	22.0	22.7	22.8
Mexico	-4.4	-1.5	-0.1	0.8	1.3	1.7	2.6	3.0	3.3	3.7
Netherlands	32.9	27.2	27.1	27.1	27.1	26.8	26.5	25.0	24.9	22.8
New Zealand	18.6	18.9	15.5	14.3	13.0	13.1	13.3	13.4	13.5	13.6
Norway	26.8	25.7	25.6	25.6	25.7	25.6	25.6	25.2	25.0	24.5
Poland	26.5	27.4	23.3	23.4	23.6	23.7	23.8	24.0	24.1	24.2
Portugal	17.4	16.9	15.7	16.1	16.2	16.6	19.8	19.4	21.1	21.2
Slovak Republic	18.0	18.3	17.2	17.6	19.3	19.3	19.3	19.5	19.7	20.0
Slovenia	32.3	30.2	30.0	28.7	28.8	28.7	28.6	28.7	28.7	28.8
Spain	15.0	16.4	14.8	17.5	17.9	18.4	18.5	18.5	16.7	16.8
Sweden	31.7	28.5	22.9	22.0	22.1	22.2	22.4	21.8	22.0	22.2
Switzerland	14.9	14.6	14.3	14.4	14.5	14.3	14.4	14.1	14.0	14.0
Turkey[2]	27.2	29.3	23.2	23.6	23.7	23.8	24.2	24.5	24.7	24.2
United Kingdom	22.8	23.9	22.4	22.6	21.7	21.2	20.0	19.4	19.2	19.1
United States	22.6	22.1	21.3	21.5	20.9	20.9	22.8	22.9	23.0	23.0
Unweighted average										
OECD-Average	**22.2**	**21.4**	**20.4**	**20.6**	**21.1**	**21.3**	**21.5**	**21.4**	**21.3**	**21.2**
OECD-EU 22	**25.4**	**24.1**	**23.3**	**23.6**	**24.4**	**24.6**	**24.7**	**24.4**	**24.3**	**24.0**

1. Information on data for Israel: http://oe.cd/israel-disclaimer.
2. Wage figures are based on the old definition of average worker (ISIC D, rev3.) for years 2000 to 2006.

StatLink http://dx.doi.org/10.1787/888933461375

Table 6.2a. **Income tax plus employee and employer contributions less cash benefits, single persons at 100% of average earnings**

Tax burden as a % of labour costs, single persons without children

	2000	2006	2009	2010	2011	2012	2013	2014	2015	2016
Australia	31.0	28.3	26.7	26.8	26.7	27.3	27.4	27.7	28.4	28.6
Austria	47.3	48.5	47.9	48.2	48.5	48.8	49.2	49.4	49.6	47.1
Belgium	57.1	55.5	55.7	55.9	56.1	56.0	55.7	55.6	55.3	54.0
Canada	32.9	31.8	30.5	30.4	30.7	30.8	31.0	31.6	31.5	31.4
Chile	7.0	7.0	7.0	7.0	7.0	7.0	7.0	7.0	7.0	7.0
Czech Republic	42.6	42.5	42.0	42.1	42.6	42.5	42.4	42.6	42.8	43.0
Denmark	42.1	38.9	37.6	36.4	36.6	36.7	36.4	36.3	36.4	36.5
Estonia	41.3	39.0	39.2	40.1	40.3	40.4	39.9	40.0	39.0	38.9
Finland	47.5	44.0	42.5	42.3	42.3	42.5	43.1	43.6	43.5	43.8
France	50.4	49.7	49.8	49.9	50.0	50.1	48.8	48.4	48.4	48.1
Germany	52.9	52.3	50.8	49.0	49.7	49.6	49.2	49.3	49.4	49.4
Greece	39.1	42.3	41.3	40.1	43.2	42.9	41.6	40.5	39.2	40.2
Hungary	54.7	51.9	53.1	46.6	49.5	49.5	49.0	49.0	49.0	48.2
Iceland	28.8	31.8	30.5	33.4	34.1	33.8	34.1	33.7	34.3	34.0
Ireland	28.9	23.0	24.7	25.8	25.8	26.9	27.6	27.9	27.3	27.1
Israel[1]	29.6	24.3	21.3	20.7	20.8	20.4	20.4	21.1	21.6	22.1
Italy	47.1	46.1	46.8	47.2	47.6	47.7	47.8	47.8	47.9	47.8
Japan	29.8	28.8	29.2	30.2	30.8	31.3	31.6	32.0	32.3	32.4
Korea	16.4	18.2	19.5	20.1	20.5	21.0	21.5	21.7	22.0	22.2
Latvia	43.2	42.7	40.9	44.0	44.2	44.3	43.7	43.0	42.5	42.6
Luxembourg	35.8	34.0	33.9	34.3	36.3	36.0	37.2	37.6	38.4	38.4
Mexico	12.7	15.1	15.3	16.0	18.7	19.0	19.3	19.5	19.8	20.1
Netherlands	40.0	38.4	38.0	38.1	38.0	38.8	41.5	39.8	37.0	37.5
New Zealand	19.4	20.4	18.1	17.0	15.9	16.4	16.9	17.2	17.6	17.9
Norway	38.6	37.4	37.3	37.3	37.6	37.4	37.4	36.9	36.6	36.2
Poland	38.2	39.0	34.1	34.2	34.3	35.5	35.6	35.7	35.7	35.8
Portugal	37.3	37.5	36.5	37.1	38.0	37.6	41.4	41.2	42.1	41.5
Slovak Republic	41.9	38.3	37.7	37.9	38.8	39.6	41.1	41.3	41.4	41.5
Slovenia	46.3	45.3	42.2	42.5	42.6	42.5	42.4	42.5	42.6	42.7
Spain	38.6	39.1	38.3	39.7	40.0	40.6	40.7	40.7	39.4	39.5
Sweden	50.1	47.8	43.2	42.8	42.8	42.9	43.0	42.5	42.6	42.8
Switzerland	22.9	22.1	22.0	22.1	22.3	22.1	22.2	21.9	21.8	21.8
Turkey[2]	40.4	42.7	36.7	37.0	37.0	37.1	37.4	38.1	38.2	38.1
United Kingdom	32.6	34.0	32.4	32.6	32.5	32.1	31.4	31.0	30.8	30.8
United States	30.8	30.6	30.3	30.7	29.9	29.8	31.5	31.6	31.6	31.7
Unweighted average										
OECD-Average	**37.0**	**36.2**	**35.2**	**35.3**	**35.8**	**35.9**	**36.2**	**36.2**	**36.1**	**36.0**
OECD-EU 22	**43.4**	**42.3**	**41.3**	**41.2**	**41.8**	**42.0**	**42.2**	**42.1**	**41.8**	**41.7**

1. Information on data for Israel: http://oe.cd/israel-disclaimer.
2. Wage figures are based on the old definition of average worker (ISIC D, rev3.) for years 2000 to 2006.

StatLink http://dx.doi.org/10.1787/888933461388

Table 6.2b. **Income tax, single persons at 100% of the average earnings**

Tax burden as a % of gross wage earnings, single persons without children

	2000	2006	2009	2010	2011	2012	2013	2014	2015	2016
Australia	26.6	24.0	22.1	22.3	22.3	23.0	23.1	23.4	24.1	24.3
Austria	12.9	15.4	14.7	15.0	15.5	15.9	16.3	16.6	17.0	13.9
Belgium	29.0	27.9	28.3	28.7	28.8	28.7	28.4	28.4	28.0	26.8
Canada	19.2	16.3	15.2	15.1	15.2	15.3	15.3	15.7	15.6	15.4
Chile	0.0	0.0	0.0	0.0	0.0	0.0	0.0	0.0	0.0	0.0
Czech Republic	10.0	9.9	11.3	11.5	12.1	11.9	11.9	12.1	12.3	12.6
Denmark	32.9	30.6	37.2	36.3	36.4	36.5	36.1	36.0	36.1	36.2
Estonia	21.9	18.1	16.8	16.7	16.9	17.1	17.5	17.6	16.8	16.7
Finland	26.9	23.8	23.0	22.3	22.2	21.8	22.5	22.6	22.6	22.0
France	15.7	14.0	14.1	14.2	14.2	14.4	14.5	14.6	14.7	14.8
Germany	22.7	20.8	20.6	18.7	18.9	19.0	19.0	19.0	19.1	19.0
Greece	6.1	10.1	8.8	7.2	10.8	10.1	9.1	9.1	8.7	9.6
Hungary	23.2	20.9	20.8	14.4	17.6	16.6	16.0	16.0	16.0	15.0
Iceland	25.3	27.7	25.7	27.1	27.9	28.2	28.6	28.2	29.0	28.9
Ireland	17.2	11.6	13.5	14.7	14.7	15.9	15.8	16.2	15.5	15.2
Israel[1]	18.0	12.6	9.7	9.0	9.1	8.7	8.6	9.1	9.4	9.9
Italy	19.9	19.6	20.2	20.7	21.3	21.5	21.6	21.5	21.6	21.6
Japan	6.4	7.2	7.9	7.6	7.6	7.6	7.6	7.7	7.8	7.8
Korea	2.2	3.4	4.1	4.5	4.4	4.9	5.2	5.3	5.6	5.7
Latvia	18.9	19.9	17.6	21.5	19.7	19.8	19.1	19.1	18.4	18.6
Luxembourg	17.0	14.9	14.0	14.6	15.3	15.8	17.2	17.7	18.0	18.1
Mexico	1.0	3.6	4.1	4.8	7.9	8.2	8.5	8.8	9.1	9.5
Netherlands	9.6	13.2	16.6	16.2	16.4	17.0	16.9	16.1	17.3	16.9
New Zealand	19.4	20.4	18.1	17.0	15.9	16.4	16.9	17.2	17.6	17.9
Norway	22.9	21.3	21.5	21.5	21.6	21.4	21.4	20.5	20.2	19.7
Poland	6.6	6.5	6.6	6.7	6.8	6.9	6.9	7.1	7.1	7.2
Portugal	11.4	11.7	10.5	11.2	12.3	11.8	16.5	16.2	17.3	16.6
Slovak Republic	7.8	8.7	8.0	8.3	9.4	9.4	9.4	9.5	9.7	9.8
Slovenia	13.5	12.7	10.8	11.2	11.3	11.1	11.0	11.1	11.2	11.3
Spain	13.5	14.1	13.4	15.4	15.7	16.5	16.6	16.6	14.9	15.0
Sweden	26.7	23.9	18.4	17.8	17.9	17.9	18.1	17.4	17.6	17.9
Switzerland	11.3	11.3	11.2	11.3	11.2	11.0	11.1	10.7	10.7	10.7
Turkey[2]	14.7	15.4	11.3	11.6	11.6	11.8	12.0	12.3	12.4	12.3
United Kingdom	17.4	17.7	16.1	16.2	15.6	15.4	14.6	14.3	14.1	14.0
United States	17.3	16.8	16.5	17.0	18.0	18.0	17.8	18.0	18.1	18.3
Unweighted average										
OECD-Average	**16.1**	**15.6**	**15.1**	**15.1**	**15.5**	**15.6**	**15.7**	**15.8**	**15.8**	**15.7**
OECD-EU 22	**17.3**	**16.6**	**16.4**	**16.3**	**16.8**	**16.9**	**17.0**	**17.0**	**17.0**	**16.8**

1. Information on data for Israel: http://oe.cd/israel-disclaimer.
2. Wage figures are based on the old definition of average worker (ISIC D, rev3.) for years 2000 to 2006.

StatLink http://dx.doi.org/10.1787/888933461391

Table 6.2c. Income tax plus employee contributions less cash benefits, single persons at 100% of average earnings

Tax burden as a % of gross wage earnings, single persons without children

	2000	2006	2009	2010	2011	2012	2013	2014	2015	2016
Australia	26.6	24.0	22.1	22.3	22.3	23.0	23.1	23.4	24.1	24.3
Austria	31.0	33.4	32.8	33.1	33.6	33.9	34.4	34.7	35.0	31.9
Belgium	43.0	41.9	42.3	42.7	42.8	42.7	42.4	42.4	42.0	40.7
Canada	25.1	23.8	22.5	22.4	22.5	22.6	22.7	23.3	23.2	23.1
Chile	7.0	7.0	7.0	7.0	7.0	7.0	7.0	7.0	7.0	7.0
Czech Republic	22.5	22.4	22.3	22.5	23.1	22.9	22.9	23.1	23.3	23.6
Denmark	41.9	38.6	37.2	35.9	36.1	36.2	35.8	35.6	35.9	36.0
Estonia	21.9	18.7	18.6	19.5	19.7	19.9	19.5	19.6	18.4	18.3
Finland	33.9	30.6	29.3	29.4	29.4	29.4	30.1	30.6	30.9	30.8
France	29.2	27.7	27.8	27.8	27.9	28.1	28.3	28.6	28.9	29.1
Germany	43.2	42.5	41.2	39.2	39.8	39.8	39.4	39.5	39.6	39.7
Greece	22.0	26.1	24.8	23.2	27.0	26.6	25.6	25.1	24.2	25.4
Hungary	35.7	35.2	37.8	31.4	35.1	35.1	34.5	34.5	34.5	33.5
Iceland	25.4	27.8	26.2	27.6	28.4	28.7	29.1	28.6	29.3	29.2
Ireland	20.3	14.7	16.7	17.9	17.8	19.1	19.8	20.2	19.5	19.2
Israel[1]	26.1	20.3	17.7	17.0	17.0	16.6	16.4	17.0	17.3	17.8
Italy	29.0	28.7	29.7	30.2	30.8	31.0	31.1	31.0	31.1	31.1
Japan	19.7	19.4	20.0	20.6	21.0	21.3	21.5	21.8	22.1	22.2
Korea	8.9	10.6	11.7	12.3	12.5	13.0	13.5	13.6	14.0	14.1
Latvia	27.9	28.9	26.6	30.5	30.7	30.8	30.1	29.6	28.9	29.1
Luxembourg	28.7	26.6	26.2	26.8	28.4	28.1	29.5	30.0	30.8	31.0
Mexico	2.5	5.0	5.4	6.1	9.2	9.6	9.8	10.1	10.4	10.8
Netherlands	33.6	32.5	31.8	31.7	31.7	32.1	35.8	33.4	30.4	30.4
New Zealand	19.4	20.4	18.1	17.0	15.9	16.4	16.9	17.2	17.6	17.9
Norway	30.7	29.1	29.3	29.3	29.4	29.2	29.2	28.7	28.4	27.9
Poland	27.8	28.7	24.4	24.5	24.6	24.7	24.8	24.9	24.9	25.0
Portugal	22.4	22.7	21.5	22.2	23.3	22.8	27.5	27.2	28.3	27.6
Slovak Republic	19.8	22.1	21.4	21.7	22.8	22.8	22.8	22.9	23.1	23.2
Slovenia	35.6	34.8	32.9	33.3	33.4	33.2	33.1	33.2	33.3	33.4
Spain	19.8	20.5	19.8	21.7	22.0	22.9	22.9	23.0	21.3	21.4
Sweden	33.7	30.9	25.4	24.8	24.8	24.9	25.1	24.4	24.6	24.9
Switzerland	17.8	17.4	17.2	17.4	17.5	17.2	17.3	17.0	16.9	16.9
Turkey[2]	28.7	30.4	26.3	26.6	26.6	26.8	27.0	27.3	27.4	27.3
United Kingdom	25.8	26.9	25.2	25.4	25.1	24.7	24.0	23.6	23.4	23.3
United States	24.9	24.4	24.2	24.6	23.6	23.6	25.5	25.6	25.8	26.0
Unweighted average										
OECD-Average	**26.1**	**25.6**	**24.7**	**24.7**	**25.2**	**25.3**	**25.7**	**25.6**	**25.6**	**25.5**
OECD-EU 22	**29.5**	**28.9**	**28.0**	**28.0**	**28.6**	**28.7**	**29.1**	**29.0**	**28.8**	**28.6**

1. Information on data for Israel: http://oe.cd/israel-disclaimer.
2. Wage figures are based on the old definition of average worker (ISIC D, rev3.) for years 2000 to 2006.

StatLink http://dx.doi.org/10.1787/888933461402

Table 6.3a. Income tax plus employee and employer contributions less cash benefits, single persons at 167% of average earnings

Tax burden as a % of labour costs, single persons without children

	2000	2006	2009	2010	2011	2012	2013	2014	2015	2016
Australia	38.8	34.7	32.6	32.4	32.2	33.1	33.2	33.4	34.0	34.1
Austria	50.4	51.6	51.2	51.4	51.5	51.4	51.9	52.0	52.1	50.8
Belgium	62.6	60.8	60.9	61.0	61.1	61.0	60.8	60.8	60.7	59.9
Canada	35.2	33.2	32.6	32.7	32.8	33.0	33.1	33.3	33.3	32.7
Chile	7.5	7.0	7.0	7.6	7.7	7.9	7.8	7.9	7.9	8.0
Czech Republic	44.8	46.1	44.6	44.7	45.0	44.9	44.9	45.0	45.1	45.2
Denmark	50.0	47.9	47.1	43.2	43.5	43.7	42.9	42.3	42.4	42.4
Estonia	42.5	40.5	40.3	41.2	41.3	41.4	40.8	40.9	39.9	39.8
Finland	53.2	49.9	48.3	48.2	48.3	48.5	48.9	49.4	49.4	49.8
France	52.5	53.3	53.6	53.6	53.8	54.0	54.1	54.3	54.3	54.4
Germany	56.2	55.0	53.1	51.5	51.3	51.3	51.3	51.4	51.3	51.4
Greece	45.1	49.1	46.0	45.6	48.6	48.2	49.3	48.3	45.6	45.8
Hungary	59.2	56.7	58.3	53.1	51.6	50.7	49.0	49.0	49.0	48.2
Iceland	39.6	34.6	34.1	37.8	38.4	38.3	38.6	38.1	38.6	38.7
Ireland	39.4	34.0	35.2	36.4	38.0	38.9	39.2	39.5	38.7	38.0
Israel[1]	38.1	33.8	30.0	29.5	29.2	28.6	29.2	30.0	30.6	31.3
Italy	51.1	50.9	52.0	52.5	53.0	53.2	53.3	53.6	54.2	54.1
Japan	31.6	31.6	32.3	33.3	33.8	34.2	34.5	34.7	34.9	35.0
Korea	20.5	21.8	21.8	21.7	22.2	22.6	23.0	23.5	24.2	24.5
Latvia	44.4	43.6	41.9	44.7	45.0	45.0	44.4	43.8	43.2	43.3
Luxembourg	44.1	41.1	41.4	41.6	43.7	43.3	44.4	44.6	45.3	45.3
Mexico	19.5	22.0	20.9	21.4	21.6	22.0	22.2	22.6	22.8	23.1
Netherlands	44.9	41.4	41.8	41.8	41.8	42.5	42.3	51.0	42.3	42.1
New Zealand	24.2	26.2	24.6	23.3	22.0	22.4	22.8	23.1	23.3	23.6
Norway	45.2	43.0	43.0	43.0	43.2	43.1	43.0	42.5	42.3	42.0
Poland	39.1	40.1	34.9	35.0	35.0	36.2	36.2	36.3	36.3	36.4
Portugal	42.3	43.3	42.2	43.1	44.6	43.6	47.7	47.4	48.0	47.0
Slovak Republic	45.2	40.4	40.1	40.3	40.8	41.6	43.3	43.4	43.4	43.5
Slovenia	51.0	51.7	47.1	47.6	47.7	47.5	46.1	46.4	46.5	46.1
Spain	41.0	42.6	41.6	42.4	42.5	43.5	44.3	45.0	43.8	43.7
Sweden	55.7	54.5	51.2	51.0	50.9	50.7	50.8	50.6	50.7	51.4
Switzerland	27.4	26.4	26.5	26.6	26.8	26.7	26.7	26.4	26.3	26.3
Turkey[2]	35.0	44.4	39.2	39.8	40.0	40.2	40.6	41.5	41.8	42.0
United Kingdom	35.8	37.8	36.9	37.2	37.9	37.8	37.6	37.3	37.3	37.3
United States	37.1	35.6	35.6	35.9	34.7	34.6	36.3	36.4	36.4	36.5
Unweighted average										
OECD-Average	**41.4**	**40.8**	**39.7**	**39.8**	**40.1**	**40.2**	**40.4**	**40.7**	**40.5**	**40.4**
OECD-EU 22	**47.8**	**46.9**	**45.9**	**45.8**	**46.2**	**46.3**	**46.5**	**46.9**	**46.3**	**46.2**

1. Information on data for Israel: http://oe.cd/israel-disclaimer.
2. Wage figures are based on the old definition of average worker (ISIC D, rev3.) for years 2000 to 2006.

StatLink http://dx.doi.org/10.1787/888933461414

Table 6.3b. **Income tax, single persons at 167% of average earnings**

Tax burden as a % of gross wage earnings, single persons without children

	2000	2006	2009	2010	2011	2012	2013	2014	2015	2016
Australia	34.9	30.8	28.3	28.2	28.2	29.2	29.2	29.4	30.1	30.2
Austria	20.4	22.5	22.0	22.2	22.5	22.8	23.0	23.2	23.4	21.0
Belgium	36.0	34.7	35.2	35.5	35.5	35.5	35.2	35.2	35.1	34.5
Canada	25.6	22.3	21.6	21.7	21.8	21.8	21.8	22.2	22.1	21.4
Chile	0.5	0.0	0.0	0.6	0.7	0.9	0.8	0.9	0.9	1.0
Czech Republic	13.0	14.7	14.8	14.9	15.3	15.2	15.2	15.3	15.4	15.6
Denmark	40.9	39.7	46.9	42.9	43.2	43.4	42.6	41.9	42.1	42.2
Estonia	23.6	20.0	18.3	18.2	18.3	18.4	18.7	18.8	18.0	17.9
Finland	34.0	31.0	30.0	29.5	29.4	29.0	29.6	29.7	29.8	29.4
France	21.2	19.9	20.3	20.3	20.5	20.7	20.8	20.8	20.9	20.9
Germany	31.7	28.9	28.6	27.1	27.5	27.6	27.5	27.5	27.7	27.5
Greece	13.8	18.8	14.8	14.4	17.7	16.9	18.8	18.9	16.7	16.6
Hungary	30.3	27.6	27.6	22.8	20.3	18.1	16.0	16.0	16.0	15.0
Iceland	36.6	30.7	29.7	32.1	32.7	33.2	33.6	33.2	33.8	34.0
Ireland	28.7	23.7	24.7	26.0	27.8	28.8	28.7	29.0	28.1	27.4
Israel[1]	26.3	20.7	16.9	16.4	16.0	15.4	15.7	16.4	16.8	17.3
Italy	25.3	25.9	27.1	27.7	28.3	28.5	28.7	29.2	29.9	29.9
Japan	10.6	11.7	12.4	12.0	12.0	12.2	12.1	12.4	12.6	12.7
Korea	6.7	8.6	8.6	8.6	8.5	8.8	9.2	9.6	10.3	10.6
Latvia	20.4	21.0	18.9	22.4	20.7	20.8	20.0	20.0	19.3	19.4
Luxembourg	26.2	22.8	22.3	22.6	23.6	23.9	25.2	25.5	25.7	25.8
Mexico	8.0	12.1	11.5	11.9	12.3	12.7	13.0	13.3	13.6	14.0
Netherlands	25.4	25.7	28.8	28.4	28.6	29.2	28.6	29.2	29.1	27.9
New Zealand	24.2	26.2	24.6	23.3	22.0	22.4	22.8	23.1	23.3	23.6
Norway	30.4	27.6	27.9	27.9	28.0	27.8	27.8	26.9	26.6	26.2
Poland	7.7	7.9	7.5	7.5	7.6	7.7	7.7	7.8	7.8	7.8
Portugal	17.6	18.8	17.4	18.5	20.4	19.2	24.2	23.9	24.6	23.4
Slovak Republic	12.4	11.9	11.4	11.6	12.3	12.3	12.2	12.3	12.4	12.5
Slovenia	19.1	18.7	16.5	17.0	17.2	17.0	15.4	15.6	15.8	15.3
Spain	18.5	19.1	19.2	20.6	21.0	22.5	22.5	22.5	21.1	21.0
Sweden	36.3	35.2	31.1	30.9	30.8	30.5	30.6	30.4	30.4	31.4
Switzerland	16.2	16.3	16.1	16.3	16.1	16.0	16.1	15.7	15.6	15.5
Turkey[2]	18.0	17.4	14.2	14.9	15.1	15.3	15.9	16.3	16.6	16.9
United Kingdom	23.1	24.2	21.9	22.4	22.4	22.6	22.6	22.3	22.3	22.3
United States	24.3	22.6	22.6	22.9	23.5	23.5	23.4	23.4	23.6	23.7
Unweighted average										
OECD-Average	**22.5**	**21.7**	**21.1**	**21.1**	**21.4**	**21.4**	**21.6**	**21.7**	**21.6**	**21.5**
OECD-EU 22	**23.9**	**23.3**	**23.0**	**22.9**	**23.2**	**23.2**	**23.4**	**23.4**	**23.3**	**22.9**

1. Information on data for Israel: http://oe.cd/israel-disclaimer.
2. Wage figures are based on the old definition of average worker (ISIC D, rev3.) for years 2000 to 2006.

StatLink http://dx.doi.org/10.1787/888933461423

Table 6.3c. Income tax plus employee contributions less cash benefits, single persons at 167% of average earnings

Tax burden as a % of gross wage earnings, single persons without children

	2000	2006	2009	2010	2011	2012	2013	2014	2015	2016
Australia	34.9	30.8	28.3	28.2	28.2	29.2	29.2	29.4	30.1	30.2
Austria	36.3	38.6	38.1	38.3	38.5	38.6	39.0	39.2	39.4	37.5
Belgium	50.1	48.8	49.2	49.5	49.6	49.5	49.2	49.2	49.1	48.5
Canada	29.3	27.2	26.5	26.6	26.7	26.8	26.8	27.1	27.0	26.3
Chile	7.5	7.0	7.0	7.6	7.7	7.9	7.8	7.9	7.9	8.0
Czech Republic	25.5	27.2	25.8	25.9	26.3	26.2	26.2	26.3	26.4	26.6
Denmark	49.9	47.7	46.9	42.9	43.2	43.4	42.6	41.9	42.1	42.2
Estonia	23.6	20.6	20.1	21.0	21.1	21.2	20.7	20.8	19.6	19.5
Finland	41.1	37.8	36.4	36.6	36.6	36.7	37.3	37.8	38.1	38.2
France	33.1	33.0	33.4	33.4	33.6	33.8	33.9	34.2	34.4	34.5
Germany	48.8	47.1	45.5	43.8	43.8	43.8	43.7	43.8	43.8	43.9
Greece	29.7	34.8	30.8	30.4	34.0	33.4	35.3	34.9	32.2	32.4
Hungary	42.8	41.9	44.6	39.8	37.8	36.6	34.5	34.5	34.5	33.5
Iceland	36.7	30.8	30.0	32.4	33.0	33.5	33.9	33.4	34.0	34.2
Ireland	32.1	26.9	28.2	29.6	31.3	32.3	32.7	33.0	32.1	31.4
Israel[1]	35.0	30.1	26.5	26.0	25.6	24.9	25.2	26.0	26.3	26.9
Italy	34.5	35.2	36.6	37.3	37.9	38.1	38.3	38.8	39.5	39.5
Japan	22.6	23.1	24.0	24.5	24.8	25.1	25.3	25.6	25.9	25.9
Korea	13.4	15.1	15.1	15.0	15.3	15.7	16.2	16.6	17.3	17.7
Latvia	29.4	30.0	27.9	31.4	31.7	31.8	31.0	30.5	29.8	29.9
Luxembourg	37.9	34.6	34.6	34.9	36.8	36.3	37.6	37.9	38.6	38.6
Mexico	10.1	13.7	13.0	13.4	13.8	14.1	14.4	14.8	15.1	15.4
Netherlands	40.6	37.5	37.9	37.7	37.8	38.3	38.6	47.6	38.3	37.9
New Zealand	24.2	26.2	24.6	23.3	22.0	22.4	22.8	23.1	23.3	23.6
Norway	38.2	35.4	35.7	35.7	35.8	35.6	35.6	35.1	34.8	34.4
Poland	28.9	30.1	25.3	25.4	25.4	25.5	25.5	25.6	25.6	25.7
Portugal	28.6	29.8	28.4	29.5	31.4	30.2	35.2	34.9	35.6	34.4
Slovak Republic	24.4	25.0	24.6	24.8	25.4	25.5	25.6	25.7	25.8	25.9
Slovenia	41.2	40.8	38.6	39.1	39.3	39.1	37.5	37.7	37.9	37.4
Spain	24.4	25.3	25.2	26.5	26.8	28.3	28.5	28.7	27.3	27.3
Sweden	41.1	39.8	35.8	35.6	35.5	35.3	35.4	35.1	35.2	36.1
Switzerland	22.7	22.1	22.1	22.2	22.3	22.2	22.2	21.9	21.7	21.7
Turkey[2]	26.9	32.4	29.2	29.9	30.1	30.3	30.9	31.3	31.6	31.9
United Kingdom	28.8	30.6	29.7	30.0	30.4	30.4	30.1	29.8	29.8	29.8
United States	31.9	30.2	30.3	30.6	29.1	29.2	31.0	31.1	31.2	31.3
Unweighted average										
OECD-Average	**31.6**	**31.1**	**30.2**	**30.2**	**30.5**	**30.6**	**30.9**	**31.2**	**30.9**	**30.8**
OECD-EU 22	**35.1**	**34.7**	**33.8**	**33.8**	**34.3**	**34.3**	**34.5**	**34.9**	**34.3**	**34.1**

1. Information on data for Israel: http://oe.cd/israel-disclaimer.
2. Wage figures are based on the old definition of average worker (ISIC D, rev3.) for years 2000 to 2006.

StatLink http://dx.doi.org/10.1787/888933461438

Table 6.4a. **Income tax plus employee and employer contributions less cash benefits, single parent at 67% of average earnings**

Tax burden as a % of labour costs, single parent with two children

	2000	2006	2009	2010	2011	2012	2013	2014	2015	2016
Australia	4.0	-1.2	-7.2	-6.5	-5.7	-3.2	-2.6	-1.8	-1.4	-1.1
Austria	25.2	26.7	25.5	26.1	27.2	28.0	28.8	29.2	29.6	27.0
Belgium	36.4	35.6	35.7	36.8	37.0	36.9	36.2	36.1	35.6	33.6
Canada	-0.4	-0.2	-9.7	-7.4	-7.0	-6.5	-6.1	-4.7	-15.4	-14.9
Chile	2.8	3.0	3.3	6.0	6.0	6.1	6.1	6.1	6.1	6.1
Czech Republic	12.7	19.2	15.6	15.8	25.4	24.2	24.1	24.8	24.6	25.0
Denmark	12.4	10.6	10.7	9.1	9.7	9.7	9.2	7.2	7.5	7.7
Estonia	18.5	18.2	22.7	24.1	25.2	26.3	26.6	27.4	21.7	21.2
Finland	28.3	26.7	25.6	25.5	25.7	25.6	26.8	27.3	27.3	27.5
France	34.5	38.1	38.5	38.8	38.9	38.8	37.1	36.6	35.8	24.5
Germany	31.8	33.8	31.2	29.8	31.0	31.2	30.9	31.2	30.7	31.0
Greece	35.4	36.7	35.7	34.4	38.8	38.6	33.4	32.1	30.8	31.7
Hungary	34.0	26.0	29.8	27.4	20.2	23.0	25.5	26.4	27.2	25.3
Iceland	5.9	15.5	12.2	16.7	19.0	17.0	19.0	18.1	20.4	21.6
Ireland	-0.7	-30.5	-29.4	-27.8	-26.2	-21.9	-20.7	-19.6	-19.1	-18.8
Israel[1]	3.3	2.2	1.8	1.6	0.8	0.5	1.2	2.9	2.8	-0.4
Italy	29.5	28.0	26.9	28.1	29.0	29.4	29.0	26.2	25.4	25.3
Japan	26.3	21.7	21.5	18.6	19.8	23.5	23.8	24.3	24.7	24.9
Korea	14.4	15.7	16.3	16.7	17.1	17.3	17.5	16.9	17.0	17.0
Latvia	24.0	31.1	27.1	29.5	29.5	30.1	29.9	25.5	25.0	25.5
Luxembourg	4.4	3.3	-0.4	0.6	3.1	3.5	5.1	6.1	7.3	7.5
Mexico	7.6	10.6	11.9	12.9	13.2	13.6	14.4	14.7	15.0	15.3
Netherlands	26.4	13.0	11.4	12.2	12.1	12.2	12.8	12.5	10.6	7.6
New Zealand	-3.0	-15.1	-17.1	-17.7	-18.3	-18.2	-16.9	-15.8	-14.4	-13.0
Norway	16.4	19.5	20.6	20.9	21.6	21.7	22.0	22.0	22.1	22.0
Poland	29.8	35.5	28.4	28.4	28.4	29.6	29.6	29.6	29.6	29.6
Portugal	26.6	24.9	19.5	20.6	22.3	23.1	25.5	25.0	25.3	21.4
Slovak Republic	25.3	21.6	21.6	21.9	23.6	24.5	26.4	26.9	27.3	27.8
Slovenia	13.4	15.1	12.5	12.4	12.8	13.0	13.1	9.9	10.1	10.4
Spain	28.6	30.3	28.4	29.2	29.9	30.3	30.4	30.6	24.2	24.4
Sweden	39.9	36.8	33.0	32.3	32.6	32.9	33.2	33.0	33.2	33.6
Switzerland	6.5	5.7	4.4	4.7	5.0	5.0	4.6	4.1	4.0	3.9
Turkey[2]	39.1	41.8	32.7	33.0	33.1	33.2	33.6	34.4	34.6	33.9
United Kingdom	15.3	14.4	8.5	9.3	7.1	6.7	5.7	4.6	5.2	6.2
United States	10.7	8.5	7.4	8.9	8.9	9.8	11.3	12.0	12.1	12.7
Unweighted average										
OECD-Average	**19.0**	**17.8**	**15.9**	**16.4**	**17.1**	**17.6**	**17.9**	**17.8**	**17.2**	**16.6**
OECD-EU 22	**24.2**	**22.5**	**20.8**	**21.1**	**22.0**	**22.5**	**22.7**	**22.2**	**21.6**	**20.7**

1. Information on data for Israel: http://oe.cd/israel-disclaimer.
2. Wage figures are based on the old definition of average worker (ISIC D, rev3.) for years 2000 to 2006.

StatLink http://dx.doi.org/10.1787/888933461444

Table 6.4b. **Income tax, single parent at 67% of average earnings**

Tax burden as a % of gross wage earnings, single parent with two children

	2000	2006	2009	2010	2011	2012	2013	2014	2015	2016
Australia	15.5	20.3	14.0	14.3	14.3	15.4	17.3	17.7	18.5	18.8
Austria	5.8	6.5	5.4	5.8	6.4	6.9	7.5	7.8	8.3	5.0
Belgium	16.7	16.2	16.4	17.2	17.3	17.2	16.6	16.5	16.0	14.1
Canada	6.6	4.9	0.5	1.0	1.1	1.1	1.1	1.5	3.5	3.5
Chile	0.0	0.0	0.0	0.0	0.0	0.0	0.0	0.0	0.0	0.0
Czech Republic	2.3	-1.1	-4.4	-4.9	-3.6	-5.4	-5.4	-4.7	-5.2	-4.9
Denmark	28.9	27.6	34.8	34.0	34.2	34.3	33.8	32.0	32.2	32.3
Estonia	19.9	8.7	9.2	9.3	10.0	10.6	11.3	11.8	11.2	11.2
Finland	20.9	17.6	16.5	15.7	15.5	14.9	15.9	15.8	15.2	14.4
France	7.1	7.2	7.4	7.5	7.5	7.6	7.6	7.6	7.9	7.9
Germany	-2.6	-1.3	-2.6	-4.0	-3.2	-2.7	-2.6	-2.2	-2.9	-2.8
Greece	1.4	3.0	1.7	0.0	5.1	4.5	3.2	3.2	3.0	3.7
Hungary	10.3	9.0	11.8	10.8	0.0	3.4	3.8	4.3	4.7	1.5
Iceland	20.0	23.9	20.8	21.5	22.6	23.1	23.7	23.3	24.5	25.0
Ireland	2.3	0.0	1.7	2.0	3.8	4.0	4.0	4.0	3.3	2.5
Israel[1]	1.1	0.0	0.0	0.0	0.0	0.0	0.0	0.0	0.0	-3.5
Italy	10.0	7.4	8.5	9.3	10.2	10.6	9.8	6.0	4.7	4.7
Japan	2.4	2.8	2.9	2.7	4.1	6.1	6.1	6.1	6.2	6.2
Korea	0.1	0.7	0.6	0.7	0.7	0.8	0.7	0.0	0.0	0.0
Latvia	5.4	12.5	6.0	9.0	6.8	7.3	6.9	1.9	3.2	3.4
Luxembourg	0.0	0.0	-0.8	-0.3	0.3	0.9	2.2	2.8	3.3	3.5
Mexico	-5.7	-2.7	-1.4	-0.4	0.0	0.4	1.4	1.8	2.1	2.5
Netherlands	3.0	2.2	3.5	3.5	3.5	3.3	3.4	3.1	5.8	4.5
New Zealand	18.6	18.9	17.2	15.9	14.5	14.6	14.8	14.8	14.9	15.0
Norway	13.3	14.1	14.1	14.1	14.2	14.0	14.0	13.4	13.2	12.9
Poland	2.5	2.6	0.0	0.0	0.0	0.0	0.0	0.0	0.0	0.0
Portugal	3.4	2.2	0.1	0.6	0.6	1.2	3.9	3.5	3.8	0.0
Slovak Republic	3.3	-3.7	-4.0	-3.5	-1.6	-1.7	-1.7	-1.3	-0.9	-0.4
Slovenia	3.4	0.7	1.0	0.0	0.0	0.0	0.0	0.0	0.0	0.1
Spain	0.4	2.6	0.7	1.7	2.6	3.1	3.3	3.5	-4.8	-4.6
Sweden	24.7	21.5	15.9	15.0	15.1	15.2	15.3	14.8	15.0	15.2
Switzerland	4.0	3.7	3.3	3.4	3.2	2.8	2.4	2.2	2.1	2.1
Turkey[2]	13.2	14.3	6.6	7.0	7.0	7.2	7.6	8.0	8.2	7.4
United Kingdom	8.6	5.0	-0.7	0.0	-2.3	-2.6	-3.7	-4.5	-4.0	-3.2
United States	-5.0	-7.7	-8.8	-7.4	-5.4	-4.4	-4.5	-4.0	-3.3	-2.6
Unweighted average										
OECD-Average	**7.5**	**6.8**	**5.7**	**5.8**	**5.8**	**6.1**	**6.3**	**6.0**	**6.0**	**5.6**
OECD-EU 22	**8.1**	**6.7**	**5.8**	**5.9**	**5.8**	**6.0**	**6.1**	**5.7**	**5.4**	**4.9**

1. Information on data for Israel: http://oe.cd/israel-disclaimer.
2. Wage figures are based on the old definition of average worker (ISIC D, rev3.) for years 2000 to 2006.

StatLink http://dx.doi.org/10.1787/888933461454

Table 6.4c. **Income tax plus employee contributions less cash benefits, single parent at 67% of average earnings**

Tax burden as a % of gross wage earnings, single parent with two children

	2000	2006	2009	2010	2011	2012	2013	2014	2015	2016
Australia	-2.1	-7.2	-14.0	-13.2	-12.0	-9.3	-8.6	-7.9	-7.4	-7.1
Austria	2.0	5.4	3.8	4.6	6.0	7.0	8.1	8.6	9.3	5.8
Belgium	16.1	17.3	17.6	18.9	19.1	19.0	18.4	18.3	17.8	15.8
Canada	-11.8	-11.8	-22.2	-19.6	-19.5	-19.1	-18.8	-17.2	-29.2	-28.7
Chile	2.8	3.0	3.3	6.0	6.0	6.1	6.1	6.1	6.1	6.1
Czech Republic	-17.9	-9.0	-13.1	-12.9	0.0	-1.6	-1.7	-0.8	-1.0	-0.5
Denmark	11.9	9.8	9.9	8.0	8.6	8.5	7.9	5.8	6.3	6.6
Estonia	-8.5	-9.1	-3.5	-2.1	-0.5	0.9	1.6	2.7	-4.8	-5.4
Finland	9.7	9.1	8.5	8.9	9.0	8.7	10.1	10.5	11.0	10.7
France	13.5	14.4	14.6	14.8	14.8	15.0	15.1	15.4	15.9	1.0
Germany	17.9	20.2	17.8	16.2	17.4	17.8	17.6	17.9	17.3	17.6
Greece	17.3	19.0	17.7	16.0	21.3	21.0	15.1	14.5	13.8	14.7
Hungary	5.0	-0.1	7.0	6.7	-2.5	3.2	4.2	5.4	6.5	4.0
Iceland	1.4	10.6	6.8	9.5	12.0	10.5	12.8	11.9	14.4	15.8
Ireland	-9.3	-44.5	-43.3	-41.5	-39.8	-35.0	-33.7	-32.4	-31.9	-31.5
Israel[1]	-1.5	-2.9	-2.2	-2.6	-3.4	-3.6	-3.0	-1.3	-1.6	-5.1
Italy	5.5	4.9	3.5	5.1	6.3	6.8	6.2	2.5	1.4	1.4
Japan	15.7	11.4	11.4	7.5	8.4	12.5	12.6	13.0	13.4	13.5
Korea	6.8	7.9	8.2	8.5	8.7	8.9	9.0	8.3	8.4	8.4
Latvia	3.5	14.4	9.5	12.4	12.5	13.2	13.0	7.8	7.3	7.9
Luxembourg	-6.4	-7.8	-12.0	-10.9	-8.8	-8.4	-6.5	-5.4	-4.1	-3.8
Mexico	-4.4	-1.5	-0.1	0.8	1.3	1.7	2.6	3.0	3.3	3.7
Netherlands	14.5	5.1	3.1	3.6	3.8	3.3	4.2	3.0	1.0	-2.8
New Zealand	-3.0	-15.1	-17.1	-17.7	-18.3	-18.2	-16.9	-15.8	-14.4	-13.0
Norway	5.7	8.8	10.5	10.8	11.4	11.5	11.9	11.9	12.0	11.8
Poland	18.0	24.7	17.8	17.8	17.8	17.8	17.8	17.8	17.8	17.8
Portugal	9.1	7.1	0.3	1.7	3.8	4.9	7.8	7.2	7.5	2.7
Slovak Republic	-3.1	1.0	1.0	1.5	3.5	3.5	3.4	4.1	4.6	5.2
Slovenia	-2.0	-1.1	-1.6	-1.7	-1.3	-1.0	-0.8	-4.6	-4.4	-4.0
Spain	6.8	8.9	7.0	8.1	8.9	9.5	9.6	9.8	1.5	1.8
Sweden	20.1	16.4	12.0	11.1	11.4	11.8	12.2	11.9	12.2	12.7
Switzerland	0.3	0.0	-1.3	-1.1	-0.9	-0.9	-1.3	-1.9	-2.0	-2.1
Turkey[2]	27.2	29.3	21.6	22.0	22.0	22.2	22.6	23.0	23.2	22.4
United Kingdom	7.7	6.1	-0.2	0.6	-1.8	-2.0	-3.1	-4.1	-3.5	-2.4
United States	2.6	-0.1	-1.2	0.2	0.2	1.3	3.1	3.7	4.3	5.0
Unweighted average										
OECD-Average	**4.9**	**4.1**	**2.3**	**2.8**	**3.6**	**4.2**	**4.5**	**4.4**	**3.8**	**3.0**
OECD-EU 22	**6.0**	**5.1**	**3.5**	**4.0**	**5.0**	**5.6**	**5.7**	**5.3**	**4.6**	**3.4**

1. Information on data for Israel: http://oe.cd/israel-disclaimer.
2. Wage figures are based on the old definition of average worker (ISIC D, rev3.) for years 2000 to 2006.

StatLink http://dx.doi.org/10.1787/888933461466

Table 6.5a. **Income tax plus employee and employer contributions less cash benefits, married couple at 100% of average earnings**

Tax burden as a % of labour costs, one-earner married couple with two children

	2000	2006	2009	2010	2011	2012	2013	2014	2015	2016
Australia	23.4	17.1	14.2	14.6	15.2	16.8	16.9	17.4	17.8	18.1
Austria	35.2	37.0	36.0	36.4	37.3	37.9	38.6	38.9	39.2	36.5
Belgium	42.6	40.3	40.4	41.2	41.4	41.3	40.7	40.6	40.3	38.6
Canada	23.1	21.5	16.6	17.7	18.1	18.4	18.6	19.3	11.0	11.9
Chile	6.1	6.1	6.2	6.3	7.0	7.0	7.0	7.0	7.0	7.0
Czech Republic	22.0	26.0	20.9	21.1	26.8	26.1	26.1	26.7	26.7	27.2
Denmark	28.8	27.2	26.9	25.4	25.9	26.2	25.9	25.6	25.9	26.1
Estonia	32.8	27.3	29.8	31.0	31.8	32.4	32.4	32.9	28.6	28.1
Finland	40.3	37.9	37.2	37.0	37.2	37.3	38.1	38.6	38.9	39.2
France	41.3	42.4	42.7	42.9	43.0	43.1	41.1	40.5	40.5	40.0
Germany	35.3	35.8	33.5	32.6	33.8	34.0	33.6	33.7	33.9	34.0
Greece	40.7	43.7	41.6	40.4	44.2	43.9	40.5	39.4	37.6	38.3
Hungary	43.9	41.1	43.2	36.7	33.0	34.2	34.2	34.8	35.3	33.7
Iceland	13.1	19.8	15.0	19.2	21.3	19.6	21.3	20.9	23.1	23.9
Ireland	15.5	1.9	2.8	4.7	5.6	8.0	9.3	9.7	9.3	8.3
Israel[1]	25.5	21.1	18.3	17.5	17.1	16.6	17.0	18.7	18.9	19.4
Italy	39.3	36.6	36.9	37.8	38.5	38.8	38.4	38.5	38.7	38.6
Japan	26.4	23.6	23.6	22.1	23.1	25.7	26.0	26.5	27.0	27.1
Korea	15.7	16.8	17.1	17.8	18.0	18.5	19.1	19.4	19.8	20.0
Latvia	31.4	35.7	32.5	34.8	35.0	35.4	35.1	31.9	31.4	31.7
Luxembourg	11.7	9.6	11.1	11.6	13.7	13.6	14.6	15.2	16.0	16.1
Mexico	12.7	15.1	15.3	16.0	18.7	19.0	19.3	19.5	19.8	20.1
Netherlands	29.9	29.1	29.7	30.8	31.1	32.4	35.6	34.2	31.6	32.2
New Zealand	13.6	0.5	-0.3	-0.9	-1.1	0.6	2.4	3.8	4.9	6.2
Norway	28.4	30.0	30.6	30.7	31.2	31.1	31.2	32.0	31.8	31.6
Poland	33.3	37.4	28.4	28.4	28.4	29.6	29.9	30.3	30.6	30.8
Portugal	30.2	28.3	25.4	26.3	27.3	27.9	30.2	29.8	30.7	28.2
Slovak Republic	30.8	23.0	22.8	22.9	24.9	25.8	27.6	28.1	28.5	28.9
Slovenia	25.0	24.2	22.1	22.9	23.2	23.2	23.2	23.5	23.6	23.9
Spain	32.3	33.6	32.4	34.0	34.3	34.7	34.8	34.9	33.7	33.8
Sweden	44.3	41.6	37.7	37.2	37.4	37.6	37.9	37.4	37.7	38.0
Switzerland	11.7	11.0	10.1	10.3	10.3	10.1	9.8	9.3	9.2	9.1
Turkey[2]	40.4	42.7	35.2	35.4	35.5	35.6	35.8	36.6	36.7	36.4
United Kingdom	27.8	28.0	26.2	26.5	26.4	27.5	26.8	26.4	25.8	25.8
United States	21.2	18.6	17.4	18.5	18.5	18.6	20.3	20.6	20.6	20.8
Unweighted average										
OECD-Average	**27.9**	**26.6**	**25.1**	**25.4**	**26.1**	**26.5**	**26.8**	**26.9**	**26.6**	**26.6**
OECD-EU 22	**32.5**	**31.3**	**30.0**	**30.1**	**30.9**	**31.4**	**31.6**	**31.4**	**31.1**	**30.8**

1. Information on data for Israel: http://oe.cd/israel-disclaimer.
2. Wage figures are based on the old definition of average worker (ISIC D, rev3.) for years 2000 to 2006.

StatLink http://dx.doi.org/10.1787/888933461476

Table 6.5b. **Income tax, married couple at 100% of average earnings**

Tax burden as a % of gross wage earnings, one-earner married couple with two children

	2000	2006	2009	2010	2011	2012	2013	2014	2015	2016
Australia	25.6	24.0	20.9	21.1	21.1	21.8	23.1	23.4	24.1	24.3
Austria	11.7	13.5	12.5	12.8	13.3	13.8	14.3	14.6	15.0	11.7
Belgium	18.9	16.5	17.0	17.7	17.8	17.7	17.2	17.1	16.7	15.1
Canada	15.0	11.6	8.2	8.5	8.7	8.8	8.8	8.8	10.0	10.6
Chile	0.0	0.0	0.0	0.0	0.0	0.0	0.0	0.0	0.0	0.0
Czech Republic	4.0	-2.6	-5.1	-5.3	-4.2	-5.2	-5.2	-4.5	-4.6	-4.2
Denmark	26.3	25.5	32.8	32.1	32.4	32.5	32.2	32.0	32.2	32.2
Estonia	17.9	8.7	9.2	9.2	9.9	10.5	11.3	11.8	11.2	11.0
Finland	26.9	23.8	23.0	22.3	22.2	21.8	22.5	22.6	22.5	21.9
France	7.3	7.8	8.3	8.3	8.4	8.5	7.9	7.9	7.9	7.9
Germany	1.5	1.1	0.2	-0.6	0.1	0.6	0.6	0.8	0.9	0.9
Greece	8.2	11.9	9.2	7.7	12.0	11.4	10.4	10.4	9.7	10.1
Hungary	18.4	20.9	20.8	14.4	8.5	8.2	7.8	8.1	8.4	5.9
Iceland	16.1	20.1	15.8	17.0	18.5	19.1	19.9	19.5	21.0	21.5
Ireland	7.0	3.6	5.0	6.2	7.0	8.0	7.9	8.2	7.9	6.8
Israel[1]	18.0	12.6	9.7	9.0	9.1	8.7	8.6	9.1	9.4	9.9
Italy	15.6	12.4	13.2	13.9	14.7	15.0	14.5	14.6	14.7	14.7
Japan	2.5	3.8	4.1	3.9	4.9	6.2	6.1	6.3	6.4	6.4
Korea	1.5	1.9	1.4	1.9	1.7	2.1	2.5	2.7	3.1	3.3
Latvia	11.1	15.9	10.9	13.9	11.9	12.3	11.7	8.4	8.9	9.1
Luxembourg	2.3	0.8	4.2	4.5	4.9	5.2	5.9	6.2	6.4	6.5
Mexico	1.0	3.6	4.1	4.8	7.9	8.2	8.5	8.8	9.1	9.5
Netherlands	4.8	12.8	16.3	15.9	16.2	16.8	16.5	15.7	16.7	16.4
New Zealand	19.4	20.4	18.4	17.0	15.9	16.4	16.9	17.2	17.6	17.9
Norway	18.1	18.8	19.0	19.0	19.1	18.9	18.9	19.3	19.0	18.6
Poland	4.8	4.7	0.0	0.0	0.0	0.0	0.3	0.8	1.1	1.4
Portugal	6.2	4.3	2.8	3.3	3.4	3.9	6.3	6.1	7.3	4.3
Slovak Republic	4.8	-4.8	-5.2	-5.1	-2.7	-2.7	-2.8	-2.3	-1.9	-1.5
Slovenia	4.8	2.2	2.5	2.9	3.0	2.8	2.7	2.8	2.9	3.0
Spain	5.2	7.0	5.8	7.9	8.3	8.9	9.0	9.1	7.6	7.7
Sweden	26.7	23.9	18.4	17.8	17.9	17.9	18.1	17.4	17.6	17.9
Switzerland	6.2	6.0	5.7	5.9	5.4	4.9	4.5	4.3	4.2	4.2
Turkey[2]	14.7	15.4	9.5	9.8	9.8	9.9	10.2	10.5	10.6	10.3
United Kingdom	17.4	15.9	14.5	14.6	14.0	15.4	14.6	14.3	13.5	13.4
United States	6.8	3.7	2.5	3.6	5.6	5.8	5.7	5.9	6.2	6.5
Unweighted average										
OECD-Average	**11.3**	**10.5**	**9.6**	**9.6**	**9.9**	**10.1**	**10.2**	**10.2**	**10.4**	**10.1**
OECD-EU 22	**11.4**	**10.3**	**9.8**	**9.7**	**10.0**	**10.1**	**10.2**	**10.1**	**10.1**	**9.6**

1. Information on data for Israel: http://oe.cd/israel-disclaimer.
2. Wage figures are based on the old definition of average worker (ISIC D, rev3.) for years 2000 to 2006.

StatLink http://dx.doi.org/10.1787/888933461488

Table 6.5c. **Income tax plus employee contributions less cash benefits, married couple at 100% of average earnings**

Tax burden as a % of gross wage earnings, one-earner married couple with two children

	2000	2006	2009	2010	2011	2012	2013	2014	2015	2016
Australia	18.4	12.1	8.7	9.3	10.1	11.9	12.0	12.4	12.9	13.2
Austria	15.1	18.7	17.4	17.9	19.0	19.8	20.7	21.1	21.0	18.2
Belgium	23.7	22.1	22.4	23.6	23.7	23.6	23.0	22.9	22.6	20.9
Canada	14.2	12.3	7.0	8.2	8.5	8.7	8.8	9.6	0.2	1.2
Chile	6.1	6.1	6.2	6.3	7.0	7.0	7.0	7.0	7.0	7.0
Czech Republic	-5.3	0.0	-6.0	-5.7	1.9	1.0	0.9	1.8	1.8	2.4
Denmark	28.6	26.8	26.4	24.9	25.3	25.5	25.1	24.9	25.3	25.5
Estonia	10.6	3.1	6.1	7.3	8.3	9.1	9.4	10.0	4.5	3.8
Finland	24.8	23.1	22.7	23.0	23.1	23.0	23.9	24.4	25.2	25.2
France	16.1	17.1	17.6	17.7	17.8	18.0	17.5	17.7	17.9	18.1
Germany	22.0	22.6	20.6	19.6	20.8	21.0	20.8	20.9	21.1	21.3
Greece	24.1	27.9	25.2	23.7	28.2	27.9	24.1	23.6	22.3	23.0
Hungary	20.5	20.7	24.7	18.7	14.0	15.4	15.4	16.2	16.9	14.8
Iceland	8.9	15.2	9.7	12.2	14.5	13.3	15.2	14.9	17.4	18.3
Ireland	5.4	-8.7	-7.6	-5.5	-4.5	-1.8	-0.4	0.0	-0.4	-1.6
Israel[1]	21.8	16.9	14.5	13.6	13.2	12.6	12.9	14.5	14.5	14.9
Italy	18.6	16.2	16.7	17.8	18.8	19.1	18.6	18.8	19.1	19.1
Japan	15.8	13.6	13.8	11.3	12.2	15.0	15.1	15.6	16.0	16.1
Korea	8.2	9.1	9.0	9.7	9.8	10.3	10.8	11.1	11.5	11.7
Latvia	12.8	20.2	16.2	19.1	19.3	19.8	19.4	15.8	15.2	15.5
Luxembourg	1.9	-0.6	0.8	1.5	3.1	3.0	4.1	4.8	5.7	5.9
Mexico	2.5	5.0	5.4	6.1	9.2	9.6	9.8	10.1	10.4	10.8
Netherlands	22.4	22.3	22.6	23.6	24.0	25.1	29.3	27.1	24.3	24.6
New Zealand	13.6	0.5	-0.3	-0.9	-1.1	0.6	2.4	3.8	4.9	6.2
Norway	19.3	20.7	21.7	21.8	22.2	22.1	22.3	23.2	23.0	22.7
Poland	22.1	26.9	17.8	17.8	17.8	17.8	18.1	18.6	18.9	19.2
Portugal	13.6	11.2	7.7	8.8	10.1	10.8	13.7	13.1	14.3	11.2
Slovak Republic	4.4	2.8	2.5	2.6	5.2	5.1	5.0	5.6	6.2	6.7
Slovenia	10.1	9.8	9.6	10.4	10.8	10.8	10.8	11.2	11.3	11.6
Spain	11.5	13.3	12.2	14.2	14.7	15.2	15.3	15.4	13.9	14.1
Sweden	26.0	22.8	18.1	17.4	17.7	17.9	18.3	17.8	18.1	18.5
Switzerland	5.9	5.6	4.6	4.9	4.7	4.5	4.1	3.6	3.5	3.4
Turkey[2]	28.7	30.4	24.5	24.8	24.8	24.9	25.2	25.5	25.6	25.3
United Kingdom	20.6	20.3	18.4	18.7	18.3	19.7	19.0	18.5	17.8	17.8
United States	14.4	11.4	10.1	11.2	11.2	11.4	13.3	13.6	13.9	14.1
Unweighted average										
OECD-Average	**15.1**	**14.2**	**12.8**	**13.0**	**13.8**	**14.2**	**14.6**	**14.7**	**14.4**	**14.3**
OECD-EU 22	**15.9**	**15.4**	**14.2**	**14.4**	**15.3**	**15.8**	**16.0**	**15.9**	**15.6**	**15.3**

1. Information on data for Israel: http://oe.cd/israel-disclaimer.
2. Wage figures are based on the old definition of average worker (ISIC D, rev3.) for years 2000 to 2006.

StatLink http://dx.doi.org/10.1787/888933461497

Table 6.6a. **Income tax plus employee and employer contributions less cash benefits, married couple with two children, at 100% and 33% of average earnings**

Tax burden as a % of labour costs, two-earner married couple with two children

	2000	2006	2009	2010	2011	2012	2013	2014	2015	2016
Australia	24.6	20.5	18.0	18.0	17.9	18.8	19.9	20.9	22.7	24.4
Austria	36.3	37.8	36.4	36.7	37.4	37.8	38.3	38.5	38.5	36.3
Belgium	44.3	41.2	41.5	42.2	42.4	42.4	41.9	41.7	41.3	38.8
Canada	26.9	25.4	23.0	23.2	23.4	23.7	24.0	24.2	19.9	20.5
Chile	4.8	4.9	4.5	4.8	4.8	4.8	4.8	4.7	4.7	4.6
Czech Republic	31.0	33.5	30.2	30.3	33.2	32.6	32.5	32.9	32.8	33.0
Denmark	33.1	31.2	30.8	29.5	29.9	30.1	29.8	29.5	29.8	29.8
Estonia	35.6	31.1	33.1	34.1	34.5	35.0	34.8	35.2	31.7	31.5
Finland	39.3	36.4	35.2	35.0	35.0	34.9	35.6	36.1	36.0	36.1
France	40.5	40.0	40.4	40.6	40.7	41.0	39.4	37.5	37.8	37.5
Germany	41.2	41.0	38.9	37.7	38.6	38.7	38.3	38.5	38.6	38.8
Greece	39.1	41.4	39.8	38.9	42.4	42.2	39.8	38.7	37.1	37.8
Hungary	44.8	40.2	42.1	36.4	34.4	35.4	36.2	38.3	38.7	37.3
Iceland	20.2	26.0	22.5	26.2	27.7	26.9	28.0	27.7	29.1	29.6
Ireland	20.3	8.6	8.7	10.6	12.3	13.4	14.4	14.6	13.9	13.4
Israel[1]	21.7	17.9	15.5	14.9	13.5	13.0	13.2	15.8	15.9	16.3
Italy	41.1	39.1	38.9	39.6	40.2	40.5	40.3	38.9	38.5	38.4
Japan	27.7	24.8	24.9	24.0	25.1	27.2	27.5	28.0	28.4	28.5
Korea	15.3	16.6	17.1	17.8	18.0	18.6	19.0	19.2	19.5	19.6
Latvia	32.8	36.3	33.3	36.3	36.3	36.6	36.3	33.7	33.3	33.6
Luxembourg	15.8	14.3	15.4	15.9	18.0	17.9	19.0	19.6	20.5	20.5
Mexico	9.8	12.8	13.5	14.1	16.3	16.7	17.0	17.3	17.6	18.0
Netherlands	34.3	29.6	29.2	29.5	29.5	29.8	32.5	30.9	28.6	27.9
New Zealand	18.5	9.5	8.0	7.4	7.0	8.6	10.0	11.1	12.0	13.0
Norway	30.8	31.3	31.5	31.6	32.0	31.8	31.7	31.3	31.1	30.8
Poland	34.6	37.8	28.9	29.3	29.7	31.1	31.3	31.7	31.9	32.1
Portugal	30.6	29.5	27.7	28.2	28.4	28.9	31.2	30.8	31.1	29.8
Slovak Republic	35.1	28.8	26.7	27.2	29.4	30.3	33.0	33.4	31.7	31.9
Slovenia	33.7	32.2	30.0	30.4	30.6	30.6	30.5	30.7	30.8	30.9
Spain	35.0	35.5	34.6	35.7	35.9	36.4	36.4	36.5	35.5	35.6
Sweden	44.7	41.6	37.3	36.8	36.9	37.1	37.4	36.9	37.1	37.4
Switzerland	14.6	13.7	13.1	13.3	13.3	13.1	12.8	12.3	12.2	12.1
Turkey[2]	39.7	42.3	34.1	34.3	34.4	34.4	34.7	35.4	35.5	35.0
United Kingdom	25.5	26.0	24.4	24.7	24.8	24.4	23.3	22.6	22.4	22.4
United States	25.0	23.0	22.6	23.0	22.6	22.7	24.3	24.6	24.4	24.5
Unweighted average										
OECD-Average	**29.9**	**28.6**	**27.2**	**27.4**	**27.9**	**28.2**	**28.5**	**28.6**	**28.3**	**28.2**
OECD-EU 22	**34.9**	**33.3**	**32.0**	**32.1**	**32.8**	**33.0**	**33.3**	**33.1**	**32.6**	**32.3**

1. Information on data for Israel: http://oe.cd/israel-disclaimer.
2. Wage figures are based on the old definition of average worker (ISIC D, rev3.) for years 2000 to 2006.

StatLink http://dx.doi.org/10.1787/888933461501

Table 6.6b. Income tax, married couple with two children, at 100% and 33% of average earnings

Tax burden as a % of gross wage earnings, two-earner married couple with two children

	2000	2006	2009	2010	2011	2012	2013	2014	2015	2016
Australia	22.0	20.6	17.3	17.4	17.4	18.1	18.7	19.0	19.7	19.9
Austria	9.4	11.3	10.5	10.7	11.1	11.4	11.7	12.0	12.1	9.2
Belgium	24.0	21.9	22.3	22.9	22.8	22.6	22.1	21.9	21.4	19.3
Canada	16.3	13.5	11.0	11.1	11.2	11.2	11.2	11.1	12.0	12.5
Chile	0.0	0.0	0.0	0.0	0.0	0.0	0.0	0.0	0.0	0.0
Czech Republic	5.2	2.7	2.8	2.5	3.2	2.3	2.2	2.6	2.4	2.5
Denmark	28.8	27.6	34.9	34.1	34.3	34.4	34.1	33.9	34.0	34.1
Estonia	19.9	12.2	12.0	12.0	12.5	13.0	13.6	13.9	13.3	13.1
Finland	23.4	20.1	19.1	18.4	18.2	17.4	18.2	18.2	17.8	16.9
France	8.9	7.2	7.7	7.8	7.9	8.3	8.3	6.6	7.9	7.9
Germany	8.6	7.5	6.7	5.4	5.9	6.3	6.3	6.4	6.5	6.5
Greece	6.2	8.9	6.9	5.8	9.8	9.2	7.8	7.8	7.3	7.6
Hungary	15.8	15.7	15.9	10.8	7.3	10.1	9.9	10.1	10.3	8.2
Iceland	19.9	23.9	20.7	21.7	22.8	23.2	23.8	23.6	24.7	25.0
Ireland	12.6	5.8	6.4	7.5	8.8	9.6	9.6	9.8	9.1	8.7
Israel[1]	13.5	9.4	7.3	6.8	5.8	5.4	5.0	6.9	7.1	7.4
Italy	14.2	11.8	12.4	13.2	13.9	14.2	14.0	12.1	11.5	11.5
Japan	3.9	4.5	4.9	4.7	5.6	6.7	6.6	6.8	6.8	6.9
Korea	1.1	1.8	1.5	1.9	1.7	2.2	2.5	2.5	2.8	2.9
Latvia	11.1	15.4	10.9	14.7	12.6	12.9	12.4	9.8	10.2	10.4
Luxembourg	3.8	2.7	5.2	5.6	6.0	6.4	7.4	7.8	8.1	8.2
Mexico	-4.0	-0.8	0.0	0.7	3.2	3.6	4.0	4.4	4.7	5.2
Netherlands	7.8	10.1	12.6	12.3	12.4	12.8	13.0	12.3	13.2	12.7
New Zealand	18.5	19.5	17.2	15.9	14.8	15.2	15.7	16.0	16.2	16.5
Norway	19.1	18.7	18.7	18.7	18.8	18.5	18.4	17.4	17.1	16.7
Poland	5.3	5.2	0.6	1.0	1.4	1.7	2.0	2.4	2.6	2.8
Portugal	5.7	4.6	2.9	3.3	3.3	3.9	6.5	6.2	6.5	4.9
Slovak Republic	4.6	1.1	-1.7	-1.0	1.6	1.7	2.9	3.3	3.7	3.9
Slovenia	6.8	4.3	3.6	3.8	3.8	3.7	3.7	3.7	3.8	3.9
Spain	8.7	9.4	8.7	10.2	10.4	11.0	11.1	11.1	9.8	9.9
Sweden	25.3	21.8	16.1	15.4	15.5	15.6	15.8	15.1	15.3	15.6
Switzerland	7.6	7.3	7.1	7.3	6.8	6.5	6.1	5.8	5.7	5.7
Turkey[2]	14.0	14.9	8.2	8.5	8.5	8.6	8.9	9.1	9.3	8.6
United Kingdom	15.1	14.2	12.9	13.1	13.4	13.0	11.9	11.4	11.1	11.0
United States	10.5	8.1	7.7	8.1	9.6	9.7	9.6	9.8	10.0	10.2
Unweighted average										
OECD-Average	**11.8**	**10.9**	**10.0**	**10.1**	**10.4**	**10.6**	**10.7**	**10.6**	**10.7**	**10.5**
OECD-EU 22	**12.3**	**11.0**	**10.4**	**10.4**	**10.7**	**11.0**	**11.1**	**10.8**	**10.8**	**10.4**

1. Information on data for Israel: http://oe.cd/israel-disclaimer.
2. Wage figures are based on the old definition of average worker (ISIC D, rev3.) for years 2000 to 2006.

StatLink http://dx.doi.org/10.1787/888933461517

Table 6.6c. Income tax plus employee contributions less cash benefits, married couple with two children, at 100% and 33% of average earnings

Tax burden as a % of gross wage earnings, two-earner married couple with two children

	2000	2006	2009	2010	2011	2012	2013	2014	2015	2016
Australia	19.8	15.7	12.7	12.9	13.0	13.9	15.1	16.1	18.1	19.9
Austria	16.5	19.7	17.9	18.3	19.1	19.7	20.3	20.6	20.8	17.8
Belgium	29.3	26.5	26.6	27.5	27.5	27.4	26.8	26.6	26.1	24.0
Canada	18.6	16.8	14.2	14.4	14.6	14.8	14.9	15.2	10.3	11.0
Chile	4.8	4.9	4.5	4.8	4.8	4.8	4.8	4.7	4.7	4.6
Czech Republic	6.9	10.2	6.5	6.6	10.5	9.6	9.6	10.1	9.9	10.2
Denmark	32.7	30.6	30.2	28.7	29.0	29.2	28.7	28.5	28.8	29.0
Estonia	14.4	8.1	10.1	11.2	12.0	12.6	12.7	13.1	8.7	8.1
Finland	23.5	21.1	20.3	20.4	20.4	20.1	20.9	21.4	21.6	21.3
France	18.8	17.6	18.1	18.2	18.4	18.8	19.0	17.5	19.0	19.1
Germany	29.1	28.9	27.1	25.7	26.5	26.7	26.4	26.6	26.8	26.9
Greece	22.1	24.9	22.9	21.8	26.0	25.7	23.3	22.8	21.7	22.3
Hungary	20.5	19.1	23.0	18.3	15.8	20.2	20.2	20.7	21.2	19.4
Iceland	16.4	21.7	17.8	19.9	21.4	21.2	22.4	22.2	23.8	24.4
Ireland	11.4	-0.7	-0.6	1.5	3.4	4.6	5.6	5.9	5.1	4.6
Israel[1]	17.8	13.6	11.8	11.1	9.7	9.2	9.2	11.8	11.8	12.1
Italy	21.0	19.6	19.3	20.2	21.0	21.4	21.1	19.3	18.7	18.7
Japan	17.3	14.9	15.2	13.5	14.5	16.7	16.8	17.3	17.6	17.7
Korea	7.8	9.0	9.1	9.7	9.8	10.3	10.7	10.8	11.1	11.3
Latvia	14.6	20.9	17.1	20.9	20.9	21.3	20.9	18.0	17.5	17.9
Luxembourg	6.3	4.6	5.6	6.3	7.9	7.8	9.1	9.7	10.7	10.9
Mexico	-2.6	0.6	1.4	2.0	4.5	4.9	5.3	5.7	6.1	6.5
Netherlands	26.6	23.2	22.5	22.6	22.7	22.7	25.9	23.4	21.0	19.8
New Zealand	18.5	9.5	8.0	7.4	7.0	8.6	10.0	11.1	12.0	13.0
Norway	21.9	22.1	22.7	22.8	23.0	22.8	22.8	22.3	22.2	21.8
Poland	23.6	27.4	18.4	18.8	19.3	19.5	19.8	20.2	20.5	20.7
Portugal	14.1	12.8	10.5	11.2	11.4	12.1	14.8	14.4	14.7	13.1
Slovak Republic	10.4	10.2	7.5	8.1	10.9	10.9	12.1	12.6	12.1	12.4
Slovenia	21.2	19.7	18.8	19.2	19.4	19.4	19.3	19.5	19.6	19.7
Spain	15.1	15.7	15.0	16.5	16.8	17.4	17.4	17.5	16.2	16.3
Sweden	26.5	22.7	17.6	16.9	17.1	17.3	17.7	17.1	17.4	17.8
Switzerland	9.0	8.5	7.8	8.0	7.8	7.7	7.4	6.9	6.7	6.6
Turkey[2]	28.0	29.9	23.2	23.5	23.5	23.6	23.9	24.1	24.3	23.6
United Kingdom	18.8	18.9	17.2	17.5	17.7	17.3	16.2	15.5	15.3	15.3
United States	18.2	15.7	15.3	15.7	15.2	15.4	17.3	17.5	17.7	17.9
Unweighted average										
OECD-Average	**17.7**	**16.7**	**15.3**	**15.5**	**16.1**	**16.4**	**16.8**	**16.8**	**16.6**	**16.4**
OECD-EU 22	**19.2**	**18.3**	**16.9**	**17.1**	**17.9**	**18.2**	**18.5**	**18.2**	**17.9**	**17.5**

1. Information on data for Israel: http://oe.cd/israel-disclaimer.
2. Wage figures are based on the old definition of average worker (ISIC D, rev3.) for years 2000 to 2006.

StatLink http://dx.doi.org/10.1787/888933461523

Table 6.7a. Income tax plus employee and employer contributions less cash benefits, married couple at 100% and 67% of average earnings

Tax burden as a % of labour costs, two-earner married couple with two children

	2000	2006	2009	2010	2011	2012	2013	2014	2015	2016
Australia	26.7	23.9	22.4	23.8	24.3	25.0	25.2	25.5	26.3	26.5
Austria	39.0	40.6	39.7	40.1	40.7	41.2	41.7	42.0	42.2	39.6
Belgium	50.9	48.3	48.3	48.9	49.1	49.0	48.5	48.4	48.1	46.4
Canada	29.7	28.6	26.6	26.5	26.8	27.0	27.2	27.3	24.3	24.7
Chile	5.3	5.4	5.5	6.6	6.6	6.6	6.6	6.6	6.6	6.6
Czech Republic	36.3	37.8	34.2	34.3	35.5	35.1	35.1	35.5	35.5	35.8
Denmark	36.5	33.5	32.9	31.7	32.0	32.1	31.8	31.6	31.8	31.9
Estonia	37.4	33.4	34.7	35.8	36.2	36.6	36.3	36.6	33.7	33.3
Finland	41.3	38.3	37.2	37.0	37.0	37.1	37.9	38.4	38.4	38.6
France	43.3	44.7	45.1	45.3	45.4	45.5	44.1	43.6	43.0	42.6
Germany	45.4	45.0	43.0	41.4	42.3	42.4	42.0	42.1	42.2	42.4
Greece	39.4	42.0	40.5	39.3	43.0	42.8	40.4	39.3	37.7	38.3
Hungary	47.0	42.0	44.4	39.6	37.9	39.6	40.1	40.5	40.8	39.5
Iceland	25.4	29.7	26.9	30.4	31.6	30.9	31.8	31.6	32.6	32.6
Ireland	21.8	13.8	14.6	16.2	17.8	18.8	19.9	20.2	19.7	19.1
Israel[1]	21.6	16.8	14.8	14.4	14.1	13.8	14.1	15.1	15.3	15.7
Italy	44.2	41.9	41.9	42.5	43.0	43.2	43.1	41.9	41.6	41.5
Japan	28.2	25.7	25.9	25.4	26.4	28.2	28.5	28.9	29.3	29.4
Korea	15.5	16.7	17.3	17.9	18.2	18.6	19.1	19.3	19.6	19.8
Latvia	35.5	38.1	35.4	38.2	38.3	38.6	38.2	36.0	35.5	35.7
Luxembourg	21.4	19.8	20.8	21.4	23.4	23.4	24.7	25.3	26.2	26.3
Mexico	10.6	13.3	14.0	14.7	16.5	16.8	17.3	17.6	17.9	18.2
Netherlands	38.1	32.8	31.7	31.9	31.8	32.1	33.7	32.5	30.8	29.8
New Zealand	19.0	15.9	14.7	13.9	13.2	14.7	15.9	16.3	16.5	16.7
Norway	33.0	33.1	33.3	33.4	33.7	33.7	33.7	33.4	33.2	32.8
Poland	37.7	38.5	30.4	30.7	31.0	32.3	32.5	32.8	33.0	33.1
Portugal	33.0	33.3	31.2	32.5	34.3	34.5	37.0	36.7	35.6	35.9
Slovak Republic	36.9	31.6	31.2	31.5	32.7	33.6	35.2	35.5	35.7	36.0
Slovenia	37.1	35.9	34.2	34.0	34.1	34.3	34.4	34.5	34.6	34.3
Spain	35.4	36.3	34.9	36.7	37.0	37.5	37.6	37.6	36.3	36.4
Sweden	46.0	43.3	39.1	38.6	38.7	38.8	39.1	38.7	38.8	39.1
Switzerland	17.7	16.8	16.2	16.4	16.4	16.3	16.0	15.5	15.4	15.2
Turkey[2]	39.9	42.3	35.1	35.4	35.4	35.6	35.8	36.6	36.7	36.4
United Kingdom	28.4	29.4	28.0	28.4	28.1	27.7	26.8	26.3	26.2	26.2
United States	26.9	25.2	24.9	25.3	24.6	24.7	26.3	26.6	26.4	26.5
Unweighted average										
OECD-Average	**32.3**	**31.3**	**30.0**	**30.3**	**30.8**	**31.1**	**31.4**	**31.3**	**31.1**	**30.9**
OECD-EU 22	**37.8**	**36.4**	**35.2**	**35.3**	**35.9**	**36.2**	**36.4**	**36.2**	**35.8**	**35.5**

1. Information on data for Israel: http://oe.cd/israel-disclaimer.
2. Wage figures are based on the old definition of average worker (ISIC D, rev3.) for years 2000 to 2006.

StatLink http://dx.doi.org/10.1787/888933461536

Table 6.7b. **Income tax, married couple at 100% and 67% of average earnings**

Tax burden as a % of gross wage earnings, two-earner married couple with two children

	2000	2006	2009	2010	2011	2012	2013	2014	2015	2016
Australia	23.8	22.5	18.8	19.1	19.7	20.6	20.8	21.1	21.9	22.1
Austria	10.8	13.0	12.0	12.3	12.8	13.2	13.6	14.0	14.3	11.1
Belgium	26.4	23.9	24.2	24.8	24.9	24.7	24.4	24.3	23.9	22.4
Canada	17.5	15.0	13.0	12.8	12.9	13.0	13.0	12.8	13.6	13.9
Chile	0.0	0.0	0.0	0.0	0.0	0.0	0.0	0.0	0.0	0.0
Czech Republic	6.8	5.5	5.0	4.9	5.6	5.0	4.9	5.4	5.3	5.6
Denmark	31.3	29.0	36.2	35.4	35.5	35.6	35.2	35.0	35.2	35.2
Estonia	21.1	14.4	13.8	13.7	14.1	14.5	15.0	15.3	14.6	14.5
Finland	24.5	21.3	20.4	19.7	19.5	19.0	19.9	19.9	19.7	19.0
France	10.8	10.6	11.1	11.1	11.2	11.4	11.5	11.5	11.3	11.0
Germany	13.8	12.2	11.6	9.9	10.3	10.6	10.6	10.8	10.9	10.8
Greece	6.5	9.7	7.8	6.3	10.5	9.9	8.4	8.4	7.8	8.1
Hungary	18.0	16.1	17.2	13.0	10.0	11.3	11.1	11.3	11.5	9.6
Iceland	23.2	26.2	23.8	24.8	25.8	26.1	26.6	26.3	27.2	27.3
Ireland	14.5	8.7	9.9	10.8	12.2	12.9	12.9	13.0	12.6	12.0
Israel[1]	12.5	7.5	5.8	5.4	5.5	5.2	5.1	5.5	5.6	5.9
Italy	16.8	14.8	15.7	16.3	17.0	17.3	17.0	15.5	15.0	15.0
Japan	4.5	5.2	5.6	5.5	6.2	7.0	7.0	7.1	7.1	7.2
Korea	1.3	1.8	1.6	2.0	1.9	2.2	2.5	2.6	2.9	3.1
Latvia	13.5	16.9	12.9	16.5	14.5	14.8	14.2	12.2	12.3	12.5
Luxembourg	8.2	6.9	8.8	9.3	9.8	10.3	11.6	12.1	12.4	12.5
Mexico	-1.7	1.1	1.9	2.7	4.7	5.1	5.6	6.0	6.3	6.7
Netherlands	7.9	9.6	11.9	11.7	11.8	12.1	12.0	11.4	12.7	11.9
New Zealand	19.0	19.8	17.9	16.5	15.3	15.7	16.0	16.3	16.5	16.7
Norway	20.6	19.9	20.0	20.0	20.1	19.9	20.0	19.1	18.8	18.4
Poland	6.1	6.0	2.3	2.6	2.9	3.2	3.4	3.7	3.9	4.1
Portugal	8.1	8.5	6.5	7.3	7.7	7.9	11.0	10.7	9.3	9.7
Slovak Republic	5.8	3.7	3.2	3.5	5.0	5.0	4.9	5.2	5.5	5.7
Slovenia	8.1	6.0	6.0	5.7	5.7	5.6	5.5	5.6	5.7	5.8
Spain	9.3	10.5	9.1	11.5	11.8	12.5	12.6	12.7	10.9	11.0
Sweden	25.9	22.9	17.4	16.7	16.8	16.8	17.0	16.4	16.5	16.8
Switzerland	9.8	9.6	9.4	9.5	9.1	8.8	8.5	8.1	8.0	7.9
Turkey[2]	14.1	14.9	9.4	9.7	9.8	9.9	10.2	10.5	10.7	10.3
United Kingdom	16.5	16.1	15.1	15.4	14.7	14.4	13.6	13.2	12.9	12.8
United States	12.8	10.8	10.5	10.9	12.0	12.2	12.1	12.2	12.4	12.5
Unweighted average										
OECD-Average	**13.4**	**12.6**	**11.9**	**11.9**	**12.2**	**12.4**	**12.5**	**12.4**	**12.4**	**12.3**
OECD-EU 22	**14.1**	**13.0**	**12.6**	**12.6**	**12.9**	**13.1**	**13.2**	**13.1**	**12.9**	**12.6**

1. Information on data for Israel: http://oe.cd/israel-disclaimer.
2. Wage figures are based on the old definition of average worker (ISIC D, rev3.) for years 2000 to 2006.

StatLink http://dx.doi.org/10.1787/888933461541

Table 6.7c. **Income tax plus employee contributions less cash benefits, married couple at 100% and 67% of average earnings**

Tax burden as a % of gross wage earnings, two-earner married couple with two children

	2000	2006	2009	2010	2011	2012	2013	2014	2015	2016
Australia	22.0	19.4	17.4	19.0	19.7	20.6	20.8	21.1	21.9	22.1
Austria	20.1	23.3	22.2	22.6	23.4	24.0	24.7	25.1	25.5	22.2
Belgium	35.0	32.9	33.1	33.9	34.1	33.9	33.5	33.5	33.1	31.5
Canada	21.6	20.3	18.1	18.1	18.2	18.4	18.5	18.6	15.1	15.6
Chile	5.3	5.4	5.5	6.6	6.6	6.6	6.6	6.6	6.6	6.6
Czech Republic	14.0	16.0	11.8	12.0	13.6	13.1	13.0	13.5	13.6	13.9
Denmark	36.3	33.0	32.5	31.0	31.3	31.4	31.0	30.8	31.1	31.2
Estonia	16.8	11.3	12.6	13.7	14.3	14.8	14.7	15.1	11.2	10.8
Finland	26.0	23.5	22.7	22.9	22.9	22.8	23.7	24.2	24.6	24.4
France	21.4	21.7	22.2	22.2	22.4	22.6	22.8	23.1	23.0	22.9
Germany	34.3	33.7	31.9	30.1	30.9	31.1	30.8	31.0	31.1	31.2
Greece	22.4	25.7	23.8	22.3	26.7	26.4	24.1	23.6	22.4	23.0
Hungary	24.3	21.8	26.3	22.3	20.2	23.1	23.1	23.5	23.9	22.3
Iceland	21.9	25.6	22.4	24.4	25.7	25.6	26.5	26.4	27.6	27.7
Ireland	13.6	4.6	5.4	7.2	9.0	10.0	11.3	11.6	11.1	10.4
Israel[1]	17.7	12.4	11.1	10.5	10.3	9.9	10.0	11.0	11.1	11.3
Italy	25.1	23.3	23.3	24.0	24.8	25.0	24.8	23.3	22.8	22.8
Japan	17.9	15.9	16.3	15.1	16.0	17.8	17.9	18.3	18.6	18.7
Korea	8.0	9.0	9.3	9.8	9.9	10.4	10.8	11.0	11.3	11.5
Latvia	18.1	23.1	19.7	23.3	23.4	23.7	23.3	20.8	20.3	20.6
Luxembourg	12.6	10.8	11.6	12.3	14.0	13.9	15.5	16.1	17.1	17.3
Mexico	-0.3	2.4	3.2	4.0	6.1	6.4	6.9	7.3	7.6	8.0
Netherlands	30.1	26.5	25.0	24.9	25.0	25.0	27.2	25.2	23.4	21.9
New Zealand	19.0	15.9	14.7	13.9	13.2	14.7	15.9	16.3	16.5	16.7
Norway	24.4	24.2	24.8	24.8	25.1	25.0	25.1	24.7	24.5	24.1
Poland	27.3	28.2	20.1	20.4	20.8	21.0	21.2	21.5	21.7	21.9
Portugal	17.0	17.5	14.9	16.5	18.7	18.9	22.0	21.7	20.3	20.7
Slovak Republic	12.9	13.7	13.2	13.6	15.1	15.1	15.0	15.4	15.7	16.0
Slovenia	25.1	23.7	23.6	23.4	23.5	23.7	23.8	24.0	24.1	23.8
Spain	15.6	16.9	15.5	17.8	18.2	18.9	18.9	19.0	17.2	17.4
Sweden	28.3	25.1	20.0	19.3	19.5	19.6	19.9	19.4	19.6	20.0
Switzerland	12.3	11.7	11.1	11.3	11.2	11.0	10.7	10.2	10.1	10.0
Turkey[2]	28.1	29.9	24.4	24.7	24.8	24.9	25.2	25.5	25.7	25.3
United Kingdom	21.5	22.1	20.7	21.1	20.6	20.3	19.4	18.9	18.7	18.7
United States	20.5	18.4	18.2	18.5	17.7	17.8	19.7	19.9	20.1	20.2
Unweighted average										
OECD-Average	**20.5**	**19.7**	**18.5**	**18.8**	**19.3**	**19.6**	**20.0**	**19.9**	**19.7**	**19.5**
OECD-EU 22	**22.6**	**21.7**	**20.6**	**20.8**	**21.5**	**21.7**	**22.0**	**21.8**	**21.4**	**21.1**

1. Information on data for Israel: http://oe.cd/israel-disclaimer.
2. Wage figures are based on the old definition of average worker (ISIC D, rev3.) for years 2000 to 2006.

StatLink http://dx.doi.org/10.1787/888933461558

Table 6.8a. **Income tax plus employee and employer contributions less cash benefits, married couple at 100% and 33% of average earnings**

Tax burden as a % of labour costs, two-earner married couple without children

	2000	2006	2009	2010	2011	2012	2013	2014	2015	2016
Australia	27.4	25.1	23.1	23.1	22.9	23.5	23.2	23.5	24.2	24.4
Austria	44.7	45.3	44.4	44.5	44.8	45.1	45.3	45.5	45.5	43.4
Belgium	51.2	47.8	48.1	48.5	48.7	48.7	48.2	48.1	47.6	45.2
Canada	30.0	28.7	27.3	27.2	27.5	27.7	27.8	28.4	28.4	28.3
Chile	7.0	7.0	7.0	7.0	7.0	7.0	7.0	7.0	7.0	7.0
Czech Republic	41.3	40.9	39.9	40.0	40.4	40.3	40.2	40.4	40.5	40.6
Denmark	38.1	36.2	35.5	34.4	34.6	34.8	34.5	34.3	34.5	34.5
Estonia	39.8	37.2	38.0	38.8	39.0	39.2	38.8	38.9	38.0	38.0
Finland	44.7	41.0	39.2	38.9	38.9	38.8	39.4	39.9	39.6	39.6
France	45.3	44.4	46.1	46.1	46.2	46.4	44.9	44.4	43.7	42.7
Germany	47.5	47.4	45.9	44.8	45.5	45.4	45.0	45.0	45.1	45.2
Greece	38.9	41.1	40.2	39.4	42.7	42.5	40.6	39.6	38.0	38.9
Hungary	52.7	48.3	49.5	43.8	46.8	47.4	47.7	49.0	49.0	48.2
Iceland	23.7	28.2	26.0	28.6	29.6	29.4	29.9	29.5	30.4	30.6
Ireland	23.5	16.7	17.3	18.2	19.4	20.2	20.7	20.9	20.2	19.9
Israel[1]	24.8	20.3	17.7	17.4	17.3	17.0	17.0	17.6	17.9	18.4
Italy	44.0	42.7	43.4	43.9	44.4	44.6	44.8	43.3	42.8	42.7
Japan	29.1	28.0	28.3	29.4	30.0	30.4	30.7	31.1	31.5	31.6
Korea	15.8	17.4	18.6	19.2	19.6	20.0	20.4	20.5	20.8	20.9
Latvia	41.7	41.6	39.6	43.2	43.2	43.3	42.8	42.0	41.6	41.8
Luxembourg	27.4	26.0	25.9	26.2	27.9	27.6	28.4	28.8	29.5	29.5
Mexico	9.8	12.8	13.5	14.1	16.3	16.7	17.0	17.3	17.6	18.0
Netherlands	38.0	34.1	33.9	34.2	34.1	34.6	37.2	35.4	33.2	32.8
New Zealand	18.5	19.5	16.9	15.9	14.8	15.2	15.7	16.0	16.2	16.5
Norway	36.0	35.1	34.9	34.8	35.1	34.8	34.7	34.1	33.9	33.5
Poland	37.0	37.8	33.1	33.3	33.4	34.7	34.7	34.9	35.0	35.1
Portugal	33.8	33.0	31.8	32.2	32.2	32.6	35.0	34.7	36.1	36.2
Slovak Republic	40.7	35.7	33.1	33.6	35.7	36.6	39.1	39.3	37.6	37.7
Slovenia	44.5	43.0	39.9	40.1	40.2	40.1	40.0	40.1	40.2	40.2
Spain	36.1	36.4	35.7	36.8	37.0	37.5	37.5	37.5	36.5	36.6
Sweden	49.1	46.2	41.5	41.0	41.0	41.1	41.3	40.7	40.9	41.1
Switzerland	20.8	20.1	19.7	19.8	20.1	19.9	19.9	19.7	19.6	19.6
Turkey[2]	39.7	42.3	34.8	35.0	35.1	35.1	35.4	36.1	36.2	35.8
United Kingdom	29.1	30.6	29.1	29.3	28.4	27.8	26.7	26.1	25.8	25.8
United States	29.5	28.8	28.0	28.3	27.8	27.7	29.3	29.5	29.2	29.2
Unweighted average										
OECD-Average	**34.3**	**33.3**	**32.2**	**32.3**	**32.8**	**33.0**	**33.2**	**33.1**	**33.0**	**32.8**
OECD-EU 22	**40.4**	**38.8**	**37.8**	**37.8**	**38.4**	**38.6**	**38.8**	**38.6**	**38.2**	**38.0**

1. Information on data for Israel: http://oe.cd/israel-disclaimer.
2. Wage figures are based on the old definition of average worker (ISIC D, rev3.) for years 2000 to 2006.

StatLink http://dx.doi.org/10.1787/888933461561

Table 6.8b. **Income tax, married couple at 100% and 33% of average earnings**

Tax burden as a % of gross wage earnings, two-earner married couple without children

	2000	2006	2009	2010	2011	2012	2013	2014	2015	2016
Australia	22.8	20.6	18.2	18.3	18.3	18.9	18.7	19.0	19.7	19.9
Austria	9.4	11.3	10.9	11.1	11.4	11.7	12.1	12.3	12.4	9.8
Belgium	25.9	23.9	24.2	24.7	24.6	24.5	24.0	23.8	23.3	21.2
Canada	16.3	13.5	12.1	12.1	12.3	12.3	12.3	12.8	12.6	12.5
Chile	0.0	0.0	0.0	0.0	0.0	0.0	0.0	0.0	0.0	0.0
Czech Republic	8.3	7.7	8.5	8.6	9.1	8.9	8.9	9.1	9.3	9.5
Denmark	28.8	27.6	34.9	34.1	34.3	34.4	34.1	33.9	34.0	34.1
Estonia	19.9	15.7	14.9	14.8	15.1	15.5	15.9	16.2	15.4	15.2
Finland	23.4	20.1	19.1	18.4	18.2	17.4	18.2	18.2	18.0	17.1
France	11.9	9.8	12.2	12.2	12.3	12.5	12.5	12.6	12.3	11.5
Germany	16.2	14.9	14.7	13.7	13.8	14.0	14.0	14.0	14.1	13.9
Greece	5.9	8.6	7.5	6.3	10.1	9.6	7.8	7.8	7.3	8.0
Hungary	19.4	15.7	15.9	10.8	14.1	16.5	16.0	16.0	16.0	15.0
Iceland	19.9	23.9	20.7	21.7	22.8	23.2	23.8	23.6	24.7	25.0
Ireland	12.6	5.8	6.4	7.5	8.8	9.6	9.6	9.8	9.1	8.7
Israel[1]	13.5	9.4	7.3	6.8	6.8	6.6	6.4	6.9	7.1	7.4
Italy	15.7	15.1	15.8	16.4	17.1	17.3	17.6	15.6	15.0	15.0
Japan	5.6	6.3	6.9	6.7	6.6	6.7	6.6	6.8	6.8	6.9
Korea	1.7	2.6	3.1	3.4	3.4	3.7	4.0	4.0	4.2	4.3
Latvia	16.9	18.4	15.9	20.5	18.5	18.6	18.0	17.8	17.3	17.5
Luxembourg	7.7	5.9	5.2	5.6	6.0	6.4	7.4	7.8	8.1	8.2
Mexico	-4.0	-0.8	0.0	0.7	3.2	3.6	4.0	4.4	4.7	5.2
Netherlands	7.8	10.2	12.7	12.4	12.5	13.0	13.3	12.6	13.7	13.2
New Zealand	18.5	19.5	16.9	15.9	14.8	15.2	15.7	16.0	16.2	16.5
Norway	20.1	18.7	18.7	18.7	18.8	18.5	18.4	17.4	17.1	16.7
Poland	5.3	5.2	5.4	5.6	5.8	5.9	6.0	6.2	6.2	6.3
Portugal	7.1	6.1	4.6	5.0	5.1	5.5	8.6	8.2	9.9	10.0
Slovak Republic	6.2	5.5	2.2	2.9	5.5	5.5	6.7	7.0	7.3	7.4
Slovenia	11.9	10.5	8.2	8.4	8.5	8.4	8.3	8.4	8.4	8.5
Spain	10.1	10.6	10.1	11.6	11.8	12.4	12.5	12.5	11.2	11.3
Sweden	25.3	21.8	16.1	15.4	15.5	15.6	15.8	15.1	15.3	15.6
Switzerland	9.1	9.2	8.8	8.9	8.9	8.6	8.7	8.4	8.4	8.3
Turkey[2]	14.0	14.9	9.1	9.3	9.3	9.4	9.7	9.9	10.0	9.5
United Kingdom	15.1	15.5	14.2	14.3	13.4	13.0	11.9	11.4	11.1	11.0
United States	15.5	14.4	13.6	13.8	15.2	15.2	15.1	15.2	15.3	15.4
Unweighted average										
OECD-Average	**13.3**	**12.5**	**11.9**	**11.9**	**12.3**	**12.5**	**12.6**	**12.6**	**12.6**	**12.4**
OECD-EU 22	**14.1**	**13.0**	**12.7**	**12.7**	**13.3**	**13.5**	**13.6**	**13.5**	**13.4**	**13.1**

1. Information on data for Israel: http://oe.cd/israel-disclaimer.
2. Wage figures are based on the old definition of average worker (ISIC D, rev3.) for years 2000 to 2006.

StatLink http://dx.doi.org/10.1787/888933461574

Table 6.8c. **Income tax plus employee contributions less cash benefits, married couple at 100% and 33% of average earnings**

Tax burden as a % of gross wage earnings, two-earner married couple without children

	2000	2006	2009	2010	2011	2012	2013	2014	2015	2016
Australia	22.8	20.6	18.2	18.3	18.3	18.9	18.7	19.0	19.7	19.9
Austria	27.5	29.4	28.2	28.4	28.8	29.0	29.4	29.6	29.7	27.0
Belgium	38.1	34.7	34.9	35.5	35.4	35.3	34.8	34.6	34.1	32.0
Canada	22.0	20.4	19.0	19.0	19.1	19.2	19.3	19.9	19.8	19.7
Chile	7.0	7.0	7.0	7.0	7.0	7.0	7.0	7.0	7.0	7.0
Czech Republic	20.8	20.2	19.5	19.6	20.1	19.9	19.9	20.1	20.3	20.5
Denmark	37.8	35.6	34.9	33.6	33.8	33.9	33.5	33.3	33.6	33.7
Estonia	19.9	16.3	16.6	17.6	17.9	18.3	17.9	18.2	17.0	16.8
Finland	30.4	26.8	25.2	25.3	25.2	24.8	25.6	26.0	26.1	25.7
France	25.3	23.6	25.9	25.9	26.0	26.2	26.3	26.6	26.5	25.8
Germany	36.7	36.6	35.3	34.2	34.7	34.8	34.4	34.4	34.5	34.6
Greece	21.8	24.6	23.5	22.3	26.3	26.1	24.3	23.8	22.8	23.7
Hungary	31.9	30.1	32.9	27.8	31.6	35.0	34.5	34.5	34.5	33.5
Iceland	20.1	24.1	21.5	22.4	23.5	23.9	24.5	24.2	25.2	25.5
Ireland	15.0	8.2	8.8	9.9	11.2	12.0	12.6	12.8	12.1	11.7
Israel[1]	21.1	16.1	14.2	13.7	13.7	13.4	13.2	13.7	13.9	14.3
Italy	24.9	24.3	25.3	25.9	26.6	26.8	27.1	25.1	24.5	24.5
Japan	18.9	18.6	19.1	19.6	20.1	20.4	20.5	20.9	21.1	21.2
Korea	8.4	9.8	10.7	11.2	11.4	11.9	12.3	12.3	12.6	12.7
Latvia	25.9	27.4	24.9	29.5	29.5	29.6	29.0	28.3	27.8	28.0
Luxembourg	19.2	17.6	17.3	17.7	19.1	18.6	19.6	20.0	20.8	20.9
Mexico	-2.6	0.6	1.4	2.0	4.5	4.9	5.3	5.7	6.1	6.5
Netherlands	30.8	28.1	27.7	27.7	27.7	28.0	31.0	28.5	26.0	25.2
New Zealand	18.5	19.5	16.9	15.9	14.8	15.2	15.7	16.0	16.2	16.5
Norway	27.9	26.5	26.5	26.5	26.6	26.3	26.2	25.6	25.3	24.9
Poland	26.4	27.4	23.2	23.4	23.6	23.7	23.8	24.0	24.1	24.2
Portugal	18.1	17.1	15.6	16.0	16.1	16.5	19.6	19.2	20.9	21.0
Slovak Republic	18.2	18.9	15.6	16.3	18.9	18.9	20.1	20.4	19.7	19.8
Slovenia	34.0	32.6	30.3	30.5	30.6	30.5	30.4	30.5	30.5	30.6
Spain	16.5	17.0	16.5	17.9	18.1	18.8	18.8	18.9	17.6	17.7
Sweden	32.3	28.8	23.1	22.4	22.5	22.6	22.8	22.1	22.3	22.6
Switzerland	15.6	15.3	14.8	15.0	15.2	14.9	14.9	14.7	14.6	14.6
Turkey[2]	28.0	29.9	24.1	24.3	24.3	24.4	24.7	24.9	25.0	24.5
United Kingdom	22.7	23.8	22.3	22.6	21.6	21.1	19.9	19.3	19.1	19.0
United States	23.1	22.1	21.2	21.5	20.9	20.9	22.7	22.8	22.9	23.0
Unweighted average										
OECD-Average	**23.0**	**22.3**	**21.2**	**21.3**	**21.8**	**22.1**	**22.3**	**22.2**	**22.1**	**22.0**
OECD-EU 22	**26.1**	**25.0**	**24.0**	**24.1**	**24.8**	**25.0**	**25.2**	**25.0**	**24.8**	**24.5**

1. Information on data for Israel: http://oe.cd/israel-disclaimer.
2. Wage figures are based on the old definition of average worker (ISIC D, rev3.) for years 2000 to 2006.

StatLink http://dx.doi.org/10.1787/888933461584

Table 6.9. **Annual average gross and net wage earnings, single individual no children, 2000-16**

In US dollars using PPP

	2000		2006		2009		2010		2011		2012		2013		2014		2015		2016	
	gross	net	gross	net	gross	net	gross	net	gross	net	gross	net	gross	net	gross	net	gross	net	gross	net
Australia	31 592	23 190	39 201	29 802	44 093	34 367	44 403	34 508	46 261	35 957	48 085	37 048	53 615	41 228	54 422	41 712	55 229	41 931	56 727	42 930
Austria	32 738	22 601	40 844	27 186	44 894	30 174	45 803	30 656	47 743	31 725	50 032	33 052	52 617	34 527	53 807	35 146	55 118	35 804	55 680	37 934
Belgium	35 133	20 023	43 072	25 016	49 642	28 647	52 002	29 788	53 655	30 676	55 813	31 975	57 305	33 007	58 193	33 544	58 256	33 783	58 214	34 492
Canada	29 357	21 988	33 344	25 424	35 385	27 428	36 360	28 219	36 671	28 406	37 715	29 189	39 172	30 289	40 257	30 857	40 172	30 832	41 021	31 554
Chile	9 672	8 995	11 156	10 375	12 682	11 794	15 409	14 330	16 678	15 510	17 909	16 656	18 887	17 565	19 172	17 830	19 953	18 556	20 517	19 081
Czech Republic	11 221	8 697	16 197	12 567	20 694	16 082	21 054	16 327	22 126	17 016	22 748	17 542	23 611	18 211	24 523	18 858	24 937	19 122	25 893	19 789
Denmark	32 466	18 861	39 911	24 510	47 535	29 858	49 635	31 796	51 759	33 083	51 817	33 082	53 497	34 348	54 251	34 920	55 424	35 531	57 310	36 701
Estonia	8 377	6 539	14 309	11 629	18 377	14 966	19 001	15 299	20 266	16 271	21 118	16 913	22 457	18 081	23 430	18 829	24 526	20 002	25 540	20 869
Finland	26 770	17 701	35 186	24 423	42 935	30 368	43 830	30 934	44 811	31 648	45 584	32 193	46 884	32 754	47 119	32 706	47 966	33 149	48 479	33 551
France	28 693	20 327	35 045	25 333	39 601	28 574	40 669	29 344	42 180	30 399	42 808	30 770	45 113	32 365	46 257	33 018	47 071	33 477	47 817	33 904
Germany	36 448	20 702	46 168	26 540	50 117	29 466	51 939	31 577	54 898	33 076	56 272	33 893	57 693	34 945	59 563	36 053	60 504	36 545	61 750	37 260
Greece	23 416	18 257	34 355	25 397	34 992	26 309	33 520	25 729	32 799	23 955	32 483	23 840	32 762	24 391	33 086	24 798	32 641	24 730	32 974	24 602
Hungary	9 861	6 338	15 092	9 773	19 104	11 890	19 909	13 660	21 290	13 817	22 608	14 665	23 482	15 381	23 705	15 527	24 255	15 887	25 627	17 042
Iceland	31 986	23 849	45 201	32 631	41 666	30 733	39 628	28 691	41 642	29 825	44 682	31 875	48 605	34 484	50 311	35 909	54 468	38 494	59 044	41 806
Ireland	23 300	18 561	30 583	26 089	35 329	29 446	38 102	31 299	38 802	31 879	41 089	33 249	41 609	33 371	41 883	33 423	43 090	34 679	44 737	36 126
Israel[1]	27 798	20 541	27 900	22 241	30 285	24 923	30 602	25 398	31 790	26 371	32 500	27 093	33 510	28 023	35 002	29 049	36 313	30 025	37 286	30 649
Italy	26 741	18 974	30 661	21 847	35 592	25 013	36 599	25 535	38 055	26 340	39 372	27 186	40 666	28 017	41 283	28 473	42 150	29 032	42 166	29 045
Japan	32 181	25 828	39 942	32 177	41 802	33 424	42 755	33 935	44 869	35 433	46 928	36 912	47 734	37 460	48 525	37 925	49 569	38 610	50 278	39 118
Korea	26 564	24 187	39 492	35 299	41 722	36 844	43 934	38 534	43 081	37 703	45 400	39 487	46 433	40 175	47 578	41 085	48 173	41 444	48 979	42 051
Latvia	6 414	4 626	9 691	6 893	14 202	10 423	15 009	10 427	15 310	10 605	15 599	10 791	16 560	11 571	17 920	12 625	19 374	13 770	20 537	14 571
Luxembourg	37 508	26 756	47 474	34 859	53 424	39 406	53 453	39 145	55 988	40 082	57 313	41 194	59 905	42 214	62 262	43 583	63 346	43 810	65 522	45 239
Mexico	7 977	7 779	10 255	9 739	11 446	10 823	11 434	10 733	11 910	10 808	12 117	10 959	12 547	11 312	12 903	11 594	12 799	11 463	13 112	11 691
Netherlands	35 799	23 764	46 772	31 574	52 416	35 751	53 040	36 249	55 363	37 811	57 253	38 852	61 641	39 579	62 212	41 437	62 042	43 206	63 549	44 200
New Zealand	24 181	19 498	27 574	21 938	31 723	25 990	32 099	26 645	33 242	27 967	34 285	28 667	36 815	30 598	37 936	31 393	38 870	32 044	39 687	32 586
Norway	32 817	22 743	45 282	32 108	50 284	35 562	51 640	36 528	54 067	38 175	55 829	39 524	58 131	41 151	57 742	41 174	56 928	40 772	60 020	43 258
Poland	12 572	9 076	15 811	11 272	18 683	14 126	20 251	15 292	21 500	16 208	22 384	16 857	23 638	17 786	25 294	19 000	26 158	19 633	27 343	20 506
Portugal	16 509	12 803	24 228	18 732	24 919	19 570	26 596	20 692	26 013	19 958	28 147	21 735	30 247	21 944	30 021	21 864	29 633	21 243	29 946	21 691
Slovak Republic	9 768	7 837	13 369	10 410	17 562	13 804	18 607	14 578	18 941	14 622	19 443	15 011	20 363	15 729	21 580	16 634	21 978	16 906	22 852	17 542
Slovenia	16 880	10 878	22 434	14 617	24 941	16 726	26 565	17 722	27 842	18 539	28 903	19 294	29 934	20 027	30 726	20 510	30 940	20 628	31 437	20 927
Spain	23 393	18 750	28 747	22 860	33 664	27 000	34 160	26 737	35 729	27 854	37 259	28 742	38 569	29 730	39 512	30 428	39 666	31 231	40 276	31 664
Sweden	28 744	19 050	35 611	24 613	40 662	30 335	40 876	30 751	42 549	31 977	44 826	33 664	46 317	34 689	46 652	35 276	46 414	35 005	47 450	35 658
Switzerland	40 731	33 473	50 467	41 687	57 131	47 283	58 132	48 027	61 635	50 853	65 996	54 617	68 582	56 693	67 615	56 130	68 974	57 304	70 077	58 246
Turkey[2]	19 677	14 023	18 576	12 936	18 174	13 394	19 623	14 407	20 398	14 964	21 545	15 781	23 053	16 824	23 935	17 413	25 123	18 247	28 099	20 438
United Kingdom	35 330	26 212	45 090	32 966	47 082	35 200	48 930	36 506	48 273	36 171	49 690	37 400	50 468	38 373	50 688	38 732	52 216	39 991	53 020	40 646
United States	33 129	24 877	39 377	29 765	44 295	33 588	45 665	34 429	46 895	35 811	47 746	36 460	48 774	36 359	50 099	37 274	51 509	38 232	52 543	38 894
OECD Average	24 736	17 952	31 383	23 007	35 059	25 980	36 035	26 698	37 287	27 471	38 666	28 462	40 320	29 520	41 127	30 135	41 880	30 718	43 015	31 607

1. Information on data for Israel: http://oe.cd/israel-disclaimer.
2. Wage figures are based on the old definition of average worker (ISIC D, rev3.) for years 2000 to 2006.

StatLink http://dx.doi.org/10.1787/888933461018

Table 6.10. **Annual average gross and net wage earnings, single individual no children, 2000-16 (national currency)**

	2000		2006		2009		2010		2011		2012		2013		2014		2015		2016	
	gross	net	gross	net	gross	net	gross	net	gross	net	gross	net	gross	net	gross	net	gross	net	gross	net
Australia	41 322	30 332	55 042	41 844	63 546	49 529	66 724	51 856	69 903	54 334	74 057	57 059	77 574	59 652	79 409	60 863	80 774	61 325	82 114	62 143
Austria	29 732	20 526	35 143	23 391	37 832	25 428	38 504	25 770	39 693	26 376	40 708	26 893	41 940	27 521	42 814	27 965	43 911	28 524	44 409	30 256
Belgium	31 644	18 035	37 674	21 880	42 149	24 324	43 423	24 873	44 636	25 520	45 886	26 288	46 197	26 609	46 451	26 776	46 479	26 954	46 570	27 593
Canada	36 038	26 992	40 191	30 644	42 516	32 955	44 400	34 459	45 469	35 221	46 940	36 329	47 946	37 074	49 821	38 188	50 350	38 644	50 997	39 227
Chile	2 770 353	2 576 428	3 594 042	3 342 459	4 478 647	4 165 142	5 508 104	5 122 537	5 804 093	5 397 806	6 218 613	5 783 310	6 604 419	6 142 110	7 019 299	6 527 948	7 557 360	7 028 345	8 003 491	7 443 247
Czech Republic	160 922	124 729	233 580	181 234	281 887	219 060	287 320	222 803	295 273	227 083	302 500	233 263	301 868	232 827	310 615	238 854	319 162	244 743	330 072	252 260
Denmark	281 700	163 652	330 900	203 212	367 051	230 550	376 073	240 914	386 457	247 013	391 951	250 237	393 463	252 625	397 600	255 926	403 600	258 738	412 555	264 195
Estonia	3 931	3 068	7 456	6 059	9 492	7 729	9 712	7 820	10 368	8 324	11 004	8 813	11 732	9 446	12 338	9 915	13 045	10 638	13 640	11 145
Finland	26 362	17 431	33 543	23 283	38 444	27 191	39 395	27 804	40 243	28 422	41 413	29 247	42 447	29 654	42 704	29 641	43 382	29 981	43 816	30 324
France	26 712	18 923	31 369	22 675	34 132	24 628	34 693	25 032	35 489	25 576	36 143	25 979	36 616	26 269	37 235	26 578	37 648	26 775	38 049	26 978
Germany	34 400	19 539	39 149	22 505	40 600	23 871	41 736	25 374	43 300	26 088	44 300	26 682	44 700	27 075	45 700	27 662	46 800	28 268	47 809	28 848
Greece	15 693	12 236	23 800	17 594	24 619	18 510	24 156	18 541	23 391	17 084	22 240	16 322	20 682	15 397	20 450	15 327	20 107	15 234	20 074	14 977
Hungary	1 086 240	698 166	1 985 412	1 285 714	2 436 408	1 516 415	2 512 020	1 723 560	2 645 712	1 717 097	2 840 112	1 842 297	2 934 744	1 922 257	3 053 364	1 999 953	3 169 128	2 075 779	3 312 081	2 202 534
Iceland	2 712 000	2 022 102	4 596 000	3 317 884	5 076 000	3 744 125	5 256 000	3 805 407	5 628 000	4 030 857	6 120 000	4 365 845	6 660 000	4 725 047	6 960 000	4 967 661	7 644 000	5 402 260	8 456 409	5 987 579
Ireland	22 008	17 532	29 931	25 533	31 802	26 507	32 308	26 540	32 264	26 508	33 819	27 366	33 754	27 071	34 178	27 275	34 674	27 906	35 592	28 741
Israel[1]	95 664	70 691	105 652	84 223	120 028	98 777	121 581	100 905	125 405	104 026	128 550	107 163	128 664	107 597	134 748	111 832	137 990	114 096	142 247	116 928
Italy	21 550	15 291	25 241	17 985	27 419	19 270	28 243	19 705	28 872	19 984	29 440	20 328	29 983	20 657	30 347	20 931	30 654	21 114	30 642	21 106
Japan	4 987 116	4 002 481	4 979 155	4 011 225	4 828 001	3 860 274	4 773 076	3 788 423	4 821 385	3 807 417	4 893 341	3 848 998	4 835 595	3 794 828	4 972 455	3 886 313	5 083 906	3 960 010	5 110 601	3 976 218
Korea	19 849 729	18 073 190	30 495 639	27 257 957	34 410 564	30 387 885	36 929 183	32 390 144	36 816 740	32 220 027	38 811 570	33 756 834	40 353 852	34 915 409	41 428 224	35 774 131	42 908 652	36 915 462	43 857 243	37 654 050
Latvia	2 316	1 670	4 740	3 372	7 392	5 425	7 296	5 069	7 632	5 286	7 896	5 463	8 268	5 777	8 892	6 264	9 588	6 815	10 173	7 218
Luxembourg	35 875	25 591	43 539	31 969	48 183	35 540	49 387	36 167	50 674	36 278	51 971	37 354	53 630	37 792	54 920	38 443	55 858	38 631	56 197	38 801
Mexico	48 607	47 400	73 695	69 988	85 043	80 412	87 672	82 301	91 386	82 933	95 224	86 121	98 922	89 190	103 246	92 777	107 551	96 320	112 827	100 601
Netherlands	31 901	21 176	40 800	27 543	44 412	30 292	45 215	30 901	46 287	31 612	47 200	32 030	49 200	31 591	49 900	33 237	50 009	34 826	50 853	35 370
New Zealand	34 923	28 159	40 843	32 495	46 653	38 221	48 007	39 850	49 395	41 557	51 278	42 875	53 234	44 244	54 733	45 293	56 110	46 257	57 649	47 334
Norway	298 385	206 788	397 765	282 046	456 214	322 642	471 696	333 655	491 072	346 730	504 535	357 183	524 887	371 568	537 621	383 355	551 198	394 770	564 218	406 643
Poland	23 061	16 649	29 271	20 867	34 878	26 372	36 482	27 548	38 731	29 198	40 205	30 278	41 652	31 339	44 513	33 437	46 136	34 628	47 782	35 834
Portugal	10 922	8 470	15 517	11 997	15 613	12 262	16 542	12 870	16 208	12 435	17 040	13 158	17 653	12 807	17 343	12 630	17 298	12 400	17 521	12 692
Slovak Republic	5 048	4 050	7 418	5 776	9 043	7 108	9 325	7 306	9 592	7 405	9 810	7 574	10 001	7 725	10 422	8 034	10 661	8 201	10 918	8 381
Slovenia	8 894	5 732	13 684	8 916	16 079	10 783	16 915	11 284	17 373	11 568	17 538	11 707	17 673	11 824	17 948	11 981	18 092	12 062	18 292	12 176
Spain	17 319	13 882	21 168	16 833	24 164	19 380	24 786	19 400	25 515	19 892	25 894	19 975	26 027	20 062	26 191	20 169	26 475	20 845	26 710	20 999
Sweden	263 581	174 686	324 618	224 362	362 291	270 277	368 208	277 001	376 309	282 810	387 960	291 356	398 220	298 247	408 188	308 651	414 105	312 312	423 065	317 926
Switzerland	72 910	59 918	80 727	66 682	83 883	69 423	85 068	70 280	86 134	71 067	89 364	73 955	90 012	74 409	86 820	72 073	86 017	71 463	85 536	71 095
Turkey[2]	5 545	3 952	15 645	10 895	16 421	12 102	18 026	13 235	19 708	14 458	21 973	16 094	24 674	18 007	27 487	19 996	31 191	22 654	36 806	26 771
United Kingdom	24 910	18 481	31 419	22 971	33 391	24 964	34 297	25 589	34 083	25 538	34 864	26 241	35 088	26 678	35 120	26 836	35 947	27 531	36 571	28 035
United States	33 129	24 877	39 377	29 765	44 295	33 588	45 665	34 429	46 895	35 811	47 746	36 460	48 774	36 359	50 099	37 274	51 509	38 232	52 543	38 894

Note: The annual average gross wage earnings in euro area countries are expressed in euros for all years.

1. Information on data for Israel: http://oe.cd/israel-disclaimer.
2. Wage figures are based on the old definition of average worker (ISIC D, rev3.) for years 2000 to 2006.

StatLink http://dx.doi.org/10.1787/888933461003

PART III

Country details, 2016

This part of the publication provides the individual country details for 2016 that lie behind the comparative analysis. For each country, a table of detailed country results is followed by a description of the tax/benefit system.

All thirty-five country tables in this part of the report have a similar format. The left hand page of each table specifies the tax-benefit position of single persons in four cases, which differ by wage level and the presence of children (0/2). The right hand page of the table specifies the tax-benefit position of married couples, again discerning between four cases, which now differ by wage level, the presence of children (0/2) and one-/two earner situations.

All tables start with gross wage earnings (line 1) and derive taxable income for the personal income tax levied by central government (line 4), taking into account a number of standard tax allowances (line 2) and taxable cash transfers (line 3). Taxable income allows one to determine central government income tax paid (line 7); including reductions in the form of tax credits (line 6). Total payments to general government (line 10) also include state and local income taxes (line 8) and employees' compulsory social security contributions (line 9). Take-home pay (line 12) is calculated as gross wage earnings less all payments to general government, plus Universal cash transfers received from general government (line 11).

Line 13 reports employers' compulsory social security contributions (including payroll taxes).

Average tax rate (line 14) are then calculated as:

- *The share of income tax in gross wage earnings;*
- *The share of employees' social security contributions in gross wage earnings;*
- *The share of income tax and employees' social security contributions minus benefits in gross wage earnings; and;*
- *The share of income tax and all social security contributions minus benefits in gross labour costs.*

Marginal tax rates (line 15) are calculated similarly as:

- *The increase in income tax and employees' contributions minus benefits as a share of the related increase in gross wage earnings (both for the principal earner and the spouse); and;*
- *The increase in tax and all social security contributions minus benefits as a share of the related increase in gross labour costs (both for the principal earner and the spouse).*

© OECD 2017

Australia (2015-16 Income tax year)

This chapter includes data on the income taxes paid by workers, their social security contributions, the family benefits they receive in the form of cash transfers as well as the social security contributions and payroll taxes paid by their employers. Results reported include the marginal and average tax burden for eight different family types.

Methodological information is available for Personal income tax systems, compulsory social security contributions to schemes operated within the public sector, Universal cash transfers as well as recent changes in the tax/benefit system. The methodology also includes the parameter values and tax equations underlying the data.

Australia 2016

The tax/benefit position of single persons

Wage level (per cent of average wage)		67	100	167	67
Number of children		none	none	none	2
1. **Gross wage earnings**		55 016	82 114	137 130	55 016
Principal Gross wage earnings		55 016	82 114	137 130	55 016
Spouse Gross wage earnings		0	0	0	0
2. **Standard tax allowances**					
Basic allowance					
Married or head of family					
Dependent children					
Deduction for social security contributions and income taxes					
Work-related expenses					
Other					
	Total	0	0	0	0
3. **Tax credits or cash transfers included in taxable income**		0	0	0	0
4. **Central government taxable income (1 - 2 + 3)**		55 016	82 114	137 130	55 016
5. **Central government income tax liability (exclusive of tax credits)**					
Income tax		9 427	18 329	38 685	9 427
Medicare Levy		1 100	1 642	2 743	1 100
Temporary Budget Repair Levy		0	0	0	0
	Total	10 528	19 971	41 428	10 528
6. **Tax credits**					
Basic credit		175	0	0	175
Married or head of family		0	0	0	0
Children					
Other					
	Total	175	0	0	175
7. **Central government income tax finally paid (5-6)**		10 353	19 971	41 428	10 353
8. **State and local taxes**		0	0	0	0
9. **Employees' compulsory social security contributions**		0	0	0	0
10. **Total payments to general government (7 + 8 + 9)**		10 353	19 971	41 428	10 353
11. **Cash transfers from general government**					
For head of family		0	0	0	0
For two children		0	0	0	14 261
	Total	0	0	0	14 261
12. **Take-home pay (1-10+11)**		44 663	62 143	95 703	58 924
13. **Employers' payroll tax**		3 283	4 900	8 184	3 283
14. **Average rates**					
Income tax		18.8%	24.3%	30.2%	18.8%
Employees' social security contributions		0.0%	0.0%	0.0%	0.0%
Total payments less cash transfers		18.8%	24.3%	30.2%	-7.1%
Total tax wedge including employer payroll taxes		23.4%	28.6%	34.1%	-1.1%
15. **Marginal rates**					
Total payments less cash transfers: Principal earner		36.0%	39.0%	39.0%	56.0%
Total payments less cash transfers: Spouse		n.a.	n.a.	n.a.	n.a.
Total tax wedge: Principal earner		39.6%	42.4%	42.4%	58.5%
Total tax wedge: Spouse		n.a.	n.a.	n.a.	n.a.

Australia 2016

The tax/benefit position of married couples

		Wage level (per cent of average wage)	100-0	100-33	100-67	100-33
		Number of children	2	2	2	none
1.	**Gross wage earnings**		82 114	109 212	137 130	109 212
	Principal Gross wage earnings		82 114	82 114	82 114	82 114
	Spouse Gross wage earnings		0	27 098	55 016	27 098
2.	**Standard tax allowances**					
	Basic allowance					
	Married or head of family					
	Dependent children					
	Deduction for social security contributions and income taxes					
	Work-related expenses					
	Other					
		Total	0	0	0	0
3.	**Tax credits or cash transfers included in taxable income**		0	0	0	0
4.	**Central government taxable income (1 - 2 + 3)**		82 114	109 212	137 130	109 212
5.	**Central government income tax liability (exclusive of tax credits)**					
	Income tax		18 329	20 020	27 757	20 020
	Medicare Levy		1 642	2 184	2 743	2 184
	Temporary Budget Repair Levy		0	0	0	0
		Total	19 971	22 204	30 499	22 204
6.	**Tax credits**					
	Basic credit		0	445	175	445
	Married or head of family		0	0	0	0
	Children					
	Other					
		Total	0	445	175	445
7.	**Central government income tax finally paid (5-6)**		19 971	21 759	30 324	21 759
8.	**State and local taxes**		0	0	0	0
9.	**Employees' compulsory social security contributions**		0	0	0	0
10.	**Total payments to general government (7 + 8 + 9)**		19 971	21 759	30 324	21 759
11.	**Cash transfers from general government**					
	For head of family		0	0	0	0
	For two children		9 141	65	0	0
		Total	9 141	65	0	0
12.	**Take-home pay (1-10+11)**		71 284	87 517	106 806	87 453
13.	**Employers' payroll tax**		4 900	6 517	8 184	6 517
14.	**Average rates**					
	Income tax		24.3%	19.9%	22.1%	19.9%
	Employees' social security contributions		0.0%	0.0%	0.0%	0.0%
	Total payments less cash transfers		13.2%	19.9%	22.1%	19.9%
	Total tax wedge including employer payroll taxes		18.1%	24.4%	26.5%	24.4%
15.	**Marginal rates**					
	Total payments less cash transfers: Principal earner		59.0%	69.0%	39.0%	39.0%
	Total payments less cash transfers: Spouse		40.1%	51.0%	36.0%	21.0%
	Total tax wedge: Principal earner		61.3%	70.7%	42.4%	42.4%
	Total tax wedge: Spouse		43.5%	53.8%	39.6%	25.4%

The national currency is the Australian dollar (AUD). For the 2015-16 income tax year AUD 1.35 was equal to USD 1. The average worker earned AUD 82 114 in 2015-16.

1. Personal income tax system

1.1. *Federal income tax*

1.1.1. *Tax unit*

Members of the family are taxed separately.

1.1.2. *Tax allowances and credits*

1.1.2.1. Standard tax reliefs

- *Basic reliefs:* Income earned up to AUD 18 200 by resident taxpayers is subject to tax at a zero rate.
- *Standard marital status reliefs:* No relief available.
- *Relief(s) for children:* See Section 4.2 for more detail on transfers related to dependent children.
- *Relief for social security contributions* and other taxes: No such contributions are levied.
- *Reliefs for low income earners:* A tax offset worth a maximum of AUD 445 is available for low income earners called the Low Income Tax Offset. Taxpayers whose taxable income was less than AUD 37 000 in 2015-16 are eligible to receive the full amount of the offset. The offset is reduced by AUD 0.015 for every AUD 1 by which a taxpayer's taxable income exceeds AUD 37 000 and is no longer available once a taxpayer's taxable income exceeds AUD 66 667.
- *Relief for mature age workers:* No relief available.
- *Relief for recipients of certain social security benefits:* The Beneficiary Tax Offset is available for those who receive certain taxable social security benefits called 'rebatable benefits'. It is calculated to ensure that a person who receives a rebatable benefit does not pay any tax on that income. The amount of the Beneficiary Tax Offset available to an individual is determined by the total amount of the rebatable benefit(s) they receive in an income year.
- *Relief for taxpayers who maintain a dependant who is genuinely unable to work:* A taxpayer who maintains a dependant who is genuinely unable to work due to invalidity or carer obligations may be eligible for the Dependent (Invalid and Carer) Tax Offset. This tax offset is worth a maximum of AUD 2 588 in 2015-16. To qualify for the offset, the combined adjusted taxable income of the taxpayer and their spouse (where one exists) should not exceed AUD 100 000 in 2015-16. The amount of offset that may be received is reduced by AUD 1 for every AUD 4 by which the dependant's adjusted taxable income exceeds AUD 282 and is no longer available once the dependant's adjusted taxable income exceeds AUD 10 634.
- There are also tax rebates to ensure that taxpayers in receipt of a taxable Australian Government pension, as well as Australians who are of Age Pension age and who meet all

of the Age Pension eligibility criteria except the income and/or asset tests, pay less tax. The Senior Australian and Pensioner Tax Offset is worth up to AUD 2 230 for a single taxpayer, up to AUD 1 602 for each member of a senior couple not separated by illness and AUD 2 040 for each member of a senior couple separated by illness. The offset is withdrawn at the rate of AUD 0.125 for every dollar that a recipient's income exceeds their effective tax-free threshold. For a single taxpayer, this means that the offset is withdrawn from AUD 32 279 and is no longer available once income reaches AUD 50 119. For members of a couple not separated by illness, the offset is withdrawn from a combined income of AUD 57 948 and is no longer available once combined income reaches AUD 83 580.

- *Other:* No other standard relief available.

1.1.2.2. Main non-standard tax reliefs applicable to an average worker include:

- *Relief for superannuation:* Contributions to a low-income spouse's superannuation attract an 18% rebate up to a maximum rebate of AUD 540. In 2015-16, eligible individuals with incomes not exceeding AUD 37 000 effectively have the tax paid on their concessional contributions refunded, up to a maximum of AUD 500.
- *Relief for private health insurance:* For the 2015-16 income year, there are different rebate amounts depending on age and income. For individuals below 65 years without dependants and with annual income for surcharge purposes below AUD 90 000 the rebate is 27.82% from 1 July 2015 to 31 March 2016 and 26.791% from 1 April 2016 of the cost of cover for eligible private health care. For families (couples and individuals with at least one dependent child) below 65 years with annual income for surcharge purposes below AUD 180 000, the rebate is 27.82% from 1 July 2015 to 31 March 2016 and from 1 April 2016 26.791% of the cost of cover for eligible private health care. The threshold is increased by AUD 1 500 for each dependent child after the first.
- The rebate percentages are reduced for individuals and families with annual incomes above these amounts. The rebate percentages are also higher for individuals and families aged 65 years or more.
- *Relief for medical expenses:* In 2015-16, there is an offset for annual net out-of-pocket medical expenses. Eligibility for the offset is based on annual income. This offset is being phased out, so for the 2015-16 income year, it is only available to individuals who have medical expenses relating to disability aids, attendant care or aged care. Single taxpayers with an adjusted taxable income (ATI) of AUD 90 000 or less, and families with ATI below AUD 180 000 (plus AUD 1 500 for each additional dependent child after the first), are able to claim 20% of medical expenses over AUD 2 265. Single taxpayers and families with incomes above these respective amounts are able to claim 10% of medical expenses over AUD 5 343.
- Other non-standard reliefs provided as deductions are:
  - subscriptions paid in respect of membership of a trade, business or professional association or union;
  - charitable contributions of AUD 2 or more to specified funds, authorities and institutions, including public benevolent institutions, approved research institutes for scientific research, building funds for schools conducted by non-profit organisations etc.; and
  - work-related expenses including cost of replacement of tools of trade, cost of provision and of cleaning protective clothing and footwear, travelling between jobs or travelling in the course of employment.

1.1.3. *Tax schedule*

General rates of tax – resident individuals

Taxable income (AUD)		Tax at general rates on total taxable income
Not less than	Not more than	
0	18 200	NIL
18 201	37 000	NIL + 19c for each AUD in excess of AUD 18 200
37 001	80 000	AUD 3 572 + 32.50c for each AUD in excess of AUD 37 000
80 001	180 000	AUD 17 547 + 37c for each AUD in excess of AUD 80 000
180 001 and over		AUD 54 547 + 45c for each AUD in excess of AUD 180 000

For the income years 2014-15, 2015-16 and 2016-17 there will be a Temporary Budget Repair Levy imposed on high income earners. The levy is applied at the rate of 2.0% of an individual's taxable income above AUD 180 000.

To nominally contribute towards the cost of basic medical and hospital care a Medicare Levy is imposed on the taxable incomes of resident taxpayers. In 2015-16 the levy applied at the rate of 2.0% of the taxable income of an individual.

Certain thresholds are applied before the levy is imposed. In 2015-16, an individual taxpayer was not liable for the levy where their taxable income did not exceed AUD 21 335. A taxpayer in a couple or sole parent family who is not receiving Parenting Payment, (see section 4.2), does not pay the levy if the taxable family income does not exceed AUD 36 001. The threshold is increased by AUD 3 306 for each dependent child. Where an individual's taxable income exceeds AUD 21 335, or a family's income exceeds AUD 36 001 (plus AUD 3 306 for each dependent child), the levy shades in at a rate of 10% of the excess of taxable income over the threshold, until the levy is equal to 2.0% of the individual's or family's taxable income.

For 2015-16, individual senior Australians of Age Pension age were not liable to pay the levy where their taxable income did not exceed AUD 33 738. Where taxable income exceeded AUD 33 738 but did not exceed AUD 42 172, the levy liability was equal to 10% of the excess of taxable income over AUD 33 738. Pensioner families (including couples and sole parents on Parenting Payment) and senior Australian families of Age Pension age, did not become liable to pay any Medicare levy until their combined income in 2015-16 exceeded AUD 46 966 (plus AUD 3 306 for each dependent child).

Individual taxpayers who had income for surcharge purposes greater than AUD 90 000 in 2015-16 (or if a couple had a combined income greater than AUD 180 000) but who did not have a complying private health care policy, were liable for the Medicare levy surcharge, which is applied as a flat rate on their taxable income. The surcharge rates are 1%, 1.25% and 1.5% depending on the taxpayer's taxable income above these thresholds. However, affected taxpayers typically purchase a complying policy as the cost of such a policy is generally less than the surcharge. The surcharge is therefore not included in this publication.

1.2. *State and local income taxes*

In Australia no states or territories levy a tax based on a resident's income.

2. Social security contributions

2.1. *Employees' contributions*

None. There is, however, a Medicare Levy which is based upon taxable income. See Section 1.1.3.

2.2. *Employers' contributions*

No contributions are collected from employers or employees specifically for pensions, sickness, unemployment or work injury benefits, family allowances or other benefits.

Part of Australia's retirement income system is the provision of compulsory employer contributions (the Superannuation Guarantee system). In 2015-16 the Superannuation Guarantee required employers to pay 9. 5% on top of employees' gross ordinary time earnings to an approved superannuation fund, provided they earn more than AUD 450 per month (they may also choose to make contributions for workers earning less than this threshold). This threshold is not indexed. There is also a limit to the Superannuation Guarantee. In each quarter any earnings beyond a threshold are not covered by the Superannuation Guarantee. This threshold is indexed to a measure of average earnings. In the 2015-16 tax year this threshold was AUD 50 810 per quarter. The Superannuation Guarantee rate will remain at 9.5% until 2020-21.

These contributions are not reflected in the "Taxing Wages" calculations because they are not a form of taxation (they are not an unrequited transfer to general government). While employers are legislatively required to make contributions to approved superannuation funds legislated, superannuation funds are private, although subject to regulation. Employers' contributions are generally made to individual accounts and form part of employees' personal superannuation assets. Some defined benefit schemes for public sector employees and private defined benefit schemes also exist. The employee may take superannuation benefits as either a lump sum payment or pension on retirement. Accordingly, superannuation contributions are reflected in the Non-Tax Compulsory Payment calculations.

3. Other taxes

3.1. *Pay-roll tax*

Australian State Governments levy pay-roll taxes on wages, cash or in kind, provided by larger employers to their employees. The rates of pay-roll tax, thresholds and deductions differ between States. In New South Wales, the State with the largest population, the pay-roll tax rate in 2015-16 was 5.45% for employers with total Australian wages in excess of AUD 750 000. Employers are entitled to an exemption from tax, or a pro-rated pay-roll tax threshold, on wages paid in New South Wales up to a maximum of AUD 750 000. The exempt amount is reduced based on the proportion of the employer's New South Wales pay-roll to its total Australian pay-roll.

4. Universal cash transfers

4.1. *Transfers related to marital status*

There are no cash transfers made on a universal basis to married couples.

4.2. *Transfers related to dependent children*

- Family Tax Benefit (FTB) Part A is paid to a parent, guardian or an approved care organisation to help families meet the costs of raising children. For 2015-16, the base rate of FTB(A) is payable where the combined 'adjusted' taxable income of parents does not exceed AUD 94 316. The payment shades out at the rate of AUD 0.30 per AUD 1 of income over the ceiling. The base rate of payment is AUD 2 230.15 (this figure includes an end of year supplement) for a dependent child aged under 15 and for dependent full time students aged 16 to 19. The base rate of payment is increased by a Large Family Supplement (LFS) for families with four or more children. In 2015-16, the LFS is payable at a rate of AUD 324.85 for the fourth and each subsequent child.
- A higher FTB(A) benefit is available for lower income earners, and the value of this benefit is dependent on the age and number of children. For 2015-16 families may receive a maximum payment of AUD 5 412.95 (this figure includes an end of year supplement) for each child aged under 13 years and AUD 6 825.50 (this figure includes an end of year supplement) for each child aged 13 to 15 years and for each child aged 16-19 in full time secondary school. The higher benefit is also boosted by the LFS for families with four or more children. For 2015-16, the higher benefit tapers out at the rate of AUD 0.20 for each dollar of income over AUD 51 027 until the base payment is reached. However, people receiving any social security allowances or pensions automatically qualify for the maximum higher benefit. The attached calculations assume each dependant is between 5 and 12 years of age.
- Family Tax Benefit Part B (FTB(B)) is targeted at single income couple and sole parent families. Eligibility for FTB(B) is contingent upon having a FTB child under the age of 16 or a qualifying dependent full-time student up to of the end of the calendar year they turn 18. There are two separate income tests applied to the parent(s). The parent earning the higher amount (or the sole parent, in the case of single parent families) must earn AUD 100 000 or less for the financial year for the family to be eligible. A secondary earner income threshold is also applied to the parent earning the lower amount. For 2015-16, this threshold is AUD 5 402, above which the entitlement is reduced by AUD 0.20 for each dollar of income. There is no secondary earner income test applied to sole parents. For 2015-16, the maximum payment is AUD 3 139.00 if the youngest dependent child is aged between 5 and 15 (or up to the end of the calendar year they turn 18 years if the dependent child is a full-time student), and AUD 4 339.85 if there is a child under 5 years. The attached calculations assume each dependant is between 5 and 12 years of age.
- Recipients of the Family Tax Benefit may elect to receive the benefit in fortnightly instalments or as an end of year lump sum payment.
- A Newborn Supplement and Newborn Upfront Payment may be paid to families for each baby born from 1 March 2014. To be eligible families will need to be eligible for Family Tax Benefit Part A and not be accessing Parental Leave Pay for that child. For multiple births, Parental Leave Pay may be payable for one child and Newborn Supplement for the other child or children. The total value of the Newborn Supplement and Newborn Upfront Payment in 2015-16 is up to AUD 2 091.84 for the first child (and all multiple births) and up to AUD 1 046.25 for subsequent children. This supplement and upfront payment replace the previous Baby Bonus.
- On 1 January 2011 Australia's first Paid Parental Leave scheme commenced. The scheme provides two government-funded payments: Parental Leave Pay and Dad and Partner Pay.

Parental Leave Pay (PLP) provides the primary carer of a child with 18 weeks' pay at the national minimum wage (AUD 657.00 per week before tax in 2015-16), in the year following the child's birth or adoption. The primary carer must have worked for at least 10 of the 13 months prior to the birth or adoption, and for at least 330 hours in that 10 month period with no more than an eight week gap between two working days. The primary carer's adjusted taxable income must be AUD 150 000 or less in the financial year prior to the date of claim or date of birth or adoption, whichever is earlier. PLP and Newborn Supplement cannot be paid for the same child. A person cannot claim FTB(B) or the dependent spouse, child housekeeper and housekeeper tax offsets while they are receiving PLP.

- Dad and Partner Pay (DAPP) provides the father or partner of the primary carer of a child with two weeks' pay at the national minimum wage (AUD 657.00 per week before tax in 2015-16), in the year following the child's birth or adoption. The father or partner must have worked for at least 10 of the 13 months prior to the birth or adoption and for at least 330 hours in that 10 month period with no more than an eight week gap between two working days. The father or partner's adjusted taxable income must be AUD 150 000 or less in the financial year prior to the date of claim or date of birth or adoption, whichever is earlier. DAPP and PLP may be paid for the same child.
- Child Care Benefit (CCB) is a means-tested payment which assists families with the cost of approved child care. In 2015-16 CCB is payable to eligible families with incomes up to AUD 152 147 for one child in care, with the income limit rising for each additional child in care. Families with annual incomes under AUD 43 727 receive the maximum rate of CCB, which is AUD 4.17 per hour for a non-school child in care. CCB is payable for a maximum of 50 hours per week. To receive more than 24 hours of CCB per week both parents must be participating in work, training or study activities for at least 15 hours per week. The attached calculations assume no child care usage.
- Child Care Rebate (CCR) is an additional payment aimed at promoting workforce participation. CCR is not means tested. It pays 50% of out-of-pocket child care expenses (after any CCB), up to an annual cap of AUD 7 500 per child in 2015-16. Families have to participate in work, training or study related commitments at some time during a week or have an exemption. No minimum number of hours is required.
- Parenting Payment is a taxable payment payable to partnered and sole parents for low income families with a qualifying child under six and eight years of age respectively. In 2015-16 the maximum annual amount of Parenting Payment (Partnered) (PP(P)) was AUD 12 295. Only one parent in a couple can be entitled to PP(P). The maximum annual amount of Parenting Payment (Single) (PP(S)) was AUD 19 023. These payments are subject to income and assets tests. The Parenting Payment (Partnered) tapers out at a rate of AUD 0.50 per AUD 1 of income over AUD 2 652 up to AUD 6 552 and reduces at a rate of AUD 0.60 per AUD 1 for income over AUD 6 552. Under the PP(P) income test, a spouse receives a reduced Parenting Payment, tapering at a rate of AUD 0.60, when the higher earning partner's income exceeds AUD 24 310. If the spouse has little or no income (less than AUD 2 652 per annum), he or she would not receive any Parenting Payment when the higher earning partner's income exceeds AUD 45 296. PP(S) reduces by AUD 0.40 for each AUD 1 of income above AUD 4 212 plus AUD 639.60 for each child other than the first. A sole parent with two qualifying dependants may be entitled to some taxable PP(S) in 2015-16 where private income does not exceed AUD 52 409. The attached calculations assume dependants are aged six and seven.

- The Newstart allowance is a taxable payment payable to single persons and partnered individuals who are unemployed. It is also payable to a member of a couple if their youngest child is aged six years or more and to single parents if their youngest child is aged eight years or more. It is conditional on recipients fulfilling a personal Job Plan, which typically involves taking part in activities such as job seeking and training. In 2015-16 the Newstart allowance for singles without dependants was AUD 13 616 and for partnered individuals was AUD 12 295. These payments taper out at a rate of AUD 0.50 per AUD 1 for incomes between AUD 2 652 and AUD 6 552, and reduce at a rate of AUD 0.60 per AUD for incomes over AUD 6 552. The Newstart allowance for partnered individuals reduces by AUD 0.60 for each AUD 1 of their partner's income above AUD 24 310. For single principal carers with dependent child(ren), it reduces at a rate of AUD 0.40 per AUD 1 for incomes over AUD 2 652.
- A non-taxable supplementary payment called Pharmaceutical Allowance (PA) is payable to eligible persons; for example, persons who receive the PP(S). PA is added to the maximum basic rate of PP(S) before a person's PP(S) entitlement is calculated. Anyone with a PP(S) entitlement, after PA has been added, receives the full amount of PA. For 2015-16, the payment is AUD 161.20.
- A Telephone Allowance is available on a quarterly basis to eligible individuals, including individuals who receive PP(S) or PA if their PP(S) entitlement is reduced to 0. The basic rate of the Telephone Allowance is AUD 110.67 for 2015-16, with a higher rate of AUD 164.89 available for recipients of Disability Support Pension who are under the age of 21 and where a home internet service is connected in the individual's or partner's name. The attached calculations assume the standard rate is applicable.

4.2. *Other transfers*

Single Income Family Supplement

- The Single Income Family Supplement (SIFS) is a non-taxable payment for households with one main income earner.
- The SIFS phases in at a rate of AUD 0.025 for every AUD 1 above AUD 68 000 until it reaches AUD 300. Once the main earner's income exceeds AUD 120 000 the SIFS reduces by AUD 0.01 for every AUD 1. If there is a secondary earner, every AUD of their income above AUD 16 000, reduces the SIFS by AUD 0.15.

Schoolkids Bonus

- Parents or carers eligible for FTB Part A are eligible to receive Schoolkids Bonus. In 2015-16, the Bonus was worth AUD 430 for each child in primary school and AUD 856 for each child in secondary school. The Schoolkids Bonus is limited to families and individuals with an income of AUD 100 000 per year or less. It is paid in two equal instalments in January and July each year. The Schoolkids Bonus is being phased out and the final instalment will be paid in July 2016.

Income Support Bonus

- The Income Support Bonus is a non-taxable payment made to recipients of eligible social security benefits. In 2015-16, single persons received AUD 222.10 and each member of a couple received AUD 184.90.

5. Recent changes in the tax/benefit system

In 2015-16, the following changes to the benefits system commenced:

- The "additional child add-on" (of USD 3796) to the threshold for paying the base rate of FTB(A) (USD 94 316) has been abolished.
- The Large Family Supplement is now payable to families with four children (it was previously three).
- The primary earner income threshold for FTB(B) has been reduced from USD 150 000 to USD 100 000 per annum.

There were no significant changes to the personal tax system relevant to Taxing Wages in 2015-16.

6. Memorandum items

6.1. *Identification of an average worker*

The source of the information used in replying to the questionnaire was the Australian Bureau of Statistics publication *Average Weekly Earnings – Australia*, catalogue number 6302.0. The survey is now conducted on a biannual basis (it was previously conducted on a quarterly basis up to the June 2012 quarter) and is based on a representative sample of employers in each industry. As a result of this change in frequency, average weekly earnings for the 2015-16 income tax year have been calculated as the average of the two biannual figures (November 2015 and May 2016 (released in August 2016)).

In August 2009 the Australian Bureau of Statistics (ABS) redesigned the survey and replaced the industry classification based on the 1993 edition of the Australian and New Zealand Standard Industrial Classification (ANZSIC), which had been in use since 1994, with the 2006 edition of ANZSIC. The 2006 edition of ANZSIC was developed to provide a more contemporary industrial classification system, taking into account issues such as changes in the structure and composition of the economy, changing user demands and compatibility with major international classification standards. Accordingly, the average wage figure for 2010 and later years is inconsistent with that provided for previous years.

All wage and salary earners who received pay for the reference period are represented in the Survey of Average Weekly Earnings (AWE), except:

- members of the Australian permanent defence forces;
- employees of enterprises primarily engaged in agriculture, forestry and fishing;
- employees of private households;
- employees of overseas embassies, consulates, etc.;
- employees based outside Australia; and
- employees on workers' compensation who are not paid through the payroll.

Also excluded are the following persons who are not regarded as employees for the purposes of this survey:

- casual employees who did not receive pay during the reference period;
- employees on leave without pay who did not receive pay during the reference period;
- employees on strike, or stood down, who did not receive pay during the reference period;
- directors who are not paid a salary;
- proprietors/partners of unincorporated businesses;

- self-employed persons such as subcontractors, owner/drivers, consultants;
- persons paid solely by commission without a retainer; and
- employees paid under the Parental Leave Pay Scheme.

The sample for the AWE survey, like most ABS business surveys, is selected from the ABS Business Register which is primarily based on registrations with the Australian Taxation Office's (ATO) Pay As You Go Withholding (PAYGW) scheme (and prior to 1 June 2000 the Group Employer (GE) scheme). The population is updated quarterly to take account of:

- new businesses;
- businesses which have ceased employing;
- changes in employment levels;
- changes in industry; and
- other general business changes.

Earnings comprise weekly ordinary time earnings and weekly overtime earnings.

Weekly ordinary time earnings refers to one week's earnings of employees for the reference period attributable to award, standard or agreed hours of work. It is calculated before taxation and any other deductions (e.g. superannuation, board and lodging) have been made. Included in ordinary time earnings are award, workplace and enterprise bargaining payments, and other agreed base rates of pay, over award and over agreed payments, penalty payments, shift and other allowances; commissions and retainers; bonuses and similar payments related to the reference period; payments under incentive or piecework; payments under profit sharing schemes normally paid each pay period; payment for leave taken during the reference period; all workers' compensation payments made through the payroll; and salary payments made to directors. Excluded are overtime payments, retrospective pay, pay in advance, leave loadings, severance, termination and redundancy payments, and other payments not related to the reference period.

Weekly overtime earnings refers to payment for hours in excess of award, standard or agreed hours of work.

6.2. Employers' contribution to private health and pension scheme

In Australia very few employers make any contributions towards health schemes for their employees, especially where the employee is at a wage level comparable to that of an average production worker.

From a survey of employment benefits conducted by the Australian Bureau of Statistics, the findings of which were published in 2001 as *Superannuation, Australia 2000* (ABS Catalogue No. 6360.0), it was estimated that 98% of all employed persons with leave entitlements were covered by a superannuation scheme.

TAXING WAGES 2017 © OECD 2017

2016 parameter values

Average earnings/yr	Ave_earn	82 114	
Low Income Tax Offset	low_inc_cr	445	
	low_inc_lim	37 000	
	low_inc_redn	0.015	
Tax schedule	tax_sch	0.000	18 200
		0.190	37 000
		0.325	80 000
		0.370	180 000
		0.450	
Medicare levy	medic_rate	0.02	
exemption limits	sing_lim	21 335	
married	m_lim	36 001	
sing parent receiving PPS	SAPTO_lim	46 966	
+ per child	ch_lim	3 306	
shading-in rate	shade_rate	0.1	
Temporary Budget Repair Levy	TBRL_rate	0.02	
income threshold	TBRL_lim	180 000	
Part A FTB max	FTB_A_max	5 412.95	
Part A FTB basic	FTB_A_base	2 230.15	
part A income limit 1	FTB_A_lim1	51 027	
part A income limit 2	FTB_A_lim2	94 316	
reduction rate 1	FTB_A_taper1	0.2	
reduction rate 2	FTB_A_taper2	0.3	
additional limit2 per extra child	FTB_A_child	0	
Large family supplement	FTB_A_large	324.85	
Part A FTB Clean Energy Advance (CEA) max	FTB_A_CEA_max	0	
Part A FTB CEA basic	FTB_A_CEA_basic	0	
Part A FTB Energy Supplement (ES) max	FTB_A_CES_max	91.25	
Part A FTB ES basic	FTB_A_CES_basic	36.5	
Part B FTB	FTB_B	3 139.00	
part B partner income limit	FTB_B_lim	5 402	
reduction rate	FTB_B_taper	0.2	
Income limit (primary earner)	FTB_B_lim_p	100 000	
Part B FTB CEA no child <5 years old	FTB_B_CEA_5	0	
Part B FTB ES no child <5 years old	FTB_B_CES_5	51.1	
Single Income Family Supplement max rate	SIFS_max	300	
Single Income Family Supplement phase-in threshold	SIFS_in_lim_pr	68 000	
Single Income Family Supplement taper in Rate - primary earner	SIFS_in_taper_pr	0.025	
Single Income Family Supplement phase-out threshold (primary earner)	SIFS_out_lim_pr	120 000	
Single Income Family Supplement taper out rate (primary earner)	SIFS_out_taper_pr	0.01	
Single Income Family Supplement phase out threshold (secondary earner)	SIFS_out_lim_sec	16 000	
Single income family supplement phase out taper - secondary earner	SIFS_out_taper_sec	0.15	
Parenting payment single	PPS	19 022.90	
reduction rate	PPS_taper	0.4	
income limit	PPS_lim	4212	
additional limit per child	PPS_ch_lim	639.6	
Parenting payment single CEA	PPS_CEA	0	
Parenting payment single Energy Supplement (ES)	PPS_CES	312	
Pharmaceutical allowance	PA	161.2	
State pay-roll tax rate (NSW)	Pay_roll_rate	0.0545	
Additional parameters			
Newstart allowance single rate	NSAS	13 616.46	
Newstart allowance single CEA	NSAS_CEA	0	
Newstart allowance single ES	NSAS_CES	228.80	
Newstart allowance partnered rate	NSAP	12 294.88	
Newstart allowance partnered CEA	NSAP_CEA	0	

2016 parameter values

Newstart allowance partnered ES	NSAP_CES	205.40
reduction rate 1	NSA_taper1	0.5
reduction rate 2	NSA_taper2	0.6
income limit 1	NSA_lim1	2652
income limit 2	NSA_lim2	6552
Senior Australian and Pensioner Tax Offset	SAPTO	2230
Senior Australian and Pensioner Tax Offset single threshold	SAPTO_thresh	32 279
Senior Australian and Pensioner Tax Offset taper rate	SAPTO_taper	0.125
SchoolKids Bonus	SKB	430
	SKB_lim	100 000
Telephone allowance	Tele_A	110.67
Flood levy	tax_flo	
Income Support Bonus - Single	ISB_s	222.10
Income Support Bonus - partnered	ISB_p	184.90

2016 tax equations

The equations for the Australian system in 2016 are mostly repeated for each individual of a married couple. However, the spouse credit is relevant only to the calculation for the principal earner and the calculation of the Medicare levy uses shading-in rules which depend on the levels of earnings of the spouses. The basis of calculation is shown by the Range indicator in the table below.

The functions which are used in the equations (Taper, MIN, Tax etc) are described in the technical note about tax equations. Variable names are defined in the table of parameters above, within the equations table, or are the standard variables "married" and "children". A reference to a variable with the affix "_total" indicates the sum of the relevant variable values for the principal and spouse. And the affixes "_princ" and "_spouse" indicate the value for the principal and spouse respectively. Where the calculation for one earner takes into account variables for the other earner, the affix "_oth" is used. Equations for a single person are as shown for the principal, with "_spouse" values taken as 0.

	Line in country table and intermediate steps	Variable name	Range	Equation
1.	Earnings	earn		
2.	Allowances	tax_al	B	0
3.	Credits in taxable income:			
	Credits in taxable income of principal	taxbl_cr_princ	P	IF(AND(Children>0,Married=0),Taper(PPS,earn_princ,PPS_lim+PPS_ch_lim*(Children-1),PPS_taper),IF(AND(Children=0,Married=0),taper2(NSAS,earn_princ,NSA_lim1,NSA_lim2,NSA_taper1,NSA_taper2),IF(Married>0,taper3(NSAP,earn_princ,earn_spouse,NSA_lim1,NSA_lim2,NSA_taper1,NSA_taper2,0),,0)))
	Credits in taxable income of spouse	taxbl_cr_spouse	S	IF(AND(Children>0,Married=0),0,IF(AND(Children=0,Married=0),0,IF(Married>0,taper3(NSAP,earn_spouse,earn_princ,NSA_lim1,NSA_lim2,NSA_taper1,NSA_taper2,0),0)))
4.	CG taxable income	tax_inc	B	earn+taxbl_cr
5.	CG tax before credits			
	Medicare Levy	med_levy	B	medicare(tax_inc,sing_lim,m_lim,SAPTO_lim,ch_lim,shade_rate,medic_rate,Married,tax_inc_oth,Children)
	Temporary Budget Repair Levy	TBRL	B	TBRL_rate*Positive(tax_inc-TBRL_lim)
	Tax liability	liab	P	Tax(tax_inc, tax_sch)
6.	Tax credits :			
	Low income credit	low_cr	B	Taper(low_inc_cr,tax_inc,low_inc_lim,low_inc_redn)
	Senior Australian and Pensioner Tax Offset	sap_cr	P	IF(AND(taxbl_cr_princ>0,NOT(AND(Children>0,Married=0))),Tax(taxbl_cr_princ,tax_sch),IF(taxbl_cr_princ>0,Taper(SAPTO,tax_inc,SAPTO_thresh,SAPTO_taper),0)
	Beneficiary tax offset	ben_cr	B	IF(AND(taxbl_cr>0, NOT(AND(Children>0, Married=0))), Tax(taxbl_cr, tax_sch), 0)
	Total	tax_cr	B	low_cr+sap_cr+ben_cr
7.	CG tax	CG_tax	B	Positive(liab-tax_cr) + med_levy + TBRL
8.	State and local taxes	local_tax	B	0
9.	Employees' soc security	SSC	B	0
11.	Cash transfers:			
	Family Tax Benefit (Part A)	ftbA	P	IF(PA>0,((FTB_A_max+FTB_A_CES_max)*Children+IF(Children>3,(Children-3)*FTB_A_large,0)),MAX(((FTB_A_max+FTB_A_CES_max)*Children+IF(Children>3,(Children-3)*FTB_A_large,0)-Positive((princ_earn+taxbl_cr+spouse_earn+taxbl_cr_spouse)-FTB_A_lim1)*FTB_A_taper1),Positive((FTB_A_base+FTB_A_CES_basic)*Children+IF(Children>3,(Children-3)*FTB_A_large,0)-Positive((princ_earn+taxbl_cr+spouse_earn+taxbl_cr_spouse)-(FTB_A_lim2+(Positive(Children-1))*FTB_A_child))*FTB_A_taper2)))

	Line in country table and intermediate steps	Variable name	Range	Equation
	Family Tax Benefit (Part B)	ftbB	J	IF(earn_princ<FTB_B_lim_p,IF(Children>0,Taper(FTB_B+FTB_B_CES_5, earn_spouse+taxbl_cr_spouse,FTB_B_lim,FTB_B_taper),0),0)
	Pharmaceutical Allowance	PA	J	AND(Children>0,Married=0)*IF(Taper(PPS+PA+PPS_CES,earn_princ, PPS_lim+PPS_ch_lim*(Children-1),PPS_taper)>0,PA,0)
	Clean Energy Advance	CEA	J	IF(AND(Children>0,Married=0,Taper(PPS+PPS_CES,earn_princ,PPS_lim+PPS_ch_lim*(Children-1),PPS_taper)>0),PPS_CEA,IF(AND(Children=0,Married=0, taper2(NSAS+NSAS_CES,earn_princ,NSA_lim1,NSA_lim2,NSA_taper1,NSA_taper2)>0),NSAS_CEA,IF(AND(Married>0,taper3(NSAP,earn_spouse,earn_princ,NSA_lim1,NSA_lim2,NSA_taper1,NSA_taper2,NSAP_CES)>0),NSAP_CEA)))+IF(AND(taxbl_cr_princ>0,Married>0,taper2(NSAP+NSAP_CES,earn_princ,NSA_lim1,NSA_lim2,NSA_taper1,NSA_taper2)>0),NSAP_CEA,0)+IF(AND(ftbA>0,ftbA>FTB_A_base*Children+IF(Children>2,(Children-2)*FTB_A_large,0)),FTB_A_CEA_max*Children, 0)+IF(AND(ftbA>0,ftbA<=FTB_A_base*Children+IF(Children>2,(Children-2)* FTB_A_large,0)),FTB_A_CEA_basic*Children,0)+IF(ftbB>0,FTB_B_CEA_5,0)
	Energy Supplement	CES	J	IF(AND(Children>0,Married=0,Taper(PPS+PPS_CES,earn_princ,PPS_lim+PPS_ch_lim*(Children-1),PPS_taper)>0), MAX(0,Taper(PPS+PPS_CES,earn_princ, PPS_lim+PPS_ch_lim*(Children-1),PPS_taper)-Taper(PPS, earn_princ,PPS_lim+PPS_ch_lim*(Children-1),PPS_taper)),IF(AND(Children>0,Married=0,Taper (PPS+PPS_CES,earn_princ,PPS_lim+PPS_ch_lim*(Children-1),PPS_taper)=0),0,IF(AND(Children=0,Married=0,taper2(NSAS+NSAS_CES,earn_princ,NSA_lim1,NSA_lim2,NSA_taper1,NSA_taper2)>0),taper2(NSAS+NSAS_CES, earn_princ,NSA_lim1,NSA_lim2,NSA_taper1,NSA_taper2)-taper2(NSAS,earn_princ,NSA_lim1,NSA_lim2,NSA_taper1,NSA_taper2),IF(AND(Married>0,taper3(NSAP,earn_spouse,earn_princ,NSA_lim1,NSA_lim2,NSA_taper1,NSA_taper2,NSAP_CES)>0),taper3(NSAP,earn_spouse,earn_princ,NSA_lim1,NSA_lim2,NSA_taper1,NSA_taper2,NSAP_CES)-taper3(NSAP,earn_spouse,earn_princ,NSA_lim1,NSA_lim2,NSA_taper1,NSA_taper2,NSAP_CES-NSAP_CES)))))+IF(AND(Married>0, ,taper2(NSAP+NSAP_CES,earn_princ,NSA_lim1,NSA_lim2,NSA_taper1,NSA_taper2)>0), max(0, taper2(NSAP+NSAP_CES,earn_princ,NSA_lim1,NSA_lim2,NSA_taper1,NSA_taper2)- taper2(NSAP,earn_princ,NSA_lim1,NSA_lim2,NSA_taper1, NSA_taper2)),0)
	SchoolKids Bonus	SKB	J	IF(earn_princ+earn_spouse+taxbl_cr_princ+taxbl_cr_spouse<SKB_lim,IF(FTB Part A>0,SKB*Children,0),0)
	Single Income Family Supplement	SIFS	J	sifs(tax_inc_princ,tax_inc_spouse,ftbA+ftbB,SIFS_max,SIFS_in_lim_pr,SIFS_in_taper_pr,SIFS_out_lim_pr,SIFS_out_taper_pr,SIFS_out_lim_sec,SIFS_out_taper_sec)
	Income support bonus	ISB	B	IF(AND(Married=0,(taxbl_cr_princ+earn_princ+PA)>0),ISB_s,IF(AND(Married>0,taper3(NSAP, taxbl_cr_princ, earn_princ,NSA_lim1,NSA_lim2,NSA_taper1,NSA_taper2,NSAP_CES)>0),ISB_p,0))+IF(AND(Married>0,taper2(NSAP+NSAP_CES,earn_princ,NSA_lim1,NSA_lim2,NSA_taper1,NSA_taper2)>0),ISB_p,0)
	Telephone Allowance	TeleA	P	IF(Married=0,IF(Children>0,IF(Taper(PPS+PA+PPS_CES,earn_princ,PPS_lim+PPS_ch_lim*(Children-1),PPS_taper)>0,Tele_A,0),0),0)
		cash_trans	J	ftbA+ftbB+taxbl_cr_princ+PA+taxbl_cr_spouse+Tele_A +CEA=CES+SKB+SIFS+ISB
13.	Employer's State pay-roll tax	tax_empr	B	earn*Pay_roll_rate

Key to range of equation B calculated separately for both principal earner and spouse P calculated for principal only (value taken as 0 for spouse calculation) J calculated once only on a joint basis. Key refers to an optimisation of benefits i.e. Parenting payment for principal and Newstart allowance for spouse versus Parenting payment for spouse and Newstart allowance for principal.

© OECD 2017

Austria

This chapter includes data on the income taxes paid by workers, their social security contributions, the family benefits they receive in the form of cash transfers as well as the social security contributions and payroll taxes paid by their employers. Results reported include the marginal and average tax burden for eight different family types.

Methodological information is available for Personal income tax systems, Compulsory social security contributions to schemes operated within the government sector, Universal cash transfers as well as recent changes in the tax/benefit system. The methodology also includes the parameter values and tax equations underlying the data.

Austria 2016

The tax/benefit position of single persons

	Wage level (per cent of average wage)		67	100	167	67
	Number of children		none	none	none	2
1.	**Gross wage earnings**		29 754	44 409	74 163	29 754
2.	**Standard tax allowances**					
	Basic allowance		60	60	60	60
	Married or head of family					
	Dependent children		0	0	0	880
	Deduction for social security contributions and income taxes		5 349	7 983	12 232	5 349
	Work-related expenses		132	132	132	132
	Other		0	0	0	0
		Total	5 541	8 175	12 424	6 421
3.	**Tax credits or cash transfers included in taxable income**		0	0	0	0
4.	**Central government taxable income (1 - 2 + 3)**		24 213	36 233	61 739	23 333
5.	**Central government income tax liability (exclusive of tax credits)**		2 866	6 570	15 958	2 558
6.	**Tax credits**					
	Basic credit		0	0	0	0
	Married or head of family		0	0	0	669
	Children					
	Other		400	400	400	400
		Total	400	400	400	1 069
7.	**Central government income tax finally paid (5-6)**		2 466	6 170	15 558	1 489
8.	**State and local taxes**		0	0	0	0
9.	**Employees' compulsory social security contributions**					
	Gross earnings		5 349	7 983	12 232	5 349
	Taxable income					
		Total	5 349	7 983	12 232	5 349
10.	**Total payments to general government (7 + 8 + 9)**		7 815	14 153	27 790	6 838
11.	**Cash transfers from general government**					
	For head of family					
	For two children		0	0	0	5 098
		Total	0	0	0	5 098
12.	**Take-home pay (1-10+11)**		21 939	30 256	46 373	28 015
13.	**Employer's wage dependent contributions and taxes**					
	Employer's compulsory social security contributions		6 370	9 507	14 566	6 370
	payroll taxes		2 232	3 331	5 562	2 232
		Total	8 601	12 838	20 129	8 601
14.	**Average rates**					
	Income tax		8.3%	13.9%	21.0%	5.0%
	Employees' social security contributions		18.0%	18.0%	16.5%	18.0%
	Total payments less cash transfers		26.3%	31.9%	37.5%	5.8%
	Total tax wedge including employer's social security contributions		42.8%	47.1%	50.8%	27.0%
15.	**Marginal rates**					
	Total payments less cash transfers: Principal earner		43.3%	43.3%	36.9%	43.3%
	Total payments less cash transfers: Spouse		n.a.	n.a.	n.a.	n.a.
	Total tax wedge: Principal earner		56.0%	56.0%	41.3%	56.0%
	Total tax wedge: Spouse		n.a.	n.a.	n.a.	n.a.

Austria 2016

The tax/benefit position of married couples

		Wage level (per cent of average wage)	100-0	100-33	100-67	100-33
		Number of children	2	2	2	none
1.	**Gross wage earnings**		44 409	59 064	74 163	59 064
2.	**Standard tax allowances**					
	Basic allowance		60	120	120	120
	Married or head of family					
	Dependent children		880	880	1 200	0
	Deduction for social security contributions and income taxes		7 983	10 178	13 332	10 178
	Work-related expenses		132	264	264	264
	Other		0	0	0	0
		Total	9 055	11 442	14 916	10 562
3.	**Tax credits or cash transfers included in taxable income**		0	0	0	0
4.	**Central government taxable income (1 - 2 + 3)**		35 353	47 622	59 247	48 502
5.	**Central government income tax liability (exclusive of tax credits)**		6 262	6 262	9 015	6 570
6.	**Tax credits**					
	Basic credit		0	0	0	0
	Married or head of family		669	0	0	0
	Children					
	Other		400	800	800	800
		Total	1 069	800	800	800
7.	**Central government income tax finally paid (5 - 6)**		5 193	5 462	8 215	5 770
8.	**State and local taxes**		0	0	0	0
9.	**Employees' compulsory social security contributions**					
	Gross earnings		7 983	10 178	13 332	10 178
	Taxable income					
		Total	7 983	10 178	13 332	10 178
10.	**Total payments to general government (7 + 8 + 9)**		13 176	15 640	21 548	15 948
11.	**Cash transfers from general government**					
	For head of family					
	For two children		5 098	5 098	5 098	0
		Total	5 098	5 098	5 098	0
12.	**Take-home pay (1-10+11)**		36 331	48 522	57 714	43 116
13.	**Employer's wage dependent contributions and taxes**					
	Employer's compulsory social security contributions		9 507	12 645	15 877	12 645
	Payroll taxes		3 331	4 430	5 562	4 430
		Total	12 838	17 075	21 439	17 075
14.	**Average rates**					
	Income tax		11.7%	9.2%	11.1%	9.8%
	Employees' social security contributions		18.0%	17.2%	18.0%	17.2%
	Total payments less cash transfers		18.2%	17.8%	22.2%	27.0%
	Total tax wedge including employer's social security contributions		36.5%	36.3%	39.6%	43.4%
15.	**Marginal rates**					
	Total payments less cash transfers: Principal earner		43.3%	43.3%	43.3%	43.3%
	Total payments less cash transfers: Spouse		16.8%	15.0%	43.3%	15.0%
	Total tax wedge: Principal earner		56.0%	56.0%	56.0%	56.0%
	Total tax wedge: Spouse		35.5%	34.0%	56.0%	34.0%

The Austrian currency is the Euro (EUR). In 2016, EUR 0.90 was equal to USD 1. In that year, the average worker in Austria earned EUR 44 409 (Secretariat estimate).

1. Personal income tax

1.1. Central government income tax

1.1.1. Tax unit

Each person is taxed separately.

1.1.2. Tax allowances

1.1.2.1. Standard tax reliefs

- Work related expenses: a minimum tax allowance of EUR 132 is available to all employees.
- Minimum tax allowance for special expenses of EUR 60.
- Social security contributions and connected contributions (see Section 2).
- Children tax allowance of EUR 440 for one or EUR 300 for both parents per child. The parents have the choice between these opportunities.

1.1.2.2. Non-standard tax reliefs

- Mainly work-related expenses ("Werbungskosten").
- Traffic relief depending on the distance between home/address and working place and the availability of public transport.

The following allowances are deductible from income (EUR per year):

	Public transport	
	Available	Not available
more than 2 km	0	372
more than 20 km	696	1 476
more than 40 km	1 356	2 568
more than 60 km	2 016	3 672

- Tax-free wage supplements exist for dirty, hard, dangerous, night, weekend and holiday work and overtime. The supplement for 10 hours of overtime up to EUR 86 per month is tax free, the other supplements are tax free up to EUR 360 (EUR 540 for night workers) per month.
- Tax allowances for contributions to state-approved churches up to EUR 400 per year and for donations up to 10% of income to research and humanitarian purposes, environmental protection, fire brigades, civil protection, etc.

1.1.3. Rate schedule

The tax schedule from 2016 onwards is:

Income (EUR) up to	Marginal rate %
11 000	0
18 000	25
31 000	35
60 000	42
90 000	48
1 000 000	50
Above	55*

* The top marginal tax rate of 55% applies only until 2020.

There is a special taxation other than the normal tax schedule for Christmas and leave bonus to the extent that their sum does not exceed two average monthly payments (1/6 of current income) or EUR 83 333. If these bonuses before deduction of SSC are below EUR 2 100 p.a., no tax is calculated. Otherwise the tax amount is calculated according to the following formula:

Income from Christmas and leave bonus (EUR) up to	Marginal rate %
2 000	0
2 345	30
25 000	6
50 000	27
83 333	35.75
Above	50/55

If income for Christmas and leave bonus exceeds EUR 83 333, the exceeding amount is added to current income and taxed accordingly (MTR of 50% or 55%, see above).

1.1.4. *Tax credits*

The following tax credits exist:

- Traffic (commuting) tax credit of EUR 400. If after overall tax calculation of current income the tax amount is negative a refund of social security contributions applies. The refund amounts to the absolute value of the negative result of the tax calculation for current income, limited to 50% of overall social security contributions paid, respectively EUR 400. For commuters with a traffic allowance (see 1.1.2.2) the maximum amount is EUR 500.
- Additional traffic tax credit in case of entitlement to traffic relief according to the distance between home/address and working place (see 1.1.2.2). In this case employees are entitled to an additional traffic tax credit of EUR 2 per km distance from home to working place.
- Sole earner's and sole parent's tax credit for families with children. The sole earner's credit is not given when a spouse's income exceeds EUR 6 000. This tax credit is EUR 494 for one child and increases by EUR 175 for the second and by EUR 220 for the third and every additional child. This tax credit is non-wastable and can be paid out as a negative income tax (in addition to the refund of social security contributions in respect of the traffic tax credit).
- Children's tax credit EUR 700.8 (58.40 per month) per child. As this tax credit is paid together with children allowances and not connected with income tax assessment. Therefore it is treated as a transfer in this Report (similar treatment as in *Revenue Statistics*).

- Tax credit for retired persons. The tax credit amounts to EUR 764 for sole earners with income up to EUR 19 930 and if the spouse's income does not exceed EUR 2 200. Otherwise the tax credit is EUR 400. The tax credit is linearly reduced to 0 between EUR 17 000 (EUR 19 930 for sole earners) and EUR 25 000 of income. If after overall tax calculation on current income the tax amount is negative a refund of social security contributions applies. The refund amounts to is limited to 50% of overall social security contributions paid, respectively to EUR 110.

1.2. State and local income taxes

None.

2. Compulsory social security contributions to schemes operated within the government sector

2.1. Employee and employer social security contributions

	Ceilings (EUR)		Rates (%)	
	Regular wage per month	Christmas and leave bonus	Employee (2)	Employer (3)
Health insurance	4 860	9 720	3.87	3.78
Unemployment insurance	4 860	9 720	(4)	3.00
Pension insurance	4 860	9 720	10.25	12.55
Accident insurance	4 860	9 720	–	1.30
Contribution to the labour chamber	4 860	1	0.50	–
Contribution for the promotion of residential building	4 860	1	0.50	0.50
Addition to secure wage payments in the case of bankruptcy	4 860	9 720	–	0.35

1. No contributions on Christmas and leave bonus. In Revenue Statistics, the contribution to the labour chamber is accounted under Taxes on Income of Individuals (1110) the total of the contribution for the promotion of residential buildings is included in Taxes on payroll (3000).
2. There is a threshold for employee contributions of EUR 415.72 per month.
3. A new program has been introduced as of 1 January 2004 for severance payments. Employers are required to pay 1.53% of gross wages for those whose employment starts after 1 January 2003 or where the employer and employee opt to participate in the new program. This contribution is seen as a non-tax compulsory wage-related payment.
4. Employees' unemployment insurance rate is reduced for low earnings. In 2015, it is zero for monthly earnings up to EUR 1 311, 1% up to EUR 1 430, 2% up to EUR 1 609 and 3% above.

2.2. Payroll taxes

There are two payroll taxes which are levied on employers for all private sector employees with a monthly gross wage total of more than EUR 1 095: the contribution to the Family Burden Equalisation Fund (4.5%) and the Community Tax (3%). The wage-dependent part of the contribution to the Austrian Economic Chamber (listed under heading 1000, taxes on profits, in the *Revenue Statistics*) which is levied, together with the contributions to the Family Burden Equalisation Fund, at different rates depending upon the Länder Chamber (the average rate is approximately 0.4%) is not taken into account. The contribution for the promotion of residential buildings (listed under heading 3000, taxes on payroll, in *Revenue Statistics*) is included in the social security contributions shown above as it is levied by the Health Insurance Companies on monthly income (current) along with the other social security contribution amounts.

3. Universal cash transfers

3.1. Transfers related to marital status

No recurrent payments.

3.2. Transfers for dependent children

A family allowance is granted for each child. The monthly payment is EUR 111.80 for the first child, EUR 125.60 for the second, EUR 149.00 for the third and EUR 164.80 for each subsequent child. It is increased by EUR 7.80 for children above 3 years, EUR 27.00 for children above 10 years of age and by EUR 50.20 for students (above 19). In the calculation the weighted average is applied.

Parents of children under the age of 3 years are entitled to a childcare transfer, introduced in 2002. Beginning 2010, the flexibility of the childcare transfer was increased significantly. The entitled parent can choose between following alternatives: EUR 14.53 per day until the 36th month of birth (whereas on parent has to consume at least 6 month), EUR 20.80 (24 months; 20 plus 4), EUR 26.60 (18 months; 15 plus 3) or EUR 33.00 (14 months; 12 plus 2). Additionally instead of the fixed amounts the parents can opt for 80% of the last net-earning, limited to EUR 66 a day (14 months; 12 plus 2).

The children's tax credit (EUR 50.90 per month, see § 1.1.4) is paid out together with the family allowance and therefore treated as a transfer.

There is a supplement to the family allowance of EUR 20.00 per month for the third and every additional child, if the family taxable income (i.e. the sum of the tax base for the progressive income tax schedule) of the preceding year did not exceed EUR 55 000. This supplement is paid out on application after an tax assessment of the very year.

An additional family allowance ("13th family allowance") of EUR 100 is given for children in the age between 6 and 16 every September.

4. Main changes in tax/benefit systems since 2004

In 2004, the first step of a comprehensive tax reform came into force. The general tax credit was increased from EUR 887 to EUR 1 264 and the phasing-out rules were considerably simplified and harmonized for all groups of taxpayers.

The tax reform in 2005 brought a new income tax schedule. Apart from the top rate of 50% for income exceeding EUR 51 000, it shows the average tax rates for two amounts of income. The tax amounts for incomes between these amounts have to be calculated by linear interpolation. The formulas that have to be applied are shown in the tax law. The tax reform included some measures which were made retrospective for 2004. These measures are the increase of the sole earner and the single parent tax credit depending on the number of children (together with a higher earnings limit for the spouse of a single earner) and an increase of the traffic reliefs by about 15%. The maximum deductible amount for church contributions was increased as well. In 2006, the traffic reliefs were again increased by about 10%.

In 2007, the traffic allowances were increased by 10% (effective from 1st July) and the maximum negative tax for employees with traffic allowances was increased from EUR 110 to EUR 240 (for 2008 and 2009). For 2008, the family allowances for the third and subsequent children were increased. In 2008, the unemployment insurance contribution of low-earning employees was reduced (effective from 1st July). In 2008 up to monthly earnings of

EUR 1 100 the rate was zero, for earnings below EUR 1 200 the contribution was 1%, below EUR 1 350 2% and above the current rate of 3%. These income limits are increased according to the increase of the ceiling levels of social security contributions every year.

In September 2008, the parliament decided some measures to compensate for the strong increase of food and energy prices: inter alia, the tax exemption of overtime supplements was increased and the 13th children allowances was introduced.

The tax reform 2009 (effective from 1st January) brought an increase of the zero bracket (from EUR 10 000 to EUR 11 000), a reduction of the income tax rates (except the top rate), an upward shift of the top rate bracket (from EUR 51 000 to EUR 60 000) and several measures for families with children: children allowance (EUR 220 or EUR 132 each parent p.a.), deductibility of cost for child care (up to EUR 2 300 p.a. per child), tax-free payments (up to EUR 500 p.a.) from employers to their employees for child care and an increase of the children tax credit.

Starting with 2013 a progressive rate schedule is applied to Christmas and leave bonus instead of a flat rate regime of 6% (see 1.1.3)

The tax reform 2016 decreased all marginal tax rates significantly, notably the marginal tax rate of the first tax bracket which was reduced by 11.5 percentage points from 36.5% to 25%. Limited to the years 2016 to 2020 the top marginal tax rate is increased by 5 percentage points to 55% temporarily. These 55% apply to parts of income exceeding EUR 1 million a year.

The tax credit for employees was increased from EUR 345 to EUR 400. The non wastable tax credit (reimbursement of social security contributions) for low earnings was extended. For employees the non wastable tax credit was increased to a maximum of 50% of social security contributions up to a ceiling of EUR 400 a year. For commuters eligible for the commuter tax allowance the maximum amount of the non wastable tax credit is EUR 500. This system of a non wastable tax credit was extended to pensioners too, limited to EUR 110.

Besides the already existing broad financial support for families (payable tax credit and transfers as well as deductibility of cost for child care) the tax reform 2016 increased the tax allowances for children from EUR 220 to EUR 440 per child. If both parents claim for this tax allowance, it increases to EUR 600 (two times EUR 300).

Tax expenditures (tax allowances) for private insurances (e.g. health and pension insurances) and mortgages were abolished for new contracts beginning with 2016. For existing contracts these tax allowances are maintained for a transitional period of five years.

The ceiling level of social security contributions was increased extraordinarily by EUR 90 to EUR 4 860 per month.

5. Memorandum items

5.1. *Calculation of earnings data*

- Sector used: All private employees except apprentices employed full-time for the whole year
- Geographical coverage: Whole country
- Sex: Male and Female
- Earnings base:
  - Items excluded: Unemployment compensation
Sickness compensation

- Items included: Vacation payments
  Overtime payments
  Recurring cash payments
  Fringe benefits (taxable value)
- Basic method of calculation used: Average annual earnings
- Income tax year ends: 31 December

  Period to which the earnings calculation refers to: one year.

2016 Parameter values

Average earnings/yr	Ave_earn	44 409	Secretariat estimate
Non current income as %	non_cur_pc	14.286%	
Tax schedule for nci	nci_sch	0	2 000
		0.3	2 345
		0.06	25 000
		0.27	50 000
Maximum non-current income tax base	nci_base_max	0.3575	83 333
Work related	work_rel	132	
Allowance f."Special expenses"	Basic_al	60	
Children allowance for 2 earning parents	Child_al_2	300	
Children allowance for sole earner/parent	Child_al_1	440	
Tax free inc.	tax_free	0%	
Basic tax credit	basic_cr		
Employee's tax credit	wage_cr	0	
Max. neg. employee's tax credit	neg_wage_cr	400	
Max. neg. employee's tax credit rate	neg_wage_cr_rate	50%	
Traffic (commuting) tax credit	traffic_cr	400	
Sole earner's (parent's) tax credit	sole_cr	0	
Children suppl.to SETC: 1st child	dsole1_cr	494	
2nd child	dsole2_cr	175	
3rd+ child	dsole3_cr	220	
Spouse income not more than	sole_lim0	0	
Spouse with children	sole_lim1	6 000	
Income tax schedule	Tax_sch	0	11 000
		0.25	18 000
		0.35	31 000
		0.42	60 000
		0.48	90 000
		0.50	1 000 000
		0.55	
Ceiling f. soc. security contributions	SSC_ceil	4 860	
lower limit	SSC_low	415.72	
Employees' contr. rates	health_rate	3.87%	
	unemp_rate	0.00%	1 311
		1.00%	1 430
		2.00%	1 609
		3.00%	
	pension_rate	10.25%	
sum without unempl. and others	empl_14	14.12%	
	others_rate	1.00%	
Employers' contr.rates	health_empr	3.78%	
	unemp_empr	3.00%	
	pension_empr	12.55%	
	accident_empr	1.30%	
	payinsur_empr	0.35%	
sum without others	empr_14	20.98%	
	others_empr	0.50%	
Payroll taxes	payroll_rate	7.50%	
Child benefit: 1st child	CB_1	1 341.6	
2nd child	CB_2	1 507.2	
3rd child	CB_3	1 788.0	
4th+ child	CB_4	1 977.6	
suppl.>3years	CB03sppl	93.6	
suppl.>10years	CB10sppl	324.0	
suppl >19years	CB19sppl	602.4	
5<suppl<17	CB5to17	100	
Child tax credit	child_cr_1	700.8	

2016 Tax equations

The equations for the Austrian system are, in principle, on an individual basis. The only variable which is dependent on the marital status is the head of family (sole earner) tax credit which is also given to single people with children. For the Christmas and leave bonus (both amounting to one monthly wage or salary) there are special rules for the calculation of social security contributions (separate ceilings and slightly lower rate) and wage tax (reduced flat rate). The income tax schedule and the tax credits are applied only for "current pays". The children tax credit is in principle given to the mother (as a negative tax together with "family allowances" = transfer for children). The sole earner and the employee tax credit are connected with negative income tax rules. Therefore, the tax finally paid may be different from tax liability minus tax credits.

Bn	Variable	Code for docn equations	Excel-Function
3	earnings (%AW)	percent	0, 33%, 67%, 1 or 167% in Taxing Wages output tables (but model can be applied to all earnings levels)
4	number of children	child	0 or 2 in Taxing Wages output tables
5	Gross earnings	earn	=Ave_earn*percent
6	Current income	cearn	=(1-non_cur_pc)*earn
7	Basic allowance	allow	=(earn>14*SSC_low)*Basic_al
8	SSC on curr.inc.	SSCc	=(empl_14+unemp(earn,unemp_rate)+others_rate)* MIN(12*SSC_ceil;cearn)*(cearn>12*SSC_low)
9	Work related expenses	work_rel	=(earn>14*SSC_low)*work_rel
10	Tax-free income	taxfrinc	=tax_free*earn
11	Child allowance	Child_al_princ Child_al_spouse	IF(cearn_spouse-allow_spouse-SSCc_spouse-work_rel_spouse-taxfrinc_spouse-12600<0,Child_al_1, Child_al_2)*childIF(Child_al_princ=child*Child_al_2, Child_al_2, 0)*Child
12	Tax base for schedule	ctbase	=(cearn-allow-Child_al_princ- SSCc-work_rel-taxfrinc)+max(0;ncearn-SSCnc-nci_base_max)
13	Gross tax on current income	gtaxcur	=Tax(ctbase;tax_sch)
14	Basic tax credit	btaxcr	=0
15	Married or head of family	headcr	=(earn_sp<IF(child>0;sole_lim1;sole_lim0))*(sole_cr+(child>0)*dsole1_cr+(child>1)*dsole2_cr+(child>2)*(child-2)*dsole3_cr
16	Other	othcr	=(earn>14*SSC_low)*(wage_cr+traffic_cr)
17	Interm. tax on current income	itcur	=gtaxcur-btaxcr-headcr-othcr
18	Net tax on current income	ntaxcur	=max(gtaxcur-btaxcr-other;-neg_wage_cr_rate*SSC;-neg-wage_cr)-child>0)-headcr
19	Non current income	ncearn	=earn-cearn
20	SSC on non-curr. inc.	SSCnc	=(health_rate+unemp(earn,unemp_rate)+pension_rate)* MIN(2*SSC_ceil;ncearn)*(ncearn>2*SSC_low)
21	Non current income-SSC	ncearn_adj1	=min(ncearn-SSCnc;nci_base_max)
22	Tax schedule for nci exc. 25000	nci_sch	=min(ncearn-SSCnc;nci_base_max)
23	Taxable income	taxinc	=ctbase+ncearn_adj1
24	Tax liability excl. tax credits	inctax_ex	=gtaxcur+taxnc
25	Income tax finally paid	inctax	=ntaxcur+taxnc
26	Employee's SSC	SSC	=SSCc+SSCnc
27	Employer's SSC	SSCf	=IF(earn/14>=SSC_low;((empr_14+others_empr)*MINA(12*SSC_ceil;cearn)+empr_14*MINA(2*SSC_ceil;ncearn));earn*accident_empr)
28	Pay-roll taxes	payroll	=payroll_rate*earn

Bn	Variable	Code for docn equations	Excel-Function
29	Cash transfers	cash	=IF(child=0;0;IF(child=2;CB_1+CB_2+child*CB10sppl+child*(child_cr_1+CB5to17)))
30	Take-home pay		=earn-inctax-SSC+cash
31	Wage cost		=earn+SSCf+payroll

unemp is a Visual Basic Function which chooses lower unemployment SSC rates for low earnings
Key to range of equation B calculated separately for both principal earner and spouse P calculated for principal only (value taken as 0 for spouse calculation) J calculated once only on a joint basis.

© OECD 2017

Belgium

This chapter includes data on the income taxes paid by workers, their social security contributions, the family benefits they receive in the form of cash transfers as well as the social security contributions and payroll taxes paid by their employers. Results reported include the marginal and average tax burden for eight different family types.

Methodological information is available for Personal income tax systems, Compulsory social security contributions to schemes operated within the government sector, Universal cash transfers as well as recent changes in the tax/benefit system. The methodology also includes the parameter values and tax equations underlying the data.

Belgium 2016

The tax/benefit position of single persons

	Wage level (per cent of average wage)	67	100	167	67
	Number of children	none	none	none	2
1.	**Gross wage earnings**	31 202	46 570	77 772	31 202
2.	**Standard tax allowances**				
	Basic allowance				
	Married or head of family				
	Dependent children				
	Deduction for social security contributions and income taxes	4 078	6 087	10 165	4 078
	Work-related expenses	4 016	4 240	4 240	4 016
	Other				
	Total	8 094	10 327	14 405	8 094
3.	**Tax credits or cash transfers included in taxable income**	0	0	0	0
4.	**Central government taxable income (1 - 2 + 3)**	23 108	36 243	63 367	23 108
5.	**Central government income tax liability (exclusive of tax credits)**	7 570	13 480	26 951	7 570
6.	**Tax credits**				
	Basic credit	0	0	0	0
	Married or head of family	1 855	1 783	1 783	2 235
	Children	0	0	0	1 216
	Other				
	Total	1 855	1 783	1 783	3 451
7.	**Central government income tax finally paid (5-6)**	4 229	8 658	18 627	3 048
8.	**State and local taxes**	1 862	3 812	8 202	1 342
9.	**Employees' compulsory social security contributions**				
	Gross earnings	4 078	6 087	10 165	4 078
	Taxable income	250	420	731	250
	Total	4 328	6 507	10 896	4 328
10.	**Total payments to general government (7 + 8 + 9)**	10 419	18 977	37 725	8 718
11.	**Cash transfers from general government**				
	For head of family				
	For two children	0	0	0	3 803
	Total	0	0	0	3 803
12.	**Take-home pay (1-10+11)**	20 783	27 593	40 047	26 287
13.	**Employer's compulsory social security contributions**	8 364	13 359	22 081	8 364
14.	**Average rates**				
	Income tax	19.5%	26.8%	34.5%	14.1%
	Employees' social security contributions	13.9%	14.0%	14.0%	13.9%
	Total payments less cash transfers	33.4%	40.7%	48.5%	15.8%
	Total tax wedge including employer's social security contributions	47.5%	54.0%	59.9%	33.6%
15.	**Marginal rates**				
	Total payments less cash transfers: Principal earner	54.6%	55.9%	59.4%	54.6%
	Total payments less cash transfers: Spouse	n.a.	n.a.	n.a.	n.a.
	Total tax wedge: Principal earner	65.7%	66.7%	67.9%	65.7%
	Total tax wedge: Spouse	n.a.	n.a.	n.a.	n.a.

Belgium 2016

The tax/benefit position of married couples

		Wage level (per cent of average wage)	100-0	100-33	100-67	100-33
		Number of children	2	2	2	none
1.	**Gross wage earnings**		46 570	61 938	77 772	61 938
2.	**Standard tax allowances**					
	Basic allowance					
	Married or head of family					
	Dependent children					
	Deduction for social security contributions and income taxes		6 087	6 087	10 165	6 087
	Work-related expenses		4 240	7 536	8 256	7 536
	Other					
		Total	10 327	13 623	18 421	13 623
3.	**Tax credits or cash transfers included in taxable income**		0	0	0	0
4.	**Central government taxable income (1 - 2 + 3)**		36 243	48 315	59 351	48 315
5.	**Central government income tax liability (exclusive of tax credits)**		11 422	16 559	21 050	16 559
6.	**Tax credits**					
	Basic credit		0	640	0	640
	Married or head of family		3 710	3 638	3 638	3 638
	Children		1 103	1 089	1 089	0
	Other					
		Total	4 813	5 366	4 726	4 278
7.	**Central government income tax finally paid (5-6)**		4 892	8 118	12 081	8 923
8.	**State and local taxes**		2 154	3 856	5 320	4 211
9.	**Employees' compulsory social security contributions**					
	Gross earnings		6 087	6 087	10 165	6 087
	Taxable income		420	577	721	577
		Total	6 507	6 664	10 886	6 664
10.	**Total payments to general government (7 + 8 + 9)**		13 553	18 638	28 287	19 798
11.	**Cash transfers from general government**					
	For head of family					
	For two children		3 803	3 803	3 803	0
		Total	3 803	3 803	3 803	0
12.	**Take-home pay (1-10+11)**		36 820	47 103	53 288	42 140
13.	**Employer's compulsory social security contributions**		13 359	14 977	21 723	14 977
14.	**Average rates**					
	Income tax		15.1%	19.3%	22.4%	21.2%
	Employees' social security contributions		14.0%	10.8%	14.0%	10.8%
	Total payments less cash transfers		20.9%	24.0%	31.5%	32.0%
	Total tax wedge including employer's social security contributions		38.6%	38.8%	46.4%	45.2%
15.	**Marginal rates**					
	Total payments less cash transfers: Principal earner		55.9%	55.9%	55.9%	55.9%
	Total payments less cash transfers: Spouse		33.1%	29.6%	54.6%	29.6%
	Total tax wedge: Principal earner		66.7%	66.7%	66.7%	66.7%
	Total tax wedge: Spouse		39.5%	52.1%	65.7%	52.1%

The national currency is the Euro (EUR). In 2016, EUR 0.90 was equal to USD 1. The Secretariat has estimated that in that same year the average worker earned EUR 46 570 (Secretariat estimate).

1. Personal income tax system

1.1. Federal government income tax

1.1.1. Tax unit

Spouses are taxed separately. As from 2004, the principle of separate taxation applies to all categories of income. A non-earning spouse is taxed separately on a notional share of income that can be transferred to him or her (see "non-earning spouse allowance", below). Married couples nonetheless file joint income tax returns.

1.1.1.1. Schedule

Taxable income (EUR)	Marginal rate (%)
0-10 860	25
10 860-12 470	30
12 470-20 780	40
20 780-38 080	45
38 080-and above	50

1.1.2. Tax allowances

1.1.2.1. Deduction of social security contributions

Unless stated otherwise, social insurance contributions are deductible from gross income.

1.1.2.2. Work-related expenses

Salaried employees and self-employed professionals are entitled to a standard deduction for work-related expenses. This deduction may under no circumstances exceed respectively EUR 4 240 per spouse for salaried employees and EUR 3 980 per spouse for self-employed professionals and is computed as follows:

The lump-sum deduction for business expenses for employees has been increased as of income year 2015 and has also been revised for income year 2016. The lump-sum deduction for business expenses for self-employed professionals remains unchanged.

For salaried employees:

Gross earnings less social insurance contributions (EUR)	Rate (%)
Below 8 450	30
Between 8 450 and 19 960	11
Above 19 960	3

For self-employed professionals:

Gross earnings less social insurance contributions (EUR)	Rate (%)
Below 5 760	28.70
Between 5 760 and 11 440	10
Between 11 440 and 19 040	5
Above 19 040	3

Paid company directors are also entitled to a standard deduction for work-related expenses; this is equal to 3% of gross income (less social insurance contributions) and may not exceed EUR 2 390 per spouse.

An additional allowance may be granted to wage-earners if their workplace is more than a certain distance from their home.

Actual expenses incurred in order to acquire or retain earned income are deductible if they exceed the standard deduction. The deductibility of certain categories of work-related expenses (cars, clothing, restaurant meals and business gifts) is limited, however. Taxpayers who report actual expenses may deduct EUR 0.15 per kilometre, up to 100 km per single journey, for travel between their home and their workplace by means other than private car.

1.1.2.3. Non-earning spouse allowance (*quotient conjugal*)

A notional amount of income can be transferred between spouses if one of them earns no more than 30% of the couple's combined earned income. In this case, the amount transferred is limited to 30% of aggregate net earned income, less the individual income of the spouse to whom the notional share is transferred. This allowance is limited to EUR 10 290.

1.1.2.4. Exempt income

The base amount is:

Taxable income (S)	Fixed amount	Variable amount
0-26 510	7 420	0
26 51-26 800	7 130	26 800-S
26 800 and up	7 130	0

These amounts vary with regards to the family situation. Additional exemptions for dependent children (a handicapped child counts as two children):

- 1 child 1 520
- 2 children 3 900
- 3 children 8 740
- 4 children 14 140
- > 4 children 5 400 per additional child

Dependent child exemptions in excess of available income give rise to a reimbursable tax credit. This reimbursable tax credit is calculated at the marginal rate for the spouse with the highest income and capped at EUR 440 per dependent child.

Additional special exemptions are also granted for certain household members (in euro):

- Other dependants 1 520
- Handicapped spouse 1 520
- Other handicapped dependants 1 520
- Widow(er) with dependent child(ren) 1 520
- Single father or mother 1 520

These additional exemptions are applied first to the taxable income of the spouse having the most income, with any remainder then being applied to the income of the other spouse.

The basic exemption plus any additional exemptions for dependants and single parents is applied against each bracket from the bottom up; in other words, the lowest brackets are depleted first.

1.1.2.5. Schedule

Basic exemption plus any additional exemption (EUR)	Marginal rate (%)
0-8 760	25
8 760-12 470	30
12 470-20 780	40
20 780-38 080	45
38 080-and above	50

The basic exemption plus any additional exemptions is applied from the bottom up.

1.2. Regional and local government taxes

With the implementation of the sixth state reform, the Flemish Region, the Walloon Region and the Brussels-Capital Region have been delegated several important competences with regard to the individual income tax. As a result of this reform, as from 1 July 2014, the regional competences are:

- the possibility to levy surcharges on the federal PIT (the supplementary regional tax on the personal income tax). The surcharge may be proportional or vary with income but there are limits to ensure that the tax remains progressive);
- to grant (on the result of the surcharges) tax discounts;
- to grant tax reductions, tax increases and tax credits;
- to regulate exclusively some tax reductions.

Under the new tax model, the assumed federal income tax amount must first be calculated. The taxable base is reduced by the exempt income (see 1.1.2.4), the tax credits for pensions, unemployment, sickness and other social benefits and the tax credit for income taxed abroad. Additionally, it is reduced by the tax due on passive income for which the Federal State remains exclusively competent.

The remaining PIT liability is than split between the central government and the Regions according to a ratio of 0.7401/0.2599.

Subsequently, the Regions are allowed to levy a proportional surcharge on this reduced federal income tax. This surcharge may, within certain limits and given the matters for which the Regions are competent, vary per tax bracket. The actual rate is set at 35.117% (0.2599/(1-0.2599).

The starting point for the calculation of the municipal (and agglomeration) surcharges is the individual income tax ("impôt total", i.e. the sum of federal PIT and regional PIT), before taking into account the surcharge resulting from insufficient prepayments, the foreign tax credit, federal and regional reimbursable tax credits (among others for children and for low-income workers), prepayments and withholding taxes. The rate of this local surtax is set by each municipality, and there is no upper limit. The additional surcharge of 1% levied in the Brussels-Capital Region, in addition to the municipal surcharge, is abolished as from income year 2016.

The calculation of the regional and local surtax for the average worker study assumes that the worker lives in the Region of Brussels-Capital. The weighted average local surtax of the 19 municipalities which form the Brussels-Capital Region is 6.6%.

1.3. *Tax credits*

Refundable tax credit for low-income workers

A refundable tax credit is intended for low-income workers and company managers (subject to the employees' social security system) entitled to the employment bonus.

The refundable tax credit amounts to 28.03% as of 1 January 2016 of the "employment bonus" which is actually granted on remunerations earned during the taxable period. It cannot exceed EUR 640 per taxable period.

1.4. *Rebate on the wage withholding tax*

Employers benefit from a rebate on the wage withholding tax, at the rate of 1%. The rebate does not affect the PIT liability of the employee and the amount of the withholding tax he may credit on its PIT liability: it just reduces the amount of withholding tax paid by the employer to the tax administration. This means that the rebate operates like a wage subsidy, or like a negative payroll tax. The rebate is a standard one: it applies in an unconditional way to any wage earners in sectors C-K.

For employers who are either considered as small companies, as defined in article 15 of the Belgian Corporation Code, or natural persons meeting *mutatis mutandis* the criteria set out in the same article 15, the rate has been increased to 1.12%.

Changes affect the percentages of this rebate for remunerations paid as of 1 April 2016. Further to the reform of the employer social security contributions in the tax shift framework, the general 1% rebate on the wage withholding tax is abolished as of 1 April 2016, with the exception of the non-profit sector, where the rate remains 1% (the rate remains increased to 1.12% for SMEs of the non-profit sector); and SMEs, where the 1.12% rate is reduced to 0.12%.

2. Compulsory social security contributions to schemes operated within the government sector

2.1. *Rates and ceiling*

a. Payroll deductions

The rates of employer and employee contributions are set by law. The applicable rates (in %) are as follows (for businesses having 20 or more employees):

The schedule applicable as from 01.01.2016 is as follows:

2016	Employee	Employer	Total
Unemployment	0.87	3.16	4.03
Health insurance indemnities	1.15	2.35	3.5
Health care	3.55	3.8	7.35
Placement services		0.05	0.05
Family allowances		7	7
Pensions	7.50	8.86	16.36
Child care		0.05	0.05
Work-related illnesses		1.01	1.01
Work-related accidents		0.32	0.32
Education leave		0.05	0.05
Business closures		0.31	0.31
Wage restraint		7.59	7.59
Total	13.07	34.55	47.62

The schedule applicable as from 01.04.2016 is as follows:

2016	Employee	Employer	Total
Unemployment	0.87	3.16	4.03
Health insurance indemnities	1.15	2.35	3.5
Health care	3.55	3.8	7.35
Placement services		0.05	0.05
Family allowances		7	7
Pensions	7.50	8.86	16.36
Child care		0.05	0.05
Work-related illnesses		1.01	1.01
Work-related accidents		0.32	0.32
Education leave		0.05	0.05
Business closures		0.31	0.31
Wage restraint		7.46	7.59
Tax shift 2016		-2.27	-2.27
Total	13.07	32.15	45.22

Vacation pay is not subject to the social security contributions applicable to salaries, but a social security levy of 13.07% is deducted when the money is attributed.

b. Reduction of employer contributions

The schedule applicable as from 01.01.2014 is as follows:

Gross annual earnings (S) in EUR	Fixed amount	Variable amount
0-22 241.96	1 850.4	0.162 (22 241.96-S)
22 241.96-53 604.28	1 850.4	0
53 604.28 and up	1 850.4	0.06 (S-53 604.28)

The schedule applicable as from 01.04.2016 is as follows:

Gross annual earnings (S) in EUR	Fixed amount	Variable amount
0-27 600.00	1 752	0.1369 (27 600-S)
27 600-53 604.28	1 752	0
53 604.28 and up	1 752	0.06 (S-53 604.28)

The schedule applicable as from 01.07.2016 is as follows:

Gross annual earnings (S) in EUR	Fixed amount	Variable amount
0-28 152.00	1 752	0.1369 (28 152-S)
28 152-54 676.36	1 752	0
54 676.36 and up	1 752	0.06 (S-54 676.36)

c. Reduction of individual social security contributions

A reduction of individual social security contributions is granted monthly for low-income earners, depending on wage level. The schedule below is restated in annual terms.

The schedule applicable as from 01.08.2015 is as follows:

Gross annual salary (S) in EUR	Reduction in Euros
0 < S < 18 562.44	2 279.76
18 562.44 < S < 28 956.00	Min (2 279.76, (2 279.76-0.2193 (S-18 562.44))
S > 28 956.00	0

The schedule applicable as from 01.06.2016 is as follows:

Gross annual salary (S) in EUR	Reduction in Euros
0 < S < 18 934.68	2 325.48
18 934.68 < S < 29 535.24	Min (2 325.48, (2 325.48-0.2194 (S-18 934.68))
S > 29 535.24	0

d. Special social security contribution

All persons totally or partially subject to the social security scheme for salaried workers are liable for this special contribution. In theory, the amount of the contribution is determined according to aggregate household income. Aggregate household income is equal to combined gross earnings less ordinary social security contributions and work-related expenses. The amount of the contribution is as follows:

Taxable income (EUR)	Amount due on the lower limit	% above the lower limit
from 0 to 18 592.02	0	0
from 18 592.02 to 21 070.96	0	9
from 21 070.96 to 60 161.85	223.10	1.3
60 161.85 and above	731.29	0

e. Work accidents

All employers are required to insure their employees against accidents that occur in the workplace or while travelling to or from the workplace. The insurance is written by a private company. The usual premiums are approximately 1% of gross pay for office workers and 3.3% for labourers. The premiums are based on capped gross wages: in 2011 these premiums apply to gross wages (including holiday pay and extra-legal remunerations) with a minimum of EUR 6 068 and a maximum of EUR 37 546 (EUR 5 949 and EUR 36 810 respectively in 2010). Higher rates apply in certain industries in which risks are greater. The premium rate for construction workers, for example, varies between 7% and 8%.

2.2. Deductions according to family status or gender

None.

3. Universal cash transfers

Family allowances are granted for children. The annual amounts of these benefits (in euro) are as follows:

	< 5 years	5-6 years	7-10 years	11-12 years	12-16 years	17-18 years	>18 years
1st child	1 116.84	1 140.77	1 331.70	1 349.38	1 449.21	1 470.02	1 514.31
2nd child	2 048.79	2 072.72	2 453.45	2 471.13	2 672.97	2 692.97	2 850.91
3rd child	3 048.66	3 072.59	3 453.32	3 471.00	3 672.03	3 692.84	3 850.78

To determine the resources available to the average worker, the Taxing Wages calculations assume that one child was between seven and ten years of age and that the other child was between eleven and twelve years of age.

4. Main changes in the tax/benefit system

None.

2016 parameter values

	Ave_earn	46 570	Secretariat estimate		
Work-related expenses	work_rel_max	4 240			
	work_rel_sch	0.30	8 450		
		0.11	19 960		
		0.03			
Tax credits (exempt income)	single_cr	7 130			
	Married_cr	7 130			
	Supp_cr_base	290			
	supp_cr_thrsh1	26 510			
One child	child_cr1	1 520			
Two children	child_cr2	3 900			
Single parents	s_parent_cr	1 520			
Maximum Child Credit Payment	child_cr_max	440			
Basic Credit	basic_cr_base	0			
	basic_cr_thrsh1	4 960			
	basic_cr_thrsh2	6 620			
	basic_cr_thrsh3	16 560			
	basic_cr_thrsh4	21 520			
Basic exemption plus any additional exemption schedule		Ex_rate1			
	Ex_sch	0.25	8 760		
		0.30	12 470		
		0.40	20 780		
		0.45	38 080		
		0.50			
Income tax schedule		tax_rate1			
	tax_sch	0.25	10 860		
		0.30	12 470		
		0.40	20 780		
		0.45	38 080		
		0.50			
	quote_max	10 290			
	quote_rate	0.3			
Regional tax	red_rate	0.2599			
	reg_tax_rate	0.35117			
Local tax	local_rate	0.066			
	add_local_rate	0.00			
Unemployment	unemp_rate	0.0087			
Medical care	med_rate	0.0115			
Sickness	sickness_rate	0.0355			
Pension	pension_rate	0.0750			
Employee contribution	SSC_rt	0.1307			
	SSC_redn	0	0	2 306.43	0
	(annual)	18 779.58	18 779.58	2 306.43	0.2194
		29 293.89	18 779.58	2 306.48	0.2194
		29 293.89	0	0	0
		99 999 999	0	0	
Special annual contribution	SSC_special	0.000	18 592.02		
		0.090	21 070.96		
		0.013	60 161.85		
		0.000			
Employer contributions	SSC_empr_rt	0.3275			
	SSC_empr_redn	0	1 776.60	0.1432	26 536.49
		26 536.49	1 776.60	0	54 140.32
		54 140.328	1 776.60	-0.06	54 140.32
		9 999 999	0	0	
Structural reduction on the withholding tax on wages	PrP_redn	0.0025			
Low-income credit	LIC_rate	0.2803			
	LIC_max	640.00			
Child benefit (age 7-10)	CB_1	1 349.38			
second child (age 7-10)	CB_2	2 453.45			
third child (age 7-10)	CB_3	3 453.32			

2016 tax equations

The equations for the Belgian system in 2016 are mostly calculated on an individual basis. But central government tax for a married couple is calculated on two bases and the lower value is used. One of the bases takes account of the combined income of the couple. Also, tax credits may be used against the tax liability of the secondary earner if the principal earner is unable to use them.

The functions which are used in the equations (Taper, Tax etc.) are described in the technical note about tax equations. Variable names are defined in the table of parameters above or are the standard variables “married” and “children”. A reference to a variable with the affix “_total” indicates the sum of the relevant variable values for the principal and spouse. And the affixes “_princ” and “_spouse” indicate the value for the principal and spouse respectively. Equations for a single person are as shown for the principal with “_spouse” values taken as 0.

	Line in country table and intermediate steps	Variable name	Range	Equation
1.	Earnings	earn		
2.	Allowances:	tax_al	B	MIN(work_rel_max, Tax(earn-SSC, work_rel_sch))+SSC
3.	Credits in taxable income	taxbl_cr	B	0
4.	CG taxable income	tax_inc_int	B	earn-tax_al
	Quote part	Q	J	IF(married, Positive(MIN(tax_inc_int_total*quote_rate, quote_max)-tax_inc_int_spouse), 0)
	CG adjusted taxable income - principal	tax_inc_adj_princ	P	Positive(tax_inc_int_princ – Q)
	CG adjusted taxable income - spouse	tax_inc_adj_spouse	S	Positive(tax_inc_int_spouse + Q)
5.	CG tax before credits	CG_tax_excl	J	Tax(tax_inc_adj, tax_sch)
6.	Calculation of credits			
	Child exemption amount	child_ex_inc	P	(children=1)*child_cr1+(children=2)*child_cr2
	Family exemption amount	fam_ex_inc	B	IF(Married,married_cr,single_cr+(Children>0)*s_parent_cr)+IF(tax_inc_adj<=0,0,IF(tax_inc_adj<=supp_cr_thrsh1,supp_cr_base,MAX(0,supp_cr_base+supp_cr_thrsh1-tax_inc_adj)))
	Initial exempt income - principal	ex_inc_int_princ	P	child_ex_inc+fam_ex_inc_princ
	Initial exempt income - spouse	ex_inc_int_spouse	S	fam_ex_inc_spouse
	Transferable amount	ex_inc_tran	J	married*IF(ex_inc_int_princ<tax_inc_adj_princ, MIN(MAX((ex_inc_int_spouse-tax_inc_adj_spouse), 0), tax_inc_adj_princ-ex_inc_int_princ), -(MIN(MAX((ex_inc_int_princ-tax_inc_adj_princ), 0), MAX(0, tax_inc_adj_spouse-ex_inc_int_spouse))))
	Final exempt income - principal	ex_inc_fin_princ	P	ex_inc_int_princ+ex_inc_tran
	Final exempt income - spouse	ex_inc_fin_spouse	S	ex_inc_int_spouse-ex_inc_tran
	Tax credits	tax_credits	J	Tax(ex_inc_fin, Ex_sch)
	Basic Credit	basic_cr	B	basic_cr_base*IF(tax_inc<=basic_cr_thrsh1, 0, IF(tax_inc<=basic_cr_thrsh2, (tax_inc-basic_cr_thrsh1)/(basic_cr_thrsh2-basic_cr_thrsh1), IF(tax_inc<= basic_cr_thrsh3, 1, IF(tax_inc<=basic_cr_thrsh4, (basic_cr_thrsh4-tax_inc)/(basic_cr_thrsh4-basic_cr_thrsh3), 0)))) +IF(tax_inc=0;0;MIN(LIC_rate*(MIN(VLOOKUP(earn, SSC_redn,3), VLOOKUP(earn, SSC_redn, 3)-VLOOKUP(earn, SSC_redn, 4)*(earn-VLOOKUP(earn, SSC_redn, 2)))));LIC_max))

	Line in country table and intermediate steps	Variable name	Range	Equation
7.	CG tax			
	Tax prior to non-wasteable credits	CG_tax_init	B	Positive(CG_tax_incl-tax_credits) *(1-red_rate)
	Non-wasteable child credit	child_credit_nw	J	MIN(Tax(MIN((children=1)*child_cr1+(children=2)*Parameters!child_cr2),(positive(ex_inc_int-tax_inc_int), tax_sch), children*child_cr_max)
	Final CG tax	CG_tax_final	J	CG_tax_init-basic_cr_total-child_credit_nw
8.	State and local taxes			
	Regional tax	regional_tax	B	CG_tax_init*reg_tax_rate
	Local tax	local_tax	J	(local_rate+add_local_rate)*(CG_tax_init+regional_tax)
9.	Employees' soc security	SSC	B	Positive((earn)*SSC_rt-MIN(VLOOKUP(earn, SSC_redn,3), VLOOKUP(earn, SSC_redn, 3)-VLOOKUP(earn, SSC_redn, 4)*(earn-VLOOKUP(earn, SSC_redn, 2))))
		SSC_special	J	positive(Tax(tax_inc_total, SSC_special)
		SSC_total		SSC+SSC_special
11.	Cash transfers	cash_trans	J	(Children>0)*CB_1+(Children>1)*CB_2
13.	Employer's soc security	empr_sch	B	Positive(earn*(SSC_empr_rt- PrP_redn)-(VLOOKUP(earn, SSC_empr_redn, 2)-VLOOKUP(earn, SSC_empr_redn, 3)*(earn-VLOOKUP(earn, SSC_empr_redn, 1))))

Key to range of equation B calculated separately for both principal earner and spouse P calculated for principal only (value taken as 0 for spouse calculation) J calculated once only on a joint basis.

Taxing Wages 2017
© OECD 2017

Canada

This chapter includes data on the income taxes paid by workers, their social security contributions, the family benefits they receive in the form of cash transfers as well as the social security contributions and payroll taxes paid by their employers. Results reported include the marginal and average tax burden for eight different family types.

Methodological information is available for Personal income tax systems, Compulsory social security contributions to schemes operated within the government sector, Universal cash transfers as well as recent changes in the tax/benefit system. The methodology also includes the parameter values and tax equations underlying the data.

Canada 2016

The tax/benefit position of single persons

	Wage level (per cent of average wage)	67	100	167	67
	Number of children	none	none	none	2
1. Gross wage earnings		34 168	50 997	85 165	34 168
2. Standard tax allowances					
Basic allowance					
Married or head of family					
Dependent children					
Deduction for social security contributions and income taxes					
Work-related expenses					
Other					
	Total	0	0	0	0
3. Tax credits or cash transfers included in taxable income		0	0	0	0
4. Central government taxable income (1 - 2 + 3)		34 168	50 997	85 165	34 168
5. Central government income tax liability (exclusive of tax credits)		5 125	7 964	14 968	5 125
6. Tax credits					
Basic credit		1 895	1 895	1 895	1 895
Married or head of family		0	0	0	1 721
Other(CPP & EI)		324	496	525	324
	Total	2 219	2 391	2 420	3 940
7. Central government income tax finally paid (5-6)		2 906	5 573	12 548	1 185
8. State and local taxes		1 111	2 291	5 642	0
9. Employees' compulsory social security contributions					
Gross earnings		2 160	3 306	3 499	2 160
Taxable income (Provincial Health Care Levy)		300	600	750	300
	Total	2 460	3 906	4 249	2 460
10. Total payments to general government (7 + 8 + 9)		6 477	11 770	22 440	3 645
11. Cash transfers from general government					
For head of family		427	0	0	491
For two children		0	0	0	12 954
	Total	427	0	0	13 445
12. Take-home pay (1-10+11)		28 118	39 227	62 725	43 968
13. Employer's compulsory social security contributions		4 092	6 187	8 054	4 092
14. Average rates					
Income tax		11.8%	15.4%	21.4%	3.5%
Employees' social security contributions		7.2%	7.7%	5.0%	7.2%
Total payments less cash transfers		17.7%	23.1%	26.3%	-28.7%
Total tax wedge including employer's social security contributions		26.5%	31.4%	32.7%	-14.9%
15. Marginal rates					
Total payments less cash transfers: Principal earner		25.5%	33.6%	33.9%	46.3%
Total payments less cash transfers: Spouse		n.a.	n.a.	n.a.	n.a.
Total tax wedge: Principal earner		33.8%	39.6%	37.0%	52.3%
Total tax wedge: Spouse		n.a.	n.a.	n.a.	n.a.

Canada 2016

The tax/benefit position of married couples

			Wage level (per cent of average wage)	100-0	100-33	100-67	100-33
			Number of children	2	2	2	none
1.	**Gross wage earnings**			50 997	67 826	85 165	67 826
2.	**Standard tax allowances**						
		Basic allowance					
		Married or head of family					
		Dependent children					
		Deduction for social security contributions and income taxes					
		Work-related expenses					
		Other					
			Total	0	0	0	0
3.	**Tax credits or cash transfers included in taxable income**			0	0	0	0
4.	**Central government taxable income (1 - 2 + 3)**			50 997	67 826	85 165	67 826
5.	**Central government income tax liability (exclusive of tax credits)**			7 964	10 488	13 089	10 488
6.	**Tax credits**						
		Basic credit		1 895	3 791	3 791	3 791
		Married or head of family		1 721	0	0	0
		Other(CPP & EI)		496	642	820	642
			Total	4 112	4 433	4 610	4 433
7.	**Central government income tax finally paid (5-6)**			3 852	6 055	8 479	6 055
8.	**State and local taxes**			1 553	2 419	3 402	2 419
9.	**Employees' compulsory social security contributions**						
		Gross earnings		3 306	4 282	5 467	4 282
		Taxable income (Provincial Health Care Levy)		600	600	900	600
			Total	3 906	4 882	6 367	4 882
10.	**Total payments to general government (7 + 8 + 9)**			9 311	13 356	18 247	13 356
11.	**Cash transfers from general government**						
		For head of family		0	0	0	0
		For two children		8 721	5 914	4 926	0
			Total	8 721	5 914	4 926	0
12.	**Take-home pay (1-10+11)**			50 408	60 384	71 844	54 470
13.	**Employer's compulsory social security contributions**			6 187	8 114	10 279	8 114
14.	**Average rates**						
	Income tax			10.6%	12.5%	13.9%	12.5%
	Employees' social security contributions			7.7%	7.2%	7.5%	7.2%
	Total payments less cash transfers			1.2%	11.0%	15.6%	19.7%
	Total tax wedge including employer's social security contributions			11.9%	20.5%	24.7%	28.3%
15.	**Marginal rates**						
	Total payments less cash transfers: Principal earner			73.0%	39.3%	39.3%	33.6%
	Total payments less cash transfers: Spouse			40.7%	35.9%	31.2%	30.2%
	Total tax wedge: Principal earner			75.4%	44.7%	44.7%	39.6%
	Total tax wedge: Spouse			46.8%	43.0%	38.8%	38.0%

The national currency is the Canadian dollar (CAD). In 2016, CAD 1.33 was equal to USD 1. In that year, the average worker earned CAD 50 997 (Secretariat estimate).

1. Personal income tax systems

1.1. Central/federal government income taxes

1.1.1. Tax unit

Under the present system, tax is levied on individuals separately; certain tax reliefs depend on family circumstances.

1.1.2. Tax allowances and credits

1.1.2.1. Standard credits

- *Basic personal amount:* All taxpayers qualify for a basic personal tax credit of CAD 1 721.10.
- *Credit for Spouse or Eligible Dependant*: A taxpayer supporting a spouse or other eligible dependant receives a tax credit of CAD 1 721.10 which is reduced by 15 cents for each dollar of the dependant's income.
- *Social security contributions:* Taxpayers are entitled to claim 15% of their contributions to the Canada or Quebec Pension Plans (to a maximum credit of CAD 2 544.30 for the Canada Pension Plan and to a maximum credit of CAD 2 737.05 for the Quebec Pension Plan) and their Employment Insurance premiums (to a maximum credit of CAD 955.04 outside Quebec; the Employment Insurance premium rate is lower for Quebec residents, who also pay into the Quebec Parental Insurance Plan; the maximum combined credit for a Quebec resident is CAD 1 163.98).
- *Working Income Tax Benefit (WITB)*: The WITB provides a non-wastable tax credit equal to 25% of each dollar of earned income in excess of CAD 3 000 to a maximum credit of CAD 1 028 for single individuals without dependents and CAD 1 868 for families (couples and single parents). The credit is reduced by 15% of net family income in excess of CAD 11 675 for single individuals and CAD 16 122 for families. This is the default national design; provinces may choose to propose jurisdiction-specific changes to this design, subject to certain principles.
- *Canada Employment Tax Credit:* A tax credit of up to CAD 174.15 on employment income.

1.1.2.2. Main non-standard tax reliefs applicable to an average worker:

A number of non-standard tax reliefs are available to the average worker in Canada. The main ones are:

- *Medical expenses credit:* Taxpayers are entitled to a 15% tax credit for an amount of eligible medical expenses that exceeds the lesser of 3% of net income or CAD 2 237.
- *Charitable donations credit:* The credit is 15% on the first CAD 200 of eligible charitable donations and 29% on eligible donations in excess of CAD 200. Eligible donations are those made to registered charities, to a maximum of 75% of net income.

- *Registered pension plan contributions:* Employees who are members of a registered pension plan are entitled to deduct their contributions to the plan in respect of current and/or past service. Generally, employee contributions to a defined benefit registered pension plan are not subject to any limit; however, limits apply to the benefits that a plan may provide. Individuals can deduct their contributions to a defined contribution registered pension plan up to a limit of 18% of earned income, to a maximum of CAD 26 010.
- *Registered retirement savings plan (RRSP) premiums*: Individuals can deduct their contributions to an RRSP up to a limit of 18% of the previous year's earned income, to a maximum of CAD 25 370 a year, unless they are also accruing benefits under a registered pension plan or a deferred profit sharing plan. Members of those other plans are limited to RRSP contributions of 18% of the previous year's earned income to a maximum of CAD 25 370, minus a pension adjustment amount based on pension benefits accrued in the previous year.
- *Union and professional dues:* Individuals with annual dues paid to a trade union or an association of public servants or paying dues required to maintain a professional status recognised by statute are allowed to deduct such fees in computing taxable income.
- *Moving expenses:* Eligible moving expenses are deductible from income if the taxpayer moves at least 40 kilometres closer to a new place of employment.
- *Child care expenses:* A portion of child care expenses is deductible if incurred for the purpose of earning business or employment income, studying or taking an occupational training course or carrying on research for which a grant is received. The lower-income spouse must generally claim the deduction. The amount of the deduction is limited to the least of:
  1. the expenses incurred for the care of a child;
  2. two-thirds of the taxpayer's earned income; and
  3. CAD 8 000 for each child who is under age seven, and CAD 5 000 per child between seven and sixteen years of age (or older if has a mental or physical impairment, but not eligible for the Disability Tax Credit). The amount for a child who is eligible for Disability Tax Credit is CAD 11 000.

1.1.3. *Tax schedule*

2016 Federal income tax rates

Taxable Income (CAD)	Rate (%)
0-45 282	15
45 282-90 563	20.5
90 563-140 388	26
140 388-200 000	29
200 000 and over	33

1.2. *State and local income taxes*

1.2.1. *General description*

All provinces and territories levy their own personal income taxes. All, with the exception of Quebec, have a tax collection agreement with the federal government, and thus use the federal definition of taxable income. They are free to determine their own tax brackets, rates and credits. Quebec collects its own personal income tax and is free to determine all of the tax parameters, including taxable income. In practice, its definition of taxable income is broadly similar to the federal definition.

1.2.2. *Tax regime selected for this study*

The calculation of provincial tax for the average worker study assumes the worker lives in Ontario, the most populous of the 10 provinces and 3 territories. The main features of the Ontario tax system relevant to this report are summarised below:

Tax Schedule

Income Bracket	Rate (%)
CAD 0 to CAD 41 536	5.05
CAD 41 536 to CAD 83 075	9.15
CAD 83 075 to CAD 150 000	11.16
CAD 150 000 to CAD 220 000	12.16
Over CAD 220 000	13.16

Surtax

Provincial tax after accounting for wastable credits	Surtax Rate
Amounts Exceeding CAD 4 484	20% of the excess amount
Amounts Exceeding CAD 5 739	36% of the excess amount

Wastable tax credits

- A basic tax credit of CAD 505.56.
- A maximum credit of CAD 429.25 for a dependant spouse or eligible dependant that is withdrawn as the income of the spouse or eligible dependant exceeds CAD 850 and is completely withdrawn when the income of the spouse is at least CAD 9 350.
- 5.05% of contributions made to the Canada Pension Plan and of Employment Insurance premiums.

Tax Reduction

An earner is entitled to claim a tax reduction where the initial entitlement is equal to CAD 231 plus CAD 427 for each dependent child under the age of 19. Where someone has a spouse, only the spouse with the higher net income can claim the dependent child tax reduction. If this amount is greater or equal to the liable provincial tax, then no tax is due. If the amount is less than the liable tax, then the actual tax reduction is equal to twice the initial entitlement amount less the liable tax (if this calculation is zero or negative, the reduction is equal to zero).

2. Compulsory social security contributions to schemes operated within the government sector

2.1. Employees' contributions

2.1.1. Pensions

Generally, all employees are eligible for coverage under the Canada Pension Plan (Québec Pension Plan in the province of Québec). For 2016, all employees are required to contribute to the Canada Pension Plan at a rate of 4.95% of income up to a maximum contribution of CAD 2 544.30 (the contribution rate is 5.325% of income for the Québec

TAXING WAGES 2017 © OECD 2017

Pension Plan up to a maximum contribution of CAD 2 737.05). Income subject to contributions is earnings (wages and salaries) less a CAD 3 500 basic exemption. The maximum contribution of CAD 2 544.30 is reached at an earnings level of CAD 54 900 i.e. (CAD 54 900-CAD 3 500) × 0.0495 = CAD 2 544.30. For employees, each contribution to the CPP or QPP gives rise to a tax credit equal to 15% of the contributed amount. Employers are also required to contribute to the Canada Pension Plan on behalf of their employees at the same rate and can deduct their contributions from taxable income (refer § 2.21).

Self-employed persons must also contribute to the Canada Pension Plan (Québec Pension Plan in the province of Québec) on their own behalf. However, the self-employed are required to contribute at the combined employer/employee rate of 9.90% of earnings up to a maximum of CAD 5 088.60 (10.65% of earnings up to a maximum of CAD 5 474.10 in Quebec). The self-employed can deduct the employer portion of their contribution from income, equal to 50% of the total contribution or CAD 2 544.30 (2 737.05 in Quebec). The remaining 50%, representing the employee portion, is then claimed as a tax credit at 15%.

2.1.2. *Sickness*

There is no national sickness benefit plan administered by the federal government. However, all provinces have provincially-administered health care insurance plans. Three provinces, Quebec, Ontario, and British Columbia, levy health premiums on individuals separately from the personal income tax to help finance their health programmes.

In the case of Ontario, the premium is determined based on taxable income. Individuals who earn up to CAD 20 000 are exempt. The premium is phased in with a number of different rates to a maximum of CAD 900 for taxable income levels greater than CAD 200 600. The following table provides further details on the structure that is applicable in 2016.

The Ontario Health Premium

Taxable income	Fixed component (CAD)	Variable component
0-CAD 20 000	0	
CAD 20 000-CAD 25 000	0	6% of the taxable income in excess of CAD 20 000
CAD 25 000-CAD 36 000	300	
CAD 36 000-CAD 38 500	300	6% of the taxable income in excess of CAD 36 000
CAD 38 500-CAD 48 000	450	
CAD 48 000-CAD 48 600	450	25% of the taxable income in excess of CAD 48 000
CAD 48 600-CAD 72 000	600	
CAD 72 000-CAD 72 600	600	25% of the amount of taxable income in excess of CAD 72 600
CAD 72 600-CAD 200 000	750	
CAD 200 000-CAD 200 600	750	25% of the amount of taxable income in excess of CAD 200 000
Over CAD 200 600	900	

2.1.3. *Unemployment*

In general, all employees are eligible for Employment Insurance. Eligibility to receive benefits is determined by insurable hours worked (with a minimum entry threshold of 420 to 700 hours, depending on region and the unemployment rate at the time the claim for benefits starts). For 2016, employees outside Quebec are required to contribute at the rate of 1.88% of insurable earnings. Insurable earnings are earnings (wages and salaries) up to a maximum of CAD 50 800 per year. The maximum employee contribution is therefore CAD 955.04 per year. Employment insurance contributions give rise to a tax credit equal to

15% of the amount contributed. Employers are also required to contribute to the plan. (See Section 2.23)

Quebec residents contribute to Employment Insurance at a rate of 1.52%; the same earnings ceiling applies. They also contribute to the Quebec Parental Insurance Plan at a rate of 0.548% of insurable earnings; maximum insurance earnings for 2016 are CAD 71 500. For a Quebec resident, the maximum employee contribution (Employment Insurance plus Quebec Parental Insurance Plan) is CAD 1 163.98.

2.1.4. *Work injury*

See section 2.24.

2.2. *Employers' contributions*

2.2.1. *Pensions*

Employers are required to contribute to the Canada Pension Plan on behalf of their employees an amount equal to their employees' contributions. Thus, employers also contribute at the rate of 4.95% of earnings (less the CAD 3 500 earnings exemption) to a maximum of CAD 2 544.30. For the Quebec Pension Plan, the contribution rate is 5.325% of earnings, to a maximum of CAD 2 737.05.

2.2.2. *Sickness*

There is no national sickness benefit plan administered by the federal government. However, all provinces have provincially-administered health care insurance plans. Three provinces levy a special tax on employer payrolls to finance health services (Québec and Ontario) or health services and education (Manitoba). These payroll taxes are deductible from the employer's income subject to tax. In the case of the province of Ontario, employers pay a Employer Health Tax on the value of their payroll, tax rates varying from 0.98% on Ontario payroll less than CAD 200 000, up to 1.95% for payroll that exceeds CAD 400 000. Certain employers are eligible for a higher exemption of CAD 450 000.

2.2.3. *Unemployment*

Employers are required to contribute to the employment insurance scheme. The general employer contribution is 1.4 times the employee contribution, that is, 2.63% of insurable earnings (outside Quebec). Premiums are adjusted for employers who provide sick pay superior to payments provided under the employment insurance regime. All employment insurance contributions are deductible from the employer's income subject to tax.

2.2.4. *Work injury*

There is no national work injury benefit plan administered by the federal government. However, employers are required to contribute to a provincial workers' compensation plan which pays benefits to workers (or their families in case of death) for work-related illness or injury. The employer contribution rates, which vary by industry and province, are related to industry experience of work-related illness and injury. Premiums are deductible from the employer's income subject to tax. In the case of Ontario, employers broadly corresponding to industry Sectors B-N inclusive pay, on average, 2.95% of the wages paid to each employee to a maximum of CAD 88 000.

3. Universal cash transfers

3.1. *Transfers related to marital status*

None.

3.2. *Transfers for dependent children*

3.2.1. *Federal*

Budget 2016 announced a significant reform of child benefit. As of July 2016, the Canada Child Benefit (CCB) takes effect and will replace the Canada Child Tax Benefit and Universal Child Care Benefit (UCCB). Entitlement to the CCB for the July 2016 to June 2017 benefit year will be based on 2015 adjusted family net income. The CCB provides a maximum benefit of CAD 6 400 per child under age six and CAD 5 400 per child for those aged six through seventeen. On the portion of adjusted family net income between CAD 30 000 and CAD 65 000, the benefit will be phased out at a rate of 7% for a one-child family, 13.5% for a two-child family, 19% for a three-child family and 23% for larger families. Where adjusted family net income exceeds CAD 65 000, remaining benefits will be phased out at rates of 3.2% for a one-child family, 5.7% for a two-child family, 8% for a three-child family and 9.5% for larger families, on the portion of income above CAD 65 000.

The Goods and Services Tax Credit provides a relief of CAD 280 for each adult 19 years of age or older and CAD 147 for each dependent child under the age of 19. Single tax filers without children and with an employment income higher than CAD 9 079 receive an additional CAD 147 that is phased in at a rate of 2%. Single tax filers with children receive an additional CAD 147 that is not subject to phase-in. The credit received for the first dependent child of a single parent is also increased from CAD 147 to CAD 280. The total amount is reduced at a rate of five percent of net family income over CAD 36 455. The amount is paid directly to families.

3.2.2. *Provincial*

For each child under eighteen, qualifying families can receive up to CAD 1 376 from the Ontario Child Benefit (OCB). The benefit is withdrawn at a rate of 8% of family income that exceeds CAD 21 011.

Ontario has a Sales Tax Credit that provides a relief of up to CAD 295 for each adult and each child. It is reduced by 4% of adjusted family net income over CAD 22 718 for single people and over CAD 28 397 for families. The amount is paid directly to families.

4. Main changes in the tax/benefit system since 2009

5. Memorandum items

5.1. *Identification of an average worker*

The earnings data refer to production workers in the industries B to N. To obtain the annual average wage figure, the average weekly earnings for the year for employees (including overtime) are multiplied by 52.

5.2. *Employer contributions to private health and pension schemes*

These do exist but no information is available on the amounts involved.

The payments that relate to income from the 2016 tax year are payable between July 2017 and June 2018. The amounts shown in this Report assume indexation of 2.0% for the 2016 tax year (and 2017-18 benefit year); the actual indexation parameter will be announced in December 2016.

2016 parameter values

Average earnings/yr	Ave_earn	50 997	Secretariat estimate
Tax credits	Basic_cred	1 721.10	
Spouse	Spouse_cred	1 721.10	
withdrawal rate	Sp_crd_wth	0.15	
Threshold	Sp_crd_thrsh	0	
Canada Employment Tax Credit	Empl_crd	174.15	
Canada Child Benefit amount per child under 6	ccb_credit1	6 400	
Canada Child Benefit amount per child aged 6-17	ccb_credit2	5 400	
First threshold	ccb_crd_thrsh1	30 000	
Second threshold	ccb_crd_thrsh2	65 000	
Frist reduction rate – 1 child	ccb_1st_redn1	0.070	
Frist reduction rate – 2 children	ccb_1st_redn2	0.135	
Frist reduction rate – 3 children	ccb_1st_redn3	0.190	
Frist reduction rate – 4+ children	ccb_1st_redn4	0.230	
Second reduction rate – 1 child	ccb_2nd_redn1	0.032	
Second reduction rate – 2 children	ccb_2nd_redn2	0.057	
Second reduction rate – 3 children	ccb_2nd_redn3	0.080	
Second reduction rate – 4+ children	ccb_2nd_redn4	0.095	
Working Income Tax Benefit	WITB_phzin_thrsh	3 000	
WITB–Phase-in Rate	WITB_phzn_rt	0.25	
WITB–Maximum Credit (per Adult/Equiv.)	WITB_max	1 028	
WITB–Addl. Maximum Credit (Fam.)	WITB_max_fam	840	
WITB–Reduction Rate	WITB_phzout_rt	0.15	
WITB–Threshold	WITB_phzout_thrsh	11 675	
WITB–Addl. Threshold (Fam.)	WITB_phzn_thrsh_fam	4 447	
Federal tax schedule	Fed_sch	0.15	45 282
		0.205	90 563
		0.26	140 388
		0.29	200 000
		0.33	
High-income surtax rate	H_sur_rate	0	
threshold	H_sur_thrsh	18 500	
Canada pension plan rate	CPP_rate	0.0495	
exemption	CPP_ex	3 500	
max contrib.	CPP_max	2 544.30	
Unemployment ins.rate	Unemp_rate	0.0188	
max contrib.	Unemp_max	955.04	
tax credit rate	Unemp_crd_rate	0.15	
employer contrib. mult.	Unemp_emplr	1.4	
GST adult credit	GST_crd_ad	280	
child credit	GST_crd_ch	147	
threshold	GST_crd_thrsh	36 455	
reduction rate	GST_crd_redn	0.05	
single supplement	GST_crd_sgsp	147	
single supplement eligibility threshold	GST_sgsp_thrsh	9 079	
single supplement phase-in rate	GST_sgsp_rate	0.02	
Province: Ontario			
Tax Credits	P_basic_crd	505.56	
Spouse	P_spouse_crd	429.25	
withdrawal rate	P_sp_crd_wd	0.0505	
threshold	P_sp_crd_thr	850	
% of BFT	P_pct_bft	0.375	
Unemployment tax credit rate	P_unem_tc_rt	0.0505	
Surtax rate 1	P_sur_rt1	0.20	
threshold	P_sur_thr1	4 484	
rate 2	P_sur_rt2	0.36	

2016 parameter values

threshold	P_sur_thr2	5 739		
Tax reduction	P_tax_red	231		
amount per dependent	P_tr_chld	427		
amount per disabled dep	P_tr_dis_ch	427		
Provincial tax schedule	Prov_sch	0.0505	41 536	
		0.0915	83 075	
		0.1116	150 000	
		0.1216	220 000	
		0.1316		
Ontario Child Benefit	P_ch_amt	1 376		
amount per child	P_ch_thresh	21 011		
threshold	P_ch_redn_rate	0.08		
reduction rate				
Sales tax credits				
sales tax credit adult	P_sales_cred	295		
sales tax credit child	P_salcr_chd	295		
threshold	P_ps_thresh	22 718		
threshold seniors/families	P_ps_thr_sen	28 397		
reduction rate	P_ps_red_rt	0.04		
reduction rate seniors	P_ps_rr_sen	0.04		
Ontario Health Premium	P_hlth_sch	20 000	0	0
		25 000	0.06	0
		36 000	0	300
		38 500	0.06	300
		48 000	0	450
		48 600	0.25	450
		72 000	0	600
		72 600	0.25	600
		200 000	0	750
		200 600	0.25	750
maximum	P_hlth_max	900		
Employer Health Tax	emp_healthtax	0.0195		
Employer Workers Compensation Levy	emp_workcomp	0.0295		
Employer Workers Compensation Levy Ceiling	emp_workcomp_ceil	88 000		
Maximum number of children under the age of 7	children_und7_max	1		

2016 Tax equations

The equations for the Canadian system are mostly repeated for each individual of a married couple. But the spouse credit is relevant only to the calculation for the principal earner and the non-wastable credits are calculated only once. This is shown by the Range indicator in the table below.

The functions which are used in the equations (Taper, MIN, Tax etc) are described in the technical note about tax equations. Variable names are defined in the table of parameters above, within the equations table, or are the standard variables "married" and "children". A reference to a variable with the affix "_total" indicates the sum of the relevant variable values for the principal and spouse. And the affixes "_princ" and "_spouse" indicate the value for the principal and spouse, respectively. Equations for a single person are as shown for the principal, with "_spouse" values taken as 0.

	Line in country table and intermediate steps	Variable name	Range	Equation
1.	Earnings	earn		
2.	Allowances	tax_al	B	0
3.	Credits in taxable income	taxbl_cr		
4.	CG taxable income	tax_inc	B	Earn
5.	CG tax before credits:	Basic_Fed_tax	B	Tax(earn, Fed_sch)
	Basic Federal tax	Basic_Fed_tax	B	Tax(earn, Fed_sch)
6.	Tax credits :			
	Basic credit	basic_cr	P	Basic_cred + Empl_crd
			S	(earn_spouse>0)*Empl_crd+IF(AND(Married=1,earn_spouse>0),Basic_cred,0)+IF (AND(Married=0,tax_inc_spouse>0),Basic_cred-Taper(Spouse_cred,tax_inc_ spouse,Sp_crd_thrsh,Sp_crd_wth),0)
	Spouse credit	spouse_cr	P	IF(OR(Married=1,Children>0),Taper(Spouse_cred, tax_inc_spouse, Sp_crd_thrsh,Sp_crd_wth), 0)
	Unemployment insurance	unemp_cr	B	Unemp_crd_rate*SSC
	Total (wastable) tax credits	tax_cr	B	basic_cr+spouse_cr+unemp_cr
	Working Income Tax Benefit	WITB	P	IF(Married>0,MAX(0,MIN(WITB_max+WITB_max_fam,(WITB_phzn_rt* MAX(0, earn_total-WITB_phzin_thrsh)))-MAX(0,WITB_phzout_rt*MAX(0,earn_total-(WITB_phzout_thrsh+WITB_phzn_thrsh_fam)))), IF(Children>0,MAX(0,MIN (WITB_max+WITB_max_fam,(WITB_phzn_rt*MAX(0,earn_total-WITB_phzin_ thrsh)))-MAX(0,WITB_phzout_rt*MAX(0,earn_total-(WITB_phzout_thrsh+WITB_ phzn_thrsh_fam)))), MAX(0,MIN(WITB_max,(WITB_phzn_rt*MAX(0,earn_total-WITB_phzin_thrsh)))-MAX(0,WITB_phzout_rt*MAX(0,earn_total-WITB_phzout_ thrsh)))))
7.	CG tax	CG_tax	B	Positive(Basic_Fed_tax-tax_cr)-WITB
8.	State and local taxes			
	Liable provincial tax	Prov_tax_sch	B	Tax(earn, Prov_sch)
	Provincial tax credits	Prov_tax_cred	P	P_basic_crd+P_unem_tc_rt*SSC_princ+IF(AND(Married=0, Children>0), P_spouse_crd, Married*Taper(P_spouse_crd, earn_spouse, P_sp_crd_thr, P_sp_crd_wd))
			S	=(earn_spouse>0)*(P_unem_tc_rt*SSC_spouse)+OR(Married=1,Children>0)*P_b asic_crd
	Provincial surtax	Prov_surtax	B	P_sur_rt1*Positive(Prov_tax_sch-Prov_tax_cred-P_sur_thr1)+P_sur_rt2*Positive(Prov_tax_sch-Prov_tax_cred-P_sur_thr2)
	Provincial tax reduction	Prov_tax_redn	B	MAX(2*(P_tax_red+Children*P_tr_chld)-(Prov_tax_sch-Prov_tax_cred+Prov_surtax), 0)
	Provincial sales tax credit	Prov_tax_stcred	P	Taper(IF(Married=1, 2, 1)*P_sales_cred+Children*P_salcr_chd, earn_total, IF(Married+Children=0, P_ps_thresh,P_ps_thr_sen),P_ps_red_rt)
	Liable provincial tax	Prov_tax	B	Positive(Prov_tax_sch-Prov_tax_cred+Prov_surtax-Prov_tax_redn)

	Line in country table and intermediate steps	Variable name	Range	Equation
9.	Employees' soc security:			
	Canada Pension Plan	CPP	B	MIN(CPP_rate*Positive((earn-CPP_ex), CPP_max)
	Unemployment insurance	Unemp	B	MIN(Unemp_rate*earn, Unemp_max)
	State health premium	Prov_health	B	MIN(Hstep(tax_inc, P_hlth_sch), P_hlth_max)
	Total Employees' soc security	SSC	B	CPP+Unemp+Prov_health
11.	Cash transfers (nonwastable)			
	Canada Child Benefit	CCB	P	Taper(Taper(Children*ccb_credit2,MINA(earn_total, ccb_crd_thrsh2), ccb_crd_thrsh1, IF(children=1, ccb_1st _redn1, IF(children=2, ccb_1st _redn2, IF(children=3, ccb_1st _redn3, IF(children>3, ccb_1st _redn4, 0))))), earn_total, ccb_crd_thrsh2, IF(children=1, ccb_2nd _redn1, IF(children=2, ccb_2nd _redn2, IF(children=3, ccb_2nd _redn3, IF(children>3, ccb_2nd _redn4, 0)))))
	GST Credit - Total	GST_cr	P	Taper((GST_crd_ad+(Married=1)*(GST_crd_ad+Children*GST_crd_ch)+(Married =0)*(Children>0)*(GST_crd_ad+GST_crd_sgsp+Positive(Children-1)*GST_ crd_ch)+(Married=0)*(Children=0)*Positive(MIN(GST_crd_sgsp, (earn_total-GST_sgsp_thrsh)*GST_sgsp_rate))), earn_total, GST_crd_thrsh, GST_crd_redn)
	GST Credit - Adult	GST_cr_adult	P	Taper((GST_crd_ad+(Married=1)*(GST_crd_ad)+(Married=0)*Positive(MIN(GST_ crd_sgsp, (earn_total-GST_sgsp_thrsh)*GST_sgsp_rate))), earn_total, GST_crd_ thrsh, GST_crd_redn)
	GST Credit - Child	GST_cr_child	P	GST_cr-GST_cr_adult
	Ontario child benefit	Prov_child_ben	P	Taper(Children*P_ch_amt,earn_total,P_ch_thresh,P_ch_redn_rate)
	Ontario sales tax credit	Prov_sales_cr	P	Taper(IF(Married=1,2,1)*P_sales_cred+Children*P_salcr_chd,earn_total, IF(Married+Children=0, P_ps_thresh,P_ps_thr_sen),P_ps_red_rt)
	Total Cash Transfers	Cash_tran	P	CCB+GST_cr+Prov_child_ben+ Prov_sales_cr
13.	Employer's soc security			
	Canada Pension Plan	CPP_empr	B	CPP
	Unemployment insurance	Unemp_empr	B	Unemp*Unemp_emplr
	Ontario Employers Health Tax	Health_empr	B	earn*emp_healthtax
	Ontario Workers Compensation	Comp_empr	B	MIN(earn, emp_workcomp_ceil)*emp_workcomp
	Total Employer's soc security	SSC_empr	B	CPP_empr+Unemp_empr+Health_empr+Comp_empr

Key to range of equation B calculated separately for both principal earner and spouse P calculated for principal only (value taken as 0 for spouse calculation) J calculated once only on a joint basis

© OECD 2017

Chile

This chapter includes data on the income taxes paid by workers, their social security contributions, the family benefits they receive in the form of cash transfers as well as the social security contributions and payroll taxes paid by their employers. Results reported include the marginal and average tax burden for eight different family types.

Methodological information is available for Personal income tax systems, Compulsory social security contributions to schemes operated within the government sector, Universal cash transfers as well as recent changes in the tax/benefit system. The methodology also includes the parameter values and tax equations underlying the data.

Chile 2016

The tax/benefit position of single persons

	Wage level (per cent of average wage)	67	100	167	67
	Number of children	none	none	none	2
1.	**Gross wage earnings**	5 362 339	8 003 491	13 365 830	5 362 339
2.	**Standard tax allowances**				
	Basic allowance	0	0	0	0
	Married or head of family				
	Dependent children				
	Deduction for social security contributions and income taxes	375 364	560 244	935 608	375 364
	Work-related expenses				
	Other	630 611	941 211	1 571 822	630 611
	Total	1 005 975	1 501 455	2 507 430	1 005 975
3.	**Tax credits or cash transfers included in taxable income**	0	0	0	0
4.	**Central government taxable income (1 - 2 + 3)**	4 356 364	6 502 036	10 858 400	4 356 364
5.	**Central government income tax liability (exclusive of tax credits)**	0	0	135 070	0
6.	**Tax credits**				
	Basic credit				
	Married or head of family				
	Children	0	0	0	231 862
	Other				
	Total	0	0	0	231 862
7.	**Central government income tax finally paid (5-6)**	0	0	135 070	0
8.	**State and local taxes**	0	0	0	0
9.	**Employees' compulsory social security contributions**				
	Gross earnings	375 364	560 244	935 608	375 364
	Taxable income				
	Total	375 364	560 244	935 608	375 364
10.	**Total payments to general government (7 + 8 + 9)**	375 364	560 244	1 070 678	375 364
11.	**Cash transfers from general government**				
	For head of family				
	For two children	0	0	0	48 528
	Total	0	0	0	48 528
12.	**Take-home pay (1-10+11)**	4 986 975	7 443 247	12 295 152	5 035 503
13.	**Employer's compulsory social security contributions**	0	0	0	0
14.	**Average rates**				
	Income tax	0.0%	0.0%	1.0%	0.0%
	Employees' social security contributions	7.0%	7.0%	7.0%	7.0%
	Total payments less cash transfers	7.0%	7.0%	8.0%	6.1%
	Total tax wedge including employer's social security contributions	7.0%	7.0%	8.0%	6.1%
15.	**Marginal rates**				
	Total payments less cash transfers: Principal earner	7.0%	7.0%	10.2%	7.0%
	Total payments less cash transfers: Spouse	n.a.	n.a.	n.a.	n.a.
	Total tax wedge: Principal earner	7.0%	7.0%	10.2%	7.0%
	Total tax wedge: Spouse	n.a.	n.a.	n.a.	n.a.

Chile 2016

The tax/benefit position of married couples

		Wage level (per cent of average wage)	100-0	100-33	100-67	100-33
		Number of children	2	2	2	none
1.	**Gross wage earnings**		8 003 491	10 644 643	13 365 830	10 644 643
2.	**Standard tax allowances**					
	Basic allowance		0	0	0	0
	Married or head of family					
	Dependent children					
	Deduction for social security contributions and income taxes		560 244	745 125	935 608	745 125
	Work-related expenses					
	Other		941 211	1 251 810	1 571 822	1 251 810
		Total	1 501 455	1 996 935	2 507 430	1 996 935
3.	**Tax credits or cash transfers included in taxable income**		0	0	0	0
4.	**Central government taxable income (1 - 2 + 3)**		6 502 036	8 647 708	10 858 400	8 647 708
5.	**Central government income tax liability (exclusive of tax credits)**		0	0	0	0
6.	**Tax credits**					
	Basic credit					
	Married or head of family					
	Children		231 862	231 862	231 862	0
	Other					
		Total	231 862	231 862	231 862	0
7.	**Central government income tax finally paid (5-6)**		0	0	0	0
8.	**State and local taxes**		0	0	0	0
9.	**Employees' compulsory social security contributions**					
	Gross earnings		560 244	745 125	935 608	745 125
	Taxable income					
		Total	560 244	745 125	935 608	745 125
10.	**Total payments to general government (7 + 8 + 9)**		560 244	745 125	935 608	745 125
11.	**Cash transfers from general government**					
	For head of family					
	For two children		0	250 152	48 528	0
		Total	0	250 152	48 528	0
12.	**Take-home pay (1-10+11)**		7 443 247	10 149 670	12 478 750	9 899 518
13.	**Employer's compulsory social security contributions**		0	0	0	0
14.	**Average rates**					
	Income tax		0.0%	0.0%	0.0%	0.0%
	Employees' social security contributions		7.0%	7.0%	7.0%	7.0%
	Total payments less cash transfers		7.0%	4.6%	6.6%	7.0%
	Total tax wedge including employer's social security contributions		7.0%	4.6%	6.6%	7.0%
15.	**Marginal rates**					
	Total payments less cash transfers: Principal earner		7.0%	7.0%	7.0%	7.0%
	Total payments less cash transfers: Spouse		-2.5%	7.0%	7.0%	7.0%
	Total tax wedge: Principal earner		7.0%	7.0%	7.0%	7.0%
	Total tax wedge: Spouse		-2.5%	7.0%	7.0%	7.0%

Chile's national currency is the peso (CLP). For 2016, the average exchange rate was CLP 676.54 to USD 1. That same year, the average worker in Chile earned CLP 8 003 491 (country estimate).

Taxes allowances and tax thresholds for the Personal income tax system and upper earnings limits for social security contributions are determined using and expressed in CPI-indexed units. As of December 31, 2016, the following currency values applied to these units:

Major revenue items	Unit	CLP	USD
Social security contributions	Unidad de Fomento[1] (UF)	26 347.98	38.95
Monthly tax thresholds	Unidad Tributaria Mensual (UTM)	46.183	68.26
Annual tax thresholds	Unidad Tributaria Anual (UTA)	554.196	819.16

1. This amount is subject to daily adjustment in line with the CPI and is compared with monthly earnings in the assessment of social security contributions

1. Personal income tax system

1.1. *Central/federal government income taxes*

1.1.1. *Tax unit*

Each family member declares and pays taxes separately.

1.1.2. *Tax allowances and credits*

1.1.2.1. Standard tax reliefs

- Education tax credit: Parents with children attending preschool, primary, special or secondary education, with a total annual taxable income (both parents) of up to CLP 20 867 600 (UF 792), are entitled to a tax credit of CLP 115 931 (UF 4.4) per child, for expenses related to education. Children shall have a minimal school attendance of 85% and the school must be recognized by the State. This tax credit can be claimed by both parents, or only by one of them.

Relief for social security contributions: Employee's compulsory social insurance contributions are deductible for income tax purposes regardless of whether they are paid to government or private health insurers. (See section 2.1 below).

1.1.2.2. Main non-standard tax reliefs

- *Voluntary contributions and APV (Voluntary Pension Fund Savings):* Voluntary contributions to pension funds and voluntary pension savings fund (APV) may be deducted from taxable income, with an annual upper limit of CLP 15 808 788 (UF 600.)
- *Mortgage Interest:* Taxpayers whose annual income falls below CLP 49 877 640 (UTA 90) may deduct from their taxable income 100% of interest paid within a year for mortgage loans. This percentage is reduced in the case of taxpayers with higher incomes up to

CLP 83 129 400 (UTA 150). This relief cannot be granted along-side the *DFL2 Housing Mortgage Loan Payments* benefit, and cannot exceed CLP 4 433 568 (UTA 8) per annum.

1.1.3. *Tax schedule*

Tax rates are applied on monthly income and these taxes are retained and paid by employers. In order to estimate taxes, tax rates are applied on an annual basis, on the annual average income.

Taxable income (UTA)	Taxable income (CLP thousands)	Tax rates %
0-13.5	0-7 482	Exempt
13.5-30	7 482-16 626	4
30-50	16 626-27 710	8
50-70	27 710 -38 794	13.5
70-90	38 794-49 878	23
90-120	49 878-66 504	30.4
120-150	66 504-83 129	35.5
150 and over	83 129 and over	40

1.2. *State and local income taxes*

No taxes apply to income at state or local government level.

2. Compulsory social security contributions to schemes operated within the government sector

2.1. *Employees' contributions*

Employees have mandatorily to contribute 7% of their income to a health insurance plan subject to an upper earnings limit of CLP 23 226 813 (UF 74.3). They are free to choose whether to pay into a government-managed plan or alternatively to a private insurer (Isapres). The public insurance is based on a joint system that, in general, operates on an equal basis for all its beneficiaries, irrespective of the risk and the amount of the individual contribution. Its financing is partly covered by the contributions and partly by way of a government subsidy. Premiums paid to the plans offered by Isapres are based on the contributors' individual risk and these plans are exclusively financed with the employees' contributions. Public insurance contributions are included in the modelling as the majority of employees pay into plans managed by the government sector.

Employee social security contributions in respect of pensions and unemployment are not classified as taxes in this report; though they are included in modelling as deductions for income tax.

- The mandatory contributions to pension funds and unemployment insurance plans are not classified as taxes, since the payments are made to private institutions. In 1980, the public social security system was replaced with a privately managed individual capitalisation system. This system is obligatory to all employees who have joined the labour force since 1983 and free-lance workers since 2012, and of a voluntary nature to all contributing to the former system. The contributions to the old government operated pension fund system are not included in the modelling because they relate to a minority

Enrollment in the private health system during 2015 amounted to 18.8% of all beneficiaries.

of employees and the system will eventually disappear once the contributions and related benefit payments to those individuals remaining in it have ceased.

- The modelling allows that the contributions to pension funds and unemployment insurance managed by private institutions are deducted from gross income. In the case of their pension funds, these payments amount to 10% of their gross income, with an upper earnings limit of CLP 23 226 813 (UF 74.3). Added to that is an amount that varies depending on the managing company that covers the management of each pension fund account. The monthly unemployment insurance premium is 0.6% of the employee's gross income, with an upper earnings limit of CLP 34 824 589 (UF 111.4) limit. Employees do not pay the monthly unemployment insurance premium when they have a fixed-term contract or after 11 years of labour relationship.
- There are also mandatory contributions to managed funds by members of the police force and the army which are classified as taxes but are not included in the modelling as they relate to a minority of the overall workforce.
- If the employee has a high risk job, that person has to make an additional contribution of 2% (heavy work) or 1% (less heavy work) of their gross income to their pension fund account.

2.2. Employers' contributions

There are four categories of employer social security contribution, none of which are classified as tax revenues in this report.

- Employers make mandatory payments of 0.95% of their employees' gross income for an occupational accident and disease insurance policy subject to an upper earnings limit. For the majority of employees the payments are made to employers' associations of labour security which are private non-profit institutions. Those remaining are made to the Social Security Regularisation Unit (ISL). Although this latter organisation is controlled by the government, the funds are invested on the private institutions market. The employers also pay an additional contribution which depends on the activity and risk associated to the enterprise (it cannot exceed 3.4% of the employees' gross earnings). This additional contribution could be reduced, down to 0%, depending on the safety measures the employer implements in the enterprise. If health and safety conditions at work are not satisfactory, this additional contribution could be applied with a surcharge of up to 100%.
- In addition, employers make payments of 2.4% of each employee's income (0.8% after 11 years of labour relationship and 3% for fixed-term contracts) to finance unemployment insurance. These funds are managed privately.
- Employers have to pay a disability insurance of 1.41% of the employees' gross income, to the pension fund manager.
- If the employee has a high risk job, the employer has to pay 2% (heavy work) or 1% (less heavy work) of the employee's gross income to his pension fund account.

3. Universal cash transfers

3.1. Marital status-related transfers

No such transfers are paid.

Average cost in 2016 was 1.16% of gross income.
Rate starting of 1 July 2016.

3.2. Transfers related to dependent children

The "Family Allowance" is paid on a monthly basis to any employee making social security contributions who has dependent children. The definition of dependants includes:

- Adopted children as well as those born to the parents;
- Children up to the age of 18 or 24 years provided they are single and are regular students in an elementary, secondary, technical, specialised or higher education establishment and whose income is less than half the minimum wage for more than three months in each calendar year.
- The amount of the payment depends on the number of dependent children and the beneficiary's level of income according to the table below. The modelling assumes that the benefit is assessed on the spouse with the lower earning level where both spouses are working.

2016 Transfer by Dependant

Annual income range (CLP)	Annual payment (CLP)
0-3 195 144	125 076
3 195 144-4 666 854	76 758
4 666 854- 7 278 696	24 264
and over	0

4. Memorandum items

4.1. Identification of an average worker

- The source of information is a survey conducted by the National Statistics Institute (INE) to determine the Salary and Labour Cost Index. This nationwide survey is carried out on a monthly sample and gathers information on salaries and labour costs. It applies to companies with at least 5-worker payrolls grouped in accordance with UN ISIC Rev.3 international economic activity standard, covering workers in industry sectors C-O.
- The average gross earning was obtained by multiplying the average hourly wage by the average number of hours worked. It covers both full and part-time workers.

4.2. Employers' contribution to private health and pension schemes

- In Chile very few employers make any contributions towards health schemes for their employees, and the relevant information is not available.

L(7522) and L(7523) are not included.

Table 4. **2016 parameter values**

Average earnings/yr	Ave_earn	8 003 491	Country estimate
Allowances	Basic_al	0	
Income tax	Tax_sch	0	7 481 646
		0.04	16 625 880
		0.080	27 709 800
		0.135	38 793 720
		0.23	49 877 640
		0.304	66 503 520
		0.355	83 129 400
		0.4	
Education tax credit	edu_tax_cre	115 931	
	edu_tax_cre_lim	20 867 600	
Employees SSC	SSC_sch	0.07	23 226 813
Upper threshold		0	
Family allowance	CTR_child	0	125 076
Child element		3 195 144	76 758
		4 666 854	24 264
		7 278 696	0

2016 tax equations

The functions which are used in the equations (Taper, MIN, Tax etc) are described in the technical note about tax equations. Variable names are defined in the table of parameters above, within the equations table, or are the standard variables "married" and "children". A reference to a variable with the affix "_total" indicates the sum of the relevant variable values for the principal and spouse. And the affixes "_princ" and "_spouse" indicate the value for the principal and spouse, respectively. Equations for a single person are as shown for the principal, with "_spouse" values taken as 0.

	Line in country table and intermediate steps	Variable name	Range	Equation
1.	Earnings	earn		
2.	Allowances:	Tax_al	B	Min(Basic_al,earn)
3.	Credits in taxable income	taxbl_cr	B	0
4.	CG taxable income	tax_inc	B	Positive(earn-tax_al)
5.	CG tax before credits	CG_tax_excl	B	Tax(tax_inc, tax_sch)
6.	Tax credits :	tax_cr	P	IF(taxinc_princ+taxinc_spouse<=edu_tax_cre_lim,IF(taxinc_spouse =0,edu_tax_cre*Children,edu_tax_cre*Children*0.5),0)
			S	IF(AND(taxinc_princ+taxinc_spouse<=edu_tax_cre_lim,taxinc_spouse>0),edu_tax_cre*Children*0.5,0)
7.	CG tax	CG_tax	B	Positive(CG_tax_excl-tax_cr)
8.	State and local taxes	local_tax	B	0
9.	Employees' soc security	SSC	B	Tax(earn, SSC_sch)
11.	Family allowance	cash_trans	P/S	IF(Children=0,0, IF(earn_spouse>0, VLOOKUP (earn_spouse, CTR_child) , VLOOKUP (earn_princ, CTR_child)) * children)
13.	Employer's soc security	SSC_empr		0

Key to range of equation B calculated separately for both principal earner and spouse P calculated for principal only (value taken as 0 for spouse calculation) J calculated once only on a joint basis.

Taxing Wages 2017
© OECD 2017

Czech Republic

This chapter includes data on the income taxes paid by workers, their social security contributions, the family benefits they receive in the form of cash transfers as well as the social security contributions and payroll taxes paid by their employers. Results reported include the marginal and average tax burden for eight different family types.

Methodological information is available for Personal income tax systems, Compulsory social security contributions to schemes operated within the government sector, Universal cash transfers as well as recent changes in the tax/benefit system. The methodology also includes the parameter values and tax equations underlying the data.

Czech Republic 2016

The tax/benefit position of single persons

	Wage level (per cent of average wage)	67	100	167	67
	Number of children	none	none	none	2
1.	**Gross wage earnings**	221 148	330 072	551 220	221 148
2.	**Standard tax allowances**				
	Basic allowance				
	Married or head of family				
	Dependent children				
	Deduction for social security contributions and income taxes				
	Work-related expenses				
	Other				
	Total	0	0	0	0
3.	**Tax credits or cash transfers included in taxable income**	0	0	0	0
4.	**Central government taxable income (1 - 2 + 3 + 13)**	296 339	442 297	738 635	296 339
5.	**Central government income tax liability (exclusive of tax credits)**	44 451	66 344	110 795	44 451
6.	**Tax credits**				
	Basic credit				
	Married or head of family				
	Children				
	Other	24 840	24 840	24 840	55 248
	Total	24 840	24 840	24 840	55 248
7.	**Central government income tax finally paid (5-6)**	19 611	41 504	85 955	- 10 797
8.	**State and local taxes**	0	0	0	0
9.	**Employees' compulsory social security contributions**				
	Gross earnings	24 326	36 308	60 634	24 326
	Taxable income				
	Total	24 326	36 308	60 634	24 326
10.	**Total payments to general government (7 + 8 + 9)**	43 937	77 812	146 590	13 529
11.	**Cash transfers from general government**				
	For head of family				
	For two children	0	0	0	14 640
	Total	0	0	0	14 640
12.	**Take-home pay (1-10+11)**	177 211	252 260	404 631	222 259
13.	**Employer's compulsory social security contributions**	75 190	112 225	187 415	75 190
14.	**Average rates**				
	Income tax	8.9%	12.6%	15.6%	-4.9%
	Employees' social security contributions	11.0%	11.0%	11.0%	11.0%
	Total payments less cash transfers	19.9%	23.6%	26.6%	-0.5%
	Total tax wedge including employer's social security contributions	40.2%	43.0%	45.2%	25.0%
15.	**Marginal rates**				
	Total payments less cash transfers: Principal earner	31.1%	31.1%	31.1%	31.1%
	Total payments less cash transfers: Spouse	n.a.	n.a.	n.a.	n.a.
	Total tax wedge: Principal earner	48.6%	48.6%	48.6%	48.6%
	Total tax wedge: Spouse	n.a.	n.a.	n.a.	n.a.

Czech Republic 2016

The tax/benefit position of married couples

	Wage level (per cent of average wage)	100-0	100-33	100-67	100-33
	Number of children	2	2	2	none
1.	**Gross wage earnings**	330 072	438 996	551 220	438 996
2.	**Standard tax allowances**				
	Basic allowance				
	Married or head of family				
	Dependent children				
	Deduction for social security contributions and income taxes				
	Work-related expenses				
	Other				
	Total	0	0	0	0
3.	**Tax credits or cash transfers included in taxable income**	0	0	0	0
4.	**Central government taxable income (1 - 2 + 3 + 13)**	442 297	588 254	738 635	588 254
5.	**Central government income tax liability (exclusive of tax credits)**	66 344	88 238	110 795	88 238
6.	**Tax credits**				
	Basic credit				
	Married or head of family				
	Children				
	Other	80 088	55 248	55 248	24 840
	Total	80 088	55 248	55 248	24 840
7.	**Central government income tax finally paid (5-6)**	- 13 744	11 096	30 707	41 504
8.	**State and local taxes**	0	0	0	0
9.	**Employees' compulsory social security contributions**				
	Gross earnings	36 308	48 290	60 634	48 290
	Taxable income				
	Total	36 308	48 290	60 634	48 290
10.	**Total payments to general government (7 + 8 + 9)**	22 564	59 386	91 342	89 794
11.	**Cash transfers from general government**				
	For head of family				
	For two children	14 640	14 640	14 640	0
	Total	14 640	14 640	14 640	0
12.	**Take-home pay (1-10+11)**	322 148	394 250	474 519	349 202
13.	**Employer's compulsory social security contributions**	112 225	149 259	187 415	149 259
14.	**Average rates**				
	Income tax	-4.2%	2.5%	5.6%	9.5%
	Employees' social security contributions	11.0%	11.0%	11.0%	11.0%
	Total payments less cash transfers	2.4%	10.2%	13.9%	20.5%
	Total tax wedge including employer's social security contributions	27.2%	33.0%	35.8%	40.6%
15.	**Marginal rates**				
	Total payments less cash transfers: Principal earner	31.1%	31.1%	31.1%	31.1%
	Total payments less cash transfers: Spouse	33.8%	11.0%	31.1%	11.0%
	Total tax wedge: Principal earner	48.6%	48.6%	48.6%	48.6%
	Total tax wedge: Spouse	50.6%	33.6%	48.6%	33.6%

The national currency is the Czech koruna (CZK). In 2016, CZK 24.44 was equal to USD 1. In that year, the average worker earned CZK 330 072 (Secretariat estimate). The Secretariat's average wage estimate for 2016 that was computed on the basis of the percentage change in compensation per employee in the total economy (i.e. 3.418357%, *OECD Economic Outlook* No. 100) was higher than the country's average wage estimate of CZK 326 850 (Macroeconomic Forecast, Ministry of Finance, November 2016). Therefore, the Taxing Wages indicators based on the Secretariat's average wage estimate might not reflect the impact of legislative measures that were adopted to reduce the tax burden on the basis of the country's forecast of average wage growth rate for 2016.

1. Personal income tax system

1.1. *Central government income taxes*

1.1.1. *Tax unit*

- The tax unit is the individual.

1.1.2. *Tax allowances and tax credits*

1.1.2.1. Standard reliefs

- *Relief for social and health security contributions.* Employees' social security contributions (see Section 2.1) are not deductible for income tax purposes.

1.1.2.2. Main non-standard tax reliefs applicable to an AW

- *Charitable donations allowance:* A tax allowance of up to 10% of taxable income is available for donations made to municipalities or legal entities for the financing of social, health, cultural, humanitarian, religious, ecological and sport activities. The minimum limit for donations is the lesser of 2% of taxable income or CZK 1 000. A similar procedure shall apply for gratuitous performance to finance the removal of the consequences of a natural disaster occurring in the territory of an EU Member State, Norway or Iceland. The total deduction may not exceed 15% of the tax base. As gratuitous performance for healthcare purposes, the value of one blood donation from an unpaid donor is valued at a sum of CZK 2 000 and the value of an organ donation from a living donor is valued at a sum of CZK 20 000.
- *Interest payments:* Taxpayers may claim an allowance of up to CZK 300 000 for mortgage interest payments or other interest payments related to the purchase or the improvement of their house. The total sum of interest by which the tax base is reduced on all credits of payers in the same jointly managed household must not exceed CZK 300 000.
- *Supplementary pension scheme contributions:* In a period of taxation, the tax base may be reduced by a contribution, in the maximum total amount of CZK 12 000, paid by a taxpayer to their supplementary pension insurance with a State contribution under a contract on supplementary pension insurance with a State contribution entered into between the payer and a pension company; the sum that may be deducted in this manner equals the

total amount of contributions paid by the payer for their supplementary pension insurance with a State contribution in the period of taxation, reduced by CZK 12 000.

- *Private life insurance premiums:* Taxpayers may claim an allowance of up to CZK 12 000 for premiums paid according to a contract between the taxpayer and an insurance company if the benefit (lump sum or recurrent pension) is paid out 60 months after the signature of the contract and in the year in which the taxpayer reaches the age of 60.

1.1.2.3. Tax schedule

From January 2008, a progressive system of taxation is replaced by a single rate of 15%. The tax base, reduced by the non-taxable part of the tax base (see 1.1.2.2 – Main non-standard tax reliefs), rounded down to whole hundreds of CZK is subject to tax at the rate of 15%. After that, tax credits (see 1.1.2.4) can be used to directly reduce a person's tax liability.

1.1.2.4. Tax credits

- Credit of CZK 24 840 per taxpayer.
- Credit of CZK 24 840 per spouse (husband or wife) living with a taxpayer in a common household provided that the spouse's own income does not exceed CZK 68 000 in the taxable period.
- Credit of CZK 13 404 for first child, credit of CZK 17 004 for second child, credit of CZK 20 604 for third and each additional child (irrespective of the child's own income) living with a taxpayer in a common household on the territory of a Member State of the EU, Norway or Iceland, if the child satisfies one or more of the following criteria:
  - age below 18 year of age,
  - age below 26 year of age and receiving full-time education,
  - age below 26 year of age and physically or mentally disabled provided that the child is not in receipt of a state disability payment

If the child is a "ZTP-P" card holder (the child with a certain type of disabilities), the tax credit is CZK 26 808. The taxpayer can claim the tax credit in the form of tax reliefs or tax bonuses or their combination.

- Credit of CZK 2 520 if the taxpayer is in receipt of a partial disability pension or is entitled to both an old-age pension and a partial disability pension
- Credit of CZK 5 040 it the taxpayer is in receipt of a full disability pension, or another type of pension conditional on his full disability pension, or if the taxpayer is entitled to both old-age pension and full disability pension or deemed to be fully disabled under statutory provisions, but his application for a full disability pension was rejected for reasons other than that he was not fully disabled (handicapped).
- Credit of CZK 16 140 if the taxpayer is a "ZTP-P" card holder.
- Credit of CZK 4 020 if the taxpayer takes part in a systematic educational or training programme under statutory provisions in order to prepare for his future vocation (profession) by means of such studies or prescribed training until completion of his/her 26 or 28 years (Ph.D. programme).
- New tax abatement (credit) which can be applied in case that a maintained child of a taxpayer is placing in a pre-school facility. The tax abatement can be applied in the amount of pre-school facility fees, which is really paid for maintained child, however at maximum up to the amount of minimum wage for a maintained child. Tax abatement

may only be used if the maintained child lives with the taxpayer in a jointly managed household. Introduction of this relief is a part of the Act on provision of childcare in a child society.

The non-standard tax reliefs, tax abatement and special solidarity surcharge of 7% for income from employment and entrepreneurship exceeding 48 times the average salary within the calendar year are not included in the tax equations underlying the Taxing Wages results.

1.2. State and local income tax

There are no regional or local income taxes.

2. Compulsory social security contributions to schemes operated within the government sector

The maximum annual earnings used to calculate social security contributions are 48 times the national average monthly wage. The maximum ceiling for social security contributions is CZK 1 296 288 for the year 2016. The maximum ceiling for health insurance has not existed since 2013.

2.1. Employees' contributions

Compulsory contributions of 11% of gross wages and salaries are paid by all employees into government operated schemes. The total is made up as follows (in %):

Health insurance	4.5
Social insurance	6.5

2.2. Employers' contributions

The total contribution for employers is 34% of gross earnings.

The contribution consists of the health insurance contribution (9% of gross wages and salaries) and social insurance (25%).

3. Universal cash transfers

3.1. Transfers related to marital status

None.

3.2. Transfers for dependent children

Non-taxable child allowances are the basic income-tested benefit provided to a dependent child with the objective to contribute to the coverage of costs incurred in his upbringing and sustenance. Entitlement to the child allowance is bound with certain income criteria. The central government pays this allowance in respect of each dependent child based on the family income level and provided that family's income does not exceed 2.4 times the relevant family's living minimum (LM). Family income includes the earnings of both parents net of income tax and the employees' social security and health insurance contributions. Child allowances are provided at three levels depending on the age of the child and are paid as follows:

Family income	Up to 2.4 LM
Age of child	Total payment CZK per month
Below 6 year of age	500
6-15 years	610
15-26 years	700

The monthly family's LM for the AW-type family with children can be calculated by summing the following amounts (in CZK):

Living minimum	
Basic personal requirement	
Single	3 410
First person in household	3 140
Second and other persons who are not a dependent child	2 830
Child aged below 6	1 740
Child aged between 6 and 15	2 140
Child aged between 15 and 26	2 450
Household expenses	
One person household	3 410
Two person household	5 970
Three person household	7 710
Four person household	9 850
Five person household	12 300

The LM is required by law. In case that family income (income of persons assessed together) don't achieve the amount of family's LM can be put in a request for state social support (housing benefit, family benefits, social assistance and other). The system applies the solidarity principle between the high-income families and low-income families, as well as between the childless families and those with children.

The term "social allowance" was abolished from 1 January 2012. However, this fact has no effect on the tax-benefit system for low-income families. The system of personalized payment was simplified and extended. For examples, in case of loss of income (social allowance) some people may put in a request for increase care allowance up to CZK 2 000. This allowance is addressed for recipients who are dependent children below 18 years of age and parent of dependent children below 18 years of age if the income of the family is under 2.0 family's living minimum. Protection in the housing sector is also addressed in the context of state social support system (housing allowances-benefit) and the system of assistance in material need as additional housing. Also foster care benefits create a separate benefit system; since 1 January 2013 they have ceased to be a component of the state social support system. These allowances (housing, care and foster care) are not included in the Taxing Wages models.

3.3. *Additional transfers*

Additional allowances (means-tested benefits in material need) are paid by the central government to low income families in adverse social and financial situation. The amount transferred is derived from the LM and varies according to total family income including family allowances and own efforts, opportunities and needs are taken into account. This allowance is not included in the computation.

4. Main changes in tax/benefit systems since 2016

In 2016, there were no changes that would have a significant effect on the current calculation of Taxing Wages.

List of main changes that have no impact on the current computation of TW:

- A tax abatement (credit) which can be applied in case that a child of a taxpayer visits a nursery school (preschool children, including kindergarten up to start school attendance) is introduced. The tax credit can be applied in the amount of nursery school fees really paid for child, however at maximum up to the amount of minimum salary for a child. Introduction of this relief is a part of the Act on provision of childcare in a child society (see chapter 1.1.2.4).
- Tax credit on second and third and next child has increased based on the Amendment (CZK 17 004 for second child, CZK 20 604 for third and each additional child) – see chapter 1.1.2.4.
- A tax abatement has no effect to the tax equations underlying the TW result but has impact on collection of IT in 2016.

5. Memorandum items

5.1. *Identification of AW and valuation of earnings*

The Ministry of Finance estimates the average earnings of the AW based on the data supplied by the Czech Statistical Office. The calculation of the average earnings AW is made by CZ-NACE division, which is compatible with ISIC classifications Ver. 4.

5.2. *Employers' contributions to private pension, health and related schemes*

There are supplementary private pension schemes only, but employers 'contributions vary. Relevant information is not available.

2016 parameter values

	Ave_earn	330 072	Secretariat estimate
Income tax rate	tax_rate	0.15	
Social security – social insurance	SSs_rate	0.065	
Social security – health insurance	SSh_rate	0.045	
Employers	SSC_empr_rate	0.34	
Child Tax credit - first child	child_cr_1	13 404	
- second child	child_cr_2	17 004	
- third child	child_cr_3	20 604	
Tax credit for individuals	tax_cr_base	24 840	
Tax credit for spouse	tax_cr_spo	24 840	
Tax credit for spouse income ceiling	Tax_cr_spo_inc_ceil	68 000	
Living minimum (LM)			
	basic_adult	3 410	
	basic_household	5 970	
	basic_child	2 140	
	house_exp	1	3 410
		2	5 970
		3	7 710
		4	9 850
		5	12 300
Cash transfers	transf_1	610	
Social security, social insurance - ceiling	soc_sec_si_ceil	1 296 288	

2016 tax equations

The equations for the Czech system are on an individual basis. But the spouse tax credit is relevant only to the calculation for the principal earner and cash transfers are calculated only once. This is shown by the Range indicator in the table below.

The functions which are used in the equations (Taper, MIN, Tax etc) are described in the technical note about tax equations. Variable names are defined in the table of parameters above, within the equations table, or are the standard variables "married" and "children". A reference to a variable with the affix "_total" indicates the sum of the relevant variable values for the principal and spouse. And the affixes "_princ" and "_spouse" indicate the value for the principal and spouse, respectively. Equations for a single person are as shown for the principal, with "_spouse" values taken as 0.

		Variable name	Range	Equation
1.	Earnings	earn	B	
2.	CG taxable income	tax_inc_princ	B	Earn+(earn*SSC_empr_rate)
3.	CG tax before credits			
	CG tax before credits principal	CG_tax_excl_princ	B	Tax(tax_inc_princ, tax_rate)
4.	Tax credits:			
	Tax credit for children	tax_cr_ch	P	If (number of children>3; (number of children - 3)*child_cr_3+child_cr_1+ child_cr_2+child_cr_3; If (number of children>2;child_cr_1 +child_cr_2 + child_cr_3; If (number of children>1;child_cr_1+child_cr_2; If (number of children=0;0)))))
	Basic tax credit	tax_cr_bas	B	tax_cr_bas
	Tax credit for spouse	tax_cr_spouse	P	Married*tax_cr_spo
5.	CG tax			
	CG tax principal	CG_tax_princ	B	Max(CG_tax_excl_princ - tax_cr_bas_princ - tax_cr_spo , 0) - tax_cr_ch
6.	State and local taxes	local_tax	B	0
7.	Employees' social security	SSs SSh	B B	MIN(earn,soc_sec_si__ceil)*SSs_rate earn*SSh_rate
8.	Cash transfers			
	Net family income	net_inc	J	earn_total-CG_tax_total-SSC_total
9.	Living minimum (monthly)	LM	J	(1-Married)*basic_adult+Married*basic_household +Children*basic_child+ VLOOKUP((1+Married+Children), house_exp, 2, FALSE)
10.	Total cash transfers	cash_trans	J	Children*IF(net_inc<=(2.4)*LM*12, transf_1*12)
11.	Employer's social security	SSs_empr SSh_empr	B B	MIN(earn,soc_sec_sir_ceil)*SSs_empr_rate earn*SSh_empr_rate

Key to range of equation: B calculated separately for both principal earner and spouse; P calculated for principal only (value taken as 0 for spouse calculation); J calculated once only on a joint basis.

Taxing Wages 2017
© OECD 2017

Denmark

This chapter includes data on the income taxes paid by workers, their social security contributions, the family benefits they receive in the form of cash transfers as well as the social security contributions and payroll taxes paid by their employers. Results reported include the marginal and average tax burden for eight different family types.

Methodological information is available for Personal income tax systems, Compulsory social security contributions to schemes operated within the government sector, Universal cash transfers as well as recent changes in the tax/benefit system. The methodology also includes the parameter values and tax equations underlying the data.

Denmark 2016

The tax/benefit position of single persons

	Wage level (per cent of average wage)	67	100	167	67
	Number of children	none	none	none	2
1.	**Gross wage earnings**	276 412	412 555	688 967	276 412
2.	**Standard tax allowances**				
	Basic allowance				
	Married or head of family				
	Dependent children				
	Deduction for social security contributions and income taxes	22 113	33 004	55 117	22 113
	Work-related expenses	0	0	0	0
	Other				
	Total	22 113	33 004	55 117	22 113
3.	**Tax credits or cash transfers included in taxable income**	0	0	0	0
	Earnings tax credit deduction	22 942	28 000	28 000	38 421
	Total	- 22 942	- 28 000	- 28 000	- 38 421
4.	**Central government taxable income (1 - 2 + 3)**	231 357	351 551	605 850	215 878
5.	**Central government income tax liability (exclusive of tax credits)**	30 031	45 010	100 645	29 567
6.	**Tax credits**				
	Basic credit	5 315	5 315	5 315	5 315
	Married or head of family				
	Children				
	Other				
	Total	5 315	5 315	5 315	5 315
7.	**Central government income tax finally paid (5-6)**	46 829	72 699	150 447	46 364
8.	**State and local taxes**	46 671	76 611	139 957	42 815
9.	**Employees' compulsory social security contributions**				
	Gross earnings	0	0	0	0
	Taxable income				
	Total	0	0	0	0
10.	**Total payments to general government (7 + 8 + 9)**	93 499	149 310	290 404	89 179
11.	**Cash transfers from general government**				
	For head of family				
	For two children	0	0	0	69 452
	Green check	950	950	0	1 390
	Total	950	950	0	70 842
12.	**Take-home pay (1-10+11)**	183 863	264 195	398 563	258 075
13.	**Employer's compulsory social security contributions**	3 227	3 227	3 227	3 227
14.	**Average rates**				
	Income tax	33.8%	36.2%	42.2%	32.3%
	Employees' social security contributions	0.0%	0.0%	0.0%	0.0%
	Total payments less cash transfers	33.5%	36.0%	42.2%	6.6%
	Total tax wedge including employer's social security contributions	34.3%	36.5%	42.4%	7.7%
15.	**Marginal rates**				
	Total payments less cash transfers: Principal earner	39.7%	42.0%	55.8%	38.2%
	Total payments less cash transfers: Spouse	n.a.	n.a.	n.a.	n.a.
	Total tax wedge: Principal earner	39.7%	42.0%	55.8%	38.2%
	Total tax wedge: Spouse	n.a.	n.a.	n.a.	n.a.

Denmark 2016

The tax/benefit position of married couples

			100-0	100-33	100-67	100-33
		Wage level (per cent of average wage)	100-0	100-33	100-67	100-33
		Number of children	2	2	2	none
1.	**Gross wage earnings**		412 555	548 698	688 967	548 698
2.	**Standard tax allowances**					
	Basic allowance					
	Married or head of family					
	Dependent children					
	Deduction for social security contributions and income taxes		33 004	43 896	55 117	43 896
	Work-related expenses		0	0	0	0
	Other					
		Total	33 004	43 896	55 117	43 896
3.	**Tax credits or cash transfers included in taxable income**		0	0	0	0
	Earnings tax credit deduction		28 000	28 000	28 000	28 000
		Total	- 28 000	- 28 000	- 28 000	- 28 000
4.	**Central government taxable income (1 - 2 + 3)**		351 551	465 502	582 907	465 502
5.	**Central government income tax liability (exclusive of tax credits)**		45 010	59 801	75 041	59 801
6.	**Tax credits**					
	Basic credit		15 946	10 630	10 630	10 630
	Married or head of family					
	Children					
	Other					
		Total	15 946	10 630	10 630	10 630
7.	**Central government income tax finally paid (5-6)**		67 384	93 067	119 528	93 067
8.	**State and local taxes**		65 650	94 036	123 281	94 036
9.	**Employees' compulsory social security contributions**					
	Gross earnings		0	0	0	0
	Taxable income					
		Total	0	0	0	0
10.	**Total payments to general government (7 + 8 + 9)**		133 034	187 102	242 809	187 102
11.	**Cash transfers from general government**					
	For head of family					
	For two children		25 284	25 284	25 284	0
	Green check		2 620	2 620	2 340	2 180
		Total	27 904	27 904	27 624	2 180
12.	**Take-home pay (1-10+11)**		307 425	389 500	473 782	363 776
13.	**Employer's compulsory social security contributions**		3 227	6 454	6 454	6 454
14.	**Average rates**					
	Income tax		32.2%	34.1%	35.2%	34.1%
	Employees' social security contributions		0.0%	0.0%	0.0%	0.0%
	Total payments less cash transfers		25.5%	29.0%	31.2%	33.7%
	Total tax wedge including employer's social security contributions		26.1%	29.8%	31.9%	34.5%
15.	**Marginal rates**					
	Total payments less cash transfers: Principal earner		42.0%	42.0%	42.0%	42.0%
	Total payments less cash transfers: Spouse		39.7%	39.7%	39.7%	39.7%
	Total tax wedge: Principal earner		42.0%	42.0%	42.0%	42.0%
	Total tax wedge: Spouse		41.1%	39.7%	39.7%	39.7%

The national currency is the Kroner (DKK). In 2016, DKK 6.73 was equal to USD 1. In that year, the average worker earned DKK 412 555 (Secretariat estimate), which is calculated on the background of the extrapolated 2015 average worker income with the expected 2016 growth rate of wages on 2.2%.

1. Personal income tax system

In the Danish Personal income tax system, the income of the individual taxpayer is split into three categories:

- *Personal income,* which consists of employment income, business income, pensions, unemployment benefits etc. and with fully deductibility of Labour Market Contributions.
- *Capital income* (e.g. interest income and some capital gains) is calculated as a net amount (the sum of positive and negative capital income net of interest expenses). Dividend income and the property value of owner-occupied dwellings are taxed at different tax rates.
- *Taxable income* – the aggregate of personal income and capital income less deductions (e.g. work-related expenses etc.).

All three categories are relevant for various tax rates, see Section 1.2.1.

The employees' social security contributions and their payments to labour market supplementary pension schemes (see Section 2.1) are not included in personal income (or taxable income).

Regarding the tax unit, the earned income of each spouse is taxed separately. However, as is mentioned in Section 1.2.1, some unutilised personal allowances can be transferred between them.

1.1. Tax allowances and tax credits

1.1.1. Standard reliefs

Wage or salary earners who make expenses in order to earn their income (e.g. transport expenses, trade union membership dues, unemployment premiums) can fully deduct these expenses from taxable income.

The tax credit scheme allows the taxpayer to deduct 8.30% of earned income to a maximum of DKK 28 000 in order to calculate taxable income. Single parents get an extra employment allowance of 5.60% in 2016 with a maximum allowance of DKK 18 800. The effective value of the credit is equal to the municipality tax (24.91%) plus the 3.0% health care tax rate that is paid to the state (27.91% on average) multiplied by the value of the deduction.

1.1.2. Main non-standard tax reliefs applicable to an AW

- *Interest payments* are fully deductible from capital income.

- The *non-standard deduction for wage and salary earners:* The actual costs that are made in order to acquire income are deductible from taxable income. The main items are:
  - Contributions paid to trade unions;
  - Transportation costs: Up to 24 km. per day: no deduction. 24-120 km.: DKK 1.99 per km. Above 120 km.: DKK 1.00 per km. as a standard, but transport from municipalities placed in the outskirts of the country gives a credit of DKK 1.99 also above 120 km;
  - Other costs above DKK 5 800.
- *Contributions/premiums* paid to *private pension saving plans* are in general deductible from personal income. From 1999 onwards, contributions/premiums paid to private pension saving plans with sum payments are no longer deductible from income subject to the top tax bracket rate. From 2013 onwards, contributions/premiums paid to private pension saving plans with sum payments are no longer deductible.
- Other reliefs:
  - Alimonies, if according to contract, are deductible from taxable income;
  - Contributions to certain non-profit institutions are deductible from taxable income (limit DKK 15 200);
  - Losses incurred from unincorporated business in earlier years are, in principle, deductible from personal income.

1.1.3. *Tax credits*

Each individual is granted a personal allowance, which is converted into a wastable tax credit by applying the marginal tax rate of the first bracket of the income tax schedule. For taxpayers who are 18 years of age or are older, the tax credit amounts to:

For central government income tax	9.08% of DKK 44 000 = DKK 3 995
For central government health care tax	3.00% of DKK 44 000 = DKK 1 320
For municipal income tax	24.91% of DKK 44 000 = DKK 10 960

Special personal allowance for an individual younger than 18: DKK 33 000.

If a married person cannot utilise the personal allowance, the unutilised part is transferred to the spouse.

1.2. *Central government income taxes*

1.2.1. *Tax schedule*

Individuals pay an 8% Labour Market Contribution (*Arbejdsmarkedsbidrag* in Danish), levied on the gross wage or other income from work before the deduction of any allowance.

Before 2008, the revenue was earmarked for certain social security expenditures through the Labour market Fund, but this system was abolished from 2008, and the tax enters the budget in the same way as any other income taxes. From 2011 the last links regarding social security of the tax were removed making all taxpayers working in Denmark pay the labour market contribution. The labour market contribution is thus treated as a PIT in Taxing Wages from 2008.

Low tax bracket to the central government is assessed on the aggregate of personal income and positive net capital income at the rate of 9.08%.

From 2010 and onwards the medium tax bracket was removed.

Top tax bracket to the central government is assessed on the excess of DKK 467 300 of the aggregate of personal income and positive net capital income in excess of DKK 41 900 at the rate of 15%. If a married individual cannot utilise the total allowance of DKK 467 300, the unutilised part is *not* transferred to the spouse.

If the marginal tax rate including local tax exceeds 51.95%, the top tax bracket rate is reduced by the difference between the marginal tax rate and 51.95%.

1.2.2. *Health care tax*

Central government levies an additional health care tax of 3%. The tax base is taxable income (see Section 1).

1.3. *State and local income taxes*

1.3.1. *General description*

Local income taxes are levied only by the municipalities. The rates vary across jurisdictions.

1.3.2. *Tax base*

The tax base is taxable income (see Section 1). Tax credit varies with tax rates. The average amount is given below.

1.3.3. *Tax rates*

Lowest rate: 22.5% (municipalities);

Highest rate: 27.8% (municipalities);

Average rate: 24.91% (municipalities);

The average rate is used in this study. It is applied to the tax base less personal allowances (see Section 1.1).

2. Compulsory social security contributions to schemes operated within the government sector

2.1. *Employees' contributions*

Employees make a fixed contribution of DKK 11 290 for unemployment insurance. From 1999 onwards, the contribution for unemployment insurance is split into two: one part consists of the contribution for unemployment insurance (DKK 4 008) while the other part consists of a voluntary contribution to an early retirement scheme (DKK 5 856). In addition an administration fee of DKK 1 426 on average is added.

Contributions to the unemployment funds are not mandatory. Nevertheless, these payments have up until the implementation of ESA 2010 and the major revision of the Danish national accounts in the autumn 2014 been defined as social security contributions and classified as taxes in the Danish national accounts because there is no direct link between what members pay to the schemes and what they receive and the funds are subsidized by the state. The contributions to the unemployment funds are no longer classified as taxes in the Danish national accounts.

In addition, there is a compulsory fixed contribution to a general Labour Market Supplementary Pension Scheme of DKK 1 136 for workers who work at least 117 hours per month (for workers who work less than 117 hours but not less than 78 hours, the rate is DKK 757; for workers who work less than 78 hours but not less than 39 hours, the rate is DKK 379); their employer makes a corresponding contribution that is double this amount. Under this scheme, each employee has a plan and it should be noted that the contribution that is ascribed to this plan is determined by the level of employment and does not necessarily relate to the actual amount described above. As the employee and employer contribution is paid to a privately-managed pension scheme, these contributions are not considered to be taxes but rather as non-tax compulsory payments and are therefore not included in the tax calculations.

Also, all private sector employers contribute to Financing Contribution (DKK 614) and barsel.dk (DKK 750). Both of the payments are paid to privately managed funds. The Financing Contribution covers part of the Danish state's expenses to ATP-contributions as well as expenses to Employees' Guarantee Fund for the unemployed. Barsel.dk is a statutory scheme covering the part of the private sector labour market that is not covered by other approved maternity/paternity compensation schemes. Those contributions are considered as non-tax compulsory payments and not included in the tax calculations either.

2.2. Employers' contributions

It is compulsory for the employer to contribute to Employers' Reimbursement System (DKK 2 775), industrial injury tax (DKK 132) and Employees' Guarantee Fund (DKK 320).The employer also contributes to a Labour Market Supplementary Pension scheme, which in case of a full-time employee corresponds to a fixed amount of DKK 2 272 (being twice the fixed amount of DKK 1 136 mentioned in Section 2.1).

3. Universal cash transfers

The transfers for each dependent child are as follows:

Age group	Quarterly amount (DKK) for each child
0-2	4 470
3-6	3 537
7-17	2 784

The transfer is reduced when the income of a parent exceeds DKK 732 900. There are additional special amounts for single parents: the transfer for each dependent child is DKK 5 432 per year and a yearly transfer of DKK 5 536 regardless of the number of children. In addition, there is a state transfer of DKK 13 884 per year for each dependent child in case an "absent parent" does not contribute (this amount) to the family. This transfer is included in this Report's calculations for single parents.

Individuals older than 18 years receive a "green check" of DKK 950; this amount is increased with DKK 220 per child for up to two children. Only one partner in a married couple receives the increased "green check" for children. The "green check" is nominally fixed and is phased out at a rate of 7.5% for income above DKK 379 900. If the yearly income of the individuals is lower than DKK 222 000 the individuals receive an "additional green check" of DKK 280.

4. Main changes in tax/benefit systems

From 2000 to 2002, the low tax bracket rate has been reduced from 7% to 5.5%. The low tax bracket is assessed on the aggregate of personal income and positive net capital income.

After the parliamentary elections in 2001, the Conservative/Liberal government adopted a tax freeze policy, which implied that tax rates could not be increased, either in nominal or relative terms, during that government term. Taxes were therefore not increased during the period 2002-05. After the parliamentary elections in February 2005, the Conservative/Liberal government and the tax freeze policy were confirmed.

In order to respect the "tax freeze", the low tax bracket has been reduced by 0.36% from 2004 to 2010 as a compensation for increases in local income taxes from 33.31% in 2004 to 33.66% in 2011.

In the spring of 2003, the government agreed with one of the opposition parties to implement a tax package. The aim of this package was to decrease the level of labour taxation in Denmark, and thereby to reduce the distortions in the labour market and to improve the incentives to work. The package contained two main elements: an increase of the threshold for the medium tax bracket of nearly DKK 50 000 and the introduction of a tax credit scheme whereby the taxpayer can deduct 2.5% of earned income to a maximum of DKK 7 500 (in 2007) in the calculation of taxable income.

Before 2004, a compulsory contribution of 1% of employees' gross earnings was paid to an individual Labour Market Supplementary Pension Scheme established for the employee – this contribution is not considered as a social security contribution but rather as savings being made by the individual. However, from 2004 to 2010, this contribution was suspended and finally abolished and the deposits paid out as of April 2010.

In September 2007, the tax cuts from the 2003-package was extended. The threshold for the medium tax bracket was to be raised with DKK 57 900 in 2009 to meet with the top tax bracket threshold. The deductible tax credit was increased to 4.0% of earned income in 2008 and to 4.25% in 2009; thus raising the maximum to 12 300 in 2008 and to 13 600 in 2009. The effective value of the credit and of the personal income allowance is equal to the local income tax rate, the church tax plus the health care tax rate (31.63% on average in 2013) multiplied by the value of the deduction.

From 1 January 2007 a Local Government Reform has come into force, which changes the structure of labour taxation. The reform however had only a minimal impact on the overall level of taxation. The number of municipalities has been cut from 270 to 98 and five regions have replaced the 14 counties. The regions will not impose taxes but will be financed through state subsidies and by contributions from the municipalities. The reform implied an increase in the average municipal tax rate from 22.1% in 2006 to 24.577% in 2007. Since then, there has been a further increase in the average municipal tax to 24.907% in 2013. The county tax has been replaced by a new health care tax of 8% which is levied by central government. The health care tax rate is decreased to 6% in 2013. The levels of taxation have thus been reduced from three to two: only the central and local governments now levy taxes.

In the spring of 2009, the government and one of the opposition parties agreed upon a major tax reform to be phased in from 2010 to 2019. The reform aims at reducing the high marginal tax rates on personal income and thus to stimulate labour supply in the medium to long-term. The reform decreases income taxes by DKK 29 billion in 2010. The tax reform is planned to be revenue neutral as a whole, but was underfinanced in the short run (2010-12) in order to stimulate the economy. The main measures taken in 2010 include the reduction of the rate of the bottom tax bracket from 5.26% to 3.67%, abolition of the medium tax bracket with the 6% rate altogether, and increase the top tax bracket threshold by DKK 28 800 to DKK 389 000. The reform will decrease the lowest marginal tax rate from 42.4% to 41.0% and the highest marginal tax rate on labour income from 63.0% to 56.1%. The marginal tax rate on positive net capital income (up to 51.5 after abolition of the middle tax bracket) is further reduced for the vast majority by introduction of an extra allowance of DKK 40 000 (DKK 80 000 for married couples) for positive net capital income in the top bracket tax.

The reform is partly financed by higher energy, transport and environmental taxes to support the energy and climate policy objectives of the government, and also by increases of excise rates on health-related goods (fat, candy, sugary drinks, tobacco). These increases are partly compensated by giving a "green check" to households (see section 3). The tax reform is also partly financed by base broadening measures. The measures include a gradual reduction from 2012 to 2019 of the tax value (from 33.5% to 25.5%) of assessment oriented deductions and limitations of the tax deductibility of net interest payments over a nominal threshold of DKK 50 000 (DKK 100 000 for married couples). Also the deductibility of payments above DKK 100 000 a year to individual pension insurance schemes with less than life-long coverage has been limited, as well as tightening of the tax treatment of company cars and other fringe benefits. Furthermore, a 6% tax is imposed from 2011 on pension payments exceeding DKK 362 800.

To consolidate the budget, a *Fiscal Consolidation Agreement* was reached in May 2010, somewhat modifying the prescriptions of the Spring Package of 2009.

The specific provisions of the *Fiscal Consolidation Agreement* include:

- The suspension from 2011 until 2013 of automatic adjustments in various tax thresholds (including personal allowances).
- Postponing from 2011 to 2014 the increase of the threshold for the top income tax rate (15%) from DKK 389 900 to 409 100 (EUR 52 316 to 54 892). The increase was an element of the *2009 tax reform*.
- The labour union membership fees' tax deductibility is limited to DKK 3 000 (EUR 403) from the year 2011. The threshold is not adjusted.
- From 2011, the annual amount of child allowance is limited to DKK 35 000 (EUR 4 696), irrespective of the number of children. This was abolished by the new government by 2012. Child allowances will be gradually reduced by 5% until 2013.

As part of the Finance Act 2012 it was decided to introduce an "additional green check" to people beyond 18 years with low income (less than DKK 212 000). The "additional green check" is DKK 280.

In June 2012 a tax reform was reached. Included in the reform were changes in the earned income tax credit and the top tax bracket. The earned income tax credit is gradually raised from 4.40% in 2012 to 10.65% in 2022 (6.95% in 2013) where the maximum limit of earned income tax credit is raised from DKK 14 100 in 2012 to DKK 34 100 in 2022 (DKK 22 300 in 2013). Furthermore, a special earned income tax credit for single parents was decided from 2014. This will be gradually introduced to the amount of 6.25% in 2022 with a maximum limit of DKK 20 000. In The Tax Reform 2012 it was also decided to gradually raise the top tax bracket from DKK 389 900 in 2012 to DKK 467 000 in 2022 (DKK 421 000 in 2013).

As part of the Finance Act 2013 an agreement, The Excise Duty and Competition Package, was reached. This agreement includes a decrease in the excise duty on electricity, an abolition of the fat tax and a planned expansion in the excise duty on sugar, which will reduce expenses of both consumers and companies. This was financed by an increase in the bottom tax rate of 0.19 percentage points and a reduction in the personal allowance by DKK 900 for all persons (under and over 18 years) introduced from the income year 2013. As a consequence the marginal tax ceiling was increased from 51.5% to 51.7%. It is estimated that the abolished excise duties and the increased income taxes will have similar effects on distribution and labour supply.

Certain elements of the tax reform from 2012 were accelerated in the 2014 Budget. The employment allowance is adjusted upwards to 7.65% (2014), 8.05% (2015), 8.3% (2016) and 8.75% (2017), with a simultaneous increase of the maximum allowance from DKK 25 000 in 2014 to DKK 28 600 in 2018. The extra employment allowance for single parents is increased to 5.40% in 2014 (instead of 2.60%) with a maximum allowance of DKK 17 700.

Growth Plan 2014 contained measures to reduce the public service obligation on electricity and roll back an increase in excise duty on fossil fuel. As part of the financing of Growth Plan 2014 the low tax bracket rate is increased by 0.28 percentage point over the next five years, including 0.25 percentage point in 2015, with a parallel increase in the tax ceiling. Also, the green check and the supplementary green check are reduced over the next five years, starting in 2015.

In the autumn 2014, the new ESA 2010 guidelines (European System of National and Regional Accounts) and a major revision of the Danish national accounts were implemented which changed the classification of a few taxes. For example, the church tax and contributions to the unemployment fund are no longer classified as taxes, but as volunteer contributions (see Section 2.1).

As part of the Finance Act 2015 the tax deductibility of labour union membership fees is increased from DKK 3 000 to DKK 6 000 in 2015.

5. Memorandum items

5.1. *Identification of an AW*

The AW is identified as an average worker employed at firms which are members of the Danish Employers' Confederation.

5.2. *Employers' contribution to private schemes*

The employer must provide his employees with work injuries' insurance.

Employees typically participate in a private occupational (labour market) pension scheme to which both the employee and the employer make contributions. The employee's contribution is deductible for income tax purposes and is treated in this Report as a non-standard tax relief. The employer's contribution is not included in the gross wage income of the employee.

2016 parameter values

Average earnings	Ave_earn	412 555	Secretariat estimate
Central taxes	Health_tax_rate	0.03	
	Low_rate	0.0908	
	Medium_thrsh	0	
	Medium_rate	0	
	Top_thrsh	467 300	
	Top_rate	0.15	
	Marg_rate_ceil	0.5195	
	Adj_top_rate	0.1496	
	Temp_tax_rate	0.00	
	Temp_tax_thrsh	0	
	Personal_al	44 000	
The green check	green_check	950	
	1 child	220	
	child max	440	
	Green_check_thrsh	379 900	
	Green_check_taper_rate	0.075	
	Extra_green_check	280	
	Extra_green_check_thrsh	222 000	
Local taxes	gener_rate	0.2491	
	church_rate	0	
total local tax rate	Local_rates	0.2491	
Earned income tax credit scheme	earncredit_rate	0.083	
	earncredit_max	28 000	
for single parents	Sing_par_earncredit_rate	0.056	
	Sing_par_earncredit_max	18 800	
Child transfers	Child_3to6	14 148	
	Child_7to17	11 136	
	Child_limit	732 900	
	Child_red	0.02	
for single parents	Sing_par_basic	5 536	
	Sing_par_ch	19 316	
Individual Labour Market Pension Scheme	Pension_rate	0	
Employees soc. security:			
suppl. pension scheme	Pension	1 136	
unempl. insurance	Unemp	0	
Labour Market Contribution	Labour_market_rate	0.08	
Employer soc. security:			
suppl. pension scheme	Pension_empr	2 272	
contributions to ATP	SSC_ATP	3 227	
SSC rate	SSC_empr	0.00	
Financing Contribution	NTCP_FC	614	
barsel.dk	NTCP_barsel	750	

2016 tax equations

The equations for the Danish system in 2016 are mostly on an individual basis but there is an interaction in the calculation of Central Government tax between spouses and the child benefit is calculated only once. This is shown by the Range indicator in the table below.

The functions which are used in the equations (Taper, MIN, Tax etc) are described in the technical note about tax equations. Variable names are defined in the table of parameters above, within the equations table, or are the standard variables "married" and "children". A reference to a variable with the affix "_total" indicates the sum of the relevant variable values for the principal and spouse. And the affixes "_princ" and "_spouse" indicate the value for the principal and spouse, respectively. Equations for a single person are as shown for the principal, with "_spouse" values taken as 0.

	Line in country table and intermediate steps	Variable name	Range	Equation
1.	Earnings	earn		
2.	Allowances:	tax_al	B	Labour_market_contr+Pension_rate*earn
		earncredit	B	Min(earn*earncredit_rate, earncredit_max)+(Children>0)*(Married=0)*Min(earn*Sing_par_earncredit_rate; Sing_par_earncredit_max)
3.	Credits in taxable income	taxbl_cr	B	0
4.	CG taxable income	tax_inc	B	Positive(earn-tax_al-earncredit+taxbl_cr)
	Personal income	pers_inc	B	Positive(earn-pension_rate*earn-Labour_market_contr)
5.	CG tax before credits	CG_tax_excl_princ	P	Low_rate*tax_inc_princ+Medium_rate*Positive(tax_inc_princ-Medium_thrsh-Married*Positive(Medium_thrsh-pers_inc_spouse))+Adj_top_rate*Positive(tax_inc_princ-Top_thrsh)
		CG_health_tax_excl_princ	P	Health_tax_rate*tax_inc_princ
		CG_tax_excl_spouse	S	Low_rate*tax_inc_spouse+Medium_rate*Positive(tax_inc_spouse-Medium_thrsh)+Adj_top_rate*Positive(tax_inc_spouse-Top_thrsh)
		CG_health_tax_excl_spouse	S	(Married=1)*Health_tax_rate*tax_inc_spouse
6.	Tax credits :	tax_cr_princ	P	Personal_al*Low_rate+Married*Positive(Personal_al-pers_inc_spouse)*Low_rate
		health_tax_cr_princ	P	Health_tax_rate*(Personal_al+Married*Positive(Personal_al-tax_inc_spouse))
		tax_cr_spouse	S	Personal_al*Low_rate
		health_tax_cr_spouse	S	(Married=1)*Health_tax_rate*Personal_al
	Labour Market Contribution	Labour_market_contr	B	Labour_market_rate*earn
7.	CG tax	CG_tax	B	Positive(CG_tax_excl-tax_cr)+Positive(CG_health_tax_excl-health_tax_cr)+Labour_market_contr
8.	State and local taxes	local_tax_princ	P	Positive((Local_rates)*(tax_inc_princ-Personal_al-Married*Positive(Personal_al-tax_inc_spouse)))
		local_tax_spouse	S	(Local_rates)*Positive(tax_inc_spouse-Personal_al)
9.	Employees' soc security contribution	SSC	B	(earn>0)*Unemp
10.	Total payments	tot_payments	J	Positive(CG_tax_total+local_tax_total+SSC_total)

	Line in country table and intermediate steps	Variable name	Range	Equation
11.	Cash transfers	cash_trans	J	Positive(((Children>0)*(Child_3to6+(Children>1)*(Children-1)*Child_7to17+(Married=0)*(Sing_par_basic+Children*Sing_par_ch)))-(Positive(earn_princ-Child_limit)*Child_red)-(Positive(earn_spouse-Child_limit)*Child_red))+IF(Married=1,(Taper(green_check,pers_inc_princ,Green_check_thrsh,Green_check_taper_rate)+Taper(green_check+MIN(Children*_1_child,child_max),pers_inc_spouse,Green_check_thrsh,Green_check_taper_rate)),Taper(green_check+MIN(Children*_1_child,child_max),pers_inc_princ, Green_check_thrsh,Green_check_taper_rate))+ IF(Married=1,(IF(pers_inc_princ<Extra_green_check_thrsh,Extra_green_check,0)+IF(pers_inc_spouse<Extra_green_check_thrsh,Extra_green_check,0)),IF(pers_inc_princ<Extra_green_check_thrsh,Extra_green_check,0))
13.	Employer's soc security	SSC_empr	B	SSC_empr*earn+SSC_ATP

Key to range of equation B calculated separately for both principal earner and spouse P calculated for principal only (value taken as 0 for spouse calculation) J calculated once only on a joint basis.

Taxing Wages 2017
© OECD 2017

Estonia

This chapter includes data on the income taxes paid by workers, their social security contributions, the family benefits they receive in the form of cash transfers as well as the social security contributions and payroll taxes paid by their employers. Results reported include the marginal and average tax burden for eight different family types.

Methodological information is available for Personal income tax systems, Compulsory social security contributions to schemes operated within the government sector, Universal cash transfers as well as recent changes in the tax/benefit system. The methodology also includes the parameter values and tax equations underlying the data.

Estonia 2016

The tax/benefit position of single persons

	Wage level (per cent of average wage)	67	100	167	67
	Number of children	none	none	none	2
1.	**Gross wage earnings**	9 139	13 640	22 778	9 139
2.	**Standard tax allowances**				
	Basic allowance	2 040	2 040	2 040	3 888
	Married or head of family				
	Dependent children				
	Deduction for social security contributions and income taxes	146	218	364	146
	Work-related expenses	0	0	0	0
	Other				
	Total	2 186	2 258	2 404	4 034
3.	**Tax credits or cash transfers included in taxable income**	0	0	0	0
4.	**Central government taxable income (1 - 2 + 3)**	6 952	11 381	20 374	5 104
5.	**Central government income tax liability (exclusive of tax credits)**	1 390	2 276	4 075	1 021
6.	**Tax credits**				
	Basic credit				
	Married or head of family				
	Children	0	0	0	0
	Other				
	Total	0	0	0	0
7.	**Central government income tax finally paid (5-6)**	1 390	2 276	4 075	1 021
8.	**State and local taxes**	0	0	0	0
9.	**Employees' compulsory social security contributions**				
	Gross earnings	146	218	364	146
	Taxable income				
	Total	146	218	364	146
10.	**Total payments to general government (7 + 8 + 9)**	1 537	2 495	4 439	1 167
11.	**Cash transfers from general government**				
	For head of family				
	For two children	0	0	0	1 660
	Total	0	0	0	1 660
12.	**Take-home pay (1-10+11)**	7 602	11 145	18 339	9 632
13.	**Employer's compulsory social security contributions**	3 089	4 610	7 699	3 089
14.	**Average rates**				
	Income tax	15.2%	16.7%	17.9%	11.2%
	Employees' social security contributions	1.6%	1.6%	1.6%	1.6%
	Total payments less cash transfers	16.8%	18.3%	19.5%	-5.4%
	Total tax wedge including employer's social security contributions	37.8%	38.9%	39.8%	21.2%
15.	**Marginal rates**				
	Total payments less cash transfers: Principal earner	21.3%	21.3%	21.3%	21.3%
	Total payments less cash transfers: Spouse	n.a.	n.a.	n.a.	n.a.
	Total tax wedge: Principal earner	41.2%	41.2%	41.2%	41.2%
	Total tax wedge: Spouse	n.a.	n.a.	n.a.	n.a.

Estonia 2016

The tax/benefit position of married couples

		Wage level (per cent of average wage)	100-0	100-33	100-67	100-33
		Number of children	2	2	2	none
1.	**Gross wage earnings**		13 640	18 141	22 778	18 141
2.	**Standard tax allowances**					
	Basic allowance		5 928	5 928	5 928	4 080
	Married or head of family					
	Dependent children					
	Deduction for social security contributions and income taxes		218	290	364	290
	Work-related expenses		0	0	0	0
	Other					
		Total	6 146	6 218	6 292	4 370
3.	**Tax credits or cash transfers included in taxable income**		0	0	0	0
4.	**Central government taxable income (1 - 2 + 3)**		7 493	11 922	16 486	13 770
5.	**Central government income tax liability (exclusive of tax credits)**		1 499	2 384	3 297	2 754
6.	**Tax credits**					
	Basic credit					
	Married or head of family					
	Children		0	0	0	0
	Other					
		Total	0	0	0	0
7.	**Central government income tax finally paid (5-6)**		1 499	2 384	3 297	2 754
8.	**State and local taxes**		0	0	0	0
9.	**Employees' compulsory social security contributions**					
	Gross earnings		218	290	364	290
	Taxable income					
		Total	218	290	364	290
10.	**Total payments to general government (7 + 8 + 9)**		1 717	2 675	3 662	3 044
11.	**Cash transfers from general government**					
	For head of family					
	For two children		1 200	1 200	1 200	0
		Total	1 200	1 200	1 200	0
12.	**Take-home pay (1-10+11)**		13 123	16 666	20 317	15 096
13.	**Employer's compulsory social security contributions**		4 610	6 191	7 699	6 191
14.	**Average rates**					
	Income tax		11.0%	13.1%	14.5%	15.2%
	Employees' social security contributions		1.6%	1.6%	1.6%	1.6%
	Total payments less cash transfers		3.8%	8.1%	10.8%	16.8%
	Total tax wedge including employer's social security contributions		28.1%	31.5%	33.3%	38.0%
15.	**Marginal rates**					
	Total payments less cash transfers: Principal earner		21.3%	21.3%	21.3%	21.3%
	Total payments less cash transfers: Spouse		21.3%	21.3%	21.3%	21.3%
	Total tax wedge: Principal earner		41.2%	41.2%	41.2%	41.2%
	Total tax wedge: Spouse		41.7%	21.9%	41.2%	21.9%

The Estonian currency is the Euro (EUR). In 2016, EUR 0.90 was equal to USD 1. In 2016, the average worker in Estonia earned EUR 13 640 (Secretariat estimate).

1. Personal income tax system

1.1. *Central government income tax*

1.1.1. *Tax unit*

The tax unit is the family.

1.1.2. *Tax allowances*

1.1.2.1. Standard tax reliefs

- *A general (basic) allowance* of EUR 2 040 is deductible from individual income in 2016.
- A *child* allowance of EUR 1 848 is also deductible from income for each of the second and any subsequent children up to and including the age of 16.
- *Relief for social security contributions*: Employee's compulsory contributions for unemployment insurance are deductible for income tax purposes.
- *Tax credits*: from 2016 there is non-payable tax credit for low-income earners ("madalapalgaliste tagasimakse"). The recipient must be in the corresponding year (2016) at least 6 months 18 years old, resident, working full time (may work with multiple job contracts), his/her yearly income in 2016 must be lower than EUR 7 818, and the tax credit cannot exceed the income tax paid by the person after all tax-exempts. The formula to calculate the tax credit is the following: (rate*12 – income*0.35)/12*number of months filling the criteria. The rate of EUR 228 per month in 2016 was fixed in State Budget 2016, the first tax credits will be paid in 2017 based on 2016 income. The tax credit will impact the revenues of persons approximately below 53% of average wage.

1.1.2.2. Non-standard tax reliefs applicable to income from employment

- *II pillar pension contributions*: In 2016, these represent voluntary payments to private funds for all employees and are paid at a rate of 2% or 3% of earnings.
- Occupational accident and illness benefits that are not paid as insurance benefits are deductible from taxable income within the limit of EUR 768 per year.
- *Housing loan interest, educational costs, gifts and donations* are deductible from taxable income within upper limits of EUR 1 200 and 50% of taxable income per year.
- *Voluntary pension contributions (III pillar)*: Contributions paid by a resident to the provider of a pension plan based in Estonia or in another EU Member State according to a pension plan that is approved and entered into a special register in accordance with the pension legislation are deductible from taxable income. In 2015 such deductions are subject to an annual limit of a sum equal to 15% and maximum of EUR 6 000 of the employee's, public servant`s or members of legal person management or control body income in a calendar year.

1.1.3. *Tax schedule*

The rate of 20% applies for all levels of taxable income.

1.2. Regional and local income tax

There are no regional or local income taxes.

2. Compulsory social security insurance system

The compulsory social security insurance system consists of three schemes as follows:

- pension insurance;
- health insurance;
- unemployment insurance.

2.1. Employees' contributions

Employees pay 1.6% of their earnings in contributions for unemployment insurance. The taxable base is the total amount of the gross wage or salary including vacation payments, fringe benefits and remuneration of expenses related to work above a certain threshold. The assessment period is the calendar month.

2.2. Employers' contributions

Social security insurance contributions are also paid by employers on behalf of their employees. The taxable base and the assessment period are the same as for employees' contributions. The employers' contribution rates are applied in two parts:

- Unemployment insurance – 0.8% of employee earnings.
- Pension and health insurance – as follows for monthly earnings above EUR 390.

Scheme name	Rate of contribution (%)
Pension insurance	20.00
Health insurance	13.00
Total	33.00

In addition there is a lump sum payment for each employee of EUR 128.70 per month (split between pensions and health insurance on a 20:13 basis).

3. Payroll tax

None.

4. Universal cash transfers

4.1. Transfers related to marital status

None.

4.2. Transfers for dependent children

Estonia's family benefits are designed to provide partial coverage of the costs families incur in caring for, raising and educating their children.

The state pays family benefits to all children until they reach the age of 16. Children enrolled in basic or secondary schools or vocational education institutions operating on the basis of basic education have the right to receive family benefits until the age of 19. Applications for the allowance are made on an annual basis and the payments are not taxable. The values of these benefits in 2016 are shown in the table below. The single parent child allowance is paid for each child.

In addition there are nine other types of family benefits for which payment depends on either the age of the child(ren) and/ or the status of the person(s) looking of them: maternity benefit; childbirth allowance; parental benefit; child care allowance; conscript's child allowance; child's school allowance, child allowance for a child under guardianship or foster care; start in independent life allowance; adoption allowance (single payment). These are not included in the modelling.

Type of benefit	Annual amount of benefit (in EUR)
Child allowance (paid until children turn 16 or until the end of the academic year in which they turn 19 if they continue studying).	
For the first and second child	600.00
For the third and any subsequent children	1 200.00
Single parent's child allowance	230.16
Parents allowance for families with seven or more children	2 024.88

In addition to existing benefits, from July 1, 2013 the need-based child benefits were introduced. Need-based family benefit income threshold is based on Statistical Office relative poverty threshold published by the 1st of March in a year before current budget year. In 2016 the need-based threshold is EUR 358 in a month for the first household member. For every other at least 14-years old member the threshold is EUR 179 and for the younger members EUR 107.4 in a month. Need-based family benefit is in 2016 EUR 45 in a month for single child family and EUR 90 for families with two or more children.

5. Main changes in tax/benefit system since 2005

- The personal income tax rate was steadily reduced from 24% in 2005 to 21% in 2008. In 2015 it was reduced to 20%.
- The child tax allowance applied for the third and subsequent children for 2005 and the second and subsequent children in 2006 and 2007. It applied to all children in 2008 and then returned to the 2007 position in 2009.
- The employee unemployment contribution rate was reduced from 1% to 0.6% in 2006 and then raised in 2 stages to 2.8% at the end of 2009. The corresponding rates for employers were a reduction from 0.5 % to 0.3% in 2006 increasing to 1.4%. In 2013 the employee unemployment contribution rate was reduced from 2.8% to 2.0% and the corresponding rate for employers from 1.4% to 1.0%. In 2015 the employee unemployment contribution rate was reduced from 2.0% to 1.6% and the corresponding rate for employers from 1.0% to 0.8%.
- In addition to existing benefits, from July 1, 2013 the need-based child benefits were introduced. Further details in section 4.2 on cash transfers.
- From 2016, a non-payable tax credit for low-income earners ("madalapalgaliste tagasimakse") was introduced. Further details in section 1.1.2. on tax allowances.

6. Memorandum items

6.1. *Average gross annual wage earnings calculation*

In Estonia the gross earnings figures cover wages and salaries paid to individuals in formal employment including payment for overtime. They also include bonus payments and other payments such as pay for annual leave, paid leave up to seven days, public holidays, absences due to sickness for up to 30 days, job training, and slowdown through no fault of the person in formal employment.

The average gross wage earnings figures of all adult workers covering industry sectors B–N by NACE Rev.2 are estimated with average wage growth rate forecast of Estonian Ministry of Finance.

6.2. *Employer contributions to private pension and health schemes*

Some employer contributions are made to private health and pension schemes but there is no relevant information available on the amounts that are paid.

2016 parameter values

Average earnings/yr	Ave_earn	13 640	Secretariat estimate
Allowances	Basic_al	2 040	
	Child_al	1 848	
Income tax	Tax_rate	0.20	
Tax credit	tax_cred	2736	
	tax_cred_rt	0.35	
	tax_cred_thr	7818	
Employers SSC	SSC_rate1	0.33	
	Threshold	4 680	
	lump_sum	1 544.4	
	SSC_rate2	0.008	
Employees SSC	SSC_rate3	0.016	
Child allowances			
First & second child	CA_first&second	600	
Other children	CA_others	1 200	
Additional for children of lone parents			
	CA_onepar	230.16	
Need-based child benefits			
one child	CB_1	540	
two or more children	CB_2	1 080	
Need-based family threshold			
first member	F_thrsh_1	4 269.00	
other members above 14	F_thrsh_2	2 148.00	
other members under 14	F_thrsh_3	1 288.8	
Days in tax year	numdays	365	

2016 tax equations

The equations for the Estonian system are mostly on an individual basis.

The functions which are used in the equations (Taper, MIN, Tax etc) are described in the technical note about tax equations. Variable names are defined in the table of parameters above, within the equations table, or are the standard variables "married" and "children". A reference to a variable with the affix "_total" indicates the sum of the relevant variable values for the principal and spouse. And the affixes "_princ" and "_spouse" indicate the value for the principal and spouse, respectively. Equations for a single person are as shown for the principal, with "_spouse" values taken as 0.

	Line in country table and intermediate steps	Variable name	Range	Equation
1.	Earnings	earn		
2.	Allowances:	tax_al	J	Min(Basic_al*(1+married)+SSC_empee+(children>1)*child_al*(Children-1),earn)
3.	Credits in taxable income	taxbl_cr	B	0
4.	CG taxable income	tax_inc	B	Positive(earn-tax_al)
5.	CG tax before credits	CG_tax_excl	B	Tax_inc*tax_rate
6.	Tax credits :	tax_cr	B	IF(earn_spouse>0,IF(earn_princ+earn_spouse<tax_cred_thr*(1+Married),Positive ((tax_cred*(1+Married))-((earn_princ+earn_spouse)*tax_cred_rt)),0),IF(earn_ princ<tax_cred_thr,Positive(tax_cred-(earn_princ*tax_cred_rt)),0))
7.	CG tax	CG_tax	B	Positive(CG_tax_excl-tax_cr)
8;	State and local taxes	local_tax	B	0
9.	Employees' soc security	SSC_empee	B	earn*SSC_rate3
11.	Cash transfers	cash_trans	J	IF(Children<3,CA_firstsecond*Children,(2*CA_firstsecond)+(CA_other* (Children-2)))+(Married=0)*Children*CA_onepar+IF((earn_total-CG_tax-SSC_ empee)<(F_thrsh_1+ (F_thrsh_2*Married=1)+ (F_thrsh_3*Children)),IF (Children>1, CB_2, CB_1),0)
13.	Employer's soc security	SSC_empr	B	IF(earn>0,IF(earn>threshold,earn*SSC_rate1,lump_sum),0)+earn*SSC_rate2

Key to range of equation B calculated separately for both principal earner and spouse P calculated for principal only (value taken as 0 for spouse calculation) J calculated once only on a joint basis.

© OECD 2017

Finland

This chapter includes data on the income taxes paid by workers, their social security contributions, the family benefits they receive in the form of cash transfers as well as the social security contributions and payroll taxes paid by their employers. Results reported include the marginal and average tax burden for eight different family types.

Methodological information is available for Personal income tax systems, Compulsory social security contributions to schemes operated within the government sector, Universal cash transfers as well as recent changes in the tax/benefit system. The methodology also includes the parameter values and tax equations underlying the data.

Finland 2016

The tax/benefit position of single persons

		67	100	167	67
	Wage level (per cent of average wage)	67	100	167	67
	Number of children	none	none	none	2
1.	**Gross wage earnings**	29 357	43 816	73 172	29 357
2.	**Standard tax allowances**				
	Basic allowance				
	Married or head of family				
	Dependent children				
	Deduction for social security contributions and income taxes	2 252	3 361	5 612	2 252
	Work-related expenses	620	620	620	620
	Other				
	Total	2 872	3 981	6 232	2 872
3.	**Tax credits or cash transfers included in taxable income**	0	0	0	0
4.	**Central government taxable income (1 - 2 + 3)**	26 485	39 835	66 940	26 485
5.	**Central government income tax liability (exclusive of tax credits)**	807	3 144	8 933	807
6.	**Tax credits**				
	Basic credit	1 260	1 111	683	1 260
	Married or head of family				
	Children	0	0	0	200
	Other				
	Total	1 260	1 111	683	1 460
7.	**Central government income tax finally paid (5-6)**	143	2 175	8 393	143
8.	**State and local taxes**	4 260	7 467	13 115	4 072
9.	**Employees' compulsory social security contributions**				
	Gross earnings	2 252	3 361	5 612	2 252
	Taxable income	279	489	858	266
	Total	2 530	3 849	6 470	2 518
10.	**Total payments to general government (7 + 8 + 9)**	6 933	13 492	27 979	6 733
11.	**Cash transfers from general government**				
	For head of family				
	For two children	0	0	0	3 584
	Total	0	0	0	3 584
12.	**Take-home pay (1-10+11)**	22 423	30 324	45 194	26 207
13.	**Employer's compulsory social security contributions**	6 773	10 108	16 881	6 773
14.	**Average rates**				
	Income tax	15.0%	22.0%	29.4%	14.4%
	Employees' social security contributions	8.6%	8.8%	8.8%	8.6%
	Total payments less cash transfers	23.6%	30.8%	38.2%	10.7%
	Total tax wedge including employer's social security contributions	37.9%	43.8%	49.8%	27.5%
15.	**Marginal rates**				
	Total payments less cash transfers: Principal earner	44.3%	45.8%	49.5%	44.3%
	Total payments less cash transfers: Spouse	n.a.	n.a.	n.a.	n.a.
	Total tax wedge: Principal earner	54.8%	55.9%	59.0%	54.8%
	Total tax wedge: Spouse	n.a.	n.a.	n.a.	n.a.

Finland 2016

The tax/benefit position of married couples

	Wage level (per cent of average wage)	100-0	100-33	100-67	100-33
	Number of children	2	2	2	none
1.	**Gross wage earnings**	43 816	58 275	73 172	58 275
2.	**Standard tax allowances**				
	Basic allowance				
	Married or head of family				
	Dependent children				
	Deduction for social security contributions and income taxes	3 361	4 470	5 612	4 470
	Work-related expenses	620	1 240	1 240	1 240
	Other				
	Total	3 981	5 710	6 852	5 710
3.	**Tax credits or cash transfers included in taxable income**	0	0	0	0
4.	**Central government taxable income (1 - 2 + 3)**	39 835	52 565	66 320	52 565
5.	**Central government income tax liability (exclusive of tax credits)**	3 144	3 144	3 951	3 144
6.	**Tax credits**				
	Basic credit	1 111	2 371	2 371	2 371
	Married or head of family				
	Children	28	128	128	0
	Other				
	Total	1 139	2 499	2 499	2 371
7.	**Central government income tax finally paid (5-6)**	2 147	2 242	2 290	2 270
8.	**State and local taxes**	7 467	7 630	11 633	7 724
9.	**Employees' compulsory social security contributions**				
	Gross earnings	3 361	4 470	5 612	4 470
	Taxable income	489	499	761	505
	Total	3 849	4 969	6 373	4 975
10.	**Total payments to general government (7 + 8 + 9)**	13 464	14 841	20 297	14 969
11.	**Cash transfers from general government**				
	For head of family				
	For two children	2 419	2 419	2 419	0
	Total	2 419	2 419	2 419	0
12.	**Take-home pay (1-10+11)**	32 771	45 853	55 294	43 306
13.	**Employer's compulsory social security contributions**	10 108	13 444	16 881	13 444
14.	**Average rates**				
	Income tax	21.9%	16.9%	19.0%	17.1%
	Employees' social security contributions	8.8%	8.5%	8.7%	8.5%
	Total payments less cash transfers	25.2%	21.3%	24.4%	25.7%
	Total tax wedge including employer's social security contributions	39.2%	36.1%	38.6%	39.6%
15.	**Marginal rates**				
	Total payments less cash transfers: Principal earner	46.8%	46.8%	46.8%	45.8%
	Total payments less cash transfers: Spouse	9.5%	31.4%	44.3%	31.4%
	Total tax wedge: Principal earner	56.8%	56.8%	56.8%	55.9%
	Total tax wedge: Spouse	26.5%	44.3%	54.8%	44.3%

The national currency is the Euro (EUR). In 2016, EUR 0.90 was equal to USD 1. In that year, the average worker earned EUR 43 816 (Secretariat estimate).

1. Personal income tax system

1.1. *Central government income taxes*

1.1.1. *Tax unit*

Spouses are taxed separately for earned income.

1.1.2. *Standard tax allowances and tax credits*

1.1.2.1. Standard reliefs

- *Work-related expenses:* A standard deduction for work-related expenses equal to the amount of wage or salary, with a maximum amount of EUR 620 is granted.
- *Tax credit:* An earned income tax credit is granted against the central government income tax. If the credit exceeds the amount of central government income tax, the excess credit is deductible from the municipal income tax and the health insurance contribution for medical care. The credit is calculated on the basis of taxpayers' income from work. The credit amounts to 11.8% of income exceeding EUR 2 500, until it reaches its maximum of EUR 1 260. The amount of the credit is reduced by 1.46% of the earned income minus work related expenses exceeding EUR 33 000. The credit is fully phased out when taxpayers' income is about EUR 120 000.
- *Child tax credit:* The credit is granted to taxpayers who have children in their care and custody according to the Population Register System records. It is given for four children at most. All parents and custodians get it regardless of which one of them has the child(ren) living with them. The size of the child tax credit depends on the number of children and whether the taxpayer has joint custody or single custody: for joint custody the credit is EUR 50 per year and child, and for single custody it is EUR 100 per year and child. If net taxable income exceeds EUR 36 000 per year (earned income and capital income combined), the credit is reduced. For the part of the income exceeding the threshold, the amount to be credited is phased out by a one percentage point rate. The child tax credit is will be in force from 2015 through 2017.

1.1.2.2. Main non-standard tax reliefs applicable to an AW

- *Interest:* Interest on loans associated with the earning of taxable income, 55% of the interest on loans for the purchase of owner-occupied dwellings, and student loans guaranteed by the state can be deducted against capital income. Of the excess of interest over capital income, 30% (32% for first-time homebuyers) can be credited against income tax up to a maximum of EUR 1 400.
- *Membership fees:* Membership fees paid to employees' organisations or trade unions.

- *Travelling expenses:* Travelling expenses from the place of residence to the place of employment using the cheapest means in excess of EUR 750 up to a maximum deduction of EUR 7 000.
- *Double housing expenses*: If the place of employment is located too far from home in order to commute (distance > 100 km), the taxpayer can deduct the costs of hiring a second dwelling located near the place of work up to EUR 250 per month. This deduction can be claimed only by one person per household.
- *Other work-related outlays:* Outlays for tools, professional literature, research equipment and scientific literature, and expenses incurred in scientific or artistic work (unless compensated by scholarships).

Travelling expenses and other work-related outlays are deductible only to the extent that their total amount exceeds the amount of the standard deduction for work-related expenses.

1.1.3. *Rate schedule*

Central government income tax:

Taxable income (EUR)	Tax on lower limit (EUR)	Tax on excess income in bracket (%)
16 700-25 000	8	6.5
25 000-40 800	547.5	17.5
40 800-72 300	3 312.5	21.5
72 300	10 085	31.75

1.2. *Local income tax*

1.2.1. *Tax base and tax rates*

The tax base of the local income tax is taxable income as established for the income tax levied by central government.

Municipal tax is levied at flat rates. In 2016 the tax rate varies between 16.50 and 22.50%, the average rate being approximately 19.87%.

Municipal tax is not deductible against central government taxes. Work-related expenses and other non-standard deductions are deductible, as for purposes of the central government income tax.

1.2.2. *Tax allowances in municipal income taxation*

- An earned income tax allowance is calculated on the basis of taxpayer's income from work. The allowance amounts to 51% of income between EUR 2 500 and EUR 7 230 and 28% of the income exceeding EUR 7 230, until it reaches its maximum of EUR 3 570. The amount of the allowance is reduced by 4.5% on earned income minus work related expenses exceeding EUR 14 000.
- A basic tax allowance is granted on the basis of taxable income remaining after the other allowances have been subtracted. The maximum amount, EUR 3 020, is reduced by 18% on income exceeding the aforementioned amount.

2. Compulsory social security contributions to schemes operated within the government sector

2.1. Employee contributions

2.1.1. Rate and ceiling

In 2016, the rate of the health insurance contribution for medical care paid by an employee is 1.3%. The tax base for this contribution is net taxable income for municipal income tax purposes.

In addition there is an employees' pension insurance contribution which amounts to 5.70% of gross salary, an employees' unemployment insurance contribution equal to 1.15% of gross salary and a health insurance contribution for daily allowance equal to 0.82% of gross salary. For employees aged 53 and older, the pension insurance contribution amounts to 7.20% of gross salary. These contributions are deductible for income tax purposes.

2.1.2. Distinction by marital status or sex

The rates do not differ.

2.2. Employers' contributions

The average rate of the employers' social security contribution in 2016 is 23.07% of gross wage.

3. Universal cash transfers

3.1. Amount for marriage

None.

3.2. Amount for children

The central government pays in 2016 the following allowances (EUR):

For the first child	1 149.00
For the second child	1 269.6
For the third child	1 620.12
For the fourth child	1 855.68
Fifth and subsequent child	2 091.24

The child subsidy for a single parent is increased by an annual amount of EUR 582.6 for each child.

4. Main changes in the tax/benefit system since 2015

Adjustments for inflation and rise of earnings levels were made to the central government tax scale in 2016. Also, the top bracket of the tax scale was temporarily, for 2016 through 2017, merged into the penultimate bracket keeping the top tax rate at 31.75%.

In 2016 the public broadcasting tax is 0.68% on taxable earned income, taxes of min. EUR 70 and max. EUR 143 will be collected.

The maximum amount of the earned income tax credit in state taxation was raised from EUR 1 025 to EUR 1 260.

The maximum amount of the basic allowance in municipal taxation was raised from EUR 2 970 to EUR 3 020.

Home-loan interest counts at 55%, down from 65%, as deductible/creditable interest.

5. Memorandum items

5.1. *Calculation of average gross annual wage*

The Finnish figures are generally calculated as follows:

- Gross annual earnings are calculated at an individual level on the basis of the hour's usually worked, average hourly pay for the fourth quarter, and the share of annual periodic bonuses.
- The earnings exclude sickness and unemployment compensations, but include all normal overtime compensations, bonuses, holiday remunerations and remunerations for public holidays.

5.2. *Employer contributions to private pension and health schemes*

No information is available.

2016 parameter values

Average earnings	Ave_earn	43 816	Secretariat estimate
Expenses	Work_exp_max	620	
	Work_exp_rate	1	
Allowances	al_SSC_rate	0.0767	
State tax	Tax_min	8	
Tax schedule	Tax_sch	0	16 700
		0.065	25 000
		0.175	40 800
		0.215	72 300
		0.3175	
Broadcasting tax	brdcst_tax_rate	0.0068	
	brdcst_tax_min	70	
	brdcst_tax_max	143	
Earned income tax credit	eitc_thrsh	2 500	
	eitc_rate	0.118	
	eitc_redn_thrsh	33 000	
	eitc_redn_rate	0.0146	
	eitc_max	1 260	
Child tax credit	child_cr	50	
	child_thres	36 000	
	child_red	0.01	
Earned income tax allowance	al_thrsh	2 500	
	al_thrsh2	7 230	
	al_rate	0.51	
	al_rate2	0.28	
	al_redn_thrsh	14 000	
	al_redn_rate	0.045	
	al_max	3 570	
low income	SL_max	3 020	
	SL_rate	0.18	
Local intax	Local_rate	0.1987	
	Church_rate	0	
	Local_tot	0.1987	
Soc sec taxpayer	SSC_rate	0.013	
soc.sec empr	SSC_empr	0.2307	
Cash transfer	ch_1	1 149.00	
	ch_2	1 269.60	
	ch_3	1 620.12	
	ch_4	1 855.68	
	ch_5	2 091.24	
	ch_small	0	
	ch_lone	582.6	

2016 Tax equations

The equations for the Finnish system are mostly on an individual basis except for the child benefit which is calculated only once. This is shown by the Range indicator in the table below.

The functions which are used in the equations (Taper, MIN, Tax etc) are described in the technical note about tax equations.

Variable names are defined in the table of parameters above, within the equations table, or are the standard variables "married" and "children". A reference to a variable with the affix "_total" indicates the sum of the relevant variable values for the principal and spouse. And the affixes "_princ" and "_spouse" indicate the value for the principal and spouse, respectively. Equations for a single person are as shown for the principal, with "_spouse" values taken as 0.

	Line in country table and intermediate steps	Variable name	Range	Equation
1.	Earnings	earn		
	Work related expenses	work_rel	B	MIN(Work_exp_max, Work_exp_rate*earn)
	SSC deduction	SSC_al	B	earn*al_SSC_rate
2.	Allowances:	tax_al	B	work_rel+SSC_al
3.	Credits in taxable income	taxbl_cr	B	0
4.	CG taxable income	tax_inc	B	Positive(earn-tax_al)
5.	CG tax before credits	CG_tax_excl	B	=Tax(tax_inc, Tax_sch)+Tax_min* (tax_inc>Tax_thrsh)
6.	Tax credits :	tax_cr	B	MINA(eitc_max,eitc_rate*Positive(earn-eitc_thrsh))-MINA(eitc_max,eitc_redn_rate*Positive(earn-work_rel-eitc_redn_thrsh))
	Child tax credit	child_cr	P	taper(child_cr*(1+(married=0))*children,earn_p-work_rel,child_thres,child_red)
			S	If(tax_inc_s>0,taper(child_cr*children,earn_s-work_rel,,child_thres,child_red),0)
		broadcasting_tax	B	IF((earn-work_rel)*brdcst_tax_rate<brdcst_tax_min,0,IF((earn-work_rel)*brdcst_tax_rate>brdcst_tax_max,brdcst_tax_max,(earn-work_rel)*brdcst_tax_rate))
7.	CG tax	CG_tax	B	Positive(CG_tax_excl - tax_cr-child_cr)+broadcasting_tax
	Earned income allowance	earninc_al	B	MIN(al_max, IF(earn>al_thrsh2, al_rate*(al_thrsh2-al_thrsh1)+al_rate2*(earn-al_thrsh2), Positive(earn-al_thrsh)))- MIN(al_max, al_redn_rate* Positive(earn-work_rel-al_redn_thrsh))
	Low income	low_inc	B	Positive(MIN(earn-work_rel-low_al-SSC_al, SL_max)- SL_rate*Positive(earn-work_rel- low_al-SSC_al-SL_max))
	Taxable income (local)	tax_inc_l	B	tax_inc-earninc_al-low_inc
8.	State and local taxes	local_tax	B	Positive(tax_inc_l*Local_tot- (local_tot/(local_tot+SSC_rate))*If((Tax_cr-CG-tax_excl)>0,(Tax_cr-CG-tax_excl)+child_cr,0)
9.	Employees' soc security	SSC	B	Positive(SSC_rate*tax_inc_l - (SSC_rate/(local_tot+SSC_rate))*IF((Tax_cr-CG-tax_excl)>0,(Tax_cr-CG-tax_excl)+child_cr,0)) + SSC_prog_rate* Positive(tax_inc_l-SSC_prog_thrsh)+SSC_al
11.	Cash transfers	cash_trans	J	(Children>0)*ch_1+(Children>1)*ch_2+ (Children>2)*ch_3+ (Children>3)*ch_4+ Positive(Children-4)*ch_4 +(Married=0)*Children*ch_lone
13.	Employer's soc security	SSC_empr	B	earn*SSC_empr

Key to range of equation B calculated separately for both principal earner and spouse P calculated for principal only (value taken as 0 for spouse calculation) J calculated once only on a joint basis

© OECD 2017

France

This chapter includes data on the income taxes paid by workers, their social security contributions, the family benefits they receive in the form of cash transfers as well as the social security contributions and payroll taxes paid by their employers. Results reported include the marginal and average tax burden for eight different family types.

Methodological information is available for Personal income tax systems, Compulsory social security contributions to schemes operated within the government sector, Universal cash transfers as well as recent changes in the tax/benefit system. The methodology also includes the parameter values and tax equations underlying the data.

France 2016

The tax/benefit position of single persons

		Wage level (per cent of average wage)	67	100	167	67
		Number of children	none	none	none	2
1.	**Gross wage earnings**		25 493	38 049	63 543	25 493
2.	**Standard tax allowances**					
	Basic allowance					
	Married or head of family					
	Dependent children					
	Deduction for social security contributions and income taxes		4 923	7 348	11 822	4 923
	Work-related expenses		2 057	3 070	5 172	2 057
	Other					
		Total	6 980	10 418	16 994	6 980
3.	**Tax credits or cash transfers included in taxable income**		0	0	0	0
4.	**Central government taxable income (1 - 2 + 3)**		18 513	27 632	46 549	18 513
5.	**Central government income tax liability (exclusive of tax credits)**		2 996	5 630	13 309	2 004
6.	**Tax credits**					
	Basic credit					
	Married or head of family					
	Children					
	Other		197	0	0	0
		Total	197	0	0	0
7.	**Central government income tax finally paid (5-6)**		2 799	5 630	13 309	2 004
8.	**State and local taxes**		0	0	0	0
9.	**Employees' compulsory social security contributions**					
	Gross earnings		3 646	5 441	8 638	3 646
	Taxable income					
		Total	3 646	5 441	8 638	3 646
10.	**Total payments to general government (7 + 8 + 9)**		6 444	11 071	21 947	5 649
11.	**Cash transfers from general government**					
	In-work benefit (Gross)		0	0	0	1 112
	For two children (Gross)		0	0	0	4 308
	CRDS Deducted		0	0	0	- 27
		Total	0	0	0	5 393
12.	**Take-home pay (1-10+11)**		19 049	26 978	41 596	25 237
13.	**Employers' compulsory social security contributions**		7 940	13 907	27 658	7 940
14.	**Average rates**					
	Income tax		11.0%	14.8%	20.9%	7.9%
	Employees' social security contributions		14.3%	14.3%	13.6%	14.3%
	Total payments less cash transfers		25.3%	29.1%	34.5%	1.0%
	Total tax wedge including employer's social security contributions		43.0%	48.1%	54.4%	24.5%
15.	**Marginal rates**					
	Total payments less cash transfers: Principal earner		43.6%	43.9%	42.6%	51.6%
	Total payments less cash transfers: Spouse		n.a.	n.a.	n.a.	n.a.
	Total tax wedge: Principal earner		69.3%	58.9%	59.9%	73.6%
	Total tax wedge: Spouse		n.a.	n.a.	n.a.	n.a.

France 2016

The tax/benefit position of married couples

		Wage level (per cent of average wage)	100-0	100-33	100-67	100-33
		Number of children	2	2	2	none
1.	**Gross wage earnings**		38 049	50 606	63 543	50 606
2.	**Standard tax allowances**					
	Basic allowance					
	Married or head of family					
	Dependent children					
	Deduction for social security contributions and income taxes		7 348	9 772	12 271	9 772
	Work-related expenses		3 070	4 083	5 127	4 083
	Other					
		Total	10 418	13 856	17 398	13 856
3.	**Tax credits or cash transfers included in taxable income**		0	0	0	0
4.	**Central government taxable income (1 - 2 + 3)**		27 632	36 750	46 145	36 750
5.	**Central government income tax liability (exclusive of tax credits)**		2 991	3 978	7 243	6 303
6.	**Tax credits**					
	Basic credit					
	Married or head of family					
	Children					
	Other		0	0	254	465
		Total	0	0	254	465
7.	**Central government income tax finally paid (5-6)**		2 991	3 978	6 990	5 838
8.	**State and local taxes**		0	0	0	0
9.	**Employees' compulsory social security contributions**					
	Gross earnings		5 441	7 237	9 087	7 237
	Taxable income					
		Total	5 441	7 237	9 087	7 237
10.	**Total payments to general government (7 + 8 + 9)**		8 432	11 214	16 076	13 075
11.	**Cash transfers from general government**					
	In-work benefit (Gross)		0	0	0	0
	For two children (Gross)		1 561	1 561	1 561	0
	CRDS Deducted		- 8	- 8	- 8	0
		Total	1 554	1 554	1 554	0
12.	**Take-home pay (1-10+11)**		31 171	40 945	49 020	37 531
13.	**Employers' compulsory social security contributions**		13 907	14 871	21 847	14 871
14.	**Average rates**					
	Income tax		7.9%	7.9%	11.0%	11.5%
	Employees' social security contributions		14.3%	14.3%	14.3%	14.3%
	Total payments less cash transfers		18.1%	19.1%	22.9%	25.8%
	Total tax wedge including employer's social security contributions		40.0%	37.5%	42.6%	42.7%
15.	**Marginal rates**					
	Total payments less cash transfers: Principal earner		22.2%	22.2%	46.1%	36.4%
	Total payments less cash transfers: Spouse		22.2%	22.2%	46.1%	36.4%
	Total tax wedge: Principal earner		43.0%	43.0%	60.5%	53.4%
	Total tax wedge: Spouse		27.7%	27.7%	70.6%	40.9%

The national currency is the Euro (EUR). In 2016, EUR 0.90 equalled USD 1. In that year, the average worker earned EUR 38 049 (Secretariat estimate).

1. Personal income tax system

1.1. Tax levied by the central government on 2016 income

1.1.1. Tax unit

The tax unit is aggregate family income, but children over 18 are included only if their parents claim them as dependants. Other persons may be fiscally attached on certain conditions: unlike spouses, who are always taxed jointly, children over 18 and other members of the household may opt to be taxed separately. Beginning with the taxation of 2004 income, the law provides for joint taxation of partners in a French civil union (*pacte civil de solidarité*, or PACS), as soon as the PACS is signed. Reporting obligations for "PACSed" partners are similar to those of married couples.

Earned income is reported net of compulsory employer and employee payroll deductions, except for 2.4 percentage points worth of CSG (*contribution sociale généralisée*) and the 0.5% CRDS (*contribution pour le remboursement de la dette sociale*), which are not deductible from the income tax base.

1.1.2. Tax reliefs and tax credits

1.1.2.1. Standard tax reliefs

- Work-related expenses, corresponding to actual amounts or a standard allowance of 10% of net pay (with a minimum of EUR 426 and a ceiling of EUR 12 181 per earner).
- Family status: The "family quotient" (*quotient familial*) system takes a taxpayer's marital status and family responsibilities into account. It involves dividing net taxable income into a certain number of shares [two shares for a married (or "PACSed") couple, one share for a single person, one half-share for each dependent child, an additional half-share for the third and each subsequent dependent child, an additional half-share for single parent, and so on]: the total tax due is equal to the amount of tax corresponding to one share multiplied by the total number of shares. The tax benefit for a half-share is limited, however, to EUR 1 512 per half-share in excess of two shares for a couple, or one share for a single person, except for the first two half-shares granted for the first child of a single parent, in which case the maximum benefit is EUR 3 566.

1.1.2.2. Main non-standard reliefs available to the average worker

Certain expenditures to improve or maintain the taxpayer's primary residence, including outlays for heat insulation or heating adjustments, major capital expenditures and money spent to equip a home to produce energy from a renewable source (30% tax credits, subject to a multi-year maximum); compensatory allowances in case of divorce if paid in a lump sum (25% reduction, capped at EUR 30 500); child care costs for children under seven (50% reduction, up to annual expenditure of EUR 2 300); dependent children attending secondary school or in higher education; donations to charities or other organisations assisting those in needs; trade union dues, etc. The exemption of the employer's participation to the collective contracts of supplementary health cover is abolished in the budget act for 2014 (i.e. income earned in 2013).

1.1.3. *Tax schedule*

	Fraction of taxable income (1 share, in Euros)	Rate (in %)
1st bracket	Up to 9 710	0
2nd bracket	From 9 710 to 26 818	14
3rd bracket	From 26 818 to 71 898	30
4th bracket	From 71 898 to 152 260	41
5th bracket	From 152 260	45

A special rebate for taxpayers with a low tax liability is applied to the amount of tax resulting from the above schedule before reductions and tax credits. To be eligible, the tax on the household's income must be less than EUR 1 553 for single households and less than 2 560 for the couples. The rebate is equal to the three-quarter of the difference between this ceiling and the amount of tax before the rebate.

A special tax reduction has been established for the 2017 income tax. The reduction rate is 20% of the tax liable if the household income is less than EUR 18 500 (doubled for couples, plus EUR 3 700 for each dependent person) and it decreases linearly until zero for households whose income equals to EUR 20 500 (doubled for couples, plus EUR 3 700 for each dependent person).

If the final tax is less than EUR 61, no tax is payable.

1.1.4. *Exceptional contribution on high revenues*

An exceptional contribution on high revenues is based on the reference taxable income ("revenu fiscal de référence"). The tax rates are 3% from EUR 250 000 to EUR 500 0000 (single person), 4% over EUR 500 0000 (single person), 3% from EUR 500 000 to EUR 1 000 000 (married couple or civil union) and 4% over EUR 1 000 000 (married couple or civil unions).

1.2. *Taxes levied by decentralised authorities*

Local taxes levied on working households are:

- Residency tax (*taxe d'habitation*), which is set by local authorities;
- Property taxes on developed and undeveloped land;
- There are common rules for each type of tax, to which certain municipalities make certain adjustments.

These local taxes, the rates of which vary widely, depending on the municipality, are not assessed here.

1.3. *Universal social contribution (contribution sociale généralisée, or CSG)*

The universal social contribution (CSG) was introduced on 1 February 1991. Since 1 January 1998, the rate of CSG has been 7.5%. This rate has been applied to a base of 98.25% as of 1st January 2012. The CSG is deductible against taxable income, but at a lower rate of 5.1%.

1.4. *Contribution to the reimbursement of social debt (contribution au remboursement de la dette sociale, or CRDS)*

The contribution to the reimbursement of social debt has been in effect since 1 February 1997. Like the universal social contribution, its base has passed to 98.25% of gross pay as of 1 January 2012. The rate is set at 0.5%. Unlike social security contributions, CRDS payments are not deductible from taxable income.

2. Compulsory social security contributions to schemes operated within the government sector

Some contributions are levied on a capped portion of monthly earnings. Since 1997, this ceiling has been adjusted once a year on 1 January. In January 2016, the ceiling was EUR 3 218 (or EUR 38 616 per year).

2.1. *Employee contributions*

2.1.1. *Pension*

- 6.9% on earnings up to the ceiling (6.85% in 2015).
- 0.35% on total earnings (0.30 in 2015).

2.1.2. *Illness, pregnancy, disability, death*

- 0.75% on total earnings.

2.1.3. *Unemployment*

- 2.4% on earnings up to 4 times the ceiling.

2.1.4. *Others*

- Supplemental pension for non-managers: minimum 3.1% up to the ceiling and 8.1% between one and three times the ceiling; for managers, 3.23% up to the ceiling and 7.93% between one and four times the ceiling.
- The AGFF (Association pour la gestion du fonds de financement) contribution replaces ASF (Association pour la gestion de la structure financière), which had previously been included in "unemployment" levies. The rate of this contribution is, for non-managerial workers,0.8% of earnings up to the social security ceiling plus 0.9% of any income in excess of the ceiling but not exceeding triple the amount of the ceiling ; for managerial workers, its rate is 0.8% up to the social security ceiling plus 0.9% from one to eight times the ceiling.

2.2. *Employer contributions*

2.2.1. *Pensions*

8.55% (8.5% in 2015) of gross pay, up to the ceiling, plus a 1.85% (1.80% in 2015) levy on total pay.

The social protection scheme is named ARRCO for non-managers and AGIRC for managers.

Between four and eight times the ceiling, the repartition of the pension contributions between employee and employer contribution is not nationally decided.

2.2.2. *Illness, pregnancy, disability, death*

12.84% of total earnings.

An additional contribution of 0.3% (contribution de solidarité autonomie – (CSA) is levied on total salary.

2.2.3. *Unemployment*

4% of earnings (4.5%, 5.5% or 7% for some temporary contracts), up to four times the ceiling; in addition, 0.25% (0.3% in 2015) up to four times the ceiling to endow the salary guarantee fund (AGS).

2.2.4. *Work-related accidents*

Contribution rates for work-related accidents vary by line of business and are published annually in the official gazette (*Journal officiel de la République française*). In 2016, the average rate is 2.38%.

2.2.5. *Family allowances*

5.25% of total pay. The rate has been reduced to 3.45% up to 1.6 times the minimum wage from 2015 with the responsibility pact, up to 3.5 times the minimum wage from April 2016.

2.2.6. *Others*

- Supplemental pension: for non-managers, 4.65% up to the ceiling and 12.15% between one and three times the ceiling; for managers, 4.87% upto the ceiling and 12.97% between one and four times the ceiling.
- The AGFF contribution is 1.2% for non-managers or managers up to the ceiling, 1.3% for non-managers between one and three times the ceiling and 1.3% for managers between one and four times the ceiling. In the table, this is combined with the rates for supplemental pensions.
- Others (construction, housing, apprenticeship, further training): 2.63% of pay (for enterprises with more than 20 employees). The transport tax is not included because it varies geographically. Contributions to finance a fund dedicated to workers exposed to distressing work conditions ("Fonds Pénibilité") vary with the levels of exposure of each worker and are therefore not included.

2.2.7. *Reduction of employer-paid social insurance contributions*

Act No. 2003-47 of 17 January 2003 on salaries, working time and the development of employment (the "Fillon Act") amended how the reduction of contributions is calculated.

As a result, since 1 July 2005 the maximum reduction has been 26% (in companies with more than 20 employees) for a worker paid the minimum wage. It then declines gradually to zero at 160% of the annual minimum wage. It applies irrespective of the number of hours worked. Since 2016 the maximum reduction has been increased up to 28.42% (28.35% in 2015) for companies with more than 20 employees, and up to 28.02% (27.95% in 2015) for companies with less than 20 employees.

The Budget Act for 2007 (Article 41 V) bolsters this measure for very small enterprises with effect from 1 July 2007. For employers with between 1 and 19 employees, the maximum deduction was raised to 28.1% at the minimum wage, declining gradually – here too – to zero at 160% of the minimum wage.

In 1 January 2011 the "Fillon act" was modified and included an annualized calculation of the general tax reliefs of employer contributions. For part-time wage-earners, the relief is computed using an equivalent full-time salary and is then adjusted proportionally to the number of hours paid.

From 2015, the Responsibility Pact (Phase 1) includes new reductions of the labour cost: total exemption of all URSSAF employer contributions on the minimum wage (except unemployment contributions); reduction of 1.8 point on employer-paid contributions for family allowance (3.45% instead of 5.25% for salary up to 1.6 times the minimum wage, and up to 3.5 times from April 2016).

The gross annual minimum wage (for 1 820 hours) in 2015 was an estimated EUR 17 599.

2.2.8. *Competitive tax credit (CICE – Crédit d'impôt pour la compétitivité et l'emploi)*

As for2015, the competitive tax credit (CICE - Crédit d'impôt pour la compétitivité et l'emploi) will benefit all businesses, regardless of their legal status or economic sector, that employ salaried workers and be liable for either corporation tax or income tax, based on actual profits.

The CICE is based on all wages paid to salaried employees in a given calendar year up to 2.5 times the minimum wage (without taking into account any overtime or additional hours worked). For part-time employees and seasonal workers, the minimum wage corresponding to the working hours stipulated in the contract shall be taken into account.

The rate of the tax credit shall be 6% for wages paid in 2016.

3. Universal cash transfers

Main minimum social benefits

The RSA (revenue de solidarité active) is the minimum income benefit. However, the eight family types studied here earn too high an income to benefit from this benefit.

Main family benefits (in respect of dependent children)

- Family allowances: monthly base for family allowances (BMAF) = EUR 406.62 as of 1 April 2016. The family allowances are subject to revenue conditions since 1 July 2015 :
  - Up to 67 408 (+5 617 per child after the second child), the rate is 32% for two children and 41% per additional child. An extra amount of 16% of the BMAF is reversed if the child is over 14 (the extra amount is not incorporated into the model).
  - Between 67 408 (+5 617 per child after the second child) and 89 847 (+5 617 per child after the second child), the above rates are divided by 2.
  - Beyond 89 847 (+5 617 per child after the second child), the above rates are divided by 4.
- ASF (Allocation de soutien familial): extra child benefit for isolated parent EUR 114.46 per child per month (28.15% of the BMAF).
- ARS (Allocation de Rentrée Scolaire): The amount payable depends on the age of the child to reflect needs. The allowance is payable to families or persons with children aged 6 to 18 attending school, and whose income is below a certain level (not incorporated into the model).

Age of the child	Percentage of the BMAF in 2016
6-10 years	89.72%
11-14 years	94.67%
15-18 years	97.95%

- Family supplement (Complément Familial): 41.65% of the BMAF. Subject to revenue ceilings, this is paid to families as of the third child. An extra amount (EUR 50.61/month) is reversed for families whose incomes are below the poverty line (not incorporated into the model).
- Early childhood benefit (not incorporated in the model) known as PAJE (Prestation d'Accueil du Jeune Enfant): subject to revenue ceilings. It includes:
  - A birth grant of 229.75% of the BMAF (EUR 923.08 after deduction of the CRDS) received at the 7th month of pregnancy.
  - A benefit ("allocation de base") of 45.95% of the BMAF (EUR 183.7 after deduction of the CRDS (or EUR 91.8 depending on revenue) a month from the birth of the child until three years of age.
- The CRDS is levied on family allowances at a rate of 0.5% (no deduction). The allowances mentioned above are after deduction of the CRDS for the benefits expressed in EUR.

Housing benefits

The housing benefits are not included in the model.

In-work benefit

The November 2014 Supplementary Budget Act eliminated the earned income tax credit (*Prime pour l'emploi*, PPE) so that it could be merged with the in-work income supplement (*RSA Activité*) and become a single in-work benefit. The in-work benefit was created by the Act of 17 August 2015 on Labour-Management Dialogue and Employment, and has been in place since 1 January 2016. The in-work benefit is better targeted to promote a return to full-time work for low-paid workers.

The amount of in-work benefit is equal to a targeted income, less the maximum between resources and a lump sum.

The targeted income is determined as the sum of three elements:

- A lump sum of EUR 524.68, modulated according to the composition of the household. For instance, it is increased by 50% for couple (EUR 787.02), then 30% for each child until two (EUR) and 40% for each additional child (EUR). The amount may be increased for isolated parent (128.412% of the basic lump sum for the adult and then 42% for each child).

Number of dependents	Single	Couple
0	524.68	787.02
1	787.02	944.42
2	944.42	1 101.82
For each additional dependent	209.87	209.87

- An individual bonus of EUR 67.06 (12.782% of the basic lump sum) is planned for persons whose net income exceeds 80% of the net minimum wage; this bonus grows linearly if the net income is between 50% and 80% of the net minimum wage.
- 62% of the net professional income of the household.

Then ressources are assessed as the sum of the household income, plus the benefits (family benefits, housing benefits). A lump sum depending on the composition of the household (12% of the basic lump sum (EUR 524.68) for a single person, 16% for a couple, 16.5% for three persons or plus) is used to take into account the housing benefits.

4. Main changes in the tax system and social benefits regime since the taxation of 2015 income

- Tax system (2016 income)
- Special income tax reduction.
- Social benefits regime
- Increased reduction of employer-paid contributions for family allowance: 3.45% instead of 5.25% for salary up to 3.5 times the minimum wage from April 2016 (1.6 times before).
- Creation of a new cash transfer benefit for low income workers ("*prime d'activité*") which replace the PPE and the "RSA activité".

5. Memorandum items

To assess the degree of comparability between countries, the following additional information should be taken into account:

- Coverage is of the private and semi-public sectors of NACE sections C to K up to 2007 and NACE rev.2 sections B to N from 2008.
- The category "employees" encompasses all full-time dependent employees (excluding apprentices and interns).
- The figures presented are obtained by applying income tax and social contribution scales to gross salaries as listed in annual social data reports (DADS) in NACE.

The boundaries are defined as: minimum of 59 hours paid at gross minimum wage per hour per month and maximum of 95 hours paid at gross minimum wage per hour per month.

Capital income, unemployment benefits, pensions or minimum old-age pensions are not taken into account in this model.

The complete formula uses the minimum of this lump sum tax and the amount of housing benefits. As the model does not include housing benefits, we only use the lump sum in the formula. This method tends to minimize the amount of "prime d'activité" served.

In the previous model, for 2015 revenues, this reform only affects the income tax (no PPE in 2016) but not the benefits, since the "prime d'activité" will be served as from the beginning of 2016.

2016 parameter values

AW earnings	Ave_earn	38 049	(secretariat estimate)
Income tax			
Work expenses	work_rel_fl	426	
	work_rel_ceil	12 181	
	work_rel_rate	0.1	
Tax schedule	tax_sch	0	9 710
		0.14	26 818
		0.3	71 898
		0.41	152 260
		0.45	
	limit_demipart	1 512	
	limit_sp_demipart1	3 566	
Décote value	decote_sing	1 553	
	decote_mar	2 560	
	decote_pente	0.75	
	red_taux	0.20	
	red_seuil_1	18 500	
	red_seuil_2	20 500	
	red_seuil_dp	3 700	
	tax_min	61	
CEHR	cehr_rate1	0.03	
	cehr_rate2	0.04	
	cehr_ceil1	250 000	
	cehr_ceil2	500 000	
CSG+CRDS	CSG_CRDS_abat	0.0175	
	CSG_rat_noded	0.0240	
	CRDS_rat_noded	0.0050	
	CSG_CRDS_rat_noded	0.0290	
	CSG_rat_ded	0.0510	
	CRDS_special	0.0050	
Employee contributions			
	pension_rate	0.069	
	pension_rate2	0.0035	
Sickness	sickness_rate	0.0075	
Unemployment	unemp_rate	0.0240	
Extra pension (non-cadres) (incl. AGFF)	pens_rate_ex	0.039	
	pens_rate_ex2	0.09	
Employer contributions			
	pens_empr1	0.0855	
	pens_empr2	0.0185	
Sickness	sickness_empr	0.1284	
Authonomous Solidarity Contribution	CSA	0.0030	
Unemployment (incl. "garantie de salaire")	unemp_empr	0.0425	
Accidents	accidents_empr	0.0238	
Family Allowance	fam_empr	0.0525	
	fam_empr_2	0.0345	
Extra pension (incl. AGFF)	pens_empr_ex	0.0585	
	pens_empr_ex2	0.1345	
Others	others_empr	0.0263	
CS reduction & corporate tax credit			
Employer SSC reduction rate	SSC_empr_redrate2	0.6	
Employer SSC reduction maximum	SSC_empr_red_max	0.2842	
Employer SSC reduction SMIC reference	SSC_empr_SMIC_ref	1.6	
	SSC_empr_SMIC2	3.5	
Taux de réduction CICE	cice_red	0.06	
	cice_max	2.5	

2016 parameter values

Social transfers		
Child benefit (second child)	CB_2	1 561.42
third & subsequent	CB_3	2 000.57
First ceiling for CB	CB_c1	6 7408
Second ceiling for CB	CB_c2	89 847
Increase of ceiling per child	CB_ceiling_extra_child	5 617
Extra child benefit (isolated parent)	CB_isol	1 373.52
Prime d'activité	pa_forf	524.68
	pa_maj1	0.50
	pa_maj2	0.30
	pa_maj3	0.40
	pa_maj_isol1	0.28412
	Pa_maj_isol2	0.42804
	pa_pct	0.62
	pa_bonus	0.12782
	pa_bonus1	(59*12*SMIC_horraire)/SMIC
	pa_bonus2	(95*12*SMIC_horraire)/SMIC
	pa_forf_logement1	0.12
	pa_forf_logement2	0.16
	pa_forf_logement3	0.165
Others		
Social security contributions	SSC_ceil	38 616
Derivation of minimum income	SMIC_horaire	9.67
	SMIC_heures	1 820
	SMIC	17 599.4

2016 tax equations

The equations for the French system are mostly calculated on a family basis. Variable names are defined in the table of parameters above, within the equations table, or are the standard variables "married" and "children". A reference to a variable with the affix "_total" indicates the sum of the relevant variable values for the principal and spouse. And the affixes "_princ" and "_spouse" indicate the value for the principal and spouse, respectively. Equations for a single person are as shown for the principal, with "_spouse" values taken as 0.

	Line in country table and intermediate steps	Variable name	Range	Equation
1.	Earnings	earn		
	Quotient for tax calculation	quotient	J	1+Married+IF(Children<3, Children/2, Children-1)+0.5*(Married=0)*(Children>0)
2.	Allowances			
	CSG deductible	CSG_ded	B	CSG_rat_ded*((1-CSG_CRDS_abat)*MIN(earn;4*SSC_ceil)+Positive(earn-4*SSC_ceil))
	Salary net	earn_dec	B	earn-SSC-CSG_ded
	Work related	work_exp	B	MIN(work_rel_ceil, MAX(work_rel_rate* earn_dec, MIN(work_rel_fl, earn_dec)))
	Basic	basic_al	B	0
3.	Credits in taxable income	taxbl_cr	B	0
4.	CG taxable income	tax_inc	J	Positive(earn_dec_total-work_exp)
5.	CG tax before credits			
	Calculation according to schedule	sch_tax	J	MAX(quotient*Tax(tax_inc/quotient, tax_sch), IF(Married, 2*Tax(tax_inc/2, tax_sch)-limit_demipart*(quotient-2), Tax(tax_inc, tax_sch)-(Children>0)* (limit_sp_demipart1+limit_demipart*(quotient-2))))++cehr_rate1* MIN((cehr_ceil2-cehr_ceil1)*(1+Married);MAX(tax_inc-cehr_ceil1*(1+Married);0))+cehr_rate2 * MAX(tax_inc-cehr_ceil2*(1+Married);0)
	Adjusted for decote	adj_tax	J	SI(Married;Positive(MINA(tax_sch; (1+decote_pente)*tax_sch- decote_pente*decote_mar));Positive(MINA(tax_sch;(1+decote_pente)*tax_sch-decote_pente*decote_sing)))
	Tax liable	inc_tax	J	(adj_tax>=tax_min)*adj_tax
	CSG+CRDS (non-deductible)	CSG_CRDS_noded	B	CSG_CRDS_rat_nod*((1-CSG_CRDS_abat)*MIN(earn;4*SSC_ceil)+Positive(earn-4*SSC_ceil))
	CSG deductible	CSG_ded	B	CSG_rat_ded*((1-CSG_CRDS_abat)*MIN(earn;4*SSC_ceil)+Positive(earn-4*SSC_ceil))
6.	Tax credits :	tax_cr	J	adj_tax*SI((tax_inc<=red_seuil_1*(1+Married)+red_seuil_dp*Children);red_taux;SI(tax_inc<=red_seuil_2*(1+Married)+red_seuil_dp*Children;(tax_inc*red_taux/(red_seuil_1*(1+Married)+red_seuil_dp*Children-(red_seuil_2*(1+Married)+red_seuil_dp*Children)))+(red_taux*(red_seuil_2*(1+Married)+red_seuil_dp*Children))/(red_seuil_2*(1+Married)+red_seuil_dp*Children-(red_seuil_1*(1+ Married)+red_seuil_dp*Children));0))
7.	CG tax	CG_tax	J	inc_tax+CSG_CRDS_noded+CSG_ded-tax_cr
8.	State and local taxes	local_tax	J	0
9.	Employees' soc security	SSC	B	pension_rate*MINA(earn, SSC_ceil) +(sickness_rate+pension_rate2)*earn+unemp_rate*MINA(earn, 4*SSC_ceil) +pens_rate_ex*MINA(earn, SSC_ceil)+(earn>SSC_ceil)*pens_rate_ex2*MINA(earn-SSC_ceil, 3*SSC_ceil-SSC_ceil)
11.	Cash transfers	cash_transf_gross	J	SI(Children<2;0;(CB_2+(Children-2)*CB_3)*SI(tax_inc<=(CB_c1+CB_ceiling_extra_child*(Children-2));1;SI(tax_inc<=(CB_c2+CB_ceiling_extra_child*(Children-2));0,5;0,25)))+SI(Isolated=1;CB_isol*Children;0)

	Line in country table and intermediate steps	Variable name	Range	Equation
		in_work_benefit_gross	J	MAX(SI((Isolated=1); 12*pa_forf*(1+pa_maj_isol1+pa_maj_isol2*Children); 12*pa_forf*(1+SI(Married=1;pa_maj1;0)+pa_maj2*SI(Children<=2;Children;0)+ pa_maj3*SI(Children>2;Children-2;0)))+pa_pct*(earn_dec-CSG_CRDS_noded)+ pa_bonus*pa_forf/(pa_bonus2-pa_bonus1)*12*SI(ET(pa_bonus1*SMIC<(earn_dec_princ-CSG_CRDS_noded_princ);pa_bonus2*SMIC>(earn_dec_princ-CSG_CRDS_noded_princ));(earn_dec_princ-CSG_CRDS_noded_princ)/ SMIC-pa_bonus1;0)+pa_bonus*pa_forf/(pa_bonus2-pa_bonus1)*12*SI(ET(pa_bonus1*SMIC<(earn_dec_spouse-CSG_CRDS_noded_spouse);pa_bonus2* SMIC>(earn_dec_spouse-CSG_CRDS_noded_spouse));(earn_dec_spouse-CSG_CRDS_noded_spouse)/SMIC-pa_bonus1;0)+pa_bonus*pa_forf*12*SI((earn_dec_princ-CSG_CRDS_noded_princ)>=pa_bonus2*SMIC;1;0)+pa_bonus*pa_forf*12*SI((earn_dec_spouse-CSG_CRDS_noded_spouse)>=pa_bonus2*SMIC; 1;0)-MAX(earn_dec-CSG_CRDS_noded+(family_benefit_gross-SI(Isolated=1; CB_isol*Children;0)*(1-(22,5%/28,15%)))+((Married+Children=0)*pa_forf_logement1*pa_forf*12+ (Married+Children=1)*pa_forf_logement2*pa_forf* 1,5*12 + (Married+Children>=2)*pa_forf_logement3*pa_forf*1,8*12); SI(ET((Married=0);(Children>0)); 12*pa_forf*(1+pa_maj_isol1+pa_maj_isol2* Children);pa_forf*12*(1+SI(Married=1;pa_maj1;0)+pa_maj2*SI(Children<=2; Children;0)+pa_maj3*SI(Children>2;Children-2;0))));0)
		crds_cash_transf	J	cash_transf_gross*-1*CRDS_special
		cash_transf_net	J	cash_transf_gross+crds_cash_transf
13.	Employer's soc security	SSC_empr_gross	B	(sickness_empr + CSA + pens_empr2 + accidents_empr+others_empr)*earn +pens_empr1*MINA(earn;SSC_ceil) +pens_empr_ex*MINA(earn;SSC_ceil) +pens_empr_ex2* MAX(MIN(earn;3*SSC_ceil) - SSC_ceil;0)+unemp_empr*MIN(earn;4*SSC_ceil)) + + 3/4*SI(earn<SSC_empr_SMIC2*SMIC; fam_empr_2*earn; fam_empr*earn)+1/4*SI(earn<SSC_empr_SMIC_ref*SMIC; fam_empr_2*earn; fam_empr*earn)
		SSC_empr_reduction	B	IF(OR(earn>SSC_empr_SMIC_ref*SMIC,earn=0),0,-MIN (SSC_empr_red_max* earn,(SSC_empr_red_max/SSC_empr_redrate2)*(SSC_empr_SMIC_ref*SMIC/ earn-1)*earn)) -IF(earn<cice_max*SMIC;earn*cice_red)
		SSC_empr_final	B	SSC_empr_gross+SSC_empr_reduction

Key to range of equation B calculated separately for both principal earner and spouse P calculated for principal only (value taken as 0 for spouse calculation) J calculated once only on a joint basis.

Taxing Wages 2017
© OECD 2017

Germany

This chapter includes data on the income taxes paid by workers, their social security contributions, the family benefits they receive in the form of cash transfers as well as the social security contributions and payroll taxes paid by their employers. Results reported include the marginal and average tax burden for eight different family types.

Methodological information is available for Personal income tax systems, Compulsory social security contributions to schemes operated within the government sector, Universal cash transfers as well as recent changes in the tax/benefit system. The methodology also includes the parameter values and tax equations underlying the data.

Germany 2016

The tax/benefit position of single persons

	Wage level (per cent of average wage)	67	100	167	67
	Number of children	none	none	none	2.00
1.	**Gross wage earnings**	32 032	47 809	79 840	32 032
2.	**Standard tax allowances**				
	Basic allowance				
	Married or head of family	0	0	0	2 148
	Dependent children	0	0	0	0
	Deduction for social security contributions and income taxes	4 957	7 398	9 278	4 877
	Work-related expenses	1 000	1 000	1 000	1 000
	Other	36	36	36	36
	Total	5 993	8 434	10 314	8 061
3.	**Tax credits or cash transfers included in taxable income**	0	0	0	0
4.	**Central government taxable income (1 - 2 + 3)**	26 039	39 375	69 526	23 971
5.	**Central government income tax liability (exclusive of tax credits)**	4 496	9 076	21 950	3 660
6.	**Tax credits**				
	Basic credit				
	Married or head of family				
	Children	0	0	0	4 560
	Other				
	Total	0	0	0	4 560
7.	**Central government income tax finally paid (5-6)**	4 496	9 076	21 950	- 900
8.	**State and local taxes**	0	0	0	0
9.	**Employees' compulsory social security contributions**				
	Gross earnings	6 623	9 884	13 068	6 542
	Taxable income				
	Total	6 623	9 884	13 068	6 542
10.	**Total payments to general government (7 + 8 + 9)**	11 119	18 961	35 019	5 642
11.	**Cash transfers from general government**				
	For head of family				
	For two children	0	0	0	0
	Total	0	0	0	0
12.	**Take-home pay (1-10+11)**	20 913	28 848	44 822	26 389
13.	**Employers' compulsory social security contributions**	6 190	9 239	12 382	6 190
14.	**Average rates**				
	Income tax	14.0%	19.0%	27.5%	-2.8%
	Employees' social security contributions	20.7%	20.7%	16.4%	20.4%
	Total payments less cash transfers	34.7%	39.7%	43.9%	17.6%
	Total tax wedge including employer's social security contributions	45.3%	49.4%	51.4%	31.0%
15.	**Marginal rates**				
	Total payments less cash transfers: Principal earner	47.0%	52.4%	44.3%	44.7%
	Total payments less cash transfers: Spouse	n.a.	n.a.	n.a.	n.a.
	Total tax wedge: Principal earner	55.6%	60.1%	44.3%	53.6%
	Total tax wedge: Spouse	n.a.	n.a.	n.a.	n.a.

Germany 2016

The tax/benefit position of married couples

	Wage level (per cent of average wage)	100-0	100-33	100-67	100-33
	Number of children	2	2	2	none
1.	**Gross wage earnings**	47 809	63 585	79 840	63 585
2.	**Standard tax allowances**				
	Basic allowance				
	Married or head of family	0	0	0	0
	Dependent children	0	0	0	0
	Deduction for social security contributions and income taxes	7 278	9 680	12 155	9 839
	Work-related expenses	1 000	2 000	2 000	2 000
	Other	72	72	72	72
	Total	8 350	11 752	14 227	11 911
3.	**Tax credits or cash transfers included in taxable income**	0	0	0	0
4.	**Central government taxable income (1 - 2 + 3)**	39 459	51 833	65 613	51 674
5.	**Central government income tax liability (exclusive of tax credits)**	4 974	8 695	13 183	8 866
6.	**Tax credits**				
	Basic credit				
	Married or head of family				
	Children	4 560	4 560	4 560	0
	Other				
	Total	4 560	4 560	4 560	0
7.	**Central government income tax finally paid (5-6)**	414	4 135	8 623	8 866
8.	**State and local taxes**	0	0	0	0
9.	**Employees' compulsory social security contributions**				
	Gross earnings	9 765	12 987	16 307	13 146
	Taxable income				
	Total	9 765	12 987	16 307	13 146
10.	**Total payments to general government (7 + 8 + 9)**	10 179	17 122	24 931	22 013
11.	**Cash transfers from general government**				
	For head of family				
	For two children	0	0	0	0
	Total	0	0	0	0
12.	**Take-home pay (1-10+11)**	37 630	46 463	54 910	41 573
13.	**Employers' compulsory social security contributions**	9 239	12 288	15 429	12 288
14.	**Average rates**				
	Income tax	0.9%	6.5%	10.8%	13.9%
	Employees' social security contributions	20.4%	20.4%	20.4%	20.7%
	Total payments less cash transfers	21.3%	26.9%	31.2%	34.6%
	Total tax wedge including employer's social security contributions	34.0%	38.8%	42.4%	45.2%
15.	**Marginal rates**				
	Total payments less cash transfers: Principal earner	43.1%	46.6%	49.4%	46.9%
	Total payments less cash transfers: Spouse	44.0%	46.6%	49.4%	46.9%
	Total tax wedge: Principal earner	52.3%	55.3%	57.6%	55.5%
	Total tax wedge: Spouse	53.1%	55.3%	57.6%	55.5%

The national currency is the Euro (EUR). In 2016, EUR 0.90 was equal to USD 1. The average worker earned EUR 47 809 (Secretariat estimate).

1. Personal income tax systems

1.1. *Central/federal government income taxes*

1.1.1. *Tax unit*

Spouses may choose between two options: Joint assessment or individual assessment. The vast majority of couples benefits financially from the joint assessment by minimizing the tax burden of the household. The income of dependent children is not assessable with that of the parents. The calculations in this Report are therefore based on the assumption of joint taxation for spouses.

1.1.2. *Tax allowances and tax credits:*

1.1.2.1. Standard reliefs and work-related expenses

- *Basic reliefs*: None.
- *Standard marital status reliefs*: In the case of joint assessment, specific allowances are doubled. The income tax liability for spouses who are assessed jointly is computed as follows:
  - *Splitting method:*
    - First step: Calculating the tax base: All incomes of the spouses are summed up and the sum is divided by two.
    - Second step: The tax rate is applied to this tax base.
    - Third step: The amount calculated in step 2 is doubled.
  - Results: Given the progressive income taxation the resulting tax liability for the household is lower than the sum of individual taxation. The household as a unit benefits from this solution otherwise both parts of the couple would opt out. Principal and second earners have the same average and marginal income tax rates.
  - The splitting effect decreases by increasing convergence of the incomes of principal earner and the spouse.
- *Relief(s) for children:* As of 1 January 2016, there are increased tax credits of EUR 2 280 for the first and the second child, of EUR 2 352 for the third child and of EUR 2 652 for the fourth and subsequent children. There is a tax allowance of EUR 2 304 for the subsistence of a child and an additional EUR 1 320 for minding and education or training needs (EUR 3 624). The amount of this allowance is doubled in case of jointly assessed parents. If the value of the tax credit is less than the relief calculated applying the tax allowances, the taxpayer obtains the tax allowance instead of the tax credit. It is also doubled for lone parents in cases where the other parent does not pay alimony. This is the assumption in the calculations presented in this Report.

- *Relief for lone parents:* As of 1 January 2015, taxpayers who live alone with at least one child that entitles them to the tax allowances or tax credits for children, receive an additional allowance of EUR 1 908 (formerly EUR 1 308). This additional allowance is increased by EUR 240 for each child in case of more than one child living in the household.
- *Reliefs for social security contributions and life insurance contributions:* Social security contributions and other expenses incurred in provision for the future (e.g. life insurance) are deductible up to specific ceilings. In 2005, a new calculation scheme came into force:
  - Step 1: all contributions made to pension funds (i.e. both employee's and employer's contributions) are added up. Step 2: the resulting amount is limited to EUR 20 000. Step 3: a certain percentage is applied to this amount (starting from 60% in 2005, this percentage will be increased by 2 percentage points each year; it will reach 100% in 2025). Step 4: the resulting amount, diminished by the (tax-free) contributions of the employer, is deductible from income.
  - The tax treatment of social security expenses (health, unemployment and care insurance) changed as of 1 January 2010. Employees' annual contributions to statutory health insurance excluding sickness benefit (assumed to amount to 96% of statutory health contributions) and employees' contributions to mandatory long-term care insurance are deductible from the tax base. In case these contributions do not exceed EUR 1 900/3 800 (single/married couples), contributions to unemployment insurance and other insurances premiums can be deducted in addition up to this ceiling.
  - If the resulting sum of deductible amounts according the legislation in force since 2005 is lower than the allowance calculated under the scheme that was valid up to 2004, the former regulations are applied in favour of the taxpayer (for more details on the old scheme: see 2005 edition and section 4. of this Report).
- *Work-related expenses:* EUR 1 000 lump-sum allowance per gainfully-employed person.
- *Special expenses:* Lump sum allowance (EUR 36/72 (singles/couples)) for special expenses, e.g. for tax accountancy. The actual expenses will be fully deductible from taxable income if the taxpayer proves that these expenses exceed the lump sum allowance.

1.1.2.2. Main non-standard tax reliefs applicable to an AW

- *Contributions to pensions, life insurance, superannuation schemes:* Other expenses than the compulsory contributions to social security are deductible as reliefs for (voluntary) social security contributions up to specific ceilings (see section 1.1.2.1).
- *Medical expenses:* Partially deductible if not covered by insurance.
- *Other:* Work-related expenses that exceed the lump-sum allowance are fully deductible (no ceiling).

1.1.3. *Tax schedule*

The German tax schedule is formula-based. Taxable income is rounded down (to the EUR).

- X is the taxable income,
- T is the income tax liability,
- As of 1 January 2016 the following definitions are used in the income tax liability formulas:

$$Y = \frac{X - 8652}{10000}$$

$$Z = \frac{X - 13669}{10000}$$

The income tax liability (amounts in EUR) is calculated as follows:

1. $T = 0$ for $X \leq 8\,652$
2. $T = (993.62\,Y + 1\,400)\,Y$ for $8\,653 \leq X \leq 13\,669$
3. $T = (225.40\,Z + 2\,397)\,Z + 952.48$ for $13\,670 \leq X \leq 53\,665$
4. $T = 0.42\,X - 8\,394.14$ for $53\,666 \leq X \leq 254\,446$
5. $T = 0.45\,X - 16\,027.52$ for $254\,447 \leq X$

These formulas are used to calculate the income tax for single individuals and married couples too.

If families choose the option of being assessed separately these formulas are applied to the individual taxable income of the principal earner and the spouse. In the case of jointly assessed families these rates are applied to half of the joint taxable income (see point 1.1.2.1. Splitting method).

1.1.4. *Solidarity surcharge*

The solidarity surcharge is levied at 5.5% of the income tax liability subject to an exemption limit of EUR 972/1 944 (singles/couples). The income tax liability is calculated applying the tax allowance for children. If the income tax liability exceeds the exemption limit, the solidarity surcharge will be phased in at a higher rate of 20% of the difference between the income tax liability and the exemption limit until it equals 5.5% of the total liability.

1.2. *State and local income taxes*

None.

2. Compulsory social security contributions to schemes operated within the government sector

The amount of social security contributions depends on the wage and the insurance contribution rate. All contributions are subject to a contribution ceiling, i.e. the maximum income for which statutory insurance contributions are calculated. The contribution rates for pension, health, care and unemployment insurances are fixed by the government.

2.1. *Employees' contributions*

In general, earnings up to EUR 4 800 per year were free of employee social security contributions until 31 December 2012. As of 1 January 2013, some essential changes came into effect concerning minimally paid employment. The earnings limit increased from EUR 400 to EUR 450 per month. Persons whose mini-job started before 2013 and do not exceed the previous earnings limit of EUR 400 stay contribution-free in all classes of social insurance. Otherwise, persons who take up a new mini-job are generally subject to mandatory insurance coverage in the statutory pension scheme with the full pension contribution rate of 18.7% (in 2016). If the earnings are below the amount of EUR 175 (minimum contribution limit), a minimum contribution of EUR 32.73 has to be paid (18.7% of EUR 175). The employer's share amounts to 15% of the whole pay whereas the employee's part adds up to 3.7% (or the difference between minimum contribution and employer share).

By applying for an exemption from obligatory insurance coverage the mini-job holder may reduce his share to EUR 0.

As of 1 April 2003, there was an additional concession for employees with monthly income between EUR 400.01 and EUR 800 per month (the so-called 'sliding pay scale', EUR 4 800.12 and EUR 9 600 per year). Due to the new regulations mentioned above the earnings limits shifted to EUR 450.01 and EUR 850.00 per month (EUR 5 400.12 and EUR 10 200 per year). If the employee's income falls within this range, part of the income will be exempt from social insurance contributions. However, employers are still required to pay the regular contributions on the employee's earnings. The arrangement is purely intended to relieve the financial burden on employees. The employees' contributions to social insurance rise on a straight-line basis over the income band reaching the full rate at EUR 850 per month. Details on social security contributions for workers earning more than EUR 10 200 per year are provided below.

2.1.1. *Pensions*

Employers and employees pay each half of the contribution rate of 18.7% in 2016, that is 9.35% of the employee's gross wage earnings, up to a contribution ceiling of EUR 74 400.

2.1.2. *Sickness*

As of 1 January 2015, the applicable contribution rate is 14.6% on principle (portion of 7.3% for employers and employees). Depending on the financial situation of each sickness fund, employees are obliged to pay a supplementary contribution to the sickness fund. In 2016, this supplementary contribution amounts to 1.1% on average. Therefore, the contribution rate averages 8.4% for employees in 2016. The contribution ceiling in 2016 is EUR 50 850. While all calculations shown in this Report assume membership in the public health insurance, workers with earnings above the contribution ceiling may opt out of the mandatory public health insurance system and may choose a private insurance provider instead (those opting for a private health insurance provider are required to obtain private long-term care insurance as well).

2.1.3. *Unemployment*

Employees pay half of the insurance contributions; the employer pays the other half. In 2016, the contribution rate is 3.0% of assessable income. Employee and employer each pay 1.5%. The contribution ceiling is EUR 74 400.

2.1.4. *Care*

A long-term care insurance (a 1% contribution rate) went into effect on 1 January 1995. The rate was raised to 1.7% of the gross wage when home nursing care benefits were added six months later. As of 1 July 2008, the rate was increased to 1.95%. In 2013 and 2014, the contribution rate amounted to 2.05%. As of 1 January 2015, the contribution rate adds up to 2.35%. The employers pay half of the contributions for long-term care insurance. In other words, employers and employees both pay a rate of 1.175%. The assessable income is scaled according to the gross wage earnings but there is a contribution ceiling of EUR 50 850 in 2016.

As from 1 January 2005, child-raising is given special recognition in the law relating to statutory long-term care insurance. Childless contribution payers are required to pay a supplement of 0.25%, raising the contribution rate paid by a childless employee from 0.975% to 1.225% as of 1 July 2008. In 2013 and 2014, the contribution rate of a childless employee added up to 1.275%. As of 1 January 2015, the contribution rate amounts to 1.425% for a childless employee.

2.1.5. *Work injury*

Employer only.

2.1.6. *Family allowances*

None.

2.1.7. *Others*

None.

2.2. *Employers' contributions*

See Section 2.1.

2.2.1-2.2.4. *(Pensions, sickness, unemployment, care):*

See Section 2.1

2.2.5. *Work injury*

Germany has established a statutory occupational accident insurance. It is provided by industrial, agricultural and public-sector employers' liability insurance funds. This insurance protects employees and their families against the consequences of accidents at work and occupational illnesses. It is funded through the contributions paid by employers only. The amount of the employer's contributions depends on the sum total of employee's annual pay and the employer's respective hazard level. As it is not possible to identify a representative contribution rate, these amounts are not considered in this Report.

2.2.6. *Family allowances*

None.

2.2.7. *Others*

None.

3. Universal cash transfers

3.1. *Transfers related to marital status*

None.

3.2. *Transfers for dependent children*

None.

4. Main changes in tax/benefit systems Since 1997

The following table shows changes in the tax credit and the tax allowance for children since 1997:

Year	Child credit				Child allowance
	First child	Second child	Third child	Fourth and subsequent children	
1997	1 350	1 350	1 841	2 147	3 534
1999	1 534	1 534	1 841	2 147	3 534
2000	1 657	1 657	1 841	2 147	5 080
2002	1 848	1 848	1 848	2 148	5 808
2009*	1 968	1 968	2 040	2 340	6 024
2010	2 208	2 208	2 280	2 580	7 008
2015	2 256	2 256	2 328	2 628	7 152
2016	2 280	2 280	2 352	2 652	7 248

* plus EUR 100 one-off child credit payment for each child.

Up to 2004, the calculation of the relief for social security contributions and other expenses proceeded in three steps. First, EUR 3 068/6 136 (singles/couples) was deducted. These amounts were, however, lowered by 16% of gross wages (serving as a proxy for employers' social security contributions). This deduction was provided as a partial compensation for the self-employed who do not receive tax-free employers' social security contributions. Second, the remaining expenses were deductible up to EUR 1 334/2 668 (singles/couples). Third, half of the remaining expenses were deductible up to EUR 667/1 334 (singles/couples).

In 2004, the tax rate was reduced and the formula for calculating the income tax was changed. The relief for lone parents was reduced to EUR 1 308, the lump sum allowance for work related expenses was reduced to EUR 920.

As from 1 January 2005, the final stage of the 2000-tax reform came into effect. The bottom and top income tax rates were further reduced to 15% and 42%. Since 1998, both the bottom and top income tax rate have been reduced by about 11 percentage points while the personal allowance has been raised from EUR 6 322 to EUR 7 664. The tax cuts reduce the tax burden for all income taxpayers, affording the greatest relief to employees and families with low and medium incomes as well as to small- and medium-sized unincorporated businesses.

On 1 January 2005, the law regulating the taxation of pensions and pension expenses entered into force. The law provides a gradual transition to ex-post taxation of pensions paid by the statutory pensions insurance. In the long run, the tax treatment of capital-based employee pension schemes based on a contract between employer and employee will be reformed in the same way as the tax treatment in respect of the state pension scheme. In addition to the increased deductibility of contributions to the state and certain private pension schemes, the law contains rules which are intended to increase the attractiveness of private capital-based pension schemes and to encourage individuals to invest privately for their old-age pension.

Up to 30 June of 2005, employees paid half of the sickness insurance contributions; the employer paid the other half. As from 1 July 2005, members of the statutory health insurance scheme also pay an income-linked contribution of 0.9% to which employers do not contribute. As from 1 July 2005, all statutory health insurance funds have reduced their contribution rates by 0.9 percentage points.

In 2007, a new top income tax rate of 45% was introduced for taxable income above EUR 250 000 (EUR 500 000 for jointly assessed spouses).

In 2009, the bottom income tax rate was reduced to 14%. The basic allowance was increased to EUR 7 834. All thresholds were increased by EUR 400.

Since 1 January 2010, the basic allowance has been augmented to EUR 8 004 and all thresholds have been increased by EUR 330. Furthermore, new legislation improves the tax treatment of expenditure on health insurance and long-term care insurance. As of 1 January 2013, the basic allowance rose to EUR 8 130. As of 1 January 2014, the basic allowance was increased to EUR 8 354. As of 1 January 2015, the basic allowance amounts to EUR 8 472. The relief for lone parents now adds up to EUR 1 908. Lone parents are entitled to an extra allowance of EUR 240 for the second and each subsequent child. Since 1 January 2016, the basic allowance has been risen to EUR 8 652.

5. Memorandum items

5.1. *Average gross annual earnings calculation*

- Source of calculation: Federal Statistical Office.
- Excluding sickness and unemployment, including normal overtime and bonuses.

5.2. *Employer's contributions to private pension, etc. schemes*

No information available, though such schemes do exist.

2016 parameter values

Average earnings/yr	Ave_earn	47 809	Secretariat estimate
Tax allowances	Child_al	7 248	
Lone Parents, first child	Lone_al	1 908	
Lone parents, subsequent child	Lone_al_add	240	
Work related	Work_rel_al	1 000	
SSC allowance	SSC_dn	1 200	
	SSC_dn_rt	0.16	
	SSC_dn_lim	1 334	
	SSC_dn_lump_rt	0.2	
Allow. for special expenses	SE_al	36	
Church tax rate	Ch_tax_rt	0	
Tax formula	Tax_rate2	0.42	
	Tax_rate3	0.45	
	Tax_thrsh1	8 652	
	Tax_thrsh2	13 669	
Top Rate Tax Reduction	Reduction	8 394.14	
	Reduction2	16 027.52	
Tax Equation Rates			
tax_eqn_rates	Squared	Single	Constant
z	225.40	2 397	952.48
y	993.62	1 400	0
Income tax rate stage	tax_first_stage	8 652	
	tax_second_stage	13 669	
	tax_third_stage	53 665	
	tax_fourth_stage	254 446	
Solidarity Surcharge	surcharge	0.055	
Solidarity Exemption Limit	surcharge_limit	972	
Alternative Surcharge Rate	surcharge_alt	0.2	
Child credit	Ch_cred		
	1. ch.	2 280	
	2. ch.	2 280	
	3.ch.	2 352	
	4.ch.	2 652	

Social security	Sickness	Pension	Unemployment	Care	Alternative employer rate	SSC Factor F
period_1	12	12	12	12	12	12
period_2	0	0	0	0		
sum (Month's)	12	12	12	12	12	12
employer_1	0.073	0.0935	0.015	0.01175	0.3	0.7547
employer_2	0	0	0	0		
employee_1	0.084	0.0935	0.015	0.01175	0.037	0.7547
employee_2	0	0	0	0		
childless_1	0.084	0.0935	0.015	0.01425	0.037	0.7547
childless_2	0	0	0	0		
ceil	50 850	74 400	74 400	50 850	2 100	
SSC Floor	SSC_floor	10 200				
Intermediate SSC Ceiling	SSC_floor1	5 400				

2016 tax equations

The equations for the German system in 2016 are mostly calculated on a family basis.

The standard functions which are used in the equations are described in the technical note about tax equations. The function acttax carries out a rounded calculation for the tables but the unrounded version purtax is used in calculating the marginal rates.

For a taxpayer with children, either the child allowance is given in the tax calculation or the cash transfer is given if this is more beneficial. In practice, therefore, it is necessary to make two calculations – with and without the child allowance. Nevertheless, the calculation of solidarity surcharge is always based on the calculation which does assume that the child tax allowance is given.

Variable names are defined in the table of parameters above, within the equations table, or are the standard variables "married" and "children". The affixes "_princ" and "_spouse" on Variable names in functions indicate that the values have to be calculated for the principal and spouse, respectively. The parameter year in function SSC_Allowance is the year for which you calculate the Allowance.

	Line in country table and intermediate steps	Variable name	Range	Equation
1.	Earnings	earn		
	Quotient for tax calculation	quotient	J	1+Married
2.	Allowances:			
	Children	children_al	J	Children*Child_al
	Lone parent	lone_allce	J	Children>0)*(Married=0)*Lone_al+(Children>0)*(Married=0)*(Children-1)*Lone_al_add
	Soc sec contributions	SSC_al	J	Function: SSC_Allowance(earn_princ, earn_spouse , SSC_princ + SSC_spouse , Quotient, SSC_dn, SSC_dn_rt, SSC_dn_lim, SSC_dn_lump_rt, If(Children>0; "employee"; "childless"), year, rounded)
	Work related	work_al	J	Work_rel_al+MIN(earn_spouse,Work_rel_al)
	Allow. for special expenses	SE_al	J	SE_al*quotient
	Total	tax_al	J	children_al+SSC_al+work_al+ lone_allce + SE_al
3.	Credits in taxable income	taxbl_cr	J	0
4.	CG taxable income	tax_inc	J	earn-tax_al
5.	CG tax before credits			
	adjusted taxable income	adj	J	tax_inc/quotient
	Formula based tax schedule	tax_formula	J	Function: acttax(taxinc, rate, reduction, threshold1, threshold2, threshold3, equationrate, tax_first_stage, tax_second_stage, tax_third_stage, tax_fourth_stage, rate2, reduction2)
	Adjust for the quotient	tax_adj	J	Quotient*tax_formula
	Include solidarity surcharge	sol_surch	J	MIN(tax_adj * surcharge, Positive(tax_adj - surcharge_limit*Quotient) * surcharge_alt)
	Tax paid	CG_tax_excl	J	tax_adj+sol_surch
6.	Tax credits :	tax_cr	J	0
7.	CG tax	CG_tax	J	CG_tax_excl
8.	State and local taxes	local_tax	J	0
9.	Employees' soc security	SSC	B	Function: SSC (earn_princ, If(Children>0; "employee"; "childless"), rounded) + SSC (earn_spouse, If(Children>0; "employee"; "childless"), rounded)
11.	Cash transfers	Cash_tran	J	Children*ch_cred
13.	Employer's soc security	SSC_empr	B	Function: SSC (earn_princ, "employer", rounded) + SSC (earn_spouse, "employer", rounded)

Key to range of equation
B calculated separately for both principal earner and spouse
P calculated for principal only (value taken as 0 for spouse calculation)
J calculated once only on a joint basis

© OECD 2017

Greece

This chapter includes data on the income taxes paid by workers, their social security contributions, the family benefits they receive in the form of cash transfers as well as the social security contributions and payroll taxes paid by their employers. Results reported include the marginal and average tax burden for eight different family types.

Methodological information is available for Personal income tax systems, Compulsory social security contributions to schemes operated within the government sector, Universal cash transfers as well as recent changes in the tax/benefit system. The methodology also includes the parameter values and tax equations underlying the data.

Greece 2016

The tax/benefit position of single persons

	Wage level (per cent of average wage)	67	100	167	67
	Number of children	none	none	none	2
1.	**Gross wage earnings**	13 449	20 074	33 523	13 449
2.	**Standard tax allowances**				
	Basic allowance				
	Married or head of family				
	Dependent children				
	Deduction for social security contributions and income taxes	2 124	3 170	5 294	2 124
	Work-related expenses				
	Other				
	Total	2 124	3 170	5 294	2 124
3.	**Tax credits or cash transfers included in taxable income**	0	0	0	0
4.	**Central government taxable income (1 - 2 + 3)**	11 325	16 904	28 229	11 325
5.	**Central government income tax liability (exclusive of tax credits)**	2 492	3 719	6 786	2 492
6.	**Tax credits**				
	Basic credit	1 900	1 900	1 818	2 000
	Married or head of family				
	Children				
	Other				
	Total	1 900	1 900	1 818	2 000
7.	**Central government income tax finally paid**	592	1 927	5 556	492
8.	**State and local taxes**	0	0	0	0
9.	**Employees' compulsory social security contributions**				
	Gross earnings	2 124	3 170	5 294	2 124
	Taxable income				
	Total	2 124	3 170	5 294	2 124
10.	**Total payments to general government (7 + 8 + 9)**	2 715	5 097	10 850	2 615
11.	**Cash transfers from general government**				
	For head of family				
	For two children	0	0	0	640
	Total	0	0	0	640
12.	**Take-home pay (1-10+11)**	10 734	14 977	22 673	11 474
13.	**Employer's compulsory social security contributions**	3 342	4 989	8 331	3 342
14.	**Average rates**				
	Income tax	4.4%	9.6%	16.6%	3.7%
	Employees' social security contributions	15.8%	15.8%	15.8%	15.8%
	Total payments less cash transfers	20.2%	25.4%	32.4%	14.7%
	Total tax wedge including employer's social security contributions	36.1%	40.2%	45.8%	31.7%
15.	**Marginal rates**				
	Total payments less cash transfers: Principal earner	34.3%	36.2%	45.3%	34.3%
	Total payments less cash transfers: Spouse	n.a.	n.a.	n.a.	n.a.
	Total tax wedge: Principal earner	47.4%	48.9%	56.2%	47.4%
	Total tax wedge: Spouse	n.a.	n.a.	n.a.	n.a.

Greece 2016

The tax/benefit position of married couples

		Wage level (per cent of average wage)	100-0	100-33	100-67	100-33
		Number of children	2	2	2	none
1.	**Gross wage earnings**		22 081	29 368	36 875	29 368
2.	**Standard tax allowances**					
	Basic allowance					
	Married or head of family					
	Dependent children					
	Deduction for social security contributions and income taxes		3 487	4 638	5 823	4 638
	Work-related expenses					
	Other					
		Total	3 487	4 638	5 823	4 638
3.	**Tax credits or cash transfers included in taxable income**		0	0	0	0
4.	**Central government taxable income (1 - 2 + 3)**		18 594	24 730	31 052	24 730
5.	**Central government income tax liability (exclusive of tax credits)**		4 091	5 441	6 831	5 441
6.	**Tax credits**					
	Basic credit		2 000	4 000	4 000	3 800
	Married or head of family					
	Children					
	Other					
		Total	2 000	4 000	4 000	3 800
7.	**Central government income tax finally paid (5-6)**		2 236	2 236	2 987	2 336
8.	**State and local taxes**		0	0	0	0
9.	**Employees' compulsory social security contributions**					
	Gross earnings		3 487	4 638	5 823	4 638
	Taxable income					
		Total	3 487	4 638	5 823	4 638
10.	**Total payments to general government (7 + 8 + 9)**		5 723	6 873	8 810	6 973
11.	**Cash transfers from general government**					
	For head of family					
	For two children		640	320	320	0
		Total	640	320	320	0
12.	**Take-home pay (1-10+11)**		16 998	22 814	28 385	22 394
13.	**Employer's compulsory social security contributions**		5 487	7 298	9 164	7 298
14.	**Average rates**					
	Income tax		10.1%	7.6%	8.1%	8.0%
	Employees' social security contributions		15.8%	15.8%	15.8%	15.8%
	Total payments less cash transfers		23.0%	22.3%	23.0%	23.7%
	Total tax wedge including employer's social security contributions		38.3%	37.8%	38.3%	38.9%
15.	**Marginal rates**					
	Total payments less cash transfers: Principal earner		36.2%	36.2%	36.2%	36.2%
	Total payments less cash transfers: Spouse		20.6%	15.8%	36.2%	15.8%
	Total tax wedge: Principal earner		48.9%	48.9%	48.9%	48.9%
	Total tax wedge: Spouse		36.4%	32.6%	48.9%	32.6%

The national currency is the Euro (EUR). In 2016, EUR 0.90 was equal to USD 1. In 2016, the estimated gross earnings of the average worker are EUR 20 074 (Secretariat estimate).

1. Personal income tax system

1.1. *Central government income tax*

1.1.1. *Tax unit*

Individuals are subject to national income tax. Every individual who derives income from sources in Greece is subject to tax irrespective of his nationality, place of domicile or residence. Moreover, every individual with domicile in Greece (more than 183 days) is subject to tax on his/her worldwide income irrespective of the individual's nationality. Due consideration is given to bilateral conventions designed to obviate double taxation.

All individuals who have completed 18 years of age are obliged to file a tax return regardless of having taxable income or not. Regarding income derived by minor children, the parent who has the custody is liable for filing a tax return. The income of minor children is added to the income of the parent who has the custody and is taxed in the name of the parent who is in principle liable for tax filing. This provision does not apply to the following types of income, in respect of which the minor child has a personal tax obligation: a) employment income and b) pensions due to the death of his father or mother.The minimum imputed income, which is required to cover the taxpayer's main living expenses is EUR 3 000 for a single individual and EUR 5 000 for spouses (in the case that any real or presumptive income is declared).

Spouses file a joint return but each spouse is liable for the tax payable on his or her share of the joint income. A joint return can also file persons who have entered into a civil union – partnership. In this case the two parts have the same tax treatment as married couples. Losses incurred by one spouse or one part of a civil union-partnership may not be set off against the income of the other spouse or part. Spouses or parts of a civil union – partnership file a return separately if a) they have been divorced or have terminated the civil partnership at the time of the tax filing or b) one of the spouses or one part of the civil partnership is bankrupt or has been subject to guardianship.Taxpayer's spouse can be considered as a dependent member, provided that he/she does not have any taxable income.

Single children under the age of 18, children who are adults up to 25 years old and study at the university, or serve their military service or are registered as unemployed to the Manpower Employment Organisation (OAED), taxpayers' ascendants and spouses' relatives (up to the 3rd degree) who are orphans are deemed to be borne by the taxpayer provided that they cohabit with the taxpayer and their annual taxable income does not exceed the amount of EUR 3 000 (alimony and disability benefits and similar allowances are not included). Single disabled children (>= 67%) or spouses' disabled siblings (>= 67%) are also considered as dependent members, except if their annual income exceeds the amount of EUR 6 000 (alimony and disability benefits and similar allowances are not included).

1.1.2. Tax allowances and tax credits

1.1.2.1. Standard tax reliefs

- Social security contributions: all compulsory social security contributions and optional contributions to legally constituted funds are fully deductible from taxable gross income.

1.1.2.2. Deductions from the payable amount of tax, as calculated on the basis of the scale (Non-Standard tax credits):

A) The tax arising by the tax scale for employees and pensioners is reduced as following:

- by EUR 1 900 for annual income up to EUR 20 000, for taxpayers with no dependent children
- by EUR 1 950 for annual income up to EUR 20 000 for taxpayers with one dependent child
- by EUR 2 000 for annual income up to EUR 20 000 for taxpayers with two dependent children
- by EUR 2 100 for annual income up to EUR 20 000 for taxpayers with 3 dependent children or more;
- for income exceeding EUR 20 000, the above mentioned tax credit is being reduced by EUR 10 for every EUR 1 000 of taxable income

B) The following tax credits are deducted from the payable amount of tax, as calculated on the basis of the scale after applying the above tax allowance:

- 10% of the expenses of medical and hospital care of the taxpayer and his/her dependents provided they are not covered by Social Security Funds and they exceed 5% of the taxable income. The total credit cannot exceed EUR 3 000.
- 10% of the expenses of medical and hospital care of the taxpayer and his dependents, provided they are not covered by Social Security Funds and they exceed 5% of the taxable income. The total credit cannot exceed EUR 3 000. Hospital expenses in respect of unmarried or widowed children who suffer from an incurable disease, who are mentally retarded or are blind and whose total annual income does not exceed EUR 6 000 are also included.

C) The amount of tax derived on the basis of all scales is reduced by EUR 200 for the taxpayer himself as well as for each dependent member, provided that the taxpayer or his dependents are handicapped (over 67%) or handicapped soldiers or military personnel injured in the course of their duties or war victims or victims of terrorist attacksor in case they receive pension by the State as war victims or as handicapped.

Note: Taxpayers who reside abroad but derive taxable income from sources in Greece are not eligible for these deductions, with the exemptions of residents of the EU Member States who derive at least 90% of their total income from sources in Greece.

Spouses:

When the wife derives income taxable on the basis of the scale, then the following are deducted from her own payable amount of tax:

a) deductions related to medical and hospital expenses, donations and the lump sum of EUR 200 of the spouse;

b) deductions related to medical and hospital expenses of the spouse's children from a former marriage, her children born out of wedlock, her parents and orphaned relatives of first and second degree of kin.

If from the joint tax return submitted the wife has no income declared then the sum of her deductions (medical and hospital expenses, lump sum of EUR 200) is attributed to the payable tax of the other spouse.

1.1.2.3. Exemptions

Some forms of income, specified by Law are exempt from the tax.

Examples:

- on condition of reciprocity, income of all kinds derived abroad by foreign ambassadors and diplomatic representatives, consulate agents and employees of embassies and consulates that have the nationality of the represented State as well as by individuals working in the EU Institutions or other International Organizations;
- alimony received by the beneficiary according to the Court adjudication or notary Document;
- all forms of pensions and relief provided to war victims and their families, as well as to soldiers and military personnel injured in the course of their duties in times of peace;
- benefits and similar allowances provided to special categories of handicapped people;
- salaries, pensions etc. paid to handicapped people (over 80%);
- unemployment benefits granted by the National Employment Organisation (OAED) provided that the total annual income of the beneficiary does not exceed the amount of EUR 10 000;
- the social solidarity benefit (E.K.A.S.) of pensioners;
- financial aid to recognized political refugees, to people residing temporarily in Greece for humanitarian reasons and to persons that have submitted the relevant application to the competent Greek authorities, paid by bodies carrying out refugee aid schemes financed by the UN and the EU;
- the benefit for hazardous labor provided to employees working in the armed forces, the police, the fire and port departments as well as the special allowance to medical, nursing and ambulance staff up to 65%;

1.1.2.4. Tax calculation

Taxable income is derived from the following sources:

a) Income from employment and pensions

b) Income from business activities, which also includes income from self-employed

c) Income from agricultural activities as

d) Rental Income

e) Investment Income which includes income from dividends, interests and loyalties and

f) Income from capital gains, which includes income deriving on transfer of real estate or securities.

Net income is computed separately within each category with tax rules that vary across income categoriesIf the declared income is not accepted as the base for the tax assessment, the tax authorities can base the assessment on the presumptive income, which is the minimum amount of income required to cover the taxpayer's main living expenses.

Employment income is subject to withholding tax. The tax is withheld by the employer and is calculated by applying the taxpayer's progressive income tax schedule.

The employer calculates the withholding tax on the basis of the taxpayer's annual net salary (net of social security contributions). The withholding tax is then reduced by 1.5% of the total amount of taxes due. The resulting tax is the annual tax due, 1/14 of which constitutes the monthly withholding tax for the private sector's employees (every employee in the private sector receives 14 monthly salaries per year, i.e. 12 monthly wages plus 1 salary as Christmas bonus, ½ salary as Easter bonus and ½ salary as summer vacation bonus). For the employees of the public sector, the monthly withholding tax is calculated as 1/12 of the annual tax due, because of the fact that bonuses in the public sector have been eliminated. If the taxpayer's final tax liability (derived from the annual declared income) exceeds the aggregate of the amounts already withheld or prepaid, the remaining tax is generally payable in three equal bimonthly instalments. Any excess tax paid or withheld will be refunded.

1.1.3. *Rate schedule*

Depending on the income category the following tax schedules apply:

Income from employment and pensions is pooled together with income from business activity and is taxed at the following rates:

Income bracket (EUR)	Tax rate (%)	Tax bracket (EUR)	Total amount	
			Income (EUR)	Tax (EUR)
20 000	22%	4 400	20 000	4 400
10 000	29%	2 900	30 000	7 300
10 000	37%	3 700	40 000	11 000
Excess	45%			

The above tax scale does not apply for employment income acquired by:

- Officers working in ships of the merchant marine, whose income is taxed at a 15% flat rate and
- Low-income crew working in ships of the merchant marine, whose income is taxed at a 10% flat rate.

For deductions see above: 1.1.2.2 Deductions from the payable amount of tax, as calculated on the basis of the scale

Income from agricultural business is taxed separately but with the same tax schedule. The previously described tax credit is granted to farmers as well. In the case where a farmer is earning income from employment/pension, only one tax credit is given.

Rental Income is taxed at the following rates:

Income	Tax rate
0-12.000	15%
12.001-35.000	35%
35.001-	45%

Solidarity contribution is included in the Income Tax Code with a separate article. Income up to EUR 12 000 is not subject to solidarity contribution. For income exceeding EUR 12 000, solidarity contribution applies with the following marginal rates:

Solidarity Contribution Marginal Tax Rates

Income	Tax rate
0-12.000	0%
12.001-20.000	2.2%
20.001-30.000	5.00%
30.001-40.000	6.50%
40.001-65.000	7.50%
65.001-220.000	9.00%
220.000	10.00%

1.2. *State and local income taxes*

There are no local income taxes in Greece. Municipalities (the local authorities) receive 20% of the national income tax revenues.

2. Compulsory social security contributions to schemes operated within the government sector

The great majority of individuals who are employed in the private sector and render dependent personal services are principally, directly and compulsorily insured in the Social Insurance Organisation (IKA). Apart from the main contribution, IKA compulsorily collects contributions for other minor Funds created for the employee's benefit (Unemployment Benefits Funds, etc.). A subsidiary Social Insurance Fund (ETEA) for employees who are principally insured in IKA has been established since 2012.

The average rates of contributions payable by white-collar employees as a percentage of gross earnings are as follows (%):

Between 1st January and 31st May, 2016

	Employer	Employee	Total
1. Social Insurance Organisation (IKA)	17.88	9.22	27.10
2. Subsidiary Social Insurance Fund (ETEA)	3.00	3.00	6.00
3. Other Funds	3.68	3.28	6.96
Total	**24.56**	**15.50**	**40.06**

From 1 June 2016

	Employer	Employee	Total
1. Social Insurance Organisation (IKA)	17.88	9.22	27.10
2. Subsidiary Social Insurance Fund (ETEA)	3.50	3.50	7.00
3. Other Funds	3.68	3.28	6.96
Total	**25.06**	**16.00**	**41.06**

Higher contributions are due (18.95% paid by the employee and 26.71% paid by the employer) in case of blue-collar workers who are engaged in heavy work (unhealthy, dangerous, etc. work) as they are entitled to a pension five years earlier than the other workers. In the industrial sector, the employer pays an additional occupational risk contribution at a rate of 1% because these workers are more vulnerable to labour accidents and occupational diseases.

Contributions are calculated on the basis of the monthly salary or wages paid but within the limits specified in the National General Collective Labour Agreement. Monthly gross remuneration includes salaries and wages, fringe benefits and bonuses and any profit distributions to employees. From 2013 onwards, an equalized ceiling of EUR 5 546.80 applies for all categories of employees.

Self-employed individuals must make monthly compulsory lump-sum contributions to OAEE (Free Professional Social Insurance Organisation); these contributions depend on the number of years that the self-employed has been insured (for more details, see the explanatory annex to table III.3 of the OECD's Tax Database).

All these social security contributions are fully deductible for income tax purposes.

3. Universal cash transfers

3.1. *Transfers related to marital status*

According to the National General Collective Labour Agreement, a marriage allowance, which is set at a rate of 10% of the gross salary, is granted only to workers employed by employers that belong to the contracting employer organisations. For public servants no marriage benefit is granted.

3.2. *Transfers for dependent children*

According to the Law 4093/2012 (as amended by Law 4144/2013, Law 4111/2013 and Law 4170/2013), the "Single children support allowance" replaced the previously existing family allowances and applies since 01/01/2013. The allowance's amount is calculated according to the number of dependent children as well as the income category of the household. More specifically the allowance provides for EUR 40/month per child.

Households that are entitled to the allowance are divided into four income categories according to their income:

- Income of < EUR 6 000: full allowance
- Income of EUR 6 001-12 000: 2/3 of the allowance
- Income of EUR 12 001-18 000: 1/3 of the allowance

where the income is calculated as the **net annual total family** income divided by the sum of family members (where the first spouse is weighted as 1, the 2nd spouse is weighted as 1/3 and each dependent child is weighted as 1/6).

3.3. *Benefits for families with three or more children*

Law 4141/2013 (as amended by Law 4170/2013) introduced the "Special Allowance for families with three or more children", which is granted to families with three or more dependent children. The Special Allowance's amount is fixed to EUR 500/year per child, provided that the total income of the household does not exceed EUR 45 000 for families with three dependent children and EUR 48 000 for families with four dependent children, while in case of larger families the amount of EUR 45 000 is increased by EUR 4 000 per additional child.

Note 1: The Special allowance for families with three or more children is not included in the net, annual, family income and is exempt from income tax since 01-01-2013 (Law 4254/2014).

Namely the Hellenic Federation of Enterprises, the Hellenic Confederation of Professionals, Craftsmen and Merchants, the National Confederation of Hellenic Commerce and the Association of Greek Tourism Enterprises.

Note 2: Both Single children support allowance and the Special allowance for families with three or more children are exempt from Special Solidarity Contribution (Law 4254/2014).

4. Main changes in the tax/benefit system since 2015

A total change in the tax schedules and rates of all sources of income has been imposed, as well as the pooling of income for income derived from wages and businesses, and the integration of Solidarity Contribution in the Income Tax Code.

5. Memorandum items

5.1. *Identification of an AW and method of calculations used*

Methodological note for the estimation of the average annual earnings per employee, for the period 2000-15.

Terminology and coverage

The average annual earnings below refer to full time employees for Sectors C to N of ISIC Rev.3.1, before 2008, and for Sectors B to N including Division 95 and excluding Divisions 37, 39 and 75 of ISIC Rev. 4, for 2008 onwards.

Data sources

In the estimation procedure of the average annual earnings per employee, for the period 2000-14 the following data are taken into account:

- Annual earnings and number of employees, as derived from the **Structure of Earnings Survey** (SES), of the years 2002, 2006 and 2010.
- Hours worked and annual average number of employees, as derived from the **Labour Force Survey** (LFS), of the years 2000-14.
- Average annual earnings indices, as derived from the Indices on **Quarterly Labour Cost Survey**, of the years 2000-14.

Secretariat average wage estimates for 2015 and 2016 are used in the calculations, since final average wage values are not available (see the Annex, *Methodology and limitations*). Those estimates are based on the percentage changes in compensation per employee that were retrieved from the *OECD Economic Outlook volume 2016 (No. 100)* and the final value for 2014 (EUR 20 450). They amount to EUR 20 107 for 2015 (-1.6749%) and to EUR 20 074 for 2016 (-0.1683%).

Annual Gross earnings per full time employee 2000-15 Greece

Year	NACE Rev 2 classification
2000	15 693
2001	15 688
2002	**17 359**
2003	19 339
2004	21 669
2005	21 902
2006	**23 800**
2007	23 893
2008	23 835
2009	24 619
2010	**24 156**
2011	23 391
2012	22 240
2013	20 682
2014	20 450
2015	Will be available end of March

Notes:

1. The Average gross Annual Earnings per **full time employee** for the period 2000 to 2015 **includes**:
   The special payments for shift and night work, as well as work during weekends and holidays;
   The total annual bonuses as well as those that are regularly paid on a monthly basis, the 13th salary (Christmas salary, where applicable) and 14th salary (Easter and vacation payments, where applicable);
   The annual bonuses based on productivity;
   The education and working time allowance;
   The marriage and children allowance;

and excludes:
   The annual payments in kind: foods, drinks, footwear, clothes, accommodation, business cars provided, mobile phone, etc.;
   The annual premiums related to profit-sharing schemes.

2. The data for 2011 and onwards will be revised when the final results of the SES 2014 will be available.
3. The data for 2013 are revised with the final data from LFS and LCI.

Source: ELSTAT.

5.2. Main employers' contributions to private pension, health, and related schemes

Contributions to private pension and sickness schemes made by employers are not added to employees' gross earnings for tax purposes and are therefore not subject to tax. Since these contributions are not obligatory for employers, no data is provided by the National Statistical Service of Greece. Very few employers have adopted such additional insurance schemes.

2016 parameter values

Average earnings/yr	Ave_earn	20 074	Secretariat estimate
Tax credit	Child_cred	0	
Rates of family subsidies			
paid by employers	Wife_sub	0.1	
children (up to 3)	Child_sub	0	
Income tax schedule	Tax_sch	0.22	20 000
		0.29	30 000
		0.37	40 000
		0.45	
Tax deduction	Tax_cred	1 900	
	Tax_cred_1dc	1 950	
	Tax_cred_2dc	2 000	
	Tax_cred_3dc	2 100	
	Tax_cred_thrsh	20 000	
	Tax_red	10	
Solidarity contribution	Solidarity_sch	0	12 000
		0.022	20 000
		0.05	30 000
		0.065	40 000
		0.075	65 000
		0.09	220 000
		0.10	
Social security contributions	SSC_rate	0.1575	
	SSC_rate_empr	0.2481	
	SSC_ceil	77 655.20	
	SSC_ceil_use	1	
Single children support allowance	Child_all	0	480
		6 000	320
		12 000	160
		18 000	0
	Spouse_weight	0.33	
	Child_weight	0.17	

TAXING WAGES 2017 © OECD 2017

2016 tax equations

The equations for the Greek system in 2016 are mostly on an individual basis. The level of gross earnings for the principal earner is increased by the spouse and child subsidy paid by the employer.

The functions which are used in the equations (Taper, MIN, Tax etc.) are described in the technical note about tax equations. Variable names are defined in the table of parameters above, within the equations table, or are the standard variables "married" and "children". A reference to a variable with the affix "_total" indicates the sum of the relevant variable values for the principal and spouse. And the affixes "_princ" and "_spouse" indicate the value for the principal and spouse, respectively. Equations for a single person are as shown for the principal, with "_spouse" values taken as 0.

	Line in country table and intermediate steps	Variable name	Range	Equation
1.	Earnings	earn_princ	P	Ave_earn*(1+Married*Wife_sub+ MIN(Children,3)*Child_sub)
		earn_spouse	S	Ave_earn*(1+Married*Wife_sub+ MIN(Children,3)*Child_sub)
2.	Allowances:	tax_al	B	SSC
3.	Credits in taxable income	taxbl_cr		0
4.	CG taxable income	tax_inc	B	Positive(earn-tax_al)
5.	CG tax before credits	CG_tax_excl	B	Tax(tax_inc,tax_sch)-Low_rate*Positive(MIN(Effect_low_band-Low_thrsh,tax_inc-Low_thrsh))
	Solidarity contribution	sol_contr	B	=Solidarity(earn-SSC,Solidarity_sch)
6.	Tax credits :	tax_cr	**B**	Positive(IF(Children>0, tax_cred_1dc*(Children=1)+tax_cred_2dc*(Children=2)+tax_cred_3dc*(Children>2),tax_cred)-(INT(Positive(earn-tax_cred_thrsh)/1000)*tax_cred_red))
7.	CG tax	CG_tax	B	Positive(CG_tax_excl-tax_cr)+sol_contr
8.	State and local taxes	local_tax	B	0
9.	Employees' soc security	SSC	B	IF(SSC_ceil_use=1,SSC_rate*MIN(earn,SSC_ceil),SSC_rate*earn)
11.	Cash transfers			
		fam_netinc	B	earn – CG_tax - SSC
		cash_trans	B	VLOOKUP(fam_netinc,Child_all,2)*Children
13.	Employer's soc security	SSC_empr	B	IF(SSC_ceil_use=1,SSC_rate_empr*MIN(earn,SSC_ceil),SSC_rate_empr*earn)

Key to range of equation B calculated separately for both principal earner and spouse P calculated for principal only (value taken as 0 for spouse calculation) J calculated once only on a joint basis.

© OECD 2017

Hungary

This chapter includes data on the income taxes paid by workers, their social security contributions, the family benefits they receive in the form of cash transfers as well as the social security contributions and payroll taxes paid by their employers. Results reported include the marginal and average tax burden for eight different family types.

Methodological information is available for Personal income tax systems, Compulsory social security contributions to schemes operated within the government sector, Universal cash transfers as well as recent changes in the tax/benefit system. The methodology also includes the parameter values and tax equations underlying the data.

Hungary 2016

The tax/benefit position of single persons

		Wage level (per cent of average wage)	67	100	167	67
		Number of children	none	none	none	2
1.	**Gross wage earnings**		2 219 094	3 312 081	5 531 175	2 219 094
2.	**Standard tax allowances**					
	Basic allowance					
	Married or head of family					
	Dependent children		0	0	0	1 999 920
	Deduction for social security contributions and income taxes					
	Work-related expenses					
	Other					
		Total	0	0	0	1 999 920
3.	**Tax credits or cash transfers included in taxable income**		0	0	0	0
4.	**Central government taxable income (1 - 2 + 3)**		2 219 094	3 312 081	5 531 175	219 174
5.	**Central government income tax liability (exclusive of tax credits)**					
	Central government income tax liability (exclusive of tax credits)		332 864	496 812	829 676	32 876
		Total	332 864	496 812	829 676	32 876
6.	**Tax credits**					
	Basic credit		0	0	0	0
	Married or head of family					
	Children					
	Other					
		Total	0	0	0	0
7.	**Central government income tax finally paid (5-6)**		332 864	496 812	829 676	32 876
8.	**State and local taxes**		0	0	0	0
9.	**Employees' compulsory social security contributions**					
	Gross earnings		410 532	612 735	1 023 267	410 532
	Taxable income					
		Total	410 532	612 735	1 023 267	410 532
10.	**Total payments to general government (7 + 8 + 9)**		743 397	1 109 547	1 852 944	443 409
11.	**Cash transfers from general government**					
	For head of family					
	For two children		0	0	0	355 200
		Total	0	0	0	355 200
12.	**Take-home pay (1-10+11)**		1 475 698	2 202 534	3 678 232	2 130 886
13.	**Employer's wage dependent contributions and taxes**					
	Employer's compulsory social security contributions		599 155	894 262	1 493 417	599 155
	Payroll taxes		33 286	49 681	82 968	33 286
		Total	632 442	943 943	1 576 385	632 442
14.	**Average rates**					
	Income tax		15.0%	15.0%	15.0%	1.5%
	Employees' social security contributions		18.5%	18.5%	18.5%	18.5%
	Total payments less cash transfers		33.5%	33.5%	33.5%	4.0%
	Total tax wedge including employer's social security contributions		48.2%	48.2%	48.2%	25.3%
15.	**Marginal rates**					
	Total payments less cash transfers: Principal earner		33.5%	33.5%	33.5%	33.5%
	Total payments less cash transfers: Spouse		n.a.	n.a.	n.a.	n.a.
	Total tax wedge: Principal earner		48.2%	48.2%	48.2%	48.2%
	Total tax wedge: Spouse		n.a.	n.a.	n.a.	n.a.

Hungary 2016

The tax/benefit position of married couples

	Wage level (per cent of average wage)	100-0	100-33	100-67	100-33
	Number of children	2	2	2	none
1.	**Gross wage earnings**	3 312 081	4 405 068	5 531 175	4 405 068
2.	**Standard tax allowances**				
	Basic allowance				
	Married or head of family				
	Dependent children	1 999 920	1 999 920	1 999 920	0
	Deduction for social security contributions and income taxes				
	Work-related expenses				
	Other				
	Total	1 999 920	1 999 920	1 999 920	0
3.	**Tax credits or cash transfers included in taxable income**	0	0	0	0
4.	**Central government taxable income (1 - 2 + 3)**	1 312 161	2 405 148	3 531 255	4 405 068
5.	**Central government income tax liability (exclusive of tax credits)**				
	Central government income tax liability (exclusive of tax credits)	196 824	360 772	529 688	660 760
	Total	196 824	360 772	529 688	660 760
6.	**Tax credits**				
	Basic credit	0	0	0	0
	Married or head of family				
	Children				
	Other				
	Total	0	0	0	0
7.	**Central government income tax finally paid (5-6)**	196 824	360 772	529 688	660 760
8.	**State and local taxes**	0	0	0	0
9.	**Employees' compulsory social security contributions**				
	Gross earnings	612 735	814 938	1 023 267	814 938
	Taxable income				
	Total	612 735	814 938	1 023 267	814 938
10.	**Total payments to general government (7 + 8 + 9)**	809 559	1 175 710	1 552 956	1 475 698
11.	**Cash transfers from general government**				
	For head of family				
	For two children	319 200	319 200	319 200	0
	Total	319 200	319 200	319 200	0
12.	**Take-home pay (1-10+11)**	2 821 722	3 548 558	4 297 420	2 929 370
13.	**Employer's wage dependent contributions and taxes**				
	Employer's compulsory social security contributions	894 262	1 189 368	1 493 417	1 189 368
	Payroll taxes	49 681	66 076	82 968	66 076
	Total	943 943	1 255 444	1 576 385	1 255 444
14.	**Average rates**				
	Income tax	5.9%	8.2%	9.6%	15.0%
	Employees' social security contributions	18.5%	18.5%	18.5%	18.5%
	Total payments less cash transfers	14.8%	19.4%	22.3%	33.5%
	Total tax wedge including employer's social security contributions	33.7%	37.3%	39.5%	48.2%
15.	**Marginal rates**				
	Total payments less cash transfers: Principal earner	33.5%	33.5%	33.5%	33.5%
	Total payments less cash transfers: Spouse	33.5%	33.5%	33.5%	33.5%
	Total tax wedge: Principal earner	48.2%	48.2%	48.2%	48.2%
	Total tax wedge: Spouse	48.2%	48.2%	48.2%	48.2%

The national currency is the Forint (HUF). In 2016, HUF 281.52 was equal to USD 1. In 2016, the average worker earned HUF 3 312 081 (Secretariat estimate).

1. Personal income tax systems

1.1. *Central/federal government income taxes*

1.1.1. *Tax unit*

The tax unit is, in all cases, the separate individual. In exceptional cases, the employer can become subject to personal income tax, for instance in the case of benefits in kind.

1.1.2. *Tax allowances and tax credits*

1.1.2.1. Standard reliefs

- *Basic reliefs*: None.
- *Standard marital status reliefs*: None.
- *Employee Tax credit:* Since 1 January 2012 there is no employee tax credit.
- *Family tax allowance:* For families having children, the basis of income tax can be reduced by the family tax allowance, which amounts to HUF 66 670 per month (for families having one child), HUF 83 330 per month/each dependent (for families having two children) or HUF 220 000 per month/each dependent (for families having at least three children). This tax allowance can be applied by a pregnant woman (or her husband) as from the 91st day after conception until birth of the child. The tax allowance may be claimed by one spouse or be split between the spouses. As of 1st January 2014 the family tax allowance was extended: families whose combined PIT base is not sufficient to claim the maximum amount of the family tax allowance can deduct the remaining sum from the 7% health insurance contribution and the 10% pension contribution. This measure does not affect the eligibility for social security benefits (pensions, healthcare, transfers, etc.).

1.1.2.2. Main non-standard tax reliefs

- *Trade Union membership dues:* Membership dues and contributions paid to trade unions and other corporate bodies of employees are deductible without any restriction.
- Tax credits are made available for physical disability or agricultural activities. Tax deduction is available for those having income from abroad.
- From 1st January 2015 for newly married couples (where it's the first marriage for at least one of the parties) the basis of income tax can be reduced by HUF 33 335 per month for one person of the couple for 24 months.

1.1.3. *Tax schedule*

The rate of personal income tax amounts to 15%.

1.2. *State and local income taxes*

In Hungary there is no local Personal income tax system supplementing the central one.

2. Compulsory social security contributions to schemes operated within the government sector

2.1. Employees' contributions

2.1.1. Pensions

The rate of pension contribution amounts to 10% of gross earnings.

2.1.2. Sickness

The rate of health security contribution amounts to 7% of gross earnings.

2.1.3. Unemployment

The worker must pay, as employees' contribution, 1.5% of gross earnings.

2.1.4. Others

None. The average worker does not have any obligation to pay other contributions than the above mentioned. However, the contribution rates may be different for certain types of income or for certain groups of income recipients (e.g. employees with pensioner status). None of these exceptions are applicable to the workers taken into consideration in this report.

2.2. Employers' contributions

2.2.1. Pensions

None.

2.2.2. Sickness

None.

2.2.3. Unemployment

None.

2.2.4. Others

From 2012 the employers' social security contributions were merged into the new payroll tax, called social contribution tax. This change is of legal nature, the combined rate remains 27% while the revenue is divided among the pension, health care and labour-market funds.

The employer contributions also include a payroll tax: the training levy amounts to 1.5% of gross earnings.

From 1 January 2013, the Job Protection Act (JPA) introduced new targeted reliefs in the employers' contributions (social contribution tax and training levy) to incentivise the employment of the most disadvantageous groups on the labour market. This measure reduces the standard rate of the employers' contributions up to a cap of HUF 100 000 per month. The JPA introduced a permanent reduction of the employers' tax rate by 14.5% for:

- employees under 25 years of age,
- employees over 55 years of age,
- employees working in elementary occupations,
- employees working in agricultural occupations.

It also introduced temporary reductions (28.5% in the first two years of the employment, and 14.5% in the third year) for:

- long term unemployed re-entering the labour market,
- people returning to work after child-care leave,
- career starters.

From 1 January 2015 the budgetary institutions are not eligible for the JPA tax allowances anymore.

The targeted reliefs in the employers' contributions are not considered in the Taxing Wages model.

Social security contributions will have to be paid on other benefits than gross earnings (e.g., grants in kind) and payments (e.g., certain kind of contracts).

3. Universal cash transfers

3.1. *Transfers related to marital status*

None.

3.2. *Transfers for dependent children*

Effective from 1 January 2008:

Type of family	HUF per month
For a couple with one child	12 200
For a single earner with one child	13 700
For a couple with two children, per child	13 300
For a single earner with two children, per child	14 800
For a couple with 3 or more children, per child	16 000
For a single earner with 3 or more children, per child	17 000
For a couple with permanently sick and disabled child	23 300
For a single earner with permanently sick and disabled child	25 900

4. Main changes in the tax/benefit system since 2010

- The tax base correction was phased out in two steps.
- The employee tax credit was abolished.
- The employees' health care contribution was increased.
- The employers' social security contributions were merged into the social contribution tax (legal change only, rates and base remained unchanged).
- Health contributions on benefits in kind were increased.
- As a temporary measure, a wage compensation scheme was in effect in the form of an employers' SSC credit.
- Targeted employment incentives to boost the employment levels of groups at the margin of the labour force.
- The child tax allowance was extended in 2014 by allowing the deduction of the allowance from employees' SSC.
- The rate of the PIT decreased by 1 percentage point in 2016.
- The rate of family tax benefit for families with two children is gradually increased from 2016 so that it will be doubled by 2019.

5. Memorandum items

5.1. *Employer contributions to private social security arrangements*

In Hungary the law dealing with the voluntary mutual insurance funds (like pension funds) was enacted on 6 December 1993. Based on the rules for 2016, the monthly contribution paid to a voluntary mutual pension fund by the employer of a private worker who participates in a voluntary mutual pension fund, limited to an amount below half of the mandatory minimum wage, is taxable according to an effective personal income tax rate of 17.85% (the nominal tax rate of 15% multiplied by 1.19) and an effective health contribution of 16.66% (the nominal tax rate of 14% multiplied by 1.19). In the case of employers' contributions paid to health funds the applicable limit is 30% of the mandatory minimum wage per month or HUF 200 000 per year and in the case of pension funds the applicable limit is 50% of the mandatory minimum wage per month or HUF 200 000 per year. Contributions in excess of these limits are taxable at an effective personal income tax rate of 17.85% and an effective health contribution of 32.12% (the nominal tax rate of 27% multiplied by 1.19) is also payable on these amounts. Sponsor's donations paid by the employer to its employees' voluntary mutual insurance fund are taxable as well. In addition, employees can apply a 20% tax credit with a limit of HUF 150 000 per year on these taxable payments. The tax authority pays the tax credit directly to a voluntary mutual insurance fund.

In general, insurance premiums (on the basis of which an employee is named as the recipient/beneficiary of insurance services) paid by the employer are taxable, and social security contributions plus training contribution are also payable. At the same time insurance premiums related to life insurance policy for accidental death, injury liability, or medical care insurance for full and permanent incapacity to work are exempted from taxation and any contributions.

As from 2008 employer pension institutions can be established. Based on the rules for 2016, the monthly contribution paid to an employer pension institution by the employer of a private worker, limited to an amount below half of the mandatory minimum wage per month or HUF 200 000 per year, is taxable according to an effective personal income tax rate of 17.85% and an effective health contribution of 16.66%. Contributions in excess of this limit are taxable at an effective personal income tax rate of 32.13% and an effective health contribution of 16.66% is also payable on these amounts.

2016 parameter values

Average earnings/yr	Ave_earn	3 312 081	Secretariat estimate		
Child allowance (per child)	child_al	1	800 040		
		2	999 960		
		3	2 640 000		
		4	2 640 000		
Income tax schedule	tax_sch	0.15			
Social security contributions	SSC_unemp	0.015			
	SSC_p	0.1			
	SSC_h	0.07			
Payroll taxes	SSC_empr	0.27			
	payroll_rate	0.015			
		# of children	1	2	3+
Transfers for children	CB_rates	0	12 200	13 300	16 000
(monthly)		1	13 700	14 800	17 000

2016 tax equations

The equations for the Hungarian system in 2016 are mostly on an individual basis. But the child allowance can be split between the spouses and cash transfers are calculated only once. This is shown by the Range indicator in the table below.

The functions which are used in the equations (Taper, MIN, Tax etc) are described in the technical note about tax equations. Variable names are defined in the table of parameters above, within the equations table, or are the standard variables "married" and "children". A reference to a variable with the affix "_total" indicates the sum of the relevant variable values for the principal and spouse. And the affixes "_princ" and "_spouse" indicate the value for the principal and spouse, respectively. Equations for a single person are as shown for the principal, with "_spouse" values taken as 0.

	Line in country table and intermediate steps	Variable name	Range	Equation
1.	Earnings	earn		
2.	Allowances:			
	Children	child_al	P	IF(Children>0, Children*VLOOKUP(Children, child_al, 2), 0)
	Total	tax_al	B	child_al
3.	Credits in taxable income	taxbl_cr	B	0
4.	CG taxable income	tax_inc	P	MAX(0,earn -tax_al)
	CG taxable income	tax_inc	S	Positive(earn_spouse-Positive(tax_al-earn_spouse-SSC_deduction_princ/tax_sch))
5.	CG tax before credits	CG_tax_excl	B	tax_inc*tax_sch
7.	CG tax	CG_tax	B	CG_tax_excl-tax_cr
8.	State and local taxes	local_tax	B	0
	Child tax allowance (Employees' SSC)	SSC_child_cr	P	=MIN(earn_princ*(SSC_h+SSC_p),Positive(tax_al-earn_princ)*tax_sch)
	Child tax allowance (Employees' SSC)		S	=MIN(earn_spouse*(SSC_h+SSC_p),Positive(-earn_princ)*tax_sch)
9.	Employees' soc security	SSC	B	earn*(SSC_unemp+ SSC_h+SSC_p)-SSC_child_cr
11.	Cash transfers	cash_trans	J	Children*(VLOOKUP((1-Married), CB_rates, MIN(Children, 3)+1)*12)
13.	Employer's soc security	SSC_empr	B	earn*SSC_empr
	Employer's payroll taxes	Payroll	B	earn*payroll_rate

Key to range of equation B calculated separately for both principal earner and spouse P calculated for principal only (value taken as 0 for spouse calculation) J calculated once only.

Taxing Wages 2017
© OECD 2017

Iceland

This chapter includes data on the income taxes paid by workers, their social security contributions, the family benefits they receive in the form of cash transfers as well as the social security contributions and payroll taxes paid by their employers. Results reported include the marginal and average tax burden for eight different family types.

Methodological information is available for Personal income tax systems, Compulsory social security contributions to schemes operated within the government sector, Universal cash transfers as well as recent changes in the tax/benefit system. The methodology also includes the parameter values and tax equations underlying the data.

Iceland 2016

The tax/benefit position of single persons

	Wage level (per cent of average wage)	67	100	167	67
	Number of children	none	none	none	2
1.	**Gross wage earnings**	5 665 794	8 456 409	14 122 203	5 665 794
2.	**Standard tax allowances**				
	Basic allowance				
	Married or head of family				
	Dependent children				
	Deduction for social security contributions and income taxes	226 632	338 256	564 888	226 632
	Work-related expenses				
	Other				
	Total	226 632	338 256	564 888	226 632
3.	**Tax credits or cash transfers included in taxable income**	0	0	0	0
4.	**Central government taxable income (1 - 2 + 3)**	5 439 162	8 118 153	13 557 315	5 439 162
5.	**Central government income tax liability (exclusive of tax credits)**	1 250 764	1 891 043	3 468 564	1 250 764
6.	**Tax credits**				
	Basic credit	623 042	623 042	623 042	623 042
	Married or head of family				
	Children				
	Other				
	Total	623 042	623 042	623 042	623 042
7.	**Central government income tax finally paid (5-6)**	627 722	1 268 001	2 845 522	627 722
8.	**State and local taxes**	785 959	1 173 073	1 959 032	785 959
9.	**Employees' compulsory social security contributions**				
	Gross earnings	27 756	27 756	27 756	27 756
	Taxable income				
	Total	27 756	27 756	27 756	27 756
10.	**Total payments to general government (7 + 8 + 9)**	1 441 437	2 468 830	4 832 310	1 441 437
11.	**Cash transfers from general government**				
	For head of family				
	For two children	0	0	0	543 689
	Total	0	0	0	543 689
12.	**Take-home pay (1-10+11)**	4 224 357	5 987 579	9 289 893	4 768 046
13.	**Employer's compulsory social security contributions**	416 436	621 546	1 037 982	416 436
14.	**Average rates**				
	Income tax	25.0%	28.9%	34.0%	25.0%
	Employees' social security contributions	0.5%	0.3%	0.2%	0.5%
	Total payments less cash transfers	25.4%	29.2%	34.2%	15.8%
	Total tax wedge including employer's social security contributions	30.5%	34.0%	38.7%	21.6%
15.	**Marginal rates**				
	Total payments less cash transfers: Principal earner	36.8%	36.8%	44.4%	46.4%
	Total payments less cash transfers: Spouse	n.a.	n.a.	n.a.	n.a.
	Total tax wedge: Principal earner	41.1%	41.1%	48.2%	50.1%
	Total tax wedge: Spouse	n.a.	n.a.	n.a.	n.a.

TAXING WAGES 2017 © OECD 2017

Iceland 2016

The tax/benefit position of married couples

		Wage level (per cent of average wage)	100-0	100-33	100-67	100-33
		Number of children	2	2	2	none
1.	**Gross wage earnings**		8 456 409	11 247 024	14 122 203	11 247 024
2.	**Standard tax allowances**					
	Basic allowance					
	Married or head of family					
	Dependent children					
	Deduction for social security contributions and income taxes		338 256	449 881	564 888	449 881
	Work-related expenses					
	Other					
		Total	338 256	449 881	564 888	449 881
3.	**Tax credits or cash transfers included in taxable income**		0	0	0	0
4.	**Central government taxable income (1 - 2 + 3)**		8 118 153	10 797 143	13 557 315	10 797 143
5.	**Central government income tax liability (exclusive of tax credits)**		1 891 043	2 498 638	3 141 807	2 498 638
6.	**Tax credits**					
	Basic credit		1 246 084	1 230 637	1 246 084	1 230 637
	Married or head of family					
	Children					
	Other					
		Total	1 246 084	1 230 637	1 246 084	1 230 637
7.	**Central government income tax finally paid (5-6)**		644 959	1 268 001	1 895 723	1 268 001
8.	**State and local taxes**		1 173 073	1 544 740	1 959 032	1 544 740
9.	**Employees' compulsory social security contributions**					
	Gross earnings		27 756	55 512	55 512	55 512
	Taxable income					
		Total	27 756	55 512	55 512	55 512
10.	**Total payments to general government (7 + 8 + 9)**		1 845 788	2 868 253	3 910 267	2 868 253
11.	**Cash transfers from general government**					
	For head of family					
	For two children		301 985	127 092	0	0
		Total	301 985	127 092	0	0
12.	**Take-home pay (1-10+11)**		6 912 606	8 505 863	10 211 936	8 378 771
13.	**Employer's compulsory social security contributions**		621 546	826 656	1 037 982	826 656
14.	**Average rates**					
	Income tax		21.5%	25.0%	27.3%	25.0%
	Employees' social security contributions		0.3%	0.5%	0.4%	0.5%
	Total payments less cash transfers		18.3%	24.4%	27.7%	25.5%
	Total tax wedge including employer's social security contributions		23.9%	29.6%	32.6%	30.6%
15.	**Marginal rates**					
	Total payments less cash transfers: Principal earner		46.4%	42.6%	36.8%	36.8%
	Total payments less cash transfers: Spouse		42.9%	41.4%	36.8%	35.6%
	Total tax wedge: Principal earner		50.1%	46.5%	41.1%	41.1%
	Total tax wedge: Spouse		46.8%	45.4%	41.1%	40.1%

The national currency is the Króna (plural: Krónur) (ISK). In 2016, ISK 120.81 was equal to USD 1. That year, the average worker is expected to earn ISK 8 456 409 (Secretariat estimate).

1. Personal income tax system

1.1. *Central government income taxes*

1.1.1. *Tax unit*

Income is taxed on an individual basis, except for capital income of married couples which is taxed jointly.

1.1.2. *Tax allowances and credits*

1.1.2.1. Standard reliefs

- *Basic tax credit*: A fixed tax credit, amounting to ISK 623 042 in 2016, is granted to all individuals 16 years and older, regardless of their marital status. The tax credit is deducted from levied central and local government taxes. Unutilised tax credits or portions thereof are wastable, i.e. non-refundable and non-transferable between tax years.
- *Standard marital status relief*: Married couples may utilise up to 100 of each spouses' unutilised portion of his/her basic tax credit.
- *Relief(s) for children*: None.
- *Relief(s) for compulsory pension contributions*: The compulsory payment to pension funds amounts to 4% of wages and is deductible. In addition, an optional payment of up to 4% of wages may also be deducted. As the additional 4% contribution is optional, it is viewed as a non-standard relief in this Report.

1.1.2.2. Main non-standard tax reliefs applicable to an AW

- *Interest payment relief*: A fully refundable tax credit is granted to purchasers of personal dwellings (homes) to recuperate a part of mortgage-related interest expenses. The maximum tax-related interest credit in 2016 is ISK 400 000 for a single person, ISK 500 000 for a single parent and ISK 600 000 for a married couple. The following constraints apply to interest rebates: 1) they cannot exceed 7.0% of the remaining debt balance incurred in buying a home for one's own use. 2) The maximum amount of interest payments that qualify for an interest rebate calculation is ISK 800 000 for an individual, ISK 1 000 000 for a single parent and ISK 1 200 000 for a couple. 3) 8.5% of taxable income is subtracted from the interest expense. 4) The rebates begin to be curtailed at a net worth threshold of ISK 4 500 000 for a single individual and a single parent and ISK 7 312 000 for a couple and are eliminated altogether at a 60% higher amount, or ISK 7 200 000 and 11 700 000, respectively. (These amounts are based on income in the year 2016 but are paid out in 2017. These numbers are estimates; final figures will be available once the 2017 budget has been passed).

The definition of average worker in Iceland includes workers in five categories. See section 5.1.

1.1.3. *Tax schedule*

The income tax base is composed of *personal income* (e.g. wages, salaries, fringe benefits, pensions, etc.), which is taxed on an individual basis, and *capital income* which is taxed jointly for married couples.

The tax on personal income is triple-rated. The central government income tax rate in 2016 is 22.68% for income up to ISK 336 035 per month. A 23.9% tax rate applies to the next ISK 500 955 or up to ISK 836 990. For income exceeding ISK 836 990 the tax rate is 31.8%. The income tax rate applies to all personal income in excess of ISK 145 659 per month (ISK 1 747 908 per year). Tax relief is provided by the basic credit described in Section 1.1.2.1.

The tax on capital income is 20%. It is levied on all capital income of individuals, such as interest, dividends, rents etc. Interest income up to ISK 125 000 per year and 30% of income from rent of residential property is tax free.

1.2. Local government income tax

The local government income tax base is the same as the central government's personal income tax base.

The local governments' income tax is single-rated, but the rate varies between 12.44 and 14.52% between municipalities. The average rate in 2016 is 14.45%.

2. Compulsory social security contributions to schemes operated within the government sector

2.1. Employees' contributions

Fee to the Retiree Investment Fund: 16 to 70 year-old individuals are subject to a fixed tax of ISK 10 956 in 2016, provided the individual's taxable income is at least ISK 1 678 002 for the year. This tax will be collected in 2017.

Fee to the broadcast media: 16 to 70 year-old individuals with taxable income over ISK 1 678 002 for the year are subject to a fixed tax of ISK 16 800 in 2016, which will be collected in 2017.

These amounts are estimates and thus subject to change as the fees are payable in 2017.

2.2. Employers' contributions

Employers have to pay a social security tax on total wages of 7.35%. In addition, 0.65% is levied on the wages of fishermen as a premium for their government accident insurance. Furthermore, a new financial activities tax was introduced in 2012, which requires financial and insurance companies to pay an additional 5.5% payroll tax in 2016.

3. Universal cash transfers

3.1. Marital status related transfers

None.

3.2. Transfers for dependent children

Child benefits are granted for each child, subject to income thresholds. In 2016 they are as follows (in ISK per year):

For each child under the age of seven:	122 879
Children under the age of eighteen at the end of 2014:	
First child	205 834
Each additional child	245 087
Benefits for single parents:	
First child	342 939
Each additional child	351 787
Income threshold for benefit curtailment:	
For couples	5 400 000
For a single parent	2 700 000
Curtailment of benefits (children under the age of seven only):	
For each child	4%
Curtailment of benefits (all children under the age of eighteen):	
For one child	4%
For two children	6%
For three children or more	8%

Note that child benefits in this Report are based on income in the year 2016 but are paid out in 2017 (see also section 4.4). These numbers are estimates and thus subject to change.

4. Main changes in the tax/benefit system since 1998

4.1. *The deductibility of the payment to pension funds*

All employees are required to participate in pension funds. The employee contribution is generally 4% of wages and the employer contribution was 6%, and increased to 8% as of beginning 2007. Both contributions are deductible from income before tax. In some cases, the contributions of employees and employers are higher. An optional, additional payment from employees of up to 4% of wages is also deductible and goes into an individual retirement account. However, from 2012 to mid-2014, this additional payment was temporarily set at 2%.

This voluntary pension savings option was first introduced in 1999 in order to encourage personal saving. At the time the contribution rate was 2% for employees and 0.2% for employers. In May 2000 these rates were doubled to 4 and 0.4%, respectively, as noted above. In addition, some employers, such as the central government, have increased their employer counter-contribution by agreement with employees. The central government contributed 1% against a voluntary employee contribution of 4% in 2001 and 2% as of the beginning of 2002. All such contributions are tax-deductible, both with the employer and the employee at the time the contribution is made. The actual pension is taxed as personal income when it is drawn. As of the beginning of 2004, the employer option of deducting the above 0.4% against the social security tax was abolished. Since such employer counter-contributions had become part of wage agreements in most cases, it was no longer felt that such a tax incentive was needed.

4.2. *Central and local income tax rates in 1997-2016*

In 1997-2007, the Government pursued a policy of reducing the marginal tax rate, as can be seen in the table below. This development was reversed in 2009 when income tax was raised by 1.35 percentage points in response to the Treasury's rising debt burden brought on by the economic crisis. At the beginning of 2010 the tax system was changed from single rated to triple rated. The tax rate was set at 24.1% for the first monthly ISK 200 000 but it was raised by 2.9% for the next ISK 450 000 and again by 6% for income in excess of ISK 650 000. In 2016, the rates are 22.68%, 23.9% and 31.8%, and the corresponding income thresholds are

ISK 336 035 and 836 990 per month; see section 1.1.3 for further details. From 1998 onwards, the central government and average local government personal income tax rates have been as follows:

	Central government general tax rate (%)	Municipal tax rate (%)	Total tax rate (%)	Central government surtax (%)
1998	27.41	11.61	39.02	7.00
1999	26.41	11.93	38.34	7.00
2000	26.41	11.96	38.37	7.00
2001	26.08	12.68	38.76	7.00
2002	25.75	12.79	38.54	7.00
2003	25.75	12.80	38.55	5.00
2004	25.75	12.83	38.58	4.00
2005	24.75	12.98	37.73	2.00
2006	23.75	12.97	36.72	0
2007	22.75	12.97	35.72	0
2008	22.75	12.97	35.72	0
2009	24.10	13.10	37.20	0
2010	24.10	13.12	37.32	2.90/6.00
2011	22.90	14.41	37.31	2.90/6.00
2012	22.90	14.44	37.34	2.90/6.00
2013	22.90	14.42	37.32	2.90/6.00
2014	22.86	14.44	37.30	2.44/6.50
2015	22.86	14.44	37.30	2.44/6.50
2016	22.68	14.45	37.13	1.22/7.90

4.3. A special tax on higher income

In 1998, the special tax on higher income was raised by 2 percentage points, from 5 to 7%. For 2003-income, it was reduced back to 5%. It was reduced to 4% for 2004 income and to 2% for 2005-income. In the fiscal year 2006, the tax was abolished. In the latter half of 2009 the special tax on higher income was introduced again at 8%. In 2010 the tax system changed to triple-rated; see sections 4.2 and 1.1.3.

4.4. A revision of child benefit system

Child benefits are granted for each child, subject to income thresholds. The amendments to tax legislation that came into effect in 2004 included a schedule for raising child benefits. As from 2007, the child benefits will be paid for children up to 18 years old instead of 16 years old. For 2009–2016, benefits are as follows (in ISK per year):

	2009	2010	2011	2012	2013	2014	2015	2016
For all children under the age of seven	61 191	61 191	61 191	100 000	100 000	115 825	119 300	122 879
Children under the age of eighteen:								
First child	152 331	152 331	152 331	167 564	167 564	194 081	199 839	205 834
Each additional child	181 323	181 323	181 323	199 455	199 455	231 019	237 949	245 087
Benefits for single parents:								
First child	253 716	253 716	253 716	279 087	279 087	323 253	332 950	342 939
Each additional child	260 262	260 262	260 262	286 288	286 288	331 593	341 541	351 787
Income threshold for benefit curtailment:								
For couples	3 600 000	3 600 000	3 600 000	4 800 000	4 800 000	4 800 000	4 800 000	5 400 000
For a single parent	1 800 000	1 800 000	1 800 000	2 400 000	2 400 000	2 400 000	2 400 000	2 700 000

	2009	2010	2011	2012	2013	2014	2015	2016
Curtailment of benefits under the age of seven:								
For each child		3%	3%	3%	3%	4%	4%	4%
Curtailment of benefits under the age of eighteen:								
For one child	2%	3%	3%	3%	3%	4%	4%	4%
For two children	5%	5%	5%	5%	5%	6%	6%	6%
For three children or more	7%	7%	7%	7%	7%	8%	8%	8%

The data for 2016 is subject to change as the benefits are not payable until 2017.

4.5. *A revision of interest rebates*

In 2004, the interest rebate was cut by 10%, effective for that year only. The ceiling on interest payments that qualify for the interest rebate was reduced from 7% to 5.5% in 2005 and the interest rate cut was reduced from 10% to 5%. As of the beginning of 2006, the ceiling was further reduced to 5%. In 2005 and again in 2007 the net worth ceiling was lifted considerably in reaction to the increase in net worth due to the house price boom in 2005-07. In 2008, as mortgage-related interest expenses surged, the ceiling on interest payments was raised back to 7% and the maximum rebate amount increased by 37%. These measures stayed in effect in 2009. In 2010 the maximum rebate amount increased by 47-62% and the net worth ceiling was reduced significantly. The rate of taxable income which is subtracted from the interest expense was increased from 6% to 8% and further to 8.5% in 2014. In addition to the ordinary interest payment relief, a temporary interest cost rebate was in effect in 2010-11; see section 1.1.2.2.

4.6. *Transferability of basic tax credit between spouses*

The basic tax credit was made transferable between spouses in stages; see section 1.1.2.1 above. In fiscal year 2001, 90% of the credit became transferable, rising to 95% in 2002 and 100% in 2003.

5. Memorandum items

5.1. *Identification of AW (only eight categories) and valuation of earnings*

The data on average earnings refers to average workers in eight categories according to the NACE rev. 2 classification which corresponds to the ISIC rev.4 system. The categories are C – Manufacturing, D – Electricity, gas, steam and air conditioning supply (from 2008), E – Water supply; sewerage, waste management and remediation activities (from 2008) F – Construction, G – Wholesale and retail trade, repair of motor vehicles, motorcycles, H – Transport, storage, and J – Information and communication K - Financial and insurance activities. Public sector employees are not included. Together, these categories comprise approximately 80% of Iceland's private sector labour force.

The original data are obtained from a monthly survey among Icelandic firms with 10 or more employees.

5.2. *Employer contributions to private pension funds, health and related schemes*

By law, all employees and employers must contribute to pension funds. These funds are private, generally linked to unions and employee associations. The private pension funds are not part of the government-run social security system, to which a payroll tax is paid as described under section 2.2 above. Compulsory and voluntary payments to such funds are described in section 4.1 above.

 TAXING WAGES 2017 © OECD 2017

2016 parameter values

Average earnings/yr	Ave_earn	8 456 409	Secretariat estimate
Pension rate for tax allowance	pension_rate	0.04	
Tax credit	Basic_crd	623 042	
	Married_propn	1	
Central income tax	tax_sch	0.2268	4 032 420
		0.239	10 043 880
		0.318	
Special tax	special_rate	0	
threshold	special_thrsh		
Local tax	local_rate	0.1445	
Church tax	church_tax	0	
Social Security Contr.	SSC_fixed	27 756	
	SSC_thrsh	1 678 002	
Employer SSC	SSC_empr	0.0735	
General child allowance:			
child allowance	CA	122 879	
Maximum number of children under 7	max_child_under7	1	
Supplement child allowance:			
Married couple case			
first child	SA_first_m	205 834	
other children	SA_others_m	245 087	
income threshold	SA_tresh_m	5 400 000	
Single parent case			
first child	SA_first_s	342 939	
other children	SA_others_s	351 787	
income threshold	SA_tresh_s	2 700 000	
reduction rate (one child)	SA_redn_1	0.04	
reduction rate (two children)	SA_redn_2	0.06	
reduction rate (tree or more children)	SA_redn_3	0.08	

2016 tax equations

The equations for the Iceland system are mostly on an individual basis. But the tax credit for married couples is relevant only to the calculation for the principal earner and child benefit is calculated only once. This is shown by the Range indicator in the table below.

The functions which are used in the equations (Taper, MIN, Tax etc) are described in the technical note about tax equations. Variable names are defined in the table of parameters above, within the equations table, or are the standard variables "married" and "children". A reference to a variable with the affix "_total" indicates the sum of the relevant variable values for the principal and spouse. And the affixes "_princ" and "_spouse" indicate the value for the principal and spouse, respectively. Equations for a single person are as shown for the principal, with "_spouse" values taken as 0.

	Line in country table and intermediate steps	Variable name	Range	Equation
1.	Earnings	earn		
2.	Allowances:	tax_al	B	earn*pension_rate
3.	Credits in taxable income	taxbl_cr	B	0
4.	CG taxable income	tax_inc	B	earn-tax_al
5.	CG tax before credits	CG_tax_excl	B	tax(tax_inc, tax_sch)
6.	Tax credits :	tax_cr	P	MIN(CG_tax_excl_princ,Basic_crd+MAX(Married*Basic_crd-CG_tax_excl_spouse-(tax_inc_spouse*local_rate),0))
			S	MIN(Married*Basic_crd, CG_tax_excl_spouse)
		special_tax	J	0
7.	CG tax	CG_tax	B	CG_tax_excl-tax_cr+special_tax
8.	State and local taxes	local_tax	P S	MAX(tax_inc_princ*local_rate-MAX(Basic_crd+ Max(Married*Basic_crd-CG_tax_excl_spouse-(tax_inc_spouse*local_rate),0)-CG_tax_excl_princ,0),0) MAX(tax_inc_spouse*local_rate-MAX(Married*Basic_crd-CG_tax_excl_spouse, 0),0)
9.	Employees' soc security	SSC	B	SSC_fixed*(earn>SSC_thrsh)
11.	Cash transfers:			
	Total family income	inc_tot	J	earn_total
	Child allowance	cash_trans	J	Positive(MIN(Children,max_child_under7)*CA-Positive(inc_total*(1-pension_rate)-IF(Married,SA_tresh_m,SA_tresh_s))*SA_redn_1) +(Children>0)*(IF(Married,SA_first_m+ Positive(Children-1)*SA_others_m,SA_first_s+ Positive(Children-1)*SA_others_s) - Positive(inc_tot*(1-pension_rate)-IF(Married,SA_tresh_m,SA_tresh_s))*IF(Children=1, SA_redn_1,IF(Children=2,SA_redn_2,SA_redn_3)))
13.	Employer's soc security	SSC_empr	B	earn*SSC_empr_rate

Key to range of equation B calculated separately for both principal earner and spouse P calculated for principal only (value taken as 0 for spouse calculation) J calculated once only on a joint basis.

© OECD 2017

Ireland

This chapter includes data on the income taxes paid by workers, their social security contributions, the family benefits they receive in the form of cash transfers as well as the social security contributions and payroll taxes paid by their employers. Results reported include the marginal and average tax burden for eight different family types.

Methodological information is available for Personal income tax systems, Compulsory social security contributions to schemes operated within the government sector, Universal cash transfers as well as recent changes in the tax/benefit system. The methodology also includes the parameter values and tax equations underlying the data.

Ireland 2016

The tax/benefit position of single persons

	Wage level (per cent of average wage)	67	100	167	67
	Number of children	none	none	none	2
1.	**Gross wage earnings**	23 846	35 592	59 438	23 846
2.	**Standard tax allowances**	0	0	0	0
3.	**Tax credits or cash transfers included in taxable income**	0	0	0	0
4.	**Central government taxable income (1 - 2 + 3)**	23 846	35 592	59 438	23 846
5.	**Central government income tax liability (exclusive of tax credits)**	4 769	7 477	17 015	4 769
6.	**Tax credits**				
	Basic credit	1 650	1 650	1 650	1 650
	Single, head of family	0	0	0	1 650
	Children				
	Other	1 650	1 650	1 650	1 650
	Total	3 300	3 300	3 300	4 950
7.	**Central government income tax finally paid (5-6)**	2 074	5 427	16 277	605
8.	**State and local taxes**	0	0	0	0
9.	**Employees' compulsory social security contributions**				
	Gross earnings	954	1 424	2 378	954
	Taxable income				
	Total	954	1 424	2 378	954
10.	**Total payments to general government (7 + 8 + 9)**	3 028	6 851	18 655	1 558
11.	**Cash transfers from general government**				
	For head of family	0	0	0	5 722
	For two children	0	0	0	3 360
	Total	0	0	0	9 082
12.	**Take-home pay (1-10+11)**	20 819	28 741	40 783	31 370
13.	**Employer's compulsory social security contributions**	2 563	3 826	6 390	2 563
14.	**Average rates**				
	Income tax	8.7%	15.2%	27.4%	2.5%
	Employees' social security contributions	4.0%	4.0%	4.0%	4.0%
	Total payments less cash transfers	12.7%	19.2%	31.4%	-31.5%
	Total tax wedge including employer's social security contributions	21.2%	27.1%	38.0%	-18.8%
15.	**Marginal rates**				
	Total payments less cash transfers: Principal earner	29.5%	49.5%	49.5%	63.8%
	Total payments less cash transfers: Spouse	n.a.	n.a.	n.a.	n.a.
	Total tax wedge: Principal earner	36.3%	54.4%	54.4%	67.3%
	Total tax wedge: Spouse	n.a.	n.a.	n.a.	n.a.

112

Ireland 2016

The tax/benefit position of married couples

	Wage level (per cent of average wage)	100-0	100-33	100-67	100-33
	Number of children	2	2	2	none
1.	**Gross wage earnings**	35 592	47 337	59 438	47 337
2.	**Standard tax allowances**	0	0	0	0
3.	**Tax credits or cash transfers included in taxable income**	0	0	0	0
4.	**Central government taxable income (1 - 2 + 3)**	35 592	47 337	59 438	47 337
5.	**Central government income tax liability (exclusive of tax credits)**	7 118	9 467	11 888	9 467
6.	**Tax credits**				
	Basic credit	3 300	3 300	3 300	3 300
	Single, head of family	0	0	0	0
	Children				
	Other	2 650	3 300	3 300	3 300
	Total	5 950	6 600	6 600	6 600
7.	**Central government income tax finally paid (5-6)**	2 419	4 118	7 143	4 118
8.	**State and local taxes**	0	0	0	0
9.	**Employees' compulsory social security contributions**				
	Gross earnings	1 424	1 424	2 378	1 424
	Taxable income				
	Total	1 424	1 424	2 378	1 424
10.	**Total payments to general government (7 + 8 + 9)**	3 843	5 542	9 520	5 542
11.	**Cash transfers from general government**				
	For head of family	1 040	0	0	0
	For two children	3 360	3 360	3 360	0
	Total	4 400	3 360	3 360	0
12.	**Take-home pay (1-10+11)**	36 149	45 155	53 278	41 795
13.	**Employer's compulsory social security contributions**	3 826	4 824	6 390	4 824
14.	**Average rates**				
	Income tax	6.8%	8.7%	12.0%	8.7%
	Employees' social security contributions	4.0%	3.0%	4.0%	3.0%
	Total payments less cash transfers	-1.6%	4.6%	10.4%	11.7%
	Total tax wedge including employer's social security contributions	8.3%	13.4%	19.1%	19.9%
15.	**Marginal rates**				
	Total payments less cash transfers: Principal earner	29.5%	29.5%	29.5%	29.5%
	Total payments less cash transfers: Spouse	23.3%	20.0%	29.5%	20.0%
	Total tax wedge: Principal earner	36.3%	36.3%	36.3%	36.3%
	Total tax wedge: Spouse	29.3%	26.3%	36.3%	26.3%

112

The national currency is the Euro (EUR). In 2016, EUR 0.90 was equal to USD 1. In that year, the average worker earned EUR 35 592 (Secretariat estimate).

1. Personal income tax systems

1.1. *Central/federal government income taxes*

1.1.1. *Tax unit*

Tax is levied on the combined income of both spouses. Either spouse may, however, opt for separate assessment, in which case the tax payable by both spouses must be the same as would be payable under joint taxation. A further option allows either spouse to opt for assessment as single persons in which case they are treated as separate units. The calculations presented in this Report are based on family taxation.

1.1.2. *Tax credits*

1.1.2.1. Standard reliefs:

- *Basic reliefs:* The single person's credit is EUR 1 650 per year.
- *Standard marital status reliefs:* The married person's credit is EUR 3 300 per year (i.e. twice the basic credit of EUR 1 650).
- *Employee credit:* With the exception of certain company directors and their spouses and the spouses of partners in partnership cases, all employees, including (subject to certain conditions) children who are full-time employees in the business of their parents, are entitled to an employee credit of EUR 1 650.
- *Earned Income credit:* Individuals in receipt of earned income are entitled to an earned income credit of EUR 550 for 2016 et seq. Note: The combined employee credit and earned income credit is limited to EUR 1 650.
- *One-Parent Family credit:* The single parent family credit is EUR 1 650.

1.1.2.2. Main non-standard tax reliefs applicable to an AW

- *Interest on qualifying loans:* This relief can no longer be claimed by new applicants but those who had claimed prior to 2012 are still eligible for relief up to 2017 inclusive. The relief varies between 25% and 15% of the following limits.

	First time mortgage holders	Other mortgage holders
Married couple	• EUR 20 000	• EUR 6 000
Widowed person	• EUR 20 000	• EUR 6 000
Single person	• EUR 10 000	• EUR 6 000

- *Medical Insurance:* Relief at the taxpayer's standard rate of tax is available for taxpayers who make a payment to an authorised insurer under a contract which provides for the payment of medical expenses resulting from sickness of the person, his wife, child or other dependants. The maximum relief is EUR 1 000 in respect of an adult and EUR 500 in respect of a child. This *relief is now granted at source and is paid to the insurance provider.*

- *Work-related Expenses:* These are relieved to the extent that they are wholly, exclusively and necessarily incurred in the performance of the duties of an employment.
- *Home Carers Allowance:* This is a tax credit of EUR 1 000 for families where one spouse works at home to care for children, the aged or incapacitated persons, where the carer spouse's income does not exceed EUR 7 199. A reduced measure of relief is granted for income between EUR 7 200 and EUR 9 200: if the income exceeds EUR 7 200 the tax credit is reduced by one half of the income of the Home Carer that exceeds this limit. This credit and the increased standard rate tax band for two income couples (see tax schedule below) are mutually exclusive but the person may opt for whichever is the more beneficial. If the Home Carer earns income of up to EUR 7 200 in his/her own right for the tax year, the full tax credit may be claimed. For the purposes of this tax credit, income means any taxable income such as income from a part-time job, dividends, etc. but does not include the Carer's Allowance payable by the Department of Social Protection.

1.1.3. *Tax schedule*

Band of taxable Income (EUR)				Rate (%)
Single/Widow(er)	Married couple (one income)	Married couple (two incomes)	One-parent families	
Up to 33 800	Up to 42 800	Up to the lesser of: 67 600; 42 800 plus the amount of the lowest income	37 800	20
Balance	Balance	Balance	Balance	40

1.1.4. *Low income exemption and marginal relief tax*

Where total income of an individual aged 65 and over is less than or equal to the income exemption limit that income is exempt from tax.

Exemption limits:

Single/Widowed	EUR 17 000
Married	EUR 34 000

The exemption limits may be increased in respect of children, as follows:

One or two children (each)	EUR 585
Subsequent children	EUR 830

The marginal relief rate of tax applies where liability to tax at the marginal relief rate is less than that which would be chargeable under the normal tax schedule and where total income is less than twice the relevant exemption limit, otherwise tax is charged under the normal tax schedule.

Marginal relief tax is charged, where applicable, at a rate of 40% on the difference between total income and the relevant exemption limit.

1.1.5. *Universal Social Charge (USC)*

The USC is charged on an individualised basis on gross income at 1% on income up to and including EUR 12 012, at 3% for income in excess of EUR 12 012 but not greater than EUR 18 668, at 5.5% for income in excess of EUR 18 668 but not greater than EUR 70 044, and at 8% above that level. The lower exemption threshold has been increased from EUR 12 012 to EUR 13 000.The USC does not apply to social welfare payments, including contributory and non-contributory social welfare State pensions.

USC rates for individuals whose total income does not exceed EUR 60 000 and who are a) aged 70 years and over or b) who hold FULL medical cards: The 33% rate applies to all income over EUR 12 012.

There is a surcharge of 3% on individuals who have income from self-employment that exceeds EUR 100 000 in a year.

1.2. *State and local income taxes*

No State or local income taxes exist in Ireland.

2. Compulsory social security contributions to schemes operated within the government sector

2.1. *Employees' contributions*

Contributions are payable at a rate of 4 percent of an employee's gross earnings less allowable superannuation contributions. No distinction is made by marital status or sex. Those earning less than EUR 352 per week are exempt. The following is a breakdown of the 2016 rate of contribution together with ceilings where applicable:

Description	Rate	Threshold (EUR)	Ceiling (EUR)
Pension and social insurance	4.00	352 per week	

2.2. *Employers' contributions*

Like employees' contributions, employers' contributions are payable as a percentage of gross employee earnings less allowable superannuation contributions. The following is a breakdown of the 2016 rate of contribution:

Description	Rate %
Occupational injuries	0.50
Redundancy contribution	0.40
Pension and social insurance	9.85
TOTAL	10.75

The employers' contribution is reduced from 10.75% to 8.5% in respect of employees earning less than EUR 376 per week.

3. Universal cash transfers

3.1. *Transfers related to marital status*

None.

3.2. *Transfers for dependent children*

These are payable to all children under the age of 16 (or under 18 years, if the child is undergoing full-time education by day or is incapacitated and likely to remain so for a prolonged period). These payments do not depend on any insurance or on the means of the claimant. Entitlements to higher rate for the third and subsequent child are being phased out over two years. The amounts payable in 2016 are as follows:

Period	Monthly rate per child	
January 2016 to December 2016	First to second child: EUR 140.00	Subsequent children: EUR 140.00

3.3. *Transfers for low income families*

A non-taxable family income supplement is payable to low income families where either the principal earner and/or the spouse are in full-time employment. Full-time employment is defined as working nineteen hours per week or more. The hours worked by the principal and the spouse can be aggregated for the purposes of this definition. When calculating income for the purposes of the relief superannuation payments, social welfare payments, tax payments, health and employment and training levies are all subtracted to arrive at disposable income.

The level of payment is dependent on the amount of family income and the number of children. The supplement payable is 60% of the difference between the family income and the income limit applicable to the family. A minimum of EUR 20 per week is payable to eligible families. No supplement is payable to families with income in excess of the relevant income limit.

The income limit for a family with two children in 2016 is EUR 612 per week.

One Parent Family Payment: This new non-taxable payment is available for men and women who for a variety of reasons are bringing up a child or children without the support of a partner. The payment which is means tested is payable in full where the person's earnings does not exceed EUR 7 618. Where earnings are between EUR 7 618 and EUR 22 100 a reduced payment is received. The amount of the full payment for 2016 is EUR 6 552 plus EUR 1 550 for each child. Because of the complex means testing system this type of person is excluded from the AW examples.

4. Other main changes in tax/benefit system since 2015

4.1. *Earned Income credit*

Individuals in receipt of earned income are entitled to an earned income credit of EUR 550 for 2016 et seq. Note: The combined employee credit and earned income credit is limited to EUR 1 650.

5. Memorandum items

5.1. *Employer contributions to private social security arrangements*

Information not available, although such schemes do exist.

2016 parameter values

Average earnings/yr	Ave_earn	35 592	Secretariat estimate
Tax allowances			
Tax Credits	Basic_al_at_standardrate	1 650	
	Married_al_at_standardrate	1 650	
	Empl_al_at_standardrate	1 650	
	Singleparent_at_standardrate	1 650	
	Carers_allow	1 000	
	Carers_thrsh1	7 200	
	Carers_thrsh2	9 200	
	Carers_taper_rt	0.5	
Exemption amount	Single_ex	0	
	Married_ex	0	
	Child_ex	0	
	Child_ex_3	0	
Marginal relief limit	Single_MR	0	
	Married_MR	0	
	Child_MR	0	
	Child_MR_3	0	
Marginal relief	marg_rel_rate	0.4	
Income tax	Single_sch	0.2	33 800
		0.4	
	Single_sch_child	0.2	37 800
		0.4	
	Married_sch_oneinc	0.2	42 800
		0.4	
	Married_sch_twoinc	0.2	67 600
		0.4	
Universal Social Charge	USC	0.01	12 012
		0.03	18 668
		0.055	70 044
		0.08	
	USC_sch_med_card	0.01	12 012
		0.03	
	USC threshold	13 000	
Maximum increase in first band	Band_increase_lim	27 400	
Social security contributions	SSC_thresh	18 304	
Employees	pension_rate	0.04	
	pension_ceil	Limit Abolished	
	Non_cum_Allc	0	
Employers	Empr_rate	0.1075	
	Empr_lower_rate	0.085	
	Empr_thrsh	19 552	
Child benefit	Empr_ceil	Limit Abolished	
	Ch_ben	1 680	
Family income supplement	Ch_ben_3	1 680	
	FIS_pay_limit	31 824	
	FIS_min	1 040	
Medical card	FIS_rate	0.6	
	single_med_card	9 568	
	married_med_card	13 858	
	Child_add_med_card	1 976	

2016 tax equations

The equations for the Irish system in 2016 are mostly on a family basis using mainly a tax credit system for the first time. But social security contributions are calculated separately for each spouse. This is shown by the Range indicator in the table below.

The functions which are used in the equations (Taper, MIN, Tax etc) are described in the technical note about tax equations. Variable names are defined in the table of parameters above, within the equations table, or are the standard variables "married" and "children". A reference to a variable with the affix "_total" indicates the sum of the relevant variable values for the principal and spouse. And the affixes "_princ" and "_spouse" indicate the value for the principal and spouse, respectively. Equations for a single person are as shown for the principal, with "_spouse" values taken as 0.

	Line in country table and intermediate steps	Variable name	Range	Equation
1.	Earnings	earn		
2.	Allowances:			(provided at standard rate (tax credit equivalent))
3.	Credits in taxable income	taxbl_cr	J	0
4.	Taxable income	tax_inc	J	earn
	New carers allowance (provided as a tax credit)	career_allow		IF((Married*Children)>0, IF(earn_spouse<=Carers_thrsh1, Carers_allow, IF(earn_spouse>Carers_thrsh2, 0, Positive (Carers_allow-Carers_taper_rt*(earn_spouse-Carers_thrsh1)))), 0)
	Preliminary Tax Liable (including carers allowance)	tax_prel	J	IF(Married=0, IF(Children=0, Tax(tax_inc, Single_sch), Tax(tax_inc, Single_sch_child)), IF(AB7=0, Tax(tax_inc, Married_sch_oneinc)-AG7, Tax(earn_principal+Positive(earn_spouse-Band_increase_lim), Married_sch_oneinc)+Tax(MIN(earn_spouse, Band_increase_lim), Married_sch_oneinc)))
5.	Tax before credits (but including carers allowance)	_tax_excl	J	IF((Married*earn_spouse)>0, MINA(tax_prel, (Tax(tax_inc, Married_sch_oneinc)-career_allow)), tax_prel)
	Universal social charge	USG	J	IF(earn>USC_threshold,IF(med_crd_fac=1,Tax(earn,USC_sch),Tax(earn,USC_sch_med_card)),0)
6.	Tax credits :	basic_cr	J	Basic_al_at_standardrate+(Married*Married_al_at_standardrate)
		single_par_cr		IF(Married=0, IF(Children>0, Singleparent_at_standardrate, 0), 0)
		other_cr		Empl_al_at_standardrate+ (IF(earn_spouse>0, Empl_al_at_standardrate, 0))
		tax_cr		basic_cr+single_par_cr+other_cr
	Exemption amount	exemp_amt	J	Single_ex+Married*Married_ex+Child_ex*MIN(2, Children)+(Children>2)*(Children-2)*Child_ex_3
	Marginal relief limit	MRL	J	Single_MR+Married*Married_MR+Child_MR*MIN(2, Children)+(Children>2)*(Children-2)*Child_MR_3
7.	Net tax	CG_tax	J	If(earn_total<=MRL, MIN(marg_rel_rate*positive(earn_total-exem_amt), positive(_tax_excl-tax_cr)), positive(_tax_excl-tax_cr))+USG
8.	State and local taxes	local_tax	J	0
	Employees' soc security			
	weekly allowance	weekly_allce	B	IF(earn=0,0,MINA(Non_cum_Allc,earn))
	Medical card factor	Med_crd_fac	J	(single_med_card+Married*(married_med_card-single_med_card)+child_add_med_card*Children<earn_princ+earn_spouse)
	employees' soc security	SSC	B	IF(earn>SSC_thresh, pension_rate*Positive(earn-weekly_allce), 0)
11.	Cash transfers			
		Child_benefit	J	Children*Ch_ben+(Children>2)*(Children-2)*(Ch_ben_3-Ch_ben)
		FIS	J	(Children>0)*IF((earn-_tax-SSC)<=FIS_pay_limit , MAXA((FIS_pay_limit-(earn-_tax-SSC))*FIS_rate, FIS_min), 0)
	Total cash transfers	cash_trans		Child_benefit+FIS
13.	Employer's soc security	SSC_empr	B	IF(earn<=Empr_thrsh, Empr_lower_rate, Empr_rate)* MIN(earn, Empr_ceil)

Key to range of equation:

B calculated separately for both principal earner and spouse

P calculated for principal only (value taken as 0 for spouse calculation)

J calculated once only on a joint basis

© OECD 2017

Israel

This chapter includes data on the income taxes paid by workers, their social security contributions, the family benefits they receive in the form of cash transfers as well as the social security contributions and payroll taxes paid by their employers. Results reported include the marginal and average tax burden for eight different family types.

Methodological information is available for Personal income tax systems, Compulsory social security contributions to schemes operated within the government sector, Universal cash transfers as well as recent changes in the tax/benefit system. The methodology also includes the parameter values and tax equations underlying the data.

The statistical data for Israel are supplied by and under the responsibility of the relevant Israeli authorities. The use of such data by the OECD is without prejudice to the status of the Golan Heights, East Jerusalem and Israeli settlements in the West Bank under the terms of international law.

Israel 2016

The tax/benefit position of single persons

	Wage level (per cent of average wage)	67	100	167	67
	Number of children	none	none	none	2
1.	**Gross wage earnings**	95 306	142 247	237 553	95 306
2.	**Standard tax allowances**				
	Basic allowance				
	Married or head of family				
	Dependent children				
	Deduction for social security contributions and income taxes				
	Work-related expenses				
	Other				
	Total	0	0	0	0
3.	**Tax credits or cash transfers included in taxable income**	0	0	0	0
4.	**Central government taxable income (1 - 2 + 3)**	95 306	142 247	237 553	95 306
5.	**Central government income tax liability (exclusive of tax credits)**	10 837	19 874	47 011	10 837
6.	**Tax credits**				
	Basic credit	5 832	5 832	5 832	7 128
	Married or head of family	0	0	0	2 592
	Children	0	0	0	5 184
	EITC	0	0	0	3 305
	Unused wastable tax credits	0	0	0	4 067
	Total	5 832	5 832	5 832	18 209
7.	**Central government income tax finally paid (5-6)**	5 005	14 042	41 179	- 3 305
8.	**State and local taxes**	0	0	0	0
9.	**Employees' compulsory social security contributions**				
	Gross earnings	5 645	11 278	22 715	5 645
	Taxable income				
	Total	5 645	11 278	22 715	5 645
10.	**Total payments to general government (7 + 8 + 9)**	10 650	25 320	63 894	2 340
11.	**Cash transfers from general government**				
	For head of family				
	For two children	0	0	0	7 170
	Total	0	0	0	7 170
12.	**Take-home pay (1-10+11)**	84 655	116 928	173 659	100 135
13.	**Employer's compulsory social security contributions**	4 388	7 909	15 057	4 388
14.	**Average rates**				
	Income tax	5.3%	9.9%	17.3%	-3.5%
	Employees' social security contributions	5.9%	7.9%	9.6%	5.9%
	Total payments less cash transfers	11.2%	17.8%	26.9%	-5.1%
	Total tax wedge including employer's social security contributions	15.1%	22.1%	31.3%	-0.4%
15.	**Marginal rates**				
	Total payments less cash transfers: Principal earner	26.0%	33.0%	43.0%	29.4%
	Total payments less cash transfers: Spouse	n.a.	n.a.	n.a.	n.a.
	Total tax wedge: Principal earner	31.2%	37.7%	47.0%	34.3%
	Total tax wedge: Spouse	n.a.	n.a.	n.a.	n.a.

Israel 2016

The tax/benefit position of married couples

	Wage level (per cent of average wage)	100-0	100-33	100-67	100-33
	Number of children	2	2	2	none
1.	**Gross wage earnings**	142 247	189 189	237 553	189 189
2.	**Standard tax allowances**				
	Basic allowance				
	Married or head of family				
	Dependent children				
	Deduction for social security contributions and income taxes				
	Work-related expenses				
	Other				
	Total	0	0	0	0
3.	**Tax credits or cash transfers included in taxable income**	0	0	0	0
4.	**Central government taxable income (1 - 2 + 3)**	142 247	189 189	237 553	189 189
5.	**Central government income tax liability (exclusive of tax credits)**	19 874	24 568	30 711	24 568
6.	**Tax credits**				
	Basic credit	5 832	12 960	12 960	12 960
	Married or head of family	0	0	0	0
	Children	0	5 184	5 184	0
	EITC	0	0	0	0
	Unused wastable tax credits	0	7 618	1 475	2 434
	Total	5 832	18 144	18 144	12 960
7.	**Central government income tax finally paid (5-6)**	14 042	14 042	14 042	14 042
8.	**State and local taxes**	0	0	0	0
9.	**Employees' compulsory social security contributions**				
	Gross earnings	11 278	12 921	16 923	12 921
	Taxable income				
	Total	11 278	12 921	16 923	12 921
10.	**Total payments to general government (7 + 8 + 9)**	25 320	26 963	30 965	26 963
11.	**Cash transfers from general government**				
	For head of family				
	For two children	4 056	4 056	4 056	0
	Total	4 056	4 056	4 056	0
12.	**Take-home pay (1-10+11)**	120 984	166 282	210 644	162 226
13.	**Employer's compulsory social security contributions**	7 909	9 529	12 297	9 529
14.	**Average rates**				
	Income tax	9.9%	7.4%	5.9%	7.4%
	Employees' social security contributions	7.9%	6.8%	7.1%	6.8%
	Total payments less cash transfers	14.9%	12.1%	11.3%	14.3%
	Total tax wedge including employer's social security contributions	19.4%	16.3%	15.7%	18.4%
15.	**Marginal rates**				
	Total payments less cash transfers: Principal earner	33.0%	33.0%	33.0%	33.0%
	Total payments less cash transfers: Spouse	3.5%	3.5%	12.0%	3.5%
	Total tax wedge: Principal earner	37.7%	37.7%	37.7%	37.7%
	Total tax wedge: Spouse	6.7%	6.7%	18.1%	6.7%

The Israeli currency is the Israeli Shekel (ILS). In 2016, ILS 3.84 was equal to USD 1. In that year, the average worker in Israel earned ILS 142 247 (Secretariat estimate).

1. Personal income tax system

1.1. *Central government income tax*

1.1.1. *Tax unit*

In general, spouses are taxed separately on their earned income, subject to the condition that its sources are independent. The household is taxed jointly if their earned income is deemed to be interdependent. Until 2014, the conditions for interdependence involved situations where one spouse worked in a business which the other spouse either owned or had certain levels of capital or management/voting rights. Since 2014, spouses could still be taxed separately, even in cases where their earned income is deemed to be interdependent, if the labour of both spouses is needed to run the business and their income is commensurate to their effort.

1.1.2. *Tax allowances and credits*

1.1.2.1. Standard tax credits

The standard tax credits are given in the form of credit points subtracted from the tax liability. Each point is worth ILS 2 592 in 2016.

- *Basic credit*: Every resident taxpayer is entitled to 2.25 credit points (ILS 5 832 in 2016).
- *Additional credit for women*: Women are entitled to a further half credit point (ILS 1 296 in 2016).
- *Child credit*: Working mothers (and fathers in one parent families) with children aged under 18 are entitled to one additional credit point per child (ILS 2 592 in 2016). In 2012 this credit was increased to 2 credit points per child aged under 5 (ILS 5 184 in 2016). Since 2012, married working fathers with children aged under 2 are also entitled to 2 credit points per child.
- *Single parent credit:* Single parents (male or female) are entitled to one additional credit point (ILS 2 592 in 2016).

1.1.2.2. Non-standard tax credits applicable to income from employment

- Tax credits are awarded for contributions to approved pension schemes, up to a ceiling which varies according to the employee's circumstances.
- Employees living in certain development areas or in conflict zones receive credits as a percentage of their income up to ceiling. In 2016, a comprehensive reform was implemented, where the average credit was decreased but the number of beneficiaries more than doubled. In 2016 the credits range from 7% in the lowest category to 20% in the highest category with ceilings of ILS 132 000 and 241 080 respectively. About 20% of the population lives in these areas.

- New immigrants are entitled to three additional credit points in their first eighteen months in Israel, two additional credit points in the following year, and one credit point in the year after.
- Discharged soldiers receive 2 credit points for three years after the completion of at least 23 months of service or 1 credit point for a shorter service.
- Graduates of academic studies receive 1 credit point for three years after the completion of a B.A. degree (or after the completion of 1 700 study hours that led to a professional certificate) and 0.5 credit point for two years after the completion of a M.A. degree.

1.1.3. *Tax schedule*

The tax schedule for earned income in 2016 is as follows:

Taxable income (ILS)	Tax rate (%)
0- 62 640	10
62 640-107 040	14
107 040-166 320	21
166 320-237 600	31
237 600-496 920	34
496 920-803 920	48
Above 803 920	50

1.2. *Regional and local income tax*

There are no regional or local income taxes.

2. Compulsory social security insurance system

Social security contributions are made up of a combination of those for National Insurance and Health Insurance. The tax rates paid by employees and employers are applied in two brackets:

- A reduced rate for income up to a level of 60% of the average wage per employee post (ILS 5 678 per month in 2016).
- A full rate for income exceeding 60% of the average wage per employee post and up to a level of around 5 times the average wage per employee post (ILS 43 240 per month in 2016).

2.1. *Employees' contributions*

The taxable base for social security insurance contributions paid by employees is the total amount of the gross wage or salary including fringe benefits. The assessment period is the calendar month. The effective employees' contribution rates in 2016 are as follows:

Insurance branch	Full rate contribution (%)	Reduced rate contribution (%)
Total for National Insurance branches	7.00	0.40
Health	5.00	3.10
Total contributions	12.00	3.50

2.2. *Employers' contributions*

Social security insurance contributions are also paid by employers on behalf of their employees. These relate to National Insurance only – employers do not pay any contributions for health insurance.

The employers' contribution rates in 2016 are as follows:

Insurance branch	Full rate contribution (%)	Reduced rate contribution (%)
Total for National Insurance branches	7.50	3.45
Health	-	-
Total contributions	7.50	3.45

3. Payroll taxes

The following payroll taxes exist in Israel but neither of them is included in the modelling as they have limited coverage:

- Wage tax on the non-profit institutions: the VAT law imposes a 7.5% on the wage-bill on the non-profit sector including Government,
- Wage tax on the financial institutions: the VAT law also imposes a 17.00% tax on the wage-bill of the financial institutions.

4. Universal cash transfers

4.1. *Transfers related to marital status*

None.

4.2. *Transfers for dependent children*

A monthly child allowance is paid to the parent (usually the mother) of unmarried children aged up to 18. The amount of the entitlement for each child depends on the date of birth of the child. Between August 2003 and June 2009, all children born after 1 June 2003 received the same benefit as the first child. But, according to the Coalition agreement signed in March 2009, the benefits for the second, third and fourth child (including those born after June 2003) were increased gradually over a period of four years (i.e. from 2009 to 2012). In August 2013 the allowance for all children born after June 2003 were decreased to ILS 140 per month per child.

In December 2015 (retroactively from May 2015) the allowance for all children were increased.

In 2016 the monthly payments per child are shown in the following table. The 'average' figure is used in the modelling.

	Children born before 1 June 2003	Children born on or after 1 June 2003
First child	150	150
Second child	188	188
Third child	188	188
Fourth child	336	188
Fifth child and above	354	150

Moreover, the government will open a closed saving account for each child and deposit ILS 50 per child per month, starting with May 2015. The savings will be liquid only at the age of 18. However, the actual deposit for the period May 2015-December 2016 will be only delivered in 36 equal instalments in January 2017-December 2019. This element is not included in the Taxing Wages modelling for 2016.

In addition a Study Grant is paid to lone parents with children aged 6 to 14. The grant is paid in one instalment, usually in September at the beginning of the school year. In 2016, the rates of grant per child were ILS 1 557 and ILS 865 respectively for children aged 6-11 and 12-14.

5. Main changes in the tax and benefit systems since 2002

- There has been a policy of gradually reducing the level of personal income taxes since 2003. This policy was expected to continue till 2016 but came to an end in 2012 with the top tax bracket increasing from 45% to 48% although the rate of one middle income tax bracket was further decreased from 23% to 21%. The rates were further increased in 2013. In 2013 a surtax of 2% was imposed on total income above ILS 811 560, effectively increasing the top marginal rate to 50%. In 2013 the value of some tax brackets weren't fully indexed to the CPI and even suffered a nominal decrease. In 2014 the value of all tax brackets and of the "credit point" weren't indexed to the CPI.
- The full contribution rate for employee social security contributions was increased gradually from 9.7% in 2002 to 12% in 2006. The reduced contribution rate was lowered from 5.76% in 2002 to 3.5% in 2006. The upper threshold for contributions was removed in July 2002 but re-instated one year later. In August 2009, as a temporary measure until December 2011, it was increased to 10 times the average wage per employee post until December 2010 and to 9 times the average wage per employed post until December 2011.
- Prior to July 2005, there was only one contribution rate for employer social security contributions and this was set at 5.93% between July 2002 and June 2005. The upper threshold for contributions was removed in July 2002 but was re-instated one year later. The current system of two tax brackets was introduced in July 2005 with a reduced contribution rate of 5.33% and a full rate of 5.68%. There has been a lowering of rates in each year between 2006 and 2009. In August 2009, as a temporary measure until March 2011, the reduced rate was increased from 3.45% to 3.85%. In April 2011 the regular rate was increased to 5.9%. It was increased again to 6.5% in January 2013, 6.75% in January 2014, 7.25% in January 2015 and 7.5% in January 2016.
- The Employers tax on wage bill of the non-profit sector excluding Government was abolished in 2008.
- In the period between August 2003 and June 2009, all children that were born on or after 1 June 2003 received the same level of benefit payment as the first child. The 2009 Coalition agreement introduced a gradual increase in the benefit payments for the second, third and fourth children in all families (including those where children were born after June 2003) over a period of four years from July 2009 to Apr 2012. In August 2013 the allowance for all children born after June 2003 was decreased to ILS 140 per month per child. In December 2015 (retroactively from May 2015) the allowance for all children were increased.

6. Memorandum items

6.1. *Average gross annual wage earnings calculation*

The average wage figures represent the amount earned for a full time post by employees working 35 hours per week or more. Until 2011 the AW data came from a combination of 2 sources – the income and expenditure survey and the labour force survey. Since 2012 the data come exclusively from the income and expenditure survey as the labour force survey has no more data on income. The Central Bureau of Statistics has now computed a new AW series based exclusively on the income and expenditure survey back from 2000.

The 2015 and 2016 data used in the modelling are estimates.

As to the economic classification, until 2012, Israel used a modified version of ISIC 3 where the B-I industries (see Table below) are a very close equivalent of C-K industries in ISIC 3.1. Israel's Central Bureau of Statistics adopted ISIC 4 in 2012 and since 2013 the Average Wage used in the modelling is based on ISIC 4.

A	Agriculture.
B	Manufacturing.
C	Electricity and water supply.
D	Construction (building and civil engineering projects).
E	Wholesale and retail trade and repairs.
F	Accommodation services and restaurants
G	Transport, storage and communication.
H	Banking, insurance and other financial institutions.
I	Business activities.
J	Public administration.
K	Education.
L	Health, welfare and social work services.
M	Community, social, personal and other services.

6.2. *Employer contributions to private pension*

Until 2007 employers were not legally obliged to pay into a pension plan for their employees. Pension rights were guaranteed in collective agreements that covered less than half of the labour force. About one million employees in Israel had no pension arrangement (mainly those earning a relatively low wage, temporary workers and those working for subcontractors).

In 2008, a compulsory employment pension was introduced for employees with a period of employment of at least 6 months. The minimum rate of contributions in January 2016 was 17.5% of the employee's salary (up to the level of the average wage of ILS 9 464 per month) and will be increased to 18.0% in July 2016 and 18/5% in January 2017. The average rate, used in the 2016 modelling, is 17.75%, about one third to be paid by the employee and two thirds by the employer.

6.3. *Earned income tax credit*

A non-wastable earned income tax credit was implemented in 2008 in selected geographical areas of Israel covering 15% of the population. Entitlement to this credit is established based on earnings in the previous year. The tax credit was extended to all areas of Israel in 2012 (based on the earnings in 2011 and therefore we already included it in the 2011 version of the model). For mothers of children up to the age of 2 and for single parents the full coverage started in 2011 (based on earnings in 2010).

Under the law, workers aged 23 or more who are parents of one or two children aged less than 18 (or workers aged 55 or more even without children), and earn at least ILS 2 050 per month (about 43% of the minimum wage) but not more than ILS 6 170 per month are eligible for a monthly increment of up to ILS 330. The corresponding figure for a family with 3 or more children is ILS 470.

Since 2016, single parents are eligible for the EITC for a wider income range – from ILS 2 050 per month to ILS 9 360 per month (for a single parents of 1-2 children) or ILS 11 400 per month (for a single parents of 3 or more children).

Since 2013 (based on earnings in 2012), these sums were increased by 50% for working mothers (and fathers in one-parent family). Families in which both parents work, and their joint income does not exceed ILS 11 860, are entitled to these benefits for each wage-earner. The grant is paid four times a year directly into the account of the eligible persons.

2016 parameter values

Average earnings/yr	Ave_earn	142 247	Secretariat estimate
Income tax	Tax_sch	0.10	62 640
		0.14	107 040
		0.21	196 320
		0.31	237 600
		0.34	496 920
		0.48	803 520
		0.50	
Employees SSC	SSC_sch	0.035	68 136
		0.12	518 880
		0	
Employers SSC	SSC_rate2	0.0345	68 136
		0.0750	518 880
		0.0000	
Child benefit	CB_firstchild	1 800	
	CB_secondchild	2 256	
	Studygrant_rate	1 557	
Wastable tax credits			
Basic element	WTC_Basic	5 832	
Lone parent	WTC_lone	2 592	
Parents/per child	WTC_Child	2 592	
Women	WTC_woman	1 296	
Negative Income tax			
Married with 1 or	NIT_sch1	0	24 600
2 children		0.161	42 708
		7.051	42 720
		0	56 880
		-0.23	74 040
Married with 3 or	NIT_sch2	0	24 600
more children		0.235	42 472
		0	42 720
		0	56 880
		-0.235	81 120
Single with 1 or	NIT_sch3	0	15 240
2 children		0.108	42 708
		2.788	42 720
		0	80 160
		-0.116	112 320
Single with 3 or	NIT_sch4	0	15 240
		0.155	42 337
		0	42 720
		0	89 520
		-0.116	136 800
	NIT_basic1	960	
	NIT_basic2	1 440	
	NIT_min	240	
	NIT_MinIncome1	24 600	
	NIT_MinIncome2	15 240	
	Nit_AddIncome1	17 040	
	Nit_AddIncome2	56 880	
	Nit_MaxIncome	142 320	
	NIT_Bonus	1.50	
Days in tax year	numdays	366	

2016 tax equations

	Line in country table and intermediate steps	Variable name	Range	Equation
1.	Earnings	earn		
2.	Allowances:	Tax_al	B	0
3.	Credits in taxable income	taxbl_cr	B	0
4.	CG taxable income	tax_inc	B	Earn
5.	CG tax before credits	CG_tax_excl	B	Tax(tax_inc, tax_sch)
6.	Tax credits (nonwastable):			
	Principal	tax_cr_princ	B	(earn>0)*(wtc_basic+(IF(married=0)*(children>0),wtc_woman+wtc_lone+(wtc_child*children))
	Spouse	tax_cr_spouse	B	(earn>0)*(wtc_basic+wtc_woman+(wtc_child*children))
	Tax credits (nonwastable)	NIT_princ	B	NIT=MAX(0,IF(Children=0,0,IF(Married=1,IF(Children<=2,NIT_basic1*(Princ_earnings>NIT_MinIncome1)+Tax(Princ_earnings,NIT_sch1),NIT_basic2*(Princ_earnings>NIT_MinIncome1)+Tax(Princ_earnings,NIT_sch2)),(IF(Children<=2,NIT_basic1*(Princ_earnings >NIT_MinIncome2)+Tax(Princ_earnings,NIT_sch3),NIT_basic2*(Princ_earnings >NIT_MinIncome2)+Tax(Princ_earnings,NIT_sch4)))))) NIT=+MAX(0,NIT+IF(Children=0,0,IF(Children<=2,-0.23,-0.235)) *MAX(0,+(Princ_earnings +Spouse_earnings)-NIT_MaxIncome-MIN(MAX(0, Princ_earnings -NIT_Addincome2),NIT_AddIncome1)-MIN(MAX(0,Spouse_earnings-NIT_Addincome2),NIT_AddIncome1))) NIT=IF(NIT<NIT_min,0,NIT)*IF(Married=1,1,NIT_Bonus)
		NIT_spouse	B	NIT=MAX(0,IF(Children=0,0,IF(Married=1,IF(Children<=2,NIT_basic1*(Spouse_earnings>NIT_MinIncome1)+Tax(Spouse_earnings,NIT_sch1),NIT_basic2*(Spouse_earnings>NIT_MinIncome1)+Tax(Spouse_earnings,NIT_sch2)),(IF(Children<=2,NIT_basic1*(Spouse_earnings>NIT_MinIncome2)+Tax(Spouse_earnings,NIT_sch3),NIT_basic2*(Spouse_earnings>NIT_MinIncome2)+Tax(Spouse_earnings,NIT_sch4)))))) NIT=+MAX(0,NIT+IF(Children=0,0,IF(Children<=2,-0.23,-0.235)) *MAX(0,+(Princ_earnings +Spouse_earnings)-NIT_MaxIncome-MIN(MAX(0, Princ_earnings -NIT_Addincome2),NIT_AddIncome1)-MIN(MAX(0,Spouse_earnings-NIT_Addincome2),NIT_AddIncome1))) NIT=IF(NIT<NIT_min,0,NIT)*NIT_Bonus
7.	CG tax	CG_tax	B	Positive(CG_tax_excl-tax_cr)-NIT
8.	State and local taxes	local_tax	B	0
9.	Employees' soc security	SSC	B	Tax(earn, SSC_sch)
11.	Cash transfers	cash_trans	J	IF(children=1,CB_firstchild,IF(Children=2,CB_firstchild+CB_secondchild)+(IF(married=0)*(children>0),Studygrant_rate*children)
13.	Employer's soc security	SSC_empr	B	Tax(earn, SSC_rate2)

Key to range of equation B calculated separately for both principal earner and spouse P calculated for principal only (value taken as 0 for spouse calculation) J calculated once only on a joint basis

© OECD 2017

Italy

This chapter includes data on the income taxes paid by workers, their social security contributions, the family benefits they receive in the form of cash transfers as well as the social security contributions and payroll taxes paid by their employers. Results reported include the marginal and average tax burden for eight different family types.

Methodological information is available for Personal income tax systems, Compulsory social security contributions to schemes operated within the government sector, Universal cash transfers as well as recent changes in the tax/benefit system. The methodology also includes the parameter values and tax equations underlying the data.

Italy 2016

The tax/benefit position of single persons

	Wage level (per cent of average wage)	67	100	167	67
	Number of children	none	none	none	2
1.	**Gross wage earnings**	20 530	30 642	51 172	20 530
2.	**Standard tax allowances**				
	Basic allowance				
	Married or head of family				
	Dependent children				
	Deduction for social security contributions and income taxes	1 948	2 908	4 907	1 948
	Work-related expenses				
	Other				
	Total	1 948	2 908	4 907	1 948
3.	**Tax credits or cash transfers included in taxable income**	0	0	0	0
4.	**Central government taxable income (1 - 2 + 3)**	18 582	27 734	46 265	18 582
5.	**Central government income tax liability (exclusive of tax credits)**	4 417	6 888	13 901	4 417
6.	**Tax credits**				
	Basic credit	1 403	990	316	1 403
	Married or head of family	0	0	0	0
	Children	0	0	0	1 579
	Other	960	0	0	960
	Total	2 363	990	316	3 942
7.	**Central government income tax finally paid (5-6)**	2 054	5 898	13 584	475
8.	**State and local taxes**	489	729	1 717	489
9.	**Employees' compulsory social security contributions**				
	Gross earnings	1 948	2 908	4 907	1 948
	Taxable income				
	Total	1 948	2 908	4 907	1 948
10.	**Total payments to general government (7 + 8 + 9)**	4 491	9 535	20 208	2 912
11.	**Cash transfers from general government**				
	For head of family				
	For two children	0	0	0	2 619
	Total	0	0	0	2 619
12.	**Take-home pay (1-10+11)**	16 039	21 106	30 964	20 237
13.	**Employer's compulsory social security contributions**	6 545	9 769	16 314	6 545
14.	**Average rates**				
	Income tax	12.4%	21.6%	29.9%	4.7%
	Employees' social security contributions	9.5%	9.5%	9.6%	9.5%
	Total payments less cash transfers	21.9%	31.1%	39.5%	1.4%
	Total tax wedge including employer's social security contributions	40.8%	47.8%	54.1%	25.3%
15.	**Marginal rates**				
	Total payments less cash transfers: Principal earner	40.4%	40.4%	51.5%	42.0%
	Total payments less cash transfers: Spouse	n.a.	n.a.	n.a.	n.a.
	Total tax wedge: Principal earner	54.8%	54.8%	63.2%	56.0%
	Total tax wedge: Spouse	n.a.	n.a.	n.a.	n.a.

Italy 2016

The tax/benefit position of married couples

		Wage level (per cent of average wage)	100-0	100-33	100-67	100-33
		Number of children	2	2	2	none
1.	**Gross wage earnings**		30 642	40 754	51 172	40 754
2.	**Standard tax allowances**					
	Basic allowance					
	Married or head of family					
	Dependent children					
	Deduction for social security contributions and income taxes		2 908	3 868	4 856	3 868
	Work-related expenses					
	Other					
		Total	2 908	3 868	4 856	3 868
3.	**Tax credits or cash transfers included in taxable income**		0	0	0	0
4.	**Central government taxable income (1 - 2 + 3)**		27 734	36 886	46 316	36 886
5.	**Central government income tax liability (exclusive of tax credits)**		6 888	8 993	11 305	8 993
6.	**Tax credits**					
	Basic credit		990	2 818	2 393	2 818
	Married or head of family		690	0	0	0
	Children		1 421	1 421	1 500	0
	Other		0	960	960	960
		Total	3 101	5 199	4 853	3 778
7.	**Central government income tax finally paid (5-6)**		3 787	3 794	6 452	5 215
8.	**State and local taxes**		729	888	1 218	888
9.	**Employees' compulsory social security contributions**					
	Gross earnings		2 908	3 868	4 856	3 868
	Taxable income					
		Total	2 908	3 868	4 856	3 868
10.	**Total payments to general government (7 + 8 + 9)**		7 424	8 549	12 527	9 970
11.	**Cash transfers from general government**					
	For head of family					
	For two children		1 579	927	847	0
		Total	1 579	927	847	0
12.	**Take-home pay (1-10+11)**		24 796	33 131	39 492	30 783
13.	**Employer's compulsory social security contributions**		9 769	12 992	16 314	12 992
14.	**Average rates**					
	Income tax		14.7%	11.5%	15.0%	15.0%
	Employees' social security contributions		9.5%	9.5%	9.5%	9.5%
	Total payments less cash transfers		19.1%	18.7%	22.8%	24.5%
	Total tax wedge including employer's social security contributions		38.6%	38.4%	41.5%	42.7%
15.	**Marginal rates**					
	Total payments less cash transfers: Principal earner		42.0%	42.0%	41.2%	40.4%
	Total payments less cash transfers: Spouse		17.6%	36.0%	41.2%	36.0%
	Total tax wedge: Principal earner		56.0%	56.0%	55.4%	54.8%
	Total tax wedge: Spouse		37.5%	51.4%	55.4%	51.4%

The national currency is the Euro (EUR). In 2016, EUR 0.90 was equal to USD 1. In that year the average worker earned EUR 30 642 (Secretariat estimate).

1. Personal income tax

1.1. *Central government income tax*

1.1.1. *Tax unit*

Spouses are taxed separately.

1.1.2. *Tax allowances and tax credits*

1.1.2.1. Tax allowances

- Social security contributions due by law

1.1.2.2. Tax credits

Italy increased the basic employee tax credit from EUR 1 840 to EUR 1 880 and as from 2014 introduced an additional refundable tax credit of EUR 960 for employees with income between EUR 8 146 and EUR 24 000, with a phase-out for income between EUR 24 000 and EUR 26 000.

Taxable income (EUR)	Fiscal bonus (EUR)
Up to 8 145	0
From 8 146 to 24 000	960
From 24 001 to 26 000	960*(26 000 – taxable income)/2 000
More than 26 000	0

- Standard tax credits (not refundable)

The PAYE tax credit is defined as a function of net income:

Taxable income (EUR)	PAYE tax credit (EUR)
Up to 8 000	1 880
From 8 001 to 28 000	Maximum tax credit + 902*(28 000 – taxable income)/20 000
From 28 001 to 55 000	Maximum tax credit*(55 000 – taxable income)/27 000
More than 55 000	0

The maximum value for the tax credit depends on the level of taxable income:

Level of taxable income (EUR)	Maximum tax credit (EUR)
From 8 001 to 15 000	978
From 15 001 to 23 000	978
From 23 001 to 24 000	978
From 24 001 to 25 000	978
From 24 001 to 26 000	978
From 26 001 to 27 700	978
From 27 701 to 28 000	978
From 28 001 to 55 000	978

- Tax credits for family dependents (not refundable)

The tax credits for family dependants, which have replaced the former tax allowances, are as follows:

Family tax credit (EUR)*	Amount (EUR)
Spouse	800 decreasing to 0 for net income over 80 000
Children	
Under three years of age	1 220 decreasing to 0 for net income over 95 000
Over three years of age	950 decreasing to 0 for net income over 95 000
Other dependent relatives	750 decreasing to 0 for net income over 80 000

* Tax credits are granted for family dependents earning less than EUR 2 840.51

The spouse tax credit is calculated as a function of net income:

Level of taxable income (EUR)	Amount of tax credit (EUR)
Up to 15 000	800-110*taxable income/15 000
From 15 001 to 29 000	690
From 29 001 to 29 200	700
From 29 201 to 34 700	710
From 34 701 to 35 000	720
From 35 001 to 35 100	710
From 35 101 to 35 200	700
From 35 201 to 40 000	690
From 40 001 to 80 000	690*(80 000-taxable income)/40 000
More than 80 000	0

The child tax credit is calculated as a function of net income:

- for families with only one child: 950*(95 000-taxable income)/95 000;
- for families with more than one child the amount of 95 000 is increased by 15 000 for each child other than the first, for every children (including the first one).

Families with more than 3 children receive an additional tax credit of EUR 200 per child.

A lone parent receives an actual tax credit for the first child equal to the maximum of the spouse tax credit and the child tax credit.

Tax credits for children have to be equally shared between the parents; different shares are no longer allowed.

If the spouse's tax liable net of the PAYE tax credit is less than his/her share (50%) in the child tax credit, the entire child tax credit is provided to the principal earner.

1.1.2.3. Main non-standard tax allowances and tax credits

- Other compulsory contributions;
- Periodical benefits allowed to the spouse fixed by judicial authority;
- Charitable donations to certain religious institutions (up to EUR 1 032.91);
- Medical and assistance expenses incurred by handicapped persons;
- Expenses to restore one's own residence at 50% for 2015 of full expenses up to EUR 96 000, apportioned into 10 annual allowances of the same amount;
- Expenses for energy requalification of buildings at 65% for 2015 of full expenses apportioned into 10 annual allowances of the same amount;
- Expenses for the replacement of covers, windows and shutters and for the installation of solar panels (only for hot water production) at 65% of full expenses (up to EUR 60 000).

For the following expenses, a tax credit of 19% of each incurred expense is allowed:

- Mortgage loan interest (up to EUR 4 000);
- Most medical expenses that exceed EUR 129.11;
- Payments to insurance funds up to EUR 1 291.14;
- Expenses to attend secondary school and university courses; in case such courses are private, the expenses allowed cannot exceed those foreseen for State courses;
- Expenses for nursery school (up to EUR 632 for each child);
- Rents paid by out of town students (up to EUR 2 633);
- Funeral charges up to EUR 1 549.37;
- Expenses for disabled persons;
- Donations to political parties (ranging from EUR 51.65 to EUR 103 291.38);
- Payments to foundations (up to EUR 2 065.83);
- Expenses related to sport activities for children between 5 and 18 years of age (up to EUR 210 per child).

1.1.3. *Tax schedule*

The following tax schedule is applied to taxable income:

Bracket (EUR)	Rate (%)
up to 15 000	23
over 15 000 up to 28 000	27
over 28 000 up to 55 000	38
over 55 000 up to 75 000	41
over 75 000	43

Decree-Law No. 138 of 13 August 2011 introduced the "Contributo di Solidarietà" for the 2011-13, (extended up to 2016), tax periods, that is a 3% "solidarity contribution" on the portion of income higher than EUR 300 000 (the amount paid is deductible from PIT base)"

1.2. *State and local taxes*

These surcharges are due only by taxpayers who pay individual income tax IRPEF (imposta sul reddito delle persone fisiche).

Regional surcharge tax

This surcharge tax has been introduced in 1997. The tax is levied by each region on resident taxpayers' total taxable income at a discretionary rate, which must fall within an established range. As from the year 2000 this range is 0.9%-1.4%.

In December 2011, with the DL 201/2011, the minimum state rate has been increased from 0.9% to 1.23%

The figure given in the 2016 parameter values table under the heading "Regional and local tax" includes the regional surcharge tax paid in the most representative city which is Rome (Lazio); the rate is 3.33% for taxable income bracket over EUR 15 000 and 1.73% for income under EUR 15 000. If the taxable income is under the threshold of EUR 35 000 the rate applicable to the total amount of taxable income is 1.73%.

Local surcharge tax

This surcharge tax has been introduced in 1999. The tax may be levied by each local government at an initial rate that cannot exceed 0.2%. If the tax is levied, the local government can increase the initial rate, on a yearly basis, up to a maximum of 0.5%. Each yearly increase cannot exceed 0.2%. As from 2012, municipalities can increase the rate up to 0.8. A 0.9 special rate can be introduced by Roma Capitale Local Government.

The figure given in the 2015 parameter values table under the heading "Regional and local tax" includes the local surcharge tax paid in the most representative city which is Rome; the rate is 0.9% in 2015.

Starting from 2011, exemption is provided to taxpayers whose total income consists of retirement income not exceeding EUR 8 000, income from land not exceeding EUR 185.92, and income from primary residence. As from 2015 the rate is not applied to taxpayers with income under EUR 12 000. The ordinary rate is applied if any one of these limits is passed.

The surcharge rates can be adjusted above the fixed roof because of the health care losses

2. Compulsory social security

2.1. Employee contributions

- Rate and ceiling
  - The average rate is 9.49% on earnings up to EUR 46 123;
  - The average rate is 10.49% on earnings over EUR 46 123 and up to EUR 100 324;
  - For earnings exceeding EUR 100 123, the employee pays a fixed amount given by (0.0949 × 46 123) + 0.1049 x (100 324-46 123).
- Distinction by marital status or sex
  - None.

2.2. Employer contributions

- Contributions equal 31.88% on earnings up to EUR 100 324. For earnings exceeding EUR 100 324, the employer pays a fixed amount given by 0.3188x 100 324.
- A General Government employer work-related accident insurance exists in Italy. It is compulsory for employers with employees and contract workers in activities involving the use of machinery and in risky activities as defined by the law. The standard premium

to be paid is calculated by applying to remuneration the rates linked to the activity in which the employee works. The rates that vary between 0 to about 13% are provided by a special classification that takes into account the different categories of risk between the various activities. It is not possible to provide a representative or average rate since the contribution rates vary depending on the industrial activities and also other factors of risk. Those contributions are not included in the Report.

3. Universal cash transfers

3.1. *Amount for spouse and for dependent children*

Cash transfers are granted for family income that is:

- composed of at least 70% wage and/or pension income;
- below a given threshold set by law each year.

Family income is the sum of the incomes of all individuals comprising the family.

Cash transfers are determined each year by INPS (Istituto Nazionale di Previdenza Sociale), the public body that collects and manages the social security contributions for dependent workers for the period beginning in July of that year (t) to June in the following year (t+1) and relate to family income earned in the previous year (t-1).

As such, the transfers granted in any given year t are determined by the family income in the previous two years. The following table provides a description of the calculations.

Transfer granted in year t	Relevant amounts as given in INPS tables
January-June	The amount of cash transfers is that given in the INPS table published in July t-1. The transfers are granted with reference to family income earned in year t-2.
July-December	The amount of cash transfers is that given in the INPS table published in July t. The transfers are granted with reference to family income earned in year t-1.

For the purposes of Taxing Wages, the cash transfers that are calculated represent those amounts that would be received by the family based on their incomes for that year even though these amounts would only begin to be paid in July of the following year.

4. Main changes

5. Memorandum item

5.1. *Identification of an AW*

The data refer to the annual earnings of average workers.

5.2. *Contributions by employers to private pension, health, etc. schemes*

In addition to the mandatory social security contributions employers may pay contributions to private pension schemes (currently about forty pension funds). Employer's contributions are included in the taxable income of the employee.

Employees may also choose to contribute to the pension funds with all or part of the retirement allowance that is otherwise withheld by the employers. In this case the employee can deduct from his taxable income an amount equal to twice the amount of the contribution paid to fund.

Employer's contributions to private health insurance schemes are not included in the taxable income of the employee up to the limit of EUR 3 615.20.

2016 parameter values

Average earnings/yr	Ave_earn	30 642	Secretariat estimate
Tax schedule	tax_sch	0.23	15 000.00
		0.27	28 000.00
		0.38	55 000.00
		0.41	75 000.00
		0.43	999 999 999.99
Sloidarity contribution	sol_tax	0.03	
	sol_inc_limit	300 000	
Tax credits			
Fiscal bonus	thre_min	8 146	
	thre_max	24 000	
	f_bonus	960	
Employment			
	emp_add	0	1 880.00
		8 000	978.00
		15 000	978.00
		23 000	978.00
		24 000	978.00
		25 000	978.00
		26 000	978.00
		27 700	978.00
		28 000	978.00
		55 000	0.00
Spouse	Spouse_cred	0	800.00
		15 000	690.00
		29 000	700.00
		29 200	710.00
		34 700	720.00
		35 000	710.00
		35 100	700.00
		35 200	690.00
		40 000	690.00
		80 000	0
limit	Sp_crd_lim	2 840.51	
Child credit	Child_credit	950	
Additional child credit	add_child	200	
Regional and local tax			
	reg_rt	0,0173	
	reg_rt_2	0,0333	
	Local_rt	0.009	
Social security contributions	SSC_sch	0.0949	46 123
		0.1049	100 324
		0.00	999 999 999.99
Employer contributions	Empr_sch	0.3188	100 324
		0.00	999 999 999.99
Cash transfers:			
family allowance schedule (t)			
married couple	trans_sch	Table is too long to be included	
single parent	Trans_sch_sp	Table is too long to be included	

2016 tax equations

The equations for the Italian system in 2016 are mostly repeated for each individual of a married couple. But the spouse credit is relevant only to the calculation for the principal earner and any child credit which the spouse is unable to use is transferred to the principal. This is shown by the Range indicator in the table below.

The functions which are used in the equations (Taper, MIN, Tax etc) are described in the technical note about tax equations. Variable names are defined in the table of parameters above, within the equations table, or are the standard variables "married" and "children". A reference to a variable with the affix "_total" indicates the sum of the relevant variable values for the principal and spouse. And the affixes "_princ" and "_spouse" indicate the value for the principal and spouse, respectively. Equations for a single person are as shown for the principal, with "_spouse" values taken as 0.

	Line in country table and intermediate steps	Variable name	Range	Equation
1.	Earnings	earn		
2.	Allowances:	tax_al	B	SSC
		Sol_tax	B	sol_tax*Positive(Gross-sol_inc_limit)
3.	Credits in taxable income	taxbl_cr	B	0
4.	CG taxable income	tax_inc	B	earn-tax_al1-sol_tax
5.	CG tax before credits	CG_tax_excl	B	Tax(tax_inc, tax_sch)
6.	Tax credits :			
	Employment credit	emp_cr_max	P	VLOOKUP(tax_inc, emp_add, 2))
		emp_cr_max_spouse	S	IF(tax_inc_spouse=0,0,(VLOOKUP(tax_inc_spouse,emp_add,2)))
		emp_cr	P	MIN(CG_tax_excl, IF(tax_inc<=8000,emp_cr_max, IF(tax_inc<=28000,emp_cr_max+902*(28000-tax_inc)/20000, IF(tax_inc>55000,emp_cr_max,emp_cr_max*(55000-tax_inc)/27000))))+
			S	MIN(CG_tax_excl_spouse, IF(tax_in_spousec<=8000,emp_cr_max_spouse, IF(tax_inc_spouse<=28000,emp_cr_max_spouse+902*(28000-tax_inc_spouse)/20000, IF(tax_inc_spouse>55000,emp_cr_max_spouse,emp_cr_max_spouse*(55000-tax_inc_spouse)/27000))))+
	Fiscal bonus	fiscal_b	B	IF(tax_inc<=thre_min,0,IF(tax_inc<=thre_max,f_bonus,IF(tax_inc<=26000,f_bonus*(26000-tax_inc)/2000)))
	Spouse credit	spouse_cr	P	IF(Married=1, IF(tax_inc_spouse>Sp_crd_lim,0, IF(tax_inc>80000,0, IF(tax_inc< 15000,800-110*tax_inc/15000, IF(tax_inc>40000,690*(80000-tax_inc)/40000, VLOOKUP(tax_inc,Spouse_cred,2))))),0)
	Child credit	child_cr_princ	P	IF(Children=0,0,IF(Married=1,(800*(95000-tax_inc)/95000+(Children-1)*800*(110000-tax_inc)/110000)*(1-child_crpct_spouse), MAX(800*(95000-tax_inc)/95000, IF(tax_inc>80000,0,IF(tax_inc<15000,800-110*tax_inc/15000, IF(tax_inc>40000,690*(80000-tax_inc)/40000, VLOOKUP(tax_inc,Spouse_cred,2)))))+(Children-1)*800*(110000-tax_inc)/110000))
		child_crfull_spouse	S	IF(Children=0,0,(spouse_cr=0)*Married*(800*(95000-tax_inc_spouse)/95000+(Children-1)*800*(110000-tax_inc_spouse)/110000))
		child_crpct_spouse	S	IF(child_crfull_spouse>0,IF((CG_tax_excl_spouse-emp_cr_spouse)/child_crfull_spouse<0.5,0,0.5),0)
		child_cr_spouse	S	child_crfull_spouse*child_crpct_spouse
	Total	tax_cr	B	MIN(emp_cr+spouse_cr+child_cr, CG_tax_excl)
7.	CG tax	CG_tax	B	Positive(CG_tax_excl-tax_cr)+sol_tax-fiscal_b
8.	State and local taxes	reg_rt	B	=IF(CG tax=0;0;IF(tax_inc<12000;0;tax_inc*local_rt))+IF(CG tax=0;0;IF(tax_inc< 35000;tax_inc*reg_rt;15000* reg_rt +(tax_inc-15000)*reg_rt2))
9.	Employees' soc security	SSC	B	Tax(earn, SSC_sch)
11.	Cash transfers		J	IF(Children=0,0,12*VLOOKUP(earn_total, IF(Married,trans_sch,trans_sch_sp),1+Children))
13.	Employer's soc security	SSC_empr	B	Tax(earn, Empr_sch)

Key to range of equation B calculated separately for both principal earner and spouse P calculated for principal only (value taken as 0 for spouse calculation) J calculated once only on a joint basis.

Taxing Wages 2017
© OECD 2017

Japan

This chapter includes data on the income taxes paid by workers, their social security contributions, the family benefits they receive in the form of cash transfers as well as the social security contributions and payroll taxes paid by their employers. Results reported include the marginal and average tax burden for eight different family types.

Methodological information is available for Personal income tax systems, Compulsory social security contributions to schemes operated within the government sector, Universal cash transfers as well as recent changes in the tax/benefit system. The methodology also includes the parameter values and tax equations underlying the data.

Japan 2016

The tax/benefit position of single persons

	Wage level (per cent of average wage)	67	100	167	67
	Number of children	none	none	none	2
1.	**Gross wage earnings**	3 424 103	5 110 601	8 534 704	3 424 103
2.	**Standard tax allowances:**				
	Basic allowance	380 000	380 000	380 000	380 000
	Married or head of family	0	0	0	0
	Dependent children	0	0	0	0
	Deduction for social security contributions and income taxes	492 135	734 530	1 128 440	492 135
	Work-related expenses	1 207 231	1 562 120	2 053 470	1 207 231
	Other				
	Total	2 079 366	2 676 650	3 561 911	2 079 366
3.	**Tax credits or cash transfers included in taxable income**	0	0	0	0
4.	**Central government taxable income (1 - 2 + 3)**	1 344 737	2 433 951	4 972 793	1 344 737
5.	**Central government income tax liability (exclusive of tax credits)**	68 649	148 959	578 967	68 649
6.	**Tax credits**				
	Basic credit				
	Married or head of family				
	Children				
	Other				
	Total	0	0	0	0
7.	**Central government income tax finally paid (5-6)**	68 649	148 959	578 967	68 649
8.	**State and local taxes**	141 974	250 895	504 779	141 974
9.	**Employees' compulsory social security contributions**				
	Gross earnings	492 135	734 530	1 128 440	492 135
	Taxable income				
	Total	492 135	734 530	1 128 440	492 135
10.	**Total payments to general government (7 + 8 + 9)**	702 757	1 134 384	2 212 187	702 757
11.	**Cash transfers from general government**				
	For head of family				
	For two children	0	0	0	240 000
	Total	0	0	0	240 000
12.	**Take-home pay (1-10+11)**	2 721 345	3 976 218	6 322 518	2 961 345
13.	**Employer's compulsory social security contributions**	517 816	772 859	1 192 451	517 816
14.	**Average rates**				
	Income tax	6.2%	7.8%	12.7%	6.2%
	Employees' social security contributions	14.4%	14.4%	13.2%	14.4%
	Total payments less cash transfers	20.5%	22.2%	25.9%	13.5%
	Total tax wedge including employer's social security contributions	31.0%	32.4%	35.0%	24.9%
15.	**Marginal rates**				
	Total payments less cash transfers: Principal earner	22.8%	27.6%	31.1%	22.8%
	Total payments less cash transfers: Spouse	n.a.	n.a.	n.a.	n.a.
	Total tax wedge: Principal earner	32.9%	37.1%	35.1%	32.9%
	Total tax wedge: Spouse	n.a.	n.a.	n.a.	n.a.

Japan 2016

The tax/benefit position of married couples

		Wage level (per cent of average wage)	100-0	100-33	100-67	100-33
		Number of children	2	2	2	none
1.	**Gross wage earnings**		5 110 601	6 797 100	8 534 704	6 797 100
2.	**Standard tax allowances**					
	Basic allowance		380 000	760 000	760 000	760 000
	Married or head of family		380 000	0	0	0
	Dependent children		0	0	0	0
	Deduction for social security contributions and income taxes		734 530	976 925	1 226 665	976 925
	Work-related expenses		1 562 120	2 236 720	2 769 351	2 236 720
	Other					
		Total	3 056 650	3 973 644	4 756 016	3 973 644
3.	**Tax credits or cash transfers included in taxable income**		0	0	0	0
4.	**Central government taxable income (1 - 2 + 3)**		2 053 951	2 823 456	3 778 689	2 823 456
5.	**Central government income tax liability (exclusive of tax credits)**		110 161	168 843	217 608	168 843
6.	**Tax credits**					
	Basic credit					
	Married or head of family					
	Children					
	Other					
		Total	0	0	0	0
7.	**Central government income tax finally paid (5-6)**		110 161	168 843	217 608	168 843
8.	**State and local taxes**		217 895	297 346	392 869	297 346
9.	**Employees' compulsory social security contributions**					
	Gross earnings		734 530	976 925	1 226 665	976 925
	Taxable income					
		Total	734 530	976 925	1 226 665	976 925
10.	**Total payments to general government (7 + 8 + 9)**		1 062 586	1 443 113	1 837 141	1 443 113
11.	**Cash transfers from general government**					
	For head of family					
	For two children		240 000	240 000	240 000	0
		Total	240 000	240 000	240 000	0
12.	**Take-home pay (1-10+11)**		4 288 016	5 593 987	6 937 563	5 353 987
13.	**Employer's compulsory social security contributions**		772 859	1 027 903	1 290 675	1 027 903
14.	**Average rates**					
	Income tax		6.4%	6.9%	7.2%	6.9%
	Employees' social security contributions		14.4%	14.4%	14.4%	14.4%
	Total payments less cash transfers		16.1%	17.7%	18.7%	21.2%
	Total tax wedge including employer's social security contributions		27.1%	28.5%	29.4%	31.6%
15.	**Marginal rates**					
	Total payments less cash transfers: Principal earner		27.6%	27.6%	27.6%	27.6%
	Total payments less cash transfers: Spouse		22.6%	21.3%	22.8%	21.3%
	Total tax wedge: Principal earner		37.1%	37.1%	37.1%	37.1%
	Total tax wedge: Spouse		32.7%	31.6%	32.9%	31.6%

The national currency is the Yen (JPY). In 2016 JPY 108.80 was equal to USD 1. In that year, the average worker is assumed to earn JPY 5 110 601 (Secretariat estimate). In Japan, the central government income tax year is a calendar year and the local government income tax year is from April to March. The calculations in this report are based on the tax rules and rates, which are applicable the 1 April.

1. Personal income tax systems

1.1. *Central government income tax*

1.1.1. *Tax unit*

Each individual is taxed separately.

1.1.2. *Allowances and tax credits*

1.1.2.1. Standard reliefs

- *Basic allowance:* a taxpayer may deduct JPY 380 000 as a basic allowance from his or her income.
- *Allowance for spouse*: allowance equal to JPY 380 000 is given to a resident taxpayer who lives with a spouse whose income does not exceed JPY 380 000.
- *Special allowance for spouse:* the allowance included in the following table is given to a resident taxpayer who lives with a spouse:

Spouse's income	Amount
0-380 000	0
380 001-399 999	380 000
400 000-449 999	360 000
450 000-499 999	310 000
500 000-549 999	260 000
550 000-599 999	210 000
600 000-649 999	160 000
650 000-699 999	110 000
700 000-749 999	60 000
750 000-759 999	30 000
760 000 or more	0

- *Allowance for dependents:* if a resident taxpayer has children and other relatives over 15 years old whose income does not exceed JPY 380 000 and who live with the resident, an allowance of JPY 380 000 is given for each dependent.
- *Special allowance for dependents:* if a resident taxpayer has dependents between 19 and 22 years old whose income does not exceed JPY 380 000 and who live with the resident, an allowance of JPY 630 000 is given for each dependent instead of the allowances for dependents mentioned above.

- *Deduction for social insurance premiums:* the whole amount of social insurance premiums for a resident taxpayer or his/her dependents shall be deducted from his/her income.
- *Employment income deduction:* the following amounts may be deducted from employment income in calculating salary income:
  - If gross employment income does not exceed JPY 1 800 000, the deduction is 40% of salaries (etc.), but the minimum amount deductible is JPY 650 000.
  - If gross employment income exceeds JPY 1 800 000, but not JPY 3 600 000, the deduction is JPY 180 000 plus 30% of salaries.
  - If gross employment income exceeds JPY 3 600 000, but not JPY 6 600 000, the deduction is JPY 540 000 plus 20% of salaries.
  - If gross employment income exceeds JPY 6 600 000, but not JPY 10 000 000, the deduction is JPY 1 200 000 plus 10% of salaries.
  - If gross employment income exceeds JPY 10 000 000, but not JPY 12 000 000, the deduction is JPY 1 700 000 plus 5% of salaries.
  - If gross employment income exceeds JPY 12 000 000, the deduction will be fixed at JPY 2 300 000.

1.1.2.2. Main non-standard tax reliefs applicable to an AW

- *Credit for housing loans:* A resident taxpayer who constructs, purchases, enlarges or rebuilds a house and finances the cost by means of a housing loan and uses the property as his or her own dwelling is entitled to an income tax credit up to the amount described below for 10 years [or 15 years] after the first use of the house, provided that the floor space is not less than 50m^2 and that at least half of the floor space is used as the owner-occupied dwelling. The base of the tax credit equals the balance of the housing loan debt amount, calculated at the end of each year, consisting of the loan obtained not only from private financial institutions but also from public institutions. This tax credit cannot be claimed by those whose total income is more than JPY 30 million.

The rates of the tax credits correspond to the year in which residence in the house commenced. The rates are as follows:

Residence starts:	From 1 January 2007 to 31 December 2007	From 1 January 2008 to 31 December 2008	From 1 January 2009 to 31 December 2010
Tax Credit Rate	For the part of remaining housing loan balance within JPY 25 million: The R.H.L.B. x 1.0%[or 0.6%] (for first 6 years [or 10 years]) The R.H.L.B. x 0.5%[or 0.4%] (for last 4 years [or 5 years])	For the part of R.H.L.B. within JPY 20 million: The R.H.L.B. x 1.0%[or 0.6%] (for first 6 years [or 10 years]) The R.H.L.B. x 0.5%[or 0.4%] (for last 4 years [or 5 years])	For the part of R.H.L.B. within JPY 50 million: The R.H.L.B. x 1.0%
Maximum tax credit amount (for each year)	JPY 250 000 [or 150 000] (for first 6 years[or 10 years]) JPY 125 000 [or 100 000] (for last 4 years [or 5 years])	JPY 200 000 [or 120 000] (for first 6 years[or 10 years]) JPY 100 000 [or 80 000] (for last 4 years [or 5 years])	JPY 500 000
Maximum tax credit amount (for the deductible period in total)	JPY 2 million	JPY 1.6 million	JPY 5 million

Residence starts:	From 1 January 2011 to 31 December 2011	From 1 January 2012 to 31 December 2012	From 1 January 2013 to 31 March 2014
Tax Credit Rate	For the part of R.H.L.B. within JPY 40 million: The R.H.L.B. x 1.0%	For the part of R.H.L.B. within JPY 30 million: The R.H.L.B. x 1.0%	For the part of R.H.L.B. within JPY 20 million: The R.H.L.B. x 1.0%
Maximum tax credit amount (for each year)	JPY 400 000	JPY 300 000	JPY 200 000
Maximum tax credit amount (for the deductible period in total)	JPY 4 million	JPY 3 million	JPY 2 million

Residence starts:	From 1 April 2014 to 30 June 2019
Tax Credit Rate	For the part of R.H.L.B. within JPY 40 million: The R.H.L.B x 1.0% If the rate of tax(consumption tax etc.) included in the amount of cost etc. of housing is other than 8% or 10%; For the part of R.H.L.B. within JPY 20 million: The R.H.L.B x 1.0%
Maximum tax credit amount (for each year)	JPY 400 000 If the rate of tax(consumption tax etc.) included in the amount of cost etc. of housing is other than 8% or 10%; JPY 200 000
Maximum tax credit amount (for the deductible period in total)	JPY 4 million If the rate of tax(consumption tax etc.) included in the amount of cost etc. of housing is other than 8% or 10%; JPY 2 million

- *Deduction for life insurance premiums:* If a resident taxpayer pays insurance premiums on life insurance contracts and the recipient of the insurance proceeds is the taxpayer, his/her spouse or other relatives living with him/her, the portion of these insurance premiums which does not exceed the maximum prescribed below, is deductible from ordinary income, retirement income or timber income.
- In addition, if a resident taxpayer pays insurance premiums for a "qualified personal pension plan (insurance type)", and the recipient of the pension payment is the taxpayer or his/her spouse under a specific condition, the portion of such premiums which does not exceed the maximum prescribed below, is deductible from ordinary income, retirement income, or timber income.
- Furthermore, if a resident taxpayer pays insurance premiums on nursing and medical insurance contacts and the taxpayer receipts the nursing and medical proceeds caused by payments for medical expenses, the portion of such premiums which does not exceed the maximum prescribed below, is deductible from ordinary income, retirement income, or timber income.

Annual premium paid (JPY)		Deduction
Over	Not over	
	20 000	Total amount of premiums paid (1)
20 000	40 000	(1) x 1/2 + JPY 10 000
40 000	80 000	(1) x 1/4 + JPY 20 000
80 000	-	JPY 40 000

- For the insurance contracts made on or after 1 January 2012 the maximum deduction is JPY 120 000. A resident taxpayer can claim the deduction up to JPY 40 000 for life insurance premiums, personal pension plan premiums and nursing and medical insurance premiums respectively.
- For the insurance contracts made on or before 31 December 2011, a resident taxpayer can claim the deduction up to JPY 50 000 for life insurance premiums, personal pension plan premiums respectively. Thus, a resident tax payer can claim the deduction up to JPY 100 000 in total.
- *Deduction for medical expenses:* If a resident taxpayer pays bills for medical or dental care for himself/herself or for his/her spouse or other relatives living with him/her and the amount of such expenses (excluding those recovered by insurance) exceeds the lesser of JPY 100 000 or 5% of the total of his/her ordinary income, retirement income and timber income, the excess amount is deductible from his/her ordinary income, retirement income or timber income. The maximum deduction is JPY 2 million.
- *Deduction for earthquake insurance premiums:* Earthquake insurance premiums up to JPY 50 000 can be deducted from income. Although the income deduction for casualty insurance premiums was basically abolished, the deduction for long-term casualty insurance premiums remains available if contracted before 31 December, 2006. The maximum deduction for long-term casualty insurance premiums is JPY 15 000. If an individual applies for both a deduction for earthquake insurance premiums and a deduction for long-term casualty premiums, the maximum deductible amount is JPY 50 000 in total.

1.1.3. *Tax schedule*

Taxable income (JPY)*		Tax rate (%)	Deductible amounts for each bracket (JPY)
Over	Not over	(A)	(B)
	1 950 000	5	-
1 950 000	3 300 000	10	97 500
3 300 000	6 950 000	20	427 500
6 950 000	9 000 000	23	636 000
9 000 000	18 000 000	33	1 536 000
18 000 000	40 000 000	40	2 796 000
40 000 000		45	4 796 000

* The fraction of taxable income that is less than JPY 1 000 is rounded down.

Tax liability is obtained by multiplying the taxable income by tax rate (A) and deducting the amount (B). For example, income tax due on taxable income of JPY 7 million is:

7 000 000 × 0.23 (A) - 636 000 (B) = JPY 974 000.

In addition, a taxpayer is required to file tax returns and make tax payments for additional 2.1% of the base income taxes from 2013 through 2037 (special income tax for reconstruction) annually together with the regular income tax of respective years.

1.2. *Local taxes (personal inhabitant's taxes)*

1.2.1. *General description of the system*

Local taxes in Japan (personal inhabitant's taxes) consist of prefectural inhabitant's tax levied by prefectures and municipal inhabitant's tax levied by cities, towns and villages.

The prefectural inhabitant's tax is collected together with the municipal inhabitant's tax by cities, towns and villages.

1.2.2. *Tax base*

Basically, personal inhabitant's taxes (prefectural and municipal inhabitant's taxes) consist of two parts; one is proportional taxable income and the other is a fixed per capita amount. The taxable income of personal inhabitant's taxes is computed on the basis of the previous year's income. The main difference from state tax (income tax) is the amount of income reliefs. For example, the amount of Basic Allowance, Allowance for Spouse, Allowance for Dependants is JPY 330 000, and the amount of specified Allowance for dependants is JPY 450 000, etc. Allowance for Dependents is available for dependent relatives 16 years or older excluding the specified dependents. Specified Allowance for dependents is available for the specified dependent relatives (between 19 and 22 years old).

1.2.3. *Tax rate*

- The standard fixed (annual) per-capita amount of Prefectural inhabitant's tax is JPY 1 500;
- The standard fixed (annual) per-capita amount of Municipal inhabitant's tax is JPY 3 500;
- The standard rate of the local taxes equals a proportional rate of 10% (Prefectural inhabitant's tax: 4%, Municipal inhabitant's tax: 6%).

Taxable income for local income tax purposes	The tax credit
JPY 2 000 000 or less	5% of the lesser of: • total amount of differences in personal reliefs between those for income tax purposes and for personal inhabitant's taxes purposes; or • taxable income amount for personal inhabitant's taxes purposes
More than JPY 2 000 000	((total amount of differences in personal reliefs between those for income tax purposes and for personal inhabitant's taxes purposes) – (taxable income amount for personal inhabitant's taxes purposes – JPY 2 000 000)) * 5%. Note: The minimum credit is JPY 2 500

Note: Local authorities do not levy the per-capita rate and the proportional rate on a taxpayer whose previous year's income does not exceed a certain amount. For example, in special wards of Tokyo, this threshold is calculated as follows:
per-capita rate: (1 + number of spouse and dependent(s) qualified for the allowance for spouse/dependents) * 350 000 (+ 210 000 in case the taxpayer has a qualified spouse or dependent(s)))
proportional rate: (1 + number of spouse and dependent(s) qualified for the allowance for spouse/dependents) * 350 000 (+ 320 000 in case the taxpayer has a qualified spouse or dependent(s)))

1.2.4. *Tax rate selected for this study*

State tax (income tax) rates as described above. The local tax (personal inhabitant's taxes) rates chosen for the purpose of this Report represent the standard rate.

The personal inhabitant's taxes rate and the income tax rate were changed in the FY 2006 tax reform. Adjusted credit (tax credit regime)was introduced in order to alleviate the tax burden increase arising from the changes in the tax rates and from the difference between the personal reliefs (Basic Allowance, Allowance for Spouse, Allowance for Dependents, Special Allowance for dependents, etc.) for national income tax purposes and for inhabitant tax purposes.

 TAXING WAGES 2017 © OECD 2017

2. Compulsory social security contribution to schemes operated within the government sector

2.1. Employees' contributions

2.1.1. *Pension*

8.914% (9.091% as from September 2016) of total remuneration (standard remuneration and bonuses). The insurable ceiling of the monthly amount of pensionable remuneration is JPY 620 000 and the insurable ceiling of the standard amount of bonus is JPY 1 500 000.

2.1.2. *Sickness*

As from April 2012 about 5.00%, (about 4.75% before March 2012), of total remuneration, (standard remuneration and bonuses). The insurable ceiling of the monthly amount of standard remuneration is JPY 1 390 000 and the insurable ceiling of the yearly amount of standard bonus is JPY 5 730 000.

2.1.3. *Unemployment*

0.4% of total remuneration for Commerce and industry in general except for Business of agriculture, forestry and fisheries, and the rice wine brewing business, and Construction business. It is 0.5% for those exceptions.

2.1.4-2.1.5. *Work injury and family allowance*

None.

2.2. Employers' contributions

2.2.1. *Pensions*

8.914% (9.091% as from September 2016) of total remuneration (standard remuneration and bonuses). The insurable ceiling of the monthly amount of pensionable remuneration is JPY 620 000 and the insurable ceiling of the standard amount of bonus is JPY 1 500 000.

2.2.2. *Sickness*

As from April 2012, about 5.00% (about 4.75% before March 2012) of total remuneration. The insurable ceiling of the monthly amount of standard remuneration is JPY 1 390 000 and the insurable ceiling of the yearly amount of standard bonus is JPY 5 730 000.

2.2.3. *Unemployment*

0.7% of total remuneration for Commerce and industry in general except for Business of agriculture, forestry and fisheries, and the rice wine brewing business, and Construction business. It is 0.8% for Business of agriculture, forestry and fisheries, and the rice wine brewing business, and 0.9% for Construction business

2.2.4. *Work injury*

0.25% to 8.8% of total remuneration, the contribution rate depending on each industry's accident rate over the last three years and other factors. There are twenty-nine rates for fifty-four industrial categories at present.

2.2.5. *Family allowance*

0.20% of total remuneration.

3. Universal cash transfers

3.1. *Transfers related to marital status*

Not available.

3.2. *Transfers for dependent children*

From April 2012 (Income caps are applied beginning from June 2012 payments):

a) For persons earning incomes below the income cap

JPY 15 000 (per month) is paid to parents/guardians for each child who is under 3 years old or for the third or subsequent child from 3 years old until he/she graduates from elementary school.

JPY 10 000 (per month) is paid to parents/guardians for each child who is for the first or second child from 3 years old until he/she graduates from elementary school or who is a junior high school student.

b) For persons earning incomes no less than the income cap

JPY 50 00 (per month) is paid to parents/guardians for each child until he/she graduates from junior high school as the Special Interim Allowances.

The income cap is set at JPY 6 220 000 (the principal's gross earnings net of certain deductions, plus JPY 380 000 per dependent).

4. Main changes in the tax/benefit systems since 1998

As part of the Fiscal Year 1999 tax reform, the highest marginal rate of the personal income tax imposed by the central government was reduced from 50% to 37%. The top rate of the local inhabitant's tax was reduced from 15% to 13%. A proportional tax reduction was granted with respect to the national income tax and the local inhabitant's tax. The amount is equal to the lesser of 20% (local inhabitant's tax: 15%) of the amount of tax before reduction or JPY 250 000 (local inhabitant's tax: JPY 40 000).

As part of the FY 2005 tax reform, the rate of the reduction was reduced from 20% to 10% (local inhabitant's tax: from 15% to 7.5%) and the ceiling was reduced from JPY 250 000 to JPY 125 000 (local inhabitant's tax from JPY 40 000 to JPY 20 000) as from 2006 (local inhabitant's tax: FY 2006). And as part of the FY 2006 tax reform, the reduction was abolished as from 2007 (local inhabitant's tax: FY 2007).

As part of the FY 2006 tax reform, the progressive rate structure of national income tax was reformed into a 6 brackets structure with tax rates ranging from 5% to 40%, and the rate of local inhabitant's tax became proportional at a rate of 10%.

As part of the FY 2012 tax reform, the upper limit on employment income deduction (JPY 2 450 000) was set for those who earn employment income more than JPY 15 000 000 as from 2013 (personal inhabitant's tax: FY 2014).

As part of the FY 2013 tax reform, the tax rate of 45% was set for the income beyond JPY 40 000 000 from 2015. By this, the progressive rate structure of income tax was reformed into a 7 brackets structure

As part of the FY 2014 tax reform, the upper limit on employment income deduction was determined to be gradually reduced. In 2016 (as for personal inhabitant's taxes, in 2017), the limit became JPY 2 300 000 in case salary income is more than JPY 12 000 000. And in 2017 (as for personal inhabitant's taxes, in 2017), the limit will become JPY 2 200 000 in case salary income is more than JPY 10 000 000.

Eligible age for transfers for dependent children was raised from three to six as from 1 June 2001, from six to nine as from 1 April 2004 and from nine to twelve as from 1 April 2006. It has been doubled to JPY 10 000 for the first and second child under the age of three as from 1 April, 2007.

As from 2010, JPY 13 000 per month is paid to parents/guardians regardless of their income for each child until he/she graduates from junior high school.

As from April 2012 (Income caps are applied beginning from June 2012 payments):

a) For persons earning incomes below the income cap

JPY 15 000 (per month) is paid to parents/guardians for each child who is under 3 years old or for the third or subsequent child from 3 years old until he/she graduates from elementary school.

JPY 10 000 (per month) is paid to parents/guardians for each child who is for the first or second child from 3 years old until he/she graduates from elementary school or who is a junior high school student.

b) For persons earning incomes no less than the income cap

JPY 5 000 (per month) is paid to parents/guardians for each child until he/she graduates from junior high school as the Special Interim Allowances.

5. Memorandum item

5.1. *Average gross annual wage earnings calculation*

The source of calculation is the *Basic Survey on Wage Structure,* published by the Ministry of Health, Labour and Welfare. This survey covers establishments with ten or more regular employees over the whole country, and contains statistical figures for monthly contractual cash earnings in June and annual special cash earnings (such as bonuses) received by various categories of workers. Male and female workers of the manufacturing, mining and quarrying, construction, wholesale and retail trade, accommodation and food service activities, financial and insurance activities, real estate activities sector are the point of departure. Their gross annual earnings have been calculated by multiplying monthly contractual cash earnings by 12 and adding any annual special cash earnings. In the *Basic Survey*, sickness and unemployment compensations are excluded from cash earnings, but average overtime and bonuses are included.

As far as the *Basic Survey* is concerned, it covers the whole country, and no special assumption is made regarding the place of residence of the average worker.

5.2. *Employer contributions to private pension and health schemes*

DB: JPY 3 528 billion (2013)

Employees' Pension Funds (EPFs): JPY 1 035 billion (2014)

DC: JPY 673 billion (2014)

Data of DB and EPFs are the total amount of employers' contribution and employees' one and there is no data of those which indicates only employers' contribution. As from January 2012, matching contribution which enables employee to pay additional contribution to employer's one became available. The amount of DC does not include the amount of matching contribution. It is regulated by law that employers' contribution must be higher than employees' one.

2016 parameter values

Average earnings/yr	Ave_earn	5 110 601	Secretariat estimate
Allowances for central tax	basic_al	380 000	
	spouse_al	380 000	
	Spouse_al_sp	0	0
		380 001	380 000
		400 000	360 000
		450 000	310 000
		500 000	260 000
		550 000	210 000
		600 000	160 000
		650 000	110 000
		700 000	60 000
		750 000	30 000
		760 000	0
spouse_al_ceil		380 000	
	child_al	0	
Employment income deduction	emp_inc_min	650 000	
	emp_inc_sch	0.4	1 800 000
		0.3	3 600 000
		0.2	6 600 000
		0.1	10 000 000
		0.05	
	emp_inc_max	2 300 000	
Central gov't tax schedule	tax_sch	0.05	1 950 000
		0.10	3 300 000
		0.20	6 950 000
		0.23	9 000 000
		0.33	18 000 000
		0.40	40 000 000
		0.45	
	surtax	1.021	
Allowances for state/local tax	s_basic_al	330 000	
	s_spouse_al	330 000	
	s_spouse_al_sp	0	0
		380 001	330 000
		450 000	310 000
		500 000	260 000
		550 000	210 000
		600 000	160 000
		650 000	110 000
		700 000	60 000
		750 000	30 000
		760 000	0
	S_spouse_al_ceil	380 000	
	s_child_al	0	
Prefectural tax	pref_per_cap	1 500	
Municipal tax	mun_per_cap	3 500	
	local_sch	0.1	
Social security contributions	SSC_pens	0.0897267	
	pens_ceil	7 440 000	
	SSC_sick	0.05	
	sick_ceil	16 680 000	
	SSC_unemp	0.004	
Employer contribution proportion	SSC_empr_unemp	0.007	
	SSC_empr_oth	0.0045	
Child transfer	Child_transfer	120 000	
	Child_transfer2	60 000	
	Child_transfer_lim	6 220 000	
	Child_transfer_lim_incr	380 000	

2016 tax equations

The equations for the Japanese system are mostly on an individual basis. But the tax allowances for the spouse and for children are relevant only to the calculation for the principal earner. This is shown by the Range indicator in the table below.

The functions which are used in the equations (Taper, MIN, Tax etc) are described in the technical note about tax equations. Variable names are defined in the table of parameters above, within the equations table, or are the standard variables "married" and "children". A reference to a variable with the affix "_total" indicates the sum of the relevant variable values for the principal and spouse. And the affixes "_princ" and "_spouse" indicate the value for the principal and spouse, respectively. Equations for a single person are as shown for the principal, with "_spouse" values taken as 0.

	Line in country table and intermediate steps	Variable name	Range	Equation
1.	Earnings	earn		
2.	Allowances:			
		tax_al	P	basic_al + Married*(earn_princ - (earn_princ>0)*MIN(emp_inc_max,MAX(emp_inc_min,Tax(earn_princ, emp_inc_sch)))<=spouse_al_ceil)*spouse_al + Married*VLOOKUP(Positive(earn_princ - (earn_princ>0)*MAX(emp_inc_min,Tax(earn_princ, emp_inc_sch))),spouse_al_sp,2,TRUE) + Children*child_al + MAX(emp_inc_min,Tax(earn_princ,emp_inc_sch)) + SSC_princ
			S	MIN(earn_spouse, basic_al + MAX(emp_inc_min, Tax(earn, emp_inc_sch)) + SSC_spouse)
3.	Credits in taxable income	taxbl_cr	B	0
4.	CG taxable income	tax_inc	B	Positive(earn-tax_al)
5.	CG tax before credits	CG_tax_excl	B	Positive(Tax(tax_inc, tax_sch))
6.	Tax credits :	tax_cr	B	0
7.	CG tax	CG_tax	B	CG_tax_excl*surtax
8.	State and local taxes			
	Local taxable income	local_tax_inc	P	Positive(earn_princ- (s_basic_al+Married*((earn_spouse-(earn_spouse>0)*MAX(emp_inc_min,Tax(earn_spouse,emp_inc_sch))<=s_spouse_al_ceil)*s_spouse_al+VLOOKUP(Positive(earn_spouse-(earn_spouse>0)*MAX(emp_inc_min,Tax(earn_spouse,emp_inc_sch))),s_spouse_al_sp,2,TRUE))+Children*s_child_al+MAX(emp_inc_min,Tax(earn_princ,emp_inc_sch))+SSC_princ))
			S	Positive(earn_spouse- (s_basic_al+(earn_spouse>0)*MAX(emp_inc_min,Tax(earn_spouse,emp_inc_sch))+SSC_spouse))
	Local tax	local_tax	P	(earn_princ-MAX(emp_inc_min,Tax(earn_princ,emp_inc_sch))>350000+(Married*(earn_princ - (earn_princ>0)*MAX(emp_inc_min,Tax(earn_princ, emp_inc_sch))<=s_spouse_al_ceil)+Children>0)*((Married*(earn_princ - (earn_princ>0)*MAX(emp_inc_min,Tax(earn_princ, emp_inc_sch))<=s_spouse_al_ceil)+Children)*350000+210000))*(pref_per_cap+mun_per_cap)+(earn_princ-MAX(emp_inc_min,Tax(earn_princ,emp_inc_sch))>350000+(Married*(earn_princ - (earn_princ>0)*MAX(emp_inc_min,Tax(earn_princ, emp_inc_sch))<=s_spouse_al_ceil)+Children>0)*((Married*(earn_princ - (earn_princ>0)*MAX(emp_inc_min,Tax(earn_princ, emp_inc_sch))<=s_spouse_al_ceil)+Children)*350000+320000))*Positive(Tax(Positive(earn_spouse-tax_al_spouse),local_sch)-IF(Positive(earn_spouse-tax_al_spouse)>2000000,MAXA(2500,((Positive(earn_spouse-tax_al_spouse)-MAX(emp_inc_min,Tax(earn_princ,emp_inc_sch)))-(Positive(earn_spouse-tax_al_spouse)-2000000))*5%),MINA((Positive(earn_spouse-tax_al_spouse)-MAX(emp_inc_min,Tax(earn_princ,emp_inc_sch))),Positive(earn_spouse-tax_al_spouse))*5%))
			S	(earn_spouse - (earn_spouse>0)*MAX(emp_inc_min,Tax(earn_spouse, emp_inc_sch))>350000)*(pref_per_cap+mun_per_cap+Positive(Tax(local_tax_inc_spouse,local_sch)-IF(local_tax_inc_spouse>2000000,MAXA(2500,((local_tax_inc_spouse-tax_inc_spouse)-(local_tax_inc_spouse-2000000))*5%),MINA((local_tax_inc_spouse-tax_inc_spouse),local_tax_inc_spouse)*5%)))

	Line in country table and intermediate steps	Variable name	Range	Equation
9.	Employees' soc security	SSC	B	SSC_pens*MIN(earn, pens_ceil)+SSC_sick*MIN(earn, sick_ceil)+SSC_unemp*earn
11.	Cash transfers	cash_trans	B	IF(Children>0,IF(Positive(princ_inc - princ_empl_inc)<Child_transfer_lim+(Child_transfer_lim_incr*Children), Child_transfer,Child_transfer2)*Children,0)
13.	Employer's social security	SSC_empr	B	SSC_pens*MIN(earn, pens_ceil)+SSC_sick*MIN(earn, sick_ceil)+(SSC_empr_unemp+SSC_empr_oth)*earn

Key to range of equation B calculated separately for both principal earner and spouse P calculated for principal only (value taken as 0 for spouse calculation).

Taxing Wages 2017
© OECD 2017

Korea

This chapter includes data on the income taxes paid by workers, their social security contributions, the family benefits they receive in the form of cash transfers as well as the social security contributions and payroll taxes paid by their employers. Results reported include the marginal and average tax burden for eight different family types.

Methodological information is available for Personal income tax systems, Compulsory social security contributions to schemes operated within the government sector, Universal cash transfers as well as recent changes in the tax/benefit system. The methodology also includes the parameter values and tax equations underlying the data.

Korea 2016

The tax/benefit position of single persons

		Wage level (per cent of average wage)	67	100	167	67
		Number of children	none	none	none	2
1.	**Gross wage earnings**		29 384 352	43 857 243	73 241 595	29 384 352
2.	**Standard tax allowances**					
	Basic allowance		1 500 000	1 500 000	1 500 000	1 500 000
	Married or head of family		0	0	0	0
	Dependent children		0	0	0	3 000 000
	Deduction for social security contributions and income taxes		1 322 296	1 973 576	2 343 600	1 322 296
	Work-related expenses					
	Other		9 657 653	13 543 590	16 276 136	10 657 653
		Total	12 479 949	17 017 166	20 119 736	16 479 949
3.	**Tax credits or cash transfers included in taxable income**		0	0	0	0
4.	**Central government taxable income (1 - 2 + 3)**		16 904 404	26 840 077	53 121 859	12 904 404
5.	**Central government income tax liability (exclusive of tax credits)**		1 455 661	2 946 012	7 529 246	855 661
6.	**Tax credits**					
	Basic credit		870 000	660 000	500 000	900 613
	Married or head of family					
	Children					
	Other					
		Total	870 000	660 000	500 000	900 613
7.	**Central government income tax finally paid (5-6)**		585 661	2 286 012	7 029 246	0
8.	**State and local taxes**		58 566	228 601	702 925	0
9.	**Employees' compulsory social security contributions**					
	Gross earnings		2 471 348	3 688 579	5 207 656	2 471 348
	Taxable income					
		Total	2 471 348	3 688 579	5 207 656	2 471 348
10.	**Total payments to general government (7 + 8 + 9)**		3 115 575	6 203 192	12 939 827	2 471 348
11.	**Cash transfers from general government**					
	For head of family		0	0	0	0
	For two children		0	0	0	0
		Total	0	0	0	0
12.	**Take-home pay (1-10+11)**		26 268 778	37 654 050	60 301 768	26 913 004
13.	**Employer's compulsory social security contributions**		3 044 343	4 543 796	6 635 867	3 044 343
14.	**Average rates**					
	Income tax		2.2%	5.7%	10.6%	0.0%
	Employees' social security contributions		8.4%	8.4%	7.1%	8.4%
	Total payments less cash transfers		10.6%	14.1%	17.7%	8.4%
	Total tax wedge including employer's social security contributions		19.0%	22.2%	24.5%	17.0%
15.	**Marginal rates**					
	Total payments less cash transfers: Principal earner		21.7%	21.0%	28.0%	8.4%
	Total payments less cash transfers: Spouse		n.a.	n.a.	n.a.	n.a.
	Total tax wedge: Principal earner		29.0%	28.5%	31.9%	17.0%
	Total tax wedge: Spouse		n.a.	n.a.	n.a.	n.a.

Korea 2016

The tax/benefit position of married couples

		Wage level (per cent of average wage)	100-0	100-33	100-67	100-33
		Number of children	2	2	2	none
1.	**Gross wage earnings**		43 857 243	58 330 133	73 241 595	58 330 133
2.	**Standard tax allowances**					
	Basic allowance		1 500 000	3 000 000	3 000 000	3 000 000
	Married or head of family		1 500 000	0	0	0
	Dependent children		3 000 000	3 000 000	3 000 000	0
	Deduction for social security contributions and income taxes		1 973 576	2 624 856	3 295 872	2 624 856
	Work-related expenses					
	Other		13 543 590	21 332 746	23 701 243	21 332 746
		Total	21 517 166	29 957 602	32 997 115	26 957 602
3.	**Tax credits or cash transfers included in taxable income**		0	0	0	0
4.	**Central government taxable income (1 - 2 + 3)**		22 340 077	28 372 531	40 244 481	31 372 531
5.	**Central government income tax liability (exclusive of tax credits)**		2 271 012	2 767 959	3 876 672	3 217 959
6.	**Tax credits**					
	Basic credit		960 000	1 239 571	1 829 198	939 571
	Married or head of family					
	Children					
	Other					
		Total	960 000	1 239 571	1 829 198	939 571
7.	**Central government income tax finally paid (5-6)**		1 311 012	1 536 012	2 047 474	2 286 012
8.	**State and local taxes**		131 101	153 601	204 747	228 601
9.	**Employees' compulsory social security contributions**					
	Gross earnings		3 688 579	4 905 811	6 159 928	4 905 811
	Taxable income					
		Total	3 688 579	4 905 811	6 159 928	4 905 811
10.	**Total payments to general government (7 + 8 + 9)**		5 130 692	6 595 423	8 412 149	7 420 423
11.	**Cash transfers from general government**					
	For head of family		0	0	0	0
	For two children		0	0	0	0
		Total	0	0	0	0
12.	**Take-home pay (1-10+11)**		38 726 550	51 734 709	64 829 446	50 909 709
13.	**Employers' compulsory social security contributions**		4 543 796	6 043 248	7 588 139	6 043 248
14.	**Average rates**					
	Income tax		3.3%	2.9%	3.1%	4.3%
	Employees' social security contributions		8.4%	8.4%	8.4%	8.4%
	Total payments less cash transfers		11.7%	11.3%	11.5%	12.7%
	Total tax wedge including employer's social security contributions		20.0%	19.6%	19.8%	20.9%
15.	**Marginal rates**					
	Total payments less cash transfers: Principal earner		21.0%	21.0%	21.0%	21.0%
	Total payments less cash transfers: Spouse		10.1%	8.4%	17.7%	8.4%
	Total tax wedge: Principal earner		28.5%	28.5%	28.5%	28.5%
	Total tax wedge: Spouse		18.6%	17.0%	25.4%	17.0%

The national currency is the Won (KRW). In 2016, KRW 1 160.59 was equal to USD 1. In this year, the average worker is expected to earn KRW 43 857 243 (Secretariat estimate).

1. Personal income tax system

1.1. *Central government income tax system*

1.1.1. *Tax unit*

Each individual is taxed on his/her own income.

Non-taxable wage income includes the:

- national pension, medical insurance, unemployment insurance and work injury insurance that are borne by employer;
- overtime payment to productive workers: up to KRW 2 400 000 of overwork payment of productive workers in manufacturing and mining sectors whose monthly wage is less than KRW 1 500 000 and whose yearly wage is less than KRW 25 000 000.

1.1.2. *Allowances and tax credits*

1.1.2.1. Standard reliefs

- *Employment income deduction:* the following deduction from gross income is provided to wage and salary income earners:

Salary	Deduction
Up to KRW 5 000 000	70%
KRW 5 000 000 to KRW 15 000 000	KRW 3 500 000 plus 40% of the salary over KRW 5 000 000
KRW 15 000 000 to KRW 45 000 000	KRW 7 500 000plus 15% of the salary over KRW 15 000 000
KRW 45 000 000 to KRW 100 000 000	KRW 12 000 000 plus 5% of the salary over KRW 45 000 000
Over KRW 100 000 000	KRW 14 750 000 plus 2% of the salary over KRW 100 000 000

- *Basic allowance*: a taxpayer can deduct KRW 1 500 000 from his/her income for each person who meets one of following conditions:
  - the taxpayer him/herself;
  - the taxpayer's spouse whose taxable income (gross earnings net of employment income deduction) is less than KRW 1 000 000;
  - the taxpayer's (including the spouse's) dependents (parents, siblings, children) within the same household whose income after accounting for the employment income deduction is less than KRW 1 000 000 and whose age is:
    1. parents: 60 years or older;
    2. brother/sister: 60 years or older or 20 years or younger;
    3. children: 20 years or younger (if both partners in the household earn wage-income, this Report assumes that the principal wage earner will claim the allowance).

- *Additional allowance:* a taxpayer can deduct KRW 1 000 000 (500 000 in the case of [c], KRW 2 000 000 in the case of [b]) from his/her gross income when the taxpayer or his/her dependents fall into one of the following categories (for this report, only cases [c] are modelled):
  - a person aged 70 years or older (a)
  - a handicapped person (b)
  - a female wage earner who is the head of a household with dependents (but without spouse) or a female wage earner with spouse when her taxable income is not more than KRW 30 million (c)
  - a single parent with descendants including adoptees (f)
- *National pension deduction*: employees can deduct 100% of their National Pension contributions
- *Working Tax credit*: wage and salary income earners obtain the following tax credit, :

Calculated tax	Amount of tax credit
Up to KRW 1 300 000	55% of calculated tax
Over KRW 1 300 000	KRW 715 000 plus 30% of the calculated tax over KRW 1 300 000

Total wage and salary income	Ceiling on credit amount
Not more than KRW 33 million	KRW 740 000
Not more than KRW 70 million	The greater of KRW 660 000 and KRW 740 000 - [(total wage and salary income - KRW 33 million) × 0.8%]
Exceeding KRW 70 million	The greater of KRW 500 000 and KRW 660 000 - [(total wage and salary income - KRW 70 million) × 50%]

1.1.2.2. Main non-standard tax reliefs

Wage and salary income earners may deduct from gross income the expenses for the following items during the tax year:

- *Insurance premiums:* the Medical insurance premium and the Unemployment insurance premium can be entirely (100%) deducted from taxable income.
- *Saving/Payment for housing:* 40% of deposits of an account for purchasing a house, which is held by a person who does not own a house, or owns only one house that is smaller than 85 square miles in size and whose price is KRW 300 million or less, 40% of repayments of loans including interest borrowed for the purpose of the lease by a person owning no house may be deducted up to three million won per year. *Credit card purchases:* Employees may deduct 15% of their credit card (30% of their debit card, prepaid card or cash receipt) purchases that exceed 25% of their total income up to lesser of KRW 3 000 000 or 20% of their total income. However, for expenditures spent for traditional markets and public transportation, the allowed deduction is equivalent to 30% of the expenditure and the ceiling is raised by an additional KRW 1 000 000 respectively.

1.1.2.3. Child tax credit

- Where a resident with taxable income has dependent children including adoption, he/she gets annual tax credit of KRW 150 000 for having a child, KRW 300 000 for having two

Overlapping of deductions for (c) and (f) is not allowed. So a taxpayer should select only one.

children and KRW 300 000 plus KRW 300 000 per an excess child over two children in case of having more than three children.

- Resident gets additional tax credit of KRW 150 000 per a child who is under 6 years of age from second child;
- Resident gets tax credit of KRW 300 000 per child for birth and adoption of the year;

1.1.2.4. Credit for Pension Insurance Premiums

- A resident who paid pension contributions to a pension account may deduct the amount equal to 12% of the premiums paid from his/her global income tax amount, only up to KRW 4 million for pension account as well as KRW 7 million for sum of the pension account and retirement -pension account
- A resident whose labour income is not exceeding KRW 55 million when he has labour income only or whose global income is not exceeding KRW 40 million would deduct 15% of the premium.

1.1.2.5. Special tax credit

- Wage and salary income earners may obtain following tax credit during the tax year:
- *Insurance premiums (a)*:12% of the general insurance premium up to KRW 1 000 000 can be deducted from his/her income tax amount.
- *Medical expenses (b)*:15% of the medical expenses exceeding 3% of taxable income can be deducted from his/her income tax amount. The medical expenses for taxpayer's dependents who are eligible for the basic deduction is limited KRW 7 000 000 and the medical expenses for the taxpayer himself, taxpayer's dependents who are aged 65 years or older and handicapped persons is not limited.
- *Educational expenses (c)*:15% of tuition fees for pre-school, elementary, middle school and college (but the graduate school fee deduction is allowed only for the taxpayer himself), either for the taxpayer himself or his/her dependents (including the taxpayer's spouse, children, and siblings), can be deducted from his/her income tax amount. The tuition fee for the taxpayer himself is not limited. For the taxpayer's dependents, the limits of tuition fees are as follows:
  - For pre-school: up to KRW 3 000 000 per child;
  - For elementary, middle and high school: up to KRW 3 000 000 per student;
  - For college/university: up to KRW 9 000 000 per student.
  - *Charities (d)*:15% of the amount of donation (in case of the donation exceeding KRW 20 million, 30% of the excess over KRW 20 million) is deducted from income tax amount. The limits of donations are as follows:
  - donations to a government body, donations for national defence, natural disaster, and certain charitable associations: up to gross income;
  - donations to public welfare or religious associations: up to 30% of gross income.
- Standard Credits: Alternatively, a taxpayer may elect to choose an annual standard credit of KRW 70 000 (KRW 130 000 for wage and salary earners and KRW 120 000 for business owners meeting certain requirements), if he or she fails to claim deductions for insurance premium, saving/payment for housing and special tax credit.

1.1.3. *Tax schedule*

Over (KRW)	Not more than (KRW)	Marginal tax rate (%)
0	12 000 000	6
12 000 000	46 000 000	15
46 000 000	88 000 000	24
88 000 000	150 000 000	35
150 000 000		38

1.2. Local income tax

1.2.1. *Tax base*

The local income tax base is the income tax paid to the central government.

1.2.2. *Tax rate*

A uniform rate of 10% is applied. However, the local government can adjust the rate between the lower limit of 5% and the upper limit of 15%.

1.2.3. *Tax rate (selected for this study)*

A country-wide rate of 10% is used in this Report.

2. Compulsory social security contribution to schemes operated within the government sector

2.1. Employees' contribution

2.1.1. *National pension*

The National pension contribution rate is 4.5% of the standardised average monthly wage income as of 2014.

The scope of the standardised average monthly wage income is from KRW 270 000 to KRW 4 210 000 as of 1 July, 2015

2.1.2. *Medical insurance*

The Medical insurance premium, which has a rate of 3.260423% (Health insurance: 3.06%, Long term care insurance: 6.55% of Health insurance premium rate), is levied on average monthly wage income as of 1 January 2016.

The scope of the average monthly wage income is from KRW 280 000 to KRW 78 100 000.

2.1.3. *Unemployment insurance*

0.65% of gross income.

2.1.4. *Industrial accident compensation insurance (premiums)*

Compulsory application, premiums paid only by employers.

2.2. Employers' contribution

2.2.1. *National pension*

The national pension contribution rate is 4.5% of the standardised average monthly wage income as of 2014.

The scope of the standardised average monthly wage income is from KRW 280 000 to KRW 4 340 000 as of 1 July, 2016.

If the average monthly wage income of a person is less than KRW 280 000, the average monthly wage income of the person is regarded as KRW 280 000 and the rate (0.045) is applied. Ifthe average monthly wage income of a person is more than KRW 4 340 000, the average monthly wage income of the person is regarded as KRW 4 340 000 and the rate (0.045) is applied; so the maximum of the national pension contribution per year is KRW 2 343 600(=KRW 4 340 000 x 0.045 x 12 months).

2.2.2. Medical insurance

The Medical insurance premium, which has a rate of 3.260423% (Health insurance: 3.06%, Long term care insurance: 6.55% of Health insurance premium rate), is levied on average monthly wage income as of 1 January, 2015.

The scope of the average monthly wage income is from KRW 280 000 to KRW 78 100 000.

2.2.3. Unemployment insurance

- the insurance premium is between 0.9% and 1.5% of total wage;
- the insurance premium selected for this study is 0.9%.

2.2.4. Work injury insurance

- the insurance premium consists of an industry-specific rate which is set by the Ministry of Employment and Labour multiplied by total wage;
- the average rate of all industries (selected for this study) is 1.70%.

3. Universal cash transfers

Child Benefit

Child benefit is paid every month to those who have children aged 5 years or younger: KRW 200 000 for a child aged 12 months or younger, KRW 150 000 for a child aged 1 to 2 years and KRW 100 000 for a child aged 2 to 5 years.

If a child attends a nursery or pre-school, childcare benefit is paid instead every month: KRW 418 000 for a child aged 0, KRW 368 000 for a child aged 1 year, KRW 304 000 for a child aged 2 years and KRW 220 000 for a child aged 3 to 5 years.

The above child benefits are not included in the Taxing Wages calculations that consider children aged between 6 and 11 inclusive.

4. Main changes in tax/benefit system since 2000

2000	Contribution to National Pension are to be deductible from 2001, upper cap of employment income deduction limit (KRW 12 000 000) is abolished from 2001
2001	Personal income tax rates are lowered by 10% (10, 20 ,30, 40% were reduced to 9, 18, 27, 36%, respectively) from 2002
2002	Limits of deduction for education fees are expanded from 2003. For pre-school: from KRW 1 000 000 to KRW 1 500 000. For elementary, middle school and high school: from KRW 1 500 000 to KRW 2 000 000. For college and university: from KRW 3 000 000 to KRW 5 000 000. Limit of deduction for interest of long-term mortgage loan for housing is expanded from KRW 3 000 000 to KRW 6 000 000 from 2003
2003	Employment income deduction and tax credit applicable to low income are increased. The deduction rate for the taxable wage income range of KRW 5 000 000 to KRW 15 000 000 is increased from 45% to 47.5%. The tax credit rate for calculated tax below KRW 500 000 is increased from 45% to 50% and the maximum tax credit is increased from KRW 400 000 to KRW 450 000.
2004	Limits of deduction for education fees are expanded. For pre-school: from KRW 1 500 000 to KRW 2 000 000. For college and university: from KRW 5 000 000 to KRW 7 000 000. Limit of deduction for interest on long-term mortgage loan for housing is expanded from KRW 6 000 000 to KRW 10 000 000. The marginal deduction rate for the taxable wage income range from KRW 5 000 000 to KRW 15 000 000 is increased from 47.5% to 50%. The tax credit rate for tax amounts below KRW 500 000 is increased from 50% to 55% and the maximum permitted tax credit goes up from KRW 450 000 to KRW 500 000.
2005	Personal income tax rates are lowered by 1% point (9, 18, 27, 36% were reduced to 8, 17, 26, 35%, respectively). Lump-sum tax relief are expanded from KRW 600 000 to KRW 1 000 000.
2007	Eligibility for the extra allowance amount has been changed. Previously, an income earner with a small number of dependents (e.g. spouse, child) eligible for basic allowance was eligible for an allowance of up to KRW 1 000 000 depending on the number of dependents. As from 2007, however, an income earner with two or more dependent children eligible for basic allowance is eligible for an allowance equivalent to KRW 500 000 if there are 2 children plus an additional KRW 1 000 000 for every additional child (e.g. 2 children: KRW 500 000; 3 children: KRW 1 500 000; 4 children: KRW 2 500 000, etc.).
2008	Tax schedule has been changed : from KRW 10 000 000, KRW 40 000 000 , KRW 80 000 000 to KRW 12 000 000, KRW 46 000 000, KRW 88 000 000; New items have been added to the additional allowance with respect to lineal descendants who are born or adopted during the concerned taxable year; Credit card purchase deduction has been changed : Employees may deduct 20% (previously 15%) of their credit/debit card purchases that exceed 20% (previously 15%) of their total income; Deduction for donations to public welfare or religious associations has been increased up to 15% of gross income. Previously, the limit was 10% of gross income.
2009	Personal income tax rates have been changed: from 8%, 17%, 26%, 35% to6%, 16%, 25%, and 35%. Employment income deduction has been changed: from 100%, 50%, 15%, and 10% 5% to 80%, 50%, 15%, and 10%. 5%
2010	Personal income tax rates have been changed: from 6%, 16%, 25%, 35% to6%, 15%, 24%, and 35%.
2012	Personal income tax rates have been changed: from6%, 15%, 24%, and 35% to 6%, 15%, 24%, 35% and 38%
2013	• A new additional allowance is added: a single parent with lineal descendants or adopted children who are eligible for basic exemption can deduct KRW 1 000 000. • Insurance premiums, medical expenses, education expenses, loans for house, designated donations, saving deposits for housing subscription, investment in employee stock ownership associations or in associations for investment in start-ups, and credit cards are allowed income deduction with a ceiling at KRW 25 000 000 in total. However, for the amount of designated donations exceeding the ceiling, deduction can be carried forward for 5 years.
2014	• Tax schedule has been changed : KRW 300 000 000 to KRW 150 000 000 • Personal and special income deductions(e.g. medical expenses, educational expenses) have been shifted toward tax credit • Employment income deduction has been changed : 80% to 70%, 50% to 40%. • The ceiling amount of earned income tax credit has been changed : KRW 500 000 to KRW 740 000 (the salary < 33 000 000), KRW 660 000 (the salary < 70 000 000)

5. Memorandum item

5.1. *Identification of the Average Worker (AW)*

Sectors used: industry Sectors B-N with reference to the International Standard Industrial Classification of All Economic Activities, Revision 4 (ISIC Rev.4)

Geographical coverage: whole country

Type of workers: wage workers (male and female).

5.2. *Method to calculate wages*

Report on Labour Force Survey at Establishments covering data in 2014 by the Ministry of Employment and Labour is used to calculate the annual wages of the AW. The statistics were obtained through a sample survey of 12 000 firms with five or more permanent employees throughout the whole country.

Basic method of calculation used: average monthly wages multiplied by 12.

5.3. *Employer's reserve for employee's retirement payment*

An employer should pay to a retiree the retirement payment which is not less than 30 days' wage and salary per one year of service (about 8.3% of gross income or more). An employer can contribute to the Retirement Payment Reserve Fund established within the company or Retirement Insurance Fund established outside the company to prepare for the retirement payment. Such contribution is treated as business expense under certain constraints. Because contribution to the Retirement Fund is not compulsory, this survey does not include such contribution except the contribution converted to employer's contribution to the national pension plan (see Section 2.21).

2016 parameter values

Average earnings/yr	Ave_earn	43 857 243	Secretariat estimate
Tax allowances	basic_al	1 500 000	
spouse	spouse_al	1 500 000	
dependents including children	dep_al	1 500 000	
additional allowance	add_all	500 000	
additional allowance 2	add2_all	1 000 000	
Employment income deduction	empdedsch	0	0.7
		5 000 000	0.4
		15 000 000	0.15
		45 000 000	0.05
		100 000 000	0.02
Earned income special credit threshold	earntaxcred	0.55	
		0.3	1 300 000
credit limit	credlimit	740 000	Ave_earn<33 000 000
		660 000	Ave_earn< 70 000 000
		500 000	Ave_earn> 70 000 000
Child tax credit	child_cred	150 000	
Lump sum tax credit	lump_cred	130 000	
	lump_thresh	1 428 571	
Tax schedule	tax_sch	0.06	12 000 000
		0.15	46 000 000
		0.24	88 000 000
		0.350.38	150 000 000
Local tax rate	local_rate	0.1	
Social security contributions	SSC_pens	0.045	
	SSC_pens_max	2 343 600	
	SSC_sick	0.03260423	
	SSC_sick_max	30 556 679.7	
	SSC_unemp	0.0065	
Employer contributions	emp_pens	0.045	
	emp_sick	0.03260423	
	emp_unemp	0.009	
	emp_inj	0.0170	

2016 tax equations

The equations for the Korean system are independent between spouses except that the principal earner has tax allowances for the spouse and for any children.

The functions which are used in the equations (Taper, MIN, Tax etc) are described in the technical note about tax equations. Variable names are defined in the table of parameters above, within the equations table, or are the standard variables married and children. A reference to a variable with the affix total indicates the sum of the relevant variable values for the principal and spouse. And the affixes princ and spouse indicate the value for the principal and spouse, respectively. Equations for a single person are as shown for the principal, with spouse values taken as 0.

	Line in country table and intermediate steps	Variable name	Range	Equation
1.	Earnings	earn		
2.	Allowances:			
	employment income	emp_al	B	Empincded(earn, empincdedsch)
	basic	bas_al	B	basic_al
	spouse	sp_al	P	Married*spouse_al*(earn_spouse-emp_al_spouse<=spouse_al)
	dependents	dp_al	P	Children*dep_al
	additional allowances	add_al_princ	P	IF(AND(Married=0,Children>0), add2_all,0)
	additional allowances	add_al_spouse	S	(earn_spouse>0)*add_all
	national pension deduction	np_de	B	Min(earn*SSC_pens, SSC_pens_max)
	Main non-standard tax relief	non-std_al	B	IF(earn*(SSC_sick+SSC_unemp)>lump_thresh,earn*(SSC_sick+SSC_unemp),0)
	Total	tax_al	B	emp_al+bas_al+sp_al+dp_al+add_al+np_al
3.	Credits in taxable income	taxbl_cr	B	0
4.	CG taxable income	tax_inc	B	Positive(earn-tax_al)
5.	CG tax before credits	CG_tax_excl	B	Tax(tax_inc, tax_sch)
6.	Tax credits :	earn_cr	B	MIN(earntaxcred(CG_tax_excl), credlimit(earn))
	earned income	child_cr	P	Children*child_cred
	special tax credit	lump_cr	B	IF(non-std_al=0, lump_cred, 0)
	child tax credit	tax_cr	B	earn_cr+child_cr+lump_cr
	lump-sum tax credit			
	Total			
7.	CG tax	CG_tax	B	CG_tax_excl-tax_cr
8.	State and local taxes	local_tax	B	local_rate*CG_tax
9.	Employees' soc security	SSC	B	MIN(earn*(SSC_pens),SSC_pens_max)+MIN(earn*(SSC_sick),SSC_sick_max)+earn*(SSC_unemp)
11.	Cash transfers	cash_trans	J	
13.	Employer's soc security	SSC_empr	B	MIN(earn*(SSC_pens),SSC_pens_max)+MIN(earn*(emp_sick),SSC_sick_max)+earn*(emp_unemp+emp_inj)

Key to range of equation:
B calculated separately for both principal earner and spouse
P calculated for principal only (value taken as 0 for spouse calculation)
S calculated for spouse only
J calculated once only on a joint basis

Taxing Wages 2017
© OECD 2017

Latvia

This chapter includes data on the income taxes paid by workers, their social security contributions, the family benefits they receive in the form of cash transfers as well as the social security contributions. Results reported include the marginal and average tax burden for eight different family types.

Methodological information is available for Personal income tax systems, Compulsory social security contributions to schemes operated within the government sector, Universal cash transfers as well as recent changes in the tax/benefit system. The methodology also includes the parameter values and tax equations underlying the data.

Latvia 2016

The tax/benefit position of single persons

	Wage level (per cent of average wage)	67	100	167	67
	Number of children	none	none	none	2
1.	**Gross wage earnings**	6 816	10 173	16 990	6 816
2.	**Standard tax allowances**				
	Basic allowance	900	900	900	900
	Married or head of family				
	Dependent children	0	0	0	4 200
	Deduction for social security contributions and income taxes	716	1 068	1 784	716
	Work-related expenses	0	0	0	0
	Other				
	Total	1 616	1 968	2 684	5 816
3.	**Tax credits or cash transfers included in taxable income**	0	0	0	0
4.	**Central government taxable income (1 - 2 + 3)**	5 200	8 205	14 306	1 000
5.	**Central government income tax liability (exclusive of tax credits)**	1 196	1 887	3 290	230
6.	**Tax credits**				
	Basic credit				
	Married or head of family				
	Children	0	0	0	0
	Other				
	Total	0	0	0	0
7.	**Central government income tax finally paid (5-6)**	1 196	1 887	3 290	230
8.	**State and local taxes**	0	0	0	0
9.	**Employees' compulsory social security contributions**				
	Gross earnings	716	1 068	1 784	716
	Taxable income				
	Total	716	1 068	1 784	716
10.	**Total payments to general government (7 + 8 + 9)**	1 912	2 955	5 074	946
11.	**Cash transfers from general government**				
	For head of family				
	For two children	0	0	0	410
	Total	0	0	0	410
12.	**Take-home pay (1-10+11)**	4 904	7 218	11 915	6 280
13.	**Employer's compulsory contributions**				
	Employer's compulsory social security contributions	1 608	2 400	4 008	1 608
	Payroll taxes	4	4	4	4
	Total	1 612	2 404	4 012	1 612
14.	**Average rates**				
	Income tax	17.5%	18.6%	19.4%	3.4%
	Employees' social security contributions	10.5%	10.5%	10.5%	10.5%
	Total payments less cash transfers	28.0%	29.1%	29.9%	7.9%
	Total tax wedge including employer's social security contributions	41.8%	42.6%	43.3%	25.5%
15.	**Marginal rates**				
	Total payments less cash transfers: Principal earner	31.1%	31.1%	31.1%	31.1%
	Total payments less cash transfers: Spouse	n.a.	n.a.	n.a.	n.a.
	Total tax wedge: Principal earner	44.2%	44.2%	44.2%	44.2%
	Total tax wedge: Spouse	n.a.	n.a.	n.a.	n.a.

Latvia 2016

The tax/benefit position of married couples

		Wage level (per cent of average wage)	100-0	100-33	100-67	100-33
		Number of children	2	2	2	none
1.	**Gross wage earnings**		10 173	13 531	16 990	13 531
2.	**Standard tax allowances**					
	Basic allowance		900	1 800	1 800	1 800
	Married or head of family					
	Dependent children		4 200	4 200	4 200	0
	Deduction for social security contributions and income taxes		1 068	1 421	1 784	1 421
	Work-related expenses		0	0	0	0
	Other					
		Total	6 168	7 421	7 784	3 221
3.	**Tax credits or cash transfers included in taxable income**		0	0	0	0
4.	**Central government taxable income (1 - 2 + 3)**		4 005	6 110	9 206	10 310
5.	**Central government income tax liability (exclusive of tax credits)**		921	1 405	2 117	2 371
6.	**Tax credits**					
	Basic credit					
	Married or head of family					
	Children		0	0	0	0
	Other					
		Total	0	0	0	0
7.	**Central government income tax finally paid (5-6)**		921	1 405	2 117	2 371
8.	**State and local taxes**		0	0	0	0
9.	**Employees' compulsory social security contributions**					
	Gross earnings		1 068	1 421	1 784	1 421
	Taxable income					
		Total	1 068	1 421	1 784	1 421
10.	**Total payments to general government (7 + 8 + 9)**		1 989	2 826	3 901	3 792
11.	**Cash transfers from general government**					
	For head of family					
	For two children		410	410	410	0
		Total	410	410	410	0
12.	**Take-home pay (1-10+11)**		8 594	11 114	13 498	9 739
13.	**Employer's compulsory contributions**					
	Employer's compulsory social security contributions		2 400	3 192	4 008	3 192
	Payroll taxes		4	9	9	9
		Total	2 404	3 201	4 016	3 201
14.	**Average rates**					
	Income tax		9.1%	10.4%	12.5%	17.5%
	Employees' social security contributions		10.5%	10.5%	10.5%	10.5%
	Total payments less cash transfers		15.5%	17.9%	20.6%	28.0%
	Total tax wedge including employer's social security contributions		31.7%	33.6%	35.7%	41.8%
15.	**Marginal rates**					
	Total payments less cash transfers: Principal earner		31.1%	31.1%	31.1%	31.1%
	Total payments less cash transfers: Spouse		24.9%	31.1%	31.1%	31.1%
	Total tax wedge: Principal earner		44.2%	44.2%	44.2%	44.2%
	Total tax wedge: Spouse		39.3%	44.2%	44.2%	44.2%

Since 2014 the Latvian currency is the Euro (EUR). In 2016, EUR 0.90 was equal to USD 1. That year, the average worker in Latvia earned EUR 10 173 per year (Secretariat estimate).

1. Personal income tax system

1.1. Central government income tax

1.1.1. Tax unit

The tax unit are individuals.

1.1.2. The main tax allowances

1.1.2.1. Standard tax reliefs:

- *A general (basic) allowance:*

In 2016, the differentiated non-taxable minimum has been introduced.

The *differentiated non-taxable minimum* will vary depending on income level: higher for lower wages, but less for higher wages. Besides it provides that in a five-year transitional period two parallel non-taxable minimums will be applied – monthly and annual.

However, in 2016 nothing changes and, as before, every month will be applied non-taxable minimum EUR 75 per month.

Differentiated non-taxable minimum criteria's

	2016	2017	2018	2019	2020
Maximum non-taxable minimum, *euro per month*	**100**	**115**	**130**	**145**	**160**
Minimum non-taxable minimum, *euro per month*	**75**	**60**	**40**	**20**	**0**
Taxable income* minimum threshold up to which the maximum annual non-taxable minimum will be applied, *euro per month*	380	400	420	440	460
Taxable income* maximum threshold up to which the annual non-taxable minimum will be applied, *euro per month*	1 000	1 100	1 200	1 350	1 500

* When calculating the taxable income not only wages, but also other income (such as dividends and income from real estate) will be taken into account. Similarly, if a person works in several jobs, the salaries will be added together and the non-taxable minimum will be applied to total revenue

Differentiated non-taxable minimum for 2016 will be applied only in 2017 when taxpayer submits annual tax return to SRS: for small income earners (up to EUR 380 per month) – EUR 100 per month or EUR 1 200 per year, for persons who receive income from EUR 380 to 1 000 per month – non-taxable minimum applying a formula gradually will decreases until at income level over EUR 1 000 per month – it remains EUR 75 per month or EUR 900 per year.

Coming years monthly applied non-taxable minimum will be gradually reduced, while the maximum applied non-taxable minimum will be increased (see table above).

- *The allowance for dependents* (which in most cases are children) of EUR 175 per month or EUR 2 100 per year (EUR 165 per month or EUR 1 980 per year in 2015) is also deductible from individual income. In addition from the list of dependents persons who are able to work has been excluded from 2016.

- To support youth employment during the summer (from June 1st to August 31st), parents can still receive tax allowance for dependents (children while it are working relation) EUR 175 per month (EUR 165 per month in 2015).
- *Relief for social security contributions*: Employee's state social security contributions are deductible for income tax purposes.
- *Tax credits*: None for employees

1.1.2.2. The main exemptions:

- capital gains on immovable property if the ownership is more than 5 years and it is place of residence more than 1 year;
- capital gains on immovable property if the ownership is more than 5 years and the last 5 years this immovable property has been the only immovable property of the payer;
- income from business or self-employed activities in field of rural tourism or agricultural manufacturing up to turnover of EUR 3 000 per taxation year, including the sums of State aid for agriculture or of the European Union aid for agriculture and rural development in amount EUR 3 000 per taxation year;
- supplementary pension capital, which is formed from the same natural person or his or her spouse, or in kinship relations to the third degree;
- scholarships regulated by special rule;
- income obtained as a result of inheritance;
- allowance (alimony);
- income from the alienation of personal property (movable objects such as furniture, clothing and other movable objects belonging to an individual intended for personal use) that is not related to business activities;
- goods and services lottery prizes;
- revenues from gifts up to EUR 1 425 from natural person, other than a close relative etc.
- revenues from gifts in full amount from natural persons, if the giver is connected to the payer by marriage or kinship to the third degree.

1.1.3. *Tax schedule*

2016 the tax rate of 23% applies for all levels of taxable income (the same rate was applied in 2015).

1.2. Regional and local income tax

No regional and local income taxes.

2. Compulsory social security contributions to schemes operated within the government sector

The state social security contribution system consists of six schemes as follows:

- state pension insurance;
- social insurance in case of unemployment;
- social insurance in respect of accidents at work and occupational diseases;

- invalidity insurance;
- maternity and sickness insurance;
- parents insurance.

In additional from 1 January 2016 is introduced a Solidarity tax. The solidarity tax represents a new progressive element in the labour taxation system. In 2014 and 2015 no social contributions were paid for wages exceeding a certain threshold (EUR 46 404 per year in 2014 and EUR 48 600 per year in 2015). From 2016 solidarity tax is applied to workers earning more than EUR 48 600 per year. Solidarity tax rate are at the same level as current social security contributions rates (10.5% and 23.59%). Solidarity tax revenue is transferred to the state budget and not tied to social services.

2.1. *Employees' contributions*

Employees pay 10.5% of their earnings in contributions. The taxable base is the total amount of the gross wage or salary including vacation payments, fringe benefits and remuneration of expenses related to work above a certain threshold. The assessment period is the calendar month.

2.2. *Employers' contributions*

Social security contributions are also paid by employers at a rate of 23.59% on behalf of their employees. The taxable base and the assessment period are the same as for employees' contributions.

The total contribution rates paid by employees and employers are applied:

Scheme name	Rate of contribution (%)
Pension insurance	23.86
Unemployment insurance	2.08
Insurance of accidents at work and occupational diseases	0.54
Invalidity insurance	3.11
Maternity and sickness insurance	3,05
Parents insurance	1.45
Total	34.09

3. Payroll tax

The Business risk fee is paid in in the state basic budget, then transferred to the Employee claim guarantee fund which is administrated by the state agency "Insolvency administration". The Insolvency administration is a public institution controlled by the Ministry of Justice.

If an enterprise is insolvent, the Insolvency Administration satisfies employee claims for their unpaid salaries, compensations for the paid annual leaves and compensations for dismissal in case of the end of the employment relationships.

The Business risk fee does not confer entitlement to any kind of social benefits.

The Business risk fee is a constant payment for a person EUR 0.36 per employee per month.

4. Universal cash transfers

4.1. *Transfers related to marital status*

None.

4.2. *Transfers for dependent children*

From 2015 support for families has been introduced through differentiated family benefits: EUR 11.38 per month for the first child, plus EUR 22.76 per month for the second child, plus EUR 34.14 per month for the third and each subsequent child. The state pays family benefits to all children until they reach the age of 15. Children enrolled in basic or secondary schools or vocational education institutions operating on the basis of basic education have the right to receive family benefits until the age of 19.

In addition there are four other types of family benefits for which payment depends on either the age of the child(ren) and/ or the status of the person(s) looking after them: maternity and paternity benefit; childbirth benefit; parental benefit; child care benefit (additional benefit for child with disabilities). These are not included in the modelling.

5. Main changes in tax/benefit system in 2016

- The allowance for dependents has been increased from EUR 165 per month in 2015 to EUR 175 per month in 2016. In addition from the list of dependents persons who are able to work has been excluded from 2016.
- The differentiated non-taxable minimum has been introduced. The differentiated non-taxable minimum will vary depending on income level: higher for lower wages, but less for higher wages. Besides it provides that in a five-year transitional period two parallel non-taxable minimums will be applied – monthly and annual.
- The solidarity tax has been introduced. Solidarity tax is applied to workers earning more than EUR 48 600 per year. Solidarity tax rate are at the same level as current social security contributions rates.

6. Memorandum items

6.1. *Average gross annual wage earnings*

In Latvia the gross earnings figures cover wages and salaries paid to individuals in formal employment including payment for overtime. They also include additional bonuses and payments and other payments such as for the annual and supplementary vacations, public holidays, sick pay (sick-leave certificate A), payment for public holidays and other days not worked, social security compulsory contributions paid by the employees and personal income tax, as well as labour remuneration subsidies.

6.2. *Employer contributions to private pension and health schemes*

Some employer contributions are made to private health and pension schemes but there is no relevant information available on the amounts that are paid.

2016 parameter values

Average earnings/yr	Ave_earn	10 173	Secretariat estimate
Allowances	Basic_al	900	
	Child_al	2 100	
Income tax	Tax_rate	0.23	
Employers SSC	SSC_rate1	0.2359	
Payroll tax - Business risk fee	payroll	4.32	
Income ceiling	Ceiling	48 600	
Employees SSC	SSC_rate2	0.105	
Child allowances	CA_first	136.56	
	CA_second	273.12	
	CA_third and each next	409.68	
Days in tax year	numdays	366	

2016 tax equations

The equations for the Latvian system are mostly on an individual basis.

The functions which are used in the equations (Taper, MIN, Tax etc) are described in the technical note about tax equations. Variable names are defined in the table of parameters above, within the equations table, or are the standard variables "married" and "children". A reference to a variable with the affix "_total" indicates the sum of the relevant variable values for the principal and spouse. And the affixes "_princ" and "_spouse" indicate the value for the principal and spouse, respectively. Equations for a single person are as shown for the principal, with "_spouse" values taken as 0.

	Line in country table and intermediate steps	Variable name	Range	Equation
1.	Earnings	earn		
2.	Allowances:	tax_al	P	=MIN(Basic_al+SSC_empee_princ+(Children>0)*(Child_al*Children);earn_princ)
			S	=Min(Basic_al+SSC_empee_spouse,earn_spouse)
3.	Credits in taxable income	taxbl_cr	B	0
4.	CG taxable income	tax_inc	B	Positive(earn-tax_al)
5.	CG tax before credits	CG_tax_excl	B	Tax_inc*tax_rate
6.	Tax credits :	tax_cr	B	0
7.	CG tax	CG_tax	B	CG_tax_excl-tax_cr
8;	State and local taxes	local_tax	B	0
9.	Employees' soc security	SSC_empee	B	= earn*SSC_rate2
11.	Cash transfers	cash_trans	J	=IF(Children<1;0;IF(Children=1;CA_first;IF(Children=2;CA_first+CA_second;IF(Children=3;CA_first+CA_second+CA_third_and_each_next;IF(Children>3;CA_first+CA _second+CA_third_and_each_next*(Children-2)))))
13.	Employer's soc security	SSC_empr	B B	=earn*SSC_rate1 =payroll

Key to range of equation B calculated separately for both principal earner and spouse P calculated for principal only (value taken as 0 for spouse calculation) J calculated once only on a joint basis.

© OECD 2017

Luxembourg

This chapter includes data on the income taxes paid by workers, their social security contributions, the family benefits they receive in the form of cash transfers as well as the social security contributions and payroll taxes paid by their employers. Results reported include the marginal and average tax burden for eight different family types.

Methodological information is available for Personal income tax systems, Compulsory social security contributions to schemes operated within the government sector, Universal cash transfers as well as recent changes in the tax/benefit system. The methodology also includes the parameter values and tax equations underlying the data.

Luxembourg 2016

The tax/benefit position of single persons

	Wage level (per cent of average wage)	67	100	167	67
	Number of children	none	none	none	2
1.	**Gross wage earnings**	37 652	56 197	93 849	37 652
2.	**Standard tax allowances**				
	Basic allowance	480	480	480	480
	Married or head of family				
	Dependent children				
	Deduction for social security contributions and income taxes	4 161	6 210	10 370	4 161
	Work-related expenses	540	540	540	540
	Other	0	0	0	0
	Total	5 181	7 230	11 390	5 181
3.	**Tax credits or cash transfers included in taxable income**	0	0	0	0
4.	**Central government rounded taxable income (1 - 2 + 3)**	32 450	48 950	82 450	32 450
5.	**Central government income tax liability (exclusive of tax credits)**	4 106	10 500	24 479	2 359
6.	**Tax credits**				
	Basic credit	300	300	300	300
	Married or head of family				
	Children				
	Other	0	0	0	750
	Total	300	300	300	1 050
7.	**Central government income tax finally paid (5-6)**	3 806	10 200	24 179	1 309
8.	**State and local taxes**	0	0	0	0
9.	**Employees' compulsory social security contributions**				
	Gross earnings	4 795	7 197	12 073	4 795
	Taxable income				
	Total	4 795	7 197	12 073	4 795
10.	**Total payments to general government (7 + 8 + 9)**	8 601	17 396	36 252	6 105
11.	**Cash transfers from general government**				
	For head of family				
	For two children	0	0	0	7 522
	Total	0	0	0	7 522
12.	**Take-home pay (1-10+11)**	29 051	38 801	57 597	39 069
13.	**Employer's compulsory social security contributions**	4 578	6 834	11 412	4 578
14.	**Average rates**				
	Income tax	10.1%	18.1%	25.8%	3.5%
	Employees' social security contributions	12.7%	12.8%	12.9%	12.7%
	Total payments less cash transfers	22.8%	31.0%	38.6%	-3.8%
	Total tax wedge including employer's social security contributions	31.2%	38.4%	45.3%	7.5%
15.	**Marginal rates**				
	Total payments less cash transfers: Principal earner	41.5%	50.1%	50.1%	44.4%
	Total payments less cash transfers: Spouse	n.a.	n.a.	n.a.	n.a.
	Total tax wedge: Principal earner	47.8%	55.5%	55.5%	50.4%
	Total tax wedge: Spouse	n.a.	n.a.	n.a.	n.a.

Luxembourg 2016

The tax/benefit position of married couples

			100-0	100-33	100-67	100-33
		Wage level (per cent of average wage)	100-0	100-33	100-67	100-33
		Number of children	2	2	2	none
1.	**Gross wage earnings**		56 197	74 742	93 849	74 742
2.	**Standard tax allowances**					
	Basic allowance		480	960	960	960
	Married or head of family					
	Dependent children					
	Deduction for social security contributions and income taxes		6 210	8 259	10 370	8 259
	Work-related expenses		540	1 080	1 080	1 080
	Other		0	4 500	4 500	4 500
		Total	7 230	14 799	16 910	14 799
3.	**Tax credits or cash transfers included in taxable income**		0	0	0	0
4.	**Central government rounded taxable income (1 - 2 + 3)**		48 950	59 900	76 900	59 900
5.	**Central government income tax liability (exclusive of tax credits)**		3 939	6 722	12 369	6 722
6.	**Tax credits**					
	Basic credit		300	600	600	600
	Married or head of family					
	Children					
	Other		0	0	0	0
		Total	300	600	600	600
7.	**Central government income tax finally paid (5-6)**		3 639	6 122	11 769	6 122
8.	**State and local taxes**		0	0	0	0
9.	**Employees' compulsory social security contributions**					
	Gross earnings		7 197	9 518	11 992	9 518
	Taxable income					
		Total	7 197	9 518	11 992	9 518
10.	**Total payments to general government (7 + 8 + 9)**		10 836	15 639	23 761	15 639
11.	**Cash transfers from general government**					
	For head of family					
	For two children		7 522	7 522	7 522	0
		Total	7 522	7 522	7 522	0
12.	**Take-home pay (1-10+11)**		52 883	66 625	77 610	59 103
13.	**Employer's compulsory social security contributions**		6 834	9 089	11 412	9 089
14.	**Average rates**					
	Income tax		6.5%	8.2%	12.5%	8.2%
	Employees' social security contributions		12.8%	12.7%	12.8%	12.7%
	Total payments less cash transfers		5.9%	10.9%	17.3%	20.9%
	Total tax wedge including employer's social security contributions		16.1%	20.5%	26.3%	29.5%
15.	**Marginal rates**					
	Total payments less cash transfers: Principal earner		32.0%	37.7%	47.2%	37.7%
	Total payments less cash transfers: Spouse		25.9%	37.7%	47.2%	37.7%
	Total tax wedge: Principal earner		39.4%	44.5%	52.9%	44.5%
	Total tax wedge: Spouse		34.0%	44.5%	52.9%	44.5%

The national currency is the Euro (EUR). In 2016, EUR 0.90 equalled USD 1. The Secretariat has estimated that in that same year the average worker earned EUR 56 197.

1. Personal income tax system

1.1. *Taxes levied by central government*

1.1.1. *Tax unit*

Spouses and partners are taxed jointly on their income. The income of minor children is included in determining the couple's taxable income. However, any earned income that children may derive from work is excluded from joint taxation.

1.1.2. *Tax reliefs and tax credits*

1.1.2.1. Standard reliefs in the form of deductions from income

- Wage-earners are entitled to a standard minimum deduction of EUR 540 for work-related expenses other than travel, unless their actual deductible expenses are higher. This deduction is doubled for spouses taxed jointly.
- The first 4 distance units (i.e. 4 * 99 = EUR 396 per year) of the lump sum deduction for travel expenses between a taxpayer's home and his working places are abolished. The maximum deduction will be limited to EUR 2 574 per year.
- Like other taxpayers, wage-earners having no special expenses (interest charges, insurance premiums or contributions other than for social security) may take a standard deduction of EUR 480 for special expenses. Actual insurance premiums are deductible up to the limit set by law.
- If both spouses have earned income and are taxed jointly, they qualify for an earned income allowance of EUR 4 500.
- Social security contributions: contributions paid to compulsory health insurance and pension schemes are deductible in full.
- Dependency insurance: the dependency contribution is not deductible for income tax purposes.

1.1.2.2. Standard reliefs in the form of tax credits

- Wage-earners and pensioners receive a refundable tax credit of EUR 300 per annum.
- Single-parents receive a refundable tax credit of EUR 750 per annum.

1.1.2.3. Non-standard allowances deductible from taxable income

- Interest charges are deductible insofar as they are not considered operating expenses or acquisition expenses, and provided they are unrelated economically to the exempt income. However, the deduction of interest charges is capped at EUR 336 per year. This ceiling is increased by EUR 336 for the taxpayer's spouse/partner and for each child.

- Taxpayers may deduct premiums paid to insurers licensed in an EU country in respect of life, death, accident, disability, illness or liability insurance, as well as dues paid to recognised mutual assistance companies. However, deductions are capped at EUR 672 per year.
- Payments to an insurance company or credit institution in respect of an individual retirement scheme are deductible. These payments are capped according to the subscriber's age and must meet certain investment policy constraints. The ceiling varies between EUR 1 500 and EUR 3 200. Each spouse/partner may take out such a contract and qualify for the respective ceilings.
- Contributions to building society savings are deductible up to the limit of EUR 672.
- Interest charges in respect of the rental value of owner-occupied housing are deductible only up to an annual ceiling. During the first five years, the ceiling is EUR 1 500; for the following five years it is EUR 1 125; thereafter it is EUR 750. These ceilings are increased by an equal amount for the taxpayer's spouse/partner, and for each qualifying child.
- As from 1 January 2009, the maximal deduction of premium related to the mortgage life insurance on the taxpayer's principal residence is EUR 6 000. This ceiling is increased by an equal amount for the taxpayer's spouse/partner and by 1 200 for each qualifying child. For taxpayers over the age of 30, the allowable deduction of EUR 6 000 is increased by 8% for each year over 30, with a ceiling of 160%.
- Upon request, taxpayers may be granted exemptions for extraordinary expenses that are unavoidable, and that considerably reduce their ability to pay taxes (e.g. uninsured health care costs, support for needy relatives, uninsured funeral costs beyond the taxpayer's means, domestic or childcare expenses, expenses for children outside the taxpayer's household, or expenses for children in a single-parent household).

1.1.3. *Tax schedule reliefs*

Income tax is determined on the basis of the following schedule (amounts in Euros):

0% for the portion of income between 11 265
8% for the portion of income between 11 265 and 13 173
10% for the portion of income between 13 173 and 15 081
12% for the portion of income between 15 081 and 16 989
14% for the portion of income between 16 989 and 18 897
16% for the portion of income between 18 897 and 20 805
18% for the portion of income between 20 805 and 22 713
20% for the portion of income between 22 713 and 24 621
22% for the portion of income between 24 621 and 26 529
24% for the portion of income between 26 529 and 28 437
26% for the portion of income between 28 437 and 30 345
28% for the portion of income between 30 345 and 32 253
30% for the portion of income between 32 253 and 34 161
32% for the portion of income between 34 161 and 36 069
34% for the portion of income between 36 069 and 37 977
36% for the portion of income between 37 977 and 39 885
38% for the portion of income between 39 885 and 41 793
39% for the portion of income between 41 793 and 100 000
40% for the portion exceeding 100 000

The income tax liability of *single* taxpayers is determined by applying the above schedule to taxable income.

The income tax liability of *married* taxpayers and partners corresponds to double the amount obtained if the above schedule is applied to half of their income (class 2).

For widow(er)s, taxpayers with a dependent child allowance and persons over 64 years of age (class 1a), tax is calculated as follows: the schedule is applied to adjusted taxable income reduced by half of the difference between that amount and EUR 45 060, with the marginal tax rate capped at 40%.

Income tax as determined by the applicable schedules is subject to a 7% "solidarity" surtax to finance the employment fund. The rate is 9% for the taxable income exceeding EUR 150 000 (tax classes 1 and 1a), respectively EUR 300 000 (tax class 2).

1.1.4. *Income exemptions*

A taxpayer may claim a deduction for a dependent child under 21 years of age who is not part of the household. This deduction is allowed for expenses actually incurred but may not exceed EUR 3 480.

1.2. *Local (municipal) taxes*

No particular income tax is levied by municipalities, which receive a direct share of the income tax revenue collected by the State. This share is equal to 18% of tax revenue.

2. Compulsory social security contributions to schemes operated within the government sector

	Employer's share (%)	Employee's share (%)	Ceiling on contributions (in euros)
a) Pension and disability insurance	8	8	115 377.84
b) Health insurance	3.05	3.05	115 377.84
c) Dependency insurance		1.4	Monthly allowance 480.74*
d) Health in the workplace	0.11		
e) Accident insurance	1.00		

* (Monthly allowance: EUR 480.74 = 0.25* social minimum salary/12). The social minimum salary in 2016 is equal to EUR 23 075.52.

No distinction is made according to family status or gender.

As from 1 January 2009 the differences in social security contributions between workers and employees are abolished.

A temporary budget balancing tax, the "impôt d'équilibrage budgétaire temporaire" (IEBT), was introduced for the year 2015. The tax rate of 0.5% will be withheld on all categories of income (professional and replacement income and non-professional income, except on supplements for overtime) for all individuals affiliated to the Luxembourg social security system.

This measure was introduced for the tax years 2015 and 2016.

3. Universal cash transfers

3.1. *For married persons*

None.

3.2. *For dependent children*

Every child raised in the Grand Duchy entitles the person on whom the child is dependent to a monthly family allowance. Family allowances are adjusted regularly for the cost of living. For 2015, the amounts are:

Effective date	As of 1 July 2006
1 eligible child	EUR 185.60
2 eligible children	EUR 440.72
3 eligible children	EUR 802.74

Starting with the fourth eligible child, the allowance is raised by EUR 361.82 per child.

The amounts indicated above are increased by EUR 16.17 for children aged 6 to 11 and by EUR 48.52 for those aged 12 years or older.

Additionally, a child bonus amounting to EUR 76.88 per child per month is paid in cash irrespective of the taxable income of the parents as from 1 January 2009. This amount is paid by the National Family Benefits Administration.

4. Main changes since 2008

4.1. *Partnerships*

The Act of 9 July 2004 introduced the notion of partnerships into tax law. The Act construes the term "partnership" as a relationship between two persons, called "partners", of opposite sex or the same sex, who live together as a couple and declare themselves as such.

As from 1 January 2008, the fiscal treatment of the partnerships is modified. The deduction for extraordinary expenses is replaced by the joint taxation of partners as it already exists for spouses.

4.2. *Introduction of tax credits*

The following changes were made as of 1 January 2009:

- Four tax allowances have been replaced by refundable tax credits. Instead of reducing their taxable income by EUR 600, wage-earners get a tax credit of EUR 300 per annum. A similar tax credit is allowed for pensioners.
- The tax exemption of EUR 1 920 for single-parent households is replaced by a tax credit of EUR 750 per annum.
- A tax credit of EUR 300 per annum is granted to self-employed persons deriving income from trade or business, income from agriculture and forestry or income from self-employment. This tax credit substitutes the allowance for business income and the agricultural allowance.

5. Memorandum item

5.1. *Identification of the average worker*

Average gross hourly wages by industry and by gender are determined on the basis of biannual surveys on industry wages and working hours. These surveys cover gross compensation for regular hours (working hours + leave time) plus overtime pay. Hourly wages include bonuses and allowances such as premiums for output, production or productivity. In contrast, non-periodic compensation (bonuses, profit-sharing) that is not paid systematically in each pay period is not included. Nevertheless, in order to allow for comparisons between countries, gross annual pay is adjusted on the basis of average non-periodic compensation as calculated from triennial surveys of labour costs.

Regarding working hours, the time taken into account is the time effectively offered, including regular working hours, overtime, night shifts and work on Sunday.

2016 parameter values

Average earnings/yr	Ave_earn	56 197	Secretariat estimate
Tax allowances: general	gen_dedn	480	
professional expenses	prof_exp	540	
travel expenses	travel_exp	0	
extra if both spouses earning	extra_dedn	4 500	
Low earner allowance	allow_1		
Low earner allowance (couples)	allow_2		
Class 1a limit	cl_1a_lim	45 060	
Tax schedule	tax_sch	0	11 265
		0.08	13 173
		0.1	15 081
		0.12	16 989
		0.14	18 897
		0.16	20 805
		0.18	22 713
		0.2	24 621
		0.22	26 529
		0.24	28 437
		0.26	30 345
		0.28	32 253
		0.3	34 161
		0.32	36 069
		0.34	37 977
		0.36	39 885
		0.38	41 793
		0.39	100 000
		0.40	
Child credit maximum	ch_cred	0	
Social Minimum Salary	min_salary	23 075.52	
Multiplier for unemployment	unemp_rate_1	1.07	
	Unemp_rate_2	1.09	
	Unemp_lim	150 000	
Social security contributions	SSC_rate	0.1105	
	SSC_ceil	115 377.84	
	infirm	0.014	
	infirm_abatement	0.25	
IEBT	iebt_rate	0.005	
Employer contributions	workhealth	0.0011	
	SSC_empr	0.1105	
	SSC_acc	0.010	
Child benefit (1 child)	CB_1	185.6	
2 children	CB_2	440.72	
extra age 6-11	CB_ex	16.17	
Child bonus	ch_bonus	922.50	
Worker tax credit	worker_credit	300	
Single parent tax credit	cr_monoparent	750	
Class 1a Discount	discount	0.50	
Maximum Marginal Rate	max_rate	0.40	

2016 tax equations

The equations for the Luxembourg system are on a joint basis except for social security contributions.

The functions which are used in the equations (Taper, MIN, Tax etc) are described in the technical note about tax equations. Variable names are defined in the table of parameters above, within the equations table, or are the standard variables "married" and "children". A reference to a variable with the affix "_total" indicates the sum of the relevant variable values for the principal and spouse. And the affixes "_princ" and "_spouse" indicate the value for the principal and spouse, respectively. Equations for a single person are as shown for the principal, with "_spouse" values taken as 0.

	Line in country table and intermediate steps	Variable name	Range	Equation
1.	Earnings	earn		
2.	Allowances:			
	Basic	basic	J	IF(earn_spouse=0, 1, 2)*gen_dedn
	work-related	work_rel	J	IF(earn_spouse=0, 1, 2)*(prof_exp)
	Other	other_al	J	(earn_spouse>0)*extra_dedn
	Total	tax_al	J	min(basic+work_rel+other_al+SSC_ded_total, earn)
3.	Credits in taxable income	taxbl_cr	J	0
	family quotient	quotient	J	1+Married
4.	CG taxable income unadjusted taxable income	tax_inc	J	earn-tax_al
5.	CG tax before credits	tax_excl	J	((Children=0)*IF(Married=0,Tax(tax_inc, tax_sch), quotient*Tax(tax_inc/quotient, tax_sch)) + (Children>0)*IF(Married=0, Taxclass1a(tax_inc, tax_sch, discount, cl_1a_lim, max_rate), quotient*Tax(tax_inc/quotient, tax_sch)))*IF(tax_inc> unemp_lim*(1+Married,unemp_rate_2,unemp_rate_1)
6.	Tax credits :	worker_cr	J	IF(earn_spouse=0,1,2)*worker_credit
		monoparent_cr	J	cr_monoparent*(AND(Married=0,Children>0))
		tax_cr	J	worker_cr+monoparent_cr
7.	CG tax	CG_tax	J	tax_excl-tax_cr
8.	State and local taxes	local_tax	J	0
9.	Employees' soc security	SSC	B	SSC_rate*MIN(earn, SSC_ceil)+infirm*Positive(earn-infirm_abatement*min_salary)+(iebt_rate*earn)
	deductible portion	SSC_ded	B	SSC_rate*MIN(earn, SSC_ceil)
11.	Cash transfers	cash_trans	J	((Children=1)*(CB_1+CB_ex)+ (Children=2)*(CB_2+2*CB_ex))*12+Children*ch_bonus
13.	Employer's soc security	SSC_empr	B	(SSC_empr+workhealth)*MIN(earn, SSC_ceil)+SSC_acc*MIN(earn, SSC_ceil)

Key to range of equation B calculated separately for both principal earner and spouse P calculated for principal only (value taken as 0 for spouse calculation) J calculated once only on a joint basis.

© OECD 2017

Mexico

This chapter includes data on the income taxes paid by workers, their social security contributions, the family benefits they receive in the form of cash transfers as well as the social security contributions and payroll taxes paid by their employers. Results reported include the marginal and average tax burden for eight different family types.

Methodological information is available for Personal income tax systems, Compulsory social security contributions to schemes operated within the government sector, Universal cash transfers as well as recent changes in the tax/benefit system. The methodology also includes the parameter values and tax equations.

Mexico 2016

The tax/benefit position of single persons

		Wage level (per cent of average wage)	67	100	167	67
		Number of children	none	none	none	2
1.	**Gross wage earnings**		75 594	112 827	188 421	75 594
2.	**Standard tax allowances**					
	Basic allowance		2 502	2 655	2 966	2 502
	Married or head of family					
	Dependent children					
	Deduction for social security contributions and income taxes					
	Work-related expenses					
	Other					
		Total	2 502	2 655	2 966	2 502
3.	**Tax credits or cash transfers included in taxable income**		0	0	0	0
4.	**Central government taxable income (1 - 2 + 3)**		73 092	110 172	185 455	73 092
5.	**Central government income tax liability (exclusive of tax credits)**		5 422	10 685	26 304	5 422
6.	**Tax credits**					
	Basic credit		3 536	0	0	3 536
	Married or head of family					
	Children					
	Other		0	0	0	0
		Total	3 536	0	0	3 536
7.	**Central government income tax finally paid (5-6)**		1 887	10 685	26 304	1 887
8.	**State and local taxes**		0	0	0	0
9.	**Employees' compulsory social security contributions**					
	Gross earnings		945	1 542	2 789	945
	Taxable income					
		Total	945	1 542	2 789	945
10.	**Total payments to general government (7 + 8 + 9)**		2 832	12 226	29 093	2 832
11.	**Cash transfers from general government**					
	For head of family					
	For two children		0	0	0	0
		Total	0	0	0	0
12.	**Take-home pay (1-10+11)**		72 762	100 601	159 328	72 762
13.	**Employers' compulsory social security contributions**		10 352	13 134	18 879	10 352
14.	**Average rates**					
	Income tax		2.5%	9.5%	14.0%	2.5%
	Employees' social security contributions		1.3%	1.4%	1.5%	1.3%
	Total payments less cash transfers		3.7%	10.8%	15.4%	3.7%
	Total tax wedge including employer's social security contributions		15.3%	20.1%	23.1%	15.3%
15.	**Marginal rates**					
	Total payments less cash transfers: Principal earner		12.1%	19.5%	22.9%	12.1%
	Total payments less cash transfers: Spouse		n.a.	n.a.	n.a.	n.a.
	Total tax wedge: Principal earner		17.5%	25.2%	28.4%	17.5%
	Total tax wedge: Spouse		n.a.	n.a.	n.a.	n.a.

Mexico 2016

The tax/benefit position of married couples

			100-0	100-33	100-67	100-33
	Wage level (per cent of average wage)		100-0	100-33	100-67	100-33
	Number of children		2	2	2	none
1.	**Gross wage earnings**		112 827	150 436	188 045	150 436
2.	**Standard tax allowances**					
	Basic allowance		2 655	4 355	5 155	4 355
	Married or head of family					
	Dependent children					
	Deduction for social security contributions and income taxes					
	Work-related expenses					
	Other					
		Total	2 655	4 355	5 155	4 355
3.	**Tax credits or cash transfers included in taxable income**		0	0	0	0
4.	**Central government taxable income (1 - 2 + 3)**		110 172	146 081	182 890	146 081
5.	**Central government income tax liability (exclusive of tax credits)**		10 685	12 716	16 066	12 716
6.	**Tax credits**					
	Basic credit		0	4 879	3 536	4 879
	Married or head of family					
	Children					
	Other		0	0	0	0
		Total	0	4 879	3 536	4 879
7.	**Central government income tax finally paid (5-6)**		10 685	7 837	12 531	7 837
8.	**State and local taxes**		0	0	0	0
9.	**Employees' compulsory social security contributions**					
	Gross earnings		1 542	2 012	2 482	2 012
	Taxable income					
		Total	1 542	2 012	2 482	2 012
10.	**Total payments to general government (7 + 8 + 9)**		12 226	9 848	15 012	9 848
11.	**Cash transfers from general government**					
	For head of family					
	For two children		0	0	0	0
		Total	0	0	0	0
12.	**Take-home pay (1-10+11)**		100 601	140 587	173 032	140 587
13.	**Employers' compulsory social security contributions**		13 134	21 017	23 461	21 017
14.	**Average rates**					
	Income tax		9.5%	5.2%	6.7%	5.2%
	Employees' social security contributions		1.4%	1.3%	1.3%	1.3%
	Total payments less cash transfers		10.8%	6.5%	8.0%	6.5%
	Total tax wedge including employer's social security contributions		20.1%	18.0%	18.2%	18.0%
15.	**Marginal rates**					
	Total payments less cash transfers: Principal earner		19.5%	19.5%	19.5%	19.5%
	Total payments less cash transfers: Spouse		-6.3%	7.4%	12.1%	7.4%
	Total tax wedge: Principal earner		25.2%	25.2%	25.2%	25.2%
	Total tax wedge: Spouse		12.1%	13.0%	17.5%	13.0%

The national currency is the peso (MXN). In 2016, MXN 18.63 was equal to USD 1. That year, the estimated earnings of the average worker are MXN 112 827 (Secretariat estimate).

1. Personal income tax

1.1. *Central government income tax*

1.1.1. *Tax unit*

Each person is taxed separately.

1.1.2. *Tax allowances and tax credits*

1.1.2.1. Standard tax reliefs

There are two basic allowances, a yearly holiday bonus and an end-of-year bonus.

- *Holiday Bonus:* Mexico's Labour Law stipulates a minimum holiday bonus of 25% of six days of the worker's wage. The maximum exemption according to the Tax Law is equivalent to 15 days of the minimum wage.
- *End-of-year bonus:* The minimum end-of-year bonus established in the Labour Law is 15 days of the worker's wage. The Tax Law exempts end-of-year-bonuses up to 30 days of the minimum wage.

1.1.2.2. Main non-standard tax reliefs

Deductions:

- Compulsory school transportation costs.
- Medical expenses (doctor and dental fees and hospital expenses): For expenses made by the taxpayer on behalf of his or her spouse and straight line relatives, the deduction is allowed only if the taxpayer's relative earns less than the minimum annual wage of his geographical area.
- Complementary contributions of certain retirement accounts are considered eligible as long as they do not exceed 10% of taxable income and MXN 133 298 (five annual minimum wages).
- Funeral expenses: for the spouse and straight-line relatives up to one annual minimum wage.
  - Charitable donations made to institutions such as:
  - Federal, state, and municipal governments.
  - Non-profit organisations involved in the fields of social beneficence, education, culture, and research and technology.

Since October 2015 there is a nationwide minimum wage. As in June 2016, the minimum wage is MXN 73.04 per day.

- Deposits on special savings accounts, payments of insurance premium of pension plans, and for the acquisition of shares of investment societies as long as they do not exceed MXN 152 000.
- Health insurance premiums for individuals, if the beneficiary is the taxpayer, and/or his family.
- Real interest expenditure of mortgage loans if the value of the property does not exceed MXN 4 071 673. Real interest expenditure is defined as the excess of interest expense over the inflation rate.
- Deduction of taxpayer's educational expenditures for himself, on behalf of his/her spouse, parents or children, among others, for the following educational levels.

Educational level	Maximum annual deduction (MXN)
Kinder Garden	14 200
Primary Education	12 900
Secondary Education	19 900
Technical Profession	17 100
High School	24 500

In 2016 the limit amount for personal deductions was increased. The new limit is the minimum between 15% of taxpayer's gross income and an amount equivalent to 5 annual minimum wages (MXN 133 298 in 2016). The limit does not apply to private school's tuition, charity donations, complementary contributions to retirement's personal accounts, professional fees, and medical expenses in the event of incapacity or disability.

1.1.2.3. Employment subsidy credit

The employment subsidy credit is decreasing on workers' income and is assigned based on a table of income brackets. For monthly income higher than MXN 7 382 no employment subsidy credit is given. Employees with an income tax lower than the credit receive in cash the difference along with their salary. The rest of the workers that receive the credit are entitled to a reduction in their tax burden. The employment subsidy credit is paid by the employers who may credit it against their tax liabilities; the credit therefore represents a fiscal cost for the government.

1.1.3. *Tax schedule and other tables*

1.1.3.1. Tax schedule

Since 2014 three additional brackets were included with a maximum marginal rate for income over MXN 3 million of 35%.

The income tax schedule and the employment subsidy credit table are updated once the accumulated inflation reaches 10%.

Taxable income (MXN)		Fixed quota (MXN)	Tax on the amount in excess of the lower limit (%)
Lower Limit	Upper Limit		
0	5 952.84	0	1.92
5 952.85	50 524.92	114.29	6.40
50 524.93	88 793.04	2 966.91	10.88
88 793.05	103 218.00	7 130.48	16.00
103 218.01	123 580.20	9 438.47	17.92
123 580.21	249 243.48	13 087.37	21.36
249 243.49	392 841.96	39 929.05	23.52
392 841.97	750 000	73 703.41	30.00
750 000.01	1 000 000.00	180 850.82	32.00
1 000 000.01	3 000 000.00	260 850.81	34.00
3 000 000.01	And over	940 850.81	35.00

1.1.3.2. Employment subsidy credit table

For taxable income in a certain income range, the employment subsidy credit is given in the third column of the following table:

Lower limit (MXN)	Upper limit (MXN)	Tax credit (MXN)
0.0	21 227.52	4 884.24
21 227.53	31 840.56	4 881.96
31 840.57	41 674.08	4 879.44
41 674.09	42 454.44	4 713.24
42 454.45	53 353.80	4 589.52
53 353.81	56 606.16	4 250.76
56 606.17	64 025.04	3 898.44
64 025.05	74 696.04	3 535.56
74 696.05	85 366.80	3 042.48
85 366.81	88 587.96	2 611.32
88 587.97	And Over	0.00

1.2. State and local income taxes

States do not levy taxes on income.

1.3. Payroll taxes

Mexico does not have a Federal pay-roll tax. However, most States apply a state pay-roll tax with an average rate of 2.31%. These taxes are not considered in this Report since there are a wide range of practices with respect to the definition of the tax base that does not allow obtaining a reliable estimation.

2. Compulsory social security contributions to schemes operated within the government sector

2.1. Employees' contributions

Social security contributions are divided as follows:

For sickness and maternity insurance, 0.625% of the workers monthly wage, plus 0.40% of the amount in excess of three times the minimal legal wage (the amount that applies within the Federal District of Mexico City MWFD). For disability and life insurance, 0.625% of the monthly wage.

In 2016 a ceiling of 25 MWFD applies to the salary that is used to calculate the social security contributions.

2.2. *Employers' contributions*

- For sickness and maternity 20.40% of the MWFD, plus 1.10% of the amount in excess of three times the MWFD, plus 1.75% of the monthly wage.
- For disability and life insurance, 1.75% of worker's monthly wage.
- For social services and nursery, 1% of worker's monthly wage.
- For insurance for work injuries of employees, 2.00% of worker's monthly wage.

In 2016 a ceiling of 25 MWDF applies to the salary that is used to calculate the social security contributions.

3. Universal cash transfers

3.1. *Transfers related to marital status*

None.

3.2. *Transfers for dependent children*

None.

4. Main changes in the tax/benefit system since 1995

The Social Security Law enacted in July 1997 changed fundamentally the financing of non-government employees' social security, which shifted from a pay-as-you-go scheme to funded individual accounts. The government does not manage these accounts; new private financial institutions were created specifically for this purpose. However, the contractual obligation is between the workers and the government, not with the private administrator of the fund, because legally they are still considered as contributions to social security, independently of who manages the fund. It should be noted that the federal government also contributes to each pension account, and guarantees a minimum pension to every beneficiary of the social security system, again independently of the administration of the fund.

5. Memorandum items

5.1. *Method used to identify an average worker and to calculate his gross earnings*

The income data refer to average workers. It should be noted that in the sample used for this survey, medium and large size firms are over-represented. In Mexico, there are no state or local government income taxes. Information on non-standard tax reliefs is not available.

Figures for 1999 and subsequent years cannot be compared with preliminary figures from previous editions of this publication for two reasons: first, the wage level of the average worker is now based on observed data instead of being estimated; second, social security contributions taken into account no longer include contributions made by employers and employees to privately managed individual accounts. Contributions no longer included in the calculation of social security contributions are specified in the table below.

The amount of the work injury fee depends on the risk level in which the company is classified. The Mexican Institute of Social Security provided a weighted average rate that considers the economic activities from C to K of the International Standard Classification.

5.2. *Main employees' and employers' contributions to private pension, health, etc. schemes*

	Account	% of workers' monthly wage
Employers' contributions	Retirement	2.00
	Discharge and old age insurance	3.15
	Housing Fund (INFONAVIT)	5.00
Employees' contributions	Discharge and old age insurance	1.125

2016 parameter values

Average earnings/yr	Ave_earn	112 827	Secretariat estimate	
(general min wage per day)	min_wage	73.04		
(general min wage per day for the Federal District of Mexico City)	min_wage_FD	73.04		
Income tax	tax_table	0.00	0	0.0192
		5 952.85	114.29	0.0640
		50 524.93	2 966.91	0.1088
		88 793.05	7 130.48	0.1600
		103 218.01	9 438.47	0.1792
		123 580.21	13 087.37	0.2136
		249 243.49	39 929.05	0.2352
		392 841.97	73 703.41	0.3000
		750 000.01	180 850.82	0.3200
		1 000 000.01	260 850.81	0.3400
		3 000 000.01	940 850.81	0.3500
Tax credit basic	Basic_crd	0.0	4 884.24	
		21 227.53	4 881.96	
		31 840.57	4 879.44	
		41 674.09	4 713.24	
		42 454.45	4 589.52	
		53 353.81	4 250.76	
		56 606.17	3 898.44	
		64 025.05	3 535.56	
		74 696.05	3 042.48	
		85 366.81	2 611.32	
		88 587.97	0.00	
Employees SSC	SSC_rate	0.0125		
	SSC_rate_sur	0.0040		
Employers SSC	SSC_empr	0.0650		
	SSC_empr_min	0.2040		
	SSC_empr_sur	0.0110		

2016 tax equations

The equations for the Mexican system in 2016 are on an individual basis.

The functions which are used in the equations (Taper, MIN, Tax etc) are described in the technical note about tax equations. Variable names are defined in the table of parameters above, within the equations table, or are the standard variables "married" and "children". A reference to a variable with the affix "_total" indicates the sum of the relevant variable values for the principal and spouse. And the affixes "_princ" and "_spouse" indicate the value for the principal and spouse, respectively. Equations for a single person are as shown for the principal, with "_spouse" values taken as 0.

	Line in country table and intermediate steps	Variable name	Range	Equation
1.	Earnings	earn		
2.	Allowances	tax_al	B	MIN(earn, MIN(earn*(6/365)*0.25, min_wage*15)+ MIN(earn*(15/365), min_wage*30))
3.	Credits in taxable income	taxbl_cr	B	0
4.	CG taxable income	tax_inc	B	Positive(earn-tax_al)
5.	CG tax before credits	CG_tax_excl	B	Tax(tax_inc, Tax_sch)
6.	Tax credits	tax_cr	B	VLOOKUP(tax_inc, Basic_crd, 2)
7.	CG tax	CG_tax	B	CG_tax_excl-tax_cr
8.	State and local taxes	local_tax	B	0
9.	Employees' soc security	SSC	B	MIN(earn*ssc_rate, min_wage_FD*25*365*ssc_rate)+MIN(Positive(earn-(3*365*min_wage_FD))*ssc_rate_sur, min_wage_FD*(25-3)*365*ssc_rate_sur)
11.	Cash transfers	cash_trans	B	0
13.	Employer's soc security	SSC_empr	B	MIN(earn*ssc_empr, min_wage_FD*25*365*ssc_empr)+365*min_wage_FD*ssc_empr_min+MIN(Positive(earn-(3*365*min_wage_FD))*ssc_empr_sur, min_wage_FD*(25-3)*365*ssc_empr_sur)
	Memorandum item: Non-wastable tax credit			
	tax expenditure component	taxexp	B	tax_cr-transfer
	cash transfer component	transfer	B	IF(CG_tax<0, -CG_tax, 0)

Key to range of equation B calculated separately for both principal earner and spouse P calculated for principal only (value taken as 0 for spouse calculation).

© OECD 2017

Netherlands

This chapter includes data on the income taxes paid by workers, their social security contributions, the family benefits they receive in the form of cash transfers as well as the social security contributions and payroll taxes paid by their employers. Results reported include the marginal and average tax burden for eight different family types.

Methodological information is available for Personal income tax systems, Compulsory social security contributions to schemes operated within the government sector, Universal cash transfers as well as recent changes in the tax/benefit system. The methodology also includes the parameter values and tax equations.

Netherlands 2016

The tax/benefit position of single persons

	Wage level (per cent of average wage)	67	100	167	67
	Number of children	none	none	none	2
1.	**Gross wage earnings**	34 072	50 853	84 925	34 072
2.	**Standard tax allowances:**				
	Basic allowance				
	Married or head of family				
	Dependent children				
	Deduction for social security contributions and income taxes	0	0	0	0
	Work-related expenses				
	Other				
	Total	0	0	0	0
3.	**Tax credits or cash transfers included in taxable income**	0	0	0	0
4.	**Central government taxable income (1 - 2 + 3)**	32 812	48 590	80 624	32 812
5.	**Central government income tax liability (exclusive of tax credits)**	3 252	9 373	23 962	3 252
6.	**Tax credits :**				
	Basic credit				
	Married or head of family				
	Children				
	Other				
	Total	1 086	777	285	1 734
7.	**Central government income tax finally paid (5-6)**	2 167	8 596	23 677	1 518
8.	**State and local taxes**	0	0	0	0
9.	**Employees' compulsory social security contributions**				
	Gross earnings	0	0	0	0
	Taxable income (net of credits)	5 599	6 888	8 537	3 488
	Total	5 599	6 888	8 537	3 488
10.	**Total payments to general government (7 + 8 + 9)**	7 766	15 484	32 214	5 006
11.	**Cash transfers from general government**				
	For head of family				
	For two children	0	0	0	5 971
	Total	0	0	0	5 971
12.	**Take-home pay (1-10+11)**	26 306	35 370	52 711	35 036
13.	**Employers' compulsory social security contributions**	3 846	5 695	6 184	3 846
14.	**Average rates**				
	Income tax	6.4%	16.9%	27.9%	4.5%
	Employees' social security contributions	16.4%	13.5%	10.1%	10.2%
	Total payments less cash transfers	22.8%	30.4%	37.9%	-2.8%
	Total tax wedge including employer's social security contributions	30.6%	37.5%	42.1%	7.6%
15.	**Marginal rates**				
	Total payments less cash transfers: Principal earner	42.5%	46.3%	52.7%	43.1%
	Total payments less cash transfers: Spouse	n.a.	n.a.	n.a.	n.a.
	Total tax wedge: Principal earner	48.2%	51.6%	52.7%	48.7%
	Total tax wedge: Spouse	n.a.	n.a.	n.a.	n.a.

Netherlands 2016

The tax/benefit position of married couples

		Wage level (per cent of average wage)	100-0	100-33	100-67	100-33
		Number of children	2	2	2	none
1.	**Gross wage earnings**		50 853	67 635	84 925	67 635
2.	**Standard tax allowances:**					
	Basic allowance					
	Married or head of family					
	Dependent children					
	Deduction for social security contributions and income taxes		0	0	0	0
	Work-related expenses					
	Other					
		Total	0	0	0	0
3.	**Tax credits or cash transfers included in taxable income**		0	0	0	0
4.	**Central government taxable income (1 - 2 + 3)**		48 590	65 026	81 402	65 026
5.	**Central government income tax liability (exclusive of tax credits)**		9 373	10 753	12 625	10 753
6.	**Tax credits :**					
	Basic credit					
	Married or head of family					
	Children					
	Other					
		Total	1 017	2 196	2 511	1 794
7.	**Central government income tax finally paid (5-6)**		8 355	8 557	10 114	8 959
8.	**State and local taxes**		0	0	0	0
9.	**Employees' compulsory social security contributions**					
	Gross earnings		0	0	0	0
	Taxable income (net of credits)		6 081	6 758	10 376	8 107
		Total	6 081	6 758	10 376	8 107
10.	**Total payments to general government (7 + 8 + 9)**		14 437	15 315	20 490	17 066
11.	**Cash transfers from general government**					
	For head of family					
	For two children		1 920	1 920	1 920	0
		Total	1 920	1 920	1 920	0
12.	**Take-home pay (1-10+11)**		38 337	54 239	66 355	50 569
13.	**Employers' compulsory social security contributions**		5 695	7 621	9 540	7 621
14.	**Average rates**					
	Income tax		16.4%	12.7%	11.9%	13.2%
	Employees' social security contributions		12.0%	10.0%	12.2%	12.0%
	Total payments less cash transfers		24.6%	19.8%	21.9%	25.2%
	Total tax wedge including employer's social security contributions		32.2%	27.9%	29.8%	32.8%
15.	**Marginal rates**					
	Total payments less cash transfers: Principal earner		46.3%	46.3%	46.3%	46.3%
	Total payments less cash transfers: Spouse		5.2%	2.6%	36.7%	8.7%
	Total tax wedge: Principal earner		51.6%	51.6%	51.6%	51.6%
	Total tax wedge: Spouse		15.0%	12.7%	43.0%	18.1%

The national currency is the Euro (EUR). In 2016, EUR 0.90 was equal to USD 1. In this year, the average worker earned EUR 50 853 (Secretariat estimate).

1. Personal income tax system (central government)

1.1. *Central government income tax*

There are three categories ('boxes') of taxable income:

- Taxable income from work and owner-occupied housing;
- Taxable income from a substantial interest in a limited liability company;
- Taxable income from savings and investments.

This description is limited to the most relevant aspects of taxable income from the first category, "taxable income from work and owner-occupied housing", because of its relevance for the AW.

1.1.1. *Tax unit*

Husbands and wives are taxed separately on their personal income, which includes income from business, profession and employment, pensions and social security benefits. Certain parts of income may be freely split between husbands and wives, such as the net-income from owner-occupied housing and the income from savings and investments.

1.1.2. *Tax allowances*

1.1.2.1. Standard allowances

Related to wage earnings:

- Employees' social security contributions (see Section 2.1.) are deductible, whereas the health insurance contribution is not deductible and is not a part of the Taxing Wages model (for more information, see the Special Feature on "non-tax compulsory payments" in the 2009 edition of the Taxing Wages Report). In the Taxing Wages model the employers' income dependant health insurance contribution was subject to income tax for the employee. In 2013 the income base for SSC and Income-Tax is harmonised. Standardising or harmonisation of the income tax base for levying SSC and Taxes was introduced in 2013 and was called the Law "WUL" i.e. harmonising the income base for SSC and Taxes (see publication CPB the Netherlands). So the income tax base is since 2013 exclusive the income dependant health care contribution and employees will no longer have to pay taxes over income dependant health care contributions, instead they pay a higher tax rate in the first tax bracket and mainly Work credit is adjusted. The tax rate in the first tax bracket has been increased from 1.95% (in 2012) till 5.85% (in 2013)

The Dutch labour market is characterized by a substantial share of part-time employees. As explained in the methodological section of this volume, the average wage measure used in the tax burden calculations refer to full-time employees only. If the wages of part-timers were taken into account, the average wage would be substantially lower.

and the Work credit is reduced for employees with a higher income such that the effect of this harmonisation is budgetary neutral.

- In 2014 this system of harmonisation remains and is operational. Only the income tax rate in the first tax bracket became 5.10%. In 2016 the tax rate in the first bracket becomes 8.40%.

1.1.2.2. Non-standard allowances applicable to AW

Related to wage earnings:

- For distances of more than 10 km between home and work, fixed amounts for travel expenses with public transportation are deductible. The maximum deduction for employees who travel by public transport is EUR 1 951 for distances of more than 80 km. If the travel expenses are reimbursed or the employer provides transport, there is no deduction; the reimbursement is untaxed (also for employees who travel by car) if it is below certain specified amounts;
- Employee contributions to private (company provided) pension schemes.

Related to owner-occupied housing:

- Excess of mortgage interest over net imputed rent.

Related to personal circumstances:

- Medical expenses and other exceptional expenses:
  - Fiscal deduction of exceptional health expenses will be reduced to the specific costs as a result of the chronic illness. As specific costs are seen medical treatment (not paid for by insurance company), diet costs, special medicine described by a doctor, extra domestic care, special expenses for clothing and transportation costs. Visual tools and insurance premiums are not seen as specific costs and are therefore no longer deductible. As from 2014, expenses for wheelchairs, scooters for the disabled and home adjustments made because of a chronic illness are no longer deductible. All expenses except for medical treatment expenses may be increased by a factor. This factor is income and age dependent. The factor amounts to 1.4 if the person is below the legal pension age and has an income on or below EUR 33 715. The factor amounts to 2.13 if the person is on or above the legal pension age and has an income on or below EUR 33 715. People with an income above EUR 33 751 cannot apply the factor.
  - For a single person: the specific expenses (after multiplication with the factor) in excess of 1.65% of income are deductible if income exceeds EUR 7 563 and is below EUR 33 751. If income is lower than or equal to EUR 7 563, the non-deductible limit is EUR 128. For a person with a partner: the joint income is used to determine the non-deductible amounts and the non-deductible limit is EUR 256.
  - If income exceeds EUR 33 751 the specific expenses in excess of 1.65% of EUR 33 751 increased with 5.75% of income above EUR 33 751 are deductible.
- Some educational expenses: in direct connection with vocational education. Expenses above the threshold of EUR 500 are deductible. Expenses above EUR 15 000 are not deductible.
- Donations to certain institutions (charity) that serve the public good are deductible if in excess of 1% of the income and in excess of EUR 60. No more than 10% of the income may be deducted in this way.

1.1.3. *Tax schedule*

The tax schedule for income from work and owner-occupied housing is as follows:

Taxable income (EUR)	Tax rate (%)	Social security contributions	
		< 65 years	*> 65 years*
0-19 922	8.40	28.15	10.25
19 922-33 715	12.25	28.15	10.25
33 715-66 421	40.40	-	-
66 421and over	52	-	-

The contributions for the general social security schemes are levied on income from work and owner-occupied housing in the first and second income tax bracket. These social security contributions are not deductible for income tax purposes. Individuals of 65 years and older pay 10.25% (for widows and orphans pensions, and exceptional medical expenses). Individuals younger than 65 years and a few month pay 28.15%, (for widows and orphans pensions, exceptional medical expenses, and old age income provision). For further information see Section 2.1.

In 2015 the SSC for specific medical expenses and long term health care is modernised. The rate (For AWBZ) is therefore reduced with 3% points and instead the tax rates in the first two brackets are raised with 3% points. The spendings for long term health care are reduced due to more responsibility for your own living in long term. These Social spendings will be used for other general social purposes and therefore the tax rates in the first two brackets are raised.

1.1.4. *Tax credits*

1.1.4.1. Standard tax credits

The tax credits are deducted partly from the income tax liability and partly from the contributions that are made to the general social security schemes (see Section 1.1.3). For most families, the share of the credit attributed to tax is related to the ratio of the tax rate to the sum of the tax rate and the social security contributions rate in the *first* bracket of the tax schedule. In 2016, this ratio was 22.98% (= 8.40%/(8.40% + 28.15%), implying that 22.98% of the (tax) credit is attributed to the personal income tax and the remaining 77.02% to social security contributions. If the individual's total tax credit is higher than the total tax and social security contributions levied on the first tax bracket, the shares of the residual amount of the tax credit that are attributed to the personal income tax and social security contributions are based on the rates of deduction in the second tax bracket in order that the employee can benefit from the full amount of the credit where the level of income allows it. As a result, the ratio of the tax rate to the sum of the tax rate and social security contribution rates is increased to 30.32% for the residual amount in 2016 (i.e. 12.25%/(28.15%+12.25%)).

Division of credits for tax and social security contributions is essential in the OECD publications. In the Netherlands no division is made in the general tax scheme between tax and SSC.

Note that the tax/benefit position tables show the total amount of social security contributions net of the credits that are claimed.

- *General tax credit*: The general tax credit is dependent on income since 2014, meaning that higher incomes receive less general tax credit. Since 2016, the general tax credit is fully phased out, meaning that higher incomes receive no general tax credit. In 2016, the maximum of the general tax credit is EUR 2 242 when no reduction is applicable (people who are on or above the legal pension age receive less general tax credit, because they do not pay social contributions for the state pension) and taxable income is below or equal to EUR 19 922. For incomes above this threshold, the general tax credit is fully phased out at a rate of 4.822% (per euro). So incomes above EUR 66 417 receive no general tax credit. So the maximum of the general credit reduction is EUR 2 242. The transfer of the general tax credit of the spouse to the principal will diminish with 6.67%-points per year in the period 2009-23, such that in 15 year time the general tax credit for a non-working (or a low earning) spouse cannot be capitalised against the tax paid by the principal.

- This reduction of the transfer of the general tax credit started in 2009. In 2023 the general tax credit can only be capitalised against the tax and social security contributions paid on own earned income. In 2012 a reduction of the general tax credit for non-working spouses born after 31 December 1962 and before 1 January 1972 is introduced. The reduction will be equal to the reduction of non-working spouses born before 1 January 1963 in year 2015. For Household types in de Taxing Wages model no difference is made between year of birth before 1963 or after 1963, idem before or after 1972. For that reason the additional reduction of the general tax credit is not added to the Taxing Wages model.
- *Work credit*: The amount of work credit depends on taxable income from work and is phased in on two trajectories; the first one runs from EUR 0 till EUR 9 147. On this first trajectory, work credit equals 1.793% of taxable income from work. On the second trajectory, which runs from EUR 9 148 till EUR 19 758, the work credit equals EUR 164 plus 27.698% of the part of income that is above EUR 9 147. So at an income of EUR 19 758, the maximum of EUR 3 103 is reached. The work credit stays at its maximum till an income of EUR 34 015. After this threshold, the work credit is fully phased out at a rate of 4% (per euro) so that incomes above EUR 111 590 receive no work credit. 2016 is the first year in which higher incomes receive no work credit.
- *Combination credit:* The combination credit is abolished in 2009.
- *Income dependant combination credit:* The additional combination credit is replaced with the income dependent combination credit. A taxpayer who is either a single parent and working or the working partner with the lowest income, and who has children below the age of 12 and has his/her taxable income from work exceeding EUR 4 881, is entitled to an income dependent combination credit of EUR 1 039 plus an extra combination credit of 6.159% of taxable income from work above EUR 4 881. The maximum total combination credit is EUR 2 769 and reached at an income level of EUR 32 970.
- The child arrangements are modernised and reduced from 10 measurements to 4 measurements. The single parents credits have stopped and instead the cash transfers become more of importance. In the TW model the adjustments mean an extra cash transfer of EUR 3 066 per year for single parents with children and a low income.
- *Single parent credit:* A single parent under certain conditions is entitled to the single parent credit of EUR 947. Has stopped in 2015 see explanation above.
- *Additional single parent credit:* A single parent who is entitled to the single parent credit receives an additional credit of 4.3% of his or her income from work, with a maximum of EUR 1 319. Has stopped in 2015, see explanation above.

The amount of the tax credit is limited to the amount of tax and premiums payable (non-refundable tax credit). If, however, a taxpayer with insufficient income to fully exploit his/her tax credit has a partner with a surplus of tax and premiums payable over his/her own tax credit, the tax credit of the former taxpayer is increased by (at most) the surplus tax and premiums payable by his/her fiscal partner. As a consequence, the tax credit of the former taxpayer will exceed tax and premiums payable, resulting in a payout of the residual tax credit to the taxpayer by the tax authority. This only applies to the work credit and the income dependent combination credit.

1.2. State and local income taxes

None.

2. Compulsory social security contributions to schemes operated within the government sector

2.1. Employees' contributions

Schemes for employees:

- Unemployment: 0% of the gross earnings below EUR 52 763 (this contribution is only for the general unemployment fund); employees do not have to pay an unemployment premium in order to reduce administration costs. Employers pay both an unemployment premium and a premium for invalidity for their employees (see par.2.2).
- For basic health insurance each adult pays an average amount of EUR 1 199 a year to a self-chosen private health insurance company. This premium is a non-tax compulsory payment and is not included in the Taxing Wages calculations but only in the NTCP calculations. Employees might obtain compensation for this nominal contribution, depending on the household's personal situation and taxable income. This is called the health care benefit. This benefit is included in the NTCP calculations as it compensates for the basic health insurance premium of on average EUR 1 199. Also 6.75% of gross earnings net of employees' pension premiums and unemployment social security contributions is paid for health care until a maximum of net earnings of EUR 52 763. Since 2013 employers contribute the Health care Fund directly for the health care of their employees, these costs remain labour costs in the Taxing Wages model. These Health care costs for employers are no longer included in the taxpayer's taxable income. The income dependent health care contribution itself, however, is not modelled (as an employer SSC) in Taxing Wages because it is seen as a Non Tax Compulsory Payment.
- Employees might obtain compensation for the nominal contribution of on average EUR 1 199 for the basic health insurance, depending on the household's personal situation and taxable income. This is called the health care benefit. The care benefit is calculated as follows:

  Single parent households: 1468 - 2.380% * 19 759 - 13.43% * (taxable income - 19 759)
- *Married couples*: number of adults * 1468 - 5.22% *19 759 - 13.43% * (taxable income principal and spouse – 19 759).
- This health care benefit is a non-tax compulsory payment and is not included in the Taxing Wages calculations but only in the "non-tax compulsory payment" calculations (see *www.oecd.org/ctp/taxingwages* for more details on non-tax compulsory payments as well as the Special Feature in the 2009 edition of the Taxing Wages Report).

TAXING WAGES 2017 © OECD 2017

- Old age pension: The age is adjusted such that elderly will receive Old Age (state) pension at the age of 66 years old in 2018 and at 67 years old in 2021. The Old age premium percentage is 17.9% of taxable income in the first and second tax bracket. This scheme does not apply to individuals aged 65 and six months (and in future aged 66 or 67) or older;
- Widows and orphans pension: 0.60% of taxable income in the first and second tax bracket;
- Exceptional medical expenses and disability: 9.65% of taxable income in the first and second tax bracket.

2.2. *Employers' contributions*

Schemes for employees:

- Unemployment: 2.44% of gross earnings below EUR 52 763for the general unemployment fund and a contribution on average of 1.78% of gross earnings below EUR 52 763 for the industrial insurance associations redundancy payments fund;
- Invalidity: 7.5% of gross earnings below EUR 52 763;
- For medical care employers contribute 6.75% of gross earnings net of employees' pension premiums and unemployment social security contributions until a maximum of gross earnings of EUR 52 763. The premium itself, however, is not modelled (either as an employee or employer SSC) in Taxing Wages. Instead, it is modelled as a NTCP from the employer to a public-man The spending of this fund mainly compensates private insurance companies for their (public) obligation to insure individuals with a high health risk.

3. Universal cash transfers

3.1. *Transfers related to marital status*

None.

3.2. *Transfers for dependent children*

Families with children receive a tax free benefit, depending on the number and age of the children. For a family with two children in the age group of 6 to 12 years, the total benefit amounts to EUR 1 920 a year. Indexation of the child benefits was frozen for three years (period 2009-11).

An additional income dependent child benefit was introduced in 2008. As of 2009, this benefit also depends on the number of children per family. A family can only claim the extra child benefit when it has children under the age of 18 years old for whom it also receives the tax free and income independent child benefit. Indexation of the extra child benefit was frozen until 2011but is used for adjustments and reductions of child arrangements. The maximum value is EUR 1 038 per year for families with one child in 2016. The maximum value is EUR 1 866 a year for families with two children. The benefit is reduced at a rate of 6.75% per euro when the family's yearly taxable income exceeds EUR 19 759 and is completely phased out for families with two children when the taxable income exceeds EUR 47 403. As from 2015 an extra benefit for single parents is introduced (independent of the number of children and the age of the children) which amounts to EUR 3 066 per year in 2016. This amount is also phased out at a rate of 6.75%.

4. Main changes in the tax/benefit systems since 2000

In 2001, the tax system was changed thoroughly. The tax rates have been lowered; the basic allowance and its supplements have been transformed into tax credits. The deduction for labour costs has also been replaced by a tax credit. Certain other deductions have been reduced or abolished. Extra tax credits for households with children were introduced.

In 2002 and 2003 the tax system was only slightly changed. The additional combination credit was introduced in 2004. The various child credits were integrated and streamlined in 2006.

Public insurance for medical care has been reformed in 2006. A new standard health insurance system was introduced. Until 2005, no public health insurance contributions were levied on income in excess of EUR 33 000. However, taxpayers earning more than EUR 33 000 were obliged to take a private insurance. These private health insurance contributions were not included in the Taxing Wages calculations because they were made to a privately-managed fund (and are therefore not taxes). Since 2006, every individual contributes a nominal contribution to a privately-managed fund (on average EUR 1 064, depending on the competition between insurance companies, a year in 2009) and, in addition for employees, a percentage of gross income (6.9%) net of employees' pension premiums and unemployment social security contributions until a maximum of gross income of EUR 32 369 (in 2009). For this last contribution, the employee receives mandatory compensation of his employer for the same amount. The premium itself, however, is not modelled (either as an employee or employer SSC) in Taxing Wages. Instead it is modelled as a non-tax compulsory payment from the employer to a public-managed health insurance fund. The spending of this fund mainly compensates private insurance companies for their (public) obligation to insure individuals with a high health risk. Taxpayers might obtain compensation for the nominal contribution to the private insurance company of on average EUR 1 064 in 2009, depending on the households personal situation and taxable income. This is called the health care benefit and is part of the NTCP (see Section 2.1).

In 2007, the tax system has not been changed, except for some parameter updates. In 2008, the child credit has been replaced by an extra child benefit.

In 2009 the general tax credit will be reduced for non-working spouses in order to cut down the capitalization of this tax credit in 2024. A non-working spouse can in 2024 capitalise the general tax credit only against his/her own earned income. In 2009 the employment credit is extended for income exceeding EUR 42 509. This credit will be reduced by maximum EUR 24, whereas the employment credit is increased for lower incomes. The income dependant combination credit is introduced in order to promote the labour participation of single parents or partners of married workers. The income-dependent combination credit has been increased considerably. The extra child benefit depends on the total income of the family and the number of children per family. The income-dependent child benefit is higher when more children under the age of 18 years are member of the family. As from 2009 onwards, employees do not have to pay an unemployment premium mainly to reduce administration costs for employers. Employers pay now both an unemployment premium and a premium for invalidity for their employees (see also par. 2.2).

In 2013 the income base for SSC and Income-Tax is harmonised. Standardising or harmonisation of the income tax base for levying SSC and Taxes is introduces in 2013 and is called the Law "WUL" i.e. Harmonising the income base for SSC and Taxes (see publication CPB the Netherlands). So the income tax base is since 2013 exclusive the income dependant health care contribution and employees will no longer have to pay taxes over income dependant health care contributions, instead they pay a higher tax rate in the first tax bracket and mainly Work credit is adjusted. The tax rate in the first tax bracket has been increased from 1.95% to 5.85% and the Work credit is reduced for employees with a higher income such that the effect of this harmonisation is budgetary neutral.

The main adjustment in 2014 is the General tax credit which is made income dependent. Higher income will receive less general credit and the reduction is 2% per euro of income between EURO 56 495 and EURO 19 645 per year. See also par 1.1.4.1.

In 2015 the child arrangements are reduced from 10 items to 4 items. For that reason Single parent credits have stopped. Cash transfers for parents with children and low income increase. And for single parents with children an extra cash benefit of EUR 3 050 is introduced to compensate the loss of single parent credits.

Not all child arrangements are part of the TW model because these are quite specific arrangements for disabled children and parents with low income with children.

Long term health care is modernised. The SSC rate for (AWBZ Dutch) reduced with 3% to 9.65% of taxable income. The tax rates in the first two brackets are raised with 3% because Social spending is still used but now for other general social purposes.

In 2016, as part of a EUR 5 billion package of tax reductions on work, the general tax credit and the work credit were phased out fully, meaning that higher incomes no longer receive the general tax credit and the work credit.

5. Memorandum items

5.1. *Identification of the AW and calculation of the AW's gross earnings*

The calculation of the annual gross earnings of an AW is based upon data on gross earnings of full-time workers in industry C-K. These data have been obtained through a yearly sample survey carried out by the Central Bureau of Statistics. Included in the AW annual salary are irregular payments, such as holiday allowances, loyalty payments and bonuses. Payments for working overtime are not included. However, the CBS has stopped carrying out the "employment and wages" survey in July 2006 due to new legislation. On Inquiry at the Central Bureau of Statistics (CBS) the information from the wage declarations by employers, delivered nowadays at the tax department, will be implemented by the CBS for the new survey about employment and wages. These changes produced a delay in delivery of the information on wages and employment for 2006.

On the base of new information on wages per industry sector, the AW is delivered to EUROSTAT in November 2009 by the CBS for years 2006 and 2007. The standard classification NACE Rev. 1 for industrial sectors C-K is used.

The new classification NACE Revision 2 (sectors B-N) will be applicable as from 2008 onwards. The estimation of the AW for 2008 according to the new classification is applicable at the beginning of May 2010. The AW for 2009 is available since November 2010. For 2008 the average annual gross earnings (full-time NACE REV 2) comes to EUR 43 146, for 2009 EUR 44 412, and EUR 45 215 in 2010. The latest information according to Eurostat is an AW in 2011 of EUR 46 287 (NACE Rev 2)

No new data is found on EU site: *http://epp.eurostat.ec.europa.eu/portal/page/portal/statistics/search_database*

The average wages from 2012 onwards include the private and the public sectors, since values on the private sectors only (sectors B to N) are not available. The values were provided by Statistics Netherlands.

5.2. *Main employers' contributions to private pension, health and related schemes*

In addition to the obligatory contributions of employees to private insurance companies, all employers pay contributions to a public-managed health fund. More information is included in the Special Feature where the contributions to the public-managed health funds are also presented.

Employers have to pay at least 70% of the gross wage of their sick employees for two years. Many employers have insured themselves privately for the risks of their employees being sick. This insurance for illness of their employees is not compulsory.

2016 parameter values

Average earnings/yr	Ave_earn	50 853	
minimum wage	min_wage	19 840	
Social security contributions	SSC_ceil	52 763	
Employees' schemes	Unemp_rate1	0	
	Unemp_franchise1	0	
Medical care	Med_rate	0.0675	
	Med_limit	999 999	
	Med_ceil	52 763	
	Med_adult	1.199	
	Med_child	0	
	Med_compensation1	0.02380	
	Med_compensation2	0.13430	
	Med_compenation 3	0.05220	
	Med_compensation 4	0.13430	
	Med_key	19.759	
	Med_adult for care benefit	1.468	
General schemes	Old_rate	0.179	
	Wid_rate	0.006	
	Ex_med_rate	0.0965	
	Gen_Schemes_thrsh	33 715	
	Unemp_empr1	0.0244	
	Unemp_empr2	0.0178	
	Unemp_unempr_franchise1	0	
	Unemp_unempr_franchise2	0	
	Inv_empr_rate	0.0750	
	Inv_empr_franchise	0	
	Med_empr	0.0675	
	Med_franchise	0	
Payroll tax	Extra_wage_tax	0	
	EWT_threshold	0	
Tax schedule	Tax_sch	0.0840	19 922
	"tax_sch_lowest"	0.1225	33 715
	"tax_thrsh_1"	0.404	66 421
	"tax_sch_2"	0.52	
Tax credits	Gen_credit_1	2 242	
	Gen_credit_2	0	
	Gen_credit1_thr	19 922	
	Gen_credit2_thr	66 417	
	Gen_credit_per	0.04822	
	Red_gen_credit	1 047	
	Emp_credit1	164	
	Emp_credit2	2 939	
	Emp_credit3	0	
	Emp_credit1_thr	9 147	
	Emp_credit2_thr	19 758	
	Emp_credit3_thr	34 015	
	Emp_credit4_thr	111 590	
	Ch_credit	nvt	
	Ch_credit_thr	nvt	
	Ch_decline	nvt	
	Ex_ch_credit	nvt	
	Ex_ch_credit_thr	nvt	
	add_ex_ch_credit	nvt	
	add_ex_ch_credit_thr	nvt	
	Comb_credit	0	
	Comb_credit_franchise	4 881	

2016 parameter values

	add_comb_credit	0
	income_dependant_comb_credit1	1 039
	income_dependant_comb_credit_max	2 769
Family cash transfers	income_dependant_comb_par_credit_per	0.06159
	Sing_par_credit	0
	Ex_sing_par_credit_per	0
	Ex_sing_par_credit_max	0
	Ch1_trans	960
	Ch2_trans	1 920
	Child_ben_1child	1 038
	Child_ben_2children	1 866
	Extra_cash_sing_par	3 066
	Child_ben_redn	0,0675
	Child_ben_ceil	19 759
Non-tax compulsory payments	dummyNTCP	0
	NTCP_pension_ee	0.0598
	NTCP_pension_er	0.1306
	NTCP_pension_franchise	13.003
	NTCP_pension_max	101.519

TAXING WAGES 2017 © OECD 2017

2016 tax equations

The equations for the tax system in the Netherlands in 2016 are repeated for each individual of a married couple. Tax credits, except a part of the general credit of the spouse, depend also on the tax paid by the principal if the spouse's income is zero or very low, and the cash transfers are calculated only once. The functions which are used in the equations (Taper, MIN, Tax etc) are described in the technical note on the tax equations. Due to the adjustment of the work credit in 2016, the function Emp_credit(Value) was altered in 2016. Variable names are defined in the table of parameters above, within the equations table, or are the standard variables "married" and "children". A reference to a variable with the affix "_total" indicates the sum of the relevant variable values for the principal and spouse. And the affix "_spouse" indicates the value for the spouse. No affix is used for the principal values. Equations for a single person are as shown for the principal, with "_spouse" values taken as 0.

	Line in country table and intermediate steps	Variable name	Range	Equation
1.	Earnings (gross)	gr_earn		
	Earnings (net)	earn	B	gr_earn
2.	Social security contributions	SSC_al	B	SSC_f(earn,Unemp_rate1,SSC_ceil,Unemp_franchise1)
3.	Credits in taxable income	taxbl_cr	B	MIN(earn-SSC_al, Med_ceil)*Med_rate
4.	CG taxable income	tax_inc	B	earn-SSC_al
5.	CG tax before credits	CG_tax_excl/ tax_liable	B	Tax(tax_inc,Tax_sch)
6.	Tax credits	tax_cr	P	MIN(CG_tax_excl+SSC_taxinc,IF((tax_inc<Gen_credit1_thr),Gen_credit_1,(Gen_credit_1-MIN(Gen_credit_per*(Gen_credit2_thr-Gen_credit1_thr),Gen_credit_per*(tax_inc-Gen_credit1_thr))))+Emp_credit(tax_inc)+IF(AND(Children>0,tax_inc>Comb_credit_franchise),IF(Married=0,income_dependant_comb_credit1+MIN(income_dependant_comb_credit_max-income_dependant_comb_credit1, income_dependant_comb_par_credit_per*(tax_inc - Comb_credit_franchise)),0)
		tax_cr_spouse	S	IF(Married>0,MIN(CG_tax_excl_spouse+SSC_taxinc_spouse+CG_tax_excl+SSC_taxinc-tax_cr,IF(tax_inc_spouse>0,IF((tax_inc_spouse<Gen_credit1_thr),Gen_credit_1,(Gen_credit_1-MIN(Gen_credit_per*(Gen_credit2_thr-Gen_credit1_thr), Gen_credit_per*(tax_inc_spouse-Gen_credit1_thr)))),Red_gen_credit)+Emp_credit(tax_inc_spouse)+IF(AND(Children>0,tax_inc_spouse>Comb_credit_franchise),income_dependant_comb_credit1+MIN(income_dependant_comb_credit_max-income_dependant_comb_credit1,income_dependant_comb_par_credit_per*(tax_inc_spouse - Comb_credit_franchise)),0)),0)
		tax_cr_inc	B	IF(tax_cr>Tax_thrsh_1*SUM(Old_rate+Wid_rate+Ex_med_rate+tax_sch_lowest), (tax_sch_2/SUM(Old_rate+Wid_rate+Ex_med_rate+tax_sch_2))*(tax_cr-(SUM(Old_rate+Wid_rate+Ex_med_rate+tax_sch_lowest)*Tax_thrsh_1))+(tax_sch_lowest/SUM(Old_rate+Wid_rate+Ex_med_rate+tax_sch_lowest))*(Tax_thrsh_1* SUM(Old_rate+Wid_rate+Ex_med_rate+tax_sch_lowest)),tax_sch_lowest/SUM(Old_rate+Wid_rate+Ex_med_rate+tax_sch_lowest)*tax_cr)
7.	CG tax	CG_tax	B	tax_liable-tax_cr_inc
8.	State and local taxes	local_tax	B	0
9.	Employees' soc security' based on earnings	SSC_earn	P	SSC_f(earn,Unemp_rate1,SSC_ceil,Unemp_franchise1)
		SSC_earn_ spouse	S	SSC_f(earn_spouse,Unemp_rate1,SSC_ceil,Unemp_franchise1)
	Based on taxable income	SSC_taxinc	B	(Old_rate+Wid_rate+Ex_med_rate)*MINA(tax_inc,Gen_Schemes_thrsh)
	Total employees' soc security	SSC_liable	J	SSC_earn+SSC_taxinc+SSC_earn_spouse+SSC_taxinc_spouse

	Line in country table and intermediate steps	Variable name	Range	Equation
		tax_cr_SSC	B	IF(tax_cr>Tax_thrsh_1*SUM(Old_rate+Wid_rate+Ex_med_rate+tax_sch_lowest),((Old_rate+Wid_rate+Ex_med_rate)/SUM(Old_rate+Wid_rate+Ex_med_rate+tax_sch_2))*(tax_cr-(SUM(Old_rate+Wid_rate+Ex_med_rate+tax_sch_lowest)*Tax_thrsh_1))+((Old_rate+Wid_rate+Ex_med_rate)/SUM(Old_rate+Wid_rate+Ex_med_rate+tax_sch_lowest))*(Tax_thrsh_1*SUM(Old_rate+Wid_rate+Ex_med_rate+tax_sch_lowest)),SUM(Old_rate+Wid_rate+Ex_med_rate)/SUM(Old_rate+Wid_rate+Ex_med_rate+tax_sch_lowest)*tax_cr)
	Total	SSC	J	SSC_liable-tax_cr_SSC
10.	Total payments	total_payments	J	CG_tax+local_tax+SSC
11.	Cash transfers	cash_trans	J	IF(Children=1,Ch1_trans,IF(Children=2,Ch2_trans,0))+IF(Children=2;1;0)*MAX(0;(Child_ben_2children+IF(Married=0;1;0)*Extra_cash_sing_par-IF((tax)inc+tax_inc_spouse)>Child_ben_ceil;1;0)*Child_ben_redn*(tax_inc+tax_inc_spouse – Child_ben_ceil)))

13.	Employer's soc security	SSC_empr	B	Function Emp_credit(Value)
				If Value <= 0 Then
				Emp_credit = 0
				ElseIf Value <= Range("Emp_credit1_thr").Value Then
				Emp_credit = (Value/Range("Emp_credit1_thr").Value) * Range("Emp_credit1").Value
				ElseIf Value <= Range("Emp_credit2_thr").Value Then
				Emp_credit = Range("Emp_credit1").Value + ((Value - Range("Emp_credit1_thr").Value)/(Range("Emp_credit2_thr").Value - Range("Emp_credit1_thr").Value)) * Range("Emp_credit2").Value
				ElseIf Value <= Range("Emp_credit3_thr").Value Then
				Emp_credit = Range("Emp_credit1").Value + Range("Emp_credit2").Value
				ElseIf Value <= Range("Emp_credit4_thr").Value Then
				Emp_credit = Range("Emp_credit1").Value + Range("Emp_credit2").Value - ((Value - Range("Emp_credit3_thr").Value)/(Range("Emp_credit4_thr").Value - Range("Emp_credit3_thr").Value)) * (Range("Emp_credit2").Value - Range("Emp_credit3").Value)
				Else
				Emp_credit = 0
				End If
				End Function

Key to range of equations B calculated separately for both principal earner and spouse P calculated for principal only (value taken as 0 for spouse calculation) J calculated once only on a joint basis.

© OECD 2017

New Zealand
(2016-17 income tax year)

This chapter includes data on the income taxes paid by workers, their social security contributions, the family benefits they receive in the form of cash transfers as well as the social security contributions and payroll taxes paid by their employers. Results reported include the marginal and average tax burden for eight different family types.

Methodological information is available for Personal income tax systems, Compulsory social security contributions to schemes operated within the government sector, Universal cash transfers as well as recent changes in the tax/benefit system. The methodology also includes the parameter values and tax equations underlying the data.

New Zealand 2016

The tax/benefit position of single persons

	Wage level (per cent of average wage)	67	100	167	67
	Number of children	none	none	none	2
1.	**Gross wage earnings**	38 625	57 649	96 274	38 625
2.	**Standard tax allowances:**				
	Basic allowance				
	Married or head of family				
	Dependent children				
	Deduction for social security contributions and income taxes				
	Work-related expenses				
	Other				
	Total	0	0	0	0
3.	**Tax credits or cash transfers included in taxable income**	0	0	0	0
4.	**Central government taxable income (1 - 2 + 3)**	38 625	57 649	96 274	38 625
5.	**Central government income tax liability (exclusive of tax credits)**	5 779	10 315	22 690	5 779
6.	**Tax credits :**				
	Basic credit	520	0	0	0
	Married or head of family				
	Children				
	Other				
	Total	520	0	0	0
7.	**Central government income tax finally paid (5-6)**	5 259	10 315	22 690	5 779
8.	**State and local taxes**	0	0	0	0
9.	**Employees' compulsory social security contributions**				
	Gross earnings	0	0	0	0
	Taxable income				
	Total	0	0	0	0
10.	**Total payments to general government (7 + 8 + 9)**	5 259	10 315	22 690	5 779
11.	**Cash transfers from general government**				
	For head of family				
	For two children	0	0	0	10 810
	Total	0	0	0	10 810
12.	**Take-home pay (1-10+11)**	33 365	47 334	73 583	43 655
13.	**Employer's compulsory social security contributions**	0	0	0	0
14.	**Average rates**				
	Income tax	13.6%	17.9%	23.6%	15.0%
	Employees' social security contributions	0.0%	0.0%	0.0%	0.0%
	Total payments less cash transfers	13.6%	17.9%	23.6%	-13.0%
	Total tax wedge including employer's social security contributions	13.6%	17.9%	23.6%	-13.0%
15.	**Marginal rates**				
	Total payments less cash transfers: Principal earner	17.5%	30.0%	33.0%	38.7%
	Total payments less cash transfers: Spouse	n.a.	n.a.	n.a.	n.a.
	Total tax wedge: Principal earner	17.5%	30.0%	33.0%	38.7%
	Total tax wedge: Spouse	n.a.	n.a.	n.a.	n.a.

New Zealand 2016

The tax/benefit position of married couples

		Wage level (per cent of average wage)	100-0	100-33	100-67	100-33
		Number of children	2	2	2	none
1.	**Gross wage earnings**		57 649	76 673	96 274	76 673
2.	**Standard tax allowances:**					
	Basic allowance					
	Married or head of family					
	Dependent children					
	Deduction for social security contributions and income taxes					
	Work-related expenses					
	Other					
		Total	0	0	0	0
3.	**Tax credits or cash transfers included in taxable income**		0	0	0	0
4.	**Central government taxable income (1 - 2 + 3)**		57 649	76 673	96 274	76 673
5.	**Central government income tax liability (exclusive of tax credits)**		10 315	12 664	16 094	12 664
6.	**Tax credits :**					
	Basic credit		0	0	0	0
	Married or head of family					
	Children					
	Other					
		Total	0	0	0	0
7.	**Central government income tax finally paid (5-6)**		10 315	12 664	16 094	12 664
8.	**State and local taxes**		0	0	0	0
9.	**Employees' compulsory social security contributions**					
	Gross earnings					
	Taxable income					
		Total	0	0	0	0
10.	**Total payments to general government (7 + 8 + 9)**		10 315	12 664	16 094	12 664
11.	**Cash transfers from general government**					
	For head of family					
	For two children		6 767	2 724	0	0
		Total	6 767	2 724	0	0
12.	**Take-home pay (1-10+11)**		54 101	66 734	80 180	64 009
13.	**Employer's compulsory social security contributions**		0	0	0	0
14.	**Average rates**					
	Income tax		17.9%	16.5%	16.7%	16.5%
	Employees' social security contributions		0.0%	0.0%	0.0%	0.0%
	Total payments less cash transfers		6.2%	13.0%	16.7%	16.5%
	Total tax wedge including employer's social security contributions		6.2%	13.0%	16.7%	16.5%
15.	**Marginal rates**					
	Total payments less cash transfers: Principal earner		51.3%	51.3%	30.0%	30.0%
	Total payments less cash transfers: Spouse		33.6%	38.7%	17.5%	17.5%
	Total tax wedge: Principal earner		51.3%	51.3%	30.0%	30.0%
	Total tax wedge: Spouse		33.6%	38.7%	17.5%	17.5%

The national currency is the New Zealand dollar (NZD). In 2016, NZD 1.44 was equal to USD 1. In that year the average worker earned NZD 57 649 (Country estimate).

1. Personal income tax system

1.1. *Central/federal government income taxes*

1.1.1. *Tax unit*

Members of the family are taxed separately.

1.1.2. *Tax allowances and tax credits*

None.

1.1.2.1. *Standard reliefs*

1.1.2.2. Main non-standard tax reliefs applicable to an average wage

None.

1.1.3. *Schedule*

- Rates of income tax for individuals:
  - On so much of the income as does not exceed NZD 14 000: 10.5%;
  - On so much of the income as exceeds NZD 14 000 but does not exceed NZD 48 000: 17.5%;
  - On so much of the income as exceeds NZD 48 000 but does not exceed NZD 70 000: 30%;
  - On so much of the income as exceeds NZD 70 000: 33%.

1.2. *State and local income taxes*

New Zealand has no state or local income tax.

2. Compulsory social security contributions to schemes operated within the government sector

New Zealand has no Compulsory social security contributions to schemes operated within the government sector.

It should be noted that there is an accident compensation scheme administered by the Accident Compensation Corporation for residents and temporary visitors to New Zealand. This scheme is funded in part by premiums paid by employees and employers. For employees, the premium represents 1.26% of their gross earnings. For employers and the self-employed, the premiums are based on a percentage of the total payroll and the applicable rate varies depending upon the associated accident risk (the average rate is 0.90%). This scheme is not considered as a compulsory social security contribution for the purposes of the Report.

3. Universal cash transfers

3.1. *Amount for marriage*

None.

3.2. *Amount for children*

The Parental Tax Credit provides NZD 220 per week for the first ten weeks of each child's life. This tax credit abates under the same regime as the Family Tax Credit, although it is unaffected until both the Family Tax Credit and In Work Tax Credit have been abated to zero.

3.3. *Family tax credit*

For an eldest child aged 16-18, the rate of the Family Tax Credit is NZD 5 303 per year, while the rate of NZD 4 822 applies if the eldest child is younger than 16. For subsequent children the rate depends on the age of the child; NZD 4 745 per year for 16-18 year-olds, NZD 3 822 per year for 13-15 year-olds and NZD 3 351 per year for children under 13 years of age. The total credit is abated by 21.25 cents on each dollar earned over NZD 36 350. The abatement is based on the combined income of the parents.

3.4. *In work tax credit*

The In Work Tax Credit is available to families with dependent children who are not receiving an income-tested benefit, veteran's pension, New Zealand Superannuation or student allowance. The level of assistance it provides is NZD 3 120 per family per year, plus an additional NZD 780 per year for fourth and subsequent children. It is only available to couple families working a total of 30 hours or more per week, or to sole parents working 20 hours or more per week. It is also affected by the abatement regime used with the Family Tax Credit, although it is unaffected until the latter has been abated to zero.

3.5. *Minimum family tax credit*

The Minimum Family Tax Credit is a scheme that ensures a guaranteed minimum family net income for all full-time earners with dependent children. The guaranteed minimum after-tax income is NZD 23 036 per year plus the Family Tax Credit and In Work Tax Credit.

3.6. *Independent Earner Tax Credit*

The Independent Earner Tax Credit of NZD 520 is available to individuals with annual net income between NZD 24 000 and NZD 48 000 that do not receive other forms of tax credits or benefits. It is abated by 13 cents on each dollar earned over NZD 44 000.

4. Main changes in tax/benefit systems over 2015/16

No changes in tax/benefit systems over 2015/16. However, for the 2016/17 there will be three changes:

- the in work tax credit will increase from NZD 3 120 per family per year to NZD 3 770;
- the abatement rate for the family tax credit, in work tax credit and parental tax credit will increase from 21.25 cents on each dollar to 22.5 cents in the dollar; and
- the minimum family tax credit guaranteed minimum after-tax income will increase from NZD 23 036 to NZD 23 764.

5. Memorandum items

5.1. *Method used to identify AW and to calculate the AW's gross earnings*

The Annual Earnings figure is derived from the *Quarterly Employment Survey* for those employees in the B-N industry groups. The annual earnings figure for the average worker is the sum of the four quarterly earnings figures, with each quarterly figure calculated by taking the average total weekly earnings and multiplying it by 13 weeks per quarter.

5.2. *Employer's contributions to private pension, health schemes, etc.*

No information available.

2016 parameter values

	Ave_earn	5 7649	Country estimate
Income tax schedule	Tax_sch	0.105	14 000
		0.175	48 000
		0.3	70 000
		0.33	
Family tax credit	Fam_sup_eld	4 822	
	Fam_sup_oth	3 351	
	Fam_sup_thrsh	36 350	
	Fam_sup_rate	0.2125	
In-work tax credit	In_work_children123	3 120	
	In_work_children4plus	780	
Minimum Family Tax Credit	Min_inc	23 036	
Independent Earner Tax Credit	IETC	520	
	IETC_thrsh1	24 000	
	IETC_thrsh2	44 000	
	IETC_rate	0.13	

2016 tax equations

The equations for the New Zealand system in 2016 are mostly repeated for each individual of a married couple. But the cash transfer is calculated only once. This is shown by the Range indicator in the table below. The functions which are used in the equations (Taper, MIN, Tax etc) are described in the technical note about tax equations. Variable names are defined in the table of parameters above, within the equations table, or are the standard variables "married" and "children". A reference to a variable with the affix "_total" indicates the sum of the relevant variable values for the principal and spouse. And the affixes "_princ" and "_spouse" indicate the value for the principal and spouse, respectively. Equations for a single person are as shown for the principal, with "_spouse" values taken as 0.

	Line in country table andintermediate steps	Variable name	Range	Equation
1.	Earnings	earn		
2.	Allowances	tax_al	B	0
3.	Credits in taxable income	taxbl_cr	B	0
4.	CG taxable income	tax_inc	B	earn
5.	CG tax before credits	CG_tax_excl	B	Tax(tax_inc, Tax_sch)
6.	Tax credits :			
	Guaranteed minimum income	GMI	J	(Children>0)*Min_inc
	Independent Earner Tax Credit	IETC_rebate	B	=AND(Children=0,earn>IETC_thrsh1)*Taper(IETC,earn,IETC_thrsh2,IETC_rate)
6.	Tax credits:	tax_cr	B	IETC_rebate
7.	CG tax	CG_tax	B	CG_tax_excl-tax_cr
8.	Local tax	local_tax	B	0
9.	Employees' soc security	SSC	B	0
11.	Cash transfers:			
	Family tax credit (unabated)	fam_tax_cr	J	Fam_sup_eld*(Children>0)+ Fam_sup_oth*Positive(Children-1)
	In-work tax credit (unabated)	in_work_tax_cr	J	(Children>0)*(In_work_children123+Positive(Children-3)*In_work_children4plus)
	Tax credits abated	tax_cr_ab	J	Taper(fam_tax_cr+in_work_tax_cr, earn_total, Fam_sup_thrsh1, Fam_sup_rate1)
	Minimum Family tax credit	min_fam_tax_cr	J	Positive(GMI-(earn_total-CG_tax_excl_totall))
	Cash transfers	cash_trans	J	tax_cr_ab + min_fam_tax_cr
13.	Employer's soc security	SSC_empr	B	0

Key to range of equation B calculated separately for both principal earner and spouse P calculated for principal only (value taken as 0 for spouse calculation) J calculated once only on a joint basis.

© OECD 2017

Norway

This chapter includes data on the income taxes paid by workers, their social security contributions, the family benefits they receive in the form of cash transfers as well as the social security contributions and payroll taxes paid by their employers. Results reported include the marginal and average tax burden for eight different family types.

Methodological information is available for Personal income tax systems, Compulsory social security contributions to schemes operated within the government sector, Universal cash transfers as well as recent changes in the tax/benefit system. The methodology also includes the parameter values and tax equations underlying the data.

Norway 2016

The tax/benefit position of single persons

		Wage level (per cent of average wage)	67	100	167	67
		Number of children	none	none	none	2
1.	**Gross wage earnings**		378 026	564 218	942 244	378 026
2.	**Standard tax allowances**					
	Basic allowance					
	Married or head of family					
	Dependent children					
	Deduction for social security contributions and income taxes					
	Work-related expenses					
	Other					
		Total	143 200	143 200	143 200	195 004
3.	**Tax credits or cash transfers included in taxable income**		0	0	0	0
4.	**Central government taxable (ordinary) income (1 - 2 + 3)**		234 826	421 018	799 044	183 022
5.	**Central government income tax liability (ordinary + personal)**		27 664	50 472	131 679	22 198
6.	**Tax credits (applicable against local tax)**					
	Basic credit					
	Married or head of family					
	Children		0	0	0	0
	Other					
		Total	0	0	0	0
7.	**Central government income tax finally paid (5-6)**		27 664	50 472	131 679	22 198
8.	**State and local taxes (net of tax credits)**		33 932	60 837	115 462	26 447
9.	**Employees' compulsory social security contributions**					
	Gross earnings		30 998	46 266	77 264	30 998
	Taxable income					
		Total	30 998	46 266	77 264	30 998
10.	**Total payments to general government (7 + 8 + 9)**		92 594	157 575	324 404	79 643
11.	**Cash transfers from general government**					
	For head of family					
	For two children		0	0	0	34 920
		Total	0	0	0	34 920
12.	**Take-home pay (1-10+11)**		285 432	406 643	617 839	333 303
13.	**Employer's compulsory social security contributions**		49 143	73 348	122 492	49 143
14.	**Average rates**					
	Income tax		16.3%	19.7%	26.2%	12.9%
	Employees' social security contributions		8.2%	8.2%	8.2%	8.2%
	Total payments less cash transfers		24.5%	27.9%	34.4%	11.8%
	Total tax wedge including employer's social security contributions		33.2%	36.2%	42.0%	22.0%
15.	**Marginal rates**					
	Total payments less cash transfers: Principal earner		34.9%	34.9%	46.9%	34.9%
	Total payments less cash transfers: Spouse		n.a.	n.a.	n.a.	n.a.
	Total tax wedge: Principal earner		42.4%	42.4%	53.0%	42.4%
	Total tax wedge: Spouse		n.a.	n.a.	n.a.	n.a.

Norway 2016

The tax/benefit position of married couples

		100-0	100-33	100-67	100-33
	Wage level (per cent of average wage)	100-0	100-33	100-67	100-33
	Number of children	2	2	2	none
1.	**Gross wage earnings**	564 218	750 410	942 244	750 410
2.	**Standard tax allowances**				
	Basic allowance				
	Married or head of family				
	Dependent children				
	Deduction for social security contributions and income taxes				
	Work-related expenses				
	Other				
	Total	167 700	275 013	286 400	275 013
3.	**Tax credits or cash transfers included in taxable income**	0	0	0	0
4.	**Central government taxable (ordinary) income (1 - 2 + 3)**	396 518	475 397	655 844	475 397
5.	**Central government income tax liability (ordinary + personal)**	47 887	56 325	78 136	56 325
6.	**Tax credits (applicable against local tax)**				
	Basic credit				
	Married or head of family				
	Children	0	0	0	0
	Other				
	Total	0	0	0	0
7.	**Central government income tax finally paid (5-6)**	47 887	56 325	78 136	56 325
8.	**State and local taxes (net of tax credits)**	57 297	68 695	94 769	68 695
9.	**Employees' compulsory social security contributions**				
	Gross earnings	46 266	61 534	77 264	61 534
	Taxable income				
	Total	46 266	61 534	77 264	61 534
10.	**Total payments to general government (7 + 8 + 9)**	151 450	186 554	250 169	186 554
11.	**Cash transfers from general government**				
	For head of family				
	For two children	23 280	23 280	23 280	0
	Total	23 280	23 280	23 280	0
12.	**Take-home pay (1-10+11)**	436 048	587 136	715 354	563 856
13.	**Employer's compulsory social security contributions**	73 348	97 553	122 492	97 553
14.	**Average rates**				
	Income tax	18.6%	16.7%	18.4%	16.7%
	Employees' social security contributions	8.2%	8.2%	8.2%	8.2%
	Total payments less cash transfers	22.7%	21.8%	24.1%	24.9%
	Total tax wedge including employer's social security contributions	31.6%	30.8%	32.8%	33.5%
15.	**Marginal rates**				
	Total payments less cash transfers: Principal earner	34.9%	34.9%	34.9%	34.9%
	Total payments less cash transfers: Spouse	18.9%	22.9%	34.9%	22.9%
	Total tax wedge: Principal earner	42.4%	42.4%	42.4%	42.4%
	Total tax wedge: Spouse	28.2%	31.8%	42.4%	31.8%

The national currency is the Kroner (NOK). In 2016, NOK 8.40 was equal to 1 USD. In that year the average worker earned NOK 564 218 (Secretariat estimate).

1. Personal income tax system

The personal income tax has two tax bases: *personal income* and *ordinary income*. Personal income is defined as income from labour and pensions. Personal income is a gross income base from which no deductions are made. Ordinary income includes all types of taxable income from labour, pensions, business and capital. Certain costs and expenses, including interest paid on debt, are deductible in the computation of ordinary income.

1.1. Central government income tax

1.1.1. Tax unit

The tax unit is in most cases the individual (tax class 1), but joint taxation (tax class 2) is also possible. Children aged below 17 are generally taxed together with their parents, but they may be taxed individually. All other income earners are taxed on an individual basis (class 1).

1.1.2. Tax allowances applicable to an AW

There are no tax allowances applicable to an AW under the central government income bracket tax. The tax base is personal income from which no deductions are allowed. As part of the overall tax rate of 25% on ordinary income, 10.55% is considered to be the central government income tax.

1.1.3. Rate schedule of the bracket tax

Rate (%)	NOK
0	0-159 800
0.44	159 800-224 900
1.70	224 900-565 400
10.70	565 400-909 500
13.70	909 500 and over

1.2. Local government income tax

The overall tax rate on ordinary income is 25%. The local government (municipal and county) income tax is 14.45% points of the overall rate. Tax on ordinary income is levied after taking into account a standard allowance of NOK 51 750 (class 1) and NOK 76 250 (class 2) in 2016. Single parents are eligible to an additional special tax allowance of NOK 51 804. The deductions in the computation of ordinary income are:

1.2.1. Standard reliefs

- Basic allowance: each individual receives a minimum allowance equal to 43% of personal income, with a minimum of NOK 4 000 and a maximum of NOK 91 450. For wage income each individual can choose a separate allowance of NOK 31 800 instead of the basic allowance. Hence, wage earners would opt to choose this separate allowance as long as it exceeds the basic allowance to which they are entitled.

1.2.2. *Non-standard reliefs*

The main non-standard allowances deductible from ordinary income are:

- Parent allowance: Documented expenses for child care limited to:
  - maximum NOK 25 000 for one child
  - plus NOK 15 000 for each subsequent child.

The allowance applies in general to the spouse who has the highest income. Unused parent allowance may be transferred to the other spouse. The allowance is also applicable to single parents.

- Travel expenses related to work exceeding NOK 22 000;
- Labour union fees up to NOK 3 850;
- Donations to voluntary organisations up to NOK 25 000;
- Contributions to individual pension agreement schemes, maximum NOK 15 000;
- Premiums and contributions to occupational pension schemes in the private and public sector, unlimited;
- Unlimited deduction for interest payments.

The main non-standard tax credits are:

- Home savings scheme (BSU): The BSU scheme aims to encourage young people (under 34 years old) to save for a future home purchase. A wastable *tax credit* of 20% of annual savings up to NOK 25 000 in special accounts is granted. Total savings may not exceed NOK 300 000.

2. Social security contributions

2.1. *Contributions to the national insurance scheme*

2.1.1. *Employees' contributions*

Employees' contributions to the National Insurance Scheme generally amount to 8.2% of personal wage income. Employees do not make contributions if their wage income is less than NOK 49 650. Once wage income exceeds this floor, an alternative calculation is made where the contributions equal 25% of the wage income in excess of the floor. The actual contributions made would represent the minimum between the alternative calculation and 8.2% of the total wage income.

Contributions from the self-employed are 11.4% of personal income attributable to labour.

2.1.2. *Employers' contributions*

Employer's social security contributions are due for all employees in both the private and the public sector. The contribution is geographically differentiated according to the municipality where the work-place is. The standard rates are 14.1%, 10.6%, 7.9%, 6.4%, 5.1% or 0% of gross wages. The highest rate applies to central parts of southern Norway. Lower rates may apply under certain circumstances. The weighted average rate is approximately 13%.

3. Universal cash transfers

3.1. *Transfers related to marital status*

None.

3.2. *Transfers for dependent children (child support)*

The following transfers are available:

NOK 11 640 per child aged 0-18 years.

Single parents receive transfers for one more child than their actual number of children.

4. Main changes in tax/benefit systems since 2002

- Most important changes related to wage taxation in 2016:
  - The general tax rate on ordinary income was reduced from 27% to 25%.
  - A bracket tax with on personal income with 4 tax brackets was introduced and replaced the former surtax on personal income.
- Most important changes related to wage taxation in 2015:
  - The threshold in surtax bracket 1 was increased by NOK 5 750.
  - The upper limit of the basic allowance for wage income/social security benefits was increased by NOK 2 100.
  - The lower threshold for the payment of employee's social security contributions was increased from NOK 39 600 to NOK 49 650.
- Most important changes related to wage taxation in 2014:
  - The general tax rate on ordinary income was reduced from 28% to 27%.
  - The employee's social security contributions were increased by 0.4 percentage points.
  - The rate in the basic allowance against wage income was increased to 43%.
  - Tax class 2 for married couples was reduced.
- Most important changes in 2013:
  - The personal allowance for labour income was increased for low income earners (below NOK 213 950) by 2 percentage points from 38% to 40% of their labour income.
  - The taxable value of second homes and commercial property for the purposes of net wealth tax was increased from 40% to 50% of estimated market value.
  - The basic allowance in the net wealth tax was increased from NOK 750 000 to NOK 870 000. Married couples will thus have a total basic allowance of NOK 1 740 000.
  - The current class 2 for sole providers was replaced by a special allowance for ordinary income which provides an equivalent tax benefit.
  - The maximum deduction for labour union fees was increased from NOK 3 750 to NOK 3 850.
- Most important changes in 2012:
  - The personal allowance for labour income was increased for low income earners (below NOK 217 000) by 2 percentage points from 36% to 38% of their labour income.
  - For self-employed the wage allowance was abolished to eliminate residual discrimination between sole proprietorships with employees and limited companies.

- In the deduction for travel expenses for travels between home and work the deduction rate per kilometre was increased for tax payers travelling between 35 000 km and 50 000 km per year.
- The maximum deduction for labour union fees was increased by NOK 90 to NOK 3 750.

- In 2011 changes to the tax system was made to provide better incentives for people to work when drawing a pension. The tax limitation rule for early-retirement and old-age pensioners was replaced by a new tax allowance for pension income. The allowance ensures that people who only receive the minimum pension will continue not to pay income tax. The allowance is scaled down against pension income, so that the marginal tax on earned income is reduced to the same level as for wage earners. The marginal tax on capital for low-income pensioners is also reduced to the same level as for other taxpayers. The new tax allowance is determined regardless of the spouse's income and married early-retirement and old-age pensioners will each have their own allowance. In addition, the pension income social security contribution is increased and the special allowance for age is discontinued.
- In 2010 a new formula-based system for determining the tax-assessed value of homes was introduced. The new tax-assessed value will be determined by multiplying the floor space of the dwelling by a square metre price based on the geographical location (neighbourhood, municipality, sparsely populated vs. densely populated area), size, age and type (detached, semi-detached, terraced, flat) of the property. For *primary homes* (owner-occupied), the per square metre rate will be set at 25% of the estimated sale price per square metre, whereas the rate for *second homes*, i.e. any other dwellings in addition to the primary home that are not defined as business or recreational properties, will be set at 40% of the estimated sale price per square metre. The current "safety valve" system is being continued so that taxpayers can appeal and have the tax-assessed value reduced to 30% of the documented fair market value (60% for second homes). In addition, the tax-assessed values of recreational properties are increased by 10%.
- Most important changes in 2009 were the abolition of the 80% rule, which primarily reduced the wealth tax of the richest. The wealth tax on equities for those who fall within the scope of the 80% rule has been more than doubled since 2005.
- The home savings scheme (BSU) was expanded in 2009 by increasing the annual savings amount to NOK 20 000 and the maximum aggregate savings amount to NOK 150 000.
- The rates of the inheritance tax were reduced and the exempted amount was increased in 2009. The instalment scheme for family businesses was expanded through the abolition of the upper limit, and the payment period was increased from 7 to 12 years.

Other changes in the personal tax base in 2009:

- The fishermen's allowance was increased from NOK 115 000 to NOK 150 000.
- The reindeer husbandry allowance was increased to the same level as the agriculture allowance.
- The allowance for labour union fees was increased by NOK 450 to NOK 3 600.
- The rate of the travel allowance was increased from NOK 1.40 per km to NOK 1.50 per km.
- The tax-free net income thresholds under the tax limitation rule were increased such as to ensure that singles and couples who receive the minimum state pension will still not be paying tax following the favourable social security settlement they benefited from in 2008.

- A tax favoured contributions to individual pension agreement schemes was reintroduced as of 2008.
- From 1 January, 2008 the employees' SSC rate for self-employed was increased from 10.7% to 11.0%.
- The upper threshold in the surtax schedule was substantially reduced from 2006 to 2007.
- The surtax rates were reduced in 2005 and 2006, as part of a reform of the dual income tax system. The basic allowance has been substantially increased.
- From 1 January, 2006 the supplementary employer's social security contribution at 12.5% for gross wage income that exceeds 16 times "G" (average "G" is estimated to be NOK 74 721 in 2010) was removed.
- From 1 January, 2006 the class 2 in the surtax was removed.
- From 1 January, 2005 the ceiling in the parent allowance for two and more children was removed, and the maximum allowance was increased with NOK 5 000 for each child after the first. From 2008 the maximum allowance will be increased with NOK 15 000 for each child after the first.
- The additional child support of NOK 7 884 for children aged 1 and 2 years was abolished as of August 1, 2003.
- An allowance of maximum NOK 6 000 for donations to voluntary organisations was introduced as of 1 January, 2003. Previously this allowance was coordinated with the allowance for labour union fees (with a combined maximum allowance). The allowance was increased to NOK 12 000 as of 1 January, 2005.
- As of 1 July, 2002 the employer's social security contribution rates for employees aged 62 years or older were reduced by 4 percentage points, although not below 0%. From 2007 the reduction was abolished.

5. Memorandum items

5.1. *Identification of an AW and calculation of earnings*

The wage series used refers to full time employees in the B-N industry group (ISIC rev.4).

The calculation of annual wage earnings is as follows:

- Weighted average monthly wage plus overtime times 12.

The average monthly wage is agreed payment for a wage earner working a normal agreed working-year. It includes bonus payments and other allowances, but not payments for overtime, sick leave, and an establishment's indirect wage costs. The sum is weighted with the number of persons employed in the different industry groups.

5.2. *Employers' contributions to private health and pension schemes*

No information available.

2016 parameter values

Average earnings/yr	Ave_earn	564 218	Secretariat estimate
Central rate (pers)	Tax1_sch	0	159 800
class 1		0.0044	224 900
		0.017	565 400
		0.107	909 500
		0.137	
class 2	Tax2_sch	0.000	159 800
		0.0044	224 900
		0.017	565 400
		0.107	909 500
		0.137	
Central rate (ord)	Cent_rate_ord	0.1055	
Local rate (ord)	Local_rate	0.1445	
Allowances	Class_al_1	51 750	
	Class_al_2	76 250	
	Special_al	51 804	
Basic relief	Basic_min	4 000	
	Basic_max	91 450	
	Basic_rel_rate	0.43	
	Basic_min_wage	31 800	
Soc security contribs	SSC_rate	0.082	
Employer	SSC_empr	0.13	
Trygd. low.lim	SSC_low_lim	49 650	
pct.rate	SSC_low_rate	0.25	
Ref. Income "G"	SSC_G	91 740	
"G" Multiple	SSC_Gmult	16	
Supplemental Rate	SSC_rate_sup	0	
Child cash transfer	Child_sup	11 640	

2016 tax equations

The equations for the system for Norway in 2016 may be calculated on an individual or joint basis for married couples. Social security contributions are calculated on an individual basis. The calculation for Class 2 is chosen for married couples whenever this gives a lower value of tax than the corresponding Class 1 calculations. The functions which are used in the equations (Taper, MIN, Tax etc) are described in the technical note about tax equations. Variable names are defined in the table of parameters above, within the equations table, or are the standard variables "married" and "children". A reference to a variable with the affix "_total" indicates the sum of the relevant variable values for the principal and spouse. And the affixes "_princ" and "_spouse" indicate the value for the principal and spouse, respectively. Equations for a single person are as shown for the principal, with "_spouse" values taken as 0.

	Line in country table and intermediate steps	Variable name	Range	Equation
1.	Earnings	earn		
2.	Allowances:	tax_al	J	IF(class=1, tax1_al_princ+tax1_al_spouse, tax2_al)
	Class 1 tax allowance (ordinary)	tax1_al_princ	P	MIN(MAX(Basic_min_wage, MIN(earn_princ*Basic_rel_rate, Basic_max)) +Class_al_1+IF(AND(Married=0,Children>0),Special_al,o), earn_princ)
	Class 1 tax allowance (ordinary)	tax1_al_spouse	S	MIN(MAX(Basic_min_wage, MIN(earn_spouse*Basic_rel_rate, Basic_max)) +Class_al_1, earn_spouse)
	Class 2 tax allowance (ordinary)	tax2_al	J	MIN(MAX(Basic_min_wage, MIN(earn_princ*Basic_rel_rate, Basic_max)), earn_princ)+MIN(MAX(Basic_min_wage, MIN(earn_spouse* Basic_rel_rate, Basic_max)), earn_spouse)+Class_al_2
3.	Credits in taxable income	taxbl_cr	J	0
4.	CG taxable income (ordinary)			
	Class 1 taxable income	tax1_inc	B	Positive(earn-tax1_al)
	Class 2 taxable income	tax2_inc	J	Positive(earn_total-tax2_al)
5.	CG tax	CG_tax		IF(class=1, CG1_tax, CG2_tax)
	Class 1 tax (personal+ordinary)	CG1_tax	B	Tax(earn, Tax1_sch)+Cent_rate_ord*tax1_inc
	Class 2 tax (personal+ordinary)	CG2_tax	J	Tax(earn_p, Tax2_sch)+ Tax(earn_s, Tax2_sch)+Cent_rate_ord*tax2_inc
6.	Tax credits :	tax_cr	P	0
7.	CG tax	CG_tax	B	CG_tax
8.	State and local taxes	local_tax	J	IF(class=1, local1_tax_total, local2_tax)
	Class 1 local tax	local1_tax	B	(Local_rate*(tax1_inc_princ+tax1_inc_spouse))-tax_cr
	Class 2 local tax	local2_tax	J	(Local_rate*tax2_inc)-tax_cr
	Favourable class	class	J	1+((CG2_tax_excl+local2_tax)<(CG1_tax_excl_total+local1_tax_total))
9.	Employees' soc security	SSC	B	MIN(earn*SSC_rate, Positive(SSC_low_rate*(earn-SSC_low_lim)))
11.	Cash transfers	cash_trans	J	(children>0)*Child_sup
13.	Employer's soc security	SSC_empr	B	earn*SSC_empr

Key to range of equation B calculated separately for both principal earner and spouse P calculated for principal only (value taken as 0 for spouse calculation) J calculated once only on a joint basis.

Taxing Wages 2017
© OECD 2017

Poland

This chapter includes data on the income tax paid by workers, their social security contributions, the family benefits they receive in the form of cash transfers as well as the social security contributions and payroll taxes paid by their employers. Results reported include the marginal and average tax burden for eight different family types.

Methodological information is available for Personal income tax systems, Compulsory social security contributions to schemes operated within the government sector, Universal cash transfers as well as recent changes in the tax/benefit system. The methodology also includes the parameter values and tax equations underlying the data.

Poland 2016

The tax/benefit position of single persons

	Wage level (per cent of average wage)	67	100	167	67
	Number of children	none	none	none	2
1.	**Gross wage earnings**	32 014	47 782	79 795	32 014
2.	**Standard tax allowances**				
	Basic allowance				
	Married or head of family				
	Dependent children				
	Deduction for social security contributions and income taxes	4 389	6 551	10 940	4 389
	Work-related expenses	1 335	1 335	1 335	1 335
	Other				
	Total	5 724	7 886	12 275	5 724
3.	**Tax credits or cash transfers included in taxable income**	0	0	0	0
4.	**Central government taxable income (1 - 2 + 3)**	26 290	39 896	67 520	26 290
5.	**Central government income tax liability (exclusive of tax credits)**	4 732	7 181	12 154	4 732
6.	**Tax credits**				
	Basic credit	556	556	556	1 112
	Married or head of family				
	Children	0	0	0	2 224
	Other (health insurance)	2 141	3 195	5 336	2 141
	Total	2 697	3 751	5 892	5 477
7.	**Central government income tax finally paid (5-6)**	2 035	3 430	6 261	0
8.	**State and local taxes**	0	0	0	0
9.	**Employees' compulsory social security contributions**				
	Gross earnings	3 221	4 807	8 027	3 221
	Taxable income	2 486	3 711	6 197	2 486
	Total	5 707	8 517	14 224	5 707
10.	**Total payments to general government (7 + 8 + 9)**	7 742	11 947	20 486	5 707
11.	**Cash transfers from general government**				
	For head of family				
	For two children	0	0	0	0
	Total	0	0	0	0
12.	**Take-home pay (1-10+11)**	24 272	35 834	59 310	26 307
13.	**Employers' compulsory social security contributions**	5 372	8 018	13 389	5 372
14.	**Average rates**				
	Income tax	6.4%	7.2%	7.8%	0.0%
	Employees' social security contributions	17.8%	17.8%	17.8%	17.8%
	Total payments less cash transfers	24.2%	25.0%	25.7%	17.8%
	Total tax wedge including employer's social security contributions	35.1%	35.8%	36.4%	29.6%
15.	**Marginal rates**				
	Total payments less cash transfers: Principal earner	26.7%	26.7%	26.7%	17.8%
	Total payments less cash transfers: Spouse	n.a.	n.a.	n.a.	n.a.
	Total tax wedge: Principal earner	37.2%	37.2%	37.2%	29.6%
	Total tax wedge: Spouse	n.a.	n.a.	n.a.	n.a.

Poland 2016

The tax/benefit position of married couples

		Wage level (per cent of average wage)	100-0	100-33	100-67	100-33
		Number of children	2	2	2	none
1.	**Gross wage earnings**		47 782	63 550	79 795	63 550
2.	**Standard tax allowances**					
	Basic allowance					
	Married or head of family					
	Dependent children					
	Deduction for social security contributions and income taxes		6 551	8 713	10 940	8 713
	Work-related expenses		1 335	2 670	2 670	2 670
	Other					
		Total	7 886	11 383	13 610	11 383
3.	**Tax credits or cash transfers included in taxable income**		0	0	0	0
4.	**Central government taxable income (1 - 2 + 3)**		39 896	52 167	66 185	52 167
5.	**Central government income tax liability (exclusive of tax credits)**		7 181	9 390	11 913	9 390
6.	**Tax credits**					
	Basic credit		1 112	1 112	1 112	1 112
	Married or head of family					
	Children		2 224	2 224	2 224	0
	Other (health insurance)		3 195	4 250	5 336	4 250
		Total	6 532	7 586	8 672	5 362
7.	**Central government income tax finally paid (5-6)**		650	1 804	3 241	4 028
8.	**State and local taxes**		0	0	0	0
9.	**Employees' compulsory social security contributions**					
	Gross earnings		4 807	6 393	8 027	6 393
	Taxable income		3 711	4 935	6 197	4 935
		Total	8 517	11 328	14 224	11 328
10.	**Total payments to general government (7 + 8 + 9)**		9 167	13 132	17 465	15 356
11.	**Cash transfers from general government**					
	For head of family					
	For two children		0	0	0	0
		Total	0	0	0	0
12.	**Take-home pay (1-10+11)**		38 614	50 417	62 330	48 193
13.	**Employers' compulsory social security contributions**		8 018	10 663	13 389	10 663
14.	**Average rates**					
	Income tax		1.4%	2.8%	4.1%	6.3%
	Employees' social security contributions		17.8%	17.8%	17.8%	17.8%
	Total payments less cash transfers		19.2%	20.7%	21.9%	24.2%
	Total tax wedge including employer's social security contributions		30.8%	32.1%	33.1%	35.1%
15.	**Marginal rates**					
	Total payments less cash transfers: Principal earner		26.7%	26.7%	26.7%	26.7%
	Total payments less cash transfers: Spouse		25.1%	26.7%	26.7%	26.7%
	Total tax wedge: Principal earner		37.2%	37.2%	37.2%	37.2%
	Total tax wedge: Spouse		35.9%	37.2%	37.2%	37.2%

The national currency is the Zloty (PLN). In 2016, PLN 3.94 was equal to USD 1. In that year, the average worker earned PLN 47 782 (Secretariat Estimate).

1. Personal income tax system

An individual being a tax resident in Poland is liable to tax on the basis of world-wide income, irrespective of the source and origin of that income. (The term "residency" is understood similarly to Article 4 paragraph 2 point a) of the OECD Model Tax Convention on Income and Capital).

1.1. *Central government income tax*

1.1.1. *Tax unit*

Individuals are taxed on their own income, but couples married during the whole calendar year can opt to be taxed on their joint income. In the latter case, the "splitting" system applies: the tax bill for a couple is twice the income tax due on half of joint income, provided the joint income does not include capital income taxed at the flat 19% rate. Single individuals with dependent children are also entitled to use the splitting system (their family quotient is two). For the purpose of this report, it is assumed that married couples are taxed on joint income.

1.1.1.1. Tax base

1.1.1.1.1. Gross employment income

For taxation purposes, taxable gross employment income in Poland includes both cash income and the value of benefits in kind. More specifically, gross employment income includes base salary, overtime payments, bonuses, awards, compensation for unused holidays, and costs that are paid in full or in part by the employer on behalf of the employee.

1.1.2. *Tax allowances and tax credits*

1.1.2.1. Standard reliefs

- Basic relief: A non-refundable tax credit of PLN 556.02 per person.
- Marital status relief: None.
- Relief for children: Yes.

However, a widowed spouse is entitled to apply the join income taxation.

It concerns a child of 18 years old or younger or a child up to 25 years old provided they are students or a disabled child irrespective of their age. The actual description in section 4.

A taxpayer can deduct from the due tax decreased by the amount of health contributions specified in the PIT Act, the amount, which is equal for each month of raising a child:

- PLN 92.67 (annually PLN 1 112.04) for the first child, if the income received by parents (married or single parent, who meets special requirements) doesn't exceed in the tax year the amount of PLN 112 000. For other parent the threshold of income is PLN 56 000;
- PLN 92.67 (annually PLN 1 112.04) for the second child;
- PLN 166.67 (annually PLN 2 000.04) for the third child;
- PLN 225.00 (annually PLN 2 700.00) for the fourth and every next child.
- Since 1 January 2015 taxpayers whose due tax is lower than the amount of relief for children, may claim for cash refund for amount of relief which has not been utilized. However, such cash refund cannot exceed the amount of deductible social security and health insurance contributions paid by taxpayer (with some exceptions).
- Relief for health insurance contributions: A tax credit is almost equal to health insurance contribution paid to the National Health Fund. The contribution is 9% of the calculation basis whereas the tax credit is 7.75% of this basis.
- Relief for other social security contributions: An allowance is provided for all social insurance contributions paid by the taxpayer.
- Relief for selected work-related expenses: Standard deductions depend on the number of workplaces and on whether place of residence and workplace are within the same town/city or not. The annual amounts in PLN (deductible from income) are:

	One workplace	Two/more workplaces
Workplace in the same town/city as place of residence	1 335.00[1]	2 002.05
Workplace in different town/city as place of residence	1 668.72	2 502.56

Note: If the actual commuting expenses exceed standard deduction, relief can be determined by the actual expenses incurred solely on personal season tickets.

1. For the purpose of the calculations in this publication, it is assumed that the worker has the same town/city as place of residence.

1.1.2.2. Main non-standard tax reliefs applicable to an average worker

Allowances:

- Expenses for the purpose of rehabilitation incurred by a taxpayer who is a disabled person, or a taxpayer, who supports the disabled;
- Equivalent of blood donations, donations made for the purposes of public benefit activity and of religious practice – in the amount of donation, no more than 6% of income;
- Donations made for charity church care - in the amount of the donation;
- Expenses incurred for the use of the Internet – a taxpayer is entitled to deduct the Internet tax allowance within the next two years, providing that during the phase preceded this period he did not deduct Internet for the use of the Internet (up to PLN 760);
- Abolished allowance (since 2007 continued on the acquired right basis) for interests payments on mortgage loans raised no later than in 2006 on acquisition of housing property on the primary market – up to the amount of interests related to the part of loan not exceeding PLN 325 990 for investments finished in 2016.

Tax credits:

- Donation made to public benefit organizations – up to 1% of due tax.
- Abolished tax credits (continued on the acquired rights basis), i.e. expenses for saving with the aim of buying a house or flat, the amount of social contributions paid on income of an unemployed person hired by a taxpayer in order to take care of their children and/or house.

1.1.3. *Tax schedule*

The tax schedule is as follows:

Tax base (in PLN)		Tax amount
Over	Below	
0	85 528	18% of the tax base, less a basic tax credit of PLN 556.02
85 528		PLN 14 839.02 + 32% of surplus over PLN 85 528

1.2. *State and local income tax*

There are no regional or local income taxes.

1.3. *Wealth tax*

There is no wealth tax.

2. Social security contributions

2.1. *Employees' contributions*

Employees pay 13.71% of the gross wage. This contribution includes:

- Pension insurance contribution – 9.76% of the gross wage. 3.65 percentage points of the pension contribution are treated as non-tax compulsory payments because these payments are either made to the OPF (1.46%) and to personal sub-account in ZUS (2.19%) or only to sub-account in ZUS (3.65%).Disability insurance contribution – 1.5% of the gross wage,
- Sickness/maternity insurance contribution – 2.45% of the gross wage,
- In case of pension and disability insurance, contributions are not paid on the part of the wage that exceeds PLN 121 650.

2.2. *Employers' contributions*

In respect of income paid under an employment contract with a Polish entity, employers have an obligation to pay social security contributions equal to 20.43% of gross wage. This value consists of:

This relief is distinct from an allowance for donations deducted from income.

Since July 2014 out of total 19.52% of social contributions 7.3% goes to subaccount in ZUS either – if voluntarily stated by insured person – 2.92% goes to account in open ended funds and 4.38% to subaccount in ZUS.

The contribution ceiling of pension and disability insurance funds for a given calendar year may not exceed thirty times the amount of the projected average monthly remuneration in the national economy for that year, as set forth in the Budgetary Act.

- 9.76 percentage points are aimed for pension insurance. 3.65 percentage points of the pension contribution are treated as non-tax compulsory payments because these payments are either made to the OPF (1.46%) and to personal sub-account in ZUS (2.19%) or only to sub-account in ZUS (3.65%).
- 6.5 percentage points are aimed for disability insurance,
- 4.17 percentage points are aimed for other insurances i.e. 1.62 percentage points (on average) accident insurance, 2.45 percentage points for Labour Found and 0.1 percentage points for the Guaranteed Employee Benefit Fund.
- In case of pension and disability insurance, contributions are not paid on the part of the wage that exceeds PLN 121 650.

3. Universal cash transfers

3.1. *Transfers related to marital status*

None.

3.2. *Transfers for dependent children*

From 1 November 2012 families where the average monthly income per household member for the previous period is no greater than PLN 539 or PLN 623 when there are one or more disabled children in the household) are entitled to family allowances. From 1 November 2015 the income criteria will be as high as PLN 674 and PLN 764. Families receive PLN 89 monthly for a child no older than 5 years, PLN 118 monthly for a child of 5 up to 18 years old, and PLN 129 monthly for a child of 18 up to 24 years old. The calculations in this Report are based on the assumption that the children are aged between 5 and 18 years.

Single parents are entitled to a supplement of PLN 185 for each child up to a maximum of PLN 370 for all children (and PLN 265 for a disabled child up to a maximum of PLN 530 for all children).

There are several supplements to family allowances:

- for large families – PLN 90 monthly for the 3rd and next children in the family;
- for education of disabled children – PLN 80 monthly for children not older than 5 years and PLN 100 for children older than 5 years.

4. Main changes in tax/benefit systems since 2012

There were no changes in taxation of wages. Tax schedule, work-related expenses, tax allowances, relieves are the same as in previous years.

There were only changes in Social Security Contribution. Since February 2014, 14.96% of the old-age insurance contribution (2.92 percentage points) are transferred by ZUS to a privately-managed fund (OPF) but since July 2014 this part of contribution will be transferred only if insured persons decides to – otherwise all 7.3 percentage points of the contributions will be passed to subaccount in ZUS.

Since July 2014 out of total 19.52% of social contributions 7.3% goes to subaccount in ZUS either – if voluntarily stated by insured person – 2.92% goes to account in open ended funds and 4.38% to subaccount in ZUS.

5. Memorandum items

5.1. Identification of AW and valuation of earnings

The Polish Central Statistical Office calculates average monthly wages and salaries for employees on the basis of reports of enterprises. The figures include overtime and bonus payments and also include information for part-time employees converted to full-time equivalents. Male and female workers are included. The information, which includes estimates for different sectors, is published in the monthly *Statistical Bulletin*.

5.2. Employers' contributions to private pension, health and related schemes

No information provided.

2016 parameter values

Average earnings/yr	Ave_earn	47 782	(Secretariat Estimate)
Work expenses	work_exp	1 335.00[1]	
Income tax schedule	tax_sch		
		0.18	85 528
		0.32	
Tax credits			
Basic credit	basic_cr	556.02	
Health insurance	health_ins	0.09	
	health_ins_credit	0.0775	
Children	Child_cr	1 112.04	
	Child_cr_lim	112 000	
Social security contributions			
Employers	SSC_empr	0.20433	
old-age pension and disability pension insurance	SSC_old	0,0976	
	SSC_old_ZUS	0.061176	
	SSC_old_ZUSII	0.0365	
	SSC_old_OPF	0	
	SSC_dis	0.065	
other insurances	SSC_a	0.0417	
Employees	SSC	0.1371	
old-age pension and disability pension insurance	SSC_old_e	0.0976	
	SSC_old_e_ZUS	0.0611	
	SSC_old_e_ZUSII	0.0365	
	SSC_old_e_OPF	0	
	SSC_dis_e	0.015	
sickness insurance	SSC_s	0.0245	
Contribution ceiling	SSC_c	121 650	
Family benefit	fam_ben	1 416	
single parent additional family benefit	fam_ben_Spsup	185	
single parent additional family benefit ceiling	fam_ben_Spsup_lim	370	
income limit	fam_ben_lim	8 088	
income limit for single parent	fam_ben_lim_sp	8 088	

1. Lump-sum annual work expenses for an employee having one workplace and living in the place (town, city) where the workplace is; employees living outside the city (town) where their workplace is may deduct 1668,72 PLN annually.

2016 tax equations

The equations for the Polish system are mostly calculated on a family basis.

The standard functions which are used in the equations (Taper, MIN, Tax etc) are described in the technical note about tax equations. Two additional functions (Tax93 and ftax) have been incorporated to carry out an iterative calculation for central government tax. These allow for the fact that the church tax is calculated as 9% of Central Government tax and is also allowed as a deduction when calculating taxable income. Variable names are defined in the table of parameters above, within the equations table, or are the standard variables "married" and "children". A reference to a variable with the affix "_total" indicates the sum of the relevant variable values for the principal and spouse. And the affixes "_princ" and "_spouse" indicate the value for the principal and spouse, respectively. Equations for a single person are as shown for the principal, with "_spouse" values taken as 0.

	Line in country table and intermediate steps	Variable name	Range	Equation
1.	Earnings	earn		
	Quotient for tax calculation	quotient	J	1+MAX(Married,(Children>0))
2.	Allowances:	tax_al	J	work_exp+MIN(earn_spouse,work_exp)+SSC+SSC_old_e_OPF*MIN(earn, SSC_c)
3.	Credits in taxable income	taxbl_cr	J	0
4.	CG taxable income	tax_inc	J	Positive(earn-tax_al)
5.	CG tax before credits	CG_tax_excl	J	quotient*Tax(tax_inc/quotient,tax_sch)
6.	Tax credits :			
	Basic credit	basic_cr	J	basic_cr*quotient
	Health insurance	health_ins_cr	B	health_ins_credit*(earn-SSC-SSC_old_e_OPF*MIN(earn, SSC_c))
	Child credit	child_cr	J	If(earn_total<Child_cr_lim,children*child_cr,0)
	Total tax credits	tax_cr	J	basic_cr+health_ins_cr+child_cr
7.	CG tax	CG_tax	J	IF(AND(ABS(Positive(CG_tax_excl-basic_cr-health_ins)-child_cr)>SSC+health_ins,Positive(CG_tax_excl-basic_cr-health_ins)-child_cr <0),-(SSC+health_ins), Positive(CG_tax_excl-basic_cr-health_ins)-child_cr)
8.	State and local taxes	local_tax	J	0
9.	Employees' soc security	health_ins	B	(earn-(MIN(earn, SSC_c)*(SSC_old_e+SSC_dis_e)+earn*SSC_s))*health_ins
.		SSC	B	(SSC_old_e_ZUS+SSC_dis_e)*MIN(earn,SSC_c)+SSC_s*earn
11.	Cash transfers	cash_tran	J	((earn_total/(1+Married+Children))<(Married*fam_ben_lim+(1-Married)*fam_ben_lim_sp))*(Children*fam_ben+(1-Married)*(Children>0)*MIN(fam_ben_Spsup*Children;fam_ben_Spsup_lim))
13.	Employer's soc security	SSC_empr	B	(SSC_old_ZUS+SSC_dis)*MIN(earn,SSC_c)+SSC_a*earn

Key to range of equation:
B calculated separately for both principal earner and spouse,
P calculated for principal only (value taken as 0 for spouse calculation),
J calculated once only on a joint basis.

© OECD 2017

Portugal

This chapter includes data on the income taxes paid by workers, their social security contributions, the family benefits they receive in the form of cash transfers as well as the social security contributions and payroll taxes paid by their employers. Results reported include the marginal and average tax burden for eight different family types.

Methodological information is available for Personal income tax systems, Compulsory social security contributions to schemes operated within the government sector, Universal cash transfers as well as recent changes in the tax/benefit system. The methodology also includes the parameter values and tax equations underlying the data.

Portugal 2016

The tax/benefit position of single persons

		Wage level (per cent of average wage)	67	100	167	67
		Number of children	none	none	none	2
1.	**Gross wage earnings**		11 739	17 521	29 261	11 739
2.	**Standard tax allowances**					
	Basic allowance		4 104	4 104	4 104	4 104
	Married or head of family					
	Dependent children					
	Deduction for social security contributions and income taxes					
	Work-related expenses		0	0	0	0
	Other					
		Total	4 104	4 104	4 104	4 104
3.	**Tax credits or cash transfers included in taxable income**		0	0	0	0
4.	**Central government taxable income (1 - 2 + 3)**		7 635	13 417	25 157	7 635
5.	**Central government income tax liability (exclusive of tax credits)**		1 197	2 903	6 834	1 191
6.	**Tax credits**					
	Basic credit		0	0	0	0
	Married or head of family					
	Children		0	0	0	1 200
	Other					
		Total	0	0	0	1 200
7.	**Central government income tax finally paid (5-6)**		1 197	2 903	6 834	0
8.	**State and local taxes**		0	0	0	0
9.	**Employees' compulsory social security contributions**					
	Gross earnings		1 291	1 927	3 219	1 291
	Taxable income					
		Total	1 291	1 927	3 219	1 291
10.	**Total payments to general government (7 + 8 + 9)**		2 488	4 830	10 053	1 291
11.	**Cash transfers from general government**					
	For head of family					
	For two children		0	0	0	969
		Total	0	0	0	969
12.	**Take-home pay (1-10+11)**		9 251	12 692	19 208	11 417
13.	**Employer's compulsory social security contributions**		2 788	4 161	6 949	2 788
14.	**Average rates**					
	Income tax		10.2%	16.6%	23.4%	0.0%
	Employees' social security contributions		11.0%	11.0%	11.0%	11.0%
	Total payments less cash transfers		21.2%	27.6%	34.4%	2.7%
	Total tax wedge including employer's social security contributions		36.3%	41.5%	47.0%	21.4%
15.	**Marginal rates**					
	Total payments less cash transfers: Principal earner		40.5%	40.5%	49.7%	11.0%
	Total payments less cash transfers: Spouse		n.a.	n.a.	n.a.	n.a.
	Total tax wedge: Principal earner		51.9%	51.9%	59.4%	28.1%
	Total tax wedge: Spouse		n.a.	n.a.	n.a.	n.a.

Portugal 2016

The tax/benefit position of married couples

			100-0	100-33	100-67	100-33
		Wage level (per cent of average wage)	100-0	100-33	100-67	100-33
		Number of children	2	2	2	none
1.	**Gross wage earnings**		17 521	23 303	29 261	23 303
2.	**Standard tax allowances**					
	Basic allowance		4 104	8 208	8 208	8 208
	Married or head of family					
	Dependent children					
	Deduction for social security contributions and income taxes					
	Work-related expenses		0	0	0	0
	Other					
		Total	4 104	8 208	8 208	8 208
3.	**Tax credits or cash transfers included in taxable income**		0	0	0	0
4.	**Central government taxable income (1 - 2 + 3)**		13 417	15 095	21 053	15 095
5.	**Central government income tax liability (exclusive of tax credits)**		1 946	2 332	4 030	2 342
6.	**Tax credits**					
	Basic credit		0	0	0	0
	Married or head of family					
	Children		1 200	1 200	1 200	0
	Other					
		Total	1 200	1 200	1 200	0
7.	**Central government income tax finally paid (5-6)**		746	1 132	2 830	2 342
8.	**State and local taxes**		0	0	0	0
9.	**Employees' compulsory social security contributions**					
	Gross earnings		1 927	2 563	3 219	2 563
	Taxable income					
		Total	1 927	2 563	3 219	2 563
10.	**Total payments to general government (7 + 8 + 9)**		2 673	3 696	6 049	4 905
11.	**Cash transfers from general government**					
	For head of family					
	For two children		718	650	0	0
		Total	718	650	0	0
12.	**Take-home pay (1-10+11)**		15 567	20 257	23 212	18 398
13.	**Employer's compulsory social security contributions**		4 161	5 535	6 949	5 535
14.	**Average rates**					
	Income tax		4.3%	4.9%	9.7%	10.0%
	Employees' social security contributions		11.0%	11.0%	11.0%	11.0%
	Total payments less cash transfers		11.2%	13.1%	20.7%	21.0%
	Total tax wedge including employer's social security contributions		28.2%	29.8%	35.9%	36.2%
15.	**Marginal rates**					
	Total payments less cash transfers: Principal earner		25.5%	39.5%	39.5%	40.5%
	Total payments less cash transfers: Spouse		18.9%	39.5%	39.5%	40.5%
	Total tax wedge: Principal earner		39.8%	51.1%	51.1%	51.9%
	Total tax wedge: Spouse		34.4%	51.1%	51.1%	51.9%

The national currency is the Euro (EUR). In 2016, EUR 0.90 equalled USD 1. The Secretariat has estimated that in that same year the average worker earned EUR 17 712 (Secretariat estimate).

1. Personal income tax system

1.1. *Taxes levied by central government*

1.1.1. *Tax unit*

The standard rule is separate taxation. However, families may opt for joint taxation. Income includes the income of any dependent children. Tax is computed on aggregate net income in the various categories of income, *i.e.* after the deductions specific to each category and standard and non-standard reliefs.

1.1.2. *Standard and non-standard reliefs and tax credits*

1.1.2.1. Standard reliefs

Standard deduction of EUR 4 104 If compulsory contributions to social protection schemes and statutory sub-schemes for health care exceed that limit, the deduction will equal the amount of those contributions.

1.1.2.2. Non-standard reliefs

For income received from 1 January 1999 onwards, the majority of the standard reliefs have been replaced by tax credits (see Section 1.1.4).

Non-standard reliefs still in effect:

- A deduction is provided for the portion of trade union dues not constituting consideration for benefits in the realm of health care, education, assistance for the elderly, housing, insurance or social security, up to 1% of the taxpayer's gross income, increased by 50%. These dues are not taken into account in the calculations underlying this Report.

1.1.3. *Social security contributions*

Social security contributions are totally deductible if they exceed EUR 4 104.00 per taxpayer, in which case the deduction for the contributions replaces the standard earned income deduction (see Section 1.1.2.1).

1.1.4. *Tax credits*

Basic credits

- EUR 600 for each dependent child. This tax credit is increased by EUR 125 for dependent children whose age does not exceed 3 years old.

The corresponding amount equals EUR 4 104.00 (72% × 12 × EUR 475.00).

- EUR 525 for each ascendant whose income does not exceed the minimum pension benefit. When there is only one ascendant, the tax credit increases by EUR 110.

Other tax credits

- 35% of household general expenses up to a limit of EUR 250, per taxpayer; this limit is increased to 45% and EUR 335, respectively, for single parents.
- Non-reimbursed health care costs, not covered by Social Security: 15% of health care costs, with a limit of EUR 1 000
- Expenditures for educating the taxpayer or the taxpayer's dependants: 30% of outlays, up to EUR 800.
- Costs for sanatoria or retirement homes for taxpayers, their ascendants and collaterals up to the third degree whose income does not exceed the national minimum wage: 25% of expenses up to EUR 403.75.
- Costs for the acquisition, construction or improvement of the taxpayers' primary, permanent residence, or for renting out property for a permanent residence: 15% of interest up to EUR 296.00. Rent paid by a tenant, for his permanent residence under an agreement typified by the law, up to EUR 502.00. This credit is applicable to contracts up to 31.12.2011. These limits are also increased by 50% for taxpayers in the first tax rate bracket, by 20% for taxpayers in the second tax rate bracket. This credit is to be phased out until 2016 (interests) and 2018 (rents).
- 20% of alimony payments compulsory under court order or court-approved agreement.
- 30% of education expenditures and 25% of life insurance premiums, up to a limit of 15% of the tax liability, for handicapped taxpayers or dependents.
- 15% of VAT paid for certain services (restaurants, lodging, hairdressers, and auto-repair) up to a limit of EUR 250. This benefit is not included on the limits referred to on the next page.

Tax credits from tax benefits

- Individual Retirement Savings Plans (PPRs): 20% of amounts invested, for unmarried taxpayers or for each spouse, up to:
  - EUR 400 for taxpayers under 35;
  - EUR 350 for taxpayers over 35 and under 50;
  - EUR 300 for taxpayers over 50.
- Social Security Individual Accounts: 20% of amounts invested, for unmarried taxpayers or for each spouse, up to a limit of EUR 350.

Donations granted on the conditions stated in the statutes governing charities (grants to central, regional or local government, special "social solidarity institutions", museums, libraries, schools, institutes, educational or research associations, public administrative bodies, etc.): 25% of donations, limited in certain cases to 15% of the donor's tax liability. However the total of tax credits related to health care costs, education and training, alimony, retirement homes, VAT paid, house expenses and tax benefits cannot exceed the values of the following amounts:

Limits are increased in 5% for each dependent.

Taxable income (EUR) (R)	Limit
Up to 7 035	Without limit
Between 7 035 and 80 000	$1000+\left[(2500-1000)*\left(\frac{80000-\textit{liable income}}{80000-7035}\right)\right]$
Over 80 000	EUR 1 000

1.1.5. *Family status – determination of taxable income*

The default status is individual taxation. Couples can opt for joint taxation based on the income-splitting system as it is described below. In the Taxing Wages calculations, the most favourable system is chosen.

1.1.6. *Tax rate schedule (applicable to 2016 income)*

Taxable income (EUR) (R)	Marginal tax rate (%) (T)	Amount to deduct (EUR) (K)
Up to 7 035	14.50	–
Over 7 035 up to 20 100	28.50	984.90
Over 20 100 up to 40 200	37.00	2 693.40
Over 40 200 up to 80 000	45.00	5 909.40
Over 80 000	48.00	8 309.40

In the case of taxpayers whose income stems primarily from dependent employment (earned income), disposable income after application of the tax rates to taxable income may not be less than, EUR 8 500.00 per taxpayer in 2016.

For residents in the Autonomous Regions of the Azores, reduced tax rates are applicable. Tax calculation formula (I = Income tax due):

- Unmarried taxpayers: $I = R \times T - K - C$

Married taxpayers can opt for joint taxation based on the income splitting method (with one or two earned incomes/see Section 1.1.5):

- $I =\{[(R : 2) \times T - K] \times 2 \} - C$

Where:

R = Taxable income, after deduction of standard and non-standard reliefs (see Sections 1.1.2 and 1.1.5.1)

T = Tax rate corresponding to the taxable income bracket

K = Amount to be deducted from each bracket

C = Tax credits (see Section 1.1.4)

Surtax:

A surtax was introduced by the 2012 State Budget and is applicable on highest income bracket. The surtax is now 2.5% applicable to taxable income between EUR 80 000 and EUR 250 000 and 5% for taxable income above EUR 250 000.

Furthermore, the surtax has been made progressive, aiming at its elimination in 2017, according to the table below, with a tax credit of 2.5% of the annual minimum wage per dependent (EUR 185.50).

Taxable income (EUR) (R)	Tax rate (%) (T)
Up to 7 070	0
Over 7 070 up to 20 000	1
Over 20 000 up to 40 000	1.75
Over 40 000 up to 80 000	3
Over 80 000	3.5

1.1.7. *Special family situations*

1.1.7.1. Handicapped taxpayer/spouse, with a disability rating of 60% or more:

- A tax credit corresponding to 4 times the 2010 minimum wage (EUR 1 900) is granted for each taxpayer or spouse.

1.1.7.2. Handicapped dependent children, with a disability rating of 60% or more:

- A tax credit corresponding to 1.5 times the social benefits index (EUR 712.50) is granted for each dependent child.

1.1.7.3. Handicapped taxpayer/spouse or dependent children, with a disability rating of 90% or more:

- An additional tax credit corresponding to 4 times the 2010 minimum wage (EUR 1 900) is granted for each taxpayer or spouse or dependent child.

1.1.8. *Non liable income*

- Lawfully granted family allowances;
- Living expenses per diem, up to the limits established for national civil servants;
- Meal allowances, up to the amount established for national civil servants, increased by 20% or 60% in the event of a meal allowance in the form of meal vouchers.

2. Compulsory social security contributions to schemes operated within the government sector

Rates and ceilings: social security contributions are levied on gross pay and are not subject to any ceiling.

2.1. *Employee contributions*

As a rule, the rate of employee contributions is 11% of gross pay, with no ceiling.

2.2. *Employer contributions*

The employer's rate of social security contributions is 23.75% of gross pay, with no ceiling.

2.3. *Areas of social protection*

- Health (sickness, disability, work accidents, work-related illness);
- Old age, survival;
- Maternity;
- Family (family allowances);
- Unemployment.

3. Universal cash benefits

3.1. *Benefits for dependent children*

The basic principle is to grant higher monthly social benefits to lower-income households.

There are six different levels of monthly allowances for dependent children, depending on the family's reference income. This reference income is determined by dividing the family's annual gross income, including vacation and Christmas allowances, by the number of dependent children plus one:

- Level 1: Families whose reference income is under 50% of 14 times the reference value (i.e. under EUR 2 934.54);
- Level 2: Families whose reference income is over 50% and under 100 percent of 14 times the reference value(i.e. over EUR 2 934.54 and under EUR 5 869.08);
- Level 3: Families whose reference income is over 100% and under 150% of 14 times the reference value (i.e. over EUR 5 869.08 and under EUR 8 803.62);
- Level 4: Families whose reference income is over 150% (i.e. over EUR 8 803.62).

Each level is also divided according to the age of the dependent child. Benefits are higher during the first 12 months of a child's life.

Monthly social benefits per child are as follows:

	Child under 12 months	Child over 12 months old	Additional benefit per child over 12 months and under 36 months in a family with 2 children	Additional benefit per child over 12 months and under 36 months in a family with 3 or more children
Level 1	145.69	36.42	36.42	84
Level 2	119.66	29.92	29.92	59.84
Level 3	94.14	27.07	27.07	54.14
Level 4	0	0	0	0

Monthly social benefits per child in a single-parent family are increased by 35%.

In September, families with dependent school children aged between 6 and 16 years receiving child benefits in level 1 receive an additional amount equal to the regular monthly benefit.

An amount equal to the cash benefits for dependent children under 12 months is attributed for each unborn child after the first month following that of the 13th week of gestation.

3.2. *Benefits for handicapped dependent children*

There is also a special family allowance scheme for handicapped children.

The above cash benefits (in Sections 3.1 and 3.2) are not taxable.

4. Main changes in the tax/benefit system since 2006

- The relief for disabled taxpayers was restructured. Former partial exemptions and allowances were replaced by tax credits.
- Tax credits for higher income households were limited or abolished;
- The fiscal autonomy of local authorities (municipalities) increased. They may set the level of their share in the revenue from personal income tax, up to 5% of their resident

taxpayers' tax liability. If this rate is set below 5%, the difference will be credited against the taxpayers' tax liability.

- Tax credits for handicapped taxpayers and dependants were increased.
- Social benefits for dependent children were increased for low income families, single-parent families and families with 2 or more children.
- Introduction of social benefits for unborn children.
- A family coefficient was introduced in 2015 and abolished in 2016.
- From 2016, the tax unit is the individual. However, couples can opt for joint taxation.

5. Memorandum items

5.1. *Method used to identify and compute gross wages of the average worker*

The operative concept of monthly compensation is that of amounts paid to full time staff before deductions for tax and compulsory contributions. It therefore includes wages and basic salaries of staff paid by the hour, by the job, or by tasks; benefits in kind or housing, if they are considered an integral part of compensation; cash subsidies for meals, housing or transport; bonuses for regular night shifts and seniority, as well as incentive pay and rewards for diligence and productivity; family allowances, compensation for overtime and work on holidays. Benefits, subsidies and bonuses are taken into account only if paid regularly at each pay period.

Payments in kind are incorporated into the concept of compensation. The statistics record such advantages in kind at their taxable value.

All managerial and supervisory workers are included in the computations.

Average annual pay is based on the average of monthly earnings for April and October multiplied by an adjustment coefficient representing the share of annual bonuses and allowances (including vacation subsidies and the Christmas allowance), which is provided by the labour cost survey.

The following formula is applied:

Average annual pay = Average monthly pay adjusted by the coefficient × 12.

5.2. *Description of the employer's main contributions to private retirement, health insurance schemes, etc.*

Outside the social security system, employers are required to insure their employees against work-related accidents (with private insurance companies). They may also provide their employees with life insurance, although this is optional.

2016 parameter values

Average earnings/yr	Ave_earn	17 521	Secretariat estimate	
Tax allowances	perc	1		
	max_al	4 104		
Tax credits				
Married (basic)	married_cred	0		
Single (basic)	single_cred	0		
Single parent	singlepar_cred	0		
Each child credit	child_cred	600		
Tax schedule	tax_sch	0.145	7 035	
		0.285	20 100	
		0.37	40 200	
		0.45	80 000	
		0.48		
	tax_floor	na		
Surtax	surtax_rate	0.025		
	surtax_rate2	0.05		
	surtax_thrs	250 000		
	add_surtax_schedule	0	7 070	
		0.01	20 000	
		0.0175	40 000	
		0.03	80 000	
		0.035		
	add_surtax_cred	0.025		
Social security contributions	SSC_rate	0.11		
ceiling	SSC_empr	0.2375		
Child benefit - Schedule	ch_ben_sch	0	473.46	1st echelon
		2 934.54	359.04	2nd echelon
		5 869.08	324.84	3rd echelon
		8 803.62	0	4th echelon
Extra child benefit for lone parents	ch_ben_lone	0.35		
Minimum Wage	MW	7 420		
Minimum Disposable Income	MinDispY	8 500		

2016 tax equations

The equations for the Portuguese system in 2016 are calculated on individual basis. Couples can opt for joint taxation based on the income-splitting system. In the Taxing Wages calculations, the two systems are modelled and the most favourable system is chosen.

The functions which are used in the equations (Taper, MIN, Tax etc) are described in the technical note about tax equations. Variable names are defined in the table of parameters above, within the equations table, or are the standard variables "married" and "children". A reference to a variable with the affix "_total" indicates the sum of the relevant variable values for the principal and spouse. And the affixes "_princ" and "_spouse" indicate the value for the principal and spouse, respectively. Equations for a single person are as shown for the principal, with "_spouse" values taken as 0.

	Line in country table and intermediate steps	Variable name	Range	Equation
1.	Earnings	earn		
2.	Allowances:	tax_al	B	MAX(MIN(perc*earn, max_al), SSC)
			J	MAX((MIN(perc*earn_princ, max_al)+MIN(perc* earn_spouse, max_al)), SSC_princ+SSC_spouse)
3.	Credits in taxable income	taxbl_cr		0
4.	CG taxable income	tax_inc	B	earn-tax_al
	Adjusted taxable income	tax_inc_adj	J	tax_inc/(1+Married)
5.	CG tax before credits	CG_tax_excl	B	IF(tax_inc>tax_floor,Tax(tax_inc,tax_sch),0)
			J	IF(tax_inc_adj>tax_floor,Tax(tax_inc_adj,tax_sch)*(1+Married),0)
6.	Tax credits :			
	Basic credit	basic_cr	B/J	0
	Child credit	child_cr	B	IF(AND(Married>0,earn_spouse>0),Children*child_cred/2,Children*child_cred)
			J	Children*child_cred
	Total	tax_cr	B/J	basic_cr+child_cr
	Surtax	surtax	B	IF(tax_inc>surtax_thrs,(surtax_rate*(surtax_thrs-TopIncBracket)+surtax_rate2*(tax_inc-surtax_thrs)),surtax_rate*Positive(tax_inc-TopIncBracket))+Positive(Tax(tax_inc,add_surtax_schedule)- ((add_surtax_cred*MW*Children)/(1+(Married*earn_spouse>0))))
			J	IF(tax_inc_adj>surtax_thrs,(surtax_rate*(surtax_thrs-TopIncBracket)+surtax_rate2*(tax_inc_adj-surtax_thrs))*(1+Married),surtax_rate*Positive(tax_inc_adj-TopIncBracket)*(1+Married))+Positive(Tax(tax_inc,add_surtax_schedule)*(1+Married))-(add_surtax_cred*MW*Children))
7.	CG tax	CG_tax	B	IF(earn-CG-tax-excl> MinDispY,Positive(CG_tax_excl-tax_cr),0)+surtax
				IF(earn-CG-tax-excl> MinDispY*(1+(Married*earn_spouse>0)),Positive(CG_tax_excl-tax_cr),0)+surtax
8.	State and local taxes	local_tax	B/J	0
9.	Employees' soc security	SSC	B	earn*SSC_rt
11.	Cash transfers	cash_trans	J	=IF(Married=0, VLOOKUP(earn/(Children+1),ch_ben_sch,2,1)*Children*(1+ch_ben_lone), VLOOKUP(earn/(Children+1),ch_ben_sch,2,1)*Children)
13.	13. Employer's soc security	SSC_empr	B	earn*SSC_empr

Key to range of equation B calculated separately for both principal earner and spouse P calculated for principal only (value taken as 0 for spouse calculation) J calculated once only on a joint basis.

Taxing Wages 2017
© OECD 2017

Slovak Republic

This chapter includes data on the income taxes paid by workers, their social security contributions, the family benefits they receive in the form of cash transfers as well as the social security contributions and payroll taxes paid by their employers. Results reported include the marginal and average tax burden for eight different family types.

Methodological information is available for Personal income tax systems, Compulsory social security contributions to schemes operated within the government sector, Universal cash transfers as well as recent changes in the tax/benefit system. The methodology also includes the parameter values and tax equations underlying the data.

Slovak Republic 2016

The tax/benefit position of single persons

	Wage level (per cent of average wage)	67	100	167	67
	Number of children	none	none	none	2
1.	**Gross wage earnings**	7 315	10 918	18 233	7 315
2.	**Standard tax allowances**				
	Basic allowance	3 803	3 803	3 803	3 803
	Married or head of family	0	0	0	0
	Dependent children	0	0	0	0
	Deduction for social security contributions and income taxes	980	1 463	2 443	980
	Work-related expenses				
	Other				
	Total	4 784	5 266	6 247	4 784
3.	**Tax credits or cash transfers included in taxable income**	0	0	0	0
4.	**Central government taxable income (1 - 2 + 3)**	2 531	5 652	11 986	2 531
5.	**Central government income tax liability (exclusive of tax credits)**	481	1 074	2 277	481
6.	**Tax credits**				
	Basic credit	0	0	0	0
	Married or head of family	0	0	0	0
	Children	0	0	0	514
	Other (ETC)	0	0	0	0
	Total	0	0	0	514
7.	**Central government income tax finally paid (5-6)**	481	1 074	2 277	- 33
8.	**State and local taxes**	0	0	0	0
9.	**Employees' compulsory social security contributions**				
	Gross earnings	980	1 463	2 443	980
	Taxable income				
	Total	980	1 463	2 443	980
10.	**Total payments to general government (7 + 8 + 9)**	1 461	2 537	4 721	947
11.	**Cash transfers from general government**				
	For head of family				
	For two children	0	0	0	564
	Total	0	0	0	564
12.	**Take-home pay (1-10+11)**	5 854	8 381	13 512	6 932
13.	**Employers' compulsory social security contributions**	2 282	3 406	5 689	2 282
14.	**Average rates**				
	Income tax	6.6%	9.8%	12.5%	-0.4%
	Employees' social security contributions	13.4%	13.4%	13.4%	13.4%
	Total payments less cash transfers	20.0%	23.2%	25.9%	5.2%
	Total tax wedge including employer's social security contributions	39.0%	41.5%	43.5%	27.8%
15.	**Marginal rates**				
	Total payments less cash transfers: Principal earner	29.9%	29.9%	29.9%	29.9%
	Total payments less cash transfers: Spouse	n.a.	n.a.	n.a.	n.a.
	Total tax wedge: Principal earner	46.5%	46.5%	46.5%	46.5%
	Total tax wedge: Spouse	n.a.	n.a.	n.a.	n.a.

Slovak Republic 2016

The tax/benefit position of married couples

		Wage level (per cent of average wage)	100-0	100-33	100-67	100-33
		Number of children	2	2	2	none
1.	**Gross wage earnings**		10 918	14 521	18 233	14 521
2.	**Standard tax allowances**					
	Basic allowance		3 803	7 068	7 607	7 068
	Married or head of family		3 803	0	0	0
	Dependent children		0	0	0	0
	Deduction for social security contributions and income taxes		1 463	1 802	2 443	1 802
	Work-related expenses					
	Other					
		Total	9 070	8 869	10 050	8 869
3.	**Tax credits or cash transfers included in taxable income**		0	0	0	0
4.	**Central government taxable income (1 - 2 + 3)**		1 848	5 652	8 183	5 652
5.	**Central government income tax liability (exclusive of tax credits)**		351	1 074	1 555	1 074
6.	**Tax credits**					
	Basic credit		0	0	0	0
	Married or head of family		0	0	0	0
	Children		514	514	514	0
	Other (ETC)		0	0	0	0
		Total	514	514	514	0
7.	**Central government income tax finally paid (5-6)**		- 163	560	1 041	1 074
8.	**State and local taxes**		0	0	0	0
9.	**Employees' compulsory social security contributions**					
	Gross earnings		1 463	1 802	2 443	1 802
	Taxable income					
		Total	1 463	1 802	2 443	1 802
10.	**Total payments to general government (7 + 8 + 9)**		1 300	2 362	3 484	2 875
11.	**Cash transfers from general government**					
	For head of family					
	For two children		564	564	564	0
		Total	564	564	564	0
12.	**Take-home pay (1-10+11)**		10 182	12 724	15 313	11 645
13.	**Employers' compulsory social security contributions**		3 406	4 170	5 689	4 170
14.	**Average rates**					
	Income tax		-1.5%	3.9%	5.7%	7.4%
	Employees' social security contributions		13.4%	12.4%	13.4%	12.4%
	Total payments less cash transfers		6.7%	12.4%	16.0%	19.8%
	Total tax wedge including employer's social security contributions		28.9%	31.9%	36.0%	37.7%
15.	**Marginal rates**					
	Total payments less cash transfers: Principal earner		29.9%	29.9%	29.9%	29.9%
	Total payments less cash transfers: Spouse		29.5%	9.4%	29.9%	9.4%
	Total tax wedge: Principal earner		46.5%	46.5%	46.5%	46.5%
	Total tax wedge: Spouse		41.8%	25.2%	46.5%	25.2%

As from 1.1.2009 Slovakia has joined the Euro zone; the national currency became the Euro (EUR). In 2016, EUR 0.90 was equal to USD 1. In that year, the average worker earned EUR 10 918 (Secretariat estimate).

1. Personal income tax system

1.1. *Central government income taxes*

1.1.1. *Tax unit*

The tax unit is the individual.

1.1.2. *Tax allowances and tax credits*

1.1.2.1. Standard reliefs

- *Basic relief*: An allowance for all taxpayers is set at 19.2 times the minimum living standard (MLS) for a basic adult as of 1 January 2016 (EUR 3 803.33). In 2016, the basic personal allowance for taxpayers with gross earnings net of employee social security contributions in excess of the threshold of EUR 19 809 per year (19 809 = 100 × MLS, which is approximately equal to an employee's monthly gross wage of EUR 1 906) is gradually withdrawn. If gross earnings net of employee social security contributions exceed EUR 19 809, the personal allowance is calculated as 44.2 times the minimum living standard minus 0.25 times gross earnings net of employee social security contributions. The basic personal allowance reaches 0 if the gross earnings net of employee social security contributions amount to EUR 35 022.31 per year (employee's monthly gross wage of approximately EUR 3 370). The value of the basic tax allowance cannot become negative.
- The regressive tax allowance is taken into account only once a year (when the tax return is filed or when the annual clearing is performed). Monthly tax prepayments during the year are therefore not affected.
- *Marital status relief*: An additional allowance is given to the principal earner in respect of a spouse living in a common household if the spouse earns no more than EUR 3 803.33. As from 1 January 2007 the value of the spouse allowance depends on the gross earnings net of employee social security contributions of both principal and spouse. As of 2013, to be entitled to spouse allowance one of the following conditions should be met:
  - spouse is taking care of (not necessarily personally) children up to 3 years (or up to 6 years if child is disabled) or
  - spouse is unemployed or
  - spouse is receiving nursing allowance or
  - spouse is disabled.
- If the principal's gross earnings net of employee social security contributions in 2016 are lower or equal to EUR 35 022.31 (= 176.8 times MLS) and the spouse's gross earnings net of employee social security contributions are lower than EUR 3 803.33, the spouse

allowance is calculated as the difference between 19.2 times MLS and the spouse's gross earnings net of employee social security contributions. If the gross earnings net of employee social security contributions of the spouse exceed EUR 3 803.33, the spouse allowance is 0. If the principal's gross earnings net of employee social security contributions exceed EUR 35 022.31 (= 176.8 times MLS), the spouse allowance is calculated as 63.4 times MLS minus 0.25 times the principal's gross earnings net of employee social security contributions. This amount is reduced by the spouse's gross earnings net of employee social security contributions. The value of the spouse allowance cannot become negative.

- The digressive tax allowance is taken into account only once a year (when the tax return is filed or when the annual clearing is performed). Monthly tax prepayments during the year are therefore not affected.
- **For the purposes of this Report,** only families with unemployed spouse are entitled to spouse allowance (spouse income does not influence any equations of spouse allowance as of 2013). Child care up to 3 years does not affect the calculation of tax wedges as according to the Taxing wages methodology any children in the household are assumed to be aged between six and eleven inclusive.
- *Relief for children:* The prior allowance for children has been replaced by a non-wastable tax credit as from January 2004. As from July 2007, the monthly tax credit is automatically indexed by MLS growth as of 1st July when also the new amount of MLS comes into force. Monthly tax credit in 2016 is EUR 21.41 per child for the whole year as MLS did not change during the year. The annual amount will be EUR 256.92. The tax credit for each dependent child is deducted from the tax liability; if the credit exceeds the tax liability, the excess will be paid to the taxpayer. In order to receive this credit, the parent must annually earn at least 6 times the minimum monthly wage, which for 2016 is set at EUR 405.0 (the total annual earnings must therefore be at least EUR 2 430.0). The credit can be taken only by one partner. It can be taken by one partner for part of the tax period (year) and by the other partner for the rest of the tax period (year); this choice will have to hold for all dependent children. (For the purposes of this Report, it is assumed that the credit is claimed by the principal wage earner).
- *Relief for social and health security contributions:* Employee's social security contributions (see Section 2.1.) are deductible for income tax purposes.

1.1.2.2. Main non-standard tax reliefs applicable to an average wage worker

- Supplementary pension insurance, special-purpose savings and life insurances repealed as from January 2011. As of 2014 allowance for supplementary pension insurance has been reintroduced. Supplementary pension contributions are tax-deductible up to the maximum limit of EUR 180 per year.
- As of 2013 voluntary contributions to the privately managed fully funded pillar up to 2% of gross earnings net of employee social security contributions are tax-deductible. Maximum yearly limit for this tax relief is calculated as: 2% x 60 x AW(t-2), where AW(t-2) average wage two years ago. It is legislated that this relief will be automatically abolished as of 2017.

1.1.2.3. Non-wastable tax credit: employee tax credit (ETC/zamestnanecká prémia)

Prior to 2015 low-income workers were eligible for employee tax credit. The employee tax credit was effective since 2009 and depended on employee's earnings and the number of months worked. In order to receive employee tax credit, earnings should be at least 6 times of the minimum wage and 12 times the minimum wage. The credit was than calculated as a 19% of the difference between the basic allowance and the tax base (gross earnings net of employee SSC). In 2016 the tax base (at the level of the minimum wage, EUR 4 367.16) is higher than the basic allowance (EUR 3 803.33) the tax credit is automatically zero (so effectively anyone can be eligible).

1.1.3. *Tax schedule*

As from 2013 the previous flat tax rate of 19% was replaced by new tax schedule with two tax brackets. The ceiling for the first bracket is set out as 176.8 times MLS (equal to EUR 35 022.31) what secure its automatic indexation. The tax schedule is as follows:

Annual taxable income (EUR)*	Rate (%)
0-35 022.31	19
35 022.31 and over	25

* Employee's social security contributions (see 1.1.2) are deductible for income tax purposes.

1.2. *State and local income tax*

Since 2016 the distribution of personal income tax (PIT) has changed and the tax revenues are redirected solely to the local governments. The share of PIT yield which is transferred to municipalities increased from 68.5% to 70%. The share of PIT yield transferred to self-governing regions increased from 29.2% to 30%.

2. Compulsory social security contributions to schemes operated within the government sector

2.1. *Employees' contributions*

Compulsory contributions of 13.4% of gross wages and salaries are paid by all employees into government operated schemes. The total is made up as follows:

Health Insurance		4.0%
Social Insurance		9.4%
of which:		
Sickness	1.4%	
Retirement	4.0%	
Disability	3.0%	
Unemployment	1.0%	

There are maximum assessment bases MSSAB (maximum threshold for contributions to apply) that apply to social security contributions. From 2004 these MSSAB are no longer fixed values but depend upon the average wages (AW). As of 2013 formulae for calculation of all maximum assessment bases has been unified. Monthly MSSAB for social security contributions are calculated as: 5 × AW(t-2), where AW(t-2) is the average wage two years ago. The average wage (AW) is determined by the Statistical Office of the Slovak Republic – for 2014 it was EUR 858 per month.

As of 2015 the health insurance contribution (HIC) allowance has been introduced. The allowance decreases the employee's and employer's assessment base for the health insurance. It amounts to EUR 380 per month (EUR 4 560 annually) and decreases with rising income up to EUR 570 (EUR 6 840 annually) when it reaches zero. With EUR 1 rise in the monthly income the monthly allowance is reduced by EUR 2. The HIC allowance is applicable only on standard employment income (not self-employed income or income based on temporary contracts). However, to determine the amount of allowance all types of incomes are assessed, to target only low income workers.

2.2. Employers' contributions

The total contribution for employers is 35.2% of gross wages and salaries. The contribution comprises the health insurance contribution (10% of gross wages and salaries) and the social insurance contribution (25.2%). The social insurance rate reflects contributions to sickness insurance (1.4%), disability insurance (3%), retirement insurance (14%), the Guaranteed Fund (0.25%), accident insurance (0.8%), for unemployment (1%) and to the Reserve Fund (4.75%). All contributions are rounded down on two decimal places.

Since January 2005, Slovakia has introduced the privately managed fully funded pillar. This means that a given proportion (9 percentage points) of social contributions paid by the employer for retirement insurance flew directly to the private pension funds and not to the Social insurance agency as in previous years. As from September 2012 pension sharing scheme has been changed. Employer's retirement contribution rate to the fully funded pillar has been reduced from 9% to 4% (for more see pension contribution sharing scheme table below). As from 2017 contribution rate to the II. pillar will automatically increase by 0.25 p.p. per year (i.e. contribution rate to the I. pillar will decrease in the same volume), stopping at 6% in 2024. Private pension funds are treated outside of general government; these contributions are therefore not taken into account in the calculations of average and marginal tax rates. For the purposes of this Report, the total contribution rate for employers in 2016 is 31.2%.

As of 2015 the health insurance contribution (HIC) allowance has been introduced (for more see 2.1).

The MSSAB also applies to the employer's SSC. The next table presents the annual values of MSSAB:

	Formula for MSSAB	Value of MSSAB
Health insurance	5.0 x AW (t-2)	51 480.00
Social insurance		
of which		
sickness, retirement, unemployment, disability, Guarantee fund, Reserve fund	5.0 x AW (t-2)	51 480.00
accident		No limit

SSC: Pension – contribution sharing in case of II. Pillar participation

Period	Percentage of gross earnings		
	I Pillar	II Pillar	Total
Previous system (up to September 2012)	9% (5% employer + 4% employee contribution)	9% (employer contribution)	18%
Current system (from September 2012)	14% (10% employer + 4% employee contribution)	4% (employer contribution)	18%

3. Universal cash transfers

3.1. *Transfers related to marital status*

None.

3.2. *Transfers for dependent children*

The central government pays an allowance in respect of each dependent child in the amount of EUR 23.52 per month in 2016. In January 2008 an extra allowance for dependent children whose parents are not eligible for the non-wastable child tax credit was introduced. The monthly amount of this allowance is EUR 11.02. For the purpose of the tax wedge calculations this allowance is not relevant, as only non-workers and taxpayers with annual earnings lower than six times the minimum monthly wage (which is the condition for eligibility for the non-wastable child tax credit) are entitled to the extra allowance.

The non-wastable tax credit mentioned in Section 1.1.2.1 is part of the social support for families with dependent children. However, it is not considered as a transfer for the purposes of this Report.

3.3. *Transfers related to social status*

To determine the claim to state social benefits (for example the allowance for housing costs), the minimum living standard amounts are relevant as they form the basis of the income test. For 2016, these amounts are:

	MLS monthly (1.1.2016-31.12.2016)
First adult	198.09
Second adult	138.19
Child	90.42

A family is entitled to a social allowance if the total combined net monthly income of the family is less than the calculated MLS for this family. The allowance varies with the family type.

The benefits available to a family in material need (valid since 1 January 2014) are:

- EUR 61.60 per month for an individual;
- EUR 117.20 per month for an individual with between one and four children;
- EUR 107.10 per month for a couple without children;
- EUR 160.40 per month for a couple with between one and four children;
- EUR 171.20 per month for an individual with more than four children;
- EUR 216.10 per month for a couple with more than four children.
- activation allowance: EUR 63.07 per month – for people who become active either by accepting qualifying employment opportunities or participating in retraining courses.
- housing allowance: EUR 55.80 per month for individual in material need, EUR 89.20 for a household in material need (if household has more than 1 person).
- protection allowance: EUR 63.07 per month for an individual in material need where employment is not possible due to such circumstances as a disability or old age, EUR 34.69 per month for individual on sick leave for at least 30 consecutive days and EUR 13.50 for a pregnant woman from 4th month of the pregnancy and lasts until the

child's age of 1 year (for the purpose of this Report, protection allowance is assumed to be EUR 63.07 for each individual).

- specific allowance: EUR 63.07 per month – entitlement arise for long-term unemployed individuals who move into work for 6 months (does not affect the calculations in this Report).
- dependent child allowance: EUR 17.20 per month for a child who properly fulfils compulsory school attendance.

4. Main changes in tax/benefit systems since 2014

The main change relate to change in PIT revenue distribution between municipalities, self-governing regions and state budget. Since the MLS has not been indexed since 2014 all allowances, credits and brackets related to MLS have not changed as well.

5. Memorandum items

5.1. *Identification of AW and valuation of earnings*

The Ministry of Finance of the Slovak republic estimates the average earnings of the AW based on the data supplied by the Statistical Office of the Slovak republic, Labour Force Survey data (LFS). Earnings data (without self-employees) are based on average wage definition including industries falling under categories B to N inclusive, with reference to International Standard Industrial Classification of All Economic Activities, Revision 4.

2016 parameter values

Average earnings/yr	Ave_earn	10 918	Secretariat estimate
Minimum living standard (MLS) 2015	basic_adult	198.09	
	basic_adult1	138.19	
	basic_child	90.42	
Basic allowance	basic_al_mult	19.2	
	basic_al	3 803.33	
	basic_al_mult1	100	
	basic_al_mult2	44.2	
	basic_al_redn	0.25	
Spouse allowance	spouse_al_limit	3 803.33	
	spouse_al_mult1	176.8	
	spouse_al_mult2	63.4	
	spouse_al_redn	0.25	
Income tax rate	Tax_sch/tax_rate	0.19	35 022.312
		0.25	
Tax credits - nonwastable	tax_cr	256.92	
	min_wage	405	
	minwage_mult	6	
	etc_thresh	4 367.16	
Employee social security contributions	SSC_rate	0.134	
	SSC_sick	0.014	
	SSC_ret	0.04	
	SSC_dis	0.03	
	SSC_unemp	0.01	
	SSC_health	0.04	
Employer social security contributions	SSC_empr	0.304	
	SSC_empsick	0.014	
	SSC_empret	0.1	
	SSC_empdis	0.03	
	SSC_empunemp	0.01	
	SSC_emphealth	0.1	
	SSC_gua	0.0025	
	SSC_acc	0.008	
	SSC_fund	0.0475	
Health Insurance Contribution allowance	HIC_treshold	4 560	
	HIC_rate	2	
Maximum assessment base	MSSAB	51 480	
Cash transfers	transf_1	282.24	
	transf_indiv	739.2	
	transf_indiv_child	1 406.4	
	transf_couple	1 285.2	
	transf_couple_child	1 924.8	
	transf_hous_indiv	669.60	
	transf_hous_couple	1 070.40	
	transf_activ	756.84	
	transf_dep	206.40	

2016 tax equations

	Line in country table and intermediate steps	Variable name	Range	Equation
1.	Earnings	earn		
2.	Allowances:			
	Basic	basic_allce	B	IF(earn-SSC<=basic_al_mult1*basic_adult,basic_al,MAXA(basic_al_mult2*basic_adult-basic_al_redn*(earn-SSC),0))
	Spouse	spouse_allce	P	IF(earn_spouse=0,1,0)*Married*Positive(IF(earn_princ-SSC_princ<=spouse_al_mult1*basic_adult, basic_al_mult*basic_adult,spouse_al_mult2*basic_adult-spouse_al_redn*(earn_princ-SSC_princ)))
	Social security contributions	SSC_al	B	SSC
	Total	tax_al	B	basic_allce+spouse_allce+SSC_al
3.	Credits in taxable income	taxbl_cr	B	0
4.	CG taxable income	tax_inc	B	Positive(earn-tax_al)
5.	CG tax before credits	CG_tax_excl	B	Tax(tax_inc,tax_sch)
6.	Tax credits:			
	Employee tax credit	etc_cr	B	IF(earn>=min_wage*minwage_mult, tax_rate*Positive(basic_al-MAX(etc_thresh, earn-SSC)), 0)
	Children	child_cr	P	(earn>=min_wage*minwage_mult)*Children*tax_cr
	Total	tax_cr	B	etc_cr+child_cr
7.	CG tax	CG_tax	B	CG_tax_excl-tax_cr
8.	State and local taxes	local_tax	B	0
9.	Employees' soc security	SSC	B	MINA(earn,MSSAB)*SSC_rate+MINA(MAX(0;(earn-MAX(0;HIC_treshold-MAX(0;(earn-HIC_treshold)*HIC_rate))));MSSAB)*SSC_health
11.	Cash transfers	cash_trans	J	Children*transf_1+Positive(IF(0,75*((earn-SSC-CG_tax_excl)/12)<(basic_adult+Married*basic_adult1+ Children*basic_child); ((1-Married)* (IF(Children>0; transf_indiv_child;transf_indiv))+ Married*(IF(Children>0;transf_couple_child; transf_couple))+IF((Married+Children)>0;transf_hous_couple;transf_hous_indiv)+(Children*transf_dep)+IF(A7>0;transf_activ;0)+IF(B7>0;transf_activ;0)-0,75*(earn-SSC-CG_tax_excl));0))
13.	Employer's soc security	SSC_empr	B	MINA(earn,MSSAB)*SSC_empr+earn*SSC_acc+MINA(MAX(0;(earn-MAX(0; HIC_treshold-MAX(0;(earn-HIC_treshold)*HIC_rate))));MSSAB)*SSC_emphealth

Key to range of equation B calculated separately for both principal earner and spouse P calculated for principal only (value taken as 0 for spouse calculation) J calculated once only on a joint basis.

© OECD 2017

Slovenia

This chapter includes data on the income taxes paid by workers, their social security contributions, the family benefits they receive in the form of cash transfers as well as the social security contributions and payroll taxes paid by their employers. Results reported include the marginal and average tax burden for eight different family types.

Methodological information is available for Personal income tax systems, Compulsory social security contributions to schemes operated within the government sector, Universal cash transfers as well as recent changes in the tax/benefit system. The methodology also includes the parameter values and tax equations underlying the data.

Slovenia 2016

The tax/benefit position of single persons

	Wage level (per cent of average wage)	67	100	167	67
	Number of children	none	none	none	2
1.	**Gross wage earnings**	12 255	18 292	30 547	12 255
2.	**Standard tax allowances**				
	Basic allowance	4 419	3 303	3 303	4 419
	Married or head of family				
	Dependent children				5 086
	Deduction for social security contributions and income taxes	2 708	4 042	6 751	2 708
	Work-related expenses	0	0	0	0
	Other				
	Total	7 127	7 345	10 054	12 213
3.	**Tax credits or cash transfers included in taxable income**	0	0	0	0
4.	**Central government taxable income (1 - 2 + 3)**	5 128	10 946	20 493	42
5.	**Central government income tax liability (exclusive of tax credits)**	821	2 073	4 664	7
6.	**Tax credits**				
	Basic credit				
	Married or head of family				
	Children	0	0	0	0
	Other				
	Total	0	0	0	0
7.	**Central government income tax finally paid (5-6)**	821	2 073	4 664	7
8.	**State and local taxes**	0	0	0	0
9.	**Employees' compulsory social security contributions**				
	Gross earnings	2 708	4 042	6 751	2 708
	Taxable income				
	Total	2 708	4 042	6 751	2 708
10.	**Total payments to general government (7 + 8 + 9)**	3 529	6 116	11 415	2 715
11.	**Cash transfers from general government**				
	For head of family				
	For two children	0	0	0	3 210
	Total	0	0	0	3 210
12.	**Take-home pay (1-10+11)**	8 726	12 176	19 132	12 750
13.	**Employer's wage dependent contributions and taxes**	1 973	2 945	4 918	1 973
	Employer's compulsory social security contributions	1 973	2 945	4 918	1 973
	Payroll taxes	0	0	0	0
14.	**Average rates**				
	Income tax	6.7%	11.3%	15.3%	0.1%
	Employees' social security contributions	22.1%	22.1%	22.1%	22.1%
	Total payments less cash transfers	28.8%	33.4%	37.4%	-4.0%
	Total tax wedge including employer's social security contributions	38.7%	42.7%	46.1%	10.4%
15.	**Marginal rates**				
	Total payments less cash transfers: Principal earner	34.6%	43.1%	54.0%	34.6%
	Total payments less cash transfers: Spouse	n.a.	n.a.	n.a.	n.a.
	Total tax wedge: Principal earner	43.6%	51.0%	60.4%	43.6%
	Total tax wedge: Spouse	n.a.	n.a.	n.a.	n.a.

Slovenia 2016

The tax/benefit position of married couples

		Wage level (per cent of average wage)	100-0	100-33	100-67	100-33
		Number of children	2	2	2	none
1.	**Gross wage earnings**		18 292	24 328	30 547	24 328
2.	**Standard tax allowances**					
	Basic allowance		3 303	8 005	7 721	8 005
	Married or head of family					
	Dependent children		5 086	5 086	5 086	
	Other dependent family member		2 437			
	Deduction for social security contributions and income taxes		4 042	5 376	6 751	5 376
	Work-related expenses		0	0	0	0
		Total	14 868	18 468	19 558	13 381
3.	**Tax credits or cash transfers included in taxable income**		0	0	0	0
4.	**Central government taxable income (1 - 2 + 3)**		3 423	5 860	10 989	10 946
5.	**Central government income tax liability (exclusive of tax credits)**		548	938	1 758	2 073
6.	**Tax credits**					
	Basic credit					
	Married or head of family					
	Children		0	0	0	0
	Other					
		Total	0	0	0	0
7.	**Central government income tax finally paid (5-6)**		548	938	1 758	2 073
8.	**State and local taxes**		0	0	0	0
9.	**Employees' compulsory social security contributions**					
	Gross earnings		4 042	5 376	6 751	5 376
	Taxable income					
		Total	4 042	5 376	6 751	5 376
10.	**Total payments to general government (7 + 8 + 9)**		4 590	6 314	8 509	7 450
11.	**Cash transfers from general government**					
	For head of family					
	For two children		2 469	1 509	1 249	0
		Total	2 469	1 509	1 249	0
12.	**Take-home pay (1-10+11)**		16 171	19 523	23 287	16 878
13.	**Employer's wage dependent contributions and taxes**		2 945	3 917	4 918	3 917
	Employer's compulsory social security contributions		2 945	3 917	4 918	3 917
	Payroll taxes		0	0	0	0
14.	**Average rates**					
	Income tax		3.0%	3.9%	5.8%	8.5%
	Employees' social security contributions		22.1%	22.1%	22.1%	22.1%
	Total payments less cash transfers		11.6%	19.7%	23.8%	30.6%
	Total tax wedge including employer's social security contributions		23.9%	30.9%	34.3%	40.2%
15.	**Marginal rates**					
	Total payments less cash transfers: Principal earner		34.6%	34.6%	34.6%	43.1%
	Total payments less cash transfers: Spouse		44.5%	22.1%	34.6%	22.1%
	Total tax wedge: Principal earner		43.6%	43.6%	43.6%	51.0%
	Total tax wedge: Spouse		52.2%	32.9%	43.6%	32.9%

The Slovenian currency is the euro (EUR). In 2016, EUR 0.90 was equal to USD 1. In that year, the average worker in Slovenia earned EUR 18 292 (Secretariat estimate).

1. Personal income tax system

1.1. *Central government income tax*

1.1.1. *Tax unit*

The tax unit is the individual.

1.1.2. *Tax allowances*

1.1.2.1. Standard tax reliefs

- *A general (basic) allowance* of EUR 3 302.70 is deductible from income in 2016. For lower income groups an additional general allowance of EUR 3 217.12 is deductible when taxable income is lower than EUR 10 866.37 and of EUR 1 115.94 when taxable income is between EUR 10 866.37 and EUR 12 570.89.
- *Family allowances* are also deductible from the tax base in the same way as for the general allowance. The allowances for 2016 are as follows:
  - EUR 2 436.92 for the first dependent child;
  - EUR 2 649.24 for the second child;
  - EUR 4 418.54 for the third child;
  - EUR 6 187.85 for the fourth child;
  - EUR 7 957.14 for the fifth child;
  - for the sixth and all additional dependent children the allowance is higher by EUR 1 769.30 relative to the amount of allowance for the preceding maintained children;
  - EUR 8 830.00 for a dependent child who requires special care;
  - EUR 2 436.92 for any other dependent family member.
- *Relief for social security contributions*: Employee's compulsory contributions for the social insurance system are deductible for income tax purposes.
- *Tax credits*: None for employees.

1.1.2.2. Non – standard tax reliefs applicable to income from employment

- *Additional voluntary pension insurance premiums*: Premiums paid by a resident to the provider of a pension plan based in Slovenia or in another EU Member State according to a pension plan that is approved and entered into a special register in accordance with the pension legislation are deductible from taxable income. In 2015 such deductions are subject to an annual limit of EUR 2 819.09 or a sum equal to 24% of the employee's contribution for compulsory pension and disability insurance if that is a lower figure.
- *Reimbursement of expenses associated with work*, such as in-work meals, transport to and from work, in-the-field supplements (per diem when an employee works outside his or

her working place) and compensation for being away from home, are exempt subject to statutory conditions and upper limits.

- *Reimbursement of expenses associated with business travel* such as: per diem allowances, transport costs (including the use of the employee's private vehicle for work purposes), and the costs of overnight accommodation, are exempt subject to statutory conditions and upper limits.
- The cost of purchasing and maintaining uniforms and personal protection work equipment defined in special regulations is exempt from income tax.
- *Compensation for the use of an employee's own tools* and other equipment (except private vehicles) necessary for the performance of work at the work place, is exempt up to a level of 2% of the monthly wage or salary of the employee, subject to an upper limit of 2% of the average gross monthly wage (AGMW).
- Long service bonuses, severance pay upon retirement and payments related to accidents, long term sickness and other unexpected events are exempt subject to statutory conditions and upper limits.
- *Severance pay* on redundancy is exempt subject to an upper limit of ten times the AGMW.
- *Compensation for the use of an employee's own possessions and property when working at home* in accordance with statutory regulations is exempt up to a level of 5% of the monthly wage or salary of the employee, subject to an upper limit of 5% of the AGMW.

1.1.3. *Tax schedule*

The tax schedule for 2016 is as follows:

Taxable income (EUR)	Tax rate (%)
Up to 8 021.34	16
8 021.34-20 400.00	27
20 400.070 907.20	41
Above 70 907.20	50

1.2. *Regional and local income tax*

There are no regional or local income taxes.

2. Compulsory social security insurance system

The compulsory social security insurance system consists of four schemes as follows:

- pension and disability insurance;
- health insurance;
- unemployment insurance;
- parental leave insurance.

2.1. *Employees' contributions*

The taxable base for social security insurance contributions paid by employees is the total amount of the gross wage or salary including vacation payments, fringe benefits and remuneration of expenses related to work above a certain threshold. The assessment period is the calendar month. Employees contribute an amount as a percentage of their remuneration as follows:

Scheme name	Rate of contribution (%)
Pension insurance	15.50
Health insurance	6.36
Unemployment insurance	0.14
Parental leave insurance	0.10
Total	22.10

2.2. *Employers' contributions*

Social security insurance contributions are also paid by employers on behalf of their employees. The taxable base and the assessment period are the same as for employees' contributions. The employers' contribution rates are as follows:

Scheme name	Rate of contribution (%)
Pension insurance	8.85
Health insurance	7.09
Unemployment insurance	0.06
Parental leave insurance	0.10
Total	16.10

The only change to these rates since 1996 has been the 0.2% increase in the employers' contribution rates for health insurance in 2002.

3. Payroll tax

None.

4. Universal cash transfers

4.1. *Transfers related to marital status*

None.

4.2. *Transfers for dependent children*

On 1.1.2012 the Exercise of Rights to Public Funds Act (*http://zakonodaja.gov.si/rpsi/r00/predpis_ZAKO4780.html*) entered into force. Regarding to a new act child allowance is a supplementary benefit for maintenance, care and education of children when the family income per family member does not exceed statutorily defined percentage of the average net wage in the previous year.

The new legislation changes family income which is the basis for the income classes from gross family income to net family income. Income includes taxable income and non-taxable income defined by the Personal Income Tax Act as for instance social benefits. Income is defined as gross income plus social benefits received but excluding the normalized cost and actual cost recognized under the law governing income tax, taxes and mandatory social security contributions levied on such income.

The new legislation also reduces the age of a child's entitlement. The right to a child benefit is held only until the child reaches 18 years. Besides, the child benefit is higher for eligible students included in higher secondary education (aged less than 18 years and with an income per family member below the average net wage).

Applications for the allowance are made on an annual basis and the payments are not taxable.

- The amount of the allowance is calculated for each child separately according to the level of net family income per family member as a percentage of the average net wage and the ranking of the child in the family. Each family is assigned to one of 8 income classes on this basis as follows:

Income class	Net family income per family member as a percentage of the average net wage
1	Up to 18%
2	18%-30%
3	30%-36%
4	36%-42%
5	42%-53%
6	53%-64%
7	64%-82%
8	82%-99%

- The relevant income is the average monthly income per family member in the calendar year prior to the claim (or one year previous if the claim is made in the month of January, February or March).
- Each child is allocated in one of 3 ranking levels (the level of payments increases with the ranking level – the lowest for the first child, higher for the second child and the highest for the third and any subsequent child). When a child lives in a one-parent family, the amount of the allowance is increased by 30%. When a pre-school child does not attend kindergarten, the amount of the allowance is increased by 20%.
- The details for the calculation of the net income per family member was prescribed by the Minister, as follows:

All income and receipts, namely net disposable income (after deduction of the normalized cost and actual cost recognized under the law governing income tax, taxes and mandatory social security contributions levied on such income) are taken into account, except those that are designed to cover the specific needs (such as allowance and attendance allowance, a large family, etc.). Property is also taken into account like immovable property, cars and other vehicles, watercraft, etc. Property is assigned a value and then it is calculated the amount of interest that would be received within one year from the value of assets deposited in a bank account in the form of time deposits.

- On 1.6.2012 the Public Finance Balance Act entered into force. Regarding to the Act the amounts of transfers for a children in fifth and sixth income classes are reduced for 10%. Moreover, transfers for children in the seventh and eighth income classes are abolished. This is a temporary measure, which applies up to the year following the year in which economic growth exceeds 2% of gross domestic product.
- Part of the Public Finance Balance Act from 2012, which reduced the amounts in the fifth and sixth income bracket by 10%, with effect from 1 January 2016 expired.
- The monthly amounts of transfers for a child **from birth to the end of primary school** in a two-parent family according to the Exercise of Rights to Public Funds Act and Public Finance Balance Act were the following for the year 2016:

Net family income per family member as a percentage of the average net wage	1st Child	2nd Child	3rd Child
	Monthly (EUR)	Monthly (EUR)	Monthly (EUR)
00	114.31	125.73	137.18
2 188.58	97.73	108.04	118.28
3 647.63	74.48	83.25	91.98
4 377.15	58.75	67.03	75.47
5 106.68	48.04	56.06	64.03
6 444.14	30.44	38.10	45.71
7 781.61	0	0	0

In 2016, the maximum annual benefit levels for children in a two-parent family were the following:

- EUR 1 371.72 for the first child;
- EUR 1 508.76 for the second child;
- EUR 1 646.16 for the third or subsequent child.

The amounts decline as the level of income per family member increases. According to the Public Finance Balance Act the benefit ceases to be available for families where the average income per member is higher than 64% of the average net wage for the year 2015.

5. Main changes in tax/benefit system since 2005

- In 2006 the taxation of income of individuals changed from global tax to a kind of a dual income tax system. Active income (from employment, business, basic agriculture and forestry, rents, royalties and other income) is taxed aggregated at progressive rates and taking into account the allowances and deductions; capital income (interest, dividends and capital gains) is taxed at proportionate rates on a scheduler basis.
- In 2007 the number of income tax brackets was reduced from five to three. At the same time, some non-standard tax reliefs for certain expenses and for interest paid on loans for housing were abolished.
- In 2008 additional general allowances were introduced for people on low incomes.
- The payroll tax was phased out at the start of 2009.
- The Exercise of Rights to Public Funds Act entered into force on 1.1.2012 changes family income which is the basis for the income classes from gross family income to net family income, which also includes social benefits received.
- Regarding to the Public Finance Balance Act which entered into force on 1.6.2012, the amounts of transfers for children in fifth and sixth income classes are reduced for 10%. Transfers for children in the seventh and eighth income classes are abolished.
- In 2013 the second bracket in the PIT schedule was broadened according to the Public Finance Balance Act. For the years 2013 and 2014 also the threshold for the third bracket (with the rate 41%) was increased and a new, top bracket with a rate 50% was introduced.
- For the year 2013 the special relief for students was reduced by 25 % compared to the tax relief in 2012 (the tax relief for 2014 amounts to EUR 2 477.03).
- Concerning rental income deriving renting of immovable and movable property a new scheduler principle of taxation was introduced in the year 2013 with proportional rate of 25%. The standardised costs were reduced from 40% to 10% of the rental income.

- The main and most important substantive change for the year 2014 and beyond eliminates the automatic adjustment of tax credits and net annual tax basis in the scale for assessing personal income tax with the growth in consumer prices.
- For the year 2014 another amendments were also introduced to the personal income tax, that is the abolishment of the tax benefits to certain groups of taxpayers (special relief for daily migrants, relief for the residents over 65 years of age).
- In 2014, the amendments to the Law on Parenthood and Family Incomes increased child benefit for each child who lives in a single-parent family. Namely, the uplift of child benefit was increased from 10 to 30%.
- The scale of assessment for income tax as a temporary measure that applies to 2013 and 2014, with the addition of a fourth class tax rate of 50% was extended for the year 2015.
- In 2015 the annual threshold between 2nd and 3rd tax bracket (above which the income tax is paid at the rate of 41%) is increased to EUR 20 400 (from EUR 18 960) for the years 2016 and 2017. The corresponding tax rate remains unchanged (i.e. 27%). The validity of the tax rate of 50% for the fourth tax bracket (for incomes above EUR 70 907) is extended also only for tax years 2016 and 2017.

6. Memorandum items

6.1. *Average gross annual wage earnings calculation*

In Slovenia the gross earnings figures cover wages and salaries paid to individuals in formal employment including payment for overtime. They also include bonus payments and other payments such as pay for annual leave, paid leave up to seven days, public holidays, absences due to sickness for up to 30 days, job training, and slowdown through no fault of the person in formal employment.

The average gross wage earnings figures of all adult workers covering industry sectors B–N are provided by the Statistical Office of the Republic of Slovenia.

6.2. *Employer contributions to private pension and health schemes*

Some employer contributions are made to private health and pension schemes but there is no relevant information available on the amounts that are paid.

2016 parameter values

Ave_earn	18 292	Secretariat estimate					
Ave_earn_1	18 092						
Ave_net_earnfam	12 158,76						
Basic_al	0	6 519.82					
	10 866,37	4 418.64					
	12 570,89	3 302.70					
Child_al1	2 436.92						
Child_al2	5 086.16						
Child_al3	9 504.70						
Child_al4	15 692.55						
Child_al5	23 649.69						
Depend_al	2 436.92						
Tax_sch	0.16	8 021.34					
	0.27	20 400.00					
	0.41	70 907.20					
	0.50						
SSC_rate1	0.221						
SSC_rate2	0.161						
		Ist child monthly	2nd child monthly	3rd child monthly	1 child-total annual	2 children-total annual	3 children-total annual
Fam_allow_mc	0	114.31	125.73	137.18	1 371.72	2 880.48	4 526.64
	2 188.58	97.73	108.04	118.28	1 172.76	2 469.24	3 888.60
	3 647.63	74.48	83.25	91.98	893.76	1 892.76	2 996.52
	4 377.15	58.75	67.03	75.47	705.00	1 509.36	2 415.00
	5 106.68	48.04	56.06	64.03	576.48	1 249.20	2 017.56
	6 444.14	30.44	38.10	45.71	365.28	822.48	1 371.00
	7 781.61	0.00	0.00	0.00	0.00	0.00	0.00
Fam_allow_spup	0.3						
		Ist child monthly	2nd child monthly	3rd child monthly	1 child-total annual	2 children-total annual	3 children-total annual
Fam_allow_sp	0	148.60	163.45	178.33	1 783.24	3 744.62	5 884.63
	2 188.58	127.05	140.45	153.76	1 524.59	3 210.01	5 055.18
	3 647.63	96.82	108.23	119.57	1 161.89	2 460.59	3 895.48
	4 377.15	76.38	87.14	98.11	916.50	1 962.17	3 139.50
	5 106.68	62.45	72.88	83.24	749.42	1 623.96	2 622.83
	6 444.14	39.57	49.53	59.42	474.86	1 069.22	1 782.30
	7 781.61	0.00	0.00	0.00	0.00	0.00	0.00
numdays	365						

TAXING WAGES 2017 © OECD 2017

2016 tax equations

	Line in country table and intermediate steps	Variable name	Range	Equation
1.	Earnings			
	Current year	earn		
	Net earnings Year-1	net_earn_1		
2.	Allowances:			
	Principal	tax_al_princ	P	VLOOKUP(earn;Basic_al;2)+SSC+IF(children=0,0,IF(children=1,child_al1,IF(children=2,child_al2,child_al3)+IF(Married=0,0,IF(S_earn=0,Depend_al,0))
	Spouse	Tax_al_ spouse	S	MINA(VLOOKUP(earn;Basic_al;2), earn)+SSC
3.	Credits in taxable income	taxbl_cr	B	0
4.	CG taxable income	tax_inc	B	Positive(earn-tax_al)
5.	CG tax before credits	CG_tax_excl	B	Tax(tax_inc, tax_sch)
6.	Tax credits (nonwastable)	Tax_cr	B	0
7.	CG tax	CG_tax	B	CG_tax_excl
8.	State and local taxes	local_tax	B	0
9.	Employees' soc security	SSC	B	earn* SSC_rate1
11.	Cash transfers	cash_trans	J	IF(Children=0,0;VLOOKUP((net_earn_1)/(1+married+children),IF(Married=0;Fam_allow_sp,Fam_allow_mc),IF(Children=1,5,IF(Children=2,6,7))))
13.	Employer's wage dependent contributions and taxes			
	Employer's soc security	SSC_empr	B	earn*SSC_rate2

Key to range of equation B calculated separately for both principal earner and spouse P calculated for principal only (value taken as 0 for spouse calculation) J calculated once only on a joint basis.

Taxing Wages 2017
© OECD 2017

Spain

This chapter includes data on the income taxes paid by workers, their social security contributions, the family benefits they receive in t-he form of cash transfers as well as the social security contributions and payroll taxes paid by their employers. Results reported include the marginal and average tax burden for eight different family types.

Methodological information is available for Personal income tax systems, Compulsory social security contributions to schemes operated within the government sector, Universal cash transfers as well as recent changes in the tax/benefit system. The methodology also includes the parameter values and tax equations underlying the data.

Spain 2016

The tax/benefit position of a single persons

		Wage level (per cent of average wage)	67	100	167	67
		Number of children	none	none	none	2
1.	**Gross wage earnings**		17 896	26 710	44 606	17 896
2.	**Standard tax allowances:**					
	Basic allowance					
	Married or head of family		0	0	0	2 150
	Dependent children					
	Deduction for social security contributions and income taxes		1 136	1 696	2 775	1 136
	Work-related expenses		2 000	2 000	2 000	2 000
	Other					
		Total	3 136	3 696	4 775	5 286
3.	**Tax credits or cash transfers included in taxable income**		0	0	0	0
4.	**Central and state government taxable income (1 - 2 + 3)**		14 760	23 014	39 831	12 610
5.	**Central and state government income tax liability (exclusive of tax credits)**		2 920	5 070	10 439	2 404
6.	**Central and state government tax credits**					
	Basic credit		1 055	1 055	1 055	3 224
	Married or head of family					
	Children					
	Other					
		Total	1 055	1 055	1 055	3 224
7.	**Central government income tax finally paid (5-6)**		933	2 008	4 692	- 1 010
8.	**State and local taxes**		933	2 008	4 692	190
9.	**Employees' compulsory social security contributions**					
	Gross earnings		1 136	1 696	2 775	1 136
	Taxable income					
		Total	1 136	1 696	2 775	1 136
10.	**Total payments to general government (7 + 8 + 9)**		3 002	5 711	12 160	317
11.	**Cash transfers from general government**					
	For head of family					
	For two children		0	0	0	0
		Total	0	0	0	0
12.	**Take-home pay (1-10+11)**		14 894	20 999	32 447	17 579
13.	**Employer's compulsory social security contributions**		5 351	7 986	13 067	5 351
14.	**Average rates**					
	Income tax		10.4%	15.0%	21.0%	-4.6%
	Employees' social security contributions		6.35%	6.35%	6.22%	6.35%
	Total payments less cash transfers		16.8%	21.4%	27.3%	1.8%
	Total tax wedge including employer's social security contributions		35.9%	39.5%	43.7%	24.4%
15.	**Marginal rates**					
	Total payments less cash transfers: Principal earner		28.8%	34.4%	37.0%	28.8%
	Total payments less cash transfers: Spouse		n.a.	n.a.	n.a.	n.a.
	Total tax wedge: Principal earner		45.2%	49.5%	37.0%	45.2%
	Total tax wedge: Spouse		n.a.	n.a.	n.a.	n.a.

Spain 2016

The tax/benefit position of married couples

		100-0	100-33	100-67	100-33
	Wage level (per cent of average wage)	100-0	100-33	100-67	100-33
	Number of children	2	2	2	none
1.	**Gross wage earnings**	26 710	35 525	44 606	35 525
2.	**Standard tax allowances**				
	Basic allowance				
	Married or head of family	3 400	0	0	0
	Dependent children				
	Deduction for social security contributions and income taxes	1 696	2 256	2 832	2 256
	Work-related expenses	2 000	7 700	4 000	7 700
	Other				
	Total	7 096	9 956	6 832	9 956
3.	**Tax credits or cash transfers included in taxable income**	0	0	0	0
4.	**Central and state government taxable income (1 - 2 + 3)**	19 614	25 569	37 774	25 569
5.	**Central and state government income tax liability (exclusive of tax credits)**	4 085	5 555	7 990	5 555
6.	**Central and state government tax credits**				
	Basic credit	2 024	2 024	3 078	1 540
	Married or head of family				
	Children				
	Other				
	Total	2 024	2 024	3 078	1 540
7.	**Central government income tax finally paid (5-6)**	1 031	1 765	2 456	2 008
8.	**State and local taxes**	1 031	1 765	2 456	2 008
9.	**Employees' compulsory social security contributions**				
	Gross earnings	1 696	2 256	2 832	2 256
	Taxable income				
	Total	1 696	2 256	2 832	2 256
10.	**Total payments to general government (7 + 8 + 9)**	3 758	5 787	7 744	6 271
11.	**Cash transfers from general government**				
	For head of family				
	For two children	0	0	0	0
	Total	0	0	0	0
12.	**Take-home pay (1-10+11)**	22 953	29 738	36 862	29 254
13.	**Employer's compulsory social security contributions**	7 986	10 622	13 337	10 622
14.	**Average rates**				
	Income tax	7.7%	9.9%	11.0%	11.3%
	Employees' social security contributions	6.35%	6.35%	6.35%	6.35%
	Total payments less cash transfers	14.1%	16.3%	17.4%	17.7%
	Total tax wedge including employer's social security contributions	33.8%	35.6%	36.4%	36.6%
15.	**Marginal rates**				
	Total payments less cash transfers: Principal earner	28.8%	34.4%	34.4%	34.4%
	Total payments less cash transfers: Spouse	23.0%	6.3%	28.8%	6.3%
	Total tax wedge: Principal earner	45.2%	49.5%	49.5%	49.5%
	Total tax wedge: Spouse	40.7%	27.9%	45.2%	27.9%

The national currency is the Euro (EUR). In 2016, EUR 0.90 was equal to USD 1. In that year the average worker earned EUR 26 710 (Secretariat estimate).

1. Personal income tax system

1.1. Central government income tax

1.1.1. Tax unit

As a general rule, the tax unit is the individual. Nevertheless, families have the options of being taxed:

- As married couples filing jointly on the combined income of both spouses and dependents.
- As heads of households (only unmarried or separated individuals with dependents).

1.1.2. Tax allowances and tax credits

1.1.2.1. Standard reliefs

- *Basic reliefs*: Married couples filing jointly may claim an allowance of EUR 3 400. This figure amounts to EUR 2 150 for heads of households.
- *Maternity tax credit*: a non-wastable tax credit addressed to working females with children under 3 years of age up to EUR 1 200.
- *Large families (3 or more children) or dependent family members with disabilities tax credits*: this additional non-wastable tax credit (up to EUR 1 200, in general, or EUR 2 400 for special large families, with 5 or more children) also may be claimed (within the Taxing Wages framework) by single-parent households with two children.
- *Relief for social security contributions*: All social security payments are fully deductible.
- *Other expenses allowance*: up to EUR 2 000, which may be increased by the same amount in case of accepting a job in a different location implying a change of residence.
- *Employment related* allowance: Net employment income (gross income - employee social security contributions) may be reduced according to the following rules:
  - Taxpayers with net employment income equal or less than EUR 11 250: EUR 3 700.
  - Taxpayers with a net employment income between EUR 11 250.01 and EUR 14 450: EUR 3 700 less the result of multiplying by 1.15625 the difference between net employment income and EUR 11 250.
- *Disabled workers allowance*: an allowance of EUR 3 500 for disabled salary earners. Those with reduced mobility may claim an augmented allowance of EUR 7 750.

As a result of the application of the above rules, net income cannot become negative.

1.1.2.2. Main non-standard reliefs applicable to an AW

- *Contributions to Pension Plans*. Contributions made by each member of the household may reduce taxable income up to the lower of the following amounts:
  - 30% of net income;

- EUR 8 000.

Moreover, those households whose second earner has net labour income below EUR 8 000 may reduce taxable income up to a maximum of EUR 2 500 on a yearly basis if the principal earner contributes to a Pension Fund for the spouse.

- *Relief for subscriptions paid in respect of membership* of a trade union and business or professional associations (last item is limited to mandatory membership) up to EUR 500.
- *Relief for expenses made for the legal defence* of the taxpayer for labour-related conflicts up to a maximum limit of EUR 300.

Other non-standard reliefs provided as deductions are:

- *Investment in the acquisition and rehabilitation of own-housing*: As a general rule, up to 1 January 2013, taxpayers were allowed to deduct from their tax liability 15% of the investment made during the year, up to a maximum of EUR 9 040.
- Furthermore, disabled taxpayers were also allowed to deduct from their tax liability 20% of the investment expenses incurred in the repairs carried out for housing adaptation to the handicapped personal needs according up to a maximum of EUR 12 080.
- With effect from 1 January 2013, the above tax credit has been abolished. Nevertheless, grandfathering rules apply for those taxpayers who before 1 January 2013 had acquired their main residence; had made some payments for it to be built; had made some payments for restoration/enlargement of their main residence or had made some payments to carry out the adaptation of the main residence of disabled people. However, in the latter two cases the works performed should be completed before 1 January 2017. For these taxpayers, the above tax credit can still be applied in accordance with the rules set up above.
- *Gifts*: 75% of the amounts (below EUR 150) donated to the State (its different levels) public universities and othe qualifying institutions. For larger gifts, 30% on the excess, which may be increased to 35% when meeting certain conditions and 10% of the amount donated non-qualifying foundations or associations.
- *Investments and expenses in goods of cultural interest*: 15% of the amounts granted to the importation, restoration, exhibition, etc. of certain goods listed in the General Register of Goods of Cultural Interest.

Each of these last two amounts cannot exceed 10% of taxable income.

1.1.2.3. Exempt income

- The base amount is EUR 5 550 per taxpayer. The same amount is granted for family units filing jointly. Taxpayers aged over 65 years may add EUR 1 150 to the former amount. Those aged over 75 years may claim additionally EUR 1 400.
- Dependent children (under 25 years): EUR 2 400 for the first dependent child; EUR 2 700 for the second one; EUR 4 000 for the third, and EUR 4 500 for any additional child.
- Child care allowance: an additional allowance of EUR 2 800 for each of the above dependent children under 3 years of age.
- In case of disabled workers and additional amount of EUR 3 000 also applies. In case of great disability prior amount reaches EUR 9 000.

Child allowances have to be shared equally between spouses when they file separately.

1.1.3. *Tax schedule*

General rates of tax – resident individuals:

Taxable income (EUR)	Tax at the lower limit (EUR)	Tax rate on taxable income in excess of the lower limit (%)
0-12 450	0	9.50
12 450-20 200	1 182.75	12.00
20 200-35 200	2 112.75	15.00
35 200-60 000	4 362.75	18.50
Over 60 000	8 950.75	22.50

1.2. *State and local income taxes*

The Regional Governments may fix their own tax schedules, based on that of the Central Government, as a reference, and within certain limits. All Regional Government tax schedules currently differ from each other (some of them include tax rates higher than the Central Government ones whilst others contain lower tax rates). Provided that, during the last years, at least one Regional Government tax schedule has matched that of the Central Government, we choose, as regional schedule more representative, that is equal to the Central Government schedule as above; this is also applied for non-resident taxpayers.

Taxable income (EUR)	Tax at the lower limit (EUR)	Tax rate on taxable income in excess of the lower limit (%)
0-12 450	0	10.00
12 450-20 200	1 182.75	12.00
20 200-35 200	2 112.75	15.00
35 200-60 000	4 362.75	18.50
Over 60 000	8 950.75	22.50

Now, there isn't any local tax rate or schedule in the Spanish PIT. However, some Local Governments (the bigger and province capital cities) receive a fixed percentage of the PIT revenues.

2. Compulsory social security contributions to schemes operated within the government sector

Social Security contributions are assessed on the basis of employees' gross earnings taking into account certain ceilings of gross employment income. In 2016, these ceilings are:

- Lower ceiling: EUR 9 172.80
- Upper Ceiling: EUR 43 704.

These ceilings are based on a full-time job. For part-time workers, ceilings are proportional to the real hours worked (the tax equations used for this Report do not take into account the lower ceiling).

2.1. *Employees' contributions*

- Old age pension/sickness and disability 4.7%
- Unemployment 1.55%
- Professional Training 0.1%

2.2. *Employers' contributions*

- Old age pension/sickness and disability 23.6%
- Unemployment/Work injuries 5.50%
- Wages fund 0.2%
- Professional Training 0.6%

3. Universal cash transfers

3.1. *Transfers related to marital status*

None.

3.2. *Transfers for dependent children*

EUR 291 for 1-child families with annual gross earnings below EUR 11 576.83; the child transfer decreases with income between EUR 11 576.83 and EUR 11 867.83; the value is 0 for gross earnings exceeding EUR 11 867.83. EUR 582 for families with 2 children with annual gross earnings below EUR 13 313.35; the child transfer decreases with income between EUR 13 313.35 and EUR 13 895.35; the value is 0 for gross earnings exceeding EUR 13 895.35.

4. Main changes in tax/benefit systems in 2016

In 2016 the Spanish Government carried out the second phase of the tax reform which started in 2015, being modified the tax schedule and improved the gifts tax credit, as aforementioned.

Moreover, since 1 March 2015 employers hiring new staff under a non-fixed term contract (signed between 1 March 2015 and 31 August 2016) may claim a partial exemption on their SSC for the first EUR 500 of monthly salaries paid to workers. This SSC concession will apply for a 24-month period. This measure is known as a "reduced rate" (Law 25/2015).

5. Memorandum items

5.1. *Identification of an AW and calculation of earnings*

Refer to the information provided in the Annex of this Report.

2016 parameter values

Average earnings/yr	Ave_earn	26 710	Secretariat estimate	
Work related allowance	wr_rate	1.15625		
	wr_lim_max	14 450		
	wr_lim_min	11 250		
	wr_allow_max	3 700		
Other deductible expenses	oth_ded_exp	2 000		
Personal & family exempt income	Per_fam_exempt_inc	5 550		
Joint taxation allowance	Joint_tax_allow_fam1	3 400		
	Joint_tax_allow_fam2	2 150		
Dependent children	dep_child	2 400		
	dep_child2	2 700		
	dep_child3	4 000		
	dep_child4	4 500		
Single parent tax credit (chld>=2)	SP_tax_credit	1 200		
Tax Schedule	tax_sch_sg	0	0	9.50%
		12 450	1 182.75	12.00%
		20 200	2 112.75	15.00%
		35 200	4 362.75	18.50%
		60 000	8 950.75	22.50%
	tax_sch_sa	0	0	9.50%
		12 450	1 182.75	12.00%
		20 200	2 112.75	15.00%
		35 200	4 362.75	18.50%
		60 000	8 950.75	22.50%
Social security contributions				
Employee:				
Pension	pension_rate	0.047		
Unemployment	unemp_rate	0.0155		
Other	oth_rate	0.001		
Employer				
Pension	pension_empr	0.236		
Unemployment	unemp_empr	0.055		
Other	oth_empr	0.008		
Ceiling and Floor	min_lim	0	9 172.8	
	top_lim	43 704		
Child benefit	SS_child_benefit	291		
	SS_child_table	1	11 576.83	11 867.83
		2	13 313.35	13 895.35
		3	17 423.84	18 224.09
		4	20 246.02	21 313.02
		5	23 068.20	24 401.95

2016 tax equations

The functions which are used in the equations (Taper, MIN, Tax etc) are described in the technical note about tax equations. Variable names are defined in the table of parameters above, within the equations table, or are the standard variables "married" and "children". A reference to a variable with the affix "_total" indicates the sum of the relevant variable values for the principal and spouse. And the affixes "_princ" and "_sp" indicate the value for the principal and spouse, respectively. Equations for a single person are as shown for the principal, with "_sp" values taken as 0.

	Line in country table and intermediate steps	Variable name	Range	Equation
1.	Earnings	earn	B	for individual taxation: earn=earn_princ, or earn=earn_sp for joint (family) taxation: earn=earn_princ+earn_sp
2.	Allowances:			
	Work related, individual	work_ind	B	IF(earn-SSC<=wr_lim_min,wr_allow_max+oth_ded_exp,IF(earn-SSC<=wr_lim_max,wr_allow_max-wr_rate*((earn-SSC)-(wr_lim_min))+oth_ded_exp,oth_ded_exp))
	Work related, family	work_fam	J	IF(AND(earn_sp=0,married=0,children=0),0,IF(earn_total-SSC_fam<=wr_lim_min,wr_allow_max+oth_ded_exp,IF(earn_total-SSC_fam=wr_lim_max,wr_allow_max-wr_rate*((earn_total-SSC_fam)-(wr_lim_min))+oth_ded_exp,oth_ded_exp)))
	Joint taxation allowance	joint_allow_fam	J	IF(AND(Married=0,Children=0),0,IF(AND(Married=0,Children>0),joint_tax_allow_fam2,joint_tax_allow_fam1))
	Personal and family exempt income, individual	ex_inc_ind	B	per_fam_exempt_inc
	Personal and family exempt income, family	ex_inc_fam	J	IF(AND(Married=0,Children=0),0,per_fam_exempt_inc)
	Children exempt income, individual	child_ex_inc_ind	P	IF(earn_sp=0, (children>0)*(dep_child+(children>1)*dep_child2+(children>2)*dep_child3+(children>3)*(children-3)*dep_child4), (children>0)*(dep_child+(children>1)*dep_child2+(children>2)*dep_child3+(children>3)*(children-3)*dep_child4)/2)
			S	IF(earn_sp=0, 0, (children>0)*(dep_child+(children>1)*dep_child2+(children>2)*dep_child3+(children>3)*(children-3)*dep_child4)/2)
	Children exempt income, family	child_ex_inc_fam	J	(children>0)*(dep_child+(children>1)*dep_child2+(children>2)*dep_child3+(children>3)*(children-3)*dep_child4)
3.	Credits in taxable income	taxbl_cr	B, J	0
4.	CG taxable income	tax_inc	B, J	IF(AND(Married=0, Children=0), tax_inc_princ, MINA(tax_inc_princ+tax_inc_sp, tax_inc_fam))
		tax_inc_ind	B	Positive(earn-(work_ind+SSC))
		tax_inc_fam	J	IF(AND(Married=0, Children), 0, Positive(earn-(work_fam+joint_allow_fam+SSC_princ+SSC_sp)))
5.	CG tax before credits	CG_tax_ind_excl	B	MAXA(0, VLOOKUP(tax_inc_ind, tax_sch_sg, 2)+(tax_inc_ind-VLOOKUP(tax_inc_ind, tax_sch_sg, 1))*VLOOKUP(tax_inc_ind, tax_sch_sg, 3))
		CG_tax_fam_excl	J	MAXA(0, VLOOKUP(tax_inc_fam, tax_sch_sg, 2)+(tax_inc_fam-VLOOKUP(tax_inc_fam, tax_sch_sg, 1))*VLOOKUP(tax_inc_fam, tax_sch_sg, 3))
6.	CG tax credits :	CG_tax_cr_ind	B	MAXA(0,VLOOKUP(ex_inc_ind+child_ex_inc_ind,tax_sch_sg,2)+ ((ex_inc_ind+child_ex_inc_ind)-VLOOKUP(ex_inc_ind+child_ex_inc_ind,tax_sch_sg,1))*VLOOKUP(ex_inc_ind+child_ex_inc_ind,tax_sch_sg,3)+IF(AND(earn>0,married=,children>=2),MIN(SP_tax_credit,(SSC+SSC_empr)),0)
		CG_tax_cr_fam	J	MAXA(0,VLOOKUP(ex_inc_fam+child_ex_inc_fam,tax_sch_sg,2)+ ((ex_inc_fam+child_ex_inc_fam)-VLOOKUP(ex_inc_fam+child_ex_inc_fam,tax_sch_sg,1))*VLOOKUP(ex_inc_fam+child_ex_inc_fam,tax_sch_sg,3)+ IF(AND(earn_total>0,married=0,children>=2),MIN(SP_tax_credit,(SSC_fam+SSC_empr_fam)),0)
7.	CG tax	CG_tax_ind	B	CG_tax_ind_excl-CG_tax_cr_ind
		CG_tax_fam	J	CG_tax_fam_excl-CG_tax_cr_fam

	Line in country table and intermediate steps	Variable name	Range	Equation
8.	State and local tax before credits	local_tax_ind_excl	B	MAXA(0, VLOOKUP(tax_inc_ind, tax_sch_sa, 2)+(tax_inc_ind-VLOOKUP(tax_inc_ind, tax_sch_sa, 1))*VLOOKUP(tax_inc_ind, tax_sch_sa, 3))
		local_tax_fam_excl	J	MAXA(0, VLOOKUP(tax_inc_fam, tax_sch_sa, 2)+(tax_inc_fam-VLOOKUP(tax_inc_fam, tax_sch_sa, 1))*VLOOKUP(tax_inc_fam, tax_sch_sa, 3))
	local tax credits	local_tax_cr_ind	B	MAXA(0,VLOOKUP(ex_inc_ind+child_ex_inc_ind,tax_sch_sa,2)+ ((ex_inc_ind+child_ex_inc_ind)-VLOOKUP(ex_inc_ind+child_ex_inc_ind,tax_sch_sa,1))* VLOOKUP(ex_inc_ind+child_ex_inc_ind,tax_sch_sa,3))
		local_tax_cr_fam	J	MAXA(0,VLOOKUP(ex_inc_fam+child_ex_inc_fam,tax_sch_sa,2)+ ((ex_inc_fam+child_ex_inc_fam)-VLOOKUP(ex_inc_fam+child_ex_inc_fam,tax_sch_sa,1))* VLOOKUP(ex_inc_fam+child_ex_inc_fam,tax_sch_sa,3))
	State and local tax	local_tax_ind	B	Positive(local_tax_ind_excl-local_tax_cr_ind)
		local_tax_fam	J	Positive(local_tax_fam_excl-local_tax_cr_fam)
9.	Employees' soc security	SSC	B	IF(AND(earn>0, earn<=min_lim), min_lim*(pension_rate+unemp_rate+oth_rate), IF(earn>=top_lim, top_lim*(pension_rate+unemp_rate+oth_rate), earn* (pension_rate+unemp_rate+oth_rate)))
		SSC_fam	J	SSC_princ+SSC_sp
11.	Cash transfers	Child_transf		IF(Children=0,0,IF(earn<=VLOOKUP(Children, SS_child_table,2),SS_child_benefit*Children, IF(earn<=VLOOKUP(Children, SS_child_table, 3), VLOOKUP (Children, SS_child_table, 3)-earn, 0)))
13.	Employer's SSC	SSC_empr		IF(AND(earn>0, earn<=min_lim), min_lim*(pension_empr+unemp_empr+ oth_umpr), IF(earn>=top_lim, top_lim*(pension_empr+unemp_empr+oth_empr), earn*(pension_empr+unemp_empr+oth_empr)))

Key to range of equation B calculated separately for both principal earner and spouse P calculated for principal only S calculated for spouse only J calculated once only on a joint basis.

Taxing Wages 2017
© OECD 2017

Sweden

This chapter includes data on the income taxes paid by workers, their social security contributions, the family benefits they receive in the form of cash transfers as well as the social security contributions and payroll taxes paid by their employers. Results reported include the marginal and average tax burden for eight different family types.

Methodological information is available for Personal income tax systems, Compulsory social security contributions to schemes operated within the government sector, Universal cash transfers as well as recent changes in the tax/benefit system. The methodology also includes the parameter values and tax equations underlying the data.

Sweden 2016

The tax/benefit position of single persons

		Wage level (per cent of average wage)	67	100	167	67
		Number of children	none	none	none	2
1.	**Gross wage earnings**		283 453	423 065	706 518	283 453
2.	**Standard tax allowances**					
	Basic allowance		19 600	13 000	13 000	19 600
	Married or head of family					
	Dependent children					
	Deduction for social security contributions and income taxes		0	0	0	0
	Work-related expenses					
	Other					
		Total	19 600	13 000	13 000	19 600
3.	**Tax credits or cash transfers included in taxable income**		0	0	0	0
4.	**Central government taxable income (1 - 2 + 3)**		263 800	410 000	693 500	263 800
5.	**Central government income tax liability (exclusive of tax credits)**		0	0	56 045	0
6.	**Tax credits**					
	Basic credit					
	Married or head of family					
	Children					
	Other		41 490	56 071	56 771	41 490
		Total	41 490	56 071	56 771	41 490
7.	**Central government income tax finally paid (5-6)**		- 41 490	- 56 071	- 726	- 41 490
8.	**State and local taxes**		84 679	131 610	222 613	84 679
9.	**Employees' compulsory social security contributions**					
	Gross earnings		19 800	29 600	33 500	19 800
	Taxable income					
		Total	19 800	29 600	33 500	19 800
10.	**Total payments to general government (7 + 8 + 9)**		62 989	105 139	255 387	62 989
11.	**Cash transfers from general government**					
	For head of family					
	For two children		0	0	0	27 000
		Total	0	0	0	27 000
12.	**Take-home pay (1-10+11)**		220 464	317 926	451 131	247 464
13.	**Employer's wage dependent contributions and taxes**					
	Employer's compulsory social security contributions		61 708	92 101	153 809	61 708
	payroll taxes		27 353	40 825	68 179	27 353
		Total	89 061	132 926	221 988	89 061
14.	**Average rates**					
	Income tax		15.2%	17.9%	31.4%	15.2%
	Employees' social security contributions		7.0%	7.0%	4.7%	7.0%
	Total payments less cash transfers		22.2%	24.9%	36.1%	12.7%
	Total tax wedge including employer's social security contributions		40.8%	42.8%	51.4%	33.6%
15.	**Marginal rates**					
	Total payments less cash transfers: Principal earner		28.5%	32.1%	60.1%	28.5%
	Total payments less cash transfers: Spouse		n.a.	n.a.	n.a.	n.a.
	Total tax wedge: Principal earner		45.6%	48.3%	69.6%	45.6%
	Total tax wedge: Spouse		n.a.	n.a.	n.a.	n.a.

Sweden 2016

The tax/benefit position of married couples

	Wage level (per cent of average wage)		100-0	100-33	100-67	100-33
	Number of children		2	2	2	none
1.	**Gross wage earnings**		423 065	562 676	706 518	562 676
2.	**Standard tax allowances:**					
	Basic allowance		13 000	47 000	32 600	47 000
	Married or head of family					
	Dependent children					
	Deduction for social security contributions and income taxes		0	0	0	0
	Work-related expenses					
	Other					
		Total	13 000	47 000	32 600	47 000
3.	**Tax credits or cash transfers included in taxable income**		0	0	0	0
4.	**Central government taxable income (1 - 2 + 3)**		410 000	515 600	673 800	515 600
5.	**Central government income tax liability (exclusive of tax credits)**		0	0	0	0
6.	**Tax credits**					
	Basic credit					
	Married or head of family					
	Children					
	Other		56 071	77 815	97 561	77 815
		Total	56 071	77 815	97 561	77 815
7.	**Central government income tax finally paid (5-6)**		- 56 071	- 77 815	- 97 561	- 77 815
8.	**State and local taxes**		131 610	165 507	216 289	165 507
9.	**Employees' compulsory social security contributions**					
	Gross earnings		29 600	39 400	49 400	39 400
	Taxable income					
		Total	29 600	39 400	49 400	39 400
10.	**Total payments to general government (7 + 8 + 9)**		105 139	127 092	168 128	127 092
11.	**Cash transfers from general government**					
	For head of family					
	For two children		27 000	27 000	27 000	0
		Total	27 000	27 000	27 000	0
12.	**Take-home pay (1-10+11)**		344 926	462 584	565 390	435 584
13.	**Employer's wage dependent contributions and taxes**					
	Employer's compulsory social security contributions		92 101	122 494	153 809	122 494
	payroll taxes		40 825	54 297	68 178	54 297
		Total	132 926	176 791	221 987	176 791
14.	**Average rates**					
	Income tax		17.9%	15.6%	16.8%	15.6%
	Employees' social security contributions		7.0%	7.0%	7.0%	7.0%
	Total payments less cash transfers		18.5%	17.8%	20.0%	22.6%
	Total tax wedge including employer's social security contributions		38.0%	37.4%	39.1%	41.1%
15.	**Marginal rates**					
	Total payments less cash transfers: Principal earner		32.1%	32.1%	32.1%	32.1%
	Total payments less cash transfers: Spouse		15.7%	28.5%	28.5%	28.5%
	Total tax wedge: Principal earner		48.3%	48.3%	48.3%	48.3%
	Total tax wedge: Spouse		35.9%	45.6%	45.6%	45.6%

The national currency is the Swedish Kronor (SEK). In 2016, SEK 8.56 was equal to USD 1. In that year, the average worker earned SEK 423 065 (Secretariat estimate).

1. Personal income tax systems

1.1. *Central government income taxes*

1.1.1. *Tax unit*

Spouses are taxed separately.

1.1.2. *Tax allowances and tax credits*

1.1.2.1. Standard reliefs

- *Basic reliefs*: A basic allowance is given for assessed earned income and varies between SEK 13 000 and SEK 34 200, depending on income. When individuals pay central government income tax, the basic allowance is at its lowest level, which equals SEK 13 000. The basic allowance depends on the assessed earned income and the basic amount, which equals SEK 44 300 in 2016.

Assessed-Earned- Income (SEK) Relative to Basic Amount (BA)	Share of BA at lower bracket	For exceeding income
-0.99	0.423	
0.99-2.72	0.423	+0.2
2.72-3.11	0.77	
3.11-7.88	0.77	-0.1
7.88-	0.293	

For taxpayers older than 65, the basic relief is calculated differently:

Assessed-Earned- Income (SEK) Relative to Basic Amount (BA)	Share of BA at lower bracket	For exceeding income
-1.11	1.11	
1.11-2.72	1.11	+0.249
2.72-3.77	1.511	
3.77-5.40	1.511	-0.1
5.40-12.43	1.348	-0.09
12.43-	0.715	

- *Standard marital status reliefs*: None.
- *Relief(s) for children*: None.
- *Work-related expenses*: None.
- *Other*: None.

1.1.2.2. Main non-standard tax reliefs applicable to an AW

- Interest on qualifying loans: Interest payments are offset against capital income. The resulting net capital income is the tax base. A tax credit is given in the case of negative capital income.
- Medical expenses: None. Other allowances are given for:
  - the amount of commuting expenses exceeding SEK 10 000;
  - other types of work-related expenses exceeding SEK 5 000; examples are the costs of tools, work-related phone calls using the taxpayer's private telephone;
  - increased living expenses while on business trips, *e.g.* such as the use of a private car if these costs are not reimbursed by the employer;
  - double housing expenses due to *temporary* work at other geographical locations (too far from home for commuting), or if the family for some reason can't move, even if the job is of a *permanent* nature;
  - travelling expenses for travelling home if the taxpayer works in another place than his/her place of residence.

1.1.3. *Tax schedule*

Taxable Income (SEK)	Tax (SEK) at lower bracket	For exceeding income, %
0-430 200	0	0
430 200-625 800	0	20
over 625 800	39 120	25

1.1.4. *Tax credits*

A tax credit equal to 100% of the compulsory social security contributions paid by the employee is granted.

For a person aged 65 or less, an annual Earned Income Tax Credit (EITC) worth up to SEK 26 471 at the average local tax rate is granted on labour income. For those older than 65, a higher credit worth up to SEK 30 000 is granted. For a person aged 65 or less the EITC is connected to the basic allowance (BAL), the basic amount (BA) and the local tax rate (LTR). For those older than 65 a simplified EITC was introduced in 2009 which is not connected to the local tax rate, the basic allowance or the basic amount. The Basic Allowance is determined in Section 1.1.2.1; the local tax rate is discussed in Section 1.2. The Basic Amount (BA) in 2016 is SEK 44 300. The Special Amount is based on the taxpayer's (gross) earned income. A phase-out of the EITC for those with incomes above around SEK 600 000 a year was introduced in 2016.

The tax credits are wastable in the sense that they cannot reduce the individual's tax payments to less than zero. The EITC is deducted from the local government income tax, whereas the tax credit for the social security contributions is deducted from other taxes as well. However the central government covers the expenses for the tax credits.

For taxpayers younger than 65, the EITC is calculated as follows:

Earned Income (EI)	EITC
-0.91 BA	(EI-BAL)*LTR
0.91 BA-2.94 BA	(0.91 BA + 0.332 * (EI-0.91 BA)-BAL)*LTR
2.94 BA-8.08 BA	(1.584 BA + 0.111 * (EI-2.94 BA)-BAL)*LTR
8.08 BA-13.54 BA	(2.155 BA-BAL)*LTR
13.54 BA-	(2.155 BA-BAL)*LTR-0.03*(EI-13.54 BA)

BA = SEK 44 300; BAL=Basic allowance, determined in Section 1.1.2.1.; LTR=local tax rate. Note that the EITC cannot be negative.

For taxpayers older than 65, the EITC is calculated differently:

Earned Income (EI)	EITC
-100 000 SEK	0.2*EI
100 001-300 000 SEK	15 000 SEK + 0.05*EI
300 001-600 000 SEK	30 000 SEK
600 001-1 600 000 SEK	30 000-0.03*(EI-600 000)
1 600 001 SEK-	0

1.2. Local government income taxes

1.2.1. General description of the systems

Sweden has both a central government and a local government personal income tax. They are completely coordinated in the assessment process and refer to the same period, i.e. the income year coincides with the calendar year.

1.2.2. Tax base

The tax base is the same as for the central government income tax. The basic allowance for individuals paying local government tax varies between SEK 13 000 and SEK 34 200; it depends on the taxpayer's income. For a taxpayer earning the AW, this basic allowance amounts to SEK 13 000 (based on an AW equal to SEK 427 905 – subject to revision with the AW).

1.2.3. Tax rates

The local government personal income tax is proportional and differs between municipalities. The average rate amounts to 32.10% in 2016, with the maximum and minimum rates being 35.11% and 29.19%, respectively.

2. Compulsory social security contributions to schemes operated within the government sector

2.1. Employees' contributions

A general pension contribution of 7% of personal income is paid by employees and the self-employed when income is equal to or greater than 42.3% of the basic amount underlying the basic allowance (see Section 1.1.2.1). The contribution cannot exceed SEK 33 500 since the general pension contributions are not paid for income over SEK 478 600 (= 8.07*59 300). The employees' contribution is offset with a tax credit.

2.2. *Employers' contributions*

The employers' contributions are calculated as a percentage of the total sum of salaries and benefits in a year. For the self-employed, the base is net business income. The rates for 2016 are listed below.

Program	Employer (%)	Self-employed (%)
Retirement pension	10.21	10.21
Survivor's pension	1.17	1.17
Parental insurance	2.60	2.60
Health insurance	4.85	4.94
Labour market	2.64	0.10
Occupational health	0.30	0.30
General wage tax	9.65	9.65
Total	31.42	28.97

In certain regions, a reduction of 10% of the base, maximum SEK 7 100 per month, is granted (SEK 18 000 per year for self-employed) (it is not included in the calculations underlying this Report). Until the 31 May 2016 employees aged under 26 have a reduced SSC rate of 25.46% (23.69% for self-employed). From the 1 June 2016 the reduced SSC rate for younger employees is abolished. For employees who are over 65 years old and born after 1937 only the retirement pension contribution (10.21%) and a special wage tax (6.15%) is applicable. For persons born in 1937 or earlier no employers' social security contributions, but a special wage tax (6.15%) is applied. On premiums for occupational pensions paid by the employer a special wage tax (24.26%) is applied.

For self-employed a general reduction of 7.5% on the SSC is applicable if the income exceeds SEK 40 000 per year. The maximal reduction is SEK 15 000 per year.

3. Universal cash transfers

3.1. *Transfers related to marital status*

None.

3.2. *Transfers for dependent children*

The transfers are tax exempt and independent of the parents' income. The transfers for each child are as follows:

First child	12 600
Second child	14 400
Third child	18 048
Fourth child	24 720
Fifth and subsequent child	27 600

4. Main changes in tax/benefit systems since 1998

A tax credit of SEK 1 320 was introduced for low- and average income earners in 1999. The credit is reduced by 1.2% of taxable income above SEK 135 000. This reduction was abolished in 2003 and was replaced by an increase in the basic allowance.

A tax credit of 25% of the social security contribution paid by employees and the self-employed was introduced in 2000. The tax credit has been gradually increased to 100% in 2006.

In 2004, a special tax credit equal to SEK 200 was provided for the statutory minimum local income tax. The special tax credit was abolished in 2005 as was the statutory minimum state income tax (a lump sum tax) of SEK 200. The central government income tax bracket is indexed with the consumer price index plus 2%. However, in 2004, 2005 and 2006 the central government income tax bracket was restricted to be indexed with the consumer price index plus 1%. In order to reduce the number of people paying the central income tax, there was an additional increase of the tax bracket in 2009. In 2016 the central government income tax bracket was restricted to be at the same level as 2015.

The child allowance was raised by SEK 1 200 per year in 2000, 2001, 2006 and in 2010 the child allowance for multiple children was raised by SEK 50 for the second child, SEK 100 for the third, SEK 150 for fourth and SEK 200 for the fifth and subsequent children.

Maximum fee for childcare was introduced in 2002.

The basic allowance has been increased in 2001, 2002, 2003, 2005 and 2006. For older people the basic allowance was increased in 2009, 2010, 2011, 2013, 2014 and 2016.

Regarding the unemployment benefit the higher benefit level of SEK 730 for the first 100 days was removed in 2007 and the maximum unemployment benefit was set to SEK 680 during the entire benefit period of 300 days (or 450 days for persons with children under the age of 18). In September 2015, the maximum unemployment benefit was raised to SEK 910 per day in day 1-100 and to SEK 760 per day in day 101-300 (or day 101-450). The compensation in the sick leave was raised from 75 to 80% in 1998. In 2003 the compensation was lowered to 77.6% and, at the same time, the number of days for which the employer is responsible was increased from 14 to 21 days. In 2005 the compensation in the sick leave and the number of days for which the employer is responsible were set to their before-2003 level.

The lowest level of compensation in the parental leave was raised on 1 July 2006 from SEK 60 to SEK 180 per day. The level was raised to SEK 225 in 2013 and once again to SEK 250 in 2016. In 2006 also the maximum income compensated for in the parental leave was raised from 7.5*Basic Amount to 10* Basic Amount.

An earned income tax credit was introduced in 2007 with the purpose of making work economically more rewarding relative to unemployment or inactivity. The earned income tax credit was increased in 2008, 2009, 2010 and 2014. In 2016 a phase-out of the EITC was introduced for persons with incomes above around SEK 600 000.

In 2007, the social security contributions for 18-24-year-old employees and self-employed were reduced. In 2009 the reduction were increased and expanded to include all aged under 26. From 1st August 2015 the reduction was reduced by half and the 1st of June 2016 the reduction was abolished. A special wage tax for persons older than 65 was abolished in 2007 for persons born after 1937 and in 2008 for persons born in 1937 or earlier. In 2016 the special wage tax for older persons was reintroduced at a rate of 6.15%.

A general reduction on the SSC for self-employed was introduced in 2010 and increased in 2014.

The deduction for premiums paid to private pension arrangements was lowered in 2015 from SEK 12 000 to SEK 1 800 and abolished in 2016.

5. Memorandum items

5.1. *Identification of an AW and calculation of earnings*

Basic data for gross earnings are taken from the series *Official Statistics of Sweden*, published by Statistics Sweden. The calculation is based upon total average monthly or hourly earnings, primarily in September of the calendar year. To arrive at the annual earnings, data have been multiplied by the normal amount of hours worked during the year or the stipulated monthly salary has been multiplied by a factor of 12.2. The figures are representative for the country as a whole. The branch classification is NACE Rev.2 B-N according to the OECD recommendation.

5.2. *Employer contributions to private health, pension, etc. schemes*

There are a handful of widespread private social security schemes. The employers' contributions to these systems for the blue-collar workers in the private sector equalled to 6.3% of wage earnings in 2007. For white-collar workers in the private sector the employers' contributions to private social security schemes was 14% in 2007. These figures are based on the statistics of labour costs in the private sector, published by Statistics Sweden.

2016 parameter values

Average earnings/yr	Ave_earn	423 065	Secretariat estimate
Central income tax			
	tax_rate	0.2	
	tax_rate2	0.05	
	tax_thrsh	430 200	
	tax_thrsh2	625 800	
Basic Allowance			
	gr1	0.99	
	gr2	2.72	
	gr3	3.11	
	gr4	7.88	
	gp1	0.423	
	gp2	0.2	
	gp3	0.1	
	gp4	0.293	
	gp5	0.77	
Local income tax			
	local_rate	0.3210	
	min_taxl	0	
Soc. security amount			
	basic_amt	44 300	
	basic_ant	59 300	
Soc. security contributions			
employee	SSC_rate	0.07	
employer	SSC_empr	0.3142	
ceiling	SSCC	8.07	
Child benefit			
	Child 1	12 600	
	Child 2	14 400	
	CB	13 500	
Tax credits			
	TC1	0	
	TC1gr1	0	
	TC1gp1	0	
	TC2gp1	1	
EITC	er_1	0.91	
	er_2	2.94	
	er_3	8.08	
	er_4	13.54	
	ep_1	1.584	
	ep_2	0.332	
	ep_3	0.111	
	ep_4	2.155	
	ep_5	0.03	
Employer payroll tax	PRT	0.0965	

2016 tax equations

The equations for the Swedish system are mostly repeated for each individual of a married couple. But the cash transfer is calculated only once. This is shown by the Range indicator in the table below.

The functions which are used in the equations (Taper, MIN, Tax etc) are described in the technical note about tax equations. Variable names are defined in the table of parameters above, within the equations table, or are the standard variables "married" and "children". A reference to a variable with the affix "_total" indicates the sum of the relevant variable values for the principal and spouse. And the affixes "_princ" and "_spouse" indicate the value for the principal and spouse, respectively. Equations for a single person are as shown for the principal, with "_spouse" values taken as 0.

1.	Earnings	earn		
		truncearn	B	TRUNC(earn, -2)
2.	Allowances:	basic_al	B	IF(truncearn<=gr_2*basic_amt, MINA(ROUNDUP(MAXA(gp_1*basic_amt, (gp_1+ gp_2*(gr_2-gr_1))*basic_amt-gp_2*MAXA(gr_2*basic_amt-truncearn, 0)), -2), truncearn), MINA(ROUNDUP(MAXA(gp_4*basic_amt, gp_5*basic_amt-gp_2* MAXA(gr_2*basic_amt-truncearn, 0)-gp_3*MAXA(truncearn-gr_3*basic_amt, 0)), -2), truncearn))
		ssc_al	B	0
	Total	tax_al	B	basic_al
3.	Credits in taxable income	taxbl_cr	B	0
4.	CG taxable income	tax_inc	B	Positive(earn-basic_al)
5.	CG tax before credits	CG_tax_excl	B	tax_rate*Positive(tax_inc-tax_thrsh)+ tax_rate2* Positive(tax_inc-tax_thrsh2)
6.	Tax credits :	ssc_credit	B	Trunc(SSC, -2)
		localtax_credit	B	0
		eitc	B	=TRUNC(MAX((((TRUNC(IF(earned_income>er_2*basic_amt; IF(earned_income> er_3*basic_amt;ep_4*basic_amt;ep_1*basic_amt+ep_3*(earned_income-er_ 2*basic_amt));MIN(earned_income;er_1*basic_amt+ep_2*(earned_income-er_ 1*basic_amt)));0))-basic_allowance)*local_rate)-(IF(earned_income>er_4*basic_ amt;ep_5*(earned_income-er_4*basic_amt);0));0);0)
		Final_eitc	B	MIN(eitc, CG_tax_excl+ local_tax- ssc_credit)
		tax_cr	B	ssc_credit+localtax_credit+final_eitc
7.	CG tax	CG_tax	B	CG_tax_excl-tax_cr
8.	State and local taxes	local_tax	B	IF(tax_inc>0, TRUNC(local_rate*tax_inc, 0)+min_taxl, 0)
9.	Employees' soc security	SSC	B	(truncearn>=gp_1*basic_amt)*MINA(ROUNDSSC(truncearn*SSC_rate), ROUNDSSC(SSCC*basic_ant*SSC_rate))
11.	Cash transfers	cash_trans	J	Children*CB
13.	Employer's contributions		B	
	Employer's SSC	SSC_empr	B	TRUNC(earn*SSC_empr)-Payroll_empr
	Employer's payroll tax	Payroll_empr	B	TRUNC(earn*PRT)
	Total	Cont_empr	B	SSC_empr+Payroll_empr

Key to range of equation B calculated separately for both principal earner and spouse P calculated for principal only (value taken as 0 for spouse calculation) J calculated once only on a joint basis.

© OECD 2017

Switzerland

This chapter includes data on the income taxes paid by workers, their social security contributions, the family benefits they receive in the form of cash transfers as well as the social security contributions and payroll taxes paid by their employers. Results reported include the marginal and average tax burden for eight different family types.

Methodological information is available for Personal income tax systems, Compulsory social security contributions to schemes operated within the government sector, Universal cash transfers as well as recent changes in the tax/benefit system. The methodology also includes the parameter values and tax equations underlying the data.

Switzerland 2016

The tax/benefit position of single persons

		Wage level (per cent of average wage)	67	100	167	67
		Number of children	none	none	none	2
1.	**Gross wage earnings**		57 309	85 536	142 845	57 309
2.	**Standard tax allowances**					
	Basic allowance					
	Married or head of family		0	0	0	0
	Dependent children		0	0	0	13 000
	Deduction for social security contributions and income taxes		6 090	10 029	18 027	6 090
	Work-related expenses		2 000	2 406	4 000	2 000
	Other		1 700	1 700	1 700	3 100
		Total	9 790	14 136	23 727	24 190
3.	**Tax credits or cash transfers included in taxable income**		0	0	0	6 000
4.	**Central government taxable income (1 - 2 + 3)**		47 500	71 400	119 100	39 100
5.	**Central government income tax liability (exclusive of tax credits)**		379	1 063	4 476	108
6.	**Tax credits**					
	Basic credit					
	Married or head of family					
	Children		0	0	0	502
	Other					
		Total	0	0	0	502
7.	**Central government income tax finally paid (5-6)**		379	1 063	4 476	0
8.	**State and local taxes**		4 073	8 053	17 678	1 209
9.	**Employees' compulsory social security contributions**					
	Gross earnings		3 567	5 325	8 892	3 567
	Taxable income					
		Total	3 567	5 325	8 892	3 567
10.	**Total payments to general government (7 + 8 + 9)**		8 020	14 441	31 045	4 776
11.	**Cash transfers from general government**					
	For head of family					
	For two children		0	0	0	6 000
		Total	0	0	0	6 000
12.	**Take-home pay (1-10+11)**		49 289	71 095	111 800	58 533
13.	**Employer's compulsory social security contributions**		3 567	5 325	8 892	3 567
14.	**Average rates**					
	Income tax		7.8%	10.7%	15.5%	2.1%
	Employees' social security contributions		6.2%	6.2%	6.2%	6.2%
	Total payments less cash transfers		14.0%	16.9%	21.7%	-2.1%
	Total tax wedge including employer's social security contributions		19.0%	21.8%	26.3%	3.9%
15.	**Marginal rates**					
	Total payments less cash transfers: Principal earner		21.7%	23.3%	32.6%	13.8%
	Total payments less cash transfers: Spouse		n.a.	n.a.	n.a.	n.a.
	Total tax wedge: Principal earner		26.3%	27.8%	36.6%	18.8%
	Total tax wedge: Spouse		n.a.	n.a.	n.a.	n.a.

Switzerland 2016

The tax/benefit position of married couples

		Wage level (per cent of average wage)	100-0	100-33	100-67	100-33
		Number of children	2	2	2	none
1.	**Gross wage earnings**		85 536	113 763	142 845	113 763
2.	**Standard tax allowances**					
	Basic allowance					
	Married or head of family		2 600	14 835	16 000	14 835
	Dependent children		13 000	13 000	13 000	0
	Deduction for social security contributions and income taxes		10 029	14 061	18 119	14 061
	Work-related expenses		2 406	2 406	2 406	2 406
	Other		4 900	4 900	4 900	3 500
		Total	32 936	49 202	54 426	34 802
3.	**Tax credits or cash transfers included in taxable income**		6 000	6 000	6 000	0
4.	**Central government taxable income (1 - 2 + 3)**		58 600	70 500	94 400	78 900
5.	**Central government income tax liability (exclusive of tax credits)**		382	739	1 688	1 027
6.	**Tax credits**					
	Basic credit					
	Married or head of family					
	Children		502	502	502	0
	Other					
		Total	502	502	502	0
7.	**Central government income tax finally paid (5-6)**		0	237	1 186	1 027
8.	**State and local taxes**		3 591	6 206	10 153	8 444
9.	**Employees' compulsory social security contributions**					
	Gross earnings		5 325	7 082	8 892	7 082
	Taxable income					
		Total	5 325	7 082	8 892	7 082
10.	**Total payments to general government (7 + 8 + 9)**		8 916	13 525	20 231	16 553
11.	**Cash transfers from general government**					
	For head of family					
	For two children		6 000	6 000	6 000	0
		Total	6 000	6 000	6 000	0
12.	**Take-home pay (1-10+11)**		82 620	106 238	128 614	97 210
13.	**Employer's compulsory social security contributions**		5 325	7 082	8 892	7 082
14.	**Average rates**					
	Income tax		4.2%	5.7%	7.9%	8.3%
	Employees' social security contributions		6.2%	6.2%	6.2%	6.2%
	Total payments less cash transfers		3.4%	6.6%	10.0%	14.6%
	Total tax wedge including employer's social security contributions		9.1%	12.1%	15.2%	19.6%
15.	**Marginal rates**					
	Total payments less cash transfers: Principal earner		17.2%	21.5%	25.0%	22.3%
	Total payments less cash transfers: Spouse		16.4%	20.6%	25.6%	21.0%
	Total tax wedge: Principal earner		22.0%	26.1%	29.4%	26.9%
	Total tax wedge: Spouse		21.3%	25.2%	30.0%	25.6%

The national currency is the Swiss franc (CHF). In 2016, CHF 0.99 equalled USD 1. The Secretariat has estimated that in that same year the average worker earned CHF 85 536 (Secretariat estimate).

Cantonal and communal income taxes are very substantial in relation to direct federal tax. Here, the canton and commune of Zurich have been selected as an example of the tax system of the 26 cantons. Local income tax is not deductible when calculating federal income tax.

1. Personal income tax systems

1.1. *Income tax collected by the federal government (Confederation)*

1.1.1. *Tax unit*

The income of spouses living together is taxed jointly, regardless of the property regime under which they were married. Income of children living under parental authority is added to the income of their custodian. Children's labour income is taxed separately and in some cases, as in Zurich, is exempt from tax.

1.1.2. *Tax reliefs and tax credits*

1.1.2.1. Standard reliefs for "postnumerando" taxation [i.e. annual taxation on the basis of actual earned income, assessed at the end of the year].

- Basic deduction

  There is a basic deduction of CHF 2 600 for married couples for direct federal tax.

- Deduction for children

  A CHF 6 500 deduction is allowed for each child under 18 years of age; the deduction is allowed for older children if they are apprentices or still in school.

- Tax credit for children

  A CHF 251 deduction from the tax liability is allowed for each child under 18 years, the deduction is allowed for older children if they are apprentices or still in school.

- Deductions for social insurance contributions and other taxes

  Premiums for old age and disability insurance (5.125% of gross earned income) and for unemployment insurance (1.1% for income up to CHF 148 200, 0.5% for income over CHF 148 200) are deductible in full. Compulsory contributions of approximately 7.73% to private pension funds are also fully deductible. Health and life insurance premiums are deductible from federal income tax up to CHF 3 500 for married persons and CHF 1 700 for taxpayers who are widow(er)s, divorced or single (such premiums are not considered social contributions). These amounts are increased by CHF 700 for each dependent child.

- Work-related expenses

  Taxpayers are allowed a deduction corresponding to 3% of net income (i.e. gross income less contributions for old age and disability insurance, unemployment insurance and work-related provident funds). This deduction may be no less than CHF 2 000 and no more than CHF 4 000.

- Deduction for two-income couples

  50% of the smaller income can be deducted, but no less than CHF 8 100 and no more than CHF 13 400.

1.1.2.2. Main non-standard reliefs available to the average worker

- Interest payments on qualifying loans

  This is the main non-standard relief available to the average worker. It is allowed for all sorts of loans.

- Medical expenses

  Expenses incurred as a result of illness, accidents or disability of the taxpayer or one of its dependants are deductible if the taxpayer bears the expenses personally and they exceed 5% of his or her net income.

1.1.3. *Tax base*

Allowable deductions from gross income	Single taxpayer (CHF)	Married taxpayer, 2 children (CHF)
Work-related expenses[1]	2 000-4 000	2 000-4 000
Personal deduction	-	2 600
Deduction for 2 dependent children	-	13 000 (6 500*2)
Social contributions		
Old age insurance	5.125%	5.125%
Unemployment insurance	1.1%[2]	1.1%[2]
Pension fund	7.73%	7.73%
Maximum deductions for health insurance premiums and loan interest[3]	1 700 plus 700 per child	3 500 plus 700 per child
Deduction for two-income couples[4]		8 100 – 13 400

1. 3% of net income, minimum CHF 2 000, maximum CHF 4 000.
2. 1.1% of income up to CHF 148 200; 0.5% of income beyond CHF 148 200.
3. For the purposes of this publication, taxpayers are assumed to always receive the relevant maximum deduction.
4. 50% of smaller income, minimum the lower of CHF 8 100 or adjusted smaller income, maximum CHF 13 400.

In addition, for the married taxpayer with 2 children, there is a tax credit for 2 dependent children amounting to CHF 502, thus reducing the tax liability by CHF 502.

1.1.4. Tax schedules

1.1.4.1. Rates for persons living alone

Taxable income (CHF)[1]	Base amount (CHF)	Plus % of excess (CHF)	
Up to 14 500	–	–	–
14 500 to 31 600		0.77	14 500
31 600 to 41 400	131.65	0.88	31 600
41 400 to 55 200	217.90	2.64	41 400
55 200 to 72 500	582.20	2.97	55 200
72 500 to 78 100	1 096.00	5.94	72 500
778 100 to 103 600	1 428.60	6.60	78 100
103 600 to 134 600	3 111.60	8.80	103 600
134 600 to 176 000	5 839.60	11.00	134 600
176 000 to 755 200	10 393.60	13.20	176 000
Over 755 200[2]	-	11.5 of total income	

1. Fractions of less than CHF 100 are disregarded.
2. The calculation model disregards this part of the schedule.

1.1.4.2. Rates for spouses living together and for widowed, separated, divorced taxpayers or unmarried taxpayers living with their own children.

Taxable income (CHF)[1]	Base amount (CHF)	Plus % of the excess (CHF)	
Up to 28 300	–	–	–
28 300 to 50 900		1	28 300
50 900 to 58 400	223	2	50 900
58 400 to 75 300	373	3	58 400
75 300 to 90 300	877	4	75 300
90 300 to 103 400	1 477	5	90 300
103 400 to 114 700	2 127	6	103 400
114 700 to 124 200	2 799	7	114 700
124 200 to 131 700	3 457	8	124 200
131 700 to 137 300	4 057	9	131 700
137 300 to 141 200	4 552	10	137 300
141 200 to 143 100	4 942	11	141 200
143 100 to 145 000	5 151	12	143 100
145 000 to 895 800	5 379	13	145 000
For 895 900	103 028.50		
Over 895 900[2]	–	11.5 of total income	

1. Fractions of less than CHF 100 are disregarded.
2. The calculation model disregards this part of the schedule.

1.2. Taxes levied by decentralised authorities (Canton and commune of Zurich)

1.2.1. General description of the system

The system of cantonal and communal taxation has the same features as that of direct federal tax.

The tax base is comprised of income from all sources.

Once the basic amount of tax is set, cantons, communes and churches levy their taxes by applying a multiple, which may change from year to year. In 2012, for example, the canton applied a multiple of 1.0, the commune of Zurich 1.19 and the reformed church 0.10. The basic amount of tax is therefore multiplied by a total of 2.29. However, following the decision no longer to include church tax in *Revenue Statistics*, it is no longer included in the calculations for *Taxing Wages*. The basic amount of tax is therefore multiplied by a total of 2.19.

1.2.2. *Tax base*

Allowable deductions from gross income	Single taxpayer (CHF)	Married taxpayer, 2 children (CHF)
Work-related expenses[1]	2 000-4 000	2 000-4 000
Personal deduction	-	-
Deduction for 2 dependent children	-	18 000 (9 000*2)
Social contributions		
Old age insurance	5.125%	5.125%
Unemployment insurance	1.1%[2]	1.1%[2]
Pension fund	7.73%	7.73%
Maximum deductions for health insurance premiums and loan interest[3]	2 600 plus 1 300 per child	5 200 plus 1 300 per child
Deduction for two-income couples		5 900

1. 3% of net income, minimum CHF 2 000 CHF, maximum CHF 4 000.
2. 1.1% of income up to CHF 148 200; 0.5% of income beyond CHF 148 200 .
3. For the purposes of this publication, taxpayers are assumed to always receive the relevant maximum deduction.

1.2.3. *Postnumerando tax rates*

Cantonal income tax (Zurich)

a) Basic income tax rates for married, divorced, widowed or single taxpayers living with children:

Taxable income (CHF)[1]	Base amount (CHF)	Plus % of the excess (CHF)	
Up to 13 500	–	0	–
13 500 to 19 600	–	2	13 500
19 160 to 27 300	122	3	19 600
27 300 to 36 700	353	4	27 300
36 700 to 47 400	729	5	36 700
47 400 to 61 300	1 264	6	47 400
61 300 to 92 100	2 098	7	61 300
92 100 to 122 900	4 254	8	92 100
122 900 to 169 300	6 718	9	122 900
169 300 to 224 700	10 984	10	169 300
224 700 to 284 800	16 434	11	224 700
284 800 to 354 100	23 045	12	284 800
Over 354 100	31 361	13	354 100

b) Basic income tax rates for other taxpayers (single without children).

Taxable income (CHF)1	Base amount (CHF)	Plus % of the excess (CHF)	
Up to 6 700	–	0	–
6 700 to 11 400	–	2	6 700
11 400 to 16 100	94	3	11 400
16 100 to 23 700	235	4	16 100
23 700 to 33 000	539	5	23 700
33 000 to 43 700	1 004	6	33 000
43 700 to 56 100	1 646	7	43 700
56 100 to 73 000	2 514	8	56 100
73 000 to 105 500	3 866	9	73 000
105 500 to 137 700	6 791	10	105 500
137 700 to 188 700	10 011	11	137 700
188 700 to 254 900	15 621	12	188 700
Over 254 900	23 565	13	254 900

1. Fractions below CHF 100 are disregarded.

c) Annual multiple as a percentage of basic tax rates:

Canton of Zurich	100
Commune of Zurich	119
Roman Catholic church tax	10 (for info.)
Reformed Church tax	10 (for info.)

A personal tax of CHF 24 is added.

1.2.4. *Tax rates used for this study*

This study uses the rates of tax levied by the federal, cantonal and communal tax authorities.

2. Compulsory social security contributions to schemes operated within the government sector

2.1. Employee contributions

2.1.1. *Retirement pensions*

5.125% of gross income for old age insurance.

2.1.2. *Health insurance*

–

2.1.3. *Unemployment*

1.1% on the portion of income up to CHF 148 200; 0.5% for income over CHF 148 200.

2.1.4. *Work-related accidents*

–

2.1.5. *Family allowances*

–

2.1.6. Other

–

2.2. Employer contributions

2.2.1. Retirement pensions

5.125% of gross income for old age insurance.

2.2.2. Health insurance

–

2.2.3. Unemployment

1.1% on the portion of income up to CHF 148 200; 0.5% for income over CHF 148 200.

2.2.4. Work-related accidents

–

2.2.5. Family allowances

The employer pays a benefit for dependent children of an employee. The effective benefits paid depend on the Canton of residence and the respective employer. As of 1 January 2009, a new Swiss-wide minimum amount of CHF 2 400 (for children up to 16 years of age and CHF 3 000 for children in education between 16 and 25 years of age) has been established. In most cases, the benefit paid exceeds this minimum. The average family benefit is estimated to amount to CHF 3 000 per child per year.

This benefit is taxable along with other components of income.

The family allowance contributions are not included in the Taxing Wages results either as they are paid to a privately-managed fund. These contributions therefore qualify as non-tax compulsory payments (see also section 5.3).

2.2.6. Other

–

3. Universal cash benefits

3.1. Benefits linked to marital status

No such benefits are paid.

3.2. Benefits for dependent children

The employer pays a benefit of, on average, approximately CHF 3 000 per year for each dependent child of an employee. This benefit is taxable along with other components of income. See 2.25.

4. Main changes in the tax/benefit system since 1998

On 1 January 1999, the canton of Zurich switched from biennial praenumerando taxation to annual postnumerando taxation on individual income. As a result, the direct federal tax is based on annual postnumerando taxation as well.

As of 1 January 2008, the basic deduction for married couples and the deduction for two-income couples were introduced. These measures are intended to minimise the marriage penalty and to reduce the high taxation of secondary earners, thereby increasing labour force participation of skilled secondary earners.

As of 1 January 2012, the tax credit for children reduces the tax liability by CHF 251 per child.

5. Memorandum item

5.1. *Identification of the average worker*

The population includes men and women working in industry, arts and crafts. The stated income is for the average of workers in the same sector. The geographical scope is the entire country, whereas the amount of tax is computed in respect of the canton and commune of Zurich.

5.2. *Method of calculation used*

- Unemployment benefits: not included;
- Sick leave payments: not included;
- Paid leave allowances: included;
- Overtime: included;
- Periodic cash bonuses: included;
- Fringe benefits: not included;
- Basic method used for calculation: monthly wages are multiplied by 12;
- Close of the income tax year: 31 December;
- Reference period for computing wages: from 1 January to 31 December of the year in question.

5.3. *Calculation of non-tax compulsory payments*

Switzerland imposes some important non-tax compulsory payments (NTCPs). These NTPCs are not included in the Taxing Wages models except when they qualify as standard personal income tax reliefs. Compulsory payments indicators, which combine the effect of taxes and NTCPs, are calculated by the OECD Secretariat and presented in the OECD Tax Database (See: *www.oecd.org/ctp/taxdatabase*). Switzerland levies the following employee and/ or employer NTCPs:

- Contributions to the second pillar of the pension system (occupational pension funds): Occupational pension funds are mandatory for salaried persons earning at least CHF 21 150 annually. Old age insurance is based on individual savings. The savings assets accumulated by the insured person on his individual savings account over the years serve to finance the old age pension. The constituted capital is converted into an annual old age pension on the basis of a conversion factor. Contribution rates depend on the occupation and the pension fund. An estimated representative rate amounts to 7.73% for employees and 10.43% for employers in 2016.
- Health insurance is compulsory for all persons domiciled in Switzerland. Every family member is insured individually, regardless of age. Health insurance contributions are lump sum contributions per capita depending on age, sex, canton of residence and insurer.

The national average rates for 2016 amount to CHF 5 138 for adults and CHF 1 184 for children per year. Health insurance premiums can be reduced depending on the contributor's income level and his family situation. Each canton has its own definition of the income thresholds and the reduction regime. The health insurance premium and reduction rates of the Canton of Zurich are used in the calculations.

- Family allowance: Employers have to make family allowance contributions. The contribution rates differ among cantons and family contribution funds. A representative rate has to be estimated, for 2016 it amounts to 1.1%.
- Accident insurance: Accident insurance is compulsory for every employee. Employees are automatically insured by their employer, whereas the employers are more or less automatically assigned to a particular insurance company depending on their branch of trade. The risk and associated costs of the respective business activity determines the insurance premiums. A representative rate would have to be estimated.

2016 parameter values

Average earnings/yr	Ave_earn	85 536	Secretariat estimate
Tax allowances	fed_child_al	6 500	
Tax credit	fed_child_cred	251	
Partner Allowance	partner_rate_fed	0.5	
	partner_min_fed	8 100	
	partner_max_fed	13 400	
Basic deduction for married couples	Married_ded_fed	2 600	
Partner income local	partner_local	5 900	
Single parent	sing_par_al	0	
Workrelated	work_exp	0.03	
	work_exp_min	2 000	
	work_exp_max	4 000	
Allowances for local tax	local_basic	0	
	local_child	9 000	
Federal tax	IFD_min_s	-	
Single	IFD_sch_s	0	14 500
		0.0077	31 600
		0.0088	41 400
		0.0264	55 200
		0.0297	72 500
		0.0594	78 100
		0.066	103 600
		0.088	134 600
		0.11	176 000
		0.132	752 200
		0.115	
Married	IFD_min_m	-	
	IFD_sch_m	0	28 300
		0.01	50 900
		0.02	58 400
		0.03	75 300
		0.04	90 300
		0.05	103 400
		0.06	114 700
		0.07	124 200
		0.08	131 700
		0.09	137 300
		0.1	141 200

2016 parameter values

		0.11	143 100
		0.12	145 000
		0.13	895 900
		0.115	
Cantonal tax	Zurich_min	24	
Single	Zurich_sch_s	0	6 700
		0.02	11 400
		0.03	16 100
		0.04	23 700
		0.05	33 000
		0.06	43 700
		0.07	56 100
		0.08	73 000
		0.09	105 500
		0.1	137 700
		0.11	188 700
		0.12	254 900
		0.13	
Married	Zurich_sch_m	0	13 500
		0.02	19 600
		0.03	27 300
		0.04	36 700
		0.05	47 400
		0.06	61 300
		0.07	92 100
		0.08	122 900
		0.09	169 300
		0.1	224 700
		0.11	284 800
		0.12	354 100
		0.13	
Canton and Commune Tax Mutiple	statetax_mult	2.19	
Social security contributions	old_age	0.05125	
Pension	pension_rate	0	
Pillar 2 pension	NTCP_old_age_max	28 200	
	NTCP_pension_ee	0.0773	
Unemployment	unemp_rate	0.011	
	unemp_rate2	0.005	
income ceiling	unemp_ciel	148 200	
Cantonal deductible limit	local_dedn	2 600	
deductible extra for child	local_dedn_c	1 300	
Max other insurance deduction			
single	max_dedn_s	1 700	
married couples	max_dedn_m	3 500	
child	max_dedn_c	700	
Child cash transfer	child_ben	3 000	

2016 tax equations

The equations for the Swiss system in 2016 are mostly calculated on a family basis.

Variable names are defined in the table of parameters above, within the equations table, or are the standard variables "married" and "children". A reference to a variable with the affix "_total" indicates the sum of the relevant variable values for the principal and spouse. And the affixes "_princ" and "_spouse" indicate the value for the principal and spouse, respectively. Equations for a single person are as shown for the principal, with "_spouse" values taken as 0.

	Line in country table and intermediate steps	Variable name	Range	Equation
1.	Earnings	earn		
2.	Allowances:	partner_al	J	IF(earn_spouse-work_al_spouse-SSC_spouse>partner_min_fed,(Married*MAX (partner_min_fed,MIN(partner_max_fed,partner_rate_fed*(earn_spouse-work_al_spouse-SSC_spouse)))),earn_spouse-work_al_spouse-SSC_spouse)+Married*Married_ded_fed
	Children	children_al	J	Children*fed_child_al+ (Children>0)*(Married=0)*sing_par_al
	Soc sec contributions	SSC_al	B	SSC + NTCP_pension_ee*IF(earn_princ>0.75*NTCP_old_age_max,MAX(0.125*NTCP_old_age_max,earn_princ-0.875*NTCP_old_age_max),0)+NTCP_pension_ee*IF(earn_spouse>0.75*NTCP_old_age_max,MAX(0.125*NTCP_old_age_max,earn_spouse-0.875*NTCP_old_age_max),0)
	Work related	work_al	B	IF(earn-SSC>work_exp_min,MAX(work_exp_min,MIN(work_exp_max,work_exp*(earn-SSC))),earn-SSC)
	Other	oth_al	J	IF(Married,IF(Children>0,max_dedn_m+Children*fed_dedn_c,max_dedn_m), IF(Children>0,max_dedn_s+Children*fed_dedn_c,max_dedn_s))
	Total	tax_al	J	partner_al+children_al+SSC_al+work_al+oth_al
3.	Credits in taxable income	taxbl_cr	J	Cash_tran
4.	CG taxable income	tax_inc	J	positive(earn_total-tax_al+taxbl_cr)
5.	CG tax before credits	CG_tax_excl	J	IF(Married+Children=0, Tax(tax_inc, IFD_sch_s)+IFD_min_s*(Tax(tax_inc, IFD_sch_s)>0), Tax(tax_inc, IFD_sch_m)+IFD_min_m*(Tax(tax_inc, IFD_sch_m)>0))
6.	Tax credits :	Children_cred	J	Child_cred*Children
7.	CG tax	CG_tax	J	Positive(CG_tax_excl- Children_cred)
8.	State and local taxes	local_tax_inc	J	MAX(earn_total+taxbl_cr-local_basic*(1+Married)-Children*local_child-work_al_total-SSC_total-(local_dedn*(1+Married)+Children*local_dedn_c)-(earn_spouse>0)*partner_local,0)
		local_tax		IF((Married+Children)>0, Tax(local_tax_inc, Zurich_sch_m)*statetax_mult+(1+Married)*Zurich_min*(Tax(local_tax_inc, Zurich_sch_m)>0), Tax(local_tax_inc, Zurich_sch_s)*statetax_mult+(Tax(local_tax_inc, Zurich_sch_s)>0)*Zurich_min)
9.	Employees' soc security	SSC	B	(old_age)*earn+IF(earn<=unemp_ciel,earn*unemp_rate,unemp_ciel*unemp_rate+(earn-unemp_ciel)*unemp_rate2)
11.	Cash transfers	Cash_tran	J	Children*child_ben
13.	Employer's soc security	SSC_empr	B	SSC

Key to range of equation B calculated separately for both principal earner and spouse P calculated for principal only (value taken as 0 for spouse calculation) J calculated once only on a joint basis.

Taxing Wages 2017
© OECD 2017

Turkey

This chapter includes data on the income taxes paid by workers, their social security contributions, the family benefits they receive in the form of cash transfers as well as the social security contributions and payroll taxes paid by their employers. Results reported include the marginal and average tax burden for eight different family types.

Methodological information is available for Personal income tax systems, Compulsory social security contributions to schemes operated within the government sector, Universal cash transfers as well as recent changes in the tax/benefit system. The methodology also includes the parameter values and tax equations underlying the data.

Turkey 2016

The tax/benefit position of single persons

		Wage level (per cent of average wage)	67	100	167	67
		Number of children	none	none	none	2
1.	**Gross wage earnings**		24 660	36 806	61 466	24 660
2.	**Standard tax allowances**					
	Basic allowance		0	0	0	0
	Married or head of family					
	Dependent children					
	Deduction for social security contributions and income taxes		3 699	5 521	9 220	3 699
	Work-related expenses					
	Other					
		Total	3 699	5 521	9 220	3 699
3.	**Tax credits or cash transfers included in taxable income**		0	0	0	0
4.	**Central government taxable income (1 - 2 + 3)**		20 961	31 285	52 246	20 961
5.	**Central government income tax liability (exclusive of tax credits)**		3 562	5 717	11 376	3 562
	Stamp tax		187	279	467	187
		Total	3 749	5 996	11 843	3 749
6.	**Tax credits**					
	Basic credit		1 482	1 482	1 482	1 927
	Married or head of family					
	Children					
	Other					
		Total	1 482	1 482	1 482	1 927
7.	**Central government income tax finally paid (5-6)**		2 267	4 514	10 361	1 822
8.	**State and local taxes**		0	0	0	0
9.	**Employees' compulsory social security contributions**					
	Gross earnings		3 699	5 521	9 220	3 699
	Taxable income					
		Total	3 699	5 521	9 220	3 699
10.	**Total payments to general government (7 + 8 + 9)**		5 966	10 035	19 581	5 521
11.	**Cash transfers from general government**					
	For head of family					
	For two children		0	0	0	0
		Total	0	0	0	0
12.	**Take-home pay (1-10+11)**		18 694	26 771	41 885	19 139
13.	**Employer's compulsory social security contributions**		4 316	6 441	10 757	4 316
14.	**Average rates**					
	Income tax		9.2%	12.3%	16.9%	7.4%
	Employees' social security contributions		15.0%	15.0%	15.0%	15.0%
	Total payments less cash transfers		24.2%	27.3%	31.9%	22.4%
	Total tax wedge including employer's social security contributions		35.5%	38.1%	42.0%	33.9%
15.	**Marginal rates**					
	Total payments less cash transfers: Principal earner		32.8%	38.7%	38.7%	32.8%
	Total payments less cash transfers: Spouse		n.a.	n.a.	n.a.	n.a.
	Total tax wedge: Principal earner		42.8%	47.8%	47.8%	42.8%
	Total tax wedge: Spouse		n.a.	n.a.	n.a.	n.a.

Turkey 2016

The tax/benefit position of married couples

			100-0	100-33	100-67	100-33
	Wage level (per cent of average wage)		100-0	100-33	100-67	100-33
	Number of children		2	2	2	none
1.	**Gross wage earnings**		36 806	48 952	61 466	48 952
2.	**Standard tax allowances**					
	Basic allowance		0	0	0	0
	Married or head of family					
	Dependent children					
	Deduction for social security contributions and income taxes		5 521	7 343	9 220	7 343
	Work-related expenses					
	Other					
		Total	5 521	7 343	9 220	7 343
3.	**Tax credits or cash transfers included in taxable income**		0	0	0	0
4.	**Central government taxable income (1 - 2 + 3)**		31 285	41 609	52 246	41 609
5.	**Central government income tax liability (exclusive of tax credits)**		5 717	7 266	9 279	7 266
	Stamp tax		279	279	279	279
		Total	5 996	7 545	9 559	7 545
6.	**Tax credits**					
	Basic credit		2 223	3 409	3 409	2 965
	Married or head of family					
	Children					
	Other					
		Total	2 223	3 409	3 409	2 965
7.	**Central government income tax finally paid (5-6)**		3 773	4 228	6 336	4 673
8.	**State and local taxes**		0	0	0	0
9.	**Employees' compulsory social security contributions**					
	Gross earnings		5 521	7 343	9 220	7 343
	Taxable income					
		Total	5 521	7 343	9 220	7 343
10.	**Total payments to general government (7 + 8 + 9)**		9 294	11 571	15 556	12 015
11.	**Cash transfers from general government**					
	For head of family					
	For two children		0	0	0	0
		Total	0	0	0	0
12.	**Take-home pay (1-10+11)**		27 512	37 381	45 910	36 937
13.	**Employer's compulsory social security contributions**		6 441	8 567	10 757	8 567
14.	**Average rates**					
	Income tax		10.3%	8.6%	10.3%	9.5%
	Employees' social security contributions		15.0%	15.0%	15.0%	15.0%
	Total payments less cash transfers		25.3%	23.6%	25.3%	24.5%
	Total tax wedge including employer's social security contributions		36.4%	35.0%	36.4%	35.8%
15.	**Marginal rates**					
	Total payments less cash transfers: Principal earner		38.7%	38.7%	38.7%	38.7%
	Total payments less cash transfers: Spouse		16.3%	28.5%	32.8%	28.5%
	Total tax wedge: Principal earner		47.8%	47.8%	47.8%	47.8%
	Total tax wedge: Spouse		28.8%	39.2%	42.8%	39.2%

The national currency unit is the "Türk Lirası" (TL). In 2016, TL 3.02 was equal to USD 1. In that year, the average worker earned TL 36 806 (Country estimate).

1. Personal income tax systems

1.1. *Central government income tax*

1.1.1. *Tax unit*

Spouses are taxed separately on earned income. This rule has been applied since 1 January 1999.

1.1.2. *Tax allowances and tax credits*

1.1.2.1. Standard reliefs:

- *Reliefs for social security contributions:* Employee's social security contributions are deductible from gross earnings. These contributions are 15% of gross income as stated by the Social Insurance Act. The contribution to the unemployment fund is included in this amount and equals 1% of gross income.
- Contributions to public pension funds established by law are deductible.
- *Work-related expenses*: None.
- *Minimum Living Relief*: The calculation of the minimum living allowance is based on the annual gross amount of the minimum wage for employees older than 16 at the beginning of the calendar year in which the income is obtained multiplied by the following rates:
  - 50% for the taxpayer him or herself;
  - 10% for the spouse who neither works nor has an income;
  - 7.5% for each of the first two children;
  - 10% for third child;
  - 5% for each additional child.

This total amount is then multiplied by the rate (15%) which is applied to the first income bracket of PIT Schedule stated in Article 103 of PIT Law, and then minimum living relief is calculated by offsetting 1/12 of the allowance amount against monthly calculated tax due on employment income. Any excess is non-refundable.

1.1.2.2. Main non-standard tax reliefs applicable to an AW

- *Reliefs for disabled*: Article 31 of PIT Law (implemented in 01.01.2004 by the law 4842) regulates tax relief for disabled persons. The employee who lost his/her working capacity with at least 80% is considered to be disabled in the 1st degree; employees are disabled in the 2nd respectively 3rd degree if they lost their working capacity with at least 60% respectively 40%. In these cases, the following amounts are deductible from monthly wages:

  - Disabled in the 1st degree: TL 900
  - Disabled in the 2nd degree: TL 460
  - Disabled in the 3rd degree: TL 210
- Legal deductions for public institutions such as OYAK (Social Aid Institution for Military Officers).
- 50% of the premiums paid by the wage-earner for life insurance policies which belong to himself (or herself), the spouse and dependent children and all of the premiums paid by the wage-earner for personal insurance policies including death, accident, health, illness, disablement, unemployment, maturity, birth, education, etc. provided that the insurance is contracted with a company establishment in or with a main office in Turkey. (The total amount of deductible premiums cannot exceed 15% of the wage that is earned in the current month. The annual amount cannot exceed the annual minimum wage.
- Membership payments made to labour unions.

1.1.3. *Tax schedule*

The tax schedule in 2016 is as follows:

Taxable income (TL)	Tax on lower threshold (TL)	Tax on excess amount above lower threshold (%)
Up to 12 600		15
12 600 up to 30 000	1 890	20
30 000 up to 110 000	5 370	27
Over 110 0000	26 970	35

1.2. *State and local income taxes*

Income tax is levied only by the central government.

1.3. *Stamp tax*

The stamp tax base is gross earnings. The tax rate is 0.759% in 2016.

2. Compulsory social security contributions to schemes operated within the government sector

2.1. *Employees' contributions*

2.11. *Pensions (disability, old age and death insurance): 9%*

2.12. *Sickness: 5%*

2.13. *Unemployment: 1%*

2.2. *Employers' contributions*

2.21. *Pensions (disability, old age and death insurance): 11%*

2.22. *Sickness: 7.5%*

2.23. *Unemployment: 2%*

2.24. *Pensions (for short term insurance branches): 2%*

In order to increase employment and reduce regional imbalances in Turkey; various incentives policies have been implemented by state, by laws 4447, 4857, 5084, 5225, 5510, 5746, 6111, 6486 by Council of Minister's Decree of 2012/3305(Unemployment Law No: 4447, Labour Law No: 4857, Investment and Employment Promotion Law No: 5084, Investment Incentives and The Law of Cultural Initiatives Law No: 5225, Social Security General Health Insurance Law No: 5510, Promotion Research and Development Activities Law No: 5746, Law On The Restricting Of Certain Receivables and Amendment To The Law Of Social Insurance and General Health Insurance and Certain Other Laws And Decree Laws No: 6111, Amendment To The Law Of Social Insurance and General Health Insurance and Certain Other Laws No: 6486, Council of Minister's Decree No: 2012/3305 on Government Subsidies for Investments).

One of the various incentives is reduction of premiums. If disability, old age and death insurance premiums paid regularly by employers as stated law 5510 article of 81 (Social Security and General Health Insurance Law), 5% of total 11% premiums are paid by state on behalf of employers. (5% discount applied in employers share). In addition to 5% discount, 6% discount is implemented from 2013 in the working places, which employ ten or more workers, located in 51 provinces, Gökçeada and Bozcaada determined by taking into account the social- development index.

There is no distinction by marital status or sex and the contributions apply to gross earnings. Compulsory social security contributions of employees and their employers are calculated according to the schemes presented above.

For employees whose gross earnings are below the base or above ceiling earnings, which are determined at least twice in a year, these contribution rates are applied to the base or ceiling amounts respectively. In 2016, the base amount is approximately TL 19 764 and the ceiling amount is approximately TL 128 466. Under the Law No. 5510 **(Social Security and General Health Insurance Law),** the base wage for social security contributions is equal to the minimum wage. Because employees cannot be less than the minimum wage, the base wage is not considered in this publication. However, the ceiling earnings are considered for the purposes of this Report.

3. Universal cash transfers

Employees obtain Universal cash transfers according to the collective labour agreements that are signed between their employer and the labour union(s). These agreements vary with the bargaining power of the different parties in the different sectors in the economy. This explains why there is no standard amount reflecting these general transfers.

4. Main changes in tax/benefit system since 2004

Personal Income Tax Law (No: 193) which is about income tax, Social Security and General Health Insurance Law (No: 5510) which is about social security contributions and Unemployment Insurance Law (No: 4447) which is about unemployment insurance fund are the main laws about tax/benefit system.

The main changes have been made to the following laws 5615, 6009, 6327 and 6645 which are as follows:

- According to Act No: 5615, the new application "*Minimum Living Relief*" began to be implemented. (See the section 1.1.2).

- According to Act No: 6009, the taxation of the wages are differentiated than the taxation of the other taxable revenue resources like trading income, income from immovable property or income from investments. By this way, it is ensured that wages (comparative to other income items) are later entered into the 3rd bracket on the income tax schedule.
- According to Act No: 6327, (published in the Official Gazette issue 28338 on 29 June 2012) there are important amendments in the Private Pension System Regulations. According to this law, any citizen of the Republic of Turkey will have the right for state subsidy for his/her paid contributions to the Private Pension Account. The contribution upper limit to favour this incentive is the annual amount of minimum wage 25% of this amount shall be transferred to the account of the insured party as a state subsidy. The state subsidy shall be earned in proportion to the amount of time within the system.
- According to Act No: 6645, "Minimum Living Relief" rate is changed from 5% to 10% which is used for third child's rate.

5. Memorandum items

5.1. *Identification of an AW*

Weighted mean, by the number of employees, of the monthly average wage information obtained from "Structure of Earnings Survey, 2010", published by TURKSTAT, according to NACE Rev.2 classification for B-N sections is calculated and B-N aggregated data is gained. (The annual average wage data is calculated by multiplying the monthly average wage values by 12).

The data from 2011-15 is reached by using 2010 = 100 base year "Hourly Earnings Index" and 2010 annual average wage data.

5.2. *Contribution to private pension and health schemes*

Business enterprises (employers) are permitted to make additional contributions for pension savings of their employees. However, these amounts of additional premiums are limited by main tax laws. Such additional pension arrangements, which are optional, are not widely used.

Monthly wage: Include the sum of monthly basic wages, over time payments, payments for shift work/ night work and other regular payments paid to employees in November 2010 by employers.

The average wage amount from 2010 is calculated as a result of a joint working performed by authorities from TURKSTAT and Ministry of Finance.

2016 parameter values

Average earnings/yr.	Ave_earn	36 806	Country estimate
Income tax	Tax_sch	0.15	12 600
		0.20	30 000
		0.27	110 000
		0.35	
Stamp tax	Stamp_rate	0.00759	
Employees SSC	SSC_rate	0.15	
	SSC_ceil	128 466	
Employers SSC	SSC_empr	0,175	
Minimum living relief	credit_rate	0.15	
	basic_allow	0.5	
	spouse_allow	0.1	
	child_allow	0.075	
	third_child_allow	0.1	
	add_child_allow	0.05	
	min_wage	19 764	

2016 tax equations

The equations for the Turkish system are on an individual basis.

The functions which are used in the equations (Taper, MIN, Tax etc) are described in the technical note about tax equations. Variable names are defined in the table of parameters above, within the equations table, or are the standard variables "married" and "children". A reference to a variable with the affix "_total" indicates the sum of the relevant variable values for the principal and spouse. And the affixes "_princ" and "_spouse" indicate the value for the principal and spouse, respectively. Equations for a single person are as shown for the principal, with "_spouse" values taken as 0.

	Line in country table and intermediate steps	Variable name	Range	Equation
1.	Earnings	earn		
2.	Allowances:	tax_al	B	SSC
3.	Credits in taxable income	taxbl_cr	B	0
4.	CG taxable income	tax_inc	B	Positive(earn-tax_al)
	Stamp tax	stamp_tax	B	earn*stamp_rate
5.	CG tax before credits	CG_tax_excl	B	Tax(tax_inc,tax_sch)
6.	Tax credits :	tax_cr	P	=credit_rate*min_wage*(basic_allow+spouse_allow*(IF(Wife=0;Married;0))+ IF (OR(Children=1;Children=2); Children*child_allow;0)+IF(Children=3;(2*child_ allow) +(Children-2)*third_child_allow;0)+IF(Children>3;(2*child_allow) +(1* third_child_allow)+(1*add_child_allow);0))
			S*	IF(spouse_earn>0,credit_rate*min_wage*basic_allow,0)
7.	CG tax	CG_tax	B	positive(CG_tax_excl-tax_cr)+stamp_tax
8.	State and local taxes	local_tax	B	0
9.	Employees' soc security	SSC	B	Min(earn,SSC_ceil)*SSC_rate
11.	Cash transfers	cash_trans	B	0
13.	Employer's soc security	SSC_empr	B	Min(earn,SSC_ceil)*SSC_empr

Key to range of equation B calculated separately for both principal earner and spouse P calculated for principal only (value taken as 0 for spouse calculation) J calculated once only on a joint basis.

* In the case where the spouse earns 33% of the average wage: Taxing Wages assumption on the working spouse earning 33% of the AW does not comply with the Turkish legislation. 33% of AW in Turkey is below the minimum wage and a person cannot be employed below minimum wage. According to the Turkish legislation, it is assumed that (because he/she doesn't obtain "wage") the spouse should not obtain income in the calculation for this case, and another minimum living allowance is not also calculated for the spouse. Minimum living allowance should be only calculated for the principle earner.

United Kingdom (2016-17 Income tax year)

This chapter includes data on the income taxes paid by workers, their social security contributions, the family benefits they receive in the form of cash transfers as well as the social security contributions and payroll taxes paid by their employers. Results reported include the marginal and average tax burden for eight different family types.

Methodological information is available for Personal income tax systems, Compulsory social security contributions to schemes operated within the government sector, Universal cash transfers as well as recent changes in the tax/benefit system. The methodology also includes the parameter values and tax equations underlying the data.

United Kingdom 2016

The tax/benefit position of single persons

		Wage level (per cent of average wage)	67	100	167	67
		Number of children	none	none	none	2
1.	**Gross wage earnings**		24 503	36 571	61 074	24 503
2.	**Standard tax allowances**					
	Basic allowance		11 000	11 000	11 000	11 000
	Married or head of family					
	Dependent children					
	Deduction for social security contributions and income taxes					
	Work-related expenses					
	Other					
		Total	11 000	11 000	11 000	11 000
3.	**Tax credits or cash transfers included in taxable income**		0	0	0	0
4.	**Central government taxable income (1 - 2 + 3)**		13 503	25 571	50 074	13 503
5.	**Central government income tax liability (exclusive of tax credits)**		2 701	5 114	13 629	2 701
6.	**Tax credits**					
	Basic credit					
	Married or head of family					
	Children		0	0	0	3 478
	Other					
		Total	0	0	0	3 478
7.	**Central government income tax finally paid (5-6)**		2 701	5 114	13 629	- 777
8.	**State and local taxes**		0	0	0	0
9.	**Employees' compulsory social security contributions**					
	Gross earnings		1 973	3 421	4 554	1 973
	Taxable income					
		Total	1 973	3 421	4 554	1 973
10.	**Total payments to general government (7 + 8 + 9)**		4 674	8 536	18 184	1 196
11.	**Cash transfers from general government**					
	For head of family					
	For two children		0	0	0	1 794
		Total	0	0	0	1 794
12.	**Take-home pay (1-10+11)**		19 829	28 035	42 890	25 100
13.	**Employer's compulsory social security contributions**		2 262	3 927	7 309	2 262
14.	**Average rates**					
	Income tax		11.0%	14.0%	22.3%	-3.2%
	Employees' social security contributions		8.1%	9.4%	7.5%	8.1%
	Total payments less cash transfers		19.1%	23.3%	29.8%	-2.4%
	Total tax wedge including employer's social security contributions		25.9%	30.8%	37.3%	6.2%
15.	**Marginal rates**					
	Total payments less cash transfers: Principal earner		32.0%	32.0%	42.0%	73.0%
	Total payments less cash transfers: Spouse		n.a.	n.a.	n.a.	n.a.
	Total tax wedge: Principal earner		40.2%	40.2%	49.0%	76.3%
	Total tax wedge: Spouse		n.a.	n.a.	n.a.	n.a.

United Kingdom 2016

The tax/benefit position of married couples

		Wage level (per cent of average wage)	100-0	100-33	100-67	100-33
		Number of children	2	2	2	none
1.	**Gross wage earnings**		36 571	48 639	61 074	48 639
2.	**Standard tax allowances**					
	Basic allowance		12 100	22 000	22 000	22 000
	Married or head of family					
	Dependent children					
	Deduction for social security contributions and income taxes					
	Work-related expenses					
	Other					
		Total	12 100	22 000	22 000	22 000
3.	**Tax credits or cash transfers included in taxable income**		0	0	0	0
4.	**Central government taxable income (1 - 2 + 3)**		24 471	26 639	39 074	26 639
5.	**Central government income tax liability (exclusive of tax credits)**		4 894	5 328	7 815	5 328
6.	**Tax credits**					
	Basic credit					
	Married or head of family					
	Children		0	0	0	0
	Other					
		Total	0	0	0	0
7.	**Central government income tax finally paid (5-6)**		4 894	5 328	7 815	5 328
8.	**State and local taxes**		0	0	0	0
9.	**Employees' compulsory social security contributions**					
	Gross earnings		3 421	3 902	5 394	3 902
	Taxable income					
		Total	3 421	3 902	5 394	3 902
10.	**Total payments to general government (7 + 8 + 9)**		8 316	9 230	13 209	9 230
11.	**Cash transfers from general government**					
	For head of family					
	For two children		1 794	1 794	1 794	0
		Total	1 794	1 794	1 794	0
12.	**Take-home pay (1-10+11)**		30 049	41 203	49 658	39 409
13.	**Employer's compulsory social security contributions**		3 927	4 473	6 189	4 473
14.	**Average rates**					
	Income tax		13.4%	11.0%	12.8%	11.0%
	Employees' social security contributions		9.4%	8.0%	8.8%	8.0%
	Total payments less cash transfers		17.8%	15.3%	18.7%	19.0%
	Total tax wedge including employer's social security contributions		25.8%	22.4%	26.2%	25.8%
15.	**Marginal rates**					
	Total payments less cash transfers: Principal earner		32.0%	32.0%	32.0%	32.0%
	Total payments less cash transfers: Spouse		7.6%	32.0%	32.0%	32.0%
	Total tax wedge: Principal earner		40.2%	40.2%	40.2%	40.2%
	Total tax wedge: Spouse		11.6%	40.2%	40.2%	40.2%

The national currency is the Pound Sterling (GBP). In 2016, GBP 0.74 was equal to USD 1. In 2016-17, the Average Worker is estimated to earn GBP 36 571 (Secretariat estimate).

1. Personal income tax system

1.1. *Central government income taxes*

1.1.1. *Tax unit*

The tax unit is the individual, but certain reliefs depend on family circumstances (see Section 1.1.2.1).

1.1.2. *Tax allowances and tax credits*

All figures shown are those applying at the start of the tax year in April.

1.1.2.1. Standard reliefs

- Basic reliefs: A personal allowance of GBP 11 000 is granted to each individual with income below GBP 100 000. The personal allowance is then tapered away by GBP 1 for every GBP 2 of income above GBP 100 000.
- Standard marital status reliefs: Marriage Allowance – Allows the transfer of 10% of an individual's personal allowance to their husband, wife or civil partner. The allowance is restricted to couples where the higher earner is a basic rate taxpayer and is only beneficial if the lower earner owes below the personal allowance. The allowance has to be claimed and is given only to those who meet the eligibility criteria.
- Working Tax Credit (WTC): A non-wastable tax credit available to low income families with or without children. It is available for families with children where one person works at least 16 hours a week (though hours must be at least 24 overall for a couple). It is also available for people with a disability who work at least 16 hours a week and for families without children where one person works at least 30 hours a week. The amount depends upon the hours worked, the ages of children, eligible childcare costs, and gross income. A family with a child 16 or under where the claimant (or, where applicable, their partner, or both claimants jointly) works at least 30 hours a week, would get a maximum credit of GBP 4 780 per year (assuming neither the adult(s) nor the child were disabled) before taking into account eligible childcare costs. This credit is reduced by 41 pence for each GBP 1 of net income above a threshold of GBP 6 420 per year. WTC was introduced on 6 April 2003.
- Relief for social security contributions and other taxes: None.

The amount of credit received is calculated by dividing separately each element of the credit by the number of days in the tax year and rounding up to the nearest penny to give a daily rate. These daily rates are then multiplied by the number of days in the relevant period (for the purposes of this Report, the tax year) and added together.

- Child Tax Credit (CTC): A non-wastable tax credit available to low and middle income families with children. It provides support for children until 1st September following their 16th birthday, and beyond that date to the age of 19 for those who continue in full-time non-advanced education. The amount depends on gross income and the number and age of the children. A family with two children would get a maximum credit GBP 6 105 per year, which is reduced by 41 pence for each GBP 1 of gross income above a threshold of GBP 16 105 if the family is not working. A lower threshold applies if the family is working; their CTC is reduced at the same rate once their WTC has been tapered to zero. CTC was introduced on 6th April 2003.

1.1.2.2. Main non-standard tax reliefs applicable to an AW.

- Work-related expenses: Flat rate expenses for tools and special clothing are allowed to certain occupational categories. Since this provision is not applicable to all manufacturing occupations, and hence average workers, and because the rates vary slightly across categories, this relief is considered here as non-standard;
- Contributions to approved superannuation schemes or personal pension schemes are deducted when calculating taxable income. Premiums on approved life assurance policies payable to life assurance companies attract 12.5% tax relief for policies entered into force before 13 March 1984.

1.1.3. *Tax schedule*

In 2016-17 all taxpayers are liable on taxable income other than savings and dividend income at the basic rate of 20% on the first GBP 32 000, 40% over the basic rate limit of GBP 32 000 and 45% over the higher rate limit of GBP 150 000. (Taxable Income is defined as gross income for income tax purposes less allowances and reliefs available at the marginal rate.) Dividend income is charged at 7.5% up to the basic rate limit of GBP 32 000, 32.5% above GBP 32 000 and 38.1% above GBP 150 000. From 2016-17, a new Dividend Allowance means that dividend taxpayers won't have to pay tax on the first GBP 5 000 of their dividend income, no matter what non-dividend income they have. Savings income is charged at 0% up to the starting rate limit on the first GBP 5 000, at 20% up to GBP 32 000, 40% above GBP 32 000 and 45% above GBP 150 000. From 2016-17, a new Personal Savings Allowance was introduced giving GBP 1 000 of savings income tax free for taxpayers with total income below the basic rate limit or GBP 500 for those with total income below the higher rate limit.

Taxable income (GBP)	Rate %
0-32 000	20
32 000-150 000	40
Over 150 000	45

1.2. *State and local income tax*

There are no regional or local income taxes.

2. Compulsory social security contributions to schemes operated within the government sector

2.1. *Employees' contributions*

National Insurance contributions are payable by employees earning more than GBP 155 in any week. These are 12% of earnings between GBP 155 and GBP 827 and 2% of earnings above GBP 827.Depending on eligibility, members of the National Insurance scheme qualify for pensions, sickness, industrial injury, unemployment benefits, etc. All employees earning under GBP 155 per week have no National Insurance contribution liability but a notional contribution will be deemed to have been paid in respect of earnings between GBP 112 and GBP 155 to protect benefit entitlement.

2.2. *Employers' contributions*

Employer's contributions are not payable for employees earning less than GBP 156 per week. The rate of employers' contributions for employees not contracted out of the additional (earnings related) scheme is 13.8% of earnings above GBP 156 per week.

3. Universal cash transfers

3.1. *Transfers related to marital status*

None (widows' benefit is covered by the government pensions scheme noted above).

3.2. *Transfers for dependent children*

A child benefit of GBP 20.70 per week is paid in respect of the first child in the family up to the age of 19 (if the child aged 16-19 is in education or training) with GBP 13.70 per week paid for each subsequent child.

From January 2013, a new tax charge has been introduced for a taxpayer who has income over GBP 50 000 and either they or their partner are in receipt of Child Benefit. For those with income between GBP 50 000 and GBP 60 000, the amount of the charge will be 1% of the Child Benefit for every GBP 100 of income over GBP 50 000. For those with income over GBP 60 000, the amount of the charge will equal the amount of Child Benefit. Where both adults are over the threshold, the liability falls on the adult with the highest adjusted net income (ANI).

4. Memorandum items

4.1. *Identification of AW and valuation of earnings*

A new Annual Survey of Hours and Earnings (ASHE) has been developed to replace the New Earnings Survey (NES) (results of which are published in *Labour Market Trends*) and shows the average weekly earnings of full-time employees in April each year. It covers men and women at adult rates in the United Kingdom (excluding Northern Ireland). The annual figure used for the gross earnings of the AW in the United Kingdom is the annual equivalent of the arithmetic average of the weekly earnings figures for April at the beginning and end of the fiscal year, as published in *Labour Market Trends*.

The earnings figures exclude the earnings of those whose pay was affected by absence (due to sickness etc.). They include overtime, payment by results and shift payments. But they do not include benefits in kind (which could in some circumstances be included in the employee's taxable income in the United Kingdom).

4.2. Employers' contributions to private pension, health etc. schemes

In 2008, there were 9.0 million active members of occupational pension schemes with two or more members in the UK, of whom 3.6 million were in the private sector and 5.4 million in the public sector.

2016 parameter values

Average earnings/yr	Ave_earn	36 571	Secretariat Estimate	
Allowances	Basic_al	11 000		
	PA taper start	100 000		
	Married_al	1 100		
	Married_rate	0		
Income tax	Tax_sch	0.2	32 000	
		0.4	150 000	
		0.45		
Employees SSC				
Primary threshold	SSC_sch	0	8 060	PT
Upper earnings limit		0.12	43 000	UEL
		0.02		
Employers SSC	SSC_rate2	0.138		
	ST	8 112		
Child benefit (first)	CB_first	20.70		
Child benefit (others)	CB_others	13.70		
	CB_1st_thres	50 000.00		
	CB_2nd_thres	60 000.00		
	CB_taper1	0.01		
	CB_taper2	100.00		
NEW TAX CREDITS				
WTC				
Basic element	WTC_Basic	1 960		
Couple/Lone parent	WTC_couple_or_lone	2 010		
30 Hour element	WTC_30hr	810		
CTC				
Family element	CTC_family	545		
Child element	CTC_child	2 780		
Baby element	CTC_baby			
Threshold	NTC_1st_thres	6 420		
	NTC_1st_taper	0.41		
Days in tax year	Numdays	365		

2016 tax equations

The equations for the UK system are mostly on an individual basis. But Child and Working tax credits are calculated on a family basis and child benefit is calculated only once. This is shown by the Range indicator in the table below.

The functions which are used in the equations (Taper, MIN, Tax etc) are described in the technical note about tax equations. Variable names are defined in the table of parameters above, within the equations table, or are the standard variables "married" and "children". A reference to a variable with the affix "_total" indicates the sum of the relevant variable values for the principal and spouse. And the affixes "_princ" and "_spouse" indicate the value for the principal and spouse, respectively. Equations for a single person are as shown for the principal, with "_spouse" values taken as 0.

	Line in country table and intermediate steps	Variable name	Range	Equation
1.	Earnings	Earn		
2.	Allowances:	tax_al	B	Tax_al IF(earn<PA_taper,IF(AND(earn<(BRL+Basic_al),earn_spouse<Basic_al, Married=1),IF(earn>earn_spouse,Basic_al+Married_al,Basic_al-Married_al),Basic_al),IF(earn>(PA_taper+(Basic_al*2)),0,MAX(0,(Basic_al-((earn-PA_taper)/2)))))
3.	Credits in taxable income	taxbl_cr	B	0
4.	CG taxable income	tax_inc	B	Positive(earn-tax_al)
5.	CG tax before credits	CG_tax_excl	B	Tax(tax_inc, tax_sch)
6.	Tax credits (nonwastable)	tax_cr	J	IF(Children>0, (Taper(ROUNDUP(CTC_family/numdays, 2)*numdays+Children*ROUNDUP(CTC_child/numdays, 2)*numdays+ROUNDUP(WTC_Basic/numdays, 2)*numdays+ROUNDUP(WTC_30hr/numdays, 2)*numdays+ROUNDUP(WTC_couple_or_lone/numdays, 2)*numdays, earn_total, NTC_1st_thres, NTC_1st_taper), Taper(ROUNDUP(WTC_Basic/numdays, 2)*numdays+ROUNDUP(WTC_30hr/numdays, 2)*numdays+IF(Married=1, ROUNDUP(WTC_couple_or_lone/numdays, 2)*numdays, 0), earn_total, NTC_1st_thres, NTC_1st_taper))
7.	CG tax	CG_tax	B	CG_tax_excl-tax_cr
8.	State and local taxes	local_tax	B	0
9.	Employees' soc security	SSC	B	Tax(earn, SSC_sch)
11.	Cash transfers	cash_trans	J	=IF(princ_earn>CB_1st_thres,IF(princ_earn>CB_2nd_thres,0,((1-(AA7-CB_1st_thres)/(CB_taper2/CB_taper1)))*(numdays/7*((Children>0)*CB_first+CB_others*Positive(Children-1)))),(numdays/7*((Children>0)*CB_first+CB_others*Positive(Children-1))))
13.	Employer's soc security	SSC_empr	B	(earn>ST)*(earn-ST)*SSC_rate2
	Memorandum item: Non-wastable tax credit			
	tax expenditure component	Taxexp	J	Tax_cr-transfer
	cash transfer component	Transfer	J	IF(CG_tax_excl<0, -CG_tax_excl, 0)

Key to range of equation B calculated separately for both principal earner and spouse P calculated for principal only (value taken as 0 for spouse calculation) J calculated once only on a joint basis

Taxing Wages 2017
© OECD 2017

United States

This chapter includes data on the income taxes paid by workers, their social security contributions, the family benefits they receive in the form of cash transfers as well as the social security contributions and payroll taxes paid by their employers. Results reported include the marginal and average tax burden for eight different family types.

Methodological information is available for Personal income tax systems, Compulsory social security contributions to schemes operated within the government sector, Universal cash transfers as well as recent changes in the tax/benefit system. The methodology also includes the parameter values and tax equations underlying the data.

United States 2016

The tax/benefit position of single persons

		Wage level (per cent of average wage)	67	100	167	67
		Number of children	none	none	none	2
1.	**Gross wage earnings**		35 204	52 543	87 747	35 204
2.	**Standard tax allowances**					
	Basic allowance		10 350	10 350	10 350	13 350
	Married or head of family					
	Dependent children		0	0	0	8 100
	Deduction for social security contributions and income taxes					
	Work-related expenses					
	Other					
		Total	10 350	10 350	10 350	21 450
3.	**Tax credits or cash transfers included in taxable income**		0	0	0	0
4.	**Central government taxable income (1 - 2 + 3)**		24 854	42 193	77 397	13 754
5.	**Central government income tax liability (exclusive of tax credits)**		3 264	6 319	15 120	1 401
6.	**Tax credits**					
	Basic credit		0	0	0	1 989
	Married or head of family					
	Children		0	0	0	2 000
	Other					
		Total	0	0	0	3 989
7.	**Central government income tax finally paid (5-6)**		3 264	6 319	15 120	- 2 588
8.	**State and local taxes**		2 157	3 310	5 651	1 669
9.	**Employees' compulsory social security contributions**					
	Gross earnings		2 693	4 020	6 713	2 693
	Taxable income					
		Total	2 693	4 020	6 713	2 693
10.	**Total payments to general government (7 + 8 + 9)**		8 114	13 649	27 484	1 773
11.	**Cash transfers from general government**					
	For head of family					
	For two children		0	0	0	0
		Total	0	0	0	0
12.	**Take-home pay (1-10+11)**		27 090	38 894	60 263	33 430
13.	**Employer's compulsory social security contributions**		3 087	4 413	7 107	3 087
14.	**Average rates**					
	Income tax		15.4%	18.3%	23.7%	-2.6%
	Employees' social security contributions		7.7%	7.7%	7.7%	7.7%
	Total payments less cash transfers		23.0%	26.0%	31.3%	5.0%
	Total tax wedge including employer's social security contributions		29.3%	31.7%	36.5%	12.7%
15.	**Marginal rates**					
	Total payments less cash transfers: Principal earner		29.3%	39.3%	39.3%	51.6%
	Total payments less cash transfers: Spouse		n.a.	n.a.	n.a.	n.a.
	Total tax wedge: Principal earner		34.3%	43.6%	43.6%	55.1%
	Total tax wedge: Spouse		n.a.	n.a.	n.a.	n.a.

United States 2016

The tax/benefit position of married couples

		Wage level (per cent of average wage)	100-0	100-33	100-67	100-33
		Number of children	2	2	2	none
1.	**Gross wage earnings**		52 543	69 882	87 747	69 882
2.	**Standard tax allowances**					
	Basic allowance		20 700	20 700	20 700	20 700
	Married or head of family					
	Dependent children		8 100	8 100	8 100	0
	Deduction for social security contributions and income taxes					
	Work-related expenses					
	Other					
		Total	28 800	28 800	28 800	20 700
3.	**Tax credits or cash transfers included in taxable income**		0	0	0	0
4.	**Central government taxable income (1 - 2 + 3)**		23 743	41 082	58 947	49 182
5.	**Central government income tax liability (exclusive of tax credits)**		2 634	5 235	7 914	6 450
6.	**Tax credits**					
	Basic credit		0	0	0	0
	Married or head of family					
	Children		2 000	2 000	2 000	0
	Other					
		Total	2 000	2 000	2 000	0
7.	**Central government income tax finally paid (5-6)**		634	3 235	5 914	6 450
8.	**State and local taxes**		2 757	3 910	5 098	4 278
9.	**Employees' compulsory social security contributions**					
	Gross earnings		4 020	5 346	6 713	5 346
	Taxable income					
		Total	4 020	5 346	6 713	5 346
10.	**Total payments to general government (7 + 8 + 9)**		7 410	12 490	17 725	16 074
11.	**Cash transfers from general government**					
	For head of family					
	For two children		0	0	0	0
		Total	0	0	0	0
12.	**Take-home pay (1-10+11)**		45 133	57 392	70 022	53 808
13.	**Employer's compulsory social security contributions**		4 413	6 134	7 500	6 134
14.	**Average rates**					
	Income tax		6.5%	10.2%	12.5%	15.4%
	Employees' social security contributions		7.7%	7.7%	7.7%	7.7%
	Total payments less cash transfers		14.1%	17.9%	20.2%	23.0%
	Total tax wedge including employer's social security contributions		20.8%	24.5%	26.5%	29.2%
15.	**Marginal rates**					
	Total payments less cash transfers: Principal earner		29.3%	29.3%	29.3%	29.3%
	Total payments less cash transfers: Spouse		29.3%	29.3%	29.3%	29.3%
	Total tax wedge: Principal earner		34.3%	34.3%	34.3%	34.3%
	Total tax wedge: Spouse		35.7%	34.3%	34.3%	34.3%

The national currency is the dollar (USD). In 2016, the average worker earned USD 52 543 (Secretariat estimate).

1. Personal income tax system

1.1. *Central/federal government income taxes*

1.1.1. *Tax unit*

Families are generally taxed in one of three ways:

- As married couples filing jointly on the combined income of both spouses;
- As married individuals filing separately and reporting actual income of each spouse; or
- As heads of households (only unmarried or separated individuals with dependents).

All others, including dependent children with sufficient income, file as single individuals.

1.1.2. *Tax allowances and tax credits*

1.1.2.1. Standard reliefs

- *Basic reliefs*: In 2016 a married couple filing a joint tax return is entitled to a standard deduction of USD 12 600. The standard deduction is USD 9 300 for heads of households and USD 6 300 for single individuals. This relief is indexed for inflation. More liberal standard deductions are available for taxpayers who are age 65 or older and taxpayers who are blind. Special rules apply to children who have sufficient income to pay tax and are also claimed as dependents by their parents.
- In addition to the standard deduction, in 2016 a USD 4 050 *personal exemption* is given to every taxpayer (including both husband and wife filing a joint return). The personal exemption is indexed annually for inflation. In 2016, there is a phase out for personal exemptions.
- Personal exemption phase out: Personal exemptions are phased out in 50 steps for taxpayers with incomes in excess of certain amounts. All of a taxpayer's exemptions are phased out simultaneously. For each USD 2 500 or fraction thereof by which income exceeds the beginning of the phase out range, personal exemptions are phased down by two percentage points.

Filing status	Beginning of phase out range (USD)
Single	259 400
Joint return	311 300
Head of household	285 350

- *Standard marital status reliefs*: Married couples generally benefit from a more favourable schedule of tax rates for joint returns of spouses (see Section 1.1.3). There are no other general tax reliefs for marriage.

- *Relief for children*: For each child and other person claimed as a dependent on a taxpayer's return, the taxpayer is entitled to a personal exemption of USD 4 050 in 2016. Low income workers with dependents are allowed a refundable (non-wastable) earned income credit. For taxpayers with one child, the credit is 34% of up to USD 9 920 of earned income in 2016. The credit phases down when income exceeds USD 18 190 (23 740 for married taxpayers) and phases out when it reaches USD 39 296 (44 846 for married taxpayers). The earned income threshold and the phase-out threshold are indexed for inflation. For taxpayers with two children, the credit is 40% of up to USD 13 930 of earned income in 2016. The credit phases down when income exceeds USD 18 190 (23 740 for married taxpayers) and phases out when it reaches USD 44 648 (50 198 for married taxpayers). For taxpayers with three or more children the credit is 45% of up to USD 13 930 of earned income. The credit phases down when income exceeds USD 18 190 (23 740 for married taxpayers) and phases out when it reaches USD 47 955 (53 505 for married taxpayers).
- Since 1998, taxpayers are permitted a tax credit for each qualifying child under the age of 17. In 2016 the maximum credit is USD 1 000. The maximum credit is reduced for taxpayers with income in excess of certain thresholds. The credit is reduced by USD 50 for each USD 1 000 of income in excess of USD 110 000 for married taxpayers (USD 75 000 for single and head of household taxpayers). These threshold amounts are not indexed for inflation. The child credit is refundable (non-wastable) to the extent of 15% of earned income in excess of USD 3 000. A taxpayer with three or more qualifying children may be allowed a supplemental refundable (non-wastable) child credit, subject to certain restrictions. The refundable credit is the excess of the taxpayer's share of social security (including Medicare) taxes over his earned income tax credit for the year not used to offset income tax liability.
- *Relief for low income workers without children*: In 1994 and thereafter, low income workers without children are eligible for the earned income credit. In 2016 low income workers without children are permitted a non-wastable earned income credit of 7.65% of up to USD 6 610 of earned income. The credit phases down when income exceeds USD 8 270 (13 820 for married taxpayers) and phases out when income reaches USD 14 880 (20 430 for married taxpayers). This credit is available for taxpayers at least 25 years old and under 65 years old.
- *Relief for social security and other taxes*. In 2016, the withholding rate for Social Security taxes for employees is 6.2%. The earned income credits described above are sometimes considered an offset to social security contributions made by eligible employees. Furthermore, only a portion of social security benefits are subject to tax.

1.1.2.2. Main non-standard reliefs applicable to an AW

- The basic non-standard relief is the deduction of certain expenses to the extent that, when itemised, they exceed in aggregate the standard deduction. For the purposes of this Report, it is assumed that workers claim the standard deduction. The principal itemised deductions claimed by individuals where the standard deduction is not being claimed are:
- *Medical and dental expenses that exceed* 10% of income (7.5% for taxpayers age 65 and over);
- State and local income taxes, real property taxes, and personal property taxes. Home mortgage interest;

- Investment interest expense up to investment income with an indefinite carry forward of disallowed investment interest expense;
- Contributions to qualified charitable organisations (including religious and educational institutions);
- *Casualty and theft losses* to the extent that each loss exceeds USD 100 and that all such losses combined exceed 10% of income; and
- Miscellaneous expenses such as non-reimbursed employee business expenses (union dues, work shoes, etc.), investment expenses, tax return preparation fees and educational expenses required by employment, to the extent that, in aggregate; they exceed 2% of income.
- In 2013, the most recent year for which such statistics are available, the 42% of taxpayers with income between USD 50 000 and USD 75 000 (the AW range) who itemised their deductions claimed average deductions as follows: medical expenses, USD 9 334; taxes paid, USD 5 472; charitable contributions, USD 2 863; interest expense, USD 7 327.
- *Contributions to pension and life insurance plans.* No relief is provided for employee contributions to employer sponsored pension plans or for life insurance premiums. However, tax relief is provided for certain retirement savings.

1.1.3. *Tax schedule*

Federal income tax rates

Taxable income bracket (USD)[1]			Marginal tax rate (%)
Single individual	Joint return of married couple	Head of household	
0 to 9 275	0 to 18 550	0 to 13 250	10
9 276 to 37 650	18 551 to 75 300	13 251 to 50 400	15
37 651 to 91 150	75 301 to 151 900	50 401 to 130 150	25
91 151 to 190 150	151 901 to 231 450	131 151 to 210 800	28
190 151 to 413 350	231 451 to 413 350	210 801 to 41 350	33
413 351 to 415 050	413 351 to 466 950	413 351 to 441 000	35
415 051 and over	466 951 and over	441 001 and over	39.6

1. The taxable income brackets are indexed for inflation.

There is a 3.8% tax on certain net investment income of individuals if their income exceeds USD 200 000 (USD 250 000 for joint returns). Net investment income includes interest, dividends, capital gains, rental and royalty income, and income from businesses trading financial instruments.

1.2. *State and local income taxes*

1.2.1. *General description of the system*

The District of Columbia and 41 of the 50 States impose some form of individual income tax. In addition, some local governments (cities and counties) impose an individual income tax, although this is not generally the case. State individual income tax structures are usually related to the federal tax structure by the use of similar definitions of taxable income, with some appropriate adjustments. This linkage is not a legal requirement but a practical convention that functions for the convenience of the taxpayer who must fill out both federal and State income tax returns.

New Hampshire and Tennessee tax only interest and dividend income received by individuals.

The AW calculations assume that the average worker lives in Detroit, Michigan. The state of Michigan permits a personal exemption of USD 4 000 for the taxpayer, the taxpayer's spouse and each child, and taxes income at the rate of 4.25%. Michigan allows taxpayers who are eligible to claim the federal earned income tax credit to claim a Michigan earned income tax credit. The Michigan earned income tax credit is a refundable (non-wastable) credit equal to 6% of the federal earned income tax credit.

The city of Detroit permits a personal exemption of USD 600 and taxes income at the rate of 2.4%.

2. Compulsory social security contributions to schemes operated within the government sector

2.1. Employees' contributions

2.1.1. Pensions

In 2015, the rate for employee contributions is 7.65% (6.2% for old age, survivors, and disability insurance, and 1.45% for old age hospital insurance). The 6.2% rate applies to earnings up to USD 118 500. Beginning in 1994, there is no limit on the amount of earnings subject to the 1.45% rate. There is an additional 0.9% tax on employee wages and salaries that exceed USD 200 000 (USD 250 000 for joint returns) as the additional hospital insurance tax on high-income taxpayers. The additional tax on wages and salaries is subject to withholding (but without regard to the earnings of the spouse) when wages from a particular job exceed USD 200 000 per year. These thresholds are not indexed for inflation.

There is no distinction by marital status or sex.

2.1.2. Other

No compulsory employee contributions exist.

2.2. Employers' contributions

2.2.1. Pensions

The rate for employers' contributions is 6.2% on earnings up to USD 118 500 and 1.45% of all earnings (without limit).

2.2.2. Unemployment

Employers are required by the federal government to pay unemployment tax of 6% on earnings up to USD 7 000. Taxes are also paid to various state-sponsored unemployment plans which may generally be credited against the required federal percentage. In 2015 the average unemployment insurance tax rate in Michigan was 3.94% of the first USD 9 500 of wages. Effective the third quarter of 2015, the taxable wage base decreased to USD 9 000 for most employers. The model considers that the Federal government allows employers to take a credit for state unemployment taxes of up to 5.4%, resulting in a net Federal tax of 0.6% on earnings up to USD 7 000.

3. Universal cash transfers

3.1. Transfers related to marital status

None.

3.2. *Transfers for dependent children*

No general cash transfers exist, although low-income mothers qualifying for categorical welfare grants may receive cash transfers.

4. Principal changes since 2011

None.

5. Memorandum items

5.1. *Identification of an AW at the wage calculation*

- The AW is identified from monthly data compiled from establishment questionnaires covering more than 40 million non-agricultural full- and part-time workers. Beginning in March 2006, data on average weekly hours and average hourly earnings cover all employees rather than solely production or non-supervisory workers. To obtain average annual wages, the product of average weekly hours (including overtime) and average hourly earnings (including overtime) is multiplied by 52 and is adjusted to reflect a full-time equivalent worker. The AW wage is estimated to be USD 51 509 for 2015.

5.2. *Employer contributions to private social security arrangements*

Employers commonly contribute to private pension plans, health insurance and life insurance. Data for these contributions are available only on a total workforce basis. It is not possible to state with accuracy the levels applicable to the AW. The following are estimates for 2015 for employees in private industry:

	Pension	Health	Life
% of workers covered	49	55	56
USD employer portion per covered employee	n.a.	7 844 (family) 3 658 (single)	n.a.

2016 parameter values

Average earnings/yr	Ave_earn	52 543	Secretariat estimate			
Standard deductions	Married_al	12 600				
	hh_al	9 300				
	single_al	6 300				
Personal exemption	pers_ex	4 000				
Dependency exemption	dep_ex	4 000				
Personal exemption reduction	ex_dedn_rate	0.02				
unit of earnings	ex_dedn_unit	2 500				
threshold single (no children)	ex_thrsh_s	259 400				
threshold single (with children)	ex_thrsh_hh	285 350				
threshold joint	ex_thrsh_m	311 300				
Federal tax schedules	Fed_sch_s	0.1	9 275			
		0.15	37 650			
Single individuals		0.25	91 150			
		0.28	1 960 150			
		0.33	413 350			
		0.35	415 050			
		0.396				
Married filing jointly	Fed_sch_m	0.1	18 550			
		0.15	75 300			
		0.25	151 900			
		0.28	231 450			
		0.33	413 350			
		0.35	466 950			
		0.396				
Head of household	Fed_sch_h	0.1	13 250			
		0.15	50 400			
		0.25	130 150			
		0.28	210 800			
		0.33	413 350			
		0.35	441 000			
		0.396				
Earned income credit	EIC_sch	rate	income limit	threshold	thresh-married	phase-out
	no children	0.0765	6 610	8 270	13 820	0.0765
	1 child	0.34	9 920	18 190	23 740	0.1598
	2 children	0.4	13 930	18 190	23 740	0.2106
	3 or more children	0.45	13 930	18 190	23 740	0.2106
Child credit	chcrd_max	1 000				
	chcrd_rdn	50				
	chcrd_thrsh_m	110 000				
	chcrd_thrsh_oth	75 000				
	chcrd_ref_perct	0.15				
	chcrd_ref_thresh	3 000				
Detroit	Detroit_ex	600				
	Detroit_rate	0.024				
Michigan	Mich_ex	3 950				
	Mich_ex_child	0				
	Mich_rate	0.0425				
Michigan's earned income tax credit	Mich_EIC_rate	0.06				
credit schedule on city tax	Mich_cr_sch	0				
		0				
		0				
maximum	Mich_cr_max	0				
Pension contributions	pens_rate_er	0.062				
	pens_rate_ee	0.062				
	hosp_rate	0.0145				

2016 parameter values

	add_hosp_rate	0.009
Ceiling for employers and employees	pens_ceil	118 500
	add_hosp_thresh_m	250 000
	add_hosp_thresh_oth	200 000
Unemployment insurance tax	Unemp_rate	0.006
	Unemp_dedn_rate	0.054
	Unemp_max	7 000
Michigan unemploy insur	Mich_unemp_rate	0.0391
	Mich_unemp_max	9 000

2016 tax equations

The equations for the US system in 2016 are mostly calculated on a family basis. There is a special function EIC which is used to calculate the earned income credit. Variable names are defined in the table of parameters above, within the equations table, or are the standard variables "married" and "children". A reference to a variable with the affix "_total" indicates the sum of the relevant variable values for the principal and spouse. And the affixes "_princ" and "_spouse" indicate the value for the principal and spouse, respectively. Equations for a single person are as shown for the principal, with "_spouse" values taken as 0.

	Line in country table and intermediate steps	Variable name	Range	Equation
1.	Earnings	earn		
2.	Allowances:	tax_al	J	IF(Married, Married_al, IF(Children=0, single_al, hh_al)) + +((1+Married)*pers_ex+ Children*dep_ex)-(ROUNDUP(Positive(earn_total-IF(Married,ex_thrsh_m,IF (Children>0,ex_thrsh_hh,ex_thrsh_s)))/ex_dedn_unit,0)*ex_dedn_rate*((1+ Married)*pers_ex+Children*dep_ex))
3.	Credits in taxable income	taxbl_cr	J	0
4.	CG taxable income	tax_inc	J	positive(earn-tax_al+taxbl_cr)
5.	CG tax before credits	CG_tax_excl	J	Tax(tax_inc, IF(Married, Fed_sch_m, IF(Children, Fed_sch_h, Fed_sch_s)))
6.	6. Tax credits :	EIC	J	EIC(Children, earn_total, EIC_sch)
		ch_crd_max	J	Children*Positive((chcrd_max-chcrd_rdn*Positive(TRUNC(earn,-3)-IF(Married>0, chcrd_thrsh_m, chcrd_thrsh_oth))/1000))
		ch_crd_tax	J	IF(ch_crd_tax>0, MIN(ch_crd_max, CG_tax_excl), 0)
		ch_crd_ref		IF(ch_crd_tax<ch_crd_max, MIN(ch_crd_max-ch_crd_tax, MAX(chcrd_ref_perct* (earn-chcrd_ref_thresh), 0)), 0)
		tax_cr	J	EIC+ch_crd_tax+ch_crd_ref
7.	CG tax	CG_tax	J	CG_tax_excl-tax_cr
8.	State and local taxes	local_tax	J	Detroit_rate* Positive(earn_total-Detroit_ex*(1+Married+Children))+ Mich_rate* Positive(earn_total - Mich_ex*(1+Married+Children) - Mich_ex_child*Children) - MIN(Mich_cr_max, Tax(AJ7, Mich_cr_sch)) -Mich_EIC_rate*EIC
9.	Employees' soc security	SSC	B	pens_rate_ee*MIN(earn, pens_ceil)+hosp_rate*earn+add_hosp_rate*Positive (earn-IF(Married,add_hosp_thresh_m,add_hosp_thresh_oth))
11.	Cash transfers	Cash_tran	J	
13.	Employer's soc security	SSC_empr	B	pens_rate_er*MIN(earn, pens_ceil)+hosp_rate*earn+MIN(earn,Unemp_max)* Unemp_rate +MIN(earn,Mich_unemp_max)*Mich_unemp_rate
	Memorandum item: non-wastable tax credits			
	tax expenditure component	taxexp		(rate_rd_crd+EIC)-transfer
	cash transfer component	transfer		IF(CG_tax<0, -CG_tax, 0)

Key to range of equation B calculated separately for both principal earner and spouse P calculated for principal only (value taken as 0 for spouse calculation) J calculated once only on a joint basis

© OECD 2017

ANNEX

Methodology and limitations

Methodology

Introduction

The personal circumstances of taxpayers vary greatly. This Report therefore adopts a specific methodology to produce comparative statistics covering taxes, benefits and labour costs across OECD member countries.[1] The framework of the methodology is as follows:

- The Report focuses on eight different family types which vary by household composition and level of earnings.
- Each household contains a full-time adult employee working in one of a broad range of industry sectors of each OECD economy. Some of the households also have a spouse working less than full-time.
- The annual income from employment is assumed to be equal to a given fraction of the average gross wage earnings of these workers.
- Additional assumptions are also made regarding other relevant personal circumstances of these wage earners in order to calculate their tax/benefit position.

The guidelines described in the following paragraphs form the basis for the calculations shown in Chapter 1 and Parts I, II and III. Table A.1 sets out the terminology that is used. Where a country has had to depart from the guidelines, this is noted in the text and/or in the country chapters contained in Part III of the Report. The number of taxpayers with the defined characteristics and the wage level of the average workers differ between OECD economies.

Taxpayer characteristics

The eight household types identified in the Report are set out in Table A.2. Any children in the household are assumed to be aged between six and eleven inclusive.

The family is assumed to have no income source other than from employment and cash benefits.

The range of industries covered

The standard assumption for calculating average wage earnings is based on Sectors B-N of the *International Standard Industrial Classification of All Economic Activities* (ISIC Revision 4, United Nations)[2] (see Table A.3). Many countries (for more detailed country information, see Table A.6) have now adopted this approach

Table A.1. **Terminology**

General terms	
Average worker (AW)	An adult full-time worker in the industry sectors covered whose wage earnings represent the average for workers.
Single persons	Unmarried men and women.
Couple with two children	Married couple with two dependent children between six to eleven years of age inclusive.
Labour costs	The sum of gross wage earnings, employers' social security contributions and payroll taxes.
Net take-home pay	Gross wage earnings less the sum of personal income tax and employee social security contributions plus cash transfers received from general government.
Personal average tax rate (tax burden)	The sum of personal income tax and employee social security contributions expressed as a percentage of gross wage earnings.
Tax wedge	The sum of personal income tax, employee and employer social security contributions plus any payroll tax less cash transfers expressed as a percentage of labour costs.
Elasticity of income after tax	Percentage change in 'after-tax' income following an increase in one currency unit of income before tax (defined more precisely as one minus a marginal tax rate divided by one minus a corresponding average tax rate).
	Terms used under the income tax
Tax reliefs	A generic term to cover all the means of giving favourable income tax treatment to potential taxpayers.
Tax allowances	Amounts deducted from gross earnings to arrive at taxable income.
Tax credits	Amounts which a taxpayer may subtract from his tax liability. They are described as payable if they can exceed tax liability (sometimes the terms 'refundable' and 'non-wastable' are used).
Standard tax reliefs	Reliefs unrelated to the actual expenses incurred by taxpayers and automatically available to all taxpayers who satisfy the eligibility rules specified in the legislation are counted as standard reliefs. These also include deductions for compulsory social security contributions.
Basic relief	Any standard tax relief available irrespective of marital or family status.
Marriage allowance	Additional tax relief given to married couples. (In some countries, this is not distinguished from the basic relief which may be doubled on marriage).
Non-standard tax reliefs	Reliefs wholly determined by reference to actual expenses incurred.
Average rate of income tax	Amount of income tax payable after accounting for any reliefs calculated on the basis of the tax provisions covered in this Report, divided by gross wage earnings.
Schedule rate	The rate which appears in the schedule of the income tax and in the schedule of social security contributions.
	Terms used under cash transfers
Cash transfers	Cash payments made by general government (agencies) paid to families usually in respect of dependent children.

StatLink http://dx.doi.org/10.1787/888933461025

Table A.2. **Characteristics of taxpayers**

Marital status	Children	Principal earner	Secondary earner
Single individual	No children	67% of average earnings	
Single individual	No children	100% of average earnings	
Single individual	No children	167% of average earnings	
Single individual	2 children	67% of average earnings	
Married couple	2 children	100% of average earnings	
Married couple	2 children	100% of average earnings	33% of average earnings
Married couple	2 children	100% of average earnings	67% of average earnings
Married couple	No children	100% of average earnings	33% of average earnings

StatLink http://dx.doi.org/10.1787/888933461031

This approach broadly corresponds to the previous calculation based on sectors C-K incl. defined in the *International Standard Industrial Classification of All Economic Activities* (ISIC Revision 3.1, United Nations) which was adopted in the 2005 edition of *Taxing Wages*. The reasons for moving to a broadened average wage definition were set out in the Special Feature of *Taxing Wages* 2003-04.

Table A.3. **International Standard Industrial Classification of All Economic Activities**

	Revision 3.1 (ISIC Rev. 3.1)
A	Agriculture, hunting and forestry
B	Fishing
C	Mining and quarrying
D	Manufacturing
E	Electricity, gas and water supply
F	Construction
G	Wholesale and retail trade; repair of motor vehicles, motorcycles and personal and household goods
H	Hotels and restaurants
I	Transport, storage and communications
J	Financial intermediation
K	Real estate, renting and business activities
L	Public administration and defence; compulsory social security
M	Education
N	Health and social work
O	Other community, social and personal service activities
P	Activities of private households as employers and undifferentiated production activities of private households
Q	Extraterritorial organisations and bodies
	Revision 4 (ISIC Rev.4)
A	Agriculture, forestry and fishing
B	Mining and quarrying
C	Manufacturing
D	Electricity, gas, steam and air conditioning supply
E	Water supply; sewerage, waste management and remediation activities
F	Construction
G	Wholesale and retail trade; repair of motor vehicles and motorcycles
H	Transportation and storage
I	Accommodation and food service activities
J	Information and communication
K	Financial and insurance activities
L	Real estate activities
M	Professional, scientific and technical activities
N	Administrative and support service activities
O	Public administration and defence; compulsory social security
P	Education
Q	Human health and social work activities
R	Arts, entertainment and recreation
S	Other service activities
T	Activities of households as employers; undifferentiated goods- and services-producing activities of households for own use
U	Activities of extraterritorial organizations and bodies

StatLink http://dx.doi.org/10.1787/888933461045

Defining gross wage earnings

This section sets out the assumptions underlying the calculation of the average earnings figures for "the average worker". The gross wage earnings data have been established using statistical data and the methodologies for calculating the earnings data in each country are set out in Table A.4. Further information on the calculation of the earnings figures is provided in the country chapters in Part III. The sources of the statistical data for each country are set out in Table A.5.

The main assumptions are as follows:

- The data relate to the average earnings in the relevant industry sectors for the country as a whole.

Table A.4. Method used to calculate average earnings

	Items included and exluded from the earnings base					Types of worker included and excluded in the average wage measure			Basic method of calculation used	Income tax year ends	Period to which the earnings calculation refers
	Sickness [1]	Vacations	Overtime	Recurring cash payments	Fringe Benefits	Supervisory workers	Managerial workers	part-time workers			
Australia	Inc	Inc	Inc	Inc	Exc	Inc	Inc	Exc	Average weekly earnings x 52	30th June	Fiscal year
Austria	Exc	Inc	Inc	Inc	Taxable value Inc	Inc	Inc	Exc	Average annual earnings	31st December	Calendar year
Belgium	Exc	Inc	Inc	Inc	Exc	Inc	Inc	Exc	Monthly earnings in October x 12 (plus recurring bonuses)	31st December	Calendar year
Canada	Exc	Inc	Inc	Inc	Exc	Inc	Inc	Inc [6]	Average weekly hours x average hourly earnings x 52	31st December	Calendar year
Chile	Exc	Inc	Inc	Inc	Exc	Inc	Inc	Inc	Hourly earnings x hours worked	31st December	Calendar year
Czech Republic	Exc	Inc	Inc	Inc	Exc	Inc	Inc	Inc [6]	Average monthly earnings x 12	31st December	Calendar year
Denmark	Exc	Inc	Exc	Inc	Exc	Inc	Inc	Inc [6]	Hourly earnings x hours worked	31st December	Calendar year
Estonia	Inc	Inc	Inc	Inc	Exc	Inc	Inc	Inc	Average earnings	31st December	Calendar year
Finland	Exc	Inc	Inc	Inc	Exc	Inc	Inc [5]	Exc	Hourly wages x usual working time or (monthly earnings x months) + vacation payments+ end of year bonuses	31st December	Calendar year
France	Exc	Inc	Inc	Inc	Exc	Inc	Inc	Exc	Annual earnings	31st December	Calendar year
Germany	Exc	Inc	Inc	Inc	Exc	Inc	Inc	Exc	Annual earnings	31st December	Calendar year
Greece	Exc	Inc	Inc	Inc [2]	Inc	Inc	Inc	Exc	Hourly earnings x hours worked	31st December	Calendar year
Hungary	Exc	Inc	Inc	Inc	Exc	Inc	Inc [5]	Exc	Average monthly earnings x 12	31st December	Calendar year
Iceland	Exc	Inc	Inc	Inc	Exc	Inc	Inc	Exc	Hourly earnings x hours worked x 12	31st December	Calendar year
Ireland	Exc	Inc	Inc	Inc	Exc	Exc	Exc	Inc	Average weekly earnings in each quarter for four quarters/4*52	31st December	Calendar year
Israel	Exc	Inc	Inc	Inc	Exc	Inc	Inc	Exc	Average earnings	31st December	Calendar year
Italy	Exc[3]	Inc	Inc	Inc	Exc [4]	Inc	Inc	Inc [6]	Average monthly earnings x 12	31st December	Calendar year
Japan	Exc	Inc	Inc	Inc	Exc	Inc	Inc	Exc	Monthly earnings in June x 12	31st December	Calendar year
Korea	Exc	Inc	Inc	Inc	Exc	Inc	Inc	Exc	Average monthly earnings x 12	31st December	Calendar year
Latvia	Inc	Inc	Inc	Inc	Exc	Inc	Inc	Exc	Average monthly earnings x 12	31st December	Calendar year
Luxembourg	Exc	Inc	Inc	Inc	Exc	Inc	Inc	Exc	Aggregate annual earnings divided by annual average number of full-time employees. Any parts of earnings that exceed the upper social contribution limit (7 times the minimum wage) are not recorded.	31st December	Calendar year
Mexico	Exc	Inc	Exc	Inc	Exc	Inc	Inc	Exc	Average monthly earnings x 12	31st December	Calendar year
Netherlands	Exc	Inc	Exc	Inc	Exc	Inc	Inc	Exc	Annual gross earnings	31st December	Calendar year
New Zealand	Exc	Inc	Inc	Inc	Exc	Inc	Inc [5]	Inc [6]	Average weekly earnings in each quarter x 13	31st March	Tax year
Norway	Exc	Exc	Inc	Inc	Exc	Inc	Inc	Inc [6]	Annual wages + estimated overtime	31st December	Calendar year
Poland	Inc	Inc	Inc	Inc	Exc	Inc	Inc	Inc [6]	Average monthly earnings x 12	31st December	Calendar year
Portugal	Exc	Inc	Inc	Inc	Inc	Inc	Inc	Exc	Weighted monthly average x 12	31st December	Calendar year

Table A.4. **Method used to calculate average earnings** *(cont.)*

	Items included and exluded from the earnings base					Types of worker included and excluded in the average wage measure			Basic method of calculation used	Income tax year ends	Period to which the earnings calculation refers
	Sickness [1]	Vacations	Overtime	Recurring cash payments	Fringe Benefits	Supervisory workers	Managerial workers	part-time workers			
Slovak Republic	Exc	Inc	Inc	Inc	Inc	Inc	Inc	Inc	Average monthly earnings x 12	31st December	Calendar year
Slovenia	Inc	Inc	Inc	Inc	Exc	Inc	Inc	Inc	Average monthly earnings * 12	31st December	Calendar year
Spain	Exc	Inc	Inc	Inc	Exc	Inc	Inc	Exc	Weighted monthly average x 12	31st December	Calendar year
Sweden	Exc	Inc	Inc	Inc	Actual value Inc	Inc	Inc	Inc [6]	Average hourly earnings in September x hours worked; and monthly earnings in September * 12	31st December	Calendar year
Switzerland	Exc	Inc	Inc	Inc	Exc	Inc	Inc	Inc [6]	Monthly earnings x 12	31st December	Calendar year
Turkey	Exc	Inc	Inc	Inc	Actual value inc	Exc	Exc	Inc	Average annual earnings	31st December	Calendar year
United Kingdom	Exc	Inc	Inc	Inc	Exc	Inc	Inc	Exc	Average gross annual earnings	5th April	Fiscal year
United States	Exc	Inc	Inc	Inc [2]	Exc	Inc	Inc	Inc [6]	Average weekly earnings x 52	31st December	Calendar year

Note: Exc = Excluded, Inc = Included, '-' = information not available.

1. Usually includes compensation paid by employer whether paid on behalf of the government or as part of a private sickness scheme.
2. Excludes profit sharing bonuses in Greece and the United States plus end of year bonuses in the United States.
3. Sickness payments are only included to the extent that they are paid by the employer. For manual workers, this is only the case during the first three days of sick leave, while payments for the fourth day onwards are made by INPS.
4. Partly: the (small) taxable part of fringe benefits is included.
5. Except for top management (Finland); except if income from profits exceeds 50% of total income (Hungary); except for proprietors (New Zealand).
6. Part-time wages are converted to full-time equivalents before calculating the average wage measure.

StatLink http://dx.doi.org/10.1787/888933461051

Table A.5. Source of earnings data, 2016

Country	Type of sample	Source
Australia	Quarterly survey of firms resulting in a representative sample of wage and salary earners in each industry.	Australian Bureau of Statistics "Average Weekly Earnings, Australia" and "Labour Force, Australia".
Austria	Annual Wage Tax Statistics.	"Lohnsteuerstatistik".
Belgium	Data collected or estimated on the basis of an annual establishment survey and social insurance registers of employees.	Statistics Division of the Ministry of Economy (Federal Public Service, Economy, SMEs, Self-employed and Energy). Same source as for Eurostat "Annual gross earnings" data.
Canada	Monthly survey of all firms.	Statistics Canada, "Survey of Employment Payrolls and Hours".
Chile	Monthly sample of businesse with 10+ employees.	National Statistics Institute of Chile (INE).
Czech Republic	Employer survey data.	National Statistical Office.
Denmark	Danish Employers Confederation survey of earnings.	Annual Report Danish Employers Confederation (Dansk Arbejds Giverforening).
Estonia	-	Statistics Estonia/Ministry of Finance.
Finland	(1) Finnish Employers Federation survey of hourly and monthly earnings; (2) Survey for unorganized employers "Structure of Earnings Statistics" published by the Central Statistical Office.	"Wages Statistics" published by the Central Statistical Office.
France	Social insurance registers covering all employers.	INSEE, "Déclarations Annuelles des Données Sociales" (DADS).
Germany	Survey carried out by the Federal Statistical Office.	National Statistical Office.
Greece	Survey carried out by National Statistics Service and Social Security Institutions.	National Statistical Service Labour Statistics. Same source as for Eurostat "Annual gross earnings" data.
Hungary	Monthly surveys among enterprises with at least five employees.	Central Statistical Office.
Iceland	Monthly survey of earnings in the private sector market.	Statistics Iceland.
Ireland	Quarterly surveys of industrial employment, earnings and hours worked.	Central Statistics Office.
Israel	-	Central Bureau of Statistics.
Italy	Quarterly indicators of wages in industry and services (OROS).	National Institute of Statistics.
Japan	Basic survey on wage structure of all establishments with more than 10 employees.	Ministry of Health, Labour and Welfare, Annual Report.
Korea	Labour Force Survey at Establishments.	Ministry of Employment and Labour.
Latvia	Average monthly wages and salaries (DSG01)	The Latvian Central Statistical Bureau.
Luxembourg	Monthly aggregated files of Social security services.	National Statistical Office and Social Security Services.
Mexico	Administrative data from the Mexican Social Security Institute (Instituto Mexicano del Seguro Social (IMSS)).	The National Minimum Wage Commission (Comisión Nacional de Salarios Mínimos (CONASAMI)).
Netherlands	Survey "Employment and Wages".	Central Bureau of Statistics, Statline.
New Zealand	The quarterly employment survey is a sample survey of significant business with an employment count of 1 or more.	Statistics New Zealand INFOS.
Norway	Sample of enterprises based on published sector statistics for 3rd quarter – except agriculture, forestry and fishing and private households.	Statistics Norway Wage.
Portugal	April and October survey of earnings carried out by the Ministry of Labour.	Ministry of Labour.
Poland	Estimates for different sectors.	Monthly Statistical Bulletin.
Slovak republic	Quarterly and annual statistical data.	Slovak Statistical Office.
Slovenia	Monthly survey of employees.	Statistical Office of the Republic of Slovenia.
Spain	Quarterly survey of firms.	Instituto Nacional de Estadistica "Encuesta Trimestral de Coste Laboral" (Labour Cost Survey).
Sweden	September survey of Swedish employers.	Statistics Sweden.
Switzerland	Swiss Statistics Office. Personnes actives occupées selon la branche économique.	La vie économique, SECO (Secrétariat d'État à l'économie) table B.8.1, *www.bfs.admin.ch/bfs/portal/fr/index/themen/03/04.html*.
Turkey	Annual Manufacturing Industry Survey.	Turkish Statistical Institute.
United Kingdom	1% sample of PAYE earnings.	Office for National Statistics, Annual Survey of Hours and Earnings (ASHE).
United States	Monthly surveys by Department of Labour on the basis of a questionnaire covering more than 40 million non-agricultural wage and salary-workers.	Employment, Hours, and Earnings from the Current Employment Statistics Survey.

StatLink http://dx.doi.org/10.1787/888933461064

TAXING WAGES 2017 © OECD 2017

- The calculations are based on the earnings of a full-time adult worker (including both manual and non-manual). They relate to the average earnings of all workers in the industry sectors covered. No account is taken of variation between males and females or due to age or region.
- The worker is assumed to be full-time employed during the entire year without breaks for sickness or unemployment. However, several countries are unable to separate and exclude part-time workers from the earnings figures (see Table A.4). Most of them report full-time equivalent wages in these cases. In four countries (Chile, Ireland, Slovak Republic and Turkey), the wages of part-time workers can be neither excluded nor converted into full-time equivalents because of the ways in which the earnings samples are constructed. As a result, average wages reported for these countries will be lower than an average of full-time workers (for example, an OECD Secretariat analysis of available Eurostat earnings data for selected European countries has shown that including part-time workers reduces average earnings by around 10%). Also, in most of the OECD countries where sickness payments are made by the employer, either on behalf of the government or on behalf of private sickness schemes, these amounts are included in the wage calculations. It is unlikely that this has a marked impact on the results since employers usually make these payments during a short period and the amounts usually correspond very closely to normal hourly wages.
- Two of the household types include a second earner at 33% of average earnings. Such individuals are more likely to be working part-time rather than full-time (as shown in the Special Feature of the 2005 edition). However, the Special Feature also showed that the assumption of all employees working full-time does not significantly affect the tax rates calculated in *Taxing Wages*, except in the case of Belgium for married couples where the spouse is earning 33% of the average wage level. This is because any special provisions made for part-time workers tend to be either of minor importance or not applicable for the household types currently presented in *Taxing Wages*.
- The earnings calculation includes all cash remuneration paid to workers in the industries covered taking into account average amounts of overtime, cash supplements (e.g. Christmas bonuses, thirteenth month) and vacation payments typically paid to workers in the covered industry sectors. However, not all countries are able to include overtime pay, vacation payments and cash bonuses according to the definition.
- The earnings figures include supervisory and/or management employees, though some countries are not able to do this. In such countries, the reported averages are lower than would otherwise be the case (for example, an OECD Secretariat analysis of available Eurostat earnings data for selected European countries has shown that excluding this type of workers can reduce average earnings by 10% to 18%).
- Fringe benefits – which include, for example, provision of food, housing or clothing by the employer either free of charge or at below market-price – are, where possible, excluded from the calculation of average earnings. This could affect comparability of tax wedges – as the reliance on fringe benefits may vary between countries and over time. However, the lack of comparability is limited as fringe benefits rarely account for more than 1-2% of labour costs and are normally more common among high-income employees than in the income ranges covered by *Taxing Wages* (33% to 167% of average earnings). Table A.4 shows that some Member countries are not able to exclude fringe benefits from the earnings figures reported and used in *Taxing Wages*. The decision to exclude was been taken because:

- these types of benefits are difficult to evaluate in a consistent way (they may be valued at the actual cost to the employer, their value to the employee or their fair market value).
- in most countries, they are of minimal importance for workers at the average wage level.
- the tax calculations would be significantly more complicated if the tax treatment of fringe benefits were to be incorporated.

- Employers' contributions to private pension, family allowance or health and life insurance schemes are excluded from the calculations, though the amounts involved can be significant. In the United States, for example, these contributions can account for more than 5% of the earnings of employees. The country chapters in Part III indicate of the existence of schemes which may be relevant for an average worker.

Calculating average gross wage earnings

Table A.4 indicates the basic calculation method used in each country while more details are, where relevant, provided in the country chapters in Part III. In principle, countries are recommended to calculate annual earnings by referring to the average of hourly earnings in each week, month or quarter, weighted by the hours worked during each period, and multiplied by the average number of hours worked during the year, assuming that the worker is neither unemployed nor sick and including periods of paid vacation. A similar procedure was recommended to calculate overtime earnings. For countries unable to separate out part-time employees from the data, it is recommended that earnings of part-time employees should if possible be converted into their full-time equivalents.

Statistical data on average gross wage earnings in 2016 are generally not available at present. For most countries, estimates of gross wage earnings of average workers in 2016 were therefore derived by the Secretariat on the basis of a uniform approach: year 2015 earnings levels are multiplied by the country-specific annual percentage change of wages for the whole economy reported in the most recently published edition of the OECD *Economic Outlook*.[3] This transparent procedure is intended to avoid any bias in the results. In some countries, there were varying different approaches;

- The final 2016 average gross wage earnings was used for Australia.
- National estimates were used for the Chile, New Zealand and Turkey as the OECD Economic Outlook does not provide percentages changes in wages for those countries.
- In some countries, average wage earnings were also estimated for prior years – Finland (2015), France (2015), Greece (2015), the Netherlands (2015), Portugal (from 2013 to 2015) and Switzerland (2007, 2009, 2011, 2013 and 2015) as no country information on average wage earnings levels was available for these years in these particular countries.

Seventeen OECD member countries have opted to provide national estimates of the level of gross wage earnings of average workers in 2016. These estimates were not used in the Taxing Wages calculations (except for the countries listed above) because of potential inconsistency with the Secretariat estimates derived for other countries. However they are included in Table A.6 to enable comparisons to be made between the estimates obtained by applying the Secretariat formula and those from national sources. In most cases, the two categories are fairly close.

Table A.7 indicates the exchange rates and purchasing power parities of national currencies for 2016 that are used to calculate comparative earnings figures across countries in the report.

Table A.6. **Estimated gross wage earnings, 2015-16 (in national currency)**

	Average wage 2015	Average wage 2016 (Secret. estimates)	Average wage 2016 (country estimates)	E0100 forecasted rates for 2016[1]
Australia[2]	80 774	81 914	82 114	1.4
Austria	43 911	44 409	44 526	1.1
Belgium	46 479	46 570	46 990	0.2
Canada	50 350	50 997	51 572	1.3
Chile[2]	7 557 360		8 003 491	
Czech Republic	319 162	330 072	326 850	3.4
Denmark	403 600	412 555		2.2
Estonia	13 045	13 640	13 714	4.6
Finland	43 382	43 816		1.0
France	37 648	38 049		1.1
Germany	46 800	47 809		2.2
Greece	20 107	20 074		-0.2
Hungary	3 169 128	3 312 081	3 321 246	4.5
Iceland	7 644 000	8 456 409		10.6
Ireland	34 674	35 592	35 897	2.6
Israel	137 990	142 247	142 130	3.1
Italy	30 654	30 642		0.0
Japan	5 083 906	5 110 601		0.5
Korea	42 908 652	43 857 243	43 931 808	2.2
Latvia	9 588	10 173	10 158	6.1
Luxembourg	55 858	56 197		0.6
Mexico	107 551	112 827	111 825	4.9
Netherlands	50 009	50 853		1.7
New Zealand[2]	56 110		57 649	
Norway	551 198	564 218		2.4
Poland	46 136	47 782		3.6
Portugal	17 298	17 521		1.3
Slovak Republic	10 661	10 918	10 970	2.4
Slovenia	18 092	18 292	18 060	1.1
Spain	26 475	26 710		0.9
Sweden	414 105	423 065	419 976	2.2
Switzerland	86 017	85 536		-0.6
Turkey[2]	31 191		36 806	
United Kingdom	35 947	36 571		1.7
United States	51 509	52 543		2.0

1. Increase of compensation per employee in the total economy (*Economic Outlook No. 100*).
2. The country AW estimate is used instead of the OECD Secretariat's AW estimate in the Taxing Wages calculations.

StatLink http://dx.doi.org/10.1787/888933461075

Coverage of taxes and benefits

The Report is concerned with personal income tax and employee and employer social security contributions payable on wage earnings. In addition, payroll taxes (see section on *Payroll taxes*) are included in the calculation of the total wedge between labour costs to the employer and the corresponding net take-home pay of the employee.

The calculation of the after-tax income includes family benefits paid by general government as cash transfers (see section on *Family cash benefits from general government*). Income tax due on capital income and non-wage labour income, several direct taxes (net wealth tax, corporate income tax) and all indirect taxes are not considered in this Report. However, all central, state and local government income taxes are included in the data.

In this Report, compulsory social security contributions paid to general government are treated as tax revenues. Being compulsory payments to general government they

Table A.7. **Purchasing power parities and exchange rates for 2016**

	Monetary unit	Exchange rates[1]	Purchasing power parities
Australia	AUD	1.35	1.45
Austria	EUR	0.90	0.80
Belgium	EUR	0.90	0.80
Canada	CAD	1.33	1.24
Chile	CLP	676.54	390.10
Czech Republic	CZK	24.44	12.75
Denmark	DKK	6.73	7.20
Estonia	EUR	0.90	0.53
Finland	EUR	0.90	0.90
France	EUR	0.90	0.80
Germany	EUR	0.90	0.77
Greece	EUR	0.90	0.61
Hungary	HUF	281.52	129.24
Iceland	ISK	120.81	143.22
Ireland	EUR	0.90	0.80
Israel	ILS	3.84	3.82
Italy	EUR	0.90	0.73
Japan	JPY	108.80	101.65
Korea	KRW	1 160.59	895.44
Latvia	EUR	0.90	0.50
Luxembourg	EUR	0.90	0.86
Mexico	MXN	18.63	8.60
Netherlands	EUR	0.90	0.80
New Zealand	NZD	1.44	1.45
Norway	NOK	8.40	9.40
Poland	PLN	3.94	1.75
Portugal	EUR	0.90	0.59
Slovak Republic	EUR	0.90	0.48
Slovenia	EUR	0.90	0.58
Spain	EUR	0.90	0.66
Sweden	SEK	8.56	8.92
Switzerland	CHF	0.99	1.22
Turkey	TRL	3.02	1.31
United Kingdom	GBP	0.74	0.69
United States	USD	1.00	1.00

1. Average of 12 months daily rates.

StatLink http://dx.doi.org/10.1787/888933461080

clearly resemble taxes. They may, however, differ from taxes in that the receipt of social security benefits depends upon appropriate contributions having been made, although the size of the benefits is not necessarily related to the amount of the contributions. Countries finance compulsory public social security programmes to a varying degree from general tax and non-tax revenue and earmarked contributions, respectively. Better comparability between countries is obtained by treating social security contributions as taxes, but they are listed under a separate heading so that their amounts can be identified in any analysis.

Calculation of personal income taxes

The method by which income tax payments are calculated is described in the country chapters in Part III. First, the tax allowances applicable to a taxpayer with the characteristics and income level related to gross annual wage earnings of an average worker are determined. Next, the schedule of tax rates is applied and the resulting tax liability is reduced by any relevant tax credits. An important issue arising in the calculation of the personal income tax liability involves determining which tax reliefs should be taken into account. Two broad categories of reliefs may be distinguished:

- *Standard tax reliefs*: reliefs which are unrelated to actual expenditures incurred by the taxpayer and are automatically available to all taxpayers who satisfy the eligibility rules specified in the legislation. Standard tax reliefs are usually fixed amounts or fixed percentages of income and are typically the most important set of reliefs in the determination of the income tax paid by workers. These reliefs are taken into account in the calculations – they include:
  - The *basic relief* which is fixed and is available to all taxpayers or all wage earners, irrespective of their marital or family status;
  - The *standard relief* which is available to taxpayers depending on their *marital status*;
  - The *standard child relief* granted to a family with two children between the ages of six to eleven inclusive;
  - The *standard relief* in respect of *work expenses*, which is usually a fixed amount or fixed percentage of (gross) wage earnings; and,
  - Tax reliefs allowed for *social security contributions* and other (sub-central government) *income taxes* are also considered as standard reliefs since they apply to all wage earners and relate to compulsory payments to general government.[4]
- *Non-standard tax reliefs*: These are reliefs which are wholly determined by reference to actual expenses incurred. They are therefore neither fixed amounts nor fixed percentages of income. Examples of non-standard tax reliefs include reliefs for interest on qualifying loans (e.g. for the purchase of a house), private insurance premiums, contributions to private pension schemes, and charitable donations. These are not taken into account in calculating the tax position of employees.

Standard reliefs are separately identified and their impact on average tax rates is calculated in the results tables shown in the Country chapters. The latter include a brief description of the main non-standard reliefs in most cases.

State and local income taxes

Personal income taxes levied by sub-central levels of government – state, provincial, cantonal or local – are included in the scope of this study. State income taxes exist in Canada, Switzerland and the United States. Since 1997, Spain has an income tax for the Autonomous Regions. Local income taxes are imposed in Belgium, Denmark, Finland, Iceland, Italy, Japan, Korea, Norway, Sweden, Switzerland and the United States. In Belgium, Canada (other than Quebec), Denmark, Iceland, Italy, Korea, Norway and Spain they are calculated as a percentage of taxable income or of the tax paid to central government. In Finland, Japan, Sweden and Switzerland, local government provides different tax reliefs from central government. In the United States, the sub-central levels of government operate a separate system of income taxation under which they have discretion over both the tax base and tax rates. Except for Canada, Spain and Switzerland, the rate schedule of these sub-central taxes consists of a single rate.

When tax rates and/or the tax base of sub-central government income taxes vary within a country, it is sometimes assumed that the average worker lives in a typical area and the income taxes (and benefits) applicable in this area are presented. This is the procedure followed in Canada, Italy, Switzerland and the United States where the tax base and tax rates vary very widely throughout the country. Belgium, Denmark, Finland, Iceland and Sweden have preferred to select the average rate of sub-central government income taxes for the country as a whole. The local rates do not vary in practice in Korea and Norway. Japan and Spain have used the widely prevalent standard schedule.

Social security contributions

Compulsory social security contributions paid by employees and employers to general government or to social security funds under the effective control of government are included in the coverage of this Report. In most countries, contributions are levied on gross earnings and earmarked to provide social security benefits. In Finland, Iceland and the Netherlands, some contributions are levied as a function of taxable income (i.e. gross wage earnings after most/all tax reliefs). Australia, Denmark and New Zealand do not levy social security contributions.

Contributions to social security schemes outside the general government sector are not included in the calculations. However, information on "non-tax compulsory payments" as well as "compulsory payment indicators" is included in the OECD Tax Database, which is accessible at *www.oecd.org/ctp/tax-database.htm.*

Payroll taxes

Payroll taxes have a tax base that is either a proportion of the payroll or a fixed amount per employee. In the OECD *Revenue Statistics,* payroll taxes are reported under heading 3000. Fifteen OECD countries report revenue from payroll taxes: Australia, Austria, Canada, Denmark, France, Hungary, Iceland, Ireland, Israel, Korea, Latvia, Mexico, Poland, Slovenia and Sweden.

Payroll taxes are included in total tax wedges reported in this publication, given that they increase the gap between gross labour costs and net take-home pay in the same way as income tax and social security contributions do. The main difference with the latter is that the payment of payroll taxes does not confer an entitlement to social security benefits. Also, the tax base of payroll taxes may differ from the tax base of employer social security contributions. For example, certain fringe benefits may only be liable to payroll tax. Because this Report presents the standard case, the payroll tax base can be – depending on the relevant legislation – gross wage (excluding fringe benefits and other items of compensation that vary per employee), gross wage plus employer social security contributions, or a fixed amount per employee.

Five of the OECD member countries include payroll taxes in the *Taxing Wages* calculations: Australia, Austria, Hungary, Latvia and Sweden. The other countries reporting payroll tax revenue in *Revenue Statistics* have not included these taxes in the calculations for the present Report for a variety of reasons.

Family cash benefits from general government

Tax reliefs and family cash transfers universally paid in respect of dependent children between the ages of six to eleven inclusive who are attending school are included in the scope of the study. If tax reliefs or cash transfers vary within this age range, the most generous provisions are adopted, except that the case of twins is explicitly disregarded. The implications of this are illustrated below – suppose the child benefit programme of a country is structured as follows:

Age group	Benefits per child
Children 6-8	100 units
Children 9-10	120 units
Children 11-14	150 units

The most favourable outcome arises in the case of 11-year old twins: 300 units. However, as the case of twins is excluded, the best outcome (given that children are between 6 and 11) now becomes 270 units (one child 11 years old, one child 9 or 10 years old). This amount would be included in the country table. Often, the amount in benefits is raised as children grow older. The calculations assume that the children have been born on 1 January so the annual amount received in child benefits may be calculated from the benefit schedule that is in place at the start of the year with any revisions to these amounts during the year being taken into account.

Relevant cash payments are those received from general government. In some cases, the cash benefits include amounts that are paid without consideration to the number of children.

Payable tax credits

Payable (non-wastable) tax credits are tax credits that can exceed tax liability, where the excess, if any, can be paid as a cash transfer to the taxpayer. In principle, these credits can be treated in different ways according to whether they are regarded as tax provisions or cash transfers or a combination of these. The Special Feature in the 2016 edition of *Revenue Statistics* discusses these alternative treatments and the conceptual and practical difficulties that arise in deciding which is the most appropriate approach for the purpose of reporting internationally comparable tax revenue figures. It also provides figures which show the impact of different treatments on tax to GDP ratios.[5]

Based on this review, the Interpretative Guide of the *Revenue Statistics* requires that

- only the portion of a payable tax credit that is claimed to reduce or eliminate a taxpayer's liability (the "tax expenditure" component)[6] should be deducted in the reporting of tax revenues;
- the part of the tax credit that exceeds a taxpayer's tax liability and is paid to the taxpayer (the "cash transfer" component) should be treated as an expenditure item and not deducted in the reporting of tax revenues.

However, additional information is provided in *Revenue Statistics* on aggregate tax expenditure components and aggregate transfer components of payable tax credits to show the effect of alternative treatments.[7]

In *Taxing Wages,* the situation is different as the full amount of the payable tax credit is taken into account in the income tax calculation.

Strict consistency with the *Revenue Statistics* would require that only the tax expenditure component be offset against derived income tax, with the excess (if any) treated as a cash transfer. However, this approach would diminish rather than strengthen the informational content of the derived results in *Taxing Wages*. In particular, limiting tax credit claims to tax expenditure amounts would yield a zero income tax liability and zero average income tax rate where cash refunds are provided. Where tax credits claims are not constrained in this way, negative income tax liabilities and negative average income tax rates would result where cash transfers are provided. Arguably, these negative amounts more clearly convey the taxpayer's position (which is improved relative to the no-tax situation). Also, not including the cash transfer portion of payable tax credits in the 'cash transfers from general government' item of the country tables permits greater transparency of the latter which focuses on "pure" cash transfers only.

However, in order to improve the informational content of country tables as regards payable tax credits, the memorandum item reporting at the bottom of the relevant country tables shows tax expenditure amounts on one line, with a second line showing cash transfer amounts. Where more than one payable tax credit program applies, the figures represent aggregates covering all the programs. Total program costs in each of the household cases considered can be derived by adding the tax expenditure and cash transfer amounts.

The calculation of marginal tax rates

In all except one case, the marginal tax rates are calculated by considering the impact of a small increase in gross earnings on personal income tax, social security contributions and cash benefits. The exception is the case of a non-working spouse where the move from zero to a small positive income is unrepresentative of income changes and therefore of little interest. So, for this case, the marginal rates for the spouse are calculated by considering the impact of an income increase from zero to 33% of the average wage.

Limitations

General limitations

The simple approach of comparing the tax/benefit position for eight model families avoids many of the conceptual and definitional problems involved in more complex international comparisons of tax burdens and transfer programmes. However, a drawback of this methodology is that the earnings of an average worker will usually occupy a different position in the overall income distribution in different economies, although the earnings relate to workers in similar jobs in various OECD Member countries.

Because of the limitations on the taxes and benefits covered in the Report, the data cannot be taken as an indication of the overall impact of the government sector on the welfare of taxpayers and their families. Complete coverage would require studies of the impact of indirect taxes, the treatment of non-wage labour income and other income components under personal income taxes and the effect of other tax allowances and cash benefits. It would also require that consideration be given to the effect on welfare of services provided by the state, either free or below cost, and the incidence of corporate and other direct taxes on earnings and prices. Such a broad coverage is not possible in an international comparison of all OECD countries. The differences between the results shown here and those of a full study of the overall impact on employees of government interventions in the economy would vary from one country to another. They would depend on the relative shares of different kinds of taxes in government revenues and on the scope and nature of government social expenditures.

The Report shows only the formal incidence of taxes on employees and employers. The final, economic incidence of taxes may be quite different, because the tax burden may be shifted from employers onto employees and *vice versa* by market adjustments to gross wages.

The income left at the disposal of a taxpayer may represent different standards of living in various countries because the range of goods and services on which the income is spent and their relative prices differ as between countries. In those countries where the general government sector provides a wide range of goods and services (generous basic old age pension, free health services, public housing, university education, etcetera), the taxpayer may be left with less cash income but may enjoy the same living standards as a taxpayer receiving a higher cash income but living in a country where there are fewer publicly provided goods and services.

As mentioned in Chapter 1 and detailed in the Special Feature of the 2005 edition of *Taxing Wages*, second earners who are earning 33% of the average wage are very likely to be working part-time, although the *Taxing Wages* methodology effectively assumes that they are working full-time. However, this only affects the accuracy of the results in *Taxing Wages* for one family type in Belgium (married couple where a second earner is earning 33% of average wages). Therefore, one should be cautious when interpreting the results for this family type for Belgium. In addition, for all countries with hour-based rules, (see the 2005 Special Feature), caution should be used in applying the results in this Report to other household types.

Some specific limitations on the income tax calculation

The exclusion of non-wage income and the limited number of tax reliefs covered mean that the average rates of income tax in the tables in this publication do not necessarily reflect the actual rates confronting taxpayers at these levels of earnings. Actual rates may be lower than the calculated rates because the latter do not take into account non-standard expense-related reliefs. On the other hand, actual rates may be higher than calculated rates because the latter do not take into account tax on non-wage income received by employees.

The decision not to calculate separately average rates of income tax taking into account the effect of non-standard tax reliefs was taken because:

- In many cases, expense-related reliefs are substitutes for direct cash subsidies. To take into account these reliefs while ignoring any corresponding direct subsidies would distort comparisons of take-home pay plus cash transfers;
- The special tax treatment of certain expenses may be linked to special treatment of any income associated with these expenses (e.g. the tax treatment of social security contributions and pension income) which is beyond the scope of this study;
- A few countries were unable to estimate the value of these reliefs and even those countries which could do so could not limit their estimates to taxpayers with the characteristics assumed in the above part on methodology; and,
- Not all countries could calculate separately the reliefs available to different family-types. Where a split is provided between single individuals and families with children, there are large differences in the value of the reliefs typically received by these two categories of households.

Limitations to time-series comparisons

The calculations of the tax burden on labour income in OECD countries reported in the 2004 and previous editions of *Taxing Wages*, are based on an average earnings measure for manual full-time workers in the manufacturing sector (the "average production worker").

Any analysis of the results over time has to take into account the fact that the earnings data do not necessarily relate to the same taxpayer throughout the period. The average earnings are calculated for each year. As such, the results do not reflect the changing earnings and tax position of particular individuals over time but rather to the position of workers earning a wage equal to average earnings in the covered industry sectors in each particular year. This, in turn, may mean that the earnings levels referred to may be at different points in the income distribution over the period covered and changes in tax rates may be influenced by these trends.

There have been changing definitions of the average worker over time. From the 2005 edition, *Taxing Wages* has reported tax calculations under a broadened average worker definition that includes all full-time employees covering industry sectors C-K (reference to ISIC Rev.3.1). The implications of adopting this new definition for time-series comparisons are discussed in the 2005 edition of Taxing Wages. As of the 2010 edition of the Taxing Wages Report, many countries have started reporting average wage earnings for full-time employees covering industry sectors B-N of the ISIC Rev.4 industry classification (which broadly corresponds to sectors C-K in ISIC Rev.3.1).

A Note on the tax equations

Each country chapter contains a section describing in a standard format the equations under-pinning the calculations required to derive the amounts of income tax, social security contributions and cash transfers. These algorithms represent in algebraic form the legal provisions described in the chapter and are consistent with the figures shown in the country and comparative tables. This section describes the conventions used in the definition of the equations and how they could be used by those wishing to implement the equations for their own research.

The earlier sections of the country chapters describe how the tax and other systems work and present the values of the parameters of those systems such as the levels of allowances and credits, and the schedule of tax rates.

In the first part of the equations section is a table showing a brief description of each parameter (such as "Basic tax credit"), the name of the parameter as used in the algebraic equation ("Basic_cred") and the actual value for the relevant year (such as "1098"). Where there is a table of values – for example a schedule of tax rates and the associated thresholds of taxable income – a name is given to the entire table (for example "tax_sch"). These variable names are those used in the equations.

After each table of parameters is the table of equations. The four columns contain information as follows:

- The first two columns give a description and a variable name for the result of the equation on that row of the table. These always include the thirteen main financial value entries in the country tables. Additional rows define any intermediate values which are calculated either to show the detail included in the tables (such as the subdivision of total tax allowances into the different categories) or values which make the calculation clearer.
- The third column shows the range of the calculation in that row. This is necessary to allow for the different way that tax may be calculated for married couples. The options are:
  - **B** The calculation is carried out separately for both the principal earner and the spouse using their individual levels of earnings. This applies in the case of independent income tax and usually also in respect of social security contributions.
  - **P** The calculation applies for the principal earner only. An example is where the principal earner can use any of the basic tax allowance of the spouse which cannot be set against the income of the spouse.

- **S** The calculation applies for the lower earning spouse only.
- **J** The calculation is carried out only once on the basis of joint income. This applies to systems of joint or family taxation and is also usual for the calculation of cash transfers in respect of children.

- The final column contains the equation itself. The equation may refer to the variables in the parameters table and to variables which result from one of the rows of the equations table itself. Use is also made of the two standard variables "Married", which have the value 1 if the family consists of a married couple and 0 in the case of a single individual, and "Children" which denotes the number of children. Sometimes there is a reference to a variable with the affix "_total" which indicates the sum of the relevant variable values for the principal earner and the spouse. Similarly, the affixes "_princ" and "_spouse" indicate the value for the principal earner and spouse, respectively.

In the equations a number of functions are used. Some of these are used in the same way as in a number of widely available 'spreadsheet' computer packages. For example, MAX(X,Y) and MIN(X,Y) find the maximum and minimum of the two values, respectively. IF(condition X,Y) chooses the expression X if the condition is true and the expression Y if it is false. Boolean expressions are also used and are taken to have the value 1 if true and 0 if false. As an example, (Children=2*CB_2 is equivalent to IF(Children=2, CB_2,0).

There are also three special functions commonly used which denote calculations often required in tax and social security systems. These are:

- Tax (taxinc, tax_sch): This calculates the result of applying the schedule of tax rates and thresholds in "tax_sch" to the value of taxable income represented by "taxinc". This function may be used in any part of the equations, not just in the income tax calculation. For some countries it is used for social security contributions or even for allowance levels which may be income dependent.
- Positive (X): This gives the result X when this value is positive and zero otherwise. It is therefore equivalent to MAX(0,X).
- Taper (value, income, threshold, rate): This gives the amount represented by "value" if "income" is less than "threshold". Otherwise, it gives "value" reduced by "rate" multiplied by (income- threshold), unless this produces a negative result in which case zero is returned. This provides the calculation which is sometimes required when a tax credit, for example, is available in full provided that total income is below a threshold but is then withdrawn at a given rate for each currency unit in excess of the threshold until it is withdrawn completely.

In some circumstances, there are country specific special functions. These functions involve programming that is designed to simplify the tax calculations. The programming underlying these functions is based on the description of the particular measure given in the relevant country chapter found in Part III. For example, the Earned Income Credit in the United States is calculated using the function called EIC.

Anyone wishing to make their own implementation of the equations will have to write functions corresponding to these special functions or make appropriate modifications to any equations that use them.

Notes

1. The statistical data for Israel are supplied by and under the responsibility of the relevant Israeli authorities. The use of such data by the OECD is without prejudice to the status of the Golan Heights, East Jerusalem and Israeli settlements in the West Bank under the terms of international law.
2. Not all national statistical agencies use ISIC Rev.3 or Rev.4 to classify industries. However, the Statistical Classification of Economic Activities in the European Community (NACE Rev.1 or Rev.2), the North American Industry Classification System (US NAICS 2012). the Australian and New Zealand Standard Industrial Classification (ANZSIC 2006) and the Korean Standard Industrial Classification (6th to 9th KISC) include a classification which broadly conforms either with industries C-K in ISIC Rev. 3 or industries B-N in ISIC Rev.4.
3. The Wage estimates reported in the *Economic Outlook* are prepared by the Economics Department (ECO) of the OECD. They are consistent with the December 2016 issue of the *Economic Outlook*.
4. In this case, the amount of tax relief is related to actual social security contributions paid by the employee or withheld from his wage – thus in this respect this item deviates from the general definition of standard tax relief under which relief is unrelated to actual expenses incurred.
5. OECD, *Revenue Statistics1965-2015*, p. 62.
6. This characterisation must be viewed as informal, as the determination of tax expenditures requires the identification of a benchmark tax system for each country, or preferably, a common international benchmark. In practice it has not been possible to reach agreement on a common international benchmark for such purposes.
7. See Table D in *OECD Revenue Statistics 2016*.

ORGANISATION FOR ECONOMIC CO-OPERATION AND DEVELOPMENT

The OECD is a unique forum where governments work together to address the economic, social and environmental challenges of globalisation. The OECD is also at the forefront of efforts to understand and to help governments respond to new developments and concerns, such as corporate governance, the information economy and the challenges of an ageing population. The Organisation provides a setting where governments can compare policy experiences, seek answers to common problems, identify good practice and work to co-ordinate domestic and international policies.

The OECD member countries are: Australia, Austria, Belgium, Canada, Chile, the Czech Republic, Denmark, Estonia, Finland, France, Germany, Greece, Hungary, Iceland, Ireland, Israel, Italy, Japan, Korea, Latvia, Luxembourg, Mexico, the Netherlands, New Zealand, Norway, Poland, Portugal, the Slovak Republic, Slovenia, Spain, Sweden, Switzerland, Turkey, the United Kingdom and the United States. The European Union takes part in the work of the OECD.

OECD Publishing disseminates widely the results of the Organisation's statistics gathering and research on economic, social and environmental issues, as well as the conventions, guidelines and standards agreed by its members.

OECD PUBLISHING, 2, rue André-Pascal, 75775 PARIS CEDEX 16
(23 2017 02 1 P) ISBN 978-92-64-27076-3 – 2017

www.ingramcontent.com/pod-product-compliance
Lightning Source LLC
LaVergne TN
LVHW080113011026
849160LV00013B/1086
* 9 7 8 9 2 6 4 2 7 0 7 6 3 *